CONTE

MW00736360

CONTENTS

CONTENTS

PREFACE

Office 2000: Brief Edition, one of the instructional tools that complements *Peter Norton's® Introduction to Computers*, covers the basic features of Office 2000. Glencoe and Peter Norton have teamed up to provide this tutorial and its ancillaries to help you become a knowledgeable, empowered end user. After you complete this tutorial, you will be able to use Office 2000 to create and modify documents and to explore the World Wide Web, including creating and using hyperlinks and producing a Web page.

OBJECTIVES OF THE *OFFICE 2000: BRIEF EDITION* TUTORIAL

Office 2000: Brief Edition presents hands-on instruction on these Microsoft Office 2000 applications: Microsoft Word 2000, Microsoft Excel 2000, Microsoft Access 2000, Microsoft PowerPoint 2000, Microsoft Outlook 2000, and integration among these application programs. The objectives of the *Office 2000: Brief Edition* tutorial are:

- To introduce the basic concepts of Windows 98. No computer knowledge is assumed in this tutorial.

- To introduce the basic concepts of Microsoft Internet Explorer 5.

- To introduce the basic concepts and skills of Microsoft Office 2000 using these applications: Microsoft Word 2000, Microsoft Excel 2000, Microsoft Access 2000, Microsoft PowerPoint 2000, and Microsoft Outlook 2000.

- To provide hands-on tutorial exercises and realistic applications of the Office 2000 features.

- To help you develop proficiency in Microsoft Office 2000 applications.

- To help you explore and navigate the World Wide Web, search the Internet, create a Web page, communicate via e-mail, and more.

- To empower you to accept responsibility for learning.

- To help you demonstrate the skills and knowledge you have acquired by creating a personal portfolio.

ORGANIZATION OF THE *OFFICE 2000: BRIEF EDITION* TUTORIAL

The *Office 2000: Brief Edition* tutorial is divided into three sections: (1) a Getting Started section that includes three lessons covering the basic concepts of Windows 98, Internet Explorer 5, and Office 2000; (2) a tutorial for Word 2000, Excel 2000, Access 2000, and PowerPoint 2000; and (3) a Managing Information section that includes two lessons covering the basic concepts of Outlook and Office 2000 integration.

- **Getting Started—Lesson 1: Windows 98 Basics.** This lesson presents the basic features of the Windows 98 operating system to enable you to work more effectively with application programs, such as Office 2000.

- **Getting Started—Lesson 2: Internet Explorer 5 Basics.** This lesson presents the basic features of Microsoft Internet Explorer 5, a program designed to help you explore the Internet, search the Internet, and view your newly created Web pages.

- **Getting Started—Lesson 3: Introducing Office 2000.** This lesson presents an overview of the Microsoft Office 2000 program—a suite of applications that allow you to create and modify documents, worksheets, databases, and presentations along with managing information.

- **The *Word 2000* tutorial.** In the *Word 2000* tutorial, you will learn the basic features of Microsoft Word 2000 and be able to create and modify documents. You will also learn to use Word 2000 to explore the World Wide Web and create hyperlinks.

- **The *Excel 2000* tutorial.** In the *Excel 2000* tutorial, you will learn the basic features of Microsoft Excel 2000 and be able to create and modify worksheets. You will also learn to use Excel 2000 to explore the World Wide Web and create a Web page.

- **The *Access 2000* tutorial.** In the *Access 2000* tutorial, you will learn the basic features of Microsoft Access 2000 and be able to create and modify databases. You will also learn to use Access 2000 to explore the World Wide Web and create hyperlinks to databases and Web sites.

- **The *PowerPoint 2000* tutorial.** In the *PowerPoint 2000* tutorial, you will learn the basic features of Microsoft PowerPoint 2000 and be able to create and modify presentations. You will also learn to use PowerPoint 2000 to explore the World Wide Web and create a Web page.

- **Managing Information—Lesson 1: Outlook Basics.** This lesson presents the basics of Outlook 2000, a personal information management program that helps you manage messages, appointments, contacts, and tasks.

- **Managing Information—Lesson 2: Integrating Office 2000.** In this lesson, you will improve your productivity skills by learning more about integrating Outlook 2000 data with Word 2000, Excel 2000, Access 2000, and PowerPoint 2000 documents in numerous hands-on activities and exercises.

In addition to the lessons and tutorials, the *Office 2000: Brief Edition* tutorial includes these items to reinforce learning:

- **Appendices.** Two appendices provide additional information. *Appendix A: Portfolio Builder* gives an overview of portfolios and provides tips on creating your personal portfolio. *Appendix B: Answers to Self Check* provides the answers to all the Self Check exercises in the entire tutorial.

- **Glossary.** Use the Glossary to look up terms that you don't understand.

- **Index.** Use the Index to find specific information in the *Office 2000: Brief Edition* tutorial.

- **Office Data CD.** Attached to the inside back cover of the *Office 2000: Brief Edition* tutorial you will find the Office Data CD. This CD contains all the files you need to complete the activities in the entire *Office 2000: Brief Edition* tutorial. A separate Student Data Disk folder appears on the CD for each of the four individual tutorials (Word, Excel, Access, and PowerPoint) and one for the Integration lessons (Integration). You must copy the folders and files from the Office Data CD to a Zip disk, to a folder on the hard drive, to a folder on the network drive, or to a floppy disk (where feasible) to be able to use the files throughout the entire tutorial. Step-by-step instructions for copying these folders from the CD appear in Getting Started—Lesson 1 in the Hands On activities called *Copying Files from a CD-ROM to a Disk* and *Setting File Attributes* (pages 31-34).

STRUCTURE AND FORMAT OF THE *OFFICE 2000: BRIEF EDITION* TUTORIAL

Many of the following features are included in the lessons throughout the *Office 2000: Brief Edition* tutorial:

- **Concepts and Objectives.** The Contents and Objectives provide an overview of the features and concepts you will learn in the lesson.

- **Explanations of important concepts.** Each lesson begins with a brief explanation of the concept or software feature covered in that lesson. The explanations help you understand "the big picture" as you learn each new feature.

- **In the Workplace.** This element appears in the margin at the beginning of each lesson and provides a brief overview of how the concepts presented in the lesson can help you succeed in the workplace.

- **New terms.** An important part of learning about computers and software is learning the terminology. Each new term in the *Office 2000: Brief Edition* tutorial appears in boldface and italic and is defined the first time it is used. As you encounter these words, read their definitions carefully. If you encounter the same word later and have forgotten the meaning, you can look up the word in the Glossary.

- **Hands On activities.** Because most of us learn best by doing, each explanation is followed by a hands-on activity that includes step-by-step instructions, which you complete at the computer. Integrated in the steps are notes and warnings to help you learn more about Windows 98, Microsoft Internet Explorer 5, and Office 2000.

- **Basics.** This element appears in the margin next to Hands On activities. The Basics element lists the general steps required to perform a particular task. Use the Basics element as a reference to quickly and easily review the steps to perform a task.

- **Hints & Tips.** This element appears in the margin and provides tips for increasing your effectiveness while using the Office 2000 program.

- **Another Way.** This element appears in the margin and provides alternative ways to perform a given task.

- **Did You Know?** Read each Did You Know?, another element that appears in the margin, to learn additional facts related to the content of the lesson or other interesting facts about computers.

- **Web Note.** Web Notes appear in the margin and contain interesting facts and Web addresses that relate to the content of the lesson and to your exploration of the World Wide Web.

- **Illustrations.** Many figures point out features on the screen and illustrate what your screen should look like after you complete important steps.

- **Using Help.** The Using Help activities reinforce the importance of using Help to explore for additional information.

- **Self Check exercises.** To check your knowledge of the concepts presented in the lesson, a self-check exercise is provided at the end of each lesson. After completing the exercise, refer to *Appendix B: Answers to Self Check* to verify your understanding of the material.

- **On the Web.** The On the Web sections included in the lessons teach you how to access and navigate the World Wide Web. Various activities show you how to insert hyperlinks into Office 2000 documents, use the Search Page, create a Web page, and more.

- **Summary.** At the end of each lesson, the Summary reviews the major topics covered in the lesson. You can use the Summary as a study guide.

- **Concepts Review.** The Concepts Review section may include five types of objective questions: a true/false exercise, a matching exercise, a completion exercise, short-answer questions, and an identification exercise.

- **Skills Review.** The Skills Review section provides simple hands-on exercises to practice each skill learned in the lesson.

- **Lesson Applications.** The Lesson Applications provide additional hands-on practice. These problems combine two or more skills learned in the lesson to modify Office 2000 documents.

- **Projects.** The Projects provide additional hands-on practice to apply your problem-solving skills. Each project allows you to create a new document or modify an existing document to incorporate one or more skills learned in the lesson. Additional *On the Web* projects reinforce the skills learned in the On the Web sections, as well as a *Project in Progress* that builds from one lesson to the next in the *Word 2000, Excel 2000, Access 2000,* and *PowerPoint 2000* tutorials.

- **Case Study.** Appearing after the last lesson in the *Word 2000, Excel 2000, Access 2000,* and *PowerPoint 2000* tutorials, the Case Study is a capstone activity that allows you to apply the various skills you have learned to plan, create, and modify documents.

ABOUT PETER NORTON

Peter Norton is a pioneering software developer and an author. *Norton Utilities, AntiVirus,* and other utility programs are installed worldwide on millions of personal computers. His books have helped countless individuals understand computers from the inside out.

Glencoe teamed up with Peter Norton to help you better understand the role computers play in your life now and in the future. As you begin to work in your chosen profession, you may use this tutorial now and later as a reference book.

Getting Started

Publishing on the Internet

You don't need to be a mechanic in order to drive a car . . .

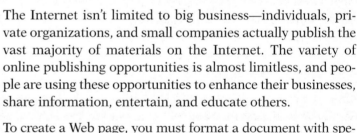

You can just turn the key and go! Back in the dark ages of online communication (about five to ten years ago!), only programming experts could post information on the Internet. But now, with the right software and an Internet account, you can publish your own materials for viewing by a worldwide audience. One of the easiest and fastest ways to publish your work online is to create your own page on the World Wide Web.

The Internet isn't limited to big business—individuals, private organizations, and small companies actually publish the vast majority of materials on the Internet. The variety of online publishing opportunities is almost limitless, and people are using these opportunities to enhance their businesses, share information, entertain, and educate others.

To create a Web page, you must format a document with special tags—called Hypertext Markup Language (HTML) tags. These tags, which surround the text they affect, make the document "readable" by the Web browser, and tell it how to display the text, whether as a heading, a table, a link, normal text, and so on.

A few years ago, you would need to be (or need to hire!) a programming expert to prepare HTML tags and ready your Web page for publication. Fortunately, now you don't have to be a computer whiz to create HTML documents. In fact, you don't even need to know anything about HTML! With the right tools, you can quickly create attractive, interesting pages that are ready to be published on the Web.

Microsoft® Office 2000, with its suite of applications including Microsoft Word, Microsoft Excel, Microsoft Access, and Microsoft PowerPoint, converts ordinary documents into HTML files. This feature lets you create any type of document, save it in HTML format, and then immediately open the document in a Web browser (such as Microsoft Internet Explorer). There you can see the page just as it would appear on the Internet if you published it. You can even make changes to the original documents, resave the documents in HTML format again, and view your changes in your browser—without typing a single HTML tag! In addition, many desktop applications (including Microsoft Office 2000) now have tools that let you embed graphics, create hyperlinks, and add other special features to your HTML documents.

You can also create feature-rich Web pages using your Web browser. Using a browser's editing tools, you can create new pages from scratch or use predesigned templates. Here's one quick and easy way to design a Web page: find a Web page you like, copy it to disk, and then open it in Edit mode in the browser. You then can use that page's HTML formatting as the basis for your page! Using a browser-based editor, you work directly with HTML tags only if you want to. If you prefer, Microsoft Office 2000 and your browser can do all the HTML formatting for you—you don't even need to "look under the hood!"

After you have created your Web pages, simply contact your Internet Service Provider (ISP). Your ISP can provide you with space on a Web server and an address where others can find your pages. Using your chosen HTML editing tools, you can update, expand, and refresh your Web site whenever you want . . . *just turn the key and go!*

LESSON 1

Windows 98 Basics

CONTENTS

OBJECTIVES

After you complete this lesson, you will be able to do the following:

■ Define the Microsoft Windows 98 operating system.

■ Start your computer system.

■ Use the mouse to point, click, double-click, right-click, drag, and display objects.

■ Activate and move desktop icons.

■ Identify the common window elements.

■ Size, minimize, maximize, restore, and scroll windows.

■ Run more than one program, switch back and forth between programs, and close programs.

■ Use menus and dialog boxes.

■ Set a default printer.

■ Find help on Windows 98 topics.

■ Use Windows Explorer to view and modify the structure of a disk; create folders and subfolders; and rename, delete, copy, and move files.

■ Change attributes of files and folders.

■ Quit Windows 98 and shut down your computer.

■ Search a Web site for information on computer products.

This lesson introduces the Windows 98 operating system—software that starts and oversees every operation you perform on your computer. You will learn about the objects that appear on your computer screen, and you will use the mouse to run programs and move graphical objects. The basic techniques you master in this lesson will enable you to work more effectively with application programs, such as Office 2000 presented in this tutorial.

THE WINDOWS 98 OPERATING SYSTEM

The computer system you work with consists of hardware and software. Usually, the hardware includes these components:

- A processor to manage, interpret, and manipulate the flow of data
- A keyboard to type information
- A mouse (or trackball) to point to objects and select options on the screen
- A monitor to see what you are doing
- A printer to produce hard copy output
- Disks to store information

Your computer system also needs both task-specific and general operational **software.** Software that helps you accomplish a specific task is called an **application** (or **application program**). You might use different applications to type a letter, to manage a budget, to balance a checkbook, or to organize a mailing list. When you are able to run more than one application program at a time, **multitasking** results. With a few quick keystrokes or a click of the mouse, you can switch from one application to another. Software that allows you to operate your hardware and use applications is called **operating system software,** or an **operating system,** for short.

Sometimes the operating system manages your computer automatically. When you turn on your computer, the operating system looks up the current date and time, sets your preferred speaker volume, and displays the selected screen color scheme. At other times, your operating system follows your instructions, such as when you duplicate a specific file or start a particular application. These computer instructions are called **commands.**

Not all personal computers use the same operating system software. Your computer's operating system determines not only the specific commands your system can execute, but also the manner in which you give those commands and otherwise interact with your computer. This human-computer interaction is called the **user interface.** It determines the look and feel of your computing experience.

Microsoft's goal for Windows 98 is to continue creating pleasing, easy-to-use operating systems—building on the success of its predecessor, Windows 95. Windows 98 integrates **Internet** access with the basic operating system, as well as supporting hardware devices and standards created since the release of Windows 95. To meet these goals, Windows 98 utilizes a **graphical user interface** (or **GUI**), where you use onscreen pictures to operate your computer.

STARTING THE COMPUTER WITH WINDOWS 98

When you turn on a computer, a complex series of events begins. First, a built-in program tests the computer. This **Power On Self Test** (or **POST**) checks the memory, keyboard, display, and disk drives of the computer system. Next, files from the hard disk containing essential operating system components are loaded. Because computer systems and setups vary greatly, you may see a series of screens informing you of the progress of the startup procedure. Finally, Windows 98 displays its opening screen. After you turn on the power, the computer gives itself the instructions it needs to start up or "pulls itself up by its bootstraps." From this figure of speech, the entire process is called **booting the system** or performing a **system boot.**

HANDS On
Windows BASICS

Booting the System

1. Turn on the computer and the monitor, if necessary.

2. Close the Welcome to Windows 98 screen, if necessary.

1. If you see a ScanDisk screen running when you boot Windows 98, the previous session was not properly shut down. Let the ScanDisk run; some of the procedures that should have been performed previously, will be run now.

2. Don't assume that a computer is turned off just because the screen is dark. As an energy saving device, the computer may just be *resting*. If the screen is black, press a key on the keyboard to see if the computer *wakes up*.

Booting the System

In this activity, you will start the computer and boot the Windows 98 operating system. If your computer is already on, you may need to restart your system. If your computer system is set up for multiple users, network access, or password security, you may have to enter information identifying you to the computer system. Check with your instructor, computer lab assistant, or network administrator for instructions.

1. Turn on the computer and the monitor.

2. Observe the booting process:

   a. Listen for the POST sound. A single beep means the system passed all the tests; a series of beeps indicates a hardware problem. If you hear a series of beeps, check the keyboard and monitor connections, read the message on the screen, or consult the computer manual to fix the problem. You may need technical help from the manufacturer, a lab assistant, or a technician.

   b. Watch the screen. After a few moments, a memory indicator may appear while the system checks its random access memory. Then, as more of the operating system loads into memory, some information may appear at the top of the screen, followed by the Windows 98 copyright screen.

You may see the Welcome to Windows 98 *window,* as shown in Figure 1.1. A window is a rectangular object that displays the contents of an icon, the options for using a program, or an area in which you create or modify a document. Windows 98 derives its name from these frames. The Welcome window displays options that provide a connection to the Internet, basic computing information, an overview of Windows 98 features, and a set of functions to improve the performance of your computer.

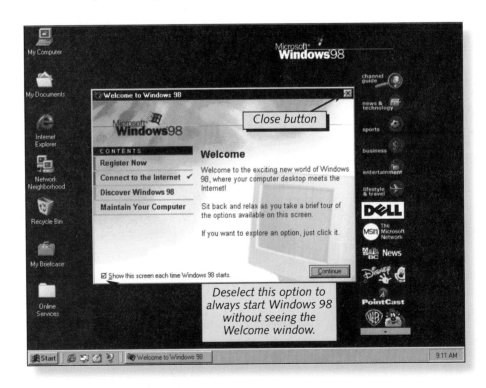

Figure 1.1
The Windows 98 Welcome screen

 *If you are using Windows 95, your desktop will differ from that shown in the figures in this tutorial. Your desktop may also vary, depending on the computer configuration and the installed programs.*

3. **If necessary, deselect the option to prevent the Welcome window from appearing each time you boot your computer.**

4. **Click the Close button ☒ in the upper-right corner of the Welcome window to close it.**

USING THE WINDOWS 98 DESKTOP

After booting Windows 98, your screen should resemble Figure 1.2. This screen, called the Windows 98 *Desktop,* is the background for your computer work. The desktop contains many of the tools for working with Windows 98. Your desktop details may vary, but you will still see the basic features discussed in this lesson.

Windows 98 has many features that integrate the operating system with the Internet. The *Web style desktop* lets you use your mouse and view your screen just as you would when you run Internet Explorer, a *browser* program that lets you access the World Wide Web. Users may choose to retain the former Windows 95 user interface, now called the *classic style desktop.*

Figure 1.2 ◄
The Windows 98 Desktop

Additionally, when you set up your screen as the *Active Desktop,* information is sent to your desktop via the Internet. This information may be news articles, weather reports, stock market quotations, or sports scores. You can get this information by specifically requesting it or you can subscribe to a service that sends you information on a regular basis.

Due to Window's high degree of customization it is rare for two desktops to look exactly the same. The desktop elements described below, however, are common to almost all screens.

- The **taskbar** has a number of buttons that you can click to select or perform an action, including the Start button [Start] on the left and the Clock button on the right.

- On the screen, you should see several small, labeled pictures or **icons**, such as My Computer, My Documents, Internet Explorer, Network Neighborhood, and Recycle Bin. These icons represent objects, such as programs, groups of programs, disk drives, documents, or specific tasks.

- The Start button [Start], when clicked, displays a menu of programs installed on the computer. A **menu** is a list of items you can choose from to select a command, set software features, or choose options.

- The **Channel bar** displays a series of icons that lets you receive information from your favorite Web sites automatically.

- When you elect to run a program or select an option, a window usually appears on your desktop.

USING THE MOUSE

You will use the **mouse** extensively in Windows 98. The mouse is the key to the graphical user interface because it lets you choose and manipulate onscreen objects without having to type on the keyboard. Although the mouse is the most popular pointing device, you may also use several other pointing devices. **Trackballs** have buttons like the mouse, but instead of moving the mouse over the desktop, you spin a large ball. Laptops often employ either a small **joystick** in the middle of the keyboard or a **touch-sensitive pad** below the keyboard. Each of these devices, however, lets you point to items on the screen and click buttons to perform actions on those items.

Your mouse probably has two or three buttons. Whenever the directions in this tutorial say *click,* use the left mouse button. If you must use the right mouse button, the directions will say *right-click* or *click the right mouse button.* (Windows 98 lets you reassign the mouse buttons so that the right button performs the actions ordinarily performed by the left button. See Help for specific information.) You can perform several actions with the mouse:

- On your screen you should see an arrow pointing toward the upper-left. This arrow is called the **mouse pointer,** or more simply, the **pointer.** Moving the mouse to position the pointer on the screen is called **pointing.** Table 1.1 shows several shapes you may notice as you point to objects on the screen. When you rest your pointer on some icons on the desktop, a description may appear.

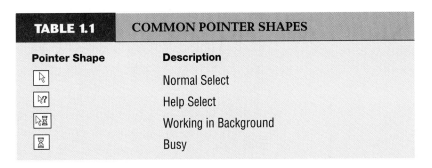

TABLE 1.1	COMMON POINTER SHAPES
Pointer Shape	**Description**
![arrow]	Normal Select
![help]	Help Select
![background]	Working in Background
![busy]	Busy

Practice using the mouse until you become comfortable with it. Although keyboard alternatives exist for most Windows 98 mouse actions, you will be more efficient if you can use both keyboard actions and the mouse.

TABLE 1.1	COMMON POINTER SHAPES—cont.
⊞	Precision Select
I	Text Select
⬉	Handwriting
⊘	Unavailable
↕	Vertical Resize
↔	Horizontal Resize
⬉	Diagonal Resize 1
⬈	Diagonal Resize 2
⊕	Move
↑	Alternate Select
🖑	Line Select

■ To **click** the mouse, point to an object and quickly press and release the left mouse button.

■ To work with an object on the screen, you must usually **select** (or **choose**) the item by clicking the object—pressing and quickly releasing the mouse button.

■ To **double-click,** point to an object and click the left mouse button twice in rapid succession without moving the pointer.

■ To **right-click,** point to an object, press the right mouse button, and then quickly release it.

■ To **drag** (or **drag-and-drop**), point to an object you want to move, press and hold the left mouse button, move the mouse to drag the object to a new location, and then release the mouse button.

HANDS On

Practicing Mouse Techniques

In this activity, you will become familiar with using the mouse to select, open, and move objects on the desktop.

1. Point to the **My Computer system icon**.

2. To select the icon, click **My Computer**.

Notice that the selected icon highlights (changes color).

3. To deselect the icon, point to an empty area of the desktop and click.

The icon deselects or returns to its original color.

4. Point to the **My Computer icon** and double-click (the left mouse button).

The My Computer window appears, as shown in Figure 1.3. When you double-click an object on the screen, such as an icon or a file name, the object's window **opens** on the screen.

Note   *If your icons are different from those shown in Figure 1.3, click the View menu and then click List. Likewise, if your window displays a toolbar and you would like to hide it, click the View menu and click Toolbars to deselect it.*

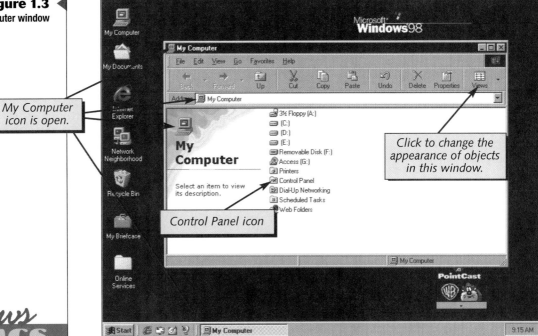

5. Double-click the **Control Panel icon**.

The Control Panel window appears. It contains a series of icons that lets you customize your computing environment.

6. Click the **Close button** ☒.

The Control Panel window disappears from the desktop. Clicking a window's Close button ☒—the X located in its upper-right corner—***closes*** the window and removes the window from the screen.

7. Point to the **My Computer icon** and press and hold the left mouse button. Move the mouse down and away from you to drag the icon from its current position to the lower-right corner of the screen. Then release the mouse button, but *not* on top of another icon.

 *If the My Computer icon won't stay where you drop it, click the right mouse button on the desktop and click Arrange Icons. If a check mark appears by Auto Arrange, click Auto Arrange to remove the check mark. Then repeat step 7.*

The icon should appear somewhere near the lower-right corner of the screen, as shown in Figure 1.4.

8. Drag the My Computer icon to its original location.

Before the advent of Windows, most PC users had to work with one program and one document at a time. Even experienced users spent a lot of time opening and closing programs.

The My Computer icon was originally here.

The My Computer icon in its new position

Figure 1.4 ◄
The moved My Computer icon

WORKING WITH WINDOWS

A window provides a view into your work and is designed to simplify tasks you perform on the computer. Options and information for each application are contained in the window, and you can easily access and use them. You can position a window on the screen and change its size using the mouse.

Two types of windows exist: *application windows* and *document windows.* An application window appears when you run a program. Document windows let you perform separate jobs within an application window. Figure 1.5 illustrates elements common to most windows. Each window contains some or all of the tools shown in Table 1.2.

Figure 1.5 ◄
Components of a typical window

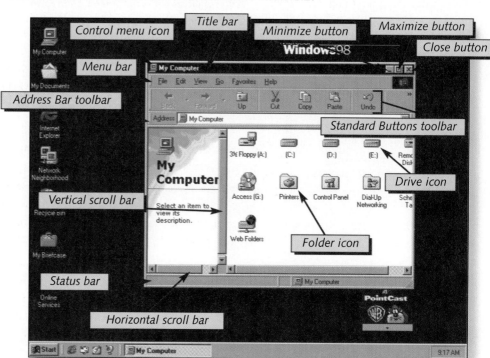

Control menu icon
Title bar
Minimize button
Maximize button
Close button
Menu bar
Address Bar toolbar
Standard Buttons toolbar
Drive icon
Vertical scroll bar
Folder icon
Status bar
Horizontal scroll bar

TABLE 1.2	COMMON WINDOW ELEMENTS
Tool	**Description**
Title bar	The shaded bar at the top of a window that displays the name of the window and contains buttons for manipulating the window.
Control menu icon	The icon ▣ at the left end of the title bar that when clicked displays the Control menu. The Control menu contains options for manipulating windows. Double-clicking the icon closes the active window.
Minimize button	The first button ▬ near the right end of the title bar that contains a horizontal line. Clicking this button reduces the window to a taskbar button.
Maximize button	The second button ▢ near the right end of the title bar that contains a box. Clicking this button enlarges the window to fill the entire screen.
Restore button	The third button ▤ that replaces the Maximize button when the window is maximized. Clicking this button returns the window to its previous size.
Close button	The button ✕ at the far right end of the title bar. This button closes the application and the window.
Window borders	The edges, or borders, of the window that you can drag to resize a window.
Window corners	The corners of a window that you can drag to enlarge or shrink both the height and width of a window at the same time.
Menu bar	The area below the title bar that displays menu names, such as File, Edit, View, and Help.
Workspace	The area in the window that displays the information with which you are working.
Scroll bars	Horizontal and vertical bars along the bottom and right sides of a window that allow you to move to and view the hidden portion of your workspace when it doesn't all fit in the window.

Moving and Sizing Windows

To move a window to a new location, point to the title bar, click and hold the left mouse button, move the mouse to drag the window, and release the button when the window is at the desired location. Some computers are set to show an outline of the window while it is being dragged. When the mouse button is released, the contents of the window appear in place of the outline.

When you point to the edge of a window, the pointer changes shape to indicate the direction in which the window edge can move. A pointer on the left or right edge of a window becomes a horizontal double-headed arrow; moving the pointer to the top or bottom edge of the window changes the pointer to a vertical double-headed arrow. By moving the pointer to one of these locations, you can drag that window edge to change the size of the window. For example, dragging the left edge of the window to the right makes a narrower window; dragging the bottom edge down makes a longer window.

If you point to one of the four corners of the window, the pointer becomes a diagonal double-headed arrow. Dragging a corner of the window stretches or shrinks two sides simultaneously. You can move a window by clicking the control menu icon and selecting the Move command. A four-way arrow appears, and you can then move the window. See Table 1.1 on page 10 for the pointers you use to size and move windows.

See Table 1.1 on page 10

HANDS On

Practicing Moving and Sizing a Window

In this activity, you will practice moving and resizing a window.

1. **Double-click the My Computer icon and click the Restore button** 🗗 **if the window is maximized.**

2. **Point to the title bar, press and hold the left mouse button, and then drag the My Computer window down to the lower-right corner of the screen, as shown in Figure 1.6. Release the mouse button to set the position of the My Computer window.**

Windows BASICS

Moving and Sizing Windows

To move a window:

1. Point to the title bar.

2. Drag the window to the desired location.

To size a window:

• Click the Maximize button, the Minimize button, or the Restore button.

• Drag the border or corner of the window to the desired size.

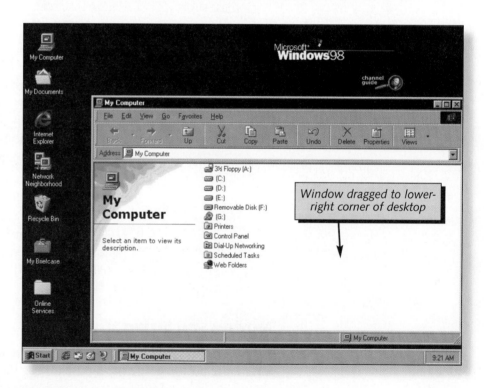

Window dragged to lower-right corner of desktop

Figure 1.6 ◄
The moved window

3. **Click the Maximize button** ▢ **on the My Computer window.**

The selected window enlarges to cover the full screen. The Maximize button ▢ changes to a Restore button 🗗.

4. **Click the Minimize button** ▬.

The My Computer window closes and its button on the taskbar appears raised, as shown in Figure 1.7.

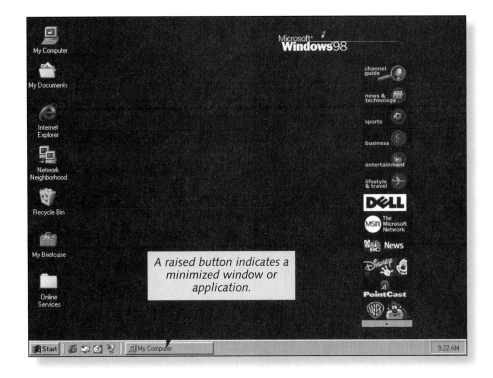

A raised button indicates a minimized window or application.

Figure 1.7
The My Computer taskbar button

5. **Click the My Computer taskbar button.**

The window reappears on the desktop.

6. **Click the Restore button  on the My Computer window.**

The window reduces to the size it was before it was maximized to full-screen size.

7. **Point to the top border of the My Computer window until the pointer changes to a vertical, double-headed arrow.**

8. **Drag the top border outline up to near the top of the screen and release the mouse button.**

The window expands vertically.

9. **Point to the left border of the window until the pointer changes to a horizontal, double-headed arrow.**

10. **Drag the left border near to the left edge of the screen so that the window expands horizontally to nearly fill the desktop.**

Arranging Icons

In an earlier activity, you learned how to use the mouse to drag an icon to a new location. You can also display icons in neat rows, using the Arrange Icons command on the *shortcut menu* that appears when you right-click the desktop or a window. Within most windows, you can change the size of the icons as well. Windows 98 allows you to view icons in two different sizes. *Large icons* are easy to distinguish, but they take up more room. *Small icons* are about a quarter of the size of large ones.

Changing the Size of an Icon

1. In an open window, right-click an empty area.

2. Point to View and click Large Icons or Small Icons.

Changing the Size of a Window's Icons

In this activity, you will modify the size of icons displayed in an open window.

1. **In the My Computer window, double-click Control Panel and size the window so it occupies one quarter of the screen.**

2. **Right-click an empty area in the Control Panel window, point to View, and click Large Icons.**

The icons change to a large display size.

3. **Right-click an empty area in the Control Panel window, point to Arrange Icons, and then click by Name on the shortcut menu.**

The icons rearrange to conform to the shape of the window. Notice that they are also arranged alphabetically by name.

4. **Right-click an empty area in the Control Panel window, point to View, and click Small Icons.**

The icons appear in a smaller display size.

Using Scroll Bars

A *scroll bar* appears along the right and/or bottom side of a window when there is not enough room to display all of the contents of the window. If the unseen information is above or below that viewed in the window, you see a *vertical scroll bar;* if the information is to the left or right, you see a *horizontal scroll bar.* Both types of scroll bars are illustrated in Figure 1.8.

Hints & Tips

A quick way to maximize an open window is to double-click its title bar. Double-clicking a maximized window is the same as clicking its Restore button.

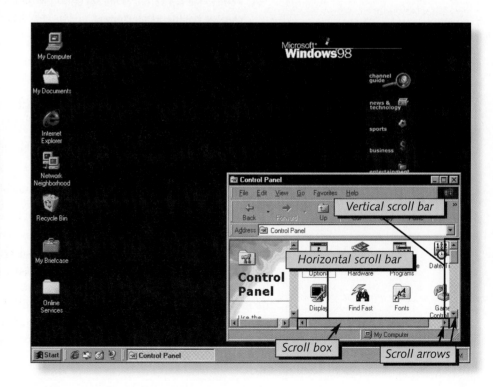

Figure 1.8 ◀
Scroll bars, arrows, and boxes

Within the scroll bar is the **scroll box,** which indicates the relative position of the screen information within its window. If the scroll box is at the top or left of the scroll bar, you are viewing the top or left part of the information. If the scroll box is at the bottom or right of the scroll bar, you are viewing the bottom or right of the information. Clicking the scroll bar shifts the display to view another screen of information. Clicking below or after the scroll box displays the next screen of information. Clicking above or before the scroll box displays the previous screen. You can also drag-and-drop the scroll box to move quickly to the desired position within a document or list of information. **Scroll arrows** at either end of the scroll bar allow slow window navigation. Clicking a scroll arrow moves one line up or down on a vertical list or right or left on a horizontal scroll bar. Pressing and holding a scroll arrow permits line-by-line scrolling in the direction the arrow points.

HANDS

Windows
BASICS

Scrolling a Window

- Click the scroll bar to view information not currently visible.

- Click below or after the scroll box to view more information.

- Click above or before the scroll box to view the previous screen of information.

- Click a scroll arrow to move one line up or down vertically or right or left horizontally.

Scrolling a Window

In this activity, you will practice using scroll bars to scroll the contents of a window.

1. With the Control Panel window open, right-click, point to **View**, and click **Large Icons**, if the option is not selected.

2. Size the window to look similar to Figure 1.8. (If necessary, right-click, point to View, and click Auto Arrange to toggle this option off.)

3. Point to the vertical scroll bar—anywhere below its scroll box—and click.

The column of icons appears to scroll upward as the scroll box moves downward.

4. If the scroll box is not already at the bottom of the vertical scroll bar, point to the vertical scroll bar below the scroll box and click as many times as is necessary to move the scroll box to the bottom of the scroll bar.

The column of icons scrolls. Notice that the last icon is visible at the bottom of the window.

5. Point to the scroll arrow at the top of the scroll bar. Press and hold the left mouse button until the scroll box moves to the top of the vertical scroll bar.

6. Right-click, point to **View**, and click **Small Icons**.

The icons change to a smaller size.

7. Click to the right of the scroll box in the horizontal scroll bar.

The contents of the window scroll to the left as the scroll box moves to the right.

8. Point to the scroll arrow to the left of the scroll bar, press and hold the left mouse button until the scroll box moves to the left end of the horizontal scroll bar.

The contents of the window scroll to the right as the box moves to the left.

9. Click the **Close button** ☒ on the Control Panel window.

RUNNING PROGRAMS

The Windows taskbar is located at the bottom of the computer screen (by default) and displays the names of the programs that are currently running. The taskbar also contains the Start button . Although you can start programs by double-clicking their icons in the My Computer window, the Start button provides a convenient way to start programs and to open documents, search for files, change system settings, access the Help feature, and shut down the computer.

Before you can run or **launch** a program, it must be installed. Thousands of programs are commonly available, but no computer is likely to have more than 10 or 20. While you can pay up to several hundred dollars for a program, Windows 98 includes a set of programs—called **accessories**—that let you perform simple tasks. WordPad—a word processing program—and Notepad—a text editing program—are two of these accessories.

In Windows 98 you can have many programs running at once, but only one window can be **active** (that is, in control) at a time. The active window is in front of any inactive windows and has a taskbar button that looks sunken or pressed in. In addition, the title bar of an active window is highlighted. If you want to switch between programs that are running in Windows, you need to activate the window for the program you want to use. The quickest way to switch between programs is to click the appropriate taskbar button.

Warning *It's easy to keep opening applications on top of one another without closing them. When you finish using an application, however, get into the habit of closing it. Unnecessarily running multiple applications will clutter your desktop and deplete system memory—which can result in slower processing times.*

HANDS On

Starting and Closing a Program

In this activity, you will start two Windows 98 accessory programs, switch between them, and close them.

1. Click the **Start button** .

The Start menu appears.

2. Point to **Programs**.

The Programs submenu appears. This menu contains the Windows 98 accessories and applications available on your computer.

3. Point to **Accessories** and the Accessories submenu appears, as shown in Figure 1.9.

4. Click **WordPad**.

The WordPad program is loaded into memory.

5. If the WordPad window doesn't cover the entire screen, click the **Maximize button** .

Starting and Closing a Program

To launch a program:

1. Click the Start button.

2. Point to Programs.

3. Point to submenus until you can click the desired program.

To switch between programs:

Click the program's taskbar button.

To close a program:

Click the Close button.

Figure 1.9
The Accessories menu

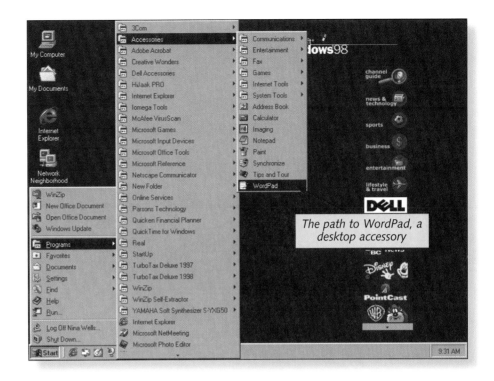

The path to WordPad, a desktop accessory

Your screen should look similar to Figure 1.10. Now WordPad is ready for you to type your text in the window's workspace. If you typed text, you would save the text as a ***document,*** a data file that the application lets you create and modify.

Figure 1.10
Blank WordPad window

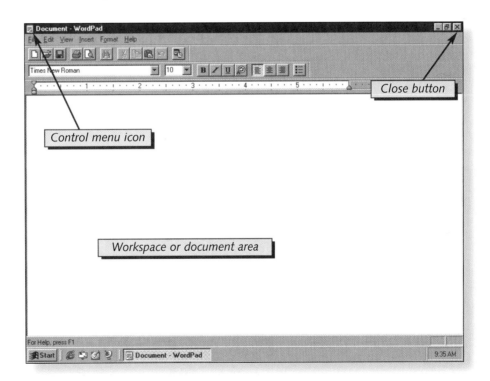

Close button

Control menu icon

Workspace or document area

To avoid distractions by other windows or by the desktop, you may want to maximize the window of the application in which you're working.

6. Click the **Start button** ![Start], point to **Programs, Accessories**, and click **Notepad**.

The Notepad window appears over the WordPad window. You now have two programs running: WordPad and Notepad.

7. Click the **WordPad button** on the taskbar.

The WordPad window once more fills the screen and becomes the active window, hiding the Notepad window.

8. Click the **Notepad button** on the taskbar.

Notepad is again in the foreground. Notice that part of the WordPad window remains visible, but the Notepad window is active.

9. Click outside the Notepad window on the WordPad window.

The WordPad window once again fills the screen, hiding the Notepad window.

10. Click the **Close button** ☒ on the WordPad title bar.

The WordPad window closes and the Notepad window reappears.

11. If a box appears asking if you want to save any changes you have made to the document, click **No**.

12. Click the **Control menu icon** ◰ in the Notepad window and click **Close**.

CHOOSING PROGRAM OPTIONS FROM THE MENU BAR

In Windows, many program features, options, and commands are hidden within a menu bar. You have already used two kinds of menus—those within the Start menu and shortcut menus. On a menu bar, menu options appear when you open the menu. When a menu is open, you can view and click the menu option you want. Menu options followed by three dots, called ellipsis (...), open a dialog box that contains additional choices. Clicking anywhere outside the menu closes it.

HANDS On

Windows BASICS

Using the Menu Bar

1. Click the menu name in the menu bar.

2. Point to and click the desired menu option.

Using the Menu Bar

In this activity, you will practice choosing from a menu bar.

1. Launch WordPad.

The WordPad window opens. The menu bar appears directly below the window's title bar.

2. Click **View**.

The View menu appears, as shown in Figure 1.11.

3. Slowly move the mouse pointer down the View menu.

Notice that each menu option is highlighted as the pointer passes over it. If you wanted to select an option, you would click while the desired option was highlighted.

4. Click outside the View menu to close it.

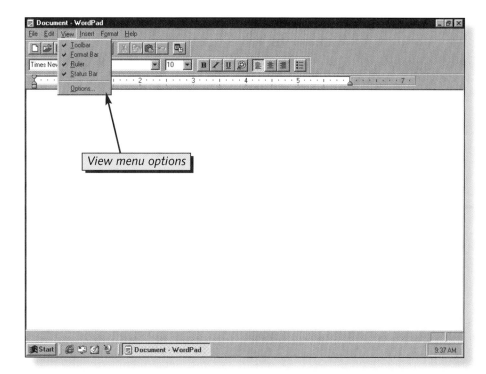

Figure 1.11
WordPad View menu

USING DIALOG BOXES

A good portion of your interaction with Windows-based programs will involve the use of **dialog boxes.** A dialog box is a special window that prompts the user for information to perform a command. You cannot proceed until you have responded to the questions in the dialog box, even if it is only to accept the suggested answers. The title bar shows the name of the dialog box. The following types of controls may appear in dialog boxes.

■ *Tabs,* similar to the tabs on paper file folders, represent different sections or categories of options that you may choose. To select a category, click the tab and that portion of the dialog box will appear in front of the other tab categories.

■ *Option buttons* are small circles that indicate a list of mutually exclusive options. In a set of option buttons, you can choose only one at a time. Clicking a different button changes your choice. The chosen option button contains a black dot.

■ *Check boxes* are small boxes that allow you to switch an option off or on. A check mark in the box means the option is on; an empty box indicates it is off. Clicking the box changes the response in a check box.

■ *Command buttons* are small labeled rectangles. You click a command button to choose an action. A button with a heavy border around it is the default button. Pressing ⌷Enter⌷ does the same thing as clicking the default button. Some command buttons open dialog boxes that offer additional choices or expand the current dialog box with advanced options.

■ *Triangle buttons* and *drop-down lists* let you choose from a predetermined set of options. You click the triangle button, point to the desired option in the list that appears, and click.

■ *Text boxes* are rectangles in which you can type information.

■ *Spinner buttons* may appear in text boxes that must contain numbers. Spinner buttons are composed of an up arrow and a down arrow. Clicking the up arrow increases the number; clicking the down arrow decreases the number.

■ A *slider control* consists of a horizontal or vertical line with progressive values and an indicator. Dragging the indicator increases or decreases the value.

Note   *Most dialog boxes use* OK *to represent a yes decision and* Cancel *to represent a no decision. In dialog boxes that contain several options, clicking* OK *saves the options you have chosen, while clicking* Cancel *closes the dialog box without saving your choices.*

HANDS On

Changing WordPad Options

1. Click the View menu, and click Options.

2. Click the Options tab.

3. Change the dialog box elements and click OK.

Examining Controls in a Dialog Box

In this activity, you will change the default options in WordPad.

1. With WordPad open, click the View menu, and then click Options.

The Options dialog box appears.

2. Click the Options tab, as shown in Figure 1.12.

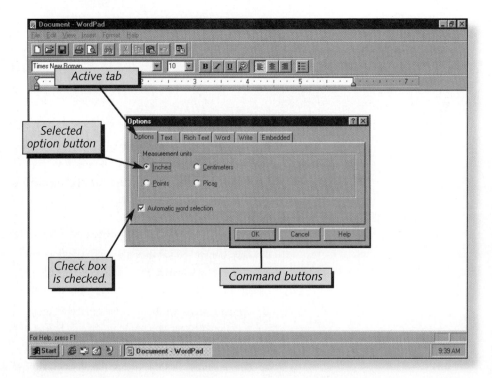

Figure 1.12 ◀
The Options dialog box

3. Click the Centimeters option button, if it is not already selected.

Notice that the black dot moves from the Inches button (or another selected button) to the Centimeters button. Remember that you can select only one option button at a time.

4. Deselect the Automatic word selection check box, if necessary.

The check mark in the box disappears, indicating that you have turned off the option.

5. Click the Cancel command button to cancel the changes and close the Options dialog box.

6. To see more dialog box features, click File and then click Print.

The Print dialog box appears.

7. Click the arrow next to the **Name list box**.

A list appears showing the names of all the printers currently installed on your system, as shown in Figure 1.13.

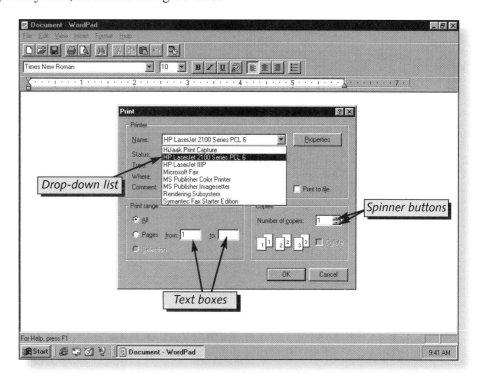

Figure 1.13 ◀
The Print dialog box

8. Click anywhere outside the list to close the list.

9. Click the **Pages option button** and type 1 in both the From and To text boxes.

This tells WordPad to print only the first page of the current document.

10. In the Number of copies box, click the up arrow of the **Number of copies box** until it changes to 5.

This tells WordPad to print five copies of the first page.

11. Click **Cancel** to cancel your changes and close the Print dialog box. Click **File** and click **Exit**.

WordPad is closed and the desktop reappears.

PRINTING YOUR WORK

Before you print from a Windows-based program, always make sure that Windows 98 and the application program you are running are set to print to the same printer. If your computer is currently connected to just one printer, someone has probably already set up that printer as the default printer. The term ***default*** applies to a printer (or folder or disk drive, for that matter) that your system automatically uses. Setting a default printer saves time by not having to specify the printer each time you want to print something. You can use a different printer any time and even change the default printer. If you are connected to more than one printer, occasionally you may need to switch between them.

HANDS ON

Windows BASICS

Setting a Default Printer

1. Click Start, Settings, Printers.

2. Right-click the desired printer and click Set as Default.

Selecting a Default Printer

To select a printer, you can use the Control Panel or the Start button ![Start] to go directly to the Printers window. In this activity, you will learn how to set a default printer using the Printers window.

1. Click the Start button ![Start]**, point to Settings, and click Printers.**

The Printers window opens, as shown in Figure 1.14. The icons in this window represent the printers that have been installed on your computer. One of the printers will have a check mark next to its icon—this is the default printer.

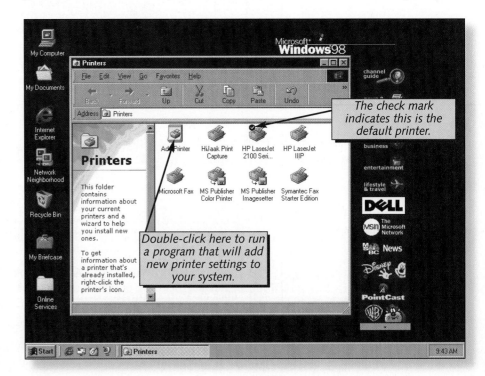

Figure 1.14
The Printers window

2. Right-click the default printer—the printer with the check mark next to the icon.

The Set as Default option has a check mark beside it. If you wanted to set another printer as the default printer, you would click this option.

3. Click anywhere outside the menu to close the shortcut menu.

4. Click the Close button ![X]**.**

GETTING HELP

Now that you know how to manipulate windows and control dialog boxes, you are ready to use the powerful *onscreen Help system* built into Windows 98. If you don't know how to do something or forget a command, you can look it up here. One of the Start menu choices is Help. This command displays the Windows Help window, as shown in Figure 1.15.

The Windows Help window is divided into two *panes*. A pane is a portion of a window. You use the left pane of the Windows Help window to locate the topic on which you want help. The right pane of the Windows Help window displays the actual information.

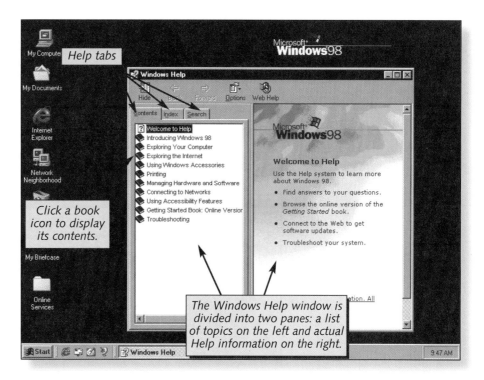

Figure 1.15
The Windows Help window

Near the top left of the Windows Help window are three tabs: Contents, Index, and Search. These tabs represent pages. The front tab is the page that is currently open, and its contents are displayed below it. In this case, the **Contents tab** is open, and you see Help topics in the window. If you click one of the topics, you either display help on that subject or a list of books contained within that book. You can click the desired book to display its contents. Sometimes, more topics are available than fit on the screen. The vertical scroll bar lets you find these topics.

Clicking the **Index tab** allows you to see an alphabetical listing of Help topics. You can get to the desired topic quickly by typing it in the text box at the top of the Index window. When you type a letter, the display scrolls to the first topic beginning with that letter. As you continue typing, you will get closer to the topic you want. You can also use the scroll bar to find the desired topic. When you've highlighted the topic you want, click the Display button to show the information on that subject.

The **Search tab** provides another way to look for information. Instead of looking for words contained within the title of the Help topic (as in the Index tab), you try to find words or phrases within the Help topics contents. Windows 98 builds a list of words in which to conduct the search. When you first use the Search feature, you see a dialog box asking how extensive to make this word list.

Figure 1.16 shows the Windows 98 Help window that appears when you select the *Start a program* topic. You can use the vertical scroll bar to scan through the Help text. You may see underlined words and phrases in the Help text. Your pointer changes to a hand pointer when you are pointing to underlined text. Some of these terms are *glossary terms.* Clicking a glossary term displays a definition of the word or phrase. Clicking other underlined words or phrases may jump to related Help screens or dialog boxes.

You can get help on items within a dialog box by right-clicking the item and selecting *What's this?*.

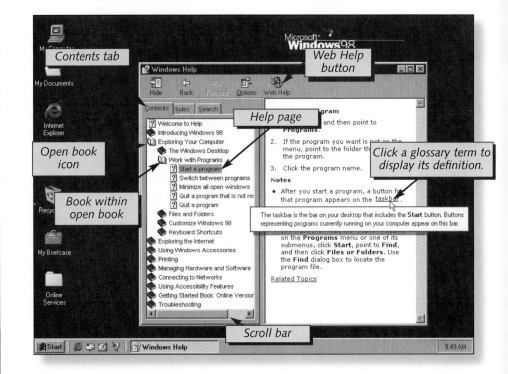

Figure 1.16
Glossary term

Windows 98 Help also provides the Web Help button ![] that connects you directly to a Microsoft Web page. There you can search for additional online information by asking specific questions.

Using Windows Help

In this activity, you will practice using the Windows 98 Help system to discover how to perform various tasks.

Using Windows Help

1. Click Start, then Help.

2. Click the tab you want to use.

3. Double-click to open book icons.

4. Type text, choose a subtopic, and click Display.

1. Click the **Start button** ![Start] and click **Help**.

The Help files load and the Windows Help window appears, as shown in Figure 1.15.

2. If necessary, click the **Contents tab** to display the list of topics.

3. Click the **Exploring Your Computer book icon**.

The books within the topic are displayed.

4. Click the **Work with Programs book icon**.

A set of Help document icons appears.

5. Click the **Start a program document icon**.

The pane on the right displays a set of numbered procedures for starting application programs, notes, and a link to related topics, as shown in Figure 1.16.

6. Click the **Index tab**.

The Windows Help set of index topics appears.

7. Type printing **in the text box.**

As you type letters, the list of Help topics scrolls down. A set of printing topics appears.

8. Click the documents subtopic and then click the Display button.

A Help window appears on the right pane with information on printing documents.

9. Click the Search tab.

The Help Search window appears.

10. Type cascade in the text box and click the List Topics button. If you receive a message that no topics are found, click OK and click List Topics again.

One topic appears in the *Select Topic to display* area.

11. Select the To display all open windows topic and click Display.

The Help document appears in the right pane with information on the selected topic, as shown in Figure 1.17.

Figure 1.17 ◄
The Windows Help Search tab

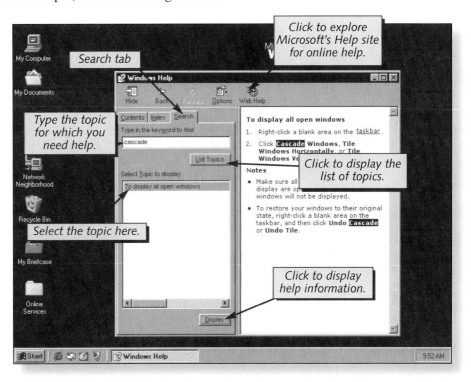

12. Click the Close button ☒.

USING WINDOWS EXPLORER

In Windows, the Programs menu is your main tool for launching programs. However, all of those programs are stored on your hard drive as files, also called **program files**. And the documents that you create using applications are also stored as files, or **document files**. Windows Explorer is the Windows 98 program you use to organize all of the files stored on your hard drive and floppy disks.

One of the primary goals of file maintenance is to keep your file structure organized, so you can find and open files easily when you need them. You can organize files by setting up *folders*—organizational structures that can contain files and subfolders. Many of the folders on your system are created during the installation of software. You can use Windows Explorer to create your own folders.

The Folders pane appears on the left side of the window. It displays the organization of the drives, folders, and subfolders available for use on your computer. A plus sign (+) in a box to the left of a folder or *drive icon* indicates that the folder or drive contains one or more subfolders. The Contents pane on the right side of the window displays the files and subfolders contained in the selected folder or drive icon in the Folders pane.

Creating a Folder and a Subfolder

In this activity, you will create a new folder on a blank disk. Make sure you have a blank, formatted disk before you start this activity.

1. Click Start [Start]**, point to Programs, and click Windows Explorer.**

The Exploring window appears on your screen.

2. If the window is not already maximized, click the Maximize button [□]**.**

Your screen looks similar to Figure 1.18. (Click the Views button to change the display until it matches Figure 1.18, if necessary.) Your list of files will be different.

Creating Folders and Subfolders

1. Click the drive and/or parent folder.

2. Click File, New, Folder.

3. Type the name of the new folder and press [Enter↵].

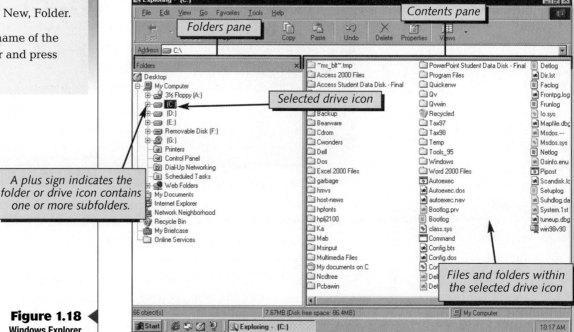

Figure 1.18 ◄
Windows Explorer

3. Insert a blank, formatted disk in the floppy drive.

4. Scroll the folders in the Folders pane and select the floppy drive icon, usually indicated as $3\frac{1}{2}$ Floppy (A:).

5. Click **File**, point to **New**, and click **Folder**.

A new folder with the name *New Folder* appears in the Contents pane.

6. Type Temporary **to replace** *New Folder,* **and then press** $\boxed{\text{Enter}\leftarrow}$.

Now you will create a folder within the ***Temporary*** folder.

7. In the Folders pane, click the **plus sign** next to the floppy drive icon.

The subfolder contained on the disk appears in the Folders pane.

8. Click the ***Temporary*** subfolder in the Folders pane.

Notice that the icon changes to an open folder to indicate that you can view the contents of the folder. However, as shown in the Contents pane, the folder is currently empty.

9. Click **File**, point to **New**, and click **Folder**.

10. Type Second Folder **to replace the** *New Folder* **name, and then press** $\boxed{\text{Enter}\leftarrow}$.

Moving and Copying Folders and Files

1. In Windows Explorer, select the file or folder to be moved.

2. Scroll the Folders pane until you can see the destination folder.

3. To move a folder or file, drag the selected item to the destination.

4. To copy a folder or file, press and hold $\boxed{\text{Ctrl}}$ and drag the selected item to the destination.

Moving and Copying Folders and Files

The tasks most frequently performed with Windows Explorer are copying and moving files or folders within a folder structure or from one disk or drive to another. You can complete these actions simply by dragging file and folder icons from one place to another in the Exploring window. Dragging a file to a different place on the same disk or drive physically moves the file. Dragging a file to a different disk or drive copies the file. In this activity, you will move a folder from one location on a disk to a new location. You will then copy a file from your hard disk drive to a disk.

1. With the disk in the floppy drive, select the ***Temporary*** folder in the Folders pane.

2. Drag the ***Second Folder*** icon in the Contents pane to the floppy drive icon in the Folders pane. When the floppy drive icon is highlighted, release the mouse button.

An information box may appear briefly while the folder is being moved. The folder named ***Second Folder*** is moved from the ***Temporary*** folder to the main folder of the floppy disk. You can see by looking in the Contents pane that the ***Temporary*** folder is now empty. The folder named ***Second Folder*** now appears in the Folders pane, on the same level as the ***Temporary*** folder.

3. Click the **plus sign** next to the C: drive icon. Scroll the Folders pane to find the Windows folder on the C: drive (or the drive where Windows 98 is installed), and double-click it. If requested in the Contents pane, click **Show Files** to display the contents of the folder.

4. Scroll past the folder icons until you see file icons. Then find and click the *Calc* file.

The file name should be highlighted.

5. Click the scroll bar if necessary to see the floppy drive icon in the Folders pane.

6. Drag the *Calc* file icon from the hard drive to the ***Temporary*** folder of the floppy drive in the Folders pane. The ***Temporary*** folder will be highlighted when the pointer is in the right place.

An information box may appear briefly while the file is being copied.

7. **To make sure the file has been copied, click the *Temporary* folder of the floppy drive in the Folders pane.**

Figure 1.19 shows the *Calc* file in the Contents pane of the *Temporary* folder.

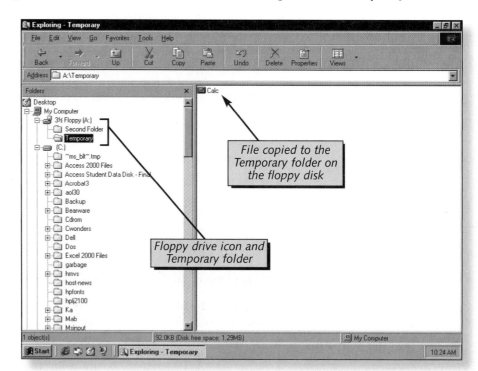

Figure 1.19 ◄
Copied file in the disk's subfolder

Renaming and Deleting Folders and Files

You can rename a file or folder at any time. Be careful, however, not to rename files or folders that you did not create—maintaining their original name may be essential to the Windows 98 operating system. When you delete files from the hard disk drive, they are temporarily stored in the Recycle Bin. You can restore the deleted file by double-clicking the Recycle Bin desktop icon. In this activity, you will rename a folder on your floppy disk to identify the files it may contain. Then you will remove files and folders that you no longer need.

1. **Click the *Second Folder* icon in the Folders pane.**

The *Second Folder* folder name is highlighted.

2. **Click within the word *Second Folder,* not on the icon itself.**

A text pointer appears within the Second Folder frame.

3. **Type Introduction Exercise and press Enter↵.**

The letters you type replace the highlighted name, and the folder has the new name.

4. **Click the *Temporary* folder on the disk and press Delete.**

A message box asks you to confirm your intention to delete the file.

5. **Click Yes or press Enter↵.**

Since this folder contains a program file, you are asked again if you want to delete it.

6. Click Yes.

The folder and the *Calc* file are removed from the floppy disk.

7. Click the *Introduction Exercise* folder, press ⌨Delete, and then click Yes.

Your disk is now blank.

Copying Data from a CD-ROM to a Disk

CD-ROMs can hold hundreds of megabytes of data. As their name implies (Compact Disc - *Read-Only* Memory), they cannot be used to modify the data they contain. Hard and floppy disks are the media generally used as personal data storage devices. To complete the lessons in this tutorial, you must copy files from your Office Data CD (in the back of this tutorial) to a Zip disk, to a folder on the hard drive, to a folder on the network drive, or to a floppy disk. You'll use these files, called the Student Data Disks, throughout the rest of this tutorial. In this activity, you will copy folders and files from the Office Data CD (in the back of this tutorial) to a Zip disk, to a folder on the hard drive, to a folder on the network drive, or to a floppy disk.

 Ask your instructor whether you should complete this hands on activity. If so, confirm exactly where you must store your Office Data CD folders and files.

If you are storing your files on a Zip disk, you'll need one Zip disk. You can copy all the Office Data CD folders and files at one time onto a Zip disk.

If you are storing your files on a hard drive or a network drive, ask your instructor for the path and folder name to use. You can copy all the Office Data CD folders and files at one time onto the hard drive or the network drive.

If you are using floppy disks, you'll need three floppy disks to copy the Excel, PowerPoint, and Word Student Disk folders each to a separate floppy disk. Because of the large folder size, you must copy the Access and the Integration Student Data Disk folders onto a Zip disk or onto the hard drive or network drive; you cannot copy these folders to a floppy disk.

Copying Data from a CD

1. Open Windows Explorer.

2. In the Folders pane, select the drive/folder of the data to copy.

3. Click Edit and click Select All.

4. Click Copy.

5. In the Folders pane, select the drive/folder where you want to store the folders/files.

6. Click Paste.

1. Insert the Office Data CD in the CD drive of your computer.

2. In the Folders pane of the Exploring window, find and select the drive icon that represents your CD drive. You may need to scroll down in the Folders pane.

3. Press ⌨Num Lock (if necessary to turn on this feature) and press * on the numeric keypad.

All subfolders on the selected drive are displayed in the Folders pane. The contents of the CD drive (the folders on the Office Data CD) will appear in the Contents pane, as shown in Figure 1.20. As you can see, five folders exist on the Office Data CD—one each for Access, Excel, PowerPoint, and Word (the four tutorials in this book) and one for the Integration lessons.

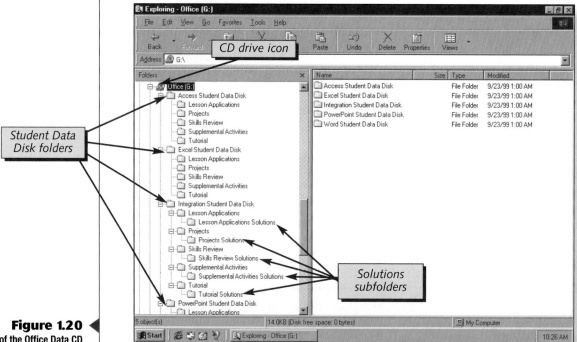

**Student Data
Disk folders**

CD drive icon

**Solutions
subfolders**

Figure 1.20 ◀
The contents of the Office Data CD

4. *If you are copying the Office Data CD folders onto a Zip disk,* you can copy all the folders at one time. Write Office Data CD on the Zip disk label and insert a blank, formatted disk into the removable disk drive. Select the **CD drive icon** if it is not already selected, then click **Edit** and click **Select All**. Proceed with step 5.

   If you are copying the Office Data CD folders onto the hard drive or the network drive, you can copy all the folders at one time. In the Folders pane, navigate to the drive and folder where you want to store the Office Data CD folders. Create a separate folder for your Office Data CD folders if necessary. (Ask your instructor if you are not sure.) Then, in the Folders pane, select the **CD drive icon**, click **Edit**, and click **Select All**. Proceed with step 5.

   If you are copying some of the Office Data CD folders to floppy disks, you can copy only the Excel, PowerPoint, and Word Student Data Disk folders each to a separate floppy disk. Because of their large folder size, you must copy the Access and Integration Student Data Disk folders onto a Zip disk or onto the hard drive or network drive. (See the previous paragraph for directions on copying folders onto the hard drive or network drive.) In the Folders pane, click the *Excel Student Data Disk* folder, click **Edit**, and click **Select All**. Write Excel Student Data Disk on the disk label and insert a blank, formatted disk into the floppy disk drive. Proceed with step 5.

5. Click **Copy** 📋 on the toolbar.

6. Scroll up, if necessary, and click the appropriate drive icon (and folder if necessary) where you want to store your files. (If you are copying the files onto a Zip disk or a floppy disk, make sure the disk is in the drive.)

7. Click **Paste** 📋 on the toolbar.

8. *If you copied the Office Data CD folders onto a Zip disk or onto the hard drive or network drive,* remove the Office Data CD from the CD drive.

   If you copied an Office Data CD folder onto a floppy disk, remove the floppy disk from the drive and repeat steps 4 through 8 to copy the PowerPoint and Word Student Data Disk folders. Consult your instructor about where to copy the Access and

WEB NOTE

You can find out ways to enhance your operating system online at Microsoft's Web site devoted to Windows 98. To learn more about the operating system, visit the Microsoft Windows 98 home page at http://www.microsoft.com /windows98.

Integration Student Data Disk folders. Then, when the copying process is complete, remove the Office Data CD from the drive.

FILE ATTRIBUTES

An *attribute* is a file or folder property that controls its use. Windows 98 files and folders can have up to four attributes: read-only, hidden, archive, and system. Hidden and system attributes are primarily used to protect those folders and files the operating system needs. The archive attribute identifies files and folders that have not been copied onto a backup, storage medium. The read-only attribute lets you view files but does not allow you to change or delete the files.

By nature of the storage medium on which they reside, CD-ROM files and folders have a read-only attribute. When you copied the files and folders from the Office Data CD in the last activity, you copied their attributes as well. To use and save changes to the files copied from the Office Data CD, you must change the attributes of the files.

HANDS On

Setting File Attributes

In this activity, you will remove the read-only attribute and add the archive attribute to the files you copied.

 Note   *Ask your instructor if you should complete this activity.*

Windows BASICS

Setting File Attributes

1. In Windows Explorer, select the file(s) or folder(s) to change.

2. Right-click a selected file or folder and click Properties.

3. Click the attribute check box to turn the attribute on or off.

1. In the Folders pane of Windows Explorer, navigate to the *Access Student Data Disk* folder and select it.

2. Click **Edit** and click **Select All**.

3. Right-click one of the selected files in the Contents pane and click **Properties** on the shortcut menu that appears.

The Properties dialog box appears.

4. On the General tab of the Properties dialog box in the Attributes area, click the **Read-only box** until the check mark disappears. Click the **Archive box** until a check mark appears in the white box.

As shown in Figure 1.21, the background of the boxes should not be shaded.

5. Click **OK**.

You have now changed the file attribute to Archive for the files in the root folder only. Each of the five folders in the *Access Student Data Disk* folder contains a file. You must also change the file attributes to Archive in these folders to be able to use the files in each folder.

6. In the Folders pane, double-click the *Access Student Data Disk* folder to display the subfolders in the Folders pane. Then click the *Lesson Applications* folder in the Folders pane. Click **Edit** and click **Select All**. Right-click one of the selected files in the Contents pane and click **Properties**. On the General tab, deselect **Read-only**, select **Archive**, and click **OK**.

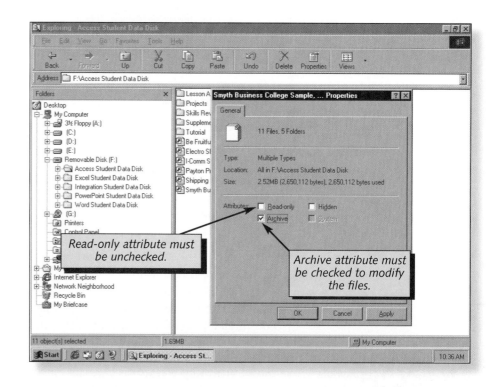

Figure 1.21
The General tab of the Properties dialog box

7. Repeat step 6 for each of these subfolders in the *Access Student Data Disk* folder: *Projects, Skills Review, Supplemental Activities,* and *Tutorial.*

All the Access files are ready to use. You can now change the file attributes for the *Integration Student Data Disk* folder.

8. In the Folders pane, double-click the *Integration Student Data Disk* folder. Then select the *Lesson Applications* folder. Click **Edit** and click **Select All**. Right-click one of the selected files in the Contents pane and click **Properties**. Deselect **Read-only**, select **Archive**, and click **OK**.

9. Change the file attributes for the files in each of the remaining subfolders in the *Integration Student Data Disk* folders: *Projects, Skills Review, Supplemental Activities,* and *Tutorial.*

You are now ready to change the file attributes for the Excel, PowerPoint, and Word Student Data Disk folders.

10. Navigate to the *Excel Student Data Disk* folder. (If you copied the *Excel Student Data Disk* folder to a floppy disk, insert the disk into the appropriate drive.)

11. Click **Edit** and click **Select All**. Right-click one of the selected files in the Contents pane and click **Properties**. On the General tab, deselect **Read-only**, select **Archive**, and click **OK**. (If you are using a floppy disk, remove the disk from the drive.)

12. Repeat steps 10 and 11 to change the file attributes of the PowerPoint and Word Student Data Disk folders. When you are finished changing all file attributes, remove the Zip disk or floppy disk from the drive, if necessary.

13. Close Windows Explorer.

All files in the Student Data Disk folders are now ready to use.

SHUTTING DOWN YOUR COMPUTER

When you are finished working with the computer, you should develop the habit of closing all open applications and using the proper procedure to shut down Windows 98. In fact, turning off the computer while applications are running is dangerous. Some of the work you have been doing may not have been saved onto disk and will be irretrievably lost. In addition, you will not have given the operating system the opportunity to erase information it may have temporarily stored on disk.

 Check with your instructor or computer lab assistant, for the "shut down" procedures in your lab or school environment.

Shutting Down

1. Click Start.

2. Click Shut Down.

3. Click Shut Down and click OK.

4. After a message appears, turn off your computer.

Shutting Down

In this activity, you will shut down the Windows 98 operating system. You will be able to start and quit Windows at any point in the lessons that follow. Instead of completing this hands on activity, you may proceed directly to the exercises for this lesson. If, however, you are finished with your computer session, shut down the computer you are using following the procedures for your lab or school environment.

1. Click Start Start.

2. Click Shut Down.

The entire screen darkens a bit, and the Shut Down Windows dialog box appears.

3. Click the Shut Down option button and click OK.

After a few moments, a message appears, informing you that you may turn off your computer.

4. Turn off the computer and the monitor.

Test your knowledge by answering the following questions. See Appendix B to check your answers.

1. Dragging a file from one folder to another folder on the same drive _____ the file.

2. The process of loading the operating system is called _____ the system.

3. Files on a CD-ROM have the _____ attribute.

4. A(n) _____ box appears when you click a menu item followed by ellipses.

5. The left side of the Windows Explorer window is the _____ pane.

ON*the*WEB

COMPUTER PRICING ONLINE

Buying a computer is a lot like buying a car. There are so many models and options from which to choose! But the choice is not just a matter of taste. Some models can meet your needs better than others. Before deciding which computer is best for you, identify the type of work for which you want to use the computer. Do you want a system for professional use, schoolwork, or home use? Do you need power or portability? Do you want a system that can expand, or will a certain set of features be enough? You must first determine the type of computer you need:

■ Personal digital assistants (PDAs) are great for managing schedules, maintaining contact lists, and taking notes on the fly.

■ If your job requires you to travel, but you still need a full-featured computer, then consider a laptop or notebook computer.

■ If you work in one place and need to perform a variety of tasks, a desktop computer is the best choice.

Several computer manufacturers have established Web sites to assist users in purchasing computer systems that precisely meet their needs. In this activity, you will use one of these Web sites to compare prices and features of high-end and budget portable and desktop computers. You must have access to the Internet and a browser to complete this activity.

1. Connect to the Internet, if you are not already connected. Ask your instructor for help, if necessary.

2. Start your Web browser by clicking the **Explorer icon** on your desktop.

 *If you are using a different browser, such as Netscape Navigator, click the icon on your desktop or click Start* **Start**, *point to Programs, and click the browser name.*

The Start Page of your Web browser appears on the screen.

3. In the Address text box, type www.dell.com and press Enter⏎.

You now must choose in which store to shop. At the Dell Web site, you can enter different stores depending on the use to which your intended computer will be put. First, you will be researching the cost and features of a computer to be used by a college student.

4. Click the **Education link**; click the **Higher Education Students, Faculty and Staff Personal Purchases link**; and click the **Desktops link**.

You will see a page of information regarding the purchase of a computer for higher education purposes.

5. Click **Choose OptiPlex**—a low cost line of desktop computers.

You will jump to a page of graphics, data, and prices on this line of computers.

6. Choose a desktop computer and click the **Customize & Price link**.

7. Click the system you want to explore.

A Web page appears that identifies the base price of this computer along with preselected options for this price. All the options are listed for the computer; you can change options as desired to customize a computer system that best meets your needs. At the same time, you can see the difference in price for any option you change.

8. Scroll down the page and notice the various options.

9. Look for Memory and click the **Memory box drop-down arrow**.

A list of memory options appears with the cost differences from the originally selected option.

10. Click a different memory option.

The new option appears in the text box.

11. Click the **Hard Drive box drop-down arrow** and click another hard drive option.

The Dell Web site offers help when you don't know which option to choose or when you just want to confirm the specifications or features of an option.

12. Scroll to the Speakers option and click the **Learn More button**.

A Web page appears that describes the features of the various speaker options.

13. Review the options, noting the one you want. Then close the window to return to the previous Web page so that you can continue choosing options for your computer system.

14. Click the **speaker option** you want.

15. Scroll to the bottom of the page. Note the price of the base computer system. Click the **Update Price button**. Then, note the difference in cost based on the options you changed.

16. Experiment with different base models, including laptops. Try to customize a computer that would meet your needs.

17. Exit your Web browser. Disconnect from the Internet, if your instructor tells you to do so.

Warning

You may proceed directly to the exercises for this lesson. If, however, you are finished with your computer session, follow the "shut down" procedures for your lab or school environment.

SUMMARY

Every computer needs an operating system. The operating system is a vital component in the computer system that includes the hardware, programs, and you. This lesson showed you how to interact with the Windows 98 operating system so that you can boot up and shut down your computer, run application software, and manage the computer's data filing system. You also learned that you can get help from Windows Help and you can click Web Help to link to the Internet for additional online help from Microsoft.

Now that you have completed this lesson, you should be able to do the following:

■ Define the components and function of the Windows 98 operating system. (Getting Started-6)

■ Turn on the computer and boot the Windows 98 operating system. (Getting Started-7)

■ Use the mouse to point, click, double-click, right-click, drag, and display objects. (Getting Started-10)

■ Identify common window elements, such as the title bar, the menu bar, drive icons, and buttons. (Getting Started-12)

■ Move and resize a window. (Getting Started-14)

■ Change the size of icons using the View menu. (Getting Started-16)

■ Use the scroll bars to bring into view contents that are out of view in a window. (Getting Started-17)

■ Launch, activate, and quit programs using the Start button and taskbar buttons. (Getting Started-18)

■ Select options from a menu bar by clicking the menu name and the option. (Getting Started-20)

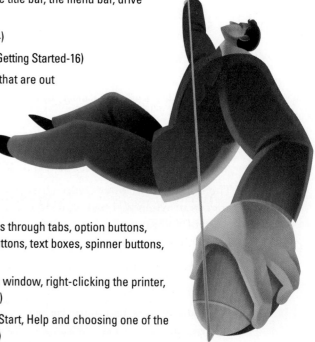

■ Identify, select, and enter data into dialog boxes through tabs, option buttons, check boxes, command buttons, drop-down buttons, text boxes, spinner buttons, and slider controls. (Getting Started-22)

■ Set your default printer by opening the Printers window, right-clicking the printer, and clicking Set as Default. (Getting Started-24)

■ Find help on any Windows 98 topic by clicking Start, Help and choosing one of the Help tabs, topics, or books. (Getting Started-26)

■ Create a folder by clicking File, New, Folder in Windows Explorer. (Getting Started-28)

■ Move or copy a folder or file by dragging within Windows Explorer. (Getting Started-29)

■ Rename or delete a folder or file by selecting the object. (Getting Started-30)

■ Copy files from a CD to a disk. (Getting Started-31)

■ Change a file's attribute(s) by right-clicking, clicking Properties, and checking the desired attributes. (Getting Started-33)

■ Shut down your computer. (Getting Started-35)

■ Search a Web site for computer-related information, comparing features and prices of various computer products. (Getting Started-36)

Lesson Summary & Exercises

CONCEPTS REVIEW

1 TRUE/FALSE

Circle T if the statement is true or F if the statement is false.

T F **1.** The Power On Self Test checks the memory, keyboard, display, and disk drives of the computer system.

T F **2.** A document window and an application window have a title bar.

T F **3.** You can never change the size of icons.

T F **4.** A Windows 98 taskbar button means that a program is active.

T F **5.** Command buttons allow you to choose an action.

T F **6.** In a dialog box that has check boxes, you can choose only one check box.

T F **7.** The classic style desktop lets you use your mouse and view your screen just as you would when you run Internet Explorer.

T F **8.** When you click a glossary term in Windows Help, a definition of the word or phrase appears.

T F **9.** You can copy files from a CD onto a hard disk and use the files without changing the file attributes.

T F **10.** The desktop is the background for your computer work.

2 MATCHING

Match each of the terms on the left with the definitions on the right.

TERMS

1. clicking
2. dialog box
3. drag-and-drop
4. active window
5. icons
6. default
7. pointing
8. taskbar
9. window
10. folder

DEFINITIONS

a. A container for files and other icons

b. Mouse action used to position the pointer in a specific location

c. Rectangular object that displays an application program, a document, and other features and that can be sized and positioned anywhere onscreen

d. Element at the bottom of the screen that contains the Start button, the clock, and a button for an open application

e. Mouse action or technique in which an object is moved from one location to another

f. The window you are currently using; the one with the colored title bar

g. Value, options, or item that is assumed if no other is specified

h. Rectangular object that displays one or more options a user can select to provide a program with the additional information necessary to carry out a command

i. Mouse action or technique in which a button is pressed (and released) once very quickly

j. Graphic pictures or onscreen objects that represent commands or programs, which carry out an operation when selected with the mouse

Lesson Summary & Exercises

3 COMPLETION

Fill in the missing word or phrase for each of the following statements.

1. For some elements onscreen in the Windows 98 environment, you can click the _____ mouse button to display a shortcut menu.

2. To help you remember and choose them, lists of commands and options appear on _____.

3. _____ appear as small images on the desktop or in windows.

4. A(n) _____ setting is one that the computer, or an applications program, uses automatically until the user specifies another.

5. To view information that exists below the last visible line at the bottom of a document window, you can use the _____.

6. Click the _____ to enlarge a window as much as possible.

7. To _____ a file or folder, select the file or folder and then type the new name.

8. _____ a file or folder's icon from one location to another to move the file or folder.

9. The _____ attribute prevents a file from being changed.

10. In Windows Help, the _____ tab displays book icons to help you find the information you need.

4 SHORT ANSWER

Write a brief answer to each of the following questions:

1. Describe the difference between the Web style desktop and the classic style desktop.

2. What is the Channel bar?

3. Identify common window elements.

4. Explain the difference among these terms: scroll bar, scroll box, and scroll arrow.

Lesson Summary & Exercises

5 IDENTIFICATION

Label each of the elements of the Windows 98 Desktop in Figure 1.22.

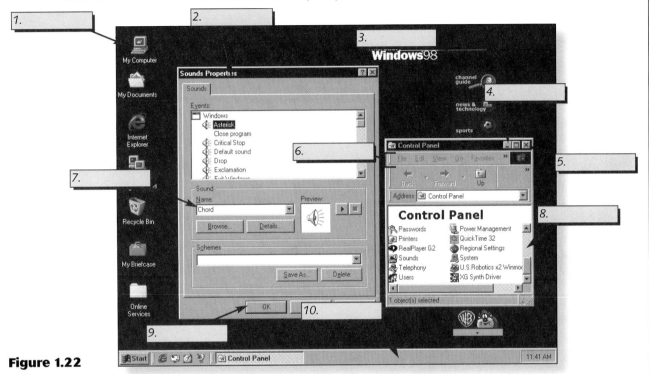

Figure 1.22

SKILLS REVIEW

Complete each of the Skills Review problems in sequential order to review your Windows 98 skills to boot the computer; master mouse skills; move and resize windows; rearrange objects within windows; scroll windows; launch, close, and switch between programs; change settings with dialog boxes and menus; set a default printer; use Windows 98 Help features; create, move, copy, rename, and delete folders; change attributes of files; and shut down your computer.

1 Boot Windows 98 and Practice Mouse Techniques

1. Turn on your computer and monitor.

2. Close the Welcome to Windows 98 window, if necessary.

3. On the Windows 98 Desktop, point to the **My Computer icon** and right-click.

4. Click **Open**.

5. Click the **Close button** ⊠.

6. Drag the My Computer icon to the middle of the desktop.

7. Double-click the **My Computer icon**.

8. Double-click the **Control Panel icon**.

9. Close the window.

10. Drag the My Computer icon back to its original location.

Lesson Summary & Exercises

2 Move and Size a Window

1. On the Windows 98 Desktop, double-click the **My Computer icon**.

2. Click the **Restore button** 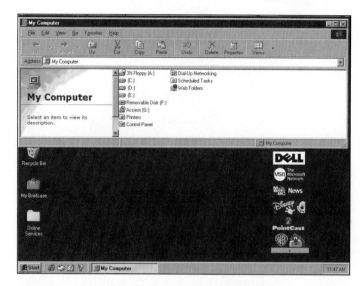.

3. Point to the My Computer window title bar. Press and hold the left mouse button and drag the window to the upper-right corner of the desktop.

4. Point to the window's borders and/or corners, press and hold the left mouse button, and drag to change the dimensions of the window. Size the window so that it occupies about half the horizontal desktop area (Figure 1.23).

5. Maximize the window. Then, restore the window.

6. Close the My Computer window.

Figure 1.23

3 Change View, Resize a Window, and Resize and Rearrange Icons

1. On the Windows 98 Desktop, open the My Computer window.

2. Double-click the **Control Panel icon**.

3. Right-click an empty area in the My Computer window.

4. Point to **View** and click **Small Icons**.

5. Right-click an empty area in the My Computer window.

6. Point to **Arrange Icons** and click **by Name**.

7. Change the **View** to **Large Icons**.

8. Rearrange the icons **by Description**.

9. Close the open windows.

4 Use Scroll Bars

1. On the Windows 98 Desktop, open the My Computer window.

2. Double-click the **Control Panel icon**.

3. Resize the Control Panel window so that both vertical and horizontal scroll bars appear.

4. Drag the horizontal scroll box to the right.

5. Click the vertical scroll arrow.

6. Close the open windows.

5 Launch, Switch Between, and Close Programs

1. Click **Start** [Start], point to **Programs**, point to **Accessories**, and click **Notepad**.

2. Click the **Maximize button** [□].

3. Click **Start** [Start], point to **Programs**, point to **Accessories**, and click **Calculator**.

4. Click the **Notepad button** on the taskbar.

5. Click the **Calculator button** on the taskbar.

6. Close the Calculator window.

7. Click the **Control menu icon** [≡] in the Notepad window. Then, click **Close**.

6 Use Menu Options and Dialog Boxes

1. Click **Start** [Start], point to **Programs**, point to **Accessories**, and click **Calculator**.

2. Click the **View menu** and click **Scientific**.

3. Click the **Close button** [X].

4. Click **Start** [Start], point to **Programs**, point to **Accessories**, and click **WordPad**.

5. Click the **View menu** and click **Options**.

6. Click the **Word tab**. Then, click the **Wrap to window option button**.

7. Verify that the Ruler check box has a check mark it in. Uncheck the other check boxes, if necessary (Figure 1.24).

8. Click the **Cancel button**; then close WordPad.

Figure 1.24

7 Select a Default Printer

1. Click **Start** [Start], point to **Settings**, and click **Printers**.

2. Right-click the printer with the check mark by its icon.

3. Click the **Set as Default option** and close the Printers window.

Lesson Summary & Exercises

8 Use Windows 98 Help

1. Click **Start** [Start] and click **Help**.
2. Click the **Contents tab**.
3. Click the **Introducing Windows 98 topic**.
4. Click the **What's New in Windows 98 subtopic**.
5. Click the **More entertaining and fun page**.
6. Read the Help information in the pane on the right.
7. Click the **Help Index tab** and type desktop in the text box.
8. Double-click the word *appearance*.
9. Read the Help information in the pane on the right.
10. Click the **Help Search tab** and type print in the text box.
11. Click **List Topics** and double-click the **Microsoft Windows Getting Started topic**.
12. Read the Help information in the pane on the right.
13. Close Windows Help.

9 Create Folders in Windows Explorer

1. Insert a blank disk into the floppy drive.
2. Click **Start** [Start], point to **Programs**, and click **Windows Explorer**.
3. Maximize the Exploring window, if necessary.
4. Scroll the Folders pane and select the floppy drive icon.
5. Click the **File menu**, point to **New**, and click **Folder**.
6. Type Memos and press [Enter◄─].
7. In the Folders pane, click the **plus sign (+)** next to the floppy drive icon.
8. Click the *Memos* folder.
9. Click the **File menu**, point to **New**, and click **Folder**.
10. Type October and press [Enter◄─].

10 Move and Copy Folders

1. With the floppy disk in the disk drive and Windows Explorer open, click the *October* folder in the Contents pane.
2. Drag the folder to the floppy drive icon.
3. Click the *Windows* folder on your C: drive.
4. Click **File**, point to **New**, and click **Folder**.
5. Type *Documents* and press [Enter◄─].
6. Drag the *Documents* folder to the floppy drive icon.
7. Delete the *Documents* folder on the C: drive in the *Windows* folder.

Lesson Summary & Exercises

11 Rename, Delete, and Change File Attributes

1. In the Exploring window, click the ***Documents*** folder on the floppy disk.

2. Click the ***Documents*** folder again and type Letters. Then press ⌷Enter⏎⌶.

3. Click the ***Memos*** folder and press ⌷Delete⌶. Click **Yes** to delete the folder.

4. Right-click the ***October*** folder and click **Properties**.

5. Click the **Read-only check box**. Then click **Cancel**.

6. Close Windows Explorer.

7. Remove the floppy disk from the computer.

12 Shut Down the Computer

1. Click **Start** ⌷Start⌶ and click **Shut Down**.

2. Click the **Shut Down option button**.

3. Click **OK**.

4. Turn off the power to your computer and monitor.

LESSON APPLICATIONS

1 Change the Date and Time

Change the time zone setting on your computer.

1. Right-click the clock on the taskbar.

2. In the Date/Time Properties dialog box, click the Time Zone tab.

3. Change the system date and the time zone setting to the (GMT-10:00) Hawaii option.

4. Verify the change to the new time setting.

5. Reset the date and time zone setting to the correct information for your location and close the Date/Time Properties dialog box.

2 Explore Windows 98 Help

Explore Windows 98 Help to find the definition of a glossary term.

1. Open Windows Help and click the Contents tab.

2. Click the Managing Hardware and Software topic and click the Tuning Up Your Computer subtopic.

3. Click the Make files open quickly Help document.

4. Read the definition of the glossary term.

5. Close Help.

Lesson Summary & Exercises

3 Use Windows Explorer

Customize the appearance of the Exploring window.

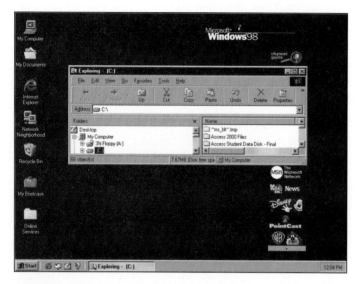

Figure 1.25

1. In Windows Explorer, modify the appearance so that the Exploring window looks similar to Figure 1.25.

2. Customize the appearance of the window to suit your preferences.

4 Work with Folders on a Disk

Create folders and subfolders on a blank disk. Then move, copy, and rename folders on the disk.

1. Create three folders on a disk: *Budgets, Expenses, Work Log*.

2. Create a subfolder named *January* within the *Budgets* folder.

3. Move the *January* subfolder in the *Budgets* folder to the *Expenses* folder.

4. Copy the *January* subfolder in the *Expenses* folder and paste to the *Work Log* folder.

5. Rename the *January* subfolder in the *Expenses* folder as *February*.

6. Delete the *January* subfolder in the *Work Log* folder.

Lesson Summary & Exercises

PROJECTS

1 Set Up a Folder Structure on a Disk

Imagine you work for an advertising company that has four clients. For each of these clients you develop brochures, radio ads, and television commercials. Using a floppy disk, create folders and subfolders that meet the following specifications:

- Create one folder within the root folder for each of your clients: *Abrams Hardware, Best Electronics, A1 Cleaners*, and *Midcity Auto*.
- Create three subfolders within each client folder: *Brochures, Radio Ads,* and *Television Commercials.*
- Change the name of the *Brochures* subfolder in the *A1 Cleaners* folder to *Newspaper Ads*.
- Remove the *Radio Ads* subfolder from the *Best Electronics* folder.

2 Explore the Web

Click the News & Technology button on the Channel bar (Figure 1.26). Click one of the channels that appear. If requested, click the Connect button to display content information from the Internet. Explore the content, but do not subscribe to and add the channel to your desktop. Point to the left of the screen to see the Channel Guide. Click the Business link, select one of the channels, and explore its contents, but again do not subscribe. Close the Channel Guide and disconnect from the Internet, if necessary. Compare the contents of the two channels you explored and report your findings to the class.

Figure 1.26

Internet Explorer 5 Basics

CONTENTS

OBJECTIVES

After you complete this lesson, you will be able to do the following:

- ■ Describe the components of Internet Explorer 5.
- ■ Start and exit the Internet Explorer 5 browser.
- ■ Identify the elements of the browser window.
- ■ Display and hide toolbars and Explorer bars.
- ■ Use the Help system.
- ■ Navigate the Web using links and toolbar buttons.
- ■ Type URLs to move to a Web page.
- ■ Print a Web page.
- ■ Add a favorite place and later return to a favorite place.
- ■ Use a search engine to find information on a topic.
- ■ Understand the use of channels and the Active Desktop.
- ■ Start and exit Outlook Express.
- ■ Send, read, and reply to mail.
- ■ Understand how Internet news is organized.

In this lesson, you will learn the basics of Microsoft Internet Explorer 5, a program designed to help you explore the variety of information on the Internet. Using Internet Explorer 5, you can surf the Web, send and receive e-mail, and create and edit Web pages. You will also explore the online Help system, which you can use to learn more about the features of Internet Explorer and to help you solve problems as you use the program.

WHAT IS INTERNET EXPLORER 5?

The Microsoft Internet Explorer 5 suite includes several programs that allow you to explore all parts of the Internet. The primary programs within the package include the Internet Explorer browser, Outlook Express, FrontPage Express, Microsoft NetMeeting, and Microsoft Chat. (This lesson focuses on only the Internet Explorer browser and Outlook Express.)

Internet Explorer Browser

The Web, unlike the other Internet services, presents information as a combination of text, pictures, sound, and animation. To view information on the Web, you need a *browser*—a tool used to navigate the Web. The Internet Explorer browser is the main program in the Internet Explorer 5 suite. The Internet Explorer browser lets you view Web pages in their visual format, search for information, set bookmarks to jump quickly to favorite pages, subscribe to Web pages and channels, download software, and much more.

Outlook Express

Outlook Express takes care of your communication needs on the Internet. Outlook Express allows you to create and send new e-mail messages, read and reply to messages from others, attach files to or download files from e-mail messages, and read and post messages to newsgroups. Although Outlook Express is automatically loaded when you install Internet Explorer, you can also use other programs to read and send e-mail and newsgroup messages.

FrontPage Express

Many individuals and companies create and publish their own Web pages. Using FrontPage Express, you can generate your own Web pages quickly and easily. Templates are available so that you can create a professional looking Web site.

Microsoft NetMeeting

If you have the right equipment, NetMeeting allows you to place and receive telephone calls to multiple users via the Internet. Not only can you hear the people you are calling but you can also see them.

Microsoft Chat

Chat rooms provide a forum for live discussions with others on the Internet. You can participate in chat rooms by viewing others' comments in standard text format or in a fun, graphical comic-strip format.

STARTING THE INTERNET EXPLORER 5 BROWSER

When you start your computer, Windows 98 will launch and you will see the desktop of your computer, as shown in Figure 2.1. If Internet Explorer is installed, you should see the icon on the desktop and on the Quick Launch bar. You may also see the Internet Explorer Channel bar.

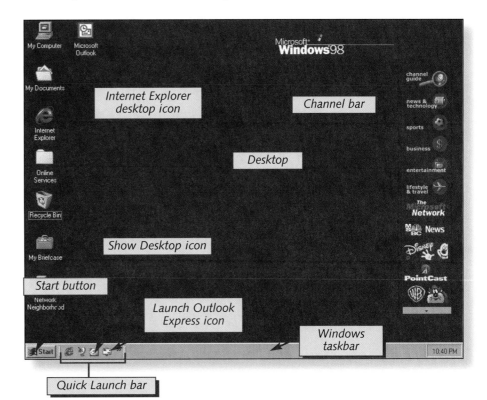

Figure 2.1
The Windows desktop

You must use Microsoft Internet Explorer 5.0 to complete the activities in this lesson. If you use a different version, the steps in the Hands On activities may still work; but you will undoubtedly see differences in the menus, toolbars, and functions as well as the figures. Access the Help menu within Explorer to determine relevant information if differences exist.

HANDS On

Launching Internet Explorer 5

In this activity, you will launch Internet Explorer 5 and connect to the Internet.

To launch the Internet Explorer browser, click the Start button, point to Programs, point to Internet Explorer, and click Personal Web Server.

1. **Double-click the Internet Explorer icon** 🄴 **on the desktop.**

2. **Depending on the Internet service provider you are using and whether you are already connected to the Internet, you may be asked if you want to connect at this time. If given the option, type a user name and password and connect to the Internet. If you receive a dialog box asking if you want to work offline, you want to work online. Ask your instructor for additional help, if necessary.**

Starting the Browser

1. Double-click the Internet Explorer icon on the desktop.

2. Connect to your Internet service provider, if necessary.

You connect to the Internet and the Internet Explorer 5 browser launches. When the browser launches, the default home page appears in your browser window. The **home page** is the Web page that your browser uses as a starting point. Although your default home page may vary from the one shown in Figure 2.2, the elements on your screen will be similar.

EXPLORING THE INTERNET EXPLORER BROWSER WINDOW

The Internet Explorer browser contains various elements that are always on the screen. You can hide or display other elements, depending on the options you select.

Title Bar

The title bar always appears at the top of the window and identifies the name of the current location. The title bar is hidden when the screen is shown in Full Screen mode.

Menu Bar

The menu bar appears directly below the title bar. Like the title bar, the menu bar is hidden in Full Screen mode. You can use the various options within the menus to issue commands. Many of the commands used most often are also available on the toolbars.

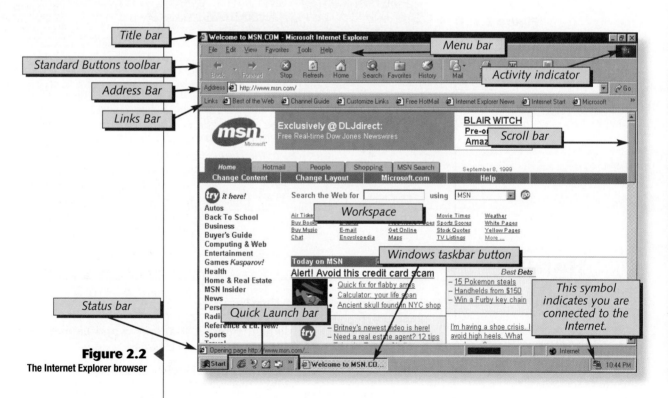

Figure 2.2
The Internet Explorer browser

Activity Indicator

The activity indicator will rotate, move, or change in appearance while a Web page is loading. Once the transaction is complete, the activity indicator is idle. Your activity indicator may use a different icon than the one shown in Figure 2.2.

Status Bar

The status bar appears at the bottom of the window. As you work on the Web, watch the status bar for reports on the progress of an action.

Quick Launch Bar

The Quick Launch bar appears within your Windows taskbar at the bottom of the screen. The Quick Launch bar provides shortcuts to access the Internet Explorer browser, Outlook Express, your desktop, and channels. The Quick Launch bar appears only if you have enabled the Active Desktop options.

Standard Buttons Toolbar

The Standard Buttons toolbar consists of several buttons that issue commonly used commands. Table 2.1 shows the buttons available on the Standard Buttons toolbar.

TABLE 2.1		THE STANDARD BUTTONS TOOLBAR
Button	**Name**	**Lets you . . .**
Back	Back	Display the last document or Web page that you retrieved during this session. Continue to press the Back button to view previously retrieved documents.
Forward	Forward	Display the next document or Web page that you retrieved during this session. You can click this button only if you have used the Back button.
Stop	Stop	Stop the downloading process of the current document or Web page. This button is useful if you change your mind about downloading a document or if the downloading process is taking too long.
Refresh	Refresh	Download a new copy of the current document or Web page. You can use this button to check for updates on the page or if you accidentally stopped the download and want to continue.
Home	Home	Display the page designated as the home page that you see when you first start Internet Explorer.
Search	Search	Display the Search Explorer bar. The Search Explorer bar appears on the left side of the window and contains options to search the Web for information.
Favorites	Favorites	Display the Favorites Explorer bar. The Favorites Explorer bar appears on the left side of the window and contains options to jump to favorite sites and documents.

TABLE 2.1		THE STANDARD BUTTONS TOOLBAR—cont.
Button	**Name**	**Lets you . . .**
	History	Display the History Explorer bar. The History Explorer bar appears on the left side of the window and contains options to jump to sites and documents that you have recently visited.
	Mail	Display a drop-down menu from which you can choose to read mail, create a new message, send a link, send a page, or read news. After you choose an option, your mail or newsreader program is launched.
	Print	Print the current Web page.
	Edit	Change the displayed page using Microsoft Word 2000 or Windows Notepad.
	Discuss	Launch the discussion groups.

Address Bar

The most common use of the Address bar is to type an address of a specific Web site. If someone has told you to visit the Web site *http://www.college net.com*, you can simply type this address in the Address bar and press Enter⏎ to go to that site. As you navigate the Web, the text in the Address bar changes to display the address of the current page.

The Address bar stores the sites that you've visited previously. You can click the Address bar drop-down list arrow to display a list of these sites. Click any of the sites in the list to go there. You can also search for Web sites using the Address bar. You can simply type a word or phrase or type find, go, or ? and then type a word that you are trying to find. Internet Explorer will use one of the search engines available and display a list of sites that contain the word.

Links Bar

The Links bar provides the quickest way to get to the Web pages you use most often. You simply click the icon of the page you want to go to, and Internet Explorer takes you there. The Links bar comes with icons to preset pages, but you can add or delete any Web pages that you wish.

Workspace

The workspace is located in the center of the window. The workspace displays the current Web page or document you are viewing. If the entire page does not fit within the window, scroll bars will appear to the right and/or bottom of the workspace so you can scroll up and down or right and left through the content of the page.

Some Web pages are broken into *frames.* Frames are panels of a page, separated by borders or scroll bars. Some framed Web pages allow you to adjust the size of each frame by dragging the border. Some framed Web pages provide scroll bars on frames so you can scroll each frame separately.

you know

When you link to your Internet service provider, you may not be connected at the optimum baud rate. If your modem is capable of a higher rate than your Internet service provider is capable of handling, you will not be able to use the full capacity of your modem.

Rearranging Toolbars

- To hide or display a toolbar, click View on the menu bar, click Toolbars, and click the name of the toolbar to hide or display.

- To change the position of a toolbar, drag the toolbar to a new location.

Displaying an Explorer Bar

Click the associated button on the Standard Buttons toolbar or click View, Explorer Bar, and an option.

Explorer Bars

Explorer bars appear on the left side of the main workspace area. The Favorites and History Explorer bars allow you to move from site to site within the bar by clicking the desired link. The Search Explorer bar allows you to access a search engine to find a word or phrase on the Web. The Folders Explorer bar allows you to access your desktop.

To display the Search, Favorites, or History Explorer bar, simply click one of the Explorer bar buttons on the Standard Buttons toolbar, or click the appropriate option from the View menu. The Search, Favorites, and History buttons display their corresponding Explorer bars. To display the Folders Explorer bar, click the Explorer Bar and Folders option on the View menu.

Displaying and Hiding Toolbars

In this activity, you will hide and display browser toolbars.

1. **Maximize the Internet Explorer browser window, if necessary.**

2. **Click View on the menu bar, point to Toolbars, and click Standard Buttons so the check mark disappears.**

 *If you don't see a check mark in front of the Standard Buttons option, click the Standard Buttons option. Then repeat step 2; this time you should see the check mark. Clicking the options on this submenu toggles between selecting and deselecting them.*

The Standard Buttons toolbar disappears from the browser window.

3. **Right-click the menu bar and click Standard Buttons.**

The Standard Buttons toolbar reappears in the window.

4. **Right-click the menu bar and verify that a check mark also appears in front of Address Bar and Links. Click anywhere to remove the submenu, if necessary.**

Displaying an Explorer Bar

In this activity, you will display and close Explorer bars.

1. **Click the Search button on the Standard Buttons toolbar.**

The Search Explorer bar appears on the left side of the window, as shown in Figure 2.3. Notice that the Search button on the toolbar is now lighter than the other buttons indicating that the Search button is active.

2. **Click the Favorites button on the Standard Buttons toolbar.**

The Search Explorer bar automatically closes and the Favorites Explorer bar displays. If you have any favorite sites stored, they will appear in the Favorites Explorer bar.

3. **Click the History button on the Standard Buttons toolbar.**

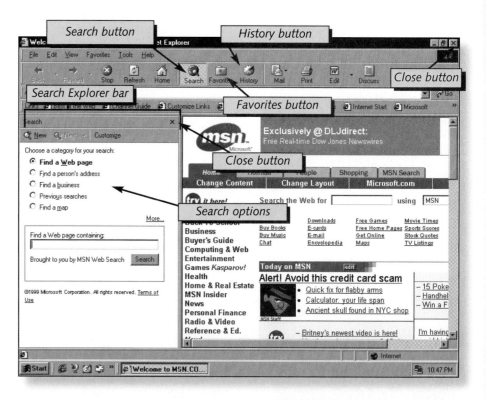

Figure 2.3
The Search Explorer bar

The History Explorer bar appears displaying the recent Web sites and pages you have visited.

4. Click the History button 🔳 **again.**

The History Explorer bar disappears and the workspace expands to the entire width of the window.

NAVIGATING THE WORLD WIDE WEB

The World Wide Web is a method for organizing the information on the Internet into a seamless system that uses links to navigate individual pages or places within pages. You can use a Web browser to transfer almost any kind of Internet resource to your own computer. Information on the World Wide Web is presented on Web pages. A **Web page** is one document that can include text and graphic images as well as sound and animation. Like a page in a book or a magazine, the layout of a Web page is limited only by the imagination of the designer. A **Web site** is a collection of related Web pages.

The Web uses hypertext to provide links between resources that may be located anywhere on the Internet. **Hypertext** is an easy-to-use method for linking related information together. Web pages may also contain text that is colored and underlined. These words or phrases are called **links** or **jumps.** When you click a link or jump, your browser may take you to another section of the same Web page, another file on the same host computer, or a file on some other computer half way around the world. Pictures can also represent links. When you point to any link or jump (whether the link is text or a picture), your pointer will change from an arrow to a hand with a pointing finger.

Your computer could catch a virus. A *virus* is a program or code created by a human that can copy itself onto files. As you save those files onto your hard drive and disks, the code copies onto other files, spreading like a virus. The virus can damage your computer, causing the computer to freeze, display error messages, or lose data.

The rules for hypertext pages are called **Hypertext Transfer Protocol (HTTP),** and the page description format used is called **Hypertext Markup Language (HTML).** As you've learned, the group of Internet resources that use hypertext is called the Web, and the tool that you use to read them is called a Web browser.

Accessing the Help System

Internet Explorer contains an online Help system to answer most questions. Some dialog boxes contain question mark icons; clicking these icons takes you to a context-sensitive Help screen. Any time you are using the Internet Explorer browser, you can access this Help system. Three methods of Help are available: Contents, Index, and Search. In this activity, you will learn about the Help system.

1. Click the **Help menu** and click **Contents and Index.**

The Internet Explorer Help window appears. You can resize and move this window as desired.

2. Click the **Contents tab** and click **Customizing Your Browser.**

The book icon next to the topic opens (Figure 2.4). A closed book icon tells you that subtopics exist. When you click the icon, the subtopics appear and the icon changes to the shape of an open book.

3. Click **Changing fonts and background colors.**

4. Read the information provided in the right pane, scrolling down as necessary.

At the bottom of this pane, you will see colored, underlined text that serve as links to other topics.

Figure 2.4
Book icons and subtopics

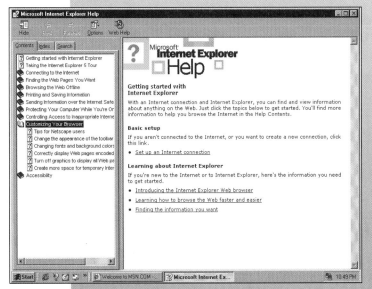

5. Click the **Index tab** and type printing in the *Type in the keyword to find* box.

Notice that as you type each letter, the highlight bar jumps to the next word beginning with that set of letters in the index listing.

6. Click the **Display button** at the bottom of the pane.

Read the text about printing a Web page in the right pane.

7. Click the **Search tab** and type offline in the keyword box and click **List Topics.**

A list of topics containing the word *offline* in the description appear in the *Select Topic to display* box.

8. Double-click the **Making pages available for offline viewing topic.**

9. Read the description of the topic in the right pane. Then close the Help window.

Navigating with Links and Buttons

- Click a link to move to the new address.

- Click the Back button to move to previous pages, one page at a time.

- Click the Forward button to move one page forward.

- Click the Stop button to cancel the downloading of a page.

After you've typed the first few letters of a URL that you've previously visited, Internet Explorer uses a feature called AutoComplete. AutoComplete tries to guess the rest of the URL so that you may not have to type the rest of the address. If AutoComplete guesses correctly, you can press Enter without typing the rest of the address.

Navigating with Links and Buttons

In this activity, you will navigate the Web by following various links and issuing commands from the Standard Buttons toolbar.

1. Slowly point to various items on your home page. As you point to various items, notice whether the pointer changes to the shape of a hand, indicating that this item is a link.

2. Click a link that appears as underlined text.

The browser moves to a new Web page (or to another part of the same page). As the transaction is taking place, you can watch the progress report in the status bar at the lower-left corner of the page.

3. Read the information on the new page. Then return to your home page by clicking the **Back button** .

Notice that the link on which you previously clicked may have changed color. This change of color differentiates the links you have used from those that you have not yet explored. Many Web pages and documents use blue text to represent links that you have not yet explored and purple text to represent links that you have explored.

4. If your home page contains any links shown as pictures, click one of them.

Again, the browser moves to the related Web page (or to another part of the same page). Notice that each time you move to a new page, the text in the Address bar changes to show the exact address of that page.

Note   *If downloading the new page seems to be taking too long or you change your mind about going to the page, click the Stop button. The transfer will stop and you can click the Back button to return to your home page.*

5. If the current page contains links, click any one of them.

6. Click the **Back button**.

The browser displays the previous page.

7. Click the **Forward button**.

The browser displays the next page. You can use the Forward and Back buttons to move between pages. The Forward button is only available after you've clicked the Back button at least once. To see updated pages, click the Refresh button.

Using URLs and Printing a Web Page

Hundreds of thousands of Web sites exist. Obviously, your home page doesn't contain links to all of these sites. One of the most direct routes to a specific site or page is to type the address in the Address bar of the browser. Every Web page has a unique *Uniform Resource Locator* or *URL*. A URL is an Internet address that is recognized by Web browsers. A URL has the following format: *protocol://domain name/path*.

Protocol identifies the kind of Internet resource. All URLs of Web pages start with HTTP (hypertext transfer protocol). (You can access other types of sites, such as FTP, telnet, and Gopher, through a Web browser by keying their types.) Both the colon (:) and the two forward slashes (//) are essential parts of every URL when the protocol is used. Older Web browsers won't recognize a URL without them. If you type a URL without a protocol in the address bar of a newer browser, such as Internet Explorer 5, the browser assumes an *http://* in front of the text. The **domain name** specifies the address of the Web site's computer. The **path** gives the exact location of a page. When you type a URL in the Address box, be careful that you type every character correctly. If any letter or punctuation mark is wrong, you won't be able to make the connection.

If you encounter information while surfing the Web that you want to print, you can produce a hard copy of any Web page or frame by clicking the Print button 🖨 on the Standard Buttons toolbar.

HANDS On

Navigating and Printing

In this activity, you will type a URL in the Address bar, navigate to that location, and print a Web page.

1. Click anywhere within the current address shown in the Address bar.

The entire address is selected.

2. Type www.glencoe.com **and press** Enter⏎.

The browser will load the Web page. Notice that the new address appears in the Address bar, as shown in Figure 2.5.

Navigating and Printing

To enter a URL:

1. Select the address in the Address bar.

2. Type the address to which you want to move and press Enter⏎.

To print a Web page:

1. Navigate to the page you want to print.

2. Click the Print button on the Standard Buttons toolbar.

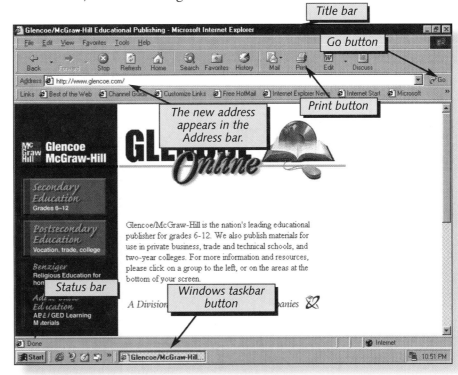

Figure 2.5
Entering a URL in the Address bar

Working with Favorites

To add a favorite:

1. Navigate to the site you want to add as a favorite place.

2. Click the Favorites menu and click Add to Favorites.

3. Click OK to accept the name and location; or, click Create In to navigate to a folder and then click OK.

To return to a favorite:

1. Click the Favorites button.

2. Click the name of the page within the Favorites Explorer bar.

Figure 2.6 ◀
The Add Favorite dialog box

---

3. Browse the site by clicking links to find information about the company.

4. Click the **Print button** 🖨 on the Standard Buttons toolbar.

The text and graphics on the current Web page will print.

RETURNING TO FAVORITE PLACES

Undoubtedly, as you explore the Web, you'll find sites that you'll want to visit again. Internet Explorer provides a convenient way to mark these sites for a quick return at any time.

Working with Favorites

In this activity, you will mark a favorite Web page, go to your home page, and then use the Favorites Explorer bar to return to the favorite page. Finally, you will delete the favorite page from the Favorites Explorer bar.

1. Type www.citynet.com in the Address bar and press `Enter←`.

The browser takes you to The CityNet site, a Web site that provides news, weather, and other information for cities throughout the United States.

2. When The CityNet page has loaded, click the **Favorites button** ⭐ and click the **Add button** 🌟Add... on the Favorites Explorer bar.

The Add Favorite dialog box appears, as shown in Figure 2.6.

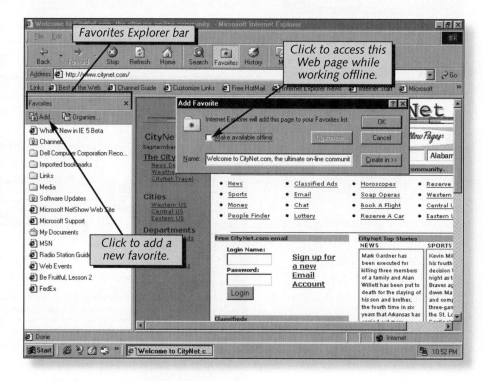

3. Click **OK** to add the page to your list of favorites.

The browser adds this Web page to your list of favorite sites, and this site appears in the Favorites Explorer bar on the left side of your workspace.

Removing Favorites

1. Click the Favorites button.

2. Right-click the name of the page within the Favorites Explorer bar.

3. Click Delete.

4. Click Yes.

Another Way

- To add a Favorite, click Favorites on the menu bar and click Add to Favorites.

- To add a Web page to your list of favorites, navigate to the page, right-click, and click Add to Favorites.

- To navigate to a Web site, type the address and click the Go button.

- To print, click File on the menu bar, click Print, and click OK in the Print dialog box.

4. Explore The CityNet site to find the names of at least two mortgage companies located in your city (or in the nearest major city). Write the names and telephone numbers of the companies on a separate sheet of paper.

5. Click the **Home button** 🏠.

6. Find and click The CityNet in the Favorites Explorer bar. If necessary, click the arrow at the bottom of the list to scroll the alphabetical listing of favorites.

The welcome page of The CityNet site reappears in the workspace.

7. Hide the Favorites Explorer bar by clicking the **Favorites button** 📁 on the Standard Buttons toolbar.

8. Explore The CityNet site to find the names of at least two restaurants where you can meet a friend in San Antonio, Texas. On a separate sheet of paper, write the names, addresses, and phone numbers of the restaurants.

9. Click the **Favorites button** 📁. Right-click The CityNet, click **Delete**, and click **Yes**.

You just removed The CityNet from the list of favorites on the computer you are using.

SEARCHING THE WEB

Internet Explorer provides several present links to sites that you can use to search for information on just about any topic imaginable or information on places, companies, people, and more. You can also customize your search settings and let Explorer do the searching for you.

Most search sites use either a subject directory method or a search engine method. A *subject directory* is a list of links to general topics arranged in alphabetical order. When you click any of the links, the links take you to a subdirectory of further links providing narrower topics. You can continue this process until you find the detailed information that you need. A *search engine* is a tool that allows you to type keywords to search for information on any topic. The result of your search displays as a list of links to Web pages. Most search engines allow you to type more than one keyword and use other symbols to narrow your search. A *keyword* is any word that you type that describes the topic for which you are searching.

When you are deciding whether to use a subject directory or search engine to find information, consider the information you already know and the number of results you want to see. For instance, if you're trying to find information on colleges located in Ohio but you don't know the names of the colleges, you might want to use a subject directory. However, if you want to find information specifically on the Denison University, you might have more success by typing these keywords into a search engine. If you want to see the most search results possible, use a search engine. Most search engines provide methods to narrow your search and thus improve the quality of your results.

Searching for Information

1. Display the Search Explorer bar.

2. Select a category for your search.

3. Type the keywords.

4. Click Search.

Searching for Information

In this activity, you will perform a search for information.

1. Click the **Search button** 🔍 on the Standard Buttons toolbar.

The Search Explorer bar appears to the left of the browser window.

2. Click the **New button** 🔍 New.

3. Select **Find a Web page**.

4. Type Mexican language schools **in the keywords box, and click Search.**

The results of your search appear in the form of links that you can click to navigate to the page described. Your search probably resulted in thousands of links, as shown in Figure 2.7. Instead of muddling through all of the links, you can type additional keywords to narrow your search.

Figure 2.7 ◀
Search results

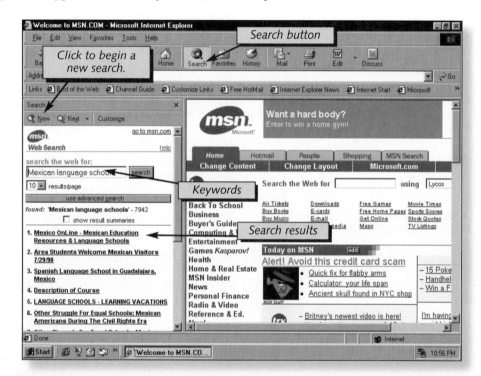

A robot or spider is an automated tool that searches for new information on the Web on a regular basis. Many search engines name their spiders. For instance, AltaVista's spider is named *Scooter* and HotBot's spider is named *Slurp*.

5. In the Search text box, type the keyword Zacatecas following *Mexican language schools* and process your search request.

By adding the keyword *Zacatecas*, your search has been narrowed to Mexican language schools located in Zacatecas. Many search engines allow you to use special symbols (such as quotation marks, a plus symbol, or a minus sign) to narrow your results even further.

6. To find out if the search engine you are using allows the use of special symbols, look for and explore a Help or an Advanced Search link that describes them.

7. From your results, click and explore one of the links that looks interesting.

USING CHANNELS AND THE ACTIVE DESKTOP

On your desktop you will likely see the Internet Explorer Channel bar on the right side of the screen. (If other program windows cover the desktop, you can minimize or close them. You may also click the Show Desktop icon on the Quick Launch bar to return quickly to the desktop.) The Internet Explorer Channel bar is a tool loaded with Internet Explorer that allows you to access channels quickly and easily. A *channel* is a Web site that is updated on a regular basis by the site's owner. You can access any of the preset channels on the Internet Explorer Channel bar by clicking them. You can also customize the Channel bar by adding and deleting existing channels. The first time you click a channel in the Internet Explorer Channel bar, you may be asked to *subscribe.* Subscribing to a Web site allows Internet Explorer to check for updated material. Unlike most other types of subscriptions, subscribing to a Web site or channel costs nothing.

Internet Explorer also offers a feature called the Active Desktop. If you currently see Web content on your desktop, the Active Desktop is already enabled and the Quick Launch bar icons appear on the Windows taskbar. After enabling the Active Desktop feature, you will be able to place information from channels that you subscribe to directly on your desktop. That means that you'll be able to view those channels not only from the Internet Explorer browser but also from your desktop. For instance, if you subscribe to a channel that provides a weather map, you can display the map directly on your desktop. Each day when you view the desktop, the map will be updated with today's weather information automatically.

USING OUTLOOK EXPRESS

Outlook Express is a program packaged with Internet Explorer that allows you to send and receive e-mail and newsgroups messages. You can start Outlook Express from the Start button or if your Active Desktop is enabled, you can click the Launch Outlook Express button on the Quick Launch bar.

E-mail is a convenient form of communication that often saves time and money. E-mail allows you to send messages at a convenient time and allows the recipients to read the messages whenever they are ready. E-mail also provides written correspondence for future reference. And, unlike mail sent through the post office, you can receive e-mail in a matter of seconds. Depending on your Internet service provider, you may be able to send messages free of charge (or send as many messages as you want for a set price).

To send an e-mail message, you must first know the address of the person to whom you want to communicate. Then, you start your mail program, choose the command to compose a new e-mail message, type the address of the recipient, type a subject (usually), and compose the text of the message. Some e-mail programs also allow you to attach a file to an e-mail message.

HANDS ON

Explorer BASICS

Using Outlook Express

To start Outlook Express:

Click Start, point to Programs, point to Internet Explorer, and click Outlook Express.

Or

Click the Launch Outlook Express button on the Quick Launch bar.

To send an e-mail message:

1. Click the New Message button.

2. Compose your message.

3. Click the Send button.

Figure 2.8 ◄
The New Message window

Launching Outlook Express and Sending an E-mail Message

In this activity, you will launch Outlook Express and create and send an e-mail message.

1. **Click the Launch Outlook Express button** 🖼️ **on the Quick Launch bar.**

Outlook Express is launched. The appearance of the main workspace in the Outlook Express area changes depending upon the option selected in the Folders list.

2. **Open the Local Folders option, if necessary, and click the Inbox folder.**

3. **Click the New Mail button** 🖼️ **on the toolbar.**

The New Message window appears, as shown in Figure 2.8.

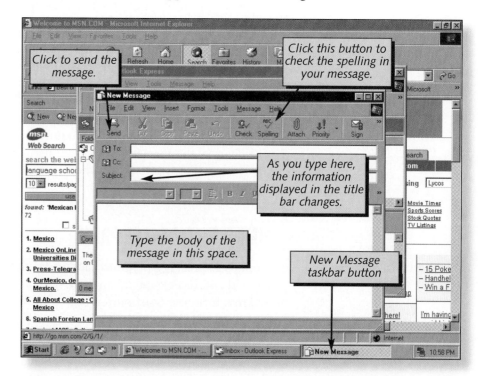

4. **Click the To box and type the full e-mail address of a fellow student or your instructor.**

5. **Press** ⎢Tab⎥ **to move the insertion point to the Cc field. If you want to send a copy of your message to another recipient, type the address in this field.**

6. **Press** ⎢Tab⎥ **again to move to the Subject field. Type** E-mail training meetings **in the Subject box and press** ⎢Tab⎥ **to move to the portion of the window where the body of the message will appear.**

The text that you typed in the Subject box appears in the title bar of the window.

7. **Type the following message as the body of your e-mail message:**

Training meetings to help you learn to use the advanced features of the Outlook Express mail program will be held next week. Please let me know by this Thursday which meeting time best fits your schedule.

Tuesday at 3 p.m.
Wednesday at 9 a.m.
Wednesday at 2 p.m.
Friday at 9 a.m.

Thank you,

(your name)

Your window should resemble the one shown in Figure 2.9.

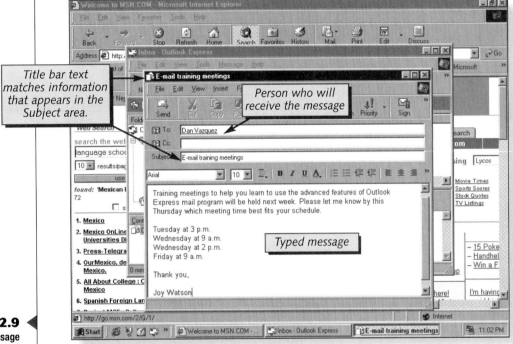

Figure 2.9
Completed e-mail message

8. **Click the Send button .**

Watch the Folders list in the left pane of the screen as your e-mail passes to the Outbox folder and then to the Sent Items folder. A number in parentheses (*1* if this is the only e-mail being sent) will appear next to the Outbox folder name. When it disappears, the message has been sent.

If you are not connected to the Internet, a dialog box may appear telling you that your message will be placed in your Outbox until you click the Send/Recv button ; click OK. A number in parentheses (*1* if this is the only e-mail in the Outbox) will appear next to the Outbox folder name. Click the Send/Recv button now to send the message. If Outlook Express asks if you want to work online and/or connect, follow the dialog boxes to do so.

Reading and Replying to an E-mail Message

To read an e-mail message:

1. Click the Inbox folder in the Folders list.

2. If necessary, click the Send/Recv button.

3. Click the message that you want to read.

4. Read the message.

To reply to an e-mail message:

1. Display the message to which you want to reply.

2. Click the Reply button on the toolbar.

3. Type the reply and click the Send button.

Reading and Replying to a Message

When somebody sends you an e-mail message, the message will appear in your Inbox. You can click the Send/Recv button [icon] to check for e-mail messages. To read a message, click the message in the Inbox folder in the Folders list. If you want to respond to a message you receive, you can use the Reply command. When you use the Reply command, the To and Subject fields are automatically filled in for you. In this activity, you will read a message and reply to it.

1. Click the **Inbox folder** in the Folders list.

A list of e-mail messages received appears in the workspace. The list displays the sender, the subject, and the date received. Information may also be displayed to indicate whether a file is attached (indicated by a paperclip icon) and the priority of the e-mail (indicated by an exclamation point). A new message displays a closed envelope icon in front of the sender's name when the message has not yet been read.

2. Click the message that you want to read.

The message appears in the bottom part of the window, similar to the one shown in Figure 2.10. The header shows the sender, recipient, and subject. If the message had never been read, the icon in front of the sender's name would change from a closed envelope to an open envelope.

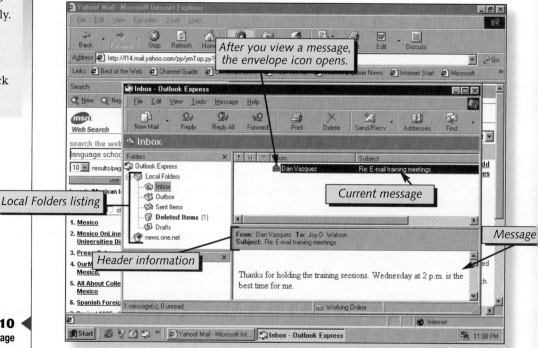

Figure 2.10
Reading an e-mail message

3. Click the Reply button ⟨ button ⟩ **on the toolbar.**

A window appears with the header already completed. The blinking insertion point appears in the message area, ready for you to type your response. As shown in Figure 2.11, the original message is displayed below the point where you will type. This message is provided for reference and to those with whom you are communicating.

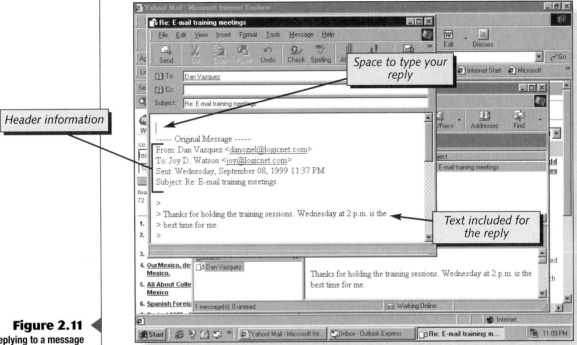

Figure 2.11
Replying to a message

4. Type the following message:

Thank you for your response, (recipient's first name). I have confirmed your spot in the class for Wednesday at 2 p.m. (or fill in another appropriate meeting time). Please provide at least 24 hours notice if you need to cancel.

(your name)

5. Click the Send button ⟨ button ⟩ **to send the reply.**

File Attachments

You can also use e-mail to send and receive files attached to e-mail messages. Attaching files to messages provides an easy way to move programs and files across the Internet to specific users. An attached file is not part of the message it accompanies, but the attached file travels through the Internet with the e-mail message. When you attach a file to an Outlook Express message, a file attachment icon appears in the message header indicating the name of the attachment.

When you receive a message with a file attached, you can simply click the file attachment icon to read it. If the file is a data file, your computer will usually choose the appropriate program to open the file.

EXPLORING INTERNET NEWS

A large and varied amount of material moves around the Internet as news. News topics range from discussions of popular television shows to announcements of new developments in every imaginable academic discipline and from requests for help repairing seventy-year-old radios to information about the latest activities in artificial intelligence. To allow people to find the discussions they want and ignore the others, Internet news is sorted into thousands of separate topics, called **newsgroups.** Some popular newsgroups might include hundreds of new messages every day, while other newsgroups devoted to more obscure subjects might handle only three or four messages a week.

With a few exceptions, newsgroups are cooperative services that do not have any formal administrators. Anybody can **post** (create and send) an **article** (also known as a message or post) that can be read by users of that newsgroup. The exceptions are **moderated newsgroups,** where all articles are screened by a person who makes sure their content is relevant to the topic of the newsgroup. To read and contribute to newsgroups on the Internet, you must use a program called a **news reader,** which obtains news articles from a computer called a **news server.** Within the universe of Internet news, tens of thousands of separate newsgroups exist. The name of each group identifies the subject under discussion and the major category in which this particular subject falls. As a general rule, the first word (or abbreviation) of a newsgroup's name is the broad general classification, and each additional word in the name is more specific. So within the major *rec* (for *recreational*) group, there could be a subgroup called *rec.food* which includes separate newsgroups devoted to recipes, restaurants, and so forth. Some of these groups are themselves broken into still smaller groups; in addition to *rec.food.drink,* there could also be separate newsgroups called *rec.food.drink.tea* and *rec.food.drink.coffee.*

EXITING MAIL AND THE BROWSER

When you finish a session on the Web, you'll usually want to close Outlook Express and Internet Explorer. Failure to close Outlook Express or Internet Explorer can lead to problems the next time you want to start the applications. Closing mail messages, Outlook Express, and Internet Explorer removes the programs from computer memory. You can close mail messages, Outlook Express, and the browser by clicking the title bar Close button or by clicking the Close command or File command on the File menu. After exiting the browser, you will see the desktop if you have no other programs running. You may then choose to disconnect from your Internet service provider.

HANDS On

Exiting Outlook Express and Internet Explorer

In this activity, you will close the Outlook Express and Internet Explorer programs.

1. Click the **Close button** ☒ on the Outlook Express window.

2. Click the **Close button** ☒ on the browser window.

3. If directed to do so by your instructor, disconnect from your Internet service provider.

Warning
You may proceed directly to the exercises for this lesson. If however, you are finished with your computer session, follow the "shut down" procedures for your lab or school environment.

Test your knowledge by answering the following questions. See Appendix B to check your answers.

T F **1.** Internet Explorer is a package of programs that allows you to explore the Internet.

T F **2.** Outlook Express is a program that you can use to send an e-mail message.

T F **3.** The Internet is only available to users of large companies.

T F **4.** The Active Desktop must be enabled to launch Internet Explorer.

T F **5.** To use the Quick Launch bar, the Active Desktop feature must be enabled.

Lesson Summary & Exercises

SUMMARY

In this lesson, you learned that Internet Explorer 5 is a package of several programs that allow you to explore all parts of the Internet. The Web browser is the main component of the Internet Explorer package. The browser lets you navigate the World Wide Web. Using the Explorer bars, you can access the Search tools, review the history of your browsing, and add sites you frequently view to a list of favorites. Additionally with Internet Explorer, you can launch Outlook Express to send and receive e-mail messages and newsgroup messages. While working with Internet Explorer, you can access the online Help system from the Help menu.

Now that you have completed this lesson, you should be able to do the following:

- Identify the primary programs that constitute the Internet Explorer 5 suite. (Getting Started-50)
- Launch the Internet Explorer browser and connect to the Internet. (Getting Started-51)
- Describe the components of the browser window. (Getting Started-52)
- Identify the buttons on the Standard Buttons toolbar. (Getting Started-53)
- Display and hide toolbars in the window. (Getting Started-55)
- Open and close the Explorer bars. (Getting Started-55)
- Access and use the online Help system. (Getting Started-57)
- Navigate the Web using links and buttons. (Getting Started-58)
- Navigate the Web using URLs. (Getting Started-59)
- Print a Web page. (Getting Started-59)
- Add a favorite. (Getting Started-60)
- Search the Web and add keywords to narrow the search. (Getting Started-62)
- Explain the Active Desktop features and how to subscribe to a channel. (Getting Started-63)
- Launch Outlook Express to send, receive, and reply to e-mail messages. (Getting Started-64)
- Send e-mail messages with attachments. (Getting Started-67)
- Explain the Internet News options. (Getting Started-68)
- Exit Outlook Express and the browser and disconnect from the Internet. (Getting Started-69)

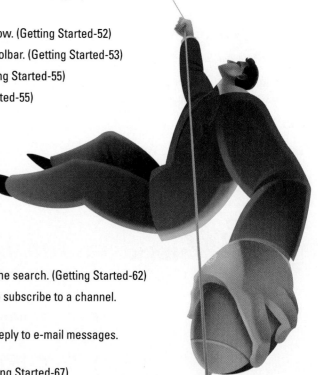

Lesson Summary & Exercises

CONCEPTS REVIEW

1 TRUE/FALSE

Circle T if the statement is true or F if the statement is false.

T F **1.** Internet Explorer 5 is only an Internet browser.

T F **2.** When the browser launches, the browser's starting point is the home page.

T F **3.** The Standard Buttons toolbar offers toolbar buttons to navigate the Web.

T F **4.** Web pages are often broken into panels of a page, called frames.

T F **5.** To open the workspace, click an option on the Standard Buttons toolbar.

T F **6.** Explorer offers an online Help system to answer most questions.

T F **7.** A Web site is a collection of related Web pages.

T F **8.** To navigate to a Web page, you can use the URL.

T F **9.** Internet Explorer 5 offers various search tools.

T F **10.** You can send and receive e-mail messages using Outlook Express.

2 MATCHING

Match each of the terms on the left with the definitions on the right.

TERMS	DEFINITIONS
1. Web page	**a.** A Web site that is updated on a regular basis by the site's owner
2. HTTP	**b.** An Internet address that is recognized by Web browsers
3. links	**c.** Any word that you type that describes the topic for which you are searching
4. URL	**d.** Create and send an article to a newsgroup
5. search engine	**e.** One document that can include text, graphic images, sound, and animation
6. subject directory	**f.** Rules for hypertext pages
7. keyword	**g.** Search tool that allows you to type keywords to search for information on any topic
8. channel	**h.** Search tool that is a list of links to general topics arranged in alphabetical order
9. newsgroups	**i.** Underlined or colored text that jumps to another section of the same document, to another file on the host computer, or to another file on a different computer
10. post	**j.** The organized news available on the Internet that allows people to find the discussions they want

Lesson Summary & Exercises

3 COMPLETION

Fill in the missing word or phrase for each of the following statements.

1. A Web site is a collection of _____ Web pages.

2. A(n) _____ is a program or code created by a human that can copy itself onto files.

3. The _____ has the format *protocol://domain name/path*.

4. When using search tools, use _____ to help narrow your search.

5. The _____ feature of Internet Explorer allows you to see Web content on your desktop.

6. Click the _____ button on the Quick Launch bar to start the mail program.

7. To create a new message, click the _____ button.

8. To send an e-mail message, you must first know the _____ of the person to whom you want to communicate.

9. In Outlook Express, the paperclip icon indicates the message has a(n) _____.

10. To display the History Explorer bar, click the History button on the _____ toolbar.

4 SHORT ANSWER

Write a brief answer to each of the following questions.

1. What is Internet Explorer?

2. How do you start the Internet Explorer browser?

3. Name four buttons on the Standard Buttons toolbar and describe their function.

4. When is the Activity Indicator idle?

5. Explain what happens when you click the Search, Favorites, or History buttons on the Standard Buttons toolbar.

6. What are three searching methods available with the online Help system?

7. What is the program that is used to send and receive e-mail messages and how do you start this program?

8. How do you create a new e-mail message?

9. What are newsgroups and who uses them?

10. How do you change the name that appears in the title bar of a new message window?

5 IDENTIFICATION

Identify each of the elements of the Internet Explorer window in Figure 2.12.

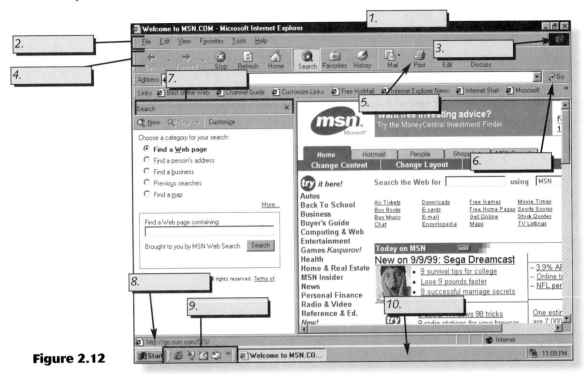

Figure 2.12

SKILLS REVIEW

Complete each of the Skills Review problems in sequential order to review your Internet Explorer skills.

1 Launch Explorer and Access Help

1. Double-click the **Internet Explorer icon** on the desktop.
2. Connect to the Internet, if your computer is not already connected.
3. Click **Help** on the menu bar and click **Contents and Index**.
4. Click the **Index tab** and type home page.
5. Double-click **changing** and read the Help information.
6. Close Help.

Lesson Summary & Exercises

2 Navigating the Web, Printing, and Adding a Favorite

1. Click a link on your home page.
2. Click the **Back button**  to return to the home page.
3. Click the **Forward button** to return to the previous page.
4. Type www.cnn.com in the Address bar and click the **Go button** .
5. Click the **Print button** to print this page.
6. Click **Favorites** on the menu bar.
7. Click **Add to Favorites** and click **OK**.

3 Searching the Web

1. Click the **Search button** .
2. Type Cincinnati in the keywords box and perform the search.
3. Narrow your search results by typing Amusement Parks in the keywords box after *Cincinnati* and perform another search.
4. Explore the search results.
5. Hide the Search Explorer bar.

4 Using Outlook Express

1. Click the **Launch Outlook Express button** in the Quick Launch bar.
2. Click the **New Mail button** .
3. Send an e-mail message to a classmate or your instructor.
4. Type Training meetings in the Subject box.
5. In the body of the e-mail message, type:

   Thank you so much for the informative training session on Outlook Express. The skills gained through this session are essential to my successful job performance.

   (your name)
6. Click the **Send button** .

5 Closing Outlook Express and Internet Explorer

1. Click the **Close button** ☒ to close Outlook Express.
2. Click the **Close button** ☒ and close the browser window.
3. Disconnect from the Internet, unless your instructor tells you to remain connected.

Lesson Summary & Exercises

LESSON APPLICATIONS

1 Use the Search Explorer Bar

Use the Search Explorer bar to explore for information.

1. Launch Internet Explorer and connect to the Internet, if necessary.
2. Click the Search button on the Standard Buttons toolbar.
3. In the keywords box, type the name of your city (or a nearby city).
4. Use advanced search features to narrow your search; include keywords such as *digital city* and *map.*
5. Explore the search results. Create and print a map from your home to the school you are attending.

2 Send an E-mail Message

Use Outlook Express to send an e-mail message.

1. Open Outlook Express.
2. Click the New Mail button.
3. Create an e-mail message to your instructor.
4. Type the answers to the Short-Answer questions in this lesson in the form of an e-mail.
5. Add an appropriate subject and send the e-mail.

PROJECTS

1 Starting Your Language School

Assume that you are thinking about starting a summer language program in Mexico to teach Spanish to English-speaking students. You want to research the competition and also find information on teaching methods. Use Internet Explorer and the Search button to discover information on the competition (specifically in Zacatecas if you desire to narrow your search) and to also learn about the teaching methods. Narrow your search as much as you desire, using search tips for the search engine you are using. Explore the search results to find a useful site and to determine the city or state name of at least one language school. Print a Web page.

Lesson Summary & Exercises

2 Searching for Cultural Information

Assume that with your summer language program (discussed in Project 1), you also want to provide cultural activities for the students. Using the Search tools on the Internet, discover the cultural activities available in the city or state of at least one school (see Project 1 for the information you recorded). Also, search for cultural or entertainment activities in this city/state. Record this information on a separate sheet of paper.

3 Searching for Exchange Rates

Use a search engine of your choice to find a Web page that computes currency exchange rates. Assume that a potential student for your language school is considering whether to travel from the United States to Mexico or to Spain to learn Spanish. Use the Web site to convert $250 (U.S. dollars) to the currency in Mexico and in Spain.

4 Sending and Receiving E-mails

Choose a classmate as a partner for this project. Assume that one of you is the individual who wants to create a summer language program (discussed in Project 1) and the other is a prospective student. The prospective student should create a brief e-mail message (addressing it to the other student) expressing an interest in attending a language experience program to learn Spanish. Request information on the costs, the types of available programs, and the dates. Be sure to include appropriate information in the header and clearly state your request in the body of the e-mail (Figure 2.13). After you send the e-mail, check the Sent Items folder to verify the e-mail has been sent.

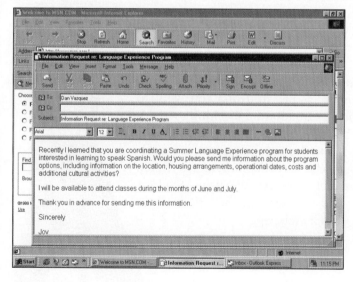

Figure 2.13

The second student (acting as the individual who wants to create the program) should reply with an appropriate response, answering the questions and providing the pertinent information in the header and body of the message.

Exchange additional e-mails in which the first student registers for the program and requests information be sent to additional classmates and the second student verifies the registration, calculates the fees, provides confirmation information, and sends e-mails to the others who are interested.

5 Testing the Students

As the plans for the language school continue to develop, you realize that you need to have a method to test the level of each entering student. Search the Web for possible methods of testing Spanish language skills and for Web sites that are in Spanish. After locating two Web sites, create and send an e-mail to your instructor listing the two sites that have content in the Spanish language.

6 Adding Favorites

While researching information to create your own language school, you remember that to travel to another country often requires permission. Search the Web to locate the information required for citizens of the United States to travel to another country. Also, search for any travel advisories that might be posted about U.S. citizens traveling to foreign countries, specifically Mexico. Since this information is subject to change often and you would need to verify travel advisories frequently, add this site to your list of favorites. Go to your home page and then return to this favorite site.

Introducing Office 2000

CONTENTS

_Office Applications

_Starting an Office Program

_Manipulating the Office Shortcut Bar

_Opening a File with the Office Shortcut Bar

_Creating a New File with the Office Shortcut Bar

_Getting Help with Office 2000

OBJECTIVES

After you complete this lesson, you will be able to do the following:

- Explain the value of each Office application.
- Explain the advantage of applications that look and act similarly.
- Move and hide the Office Shortcut Bar.
- Use the Office Shortcut Bar to open an existing document.
- Customize the Shortcut Bar.
- Use the Office Shortcut Bar to create a new document.
- Get help from Office 2000's ScreenTips, Office Assistant, Answer Wizard, Contents, and Index.

Office 2000 is a suite or collection of several major applications. Microsoft has designed each of these applications to work much the same way—they even share some of the same toolbar buttons and functions. Because of these similarities, when you are familiar with one Office application, you can learn a new application more quickly. Another advantage of Office is that, in most cases, you can share information stored in one application with another application. This means not only that less time is spent retyping information but also that a document can be enhanced with features from another application.

OFFICE APPLICATIONS

The Microsoft Office 2000 Professional Edition suite includes these major applications: Word, Excel, Access, PowerPoint, and Outlook. Each application focuses on one aspect of computer processing; however, all five applications are interactive and work together sharing files. For example, you can include a chart created in Excel (the worksheet program) in a letter created in Word (the word processing program). An Office tool called Microsoft Office Binder 2000 allows you to organize documents created in the different applications by grouping them together. In addition to the major applications, Office 2000 Professional Edition includes Internet Explorer (browser software used to view Web pages over the Internet), Small Business Tools (four programs designed to improve customer communication, streamline daily tasks, and make better business decisions), and Microsoft Publisher (desktop publishing software used to create newsletters, brochures, Web pages, and more).

Microsoft Word

Microsoft Word is a popular word processing program that enables you to create a full range of business and personal correspondence. Using Word, you can also create more complex documents, such as invoices, flyers, newsletters, and Web pages. Word extends the boundaries of word processing with its ability to add graphics, charts, colors, and tables. Other Word features include step-by-step mail merge, spelling and grammar checking, simplified table creation, and Wizards—automated assistants that lead you through more complicated document-creation tasks. Figure 3.1 shows a letter as it appears in Word.

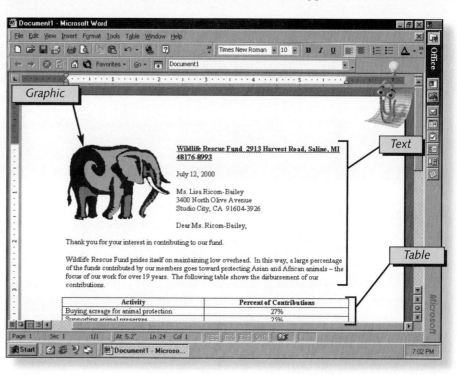

Figure 3.1 ◀
A letter displayed in Word

Microsoft Excel

Microsoft Excel offers tools to enter, analyze, report, and graph data. A worksheet resembles an accountant's ledger with information arranged in rows and columns. When you create a chart or graph, the Excel Chart Wizard guides you step by step, while you maintain control over the look of the completed chart. Its AutoFill and Repeat functions save you keystrokes when entering information. Excel's formatting capabilities allow a range of fonts, styles, and colors, as well as borders and shading. Figure 3.2 shows a worksheet and chart as they appear in Excel.

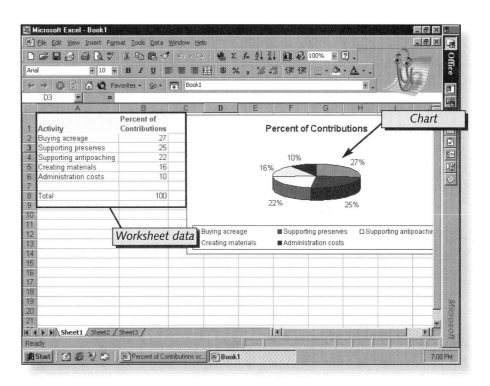

Figure 3.2
A worksheet and chart
displayed in Excel

Microsoft Access

Microsoft Access 2000 is a powerful—but understandable—database application. A database is simply an organized collection of related information arranged in tables and other associated objects. Access incorporates a number of wizards to simplify common database tasks, such as the creation of customized reports and data entry forms. Access enables you to maintain great amounts of information, retrieve that information quickly, and share it with the other Office applications. Figure 3.3 shows a report created in Access.

Microsoft PowerPoint

Used to create presentations or slides, Microsoft PowerPoint combines ease-of-use with an array of graphics and text formatting options. This presentation program incorporates many of Word's text formatting abilities. You can use charts, clip art, organization charts, and bullets to create a brief slide show or an extensive presentation that uses cutting-edge computer graphics.

You can use one of many Office programs—including Word, Excel, PowerPoint, and Access—to create a Web page. You can view any Web page that you create using an Office program in your Web browser.

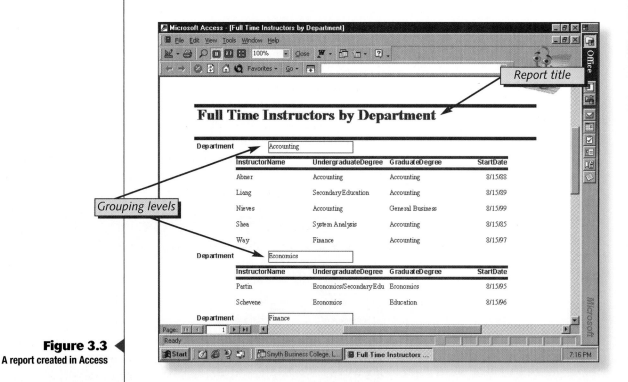

Figure 3.3
A report created in Access

One of PowerPoint's special features, called the ***Pack and Go Wizard,*** helps package presentations onto a disk to take on the road. Figure 3.4 shows a presentation slide as displayed in PowerPoint.

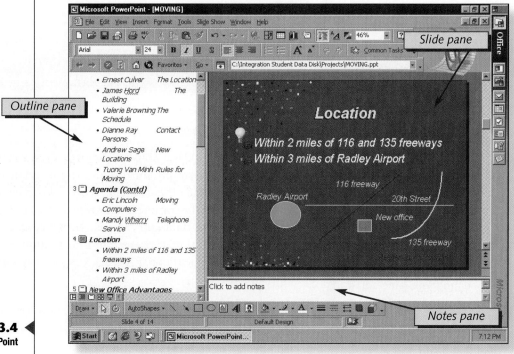

Figure 3.4
A slide displayed in PowerPoint

Microsoft Outlook

Office includes a time-management tool called Microsoft Outlook with which you can keep track of appointments, meetings, tasks, messages, contacts, and events.

Microsoft Office Binder

The Microsoft Office Binder acts like a giant paper clip that keeps together different types of documents relating to the same project. Using Binder, you can work on a document using all of the features of the applications without removing the document from the binder. For example, you can create a binder that includes a report created in Word, a financial statement created in Excel, a list of customers created in Access, and presentation material created in PowerPoint.

STARTING AN OFFICE PROGRAM

As you learned in *Lesson 1: Windows 98 Basics*, you can start a program by clicking the Start button, pointing to Programs, and clicking the program that you want to open. When you install Office 2000, the various Office programs, such as Excel and PowerPoint, are added to the Programs menu so that you can use the Start button to launch them.

Launching and Moving Between Two Programs

In this activity, you will practice opening a few of the Office 2000 applications, switching between them, and closing them.

1. Click the **Start button** and point to **Programs**.

The Programs submenu appears, as shown in Figure 3.5. Notice the Microsoft programs available on your menu. You may need to scroll through the Programs menu to see all of the available programs. Scroll by resting your pointer on the arrow at the top or bottom of the menu.

2. Click **Microsoft Word**. If a Welcome message from the Office Assistant appears, click **OK**.

Word is launched and a blank word processing document appears on the screen.

3. Click the **Start button** again, point to **Programs**, and click **Microsoft Excel**.

Excel is launched and a window containing a new worksheet covers the Word window.

Figure 3.5
The Office applications

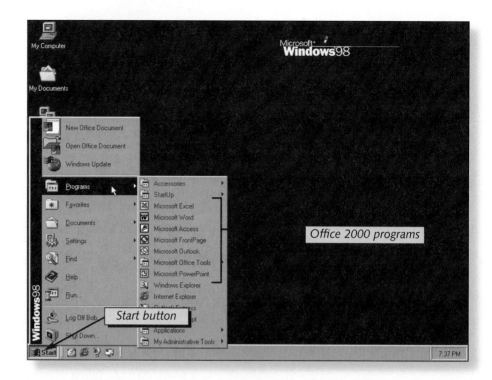

Office 2000 programs

Start button

4. Click the Document 1 - Microsoft Word taskbar button.

The Word window reappears, as shown in Figure 3.6. Remember that you can switch between programs by clicking their taskbar buttons.

Figure 3.6
Switching between programs
by using taskbar buttons

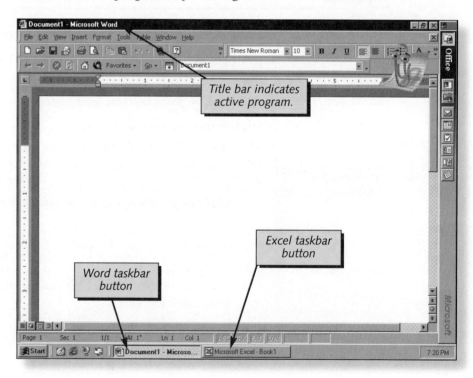

Title bar indicates active program.

Excel taskbar button

Word taskbar button

Another Way

- If your keyboard has a Start key (with a Windows symbol), press it to view the Start menu, use the arrow keys on the keyboard to make a selection, and press `Enter ←` to activate your selection.

- To switch among programs, press `Alt` + `Tab`.

- To close a program, click Exit on the File menu.

5. Click the Close button ☒ **on the Word window to exit the program.**

6. Click the Close button ☒ **on the Excel window to exit the program.**

MANIPULATING THE OFFICE SHORTCUT BAR

Office provides an even easier way to start its programs—the Office Shortcut Bar. After the Office Shortcut Bar is installed, it automatically appears each time you start Windows. At times, however, you'll want to move the Shortcut Bar to display it in a convenient location, to hide it so that it appears only when you are ready to use it, or to completely remove it from the screen for a while.

The Office Shortcut Bar must be installed in order to complete the remainder of this lesson. It is not installed during a typical installation unless you are upgrading from an Office 97 installation that used it. To install the Office Shortcut Bar, click the Start button, point to Programs, point to Microsoft Office Tools, and click Microsoft Office Shortcut Bar. If you get a message that tells you that the feature is on your CD, insert the Office 2000 CD and click OK. (If inserting the CD opens the Microsoft Office 2000 Maintenance Mode dialog box, close it.) In the Microsoft Office Shortcut Bar dialog box, click Yes to configure the Shortcut Bar to start each time Windows is loaded; the Shortcut Bar should appear on your screen.

Moving and Hiding the Shortcut Bar

In this activity, you will move the Shortcut Bar to different locations on the screen, docking it to the side of the screen and allowing it to float in the center of the screen. You'll also learn to minimize the Shortcut Bar so that it appears as a taskbar button as well as hide the Shortcut Bar so that it appears only when you need it.

1. Find the Office Shortcut Bar on your desktop. It usually appears on the right side of the screen, as shown in Figure 3.7. If it appears in a different position, drag its title bar off the right side of your screen.

2. Click the **title bar** of the Shortcut Bar (the space beside the Control menu icon) and drag the bar to the center of the screen.

The buttons now appear in a floating window.

3. Click the **title bar** on the Shortcut Bar again and drag it off the top edge of the screen. When the window's outline changes to a long, narrow rectangle, release the mouse button.

The Shortcut Bar is now docked, or attached, to the top edge of the screen.

4. Drag the Shortcut Bar back to its floating position.

5. Double-click the Shortcut Bar's **title bar**.

The Shortcut Bar moves back to the docked position. Double-clicking the title bar toggles the Shortcut Bar between its floating and docked positions.

Figure 3.7
The Office Shortcut Bar

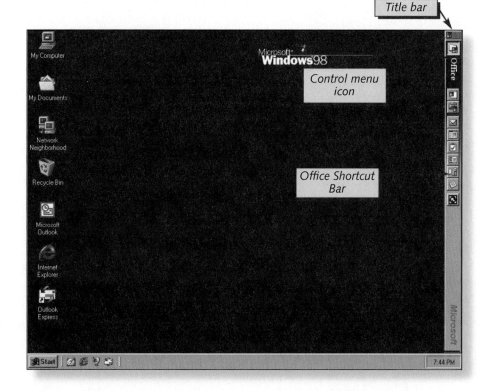

Manipulating the Office Shortcut Bar

- To dock the Shortcut Bar to any side of the screen, drag its title bar to the desired side. When its outline changes to the shape of a long rectangle, release the mouse button.

- To float the Shortcut Bar in the middle of the screen, drag its title bar to the desired location in the middle of the screen.

- To minimize the Shortcut Bar, click its Control menu icon and click Minimize.

- To hide the Shortcut Bar, click its Control menu icon and click Auto Hide.

6. Click the **Control menu icon** and click **Minimize** on the menu that appears.

The Shortcut Bar is minimized to a taskbar button.

7. Click the **Microsoft Office Shortcut Bar button** on the Windows taskbar.

The Shortcut Bar returns to its docked position. Minimizing the Shortcut Bar works well if you don't plan to use it often. Other times, you'll want to use the Shortcut Bar frequently but hide it while you're not using it.

8. Drag the Shortcut Bar to the right side of the screen so that it is docked there.

9. Click the **Control menu icon** and click **Auto Hide** on the menu.

10. Click away from the Shortcut Bar, anywhere on the desktop.

The Shortcut Bar disappears. A thin, vertical line representing its edge remains on the right edge of the screen, as shown in Figure 3.8.

11. Point to the right side of the screen.

The Shortcut Bar returns to view. Moving the mouse pointer back and forth horizontally on the screen will make the Shortcut Bar disappear and reappear.

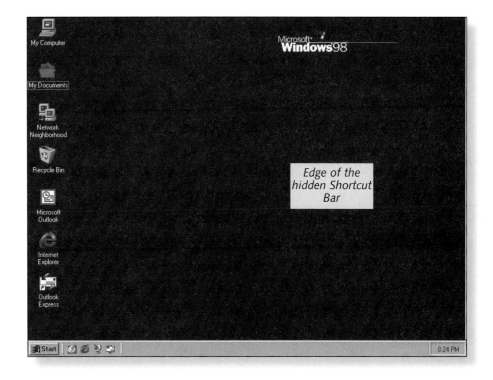

Edge of the
hidden Shortcut
Bar

Figure 3.8
Hiding the Shortcut Bar

OPENING A FILE WITH THE OFFICE SHORTCUT BAR

Now that you know how to manipulate the Office Shortcut Bar, you need to
learn how to use some of its buttons. Many of the buttons in the middle of
the toolbar take you directly to several functions of Microsoft Outlook, a
program you'll use later in this tutorial. You can use the first two buttons,
however, with any of the other Office programs. They allow you to create a
new Office document or open an existing one. You can also find these
options on your Start menu.

Opening a File

In this activity, you'll learn how to open an existing document using the
Shortcut Bar. You'll need to access the Integration Student Data Disk that
you created from the Office Data CD (in the back of this tutorial) to complete this section. If you have not yet copied the folders on the Office Data
CD, see pages 31-34 of *Lesson 1: Windows 98 Basics* for the instructions.

   1. Point to the right side of the screen so that the Office Shortcut Bar appears.

   2. Click the Open Office Document button  on the Shortcut Bar.

You see the Open Office Document dialog box, as shown in Figure 3.9. The
dialog box contains a list of all of the folders and files found on the drive last
accessed. (Your list will be different.) You need to change to the *Tutorial*
folder on your Integration Student Data Disk.

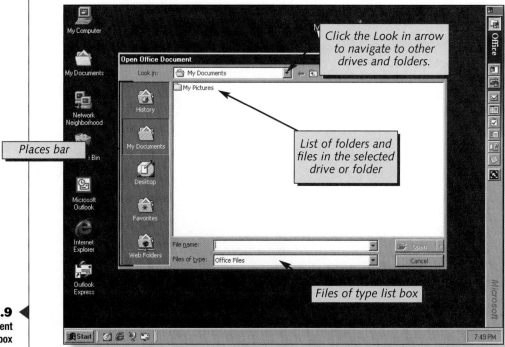

Click the Look in arrow to navigate to other drives and folders.

List of folders and files in the selected drive or folder

Places bar

Files of type list box

Figure 3.9
The Open Office Document
dialog box

3. Click the Look in drop-down arrow.

A list of drives appears.

4. Navigate to the drive and folder where you stored your Integration Student Data Disk and open the *Tutorial* folder.

Note

If you stored the Integration Student Data Disk on a Zip disk, *insert the disk in the removable drive. Click the letter that represents your removable drive and then double-click the **Tutorial** folder.*

If you stored the Integration Student Data Disk on your hard drive or a network drive, *click the letter that represents your hard drive or network drive, navigate to the Integration Student Data Disk, and then double-click the **Tutorial** folder.*

If you stored the Integration Student Data Disk in the My Documents or Favorites folder on your hard drive, *click the appropriate button in the Places bar, navigate to the Integration Student Data Disk, and double-click the **Tutorial** folder.*

The selected *Tutorial* folder appears in the Look in list box, and the names of the folders and Office files in that folder appear in the Open dialog box. You can now limit the files to display only one type of file. Notice that the Files of type list box shows Office Files and the icons next to the file names indicate the file type.

Opening a File

1. Display the Office Shortcut Bar and click the Open Office Document button.

2. Click the Look in drop-down arrow and click the drive and/or folder in which the file is located.

3. If you wish to limit the files shown, click the Files of type drop-down arrow and click the desired type of file.

4. Click the name of the file you wish to open and click Open.

Figure 3.10 ◀
Selecting a file

5. Click the **Files of type drop-down arrow** and click **Workbooks**.

Workbooks include all Excel files. The Open Office Document dialog box now shows names of the Excel files in your *Tutorial* folder.

6. Click the *Pricing* workbook name to select it.

Your Open Office Document dialog box should resemble the one in Figure 3.10.

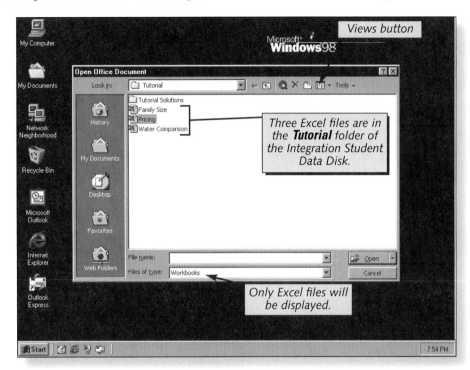

7. Click the **Open button**.

Excel is launched and the highlighted file is opened.

8. Click the **Close button** ☒ on the Excel window.

The workbook and Excel close.

The Open feature is capable of sophisticated searches for files. Using the Find option under the Tools button, you can search for a file based on its type, name, date of last modification, and text contained in it, size, and more. You can also use the Open Office Document dialog box to perform other tasks such as deleting a file, printing a file, and searching the Web. The same Open feature is available for Access, PowerPoint, and Word files.

CREATING A NEW FILE WITH THE OFFICE SHORTCUT BAR

At times, you'll work with existing documents. Other times, you'll want to create your own documents. Using the Shortcut Bar, you can quickly create a new Word document, Excel workbook, Access database, PowerPoint presentation, blank Binder, Web page, or Publisher document.

Creating a New File

1. Display the Office Shortcut Bar and click the New Office Document button.

2. Click the General tab.

3. Click the icon that represents the type of file you wish to create and click OK.

Creating a New Word Document

In this activity, you will use the New Office Document button 🖻 on the Shortcut Bar to create a new word processing document.

1. If the Office Shortcut Bar does not appear, point to the right of the screen so that it is displayed.

2. Right-click a blank background area of the Shortcut Bar and click **Auto Hide** on the menu to deselect it.

The Shortcut Bar will now remain on your screen while you work.

3. Click the **New Office Document button** 🖻 on the Shortcut Bar.

The New Office Document dialog box appears, as shown in Figure 3.11. Depending on the setup and installation of Office 2000, the tabs in your New Office Document dialog box may vary from the ones shown.

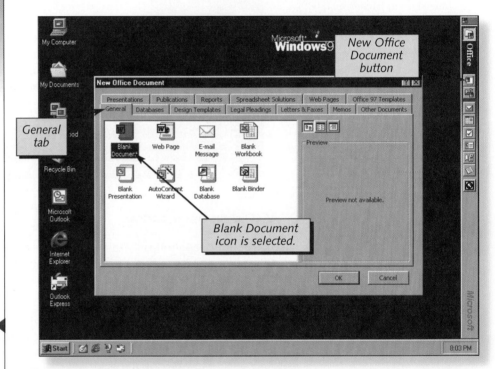

Figure 3.11
The New Office Document dialog box

4. If it is not already selected, click the **General tab**.

The other tabs contain templates, or preformatted files, which you will learn about in the individual tutorials in this book.

5. Click the **Blank Document icon** so that it is selected and then click **OK**.

Word is launched and a new, blank word processing document appears.

6. Click the **Close button** ☒ on the Word window to close the document and exit Word.

GETTING HELP WITH OFFICE 2000

While you are using any of the Office 2000 applications, you may need to reference Help for that application. Office 2000 provides an extensive online Help system—an electronic manual that you can open with the press of a key or the click of a mouse. Office 2000 provides several different Help tools: the Office Assistant, the Contents tab, the Index tab, and a tool called the Answer Wizard.

While using the Office 2000 Help system, you may find links to other topics in the form of hypertext within a Help window. Hypertext is blue, underlined text; when you point to it, the pointer changes to the shape of a hand. Click the hypertext to jump to a new Help window. After you click hypertext, its color changes from blue to purple. Another name for hypertext is *hyperlink,* because the special text links one Help frame to another. Pictures, graphic elements, and objects may also contain hyperlinks.

Within a Help window, you may also see words that appear in blue with no underlining. These words are glossary terms and are also hypertext. When you point to a glossary term, the pointer changes to the shape of a hand. Click a glossary term to display its definition. After you have accessed a glossary term, its color also changes from blue to purple. Click anywhere on the screen to cancel a glossary term and return to the Help window.

Using ScreenTips and the Office Assistant

You can access most of the Office 2000 Help tools through the *Office Assistant,* an animated character that can answer specific questions, offer tips, and provide help for features of the Office 2000 applications—sometimes even before you ask. In addition, you can access ScreenTips—helpful text boxes that provide information on various Office 2000 elements—through the Help menu. You can activate the Office Assistant in each Office 2000 application by clicking the animated character on your screen, by clicking the Help button 🔲, or by clicking the Help command on the Help menu.

Using ScreenTips and Asking the Office Assistant for Help

In this activity, you will explore Microsoft Word Help, using ScreenTips and asking the Office Assistant for help.

1. Right-click a blank background area of the Shortcut Bar and click **Auto Hide** on the menu to select it. Then click anywhere on the screen to hide the Shortcut Bar.

2. Click the **Open Office Document button** 🔲 on the Shortcut Bar. Navigate to the drive and folder where you stored your Integration Student Data Disk and open the *Tutorial* folder.

3. Click **Long Document** and click the **Open button**.

Word is launched and the highlighted file is opened.

Using ScreenTips and Office Assistant

To use ScreenTips:

1. Click *What's This?* on the Help menu.

2. Click the screen element you wish to identify.

To use the Office Assistant:

1. Click the Office Assistant.

2. Type a search topic in the *What would you like to do?* box.

3. Click the Search button.

4. Click the option that best describes the help you wish to obtain.

5. Read the text in the Help window.

Figure 3.12 ◀
A ScreenTip

You can turn off the Office Assistant when you likely will not need help. On the Help menu, click the Hide command and the Office Assistant will disappear. Click the Show command on the Help menu to return the Assistant to your screen.

4. Click the **Help menu** and click **What's This?**.

The pointer changes to include a question mark next to the arrow.

5. Click the **Print Preview button** 🔲 on the Standard toolbar.

As shown in Figure 3.12, the name and description of the Print Preview button appears.

6. Click anywhere on the screen to remove the ScreenTip. If time permits, use *What's This?* to explore other elements of the Word window.

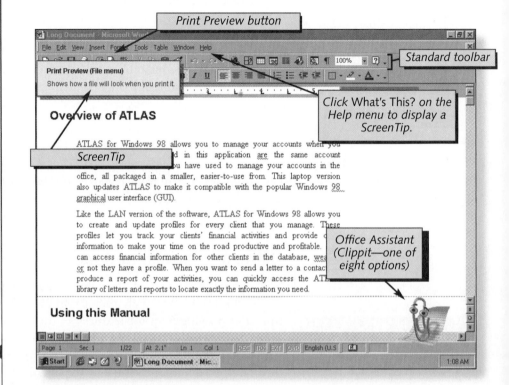

7. Click the **Office Assistant**.

If the Office Assistant is not displayed on your screen, click the Microsoft Word Help button 🔲 on the Standard toolbar. The Office Assistant asks what you would like to do.

8. In the *What would you like to do?* box, type scroll, as shown in Figure 3.13. Then, click the **Search button**.

9. Click the **Scroll through a document option**.

A Help window appears—either a full screen or a narrow screen on the left or right of the retracted document window.

10. On the Help window, point to the options.

As you point, the pointer takes the shape of a hand because this text is hypertext. When you click the hypertext, you will jump to another Help frame.

11. Click the **Scroll through a document by using the mouse hypertext**.

A Help window appears, as shown in Figure 3.14.

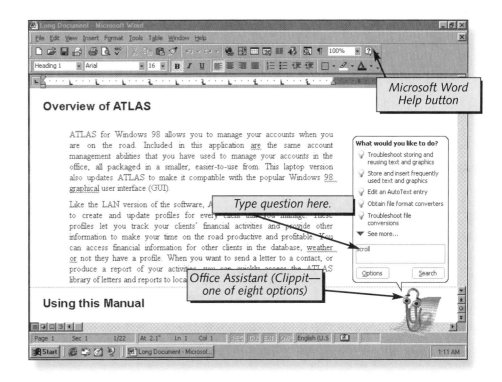

Note — *If you accidentally clicked a different link, you can go back and choose again: Click the Back button* ⬅ *at the top of the Help window.*

12. On the Help window vertical scroll bar, click the **down arrow**; then click the **scroll box** and drag it to the bottom.

13. Click the **up scroll arrow**; then click the **scroll box** and drag it to the top.

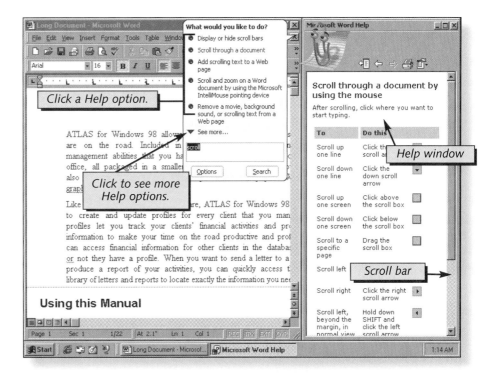

HANDS On

Using the Answer Wizard, Contents, and Index

You can use the Office Assistant at any time to obtain help with each of the Office 2000 applications. The Office Assistant also contains some other Help tools. The Answer Wizard can answer specific questions similar to the Office Assistant. You can use the Contents tab to view a listing of general Help topics for the application; this method can be useful if you don't know the name of a feature. The Index tab can find instances of specific keywords within a Help window.

Using the Answer Wizard

In this activity, you will explore Microsoft Word Help, using the Answer Wizard.

1. At the top of the Help window, click the Show button 🔳.

The Help window expands, showing the Contents, Answer Wizard, and Index tabs; and the Show button changes to a Hide button 🔳, as shown in Figure 3.15.

Figure 3.15 ◀
The expanded Help window

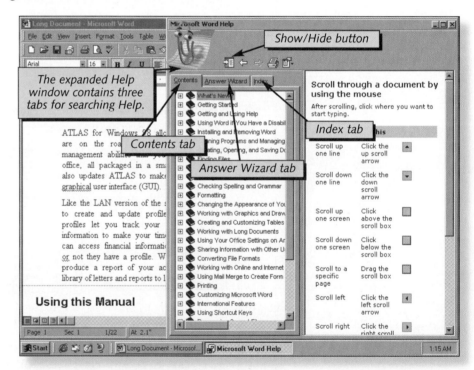

2. Click the Answer Wizard tab, if it is not on top.

3. In the *What would you like to do?* box, type find specific text **and click the Search button**.

Topics that may answer your question appear in the *Select topic to display* box.

4. In the *Select topic to display* box, select the Find and replace text or formatting topic.

5. Click the Find Text hypertext in the right pane of the Help window and read the displayed Help information.

Text in the right pane explains how to find specific text, as shown in Figure 3.16.

Figure 3.16
An Answer Wizard search

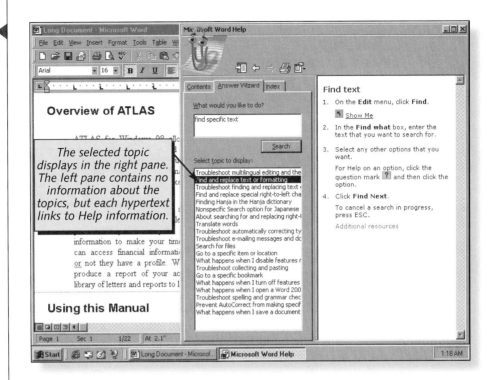

The selected topic displays in the right pane. The left pane contains no information about the topics, but each hypertext links to Help information.

The Office 2000 Help system refers to menu commands, but directions in this tutorial refer to toolbar button commands. For example, the Help window tells you to click Find on the Edit menu. This tutorial directs you to click the Find button 🔍. Both are right; toolbar buttons are quicker.

Using the Contents Tab

1. Click the Contents tab in the Help window.

2. Click the plus sign in front of the topic you wish to open.

3. Click the subtopic you wish to read

Using the Contents and Index Tabs

In this activity, you will explore Microsoft Word Help, using the Contents and Index tabs.

1. **Click the Contents tab, and click the plus sign in front of the Typing, Navigating Documents, and Selecting Text topic.**

The topic expands to show subtopics, and the closed book icon changes to an open book icon, as shown in Figure 3.17. The pane on the right shows the previous search results.

2. **Double-click the Typing topic, and click the Type text subtopic.**

3. **In the right pane, click the typing text link. Read about typing over existing text and click the link in this paragraph. Then read about switching to Overtype mode.**

4. **Click the Back button ⇐ and read the Replacing selected text as you type topic.**

5. **Click the Index tab, and in the *Type keywords* box, type print. Then, click the Search button.**

As you type each letter, the highlighted word within the *Or choose keywords* box jumps to the next word that contains the letter you just typed. The search results in 153 topics listed in the *Choose a topic* box.

Figure 3.17
The Contents tab showing a topic
and subtopics

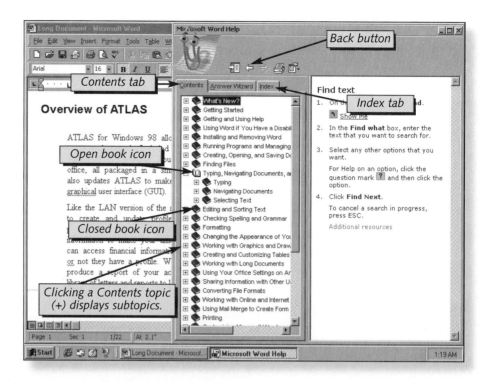

Using the Index Tab

1. Click the Index tab in
   the Help window.

2. Click or type one or
   more keywords.

3. Click the Search button.

4. In the *Choose a topic*
   box, double-click the
   topic you wish to read.

6. In the *Or choose keywords* box, scroll to the word *range* and double-click it so that
   both *print* and *range* appear in the *Type keywords* box.

A two-word search results in fewer topics than a one-word search; the list of
topics that contains both keywords appears in the *Choose a topic* box. The
first topic is displayed in the right pane.

7. Click the **Print a document topic**, and read the Help information in the right
   pane, as shown in Figure 3.18.

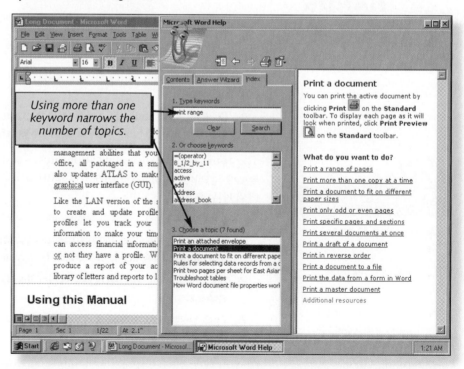

Figure 3.18
Search results involving
two keywords

8. In the right pane, click the **Print specific pages and sections link**; read the first
   two items in the Help window.

9. Click the **Hide button** ; then click the **Close button** ⊠ on the Help window.

10. Click the **Close button** ⊠ on the Word window to close the document and exit Word.

Adding Buttons to the Shortcut Bar

You can customize the Shortcut Bar to best suit your needs. Use the Office Shortcut Bar Help to learn how to add and delete buttons on the Shortcut Bar.

1. With the Shortcut Bar displayed, click the **Control menu icon**.

2. Click **Contents and Index**.

3. Click the **Contents tab**.

Figure 3.19
Learning how to add a button to the Shortcut Bar

4. Click the **plus sign** in front of the Microsoft Office Shortcut Bar topic.

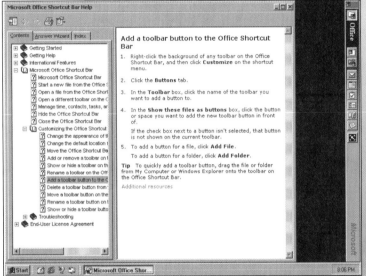

5. Click the **plus sign** in front of the Customizing the Office Shortcut Bar topic.

6. Click the **Add a toolbar button to the Office Shortcut Bar topic**.

7. Read the new text in the right pane of the Help window (Figure 3.19).

8. In the left pane of the Help window, click the **Delete a toolbar button from the Office Shortcut Bar topic**.

9. If time permits, follow the steps you just learned to add a toolbar button to the Shortcut Bar. Then delete the button.

10. Click the **Close button** ⊠ to close the Help window.

Test your knowledge by completing the following statements. See Appendix B to check your answers.

1. The Office 2000 program that allows you to create worksheets to calculate numbers is called _____.

2. The Office 2000 program that allows you to create databases to hold records of information is called _____.

3. The Office 2000 program that allows you to create word processing documents is called _____.

4. The Office 2000 program that allows you to create presentations or slides is called _____.

5. _____ _____ are words that appear in blue in a Help window and show the definition of the word when you click it.

Lesson Summary & Exercises

SUMMARY

In this lesson you learned about the suite of Office 2000 applications, including the four major programs—Word, Excel, Access, and PowerPoint. Word is a word processing program. Excel manipulates data in rows and columns for analysis, reporting, and graphing. Access is a database application. PowerPoint is a presentation or slide show creator. You can launch any of the Office applications from the Start menu or by using the Office Shortcut Bar. You can place the Shortcut Bar anywhere on your screen. Office 2000 provides several different Help tools to assist you in using each application effectively. You learned to use ScreenTips, the Office Assistant, and the Contents, Answer Wizard, and Index tabs to answer questions and further your understanding of Office 2000.

Now that you have completed this lesson, you should be able to do the following:

- Choose the correct Office application to perform a task by analyzing each program's strengths. (Getting Started-80)

- Launch an application by clicking Start ![Start], pointing to Programs, and then clicking the program name. Click the application's taskbar button to switch between running programs. (Getting Started-83)

- Move and hide the Office Shortcut Bar. (Getting Started-85)

- Open a file by clicking the Open Office Document button ![icon] on the Shortcut Bar. (Getting Started-87)

- Create a new file by clicking the New Office Document button ![icon]. (Getting Started-90)

- Display ScreenTips for various screen elements. (Getting Started-91)

- Use the Office Assistant to obtain Help. (Getting Started-92)

- Access and use the Answer Wizard, Contents, and Index tabs in the Help window. (Getting Started-94)

- Customize the Shortcut Bar. (Getting Started-97)

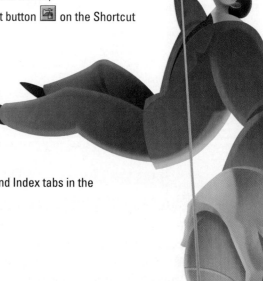

PROJECTS

1 Starting Office Programs

Use the Start button to launch Microsoft PowerPoint. Create a new presentation using the blank presentation option. Click OK to accept the selected AutoLayout. Then use the Office Shortcut Bar to create a new document in Microsoft Access. Click Blank Database and OK. Then, click Cancel in the File New Database dialog box. Use the taskbar button to switch back to PowerPoint. Close both programs.

2 Manipulating the Office Shortcut Bar

Make sure that all applications are closed or minimized so that you can see the desktop. Then, dock the Office Shortcut Bar on the left side of the screen. What happens to the desktop icons? Dock the Office Shortcut Bar on the bottom of the screen. Does it appear above or below the Windows taskbar? Double-click the Shortcut Bar's title bar. Where does it move? Leave the Shortcut Bar in its present position.

3 Creating a New Excel Workbook

Use the Shortcut Bar to create a new Excel workbook. Which Shortcut Bar button do you need to use? As you are creating the workbook and after the workbook is open, do you see any problems with the position of the Shortcut Bar? If so, name two ways that you could correct the problem.

4 Opening an Access Database and Getting Help

Dock the Office Shortcut Bar on the right side of the screen. Then click the option to hide it when you are not using it. Then use the Shortcut Bar to open the *Bobcat* database in the *Tutorial* folder of the Integration Student Data Disk. Ask the Office Assistant for help to spell check a database table. After exploring the spell check topic, close Microsoft Access Help. Display the ScreenTip for the Spelling button. Then close Excel (if it is still running from Project 3) and close Access.

5 Searching the Web

Open the Open Office Document dialog box and click the Search the Web button. Clicking this button opens your Web browser. Describe the window that appears. Connect to the Internet and explore the search engine or list of search engines that appear. After exploring, disconnect from the Internet and close the Web browser.

Word 2000

Communicating in Real Time

Software-to-software communication provides up-to-the-minute information

Software applications are increasingly being designed to work together. With a set of these applications on your computer, you can move data freely from one program to another, share different types of data among different applications, and add data from one application to documents created in a different application.

With these capabilities, you can create a report in Microsoft® Word 2000 and then insert a chart that you created in a worksheet application. You can create a logo using a graphics package and add it to the letterhead on your memo. If you distribute the memo online or on disk, you can also add other types of files—such as audio, video, or animation files—that were created in other types of applications. When you're finished, you have what is called a "complex document"—a deceivingly simple term for a powerful tool that is revolutionizing today's business communications.

A complex document's data comes from other files, called source files. Originally source files from different applications were standalone; they could not communicate with one another at all. After a few generations of software evolution, most application software could communicate with each other using an elementary, but certainly workable, method—cut, copy, and paste. You, the user, could cut or copy data from one application and paste it into another. Suppose, for example, that you are writing a research paper in Word and you want the paper to include data from an Excel worksheet. You can open the worksheet, select the data you want to use, and choose the Cut or Copy command to place the data in a temporary storage area called the Clipboard. Then you can toggle back to Word, place the

Photo: Mendola Ltd./The Stock Market

insertion point where the data should go, and choose the Paste command to add the worksheet data to the research paper. That's a fast and simple way to combine data from two different application programs—unfortunately, it's also a static, one-way conversation. When the worksheet data changes, the research paper becomes out-of-date because the copied data in the research paper remains the same. To update the research paper, you must copy and paste new worksheet data whenever that data changes.

Fortunately, application software has evolved to the point where programs can now communicate with one another in a two-way conversation by using either Dynamic Data Exchange (DDE) or Object Linking and Embedding (OLE):

- *Dynamic Data Exchange (DDE).* This works in much the same way as using the Clipboard to copy and paste data, but gives you an extra option. That is, when you paste the copied data from Excel into Word, you can establish a link back to Excel. Then if the data in your worksheet ever changes, it can be updated in the Word document without copying and pasting again. Using DDE, you can set the data in Word to update itself automatically, or you can update it manually.

- *Object Linking and Embedding (OLE).* OLE works like DDE, but instead of enabling you to update the shared data in the complex document, OLE actually inserts the shared data as an object. This lets you launch the shared data's source application from within the complex document. Suppose, for example, that you are reading your research paper in Word and see that you need to change the Excel data. Instead of opening Excel separately, changing the data, and then updating it in the Word file by either recopying it or using DDE, you simply double-click the Excel data in the Word document. A mini-Excel window appears inside the Word document, enabling you to change the Excel data in both the research paper and the original worksheet on the spot. OLE provides other advantages, as well. Suppose, for example, that you want to embed a sound file in an e-mail message. When you do this, the recipient can just double-click the sound file's icon in the message. This action launches a player that plays the file immediately. This capability frees the document's user from opening different applications.

Advances in software technology, such as DDE and OLE, give you the ability to communicate real-time information to your audience. By understanding and using these capabilities in your Word 2000 documents, you can create complex documents to communicate more effectively in today's "speed-of-light" business environment.

Photo: David Raymer/The Stock Market

Word Basics

CONTENTS

OBJECTIVES

After you complete this lesson, you will be able to do the following:

- Explain word processing.
- Start and exit Microsoft Word.
- Name the main components of the Word window and display and hide toolbars.
- Open, scroll, navigate, view, name and save, preview, print, close, and reopen documents.
- Create a folder.
- Get help from Word's Office Assistant, ScreenTips, Answer Wizard, Contents, and Index.
- Find pages, words, and phrases and insert new text and AutoText.
- Select, overtype, delete, insert, and use the Undo, Redo, Repeat, and Replace commands to edit text.
- Create and send an e-mail message.
- Name buttons on the Web toolbar and navigate a Web site.
- Connect to and disconnect from the Internet.

This lesson teaches you basic word processing terms, shows you how to launch Microsoft Word, and introduces the Word window. You will learn how to open, close, and print documents—essential skills that you will use whenever you work with Word. Also, you will explore the online Help system, which you can use to learn more about the features of Word and to help you solve problems as you use the program. Finally, you will learn how to create and send an e-mail message.

Word processing—the most common use of computers—has become a universal communication tool. Students, from elementary through graduate school, use word processing to prepare assignments. Writers, from cub reporters to Pulitzer prize-winning novelists, use word processing to compose their works. Written communication, from memos, letters, and reports to e-mail attachments and Web pages, turns the wheels of business, industry, and professions all over the globe. Whatever your career choice, word processing will be vital.

INTRODUCING MICROSOFT WORD

Microsoft Word is a powerful *word processing* program that enables you to create all kinds of documents—from short letters to long reports to complicated brochures and newsletters. Using Word, you can easily perform basic word-processing functions, such as typing, editing, printing, and saving text. In addition, many features allow you to *format* (arrange) and enhance text, making it attractive and easy to read. Word will correct typing, spelling, and grammar errors as you type and afterwards. Other Word features help you find and replace text quickly and easily. Special tools allow you to add graphics, pictures, tables, sounds, and links to any document and to the Internet. Word also offers prewritten documents that you can adapt to your needs, instead of writing from scratch.

Word provides extensive online help; the Office Assistant is always right there to answer your questions and provide tips about tasks you want to perform. You can easily navigate your documents no matter how long or short they are. You can manage your Word files by naming and renaming files, copying and deleting files, and saving documents as various file types. You can even ask Word to convert any document to a Web page—Word will guide you step-by-step to create a Web page you can publish on an intranet or the Internet. From the Word window, you can also navigate and search the World Wide Web. You can even create an e-mail message right in the Word window, send a Word document as an e-mail message, or attach a Word document to an e-mail message.

STARTING MICROSOFT WORD

Before you can start Microsoft Word, both Microsoft Word 2000 and Windows 95 (or higher version) must be installed on the computer you are using. The figures in this tutorial use Windows 98; if you are using a different version of Windows, the information appearing on your screen may vary slightly.

You must create the Student Data Disk for this tutorial from the Data CD located on the inside back cover of this tutorial. If you have not created the Student Data Disk, ask your instructor for help.

Launching Microsoft Word

In this activity, you will start Microsoft Word.

1. Turn on your computer.

If you are prompted for a username and/or password, enter the information at this time. If you do not know your username and/or password, ask your instructor for help.

Word BASICS

Launching Microsoft Word

1. Turn on your computer.

2. Click the Start button.

3. Point to Programs; click Microsoft Word.

The Windows operating system boots the computer. Your screen should resemble Figure 1.1. If the Welcome to Windows screen appears, click its Close button ⊠ to close the window.

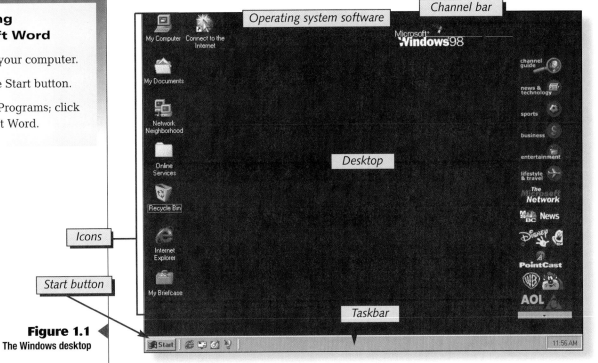

Figure 1.1
The Windows desktop

2. Click the Start button 🏁Start on the Windows taskbar.

3. Point to Programs.

The Programs menu appears similar to Figure 1.2. Depending on the applications installed on your computer, your Programs menu may be different from Figure 1.2.

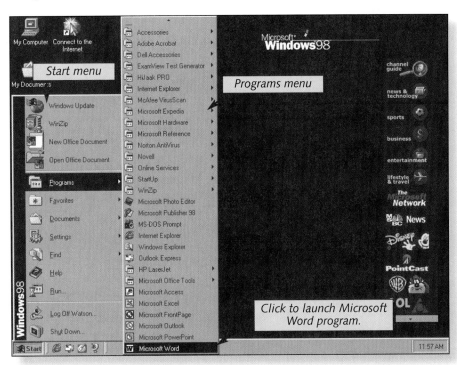

Figure 1.2
The Programs Menu

4. Click Microsoft Word.

The Word program starts and a new, blank document appears.

EXPLORING THE WORD WINDOW

The Word *application window* (screen) is shown in Figure 1.3. Your window may look slightly different, because Word allows users to *customize,* or alter, the Word window to suit their individual needs. The Word window contains many standard Windows elements, including a title bar; the Minimize, Restore, and Close buttons; a menu bar; toolbars; and the scroll bars. These items should seem familiar if you have used Windows 95, Windows 98, or any other Windows 95 or Windows 98 application.

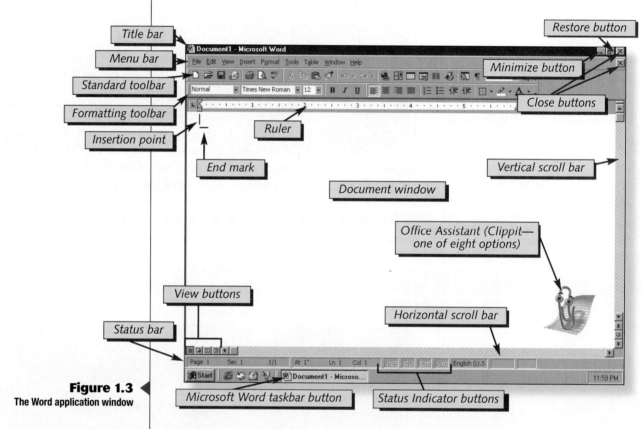

Figure 1.3
The Word application window

As shown in Figure 1.3, the document window displays the insertion point and the end mark. The *insertion point* (a blinking vertical bar) indicates where text will be inserted when you begin typing. The *end mark* (a short horizontal line) moves downward in your document each time you begin a new line.

An animated character called the Office Assistant is perhaps the most curious object in the application window. This character—part of the Help system—represents an Office Assistant for Word users. If the Office Assistant is not on your screen, press [F1]. When the figure gets in your way, drag the character to an out-of-the-way location.

Across the bottom of the screen is the taskbar, including the Start button and other buttons for **navigating** Windows. Buttons on the taskbar show which applications are open. When the Word taskbar icon is active, you know that Word is ready to use. Across the top, the **title bar** shows the name of the application and the name of the current document. Word, by default, gives a temporary name to all documents. In Figure 1.3, the document is called *Document1*.

 *When this tutorial mentions a toolbar button, a picture of the button is displayed within the text. For instance, when a step instructs you to click the Bold button* **B** *, the button will be illustrated as shown here.*

Identifying Menus and Commands

As shown in Figure 1.3, the Word **menu bar** appears below the title bar. The menu bar displays menu names found in most Windows applications, such as File, Edit, and Help. Word also includes menus just for word processing, such as Format and Table.

Menus list the **commands** available in Word. To display a menu's commands, click a menu name on the menu bar. The menu will display a **short menu,** a list of the most-used commands, with an arrow at the bottom. If you keep your pointer on the menu for a few seconds or if you click the double arrow at the bottom of the menu, an **expanded menu** appears. This expanded menu shows all commands available on that menu. The most-used commands appear when a menu opens; when the list expands, less common commands appear. Figure 1.4 shows both versions of Word's Format menu—as a short menu and an expanded menu.

Figure 1.4 ◀
The short and expanded Format menus

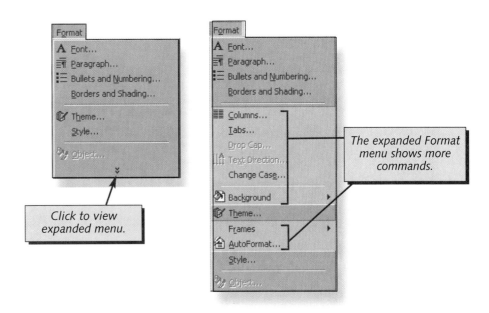

Click to view expanded menu.

The expanded Format menu shows more commands.

As you can see in Figure 1.4, seven commands appear on the initial Format menu. These seven commands are the commands used most often from this menu. The expanded menu shows eight additional commands that are not used as frequently. The backgrounds of the additional commands are a lighter shade of gray. After you use one of these additional commands, this command will be added to the short menu. This **adaptive menu** feature allows each user to customize the menus. Word will automatically customize menus as you work, placing the commands that *you* use often on the short menu.

Table 1.1 provides a brief description of the menus available on the Word menu bar.

TABLE 1.1	THE WORD MENU BAR
Menu	**Contains Commands that Let You . . .**
File	Control your document files by opening, saving, and printing them.
Edit	Rearrange text and other elements of documents by locating, copying, moving, and deleting them.
View	View documents different ways; display and hide toolbars.
Insert	Insert various elements, such as page breaks, pictures, symbols, and hyperlinks, into your documents.
Format	Determine the appearance of text in your documents; for example, the size of characters or the alignment of a paragraph.
Tools	Use Word's special word processing tools, such as a spelling and grammar checker, thesaurus, and automatic correction features.
Table	Insert, fill-in, and format an arrangement of columns and rows as tabular information in documents.
Window	Work in multiple documents at once, in one or more windows.
Help	Access Word's online Help system and the Microsoft Office Home Page on the Internet for word processing assistance and support.

Opening and Closing Menus

Now that you know the menu names and have a general idea of the commands, you should review some of the commands available from the menu bar. An ellipsis (...) after a command indicates that clicking the command will display a **dialog box** to specify details. Pointing to the arrow to the right of a command displays another list of commands called a **submenu.**

Identifying Toolbars and Buttons

Below the menu bar are Word's Standard and Formatting toolbars, as shown in Figure 1.3 on page 108. A *toolbar* contains a row of buttons for many of the most frequently used commands. Although you can access these commands on one of the menus, clicking a toolbar button is often more convenient. You can quickly identify any toolbar button by pointing to it and reading the name. The name appears in a small text box called a ***ScreenTip.***

 *If your Standard and Formatting toolbars share one row below the menu bar, you can display them as two separate toolbars by clicking Customize on the Tools menu. On the Options tab, deselect the Standard and Formatting toolbars share one row option and click Close.*

The icon on each toolbar button symbolizes the command. For example, on Word's Standard toolbar the New Blank Document button ▢ is symbolized by a piece of paper. Table 1.2 displays each button available on the Word Standard toolbar and explains the function. The Standard toolbar, like Word's menus, is adaptive. The most common buttons appear on the main toolbar, while buttons used less often are accessible by clicking More Buttons ▪ at the end of the toolbar. When you click one of these seldom-used buttons, Word adds it to the main toolbar.

The Formatting toolbar appears directly below the Standard toolbar, as shown in Figure 1.3 on page 108. This toolbar includes commands for controlling the appearance of text.

In addition to the Standard and Formatting toolbars, Word includes many other toolbars, each arranged for a different purpose. The View menu includes the Toolbars command. The Toolbars submenu allows you to control which toolbars are displayed as you work. A check mark next to a toolbar name indicates that toolbar is displayed. Clicking a check mark will ***deselect,*** or hide, that toolbar.

Identifying the Ruler and Status Bar

The ***ruler*** displays below the Standard and Formatting toolbars, as shown in Figure 1.3 on page 108, enabling you to judge measurements, such as paragraph indentions, on document pages. (If the ruler does not appear on your screen, click the View menu and click Ruler.)

The ***status bar*** displays at the bottom of the document window just above the taskbar. The status bar indicates information about a command or toolbar button, an operation in progress, or the location of the insertion point. The ***status indicators*** in the middle of the status bar turn special keys or modes (Overtype, for example) on or off. These indicator buttons display darkened when turned on and dimmed when off. Just double-click the status indicator to toggle the particular key.

Button	Name	Action
	New Blank Document	Creates a new document.
	Open	Opens a document.
	Save	Makes a permanent copy of a document to a file on disk.
	E-mail	Opens a header to send your document as an electronic mail message.
	Print	Prints the entire document.
	Print Preview	Previews the document.
	Spelling and Grammar	Checks for spelling and grammar errors.
	Cut	Removes the selected item(s) from the document to the Clipboard—a temporary storage place for information that is used by all Windows applications.
	Copy	Copies the selected item(s) and places this copy on the Clipboard.
	Paste	Pastes the selected item(s) from the Clipboard into the current location.
	Format Painter	Copies the formatting from the selected item(s) to another item(s).
	Undo	Reverses the last command.
	Redo	Repeats the last command.
	Insert Hyperlink	Inserts a link from the current document to another part of the current document, another document, or an Internet site.
	Tables and Borders	Displays or hides the Tables and Borders toolbar.
	Insert Table	Inserts a table.
	Insert Microsoft Excel Worksheet	Inserts an Excel worksheet.
	Columns	Adjusts text to a column format.
	Drawing	Displays or hides the Drawing toolbar.
	Document Map	Turns the Document map feature on or off.
	Show/Hide	Shows or hides the formatting marks.
100%	Zoom	Increases or decreases the displayed size of the document.
	Microsoft Word Help	Displays the Office Assistant—an animated character than can answer your specific questions, offer helpful tips, and provide help for any Word feature.
	Close	Closes the current document.
	Envelopes and Labels	Creates an envelope or a label.
	Find	Searches the document for specific text or item.

TABLE 1.2 THE WORD STANDARD TOOLBAR

OPENING DOCUMENTS

Anytime you want to use a document that you or someone else created, you must *open* the document. Opening a document (or file) means copying that file from disk into the memory of your computer so that you can update or view the document. To open any Word file, you can click the Open button  on the Standard toolbar or click the Open command on the File menu. Clicking the Open button displays a dialog box, where you specify the drive, folder, and file that you want to open. A *folder* is a named location where you store and organize your document files. If you've used a file recently, you may also open a file by choosing the file name from the list of recently opened files that appear near the bottom of the File menu. By default, Word lists the last four files you've opened. You can have several files open at the same time. To move between open files, click the appropriate button on the Windows taskbar.

HANDS On

Opening a File

In this activity, you will learn how to open a file on your Student Data Disk.

1. Click the Open button  **on the Standard toolbar.**

The Open dialog box displays, as shown in Figure 1.5. The Look in box shows the current folder or drive or the last folder used to open a document on your computer.

Warning *If you're sharing a computer with one or more users in a lab or school environment, the list of files displayed in the Open dialog box may not contain the file you wish to open. Continue with steps 2 and 3 to properly navigate to your files.*

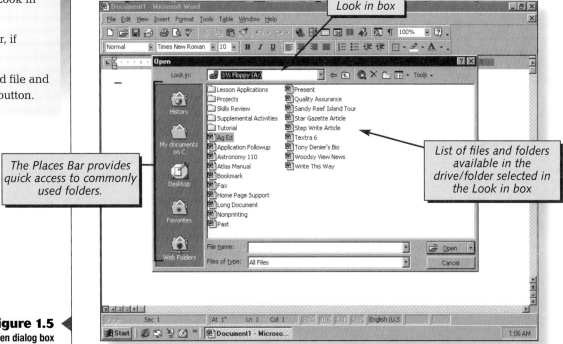

The Places Bar provides quick access to commonly used folders.

List of files and folders available in the drive/folder selected in the Look in box

Figure 1.5 ◀
The Open dialog box

Another Way

To open a file, double-click the file name in the Open dialog box. You can also click Open on the File menu.

The Places Bar in various Word dialog boxes gives you quick access to commonly used folders. For instance, in the Open dialog box, you can click the Favorites folder to see a list of the files stored in this folder. You can access files of different formats by changing the Files of type setting in the Open dialog box.

2. Verify that the Files of type is set to **All Files**.

3. Click the **Look in box arrow** to display a list of the available drives.

4. Click the drive that contains your Student Data Disk for this tutorial. If necessary, click the folder in which the Student Data Disk files are stored.

Below the Look in box you will see a list of folders and files similar to Figure 1.5.

Note *If you copied the Student Data Disk files for this tutorial onto a Zip disk or a floppy disk, you must insert the disk into the drive.*

5. Click *Long Document* in the list of file names, and click the **Open button**.

The *Long Document* file opens in Word, as shown in Figure 1.6. Keep the document open; you will work with this file later in this lesson.

Figure 1.6
The Long Document file

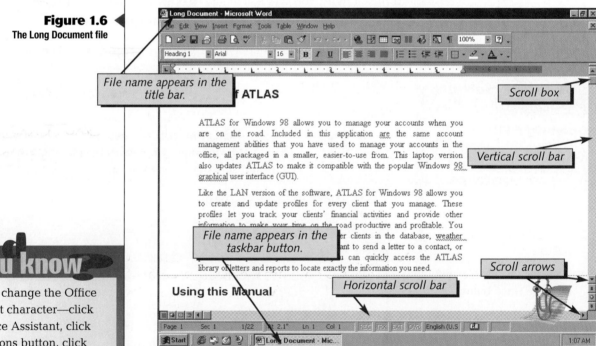

Did you know?

You can change the Office Assistant character—click the Office Assistant, click the Options button, click the Gallery tab, and select the character you want to display. You can also change the way the Office Assistant works and specify the types of tips you see—click the Office Assistant, click the Options button, click the Options tab, and select or deselect the appropriate options.

GETTING HELP WITH WORD

While you are using Word, you may need to reference the online Help system. Word provides several different Help tools: ScreenTips, the Office Assistant, the Contents tab, the Index tab, and a tool called the Answer Wizard. You can activate the Office Assistant by clicking the animated character on your screen, by clicking the Microsoft Word Help button ⊞, by clicking Microsoft Word Help on the Help menu, or by pressing ⊞. For more detailed Help instructions, review pages 91-97 in *Lesson 3: Introducing Office 2000*.

Searching for File Management Help

In this activity, you will search Help for information on file management.

1. Click the **Office Assistant**.

2. Type manage files **in the text box, and click the Search button**.

3. Click the **Manage files option**.

The Manage Files Help window displays, as shown in Figure 1.7.

4. Click the **Save a Word document link to see the many ways you can save a document**.

5. Click the **Save a new, unnamed document link, and read the information in the Help window**.

Figure 1.7
A Help window

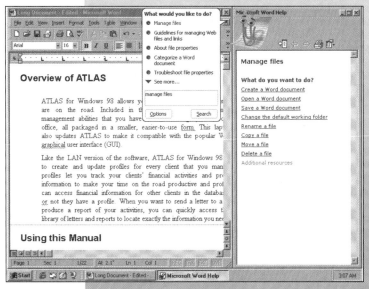

6. At the top of the screen, click the **Back button ⇐**.

7. Scroll to the bottom and click the **Save a Word document as a Web page link**.

8. When you are finished reading the steps, click the **Back button ⇐** until you return to the Manage Files screen.

9. Click **Create a Word document** and explore the topics related to templates.

10. Close the Help window. If necessary, click anywhere on your document to close the Office Assistant.

SCROLLING DOCUMENTS

Many of your documents will contain more text than you can see at once. As you work, you can move through a document to bring the hidden portions into view. You can perform this procedure, called *scrolling*, using the scroll bars, scroll arrows, and scroll box. At the right of the application window, the *vertical scroll bar*, as shown in Figure 1.6 on page 114, moves through the pages of a document. Clicking the *scroll arrows* at each end of the bar, dragging the *scroll box* within the bar, and clicking between the scroll box and a scroll arrow result in moving a document at varying speeds. The *horizontal scroll bar*, at the bottom of the document window (except in Web Layout View) moves documents from side to side.

Scrolling a Document

In this activity, you will scroll the displayed document several different ways.

1. On the horizontal scroll bar, click the **right scroll arrow**.

The window contents scroll slightly to the right, as shown in Figure 1.8.

Scrolling a Document

- Click a scroll arrow to move slightly.

- Click the scroll bar between the scroll box and arrow to move more rapidly.

- Drag the scroll box to move rapidly.

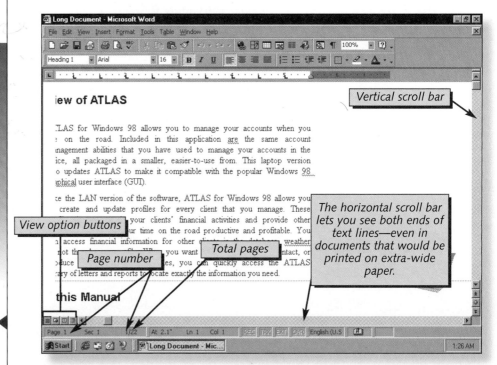

Figure 1.8 ◄
Scroll arrows move the window from side to side

Another Way

- To scroll a document, use the arrow keys on the keyboard. Pressing an arrow key moves the insertion point in the indicated direction. Press once to move up or down one line or left or right one character.

- To move immediately to the beginning of a document, press `Ctrl` + `Home`.

- To move immediately to the end of a document, press `Ctrl` + `End`.

2. Click and hold the right scroll arrow until the scroll box moves as far as possible.

The window moves continuously in the direction of the arrow, all the way to the far right edge of the page. The document disappears from the screen.

3. Click the horizontal scroll bar to the left of the scroll box until the document is visible on the screen.

The window scrolls farther and faster when you click the scroll bar than when you clicked the scroll arrows.

4. On the vertical scroll bar, drag the scroll box to the bottom of the bar.

Word scrolls to the end of the document. Notice that the page number and words appear in a ScreenTip as you drag the scroll box. The page number also shows on the status bar.

5. Click the vertical scroll bar three times, and watch the window scroll one screen at a time.

6. Drag the scroll box to about the middle of the first page.

7. Click the up arrow five times, and watch the window scroll up one line at a time.

8. Drag the scroll box to the top of the bar.

VIEWING DOCUMENTS

Word allows users to see all documents, including Web pages, in *WYSIWYG* (what you see is what you get). As shown in Figure 1.8, four view option buttons are located at the lower left in the Word window. A document might be created in Outline View and switched to other views for editing, formatting, and printing. The four views are identified in Table 1.3. You can easily reduce or magnify the document area displayed on screen by changing the Zoom setting.

TABLE 1.3	DOCUMENT VIEWING OPTIONS	
Button	**View Type**	**Typical Use**
	Normal View	The main view used for typing, editing, and formatting text.
	Web Layout View	Used mostly for editing and formatting documents to be posted as Web pages.
	Print Layout View	Used for seeing how documents will look when printed.
	Outline View	Used only for organizing and developing the content of documents.

Viewing a Document

In this activity, you will see the *Long Document* in all four views. Scrolling the document will help you observe differences in the views. You will also change the Zoom setting.

> **1.** In the View toolbar in the lower-left area of the screen, click the **Web Layout View button** 🗔.

Long lines of text and very narrow side margins characterize this view, as shown in Figure 1.9, and no lines divide the document into separate pages.

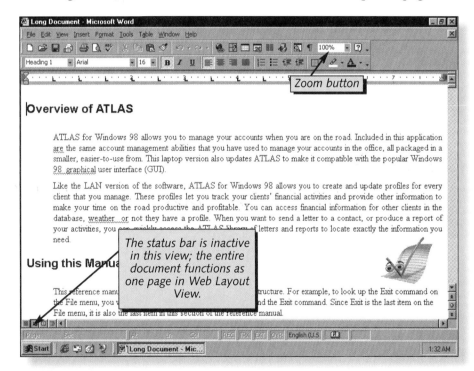

Figure 1.9
Long Document in
Web Layout View

> **2.** Scroll rapidly to the end of the document; check the status bar.

The page numbers do not appear in a ScreenTip as you scroll and the status bar is not active in Web Layout View, because on the Web, the whole document functions as one page.

[Handwritten notes at top left:]
R click Start
Click onto Explorel
See Programs. File
go to explorer.
Windows Explorer

Another Way

To view a document in a different view, click the View menu and click the desired View option.

[Handwritten notes:]
Go to Folder.
File
Doc. to Folder; New.
Foll A-D.
To build new folder (A)
Toll (B)
Hold Control
then Click
Hold Shift Ke
Then Click Top of Set
& Bottom of Set.
Release Keyboard.

WEB NOTE

One way to navigate the Web is to click hyperlinks which appear as hypertext, graphics, objects, and pictures. In Word you jump from one Help topic to another; but on the Internet, you may jump from a computer in Indiana to one in Ireland or Indonesia—just by following links.

3. Scroll to the beginning of the document; click the **Print Layout View button** 🔲.

The document takes the appearance of a printed sheet.

4. Scroll gradually to the top of page 2, and notice an actual break between pages 1 and 2.

5. Scroll slowly to the *Using ATLAS for Windows 98* heading at the top of page 3.

6. Click the **Outline View button** 🔲.

A new toolbar appears at the top of the document. A mark at the left of each line of text indicates a separate unit that you can move above or below other units by clicking the arrows in the Outlining toolbar.

7. Click the **Normal View button** 🔲.

Side margins are visible on the left and right side of text, and faint dotted lines divide the screen into pages.

8. Click the **Zoom arrow** `100%` on the Standard toolbar, and in the list box, click the **150% option**.

Word enlarges the appearance of the document.

[Handwritten:] Either / Shift & Click / Control C or more outline

9. Click the **Zoom arrow** `100%`, and click the **100% option**.

Word returns the document to its actual size.

[Handwritten:] Control X (cut) Paste, Control V

INSERTING TEXT *C*

As you point to text in a document, the pointer becomes an *I-beam pointer*. When you want to type, position the pointer where the text is to go and click. The pointer then becomes a blinking vertical bar, called the insertion point. When you type, text will begin at the insertion point. As you type, you can erase errors to the left of the insertion point by pressing [Backspace], and you can erase errors to the right of the insertion point by pressing [Delete]. When you reach the end of a complete line, text and the insertion point will move automatically to the next line. This basic word processing feature is called *word wrap.* At the end of a paragraph or wherever text must begin on a new line, press [Enter←] to insert a *hard return* that moves the insertion point to the next line.

[Handwritten:] and drag to B. (Control X) extract

Note *Insert a hard return only to move text or the insertion point to the next line, to insert blank lines into your document, to begin a new paragraph, or to apply certain Word commands. Otherwise, allow your copy to wrap with the* **soft returns** *that Word inserts automatically.*

Word involves two typing modes. When you use the *Insert mode,* the text you type appears on the blank screen or is inserted into existing text, pushing the characters after it to the right. When you use the *Overtype mode,* your text *types over* the existing text. Use the Insert mode—the default typing mode—to insert new text; use the Overtype mode to edit text. Always determine which mode is active before you type, to avoid replacing text accidentally. When Word is in the Overtype mode, the status indicator button will display OVR in black letters. When the Insert mode is active, the status indicator button will display a dimmed or gray OVR button. You can switch

(Handwritten margin notes:)
Press Insert
to put in
Words.
Push Insert
2nd Time & you
over write

Bad Spacin'
identify Problem
Site with ¶ of
Word Tool, Bar

back and forth between the modes by double-clicking the OVR button or by pressing [Insert].

As you type, Word may display a ScreenTip that suggests text you are typing, such as your name, the date, the day of the week, or a month. Word's AutoComplete feature automatically tries to complete what you are typing. If the **AutoComplete tip** is accurate, press [Enter←] or [F3] to instruct Word to insert the text into your document where the insertion point is.

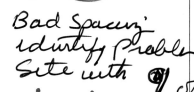

Inserting Paragraphs

In this activity, you will add two paragraphs to **Long Document**.

1. Scroll to page 2, click the space at the end of the second paragraph, and press [Enter←].

You want to use Overtype mode to type over existing text.

2. On the status bar, point to the **OVR status indicator button**.

If OVR appears in bold, black letters, Overtype mode is active. If OVR is gray or dimmed, Insert mode is active.

3. Activate the Insert mode, if necessary.

4. Type the following text: We have also included a small "map" in the upper-right corner of each page. This map indicates exactly where the described menu or dialog is in the program.

The insertion point moves to the right as you type and moves to the next line when a line is full.

5. Scroll to the top of page 3, to the beginning of the first paragraph, and click the I-beam before the word **You.**

6. Type the following paragraph and then press [Enter←]: If you are new to Windows 98, look over this section to familiarize yourself with the Windows conventions.

The insertion point pushes the existing text to the right as you type new text. Your document should now resemble Figure 1.10.

FINDING AND EDITING TEXT

The power of a word processing program becomes apparent when you want to change your text. The ease of changing, deleting, replacing, and moving text means that you can type a rough draft of your ideas quickly, going back later to refine, or edit, your document. When you work with a multi-page document like **Long Document**, you need a variety of editing features. You also need ways, besides scrolling, to locate specific text.

Locating Pages and Text

The Go To feature allows you to go to a specific page, line, section, heading, and so on. On the Go To tab in the Find and Replace dialog box, you can type a page number for Word to go directly to that page. Once there, you can direct Word to go back and forward a certain number of pages.

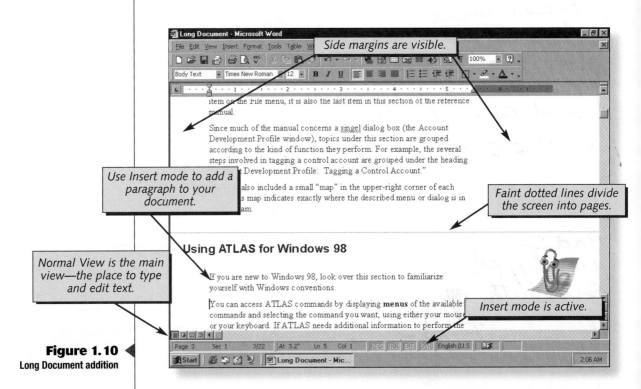

Figure 1.10
Long Document addition

When editing text, you may want to move quickly to a particular word or phrase, not knowing which page or line it's on. The Find command allows you to do so. You tell Word exactly what text to find—including the capitalization. Word searches for it and highlights the first occurrence *following the insertion point*. Then you can ask Word to continue searching the entire document, highlighting every occurrence of the text you specify.

Finding Specific Text and Pages

In this activity, you will find specific words and use the Go To feature to locate specific pages in *Long Document*. At those locations, you will type a few words in the existing text.

1. Press Ctrl **+** Home **to move to the beginning of *Long Document*.**

Word can search for specific pages and text from any point. It would search to the end of the document and continue searching the beginning of it.

2. Click the Find button 🔍 **.**

If the Find button is not on the Standard toolbar, click More Buttons ⊡ *and add Find to your toolbar. You also may click Find on the Edit menu.*

The Find and Replace dialog box appears.

3. On the Find tab, type administrator **in the Find what box, as shown in Figure 1.11.**

4. Click Find Next.

Word searches the document and highlights this word.

Figure 1.11
The Find and Replace dialog box

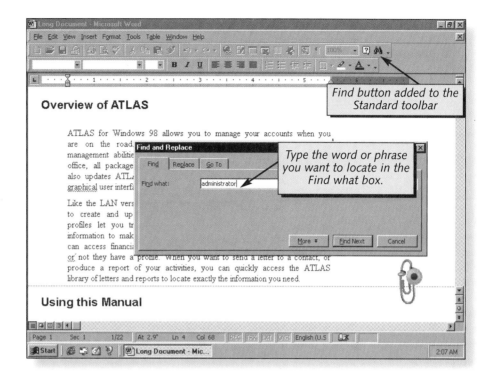

Navigating a Document

To find specific text:

1. Click the Find button on the Standard toolbar.

2. Type text in the Find what box.

3. Click Find Next.

To use the Go To feature:

1. Click the Find button; click the Go To tab.

2. Click Page in the Go to what box.

3. Type a page number or type + or - and the number of pages to go forward or back.

4. Click the Go To button.

5. Click the Document to work in it.

The Select Browse Object tool on the vertical scroll bar is a shortcut. Click the Select Browse Object button and click the Browse by Page tool. Word will go directly to the next page.

5. **Click anywhere on the document window.**

6. **Click the space before the word in the document and make sure Insert mode is active; type** central system **followed by a space.**

7. **In the Find what box, select the word** *administrator* **and type** refreshing. **Then click Find Next.**

Word stops at the phrase *refreshing LAN data*.

8. **Click Find Next again.**

9. **Click anywhere in the document, and click before the** *d* **in** *data.* **Then type** LAN **followed by a space.**

10. **In the Find and Replace dialog box, click the Go To tab. In the Go to what list box, click Page, if it is not already selected. Then type** 5 **in the Enter page number box.**

The Next button changes to a Go To button.

11. **Click the Go To button.**

Word goes directly to the top of page 5, and the status bar indicates that you are now on page 5 of 22. The insertion point is at the beginning of the page but not blinking. To type on this page, you must first click the page. If you type without clicking the page, the characters will appear in the Enter page number box on the Go To tab.

12. **In the Enter page number box, type** +4 **and click the Go To button.**

Word moves forward four pages; you are now on page 9.

13. **In the Enter page number box, type** -6 **and click the Go To button.**

Word moves back six pages; you are now on page 3.

14. **Close the Find and Replace dialog box.**

Editing Text

Sometimes you will need to insert a single word or a missing character within a word, which you can do in Insert mode. Occasionally, you will need to replace incorrect characters with correct ones by *overtyping* them. You can replace text in Overtype mode. While editing a rough draft, you will often need to **delete** characters, words, phrases, sentences, even whole paragraphs. Deleting text is a two-step procedure. First you must select the text you want to delete. Clicking a single letter selects it, and dragging the pointer over words and phrases selects them. You can select a word by double-clicking it. After you select a word, press Delete to remove it; or, type to replace the word with another word. You can also replace text in an entire document easily by using the Replace feature. In the Find and Replace dialog box, type the text to find and the text to replace with. Then for each occurrence, you can tell Word to replace the text, skip to the next occurrence, or replace all occurrences.

As you edit documents, you may be unsure about a particular word choice or the phrasing of a sentence. The Undo button reverses actions (for example, deletes the text just typed). The ScreenTip changes to Can't Undo if you cannot reverse the last action. The Redo button reverses an action that you *undo*. You can also use the Repeat command on the Edit menu to repeat an action.

Replacing Text

In this activity, you will replace incorrect letters and words.

1. Press Ctrl + Home to go to the top of the document.
2. Click the **Find button** and **type** use from. in the Find what box. Then click **Find Next**.
3. Click anywhere in the document, and then click before the *r* in the highlighted words.

If the Find and Replace dialog box covers the status bar or is in the way when you correct an error, click its title bar and drag it to another area of the window.

4. Activate the Overtype mode, if necessary, and type **or** to replace the letters *r* and *o*.
5. Find the word *weather* and overtype to make it *whether*, as shown in Figure 1.12.
6. Find the misspelled word *singel* and overtype two letters to make the word *single*.

A wavy, red line under some words (such as singel*) marks words or abbreviations not in the Word spelling dictionary. These words could be spelling errors. Similarly, a wavy, green line marks possible grammar errors. Some wavy lines will disappear as you edit the document; otherwise, ignore them for now. You will learn more about them in Lesson 2.*

7. Find the phrase *than type*; overtype the *a* with *e*.
8. In the Find and Replace dialog box, click the **Replace tab**.

The Replace tab is displayed.

9. Type Alt in the Find what box. Press Tab and type <Alt> in the Replace with box. Then click the **Find Next button**.

Figure 1.12
Word window in Overtype mode

Word BASICS

Replacing Text

To overtype:

1. Click the character you want to replace.

2. Verify that Overtype mode is active and type the character(s).

To insert:

1. Click the position where you want to add a character.

2. Verify that Insert mode is active and type the character(s).

To use Replace feature:

1. Click the Find button.

2. Click the Replace tab.

3. In the Find what box, type the word or phrase to be replaced.

4. In the Replace with box, type the replacement.

5. Click Find Next.

6. Click Replace, Replace All, or Find Next.

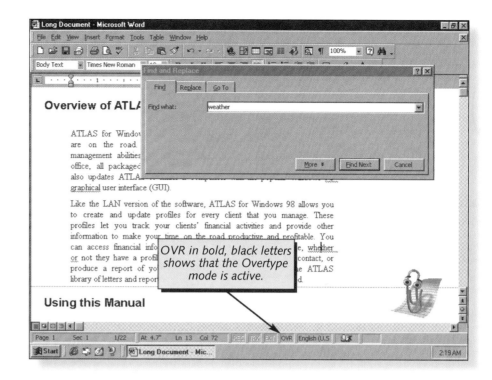

Word searches the document.

10. At the first occurrence of *Alt*, click **Replace**.

Word replaces *Alt* with *<Alt>* and continues searching the document.

11. At the second occurrence of *Alt*, click the **Find Next button**. Continue searching the entire document.

The Office Assistant indicates that the entire document was searched and no other occurrences were found.

12. Find the words *first you* and insert the word time between them.

13. Find the word *familiarize* and proofread the entire paragraph, which you typed in an earlier activity; correct any errors you see by inserting or overtyping characters.

14. Find the word *map*; proofread the paragraph and correct any errors.

Selecting and Deleting Text

In this activity, you will remove extra letters and words in *Long Document*.

1. If the Find and Replace dialog box is not open, click the **Find button** and find the word *menue.* If the Office Assistant indicates that Word has finished searching the document, click **Find Next** to continue searching.

2. Select the second *e* and press Delete to remove it.

The space occupied by the deleted character closes automatically.

3. Find the word *existing*; delete the *s* to make the word *exiting*.

4. Find the words *lap top* and delete the space between them. Then, close the Find and Replace dialog box.

Selecting and Deleting Text

To delete a character:

1. Click the letter or character.

2. Press Delete.

To delete a word:

1. Double-click the word to select it.

2. Press Delete.

To delete a phrase:

1. Click the first character.

2. Drag through the phrase to select it.

3. Press Delete.

5. Go to the first paragraph on page 7.

The word *the* is repeated in this sentence.

6. Double-click the repeated word to select it and press Delete.

7. Go to page 10, item 2, select and delete words to match this phrase: *. . . using* **backspace** *to erase. . .*

8. On page 12, edit the last bulleted item to match this phrase: *. . . alerts and to enter. . .* as shown in Figure 1.13.

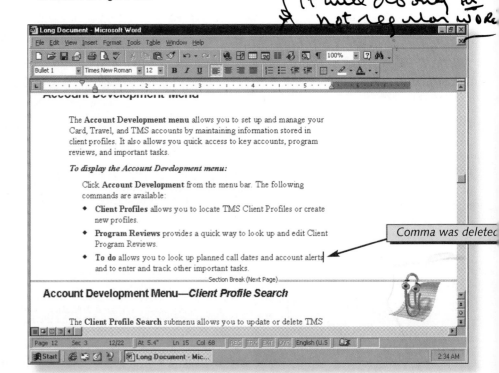

Figure 1.13
Edited Long Document

Comma was deleted

HANDS On

Undoing, Redoing, and Repeating Actions

In this activity, you will locate a specific word, select and replace it, and undo that action. After the word is restored, you will repeat the action.

1. **Open the Find and Replace dialog box. On the Find tab, click the More button, and click the Match case checkbox so that a check mark appears in it.**

Word will now skip occurrences of the text that do not match the capitalization used in the Find what box.

2. **Type** Important: **in the Find what box, as shown in Figure 1.14. Then, click Find Next.**

3. **While the word is still selected, click the document anywhere and press** Delete.

4. **Click the Undo button** ↺ **to restore the word** *Important:*.

5. **In the same sentence, select the word** *checkbox* **and then type** button.

The second word replaces the first.

6. **Click the Undo button** ↺ **to restore the word** *checkbox*. **Click the Redo button** ↻ **to restore the word** *button*. **Click the Undo button** ↺ **to restore the word** *checkbox*.

Undoing, Redoing, and Repeating Actions

1. Click the Undo button to delete text just typed, or click the Undo arrow and click the action you want to undo.

2. Click the Redo button to reverse an *Undo* action.

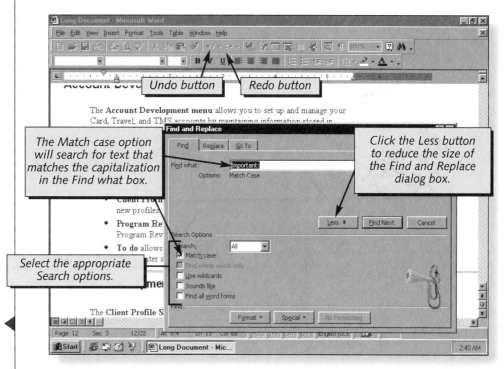

Figure 1.14
Select the Match case
search option

7. In the Find and Replace dialog box, deselect the **Match case search option**, and click the **Less button**.

8. Find the word *TIP:*, click before the word, and type ATLAS. Then, find another occurrence of *TIP:* and click before the word.

9. Click **Repeat Typing** on the Edit menu.

Word automatically repeats the last word you typed: *ATLAS*.

10. Close the Find and Replace dialog box.

SAVING DOCUMENTS

After typing and editing your document, you should *save* it. Saving a document transfers all the text from computer memory to your disk, and you can open the document later. Saving your work often is important in case something goes wrong with the computer. For example, if you have not saved your document and your computer malfunctions or someone kicks the power cord, all your work may be lost.

When you are working on a new document that you have not yet saved, Word names the file *Document1* as the default file name. When you save the file, you should give the file a more meaningful name, so you can see at a glance what information the file contains. Besides naming a file, you also must specify where to store the file (the drive and path). A file name, including the drive and path, can contain up to 255 characters, including spaces. The file name may not include any of the following characters, however: \ / < > * ? " ; : or |

After you name and save a file, clicking the Save button  on the Standard toolbar replaces the file on disk with the version currently in memory, without displaying the Save As dialog box. If you want to save the file in a different place or under a new name, click the Save As command on the File menu. The Save As dialog box appears, and you can type a new file name and/or location. When you use the Save As command, you are *not* renaming a file. Instead you are saving a copy of the file under a different name or in a different place. The original file with the original name will not be deleted. You can also create a new folder in which to save the file. To do so, select the drive (and folder, if appropriate) for the location of the new folder. Then click the Create New Folder button 🔲. Type the folder name, and click OK. You can then save the file in this newly created folder.

Warning

Save your files often—especially after making any changes. Even if you have saved a file, unsaved changes will be lost if your computer malfunctions or a power outage occurs.

HANDS On

Naming and Saving a Document

In this activity, you will save your document to your Student Data Disk in a folder named *Tutorial*.

1. Press `Ctrl` + `Home` to return to the beginning of the document.

2. On the File menu, click **Save As**.

The Save As dialog box appears.

3. If the drive that contains your Student Data Disk does not appear in the Save in box, click the **Save in arrow** and click the name of the drive.

Note *You could save the document in HTML (Web Page) format by clicking Save As Web Page on the File menu. The Save procedure is the same, but the file type is Web Page instead of Word Document.*

4. Click the *Tutorial* folder in the window below the Save in box; click the **Open button**.

The *Tutorial* folder opens and appears in the Save in box.

5. In the File name box, edit the file name to be *Long Document - Edited* as shown in Figure 1.15. Then, click the **Save button**.

Word saves the file as you specified and your open document remains in the window. The title bar and the taskbar button show the new file name.

Adding AutoText and Saving Changes

Now that your document is saved, you realize you omitted a code that you wanted to show on the last page—the file name and date. Word can insert such information automatically; the feature is called AutoText. AutoText is a handy alternative to typing repetitive text, such as the date, your name, or a frequently used phrase, like *Sincerely yours.*

Word BASICS

Naming and Saving a Document

1. Click the File menu and click Save As.

2. Select the drive (and folder if appropriate) in the Save in box.

3. Type a name for the document in the File name box.

4. Click the Save button.

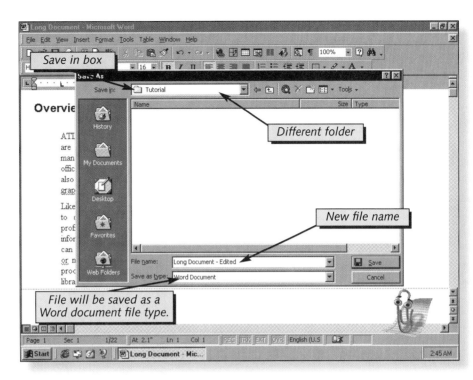

Figure 1.15
The Tutorial folder

HANDS On

Inserting AutoText

1. Display the AutoText toolbar.

2. Click where you want to insert the AutoText.

3. Click the All Entries button.

4. Point to the type of AutoText you want.

5. Click the specific AutoText option you want.

6. Hide the AutoText toolbar.

Inserting AutoText and Saving Changes

In this activity, you will add AutoText to the end of your document and then save the updated file.

1. **Press** Ctrl + End **to move immediately to the end of the document, and press** Enter ← **two times.**

2. **Click the View menu, point to Toolbars, and click AutoText.**

The AutoText toolbar appears below the Formatting toolbar.

3. **Click the All Entries button on the AutoText toolbar and point to Header/Footer.**

The All Entries menu and the Header/Footer submenu are displayed, as shown in Figure 1.16.

4. **On the Header/Footer submenu, click the Filename option.**

The name of your file is inserted at the insertion point. If you change the name of this file, Word will automatically change this text in your document.

5. **Type / after the file name, and click Date and Time on the Insert menu.**

6. **In the Date and Time dialog box, select the Update automatically box, if it is not selected.**

If a check mark already appears in this box, skip step 6. This choice will cause the date in the file to be current each time the file is opened or printed. Notice all the available formats.

7. **Click one of the options that shows the date and the time; then click OK.**

8. **Type / and then type your initials.**

9. **Click the Save button 🖫 on the Standard toolbar.**

Figure 1.16
Insert AutoText options

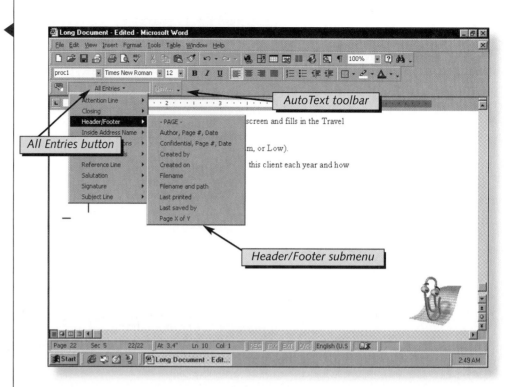

Word saves the updated file with the same name and in the *Tutorial* folder that you specified earlier.

10. Click **View**, point to **Toolbars**, and deselect **AutoText**.

PREVIEWING DOCUMENTS

Before you print any document, get into the habit of using the Print Preview button 🔍. This feature lets you look at each printed page—*before* printing—to see exactly how a document will look on the printed page. You can examine the format of up to six pages at once or only one page at a time. In Print Preview, clicking a scroll arrow displays the next or previous page. You will notice that text is too small to read; but you can see whether page breaks are satisfactory, margins are consistent size, and headings are all the same style. You can see whether you need to make any adjustments prior to printing. If you wish to read the text at a certain point in the document, click that area of the document.

Previewing a Multi-Page Document

In this activity, you will preview the current document and see whether you need to make any adjustments prior to printing.

1. Click ⌃Ctrl + ⌂Home to return to the beginning of the document, and click the **Print Preview button** 🔍 on the Standard toolbar.

The Print Preview window displays.

2. In the Preview toolbar, click the **Multiple Pages button** ▦ and then drag to select the first row of icons (1 x 3 pages). Then click.

The first three pages appear on the preview screen, as shown in Figure 1.17.

Figure 1.17 ◀
The Print Preview window

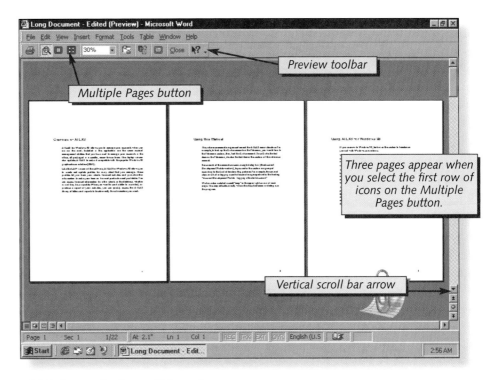

Previewing a Document

- Click the Print Preview button.

- Click the One Page button to see a page at a time.

- Click the Multiple Pages button to see 2-6 pages at once.

- Click a scroll arrow to see the next or previous page(s).

3. Click the vertical scroll bar down arrow.

The next three pages display.

4. Click the One Page button 🔲 **to view one page on the preview screen, as shown in Figure 1.18.**

Figure 1.18 ◀
One Page display

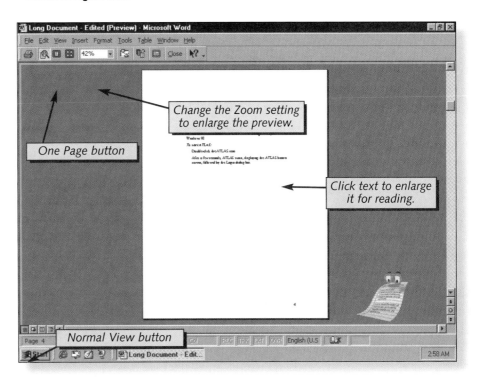

Another⧫Way

- To change the magnification setting, click the Zoom arrow and select option.

- To close the Print Preview window, click the Close button.

5. On the vertical scroll bar, click once between the scroll box and the up arrow.

The previous page displays.

6. Click the document and watch the document zoom to actual size.

7. Click the document again; then click the **Normal View button** 📄 on the View toolbar.

The Print Preview window disappears and your document displays in Normal View. Your preview of the document indicated that the layout is fine.

PRINTING DOCUMENTS

Printing is a simple task in Word. Clicking the Print button 🖨 on the Standard toolbar prints one copy (or **printout**) of all pages of your document. To print only some of the pages, click Print on the File menu. Then, in the Print dialog box, specify whether you want to print just the current page (page holding the insertion point), only text that you have highlighted (selection), or several pages. Type page numbers with a hyphen or comma between two numbers to tell Word which pages to print. If you want to cancel a print job, double-click the printer icon (on the taskbar by the clock). In the printer window, select the job you want to cancel and click Cancel Printing on the Document menu. Then close the printer window.

Printing Selected Pages

In this activity, you will print selected pages of **Long Document - Edited**.

1. On the File menu, click **Print**.

2. In the Page range box of the Print dialog box, select the **Pages option**.

3. Type 1,6,20 in the Pages text box.

Word will print the first, sixth, and twentieth page of **Long Document - Edited**.

4. Verify that **Number of copies** is set to 1, as shown in Figure 1.19. If not, click the down arrow until 1 appears in the list box. Then, click **OK**.

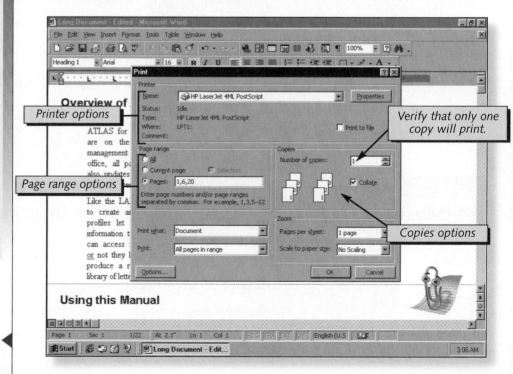

Figure 1.19 ◄
The Print dialog box

E-mail a Word Document

You can create an *e-mail* message directly in Word. You also can send a Word document as an e-mail message, or you can attach a Word document to an e-mail message. In this activity, you will explore Help to learn about the features of your mail program and how to use Word to send e-mail messages. Before you complete this activity, secure permission from your instructor.

1. Ask the Office Assistant for information on e-mail messages. Explore the **E-mail messages and documents topic** and other related links.

Figure 1.20
E-mail header in the Word window

2. Answer these questions: (a) Can I use Word to send an e-mail message?, (b) May I send a Word document by e-mail?, (c) Can I send an HTML document by e-mail?, and (d) What is an e-mail attachment?

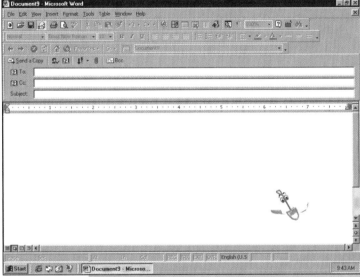

3. In a new blank document, click the **E-mail button** 🖻 on the Standard toolbar. Word displays an e-mail header (Figure 1.20).

4. In the *To* box, type an e-mail address of a friend, a student, or your instructor. (Your instructor may provide the address.) Press Tab twice to move to the *Subject* box. Word will include your e-mail address automatically in a *From* box that doesn't display in the e-mail header.

5. In the *Subject* box, type Newsletter and press Tab.

6. In the message area, type the name of the person to whom you are writing, followed by a comma. Press Enter twice and type:

   After much consideration, the Woodsy View Association decided to send its quarterly newsletter to you as an e-mail attachment. Do you prefer e-mail or snail mail?

   Press Enter twice and type your name.

7. Click the **Attach File button** 📎. Navigate to the *Woodsy View News* file on your Student Data Disk. Click **Attach**. An *Attach* box appears in the e-mail header and identifies the name and size of the attached file.

8. To send the e-mail message and the attachment, click the **Send a Copy button** Send a Copy. If you are connected to the Internet, Word will send your message to the address in the *To* box and close your document window. If you are not connected, you will receive a message asking you to connect to the Internet.

9. Open the *Woodsy View News* file on your Student Data Disk. Click the **E-mail button** 🖻. By default, the file name will appear in the *Subject* box.

10. Type an e-mail address in the *To* box and click the **Send a Copy button** Send a Copy. This time you sent the *Woodsy View News* document as the e-mail message rather than an e-mail attachment. Close the *Woodsy View News* file.

CLOSING DOCUMENTS AND EXITING WORD

When you are finished working with a document, you should *close* the file. You do not need to close your document file to open another Word document, however. Word lets you open several files at once. To have more free memory, though, you should close files that you are no longer using. When you close a document, you remove the specific document from memory but leave Word operating.

When only one document is open, two Close buttons ☒ are present: one for the document on the *menu bar* and one for Word on the *title bar*. Clicking the Close button on the menu bar will close the file. Clicking the Close button on the title bar will close Word—so be careful! When more than one document is open, click the title bar Close button to close the displayed document. Word also has a Close button 🖿 available on the Standard toolbar. Using this button avoids the problem of accidentally closing Word when you intend to close a file.

Documents that you have opened recently are added to a list near the bottom of the File menu. If you need to reopen a file you just closed, you can select the document quickly from that list. By default, Word lists the last four files; a user may choose to list up to nine files on the File menu.

When you are finished with the Word program, you should exit the program properly. Failure to close Word can lead to problems the next time you want to start the application. Exiting the program closes any open Word files and removes Word from computer memory. You can exit Word by clicking the title bar Close button ☒ or by clicking the Exit command on the File menu. After exiting Word, you will see the desktop if you have no other programs running. From there, you may choose to shut down your computer.

HANDS On

Closing and Reopening Files and Exiting Word

In this activity, you will close and reopen a file and then exit Word.

1. Click the Close button 🖿 **on the Standard toolbar.**

If the Close button 🖿 is not visible on the Standard toolbar, click More Buttons ▪ and add it. If the Office Assistant asks you whether you want to save the changes, click Yes. Word closes the document, clearing the screen completely—except for the Office Assistant.

2. Click the File menu.

The file name appears near the bottom of the menu, and the file closed most recently is listed first, as shown in Figure 1.21.

3. To reopen the file, click its file name near the bottom of the menu.

The document reappears in the Word application window.

Word
BASICS

Closing and Reopening Files and Exiting Word

To close a file:

1. Click the Close button on the Standard toolbar.

2. Respond to the Save prompt.

To reopen a file:

Click the file name on the File menu.

To exit Word:

1. Click the title bar Close button or click the File menu and click Exit.

2. Remove your Student Data Disk from the drive, if necessary.

Figure 1.21
File menu listing

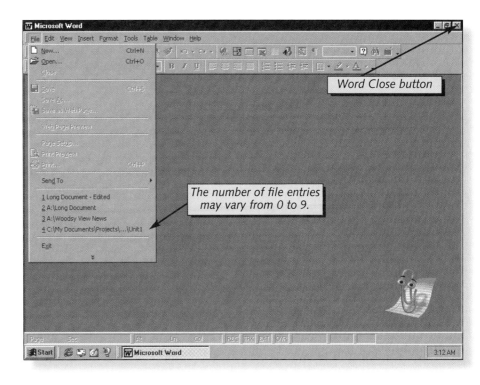

Word Close button

The number of file entries may vary from 0 to 9.

4. Click the **Close button** .

Note *If you made even a minute change—such as pressing* [Spacebar] *by mistake—the Office Assistant will ask if you want to save your changes. Click No.*

5. Click the **Close button** ☒ on the title bar.

Word disappears from the screen; the desktop appears if you have not opened any other application.

6. Remove your **Student Data Disk** from the drive, if necessary.

Test your knowledge by answering the following questions. See Appendix B to check your answers.

T   F   1. Both the Standard and Formatting toolbars are expandable and customized for individual users.

T   F   2. The Print Layout viewing option is the ideal choice for typing and editing text.

T   F   3. Double-click the Overtype button to switch between Insert and Overtype modes.

T   F   4. To scroll rapidly, drag the scroll box on the vertical scroll bar.

T   F   5. To exit Word, click the Close button or click Close on the File menu.

ON*the*WEB

EXPLORING THE WEB TOOLBAR

Every day, computer users around the world use the Internet for work, play, and research. The ***Internet*** is a worldwide network of computers that connects each Internet user's computer to all other computers in the network. Vast quantities of infinitely varied information—from simple text in the form of an e-mail message to extremely complex software—can pass through these connections. The Internet organizes information into small parcels, or pages. The most popular tool to access pages is the ***World Wide Web*** (the Web); therefore, a page of information is called a ***Web page.*** Because a page holds a specific *place* on the Web, it is also called a ***Web site.***

If you have a Web ***browser***—a software tool used to navigate the Web—you can access most Internet and all World Wide Web pages from Word's application window. Using the buttons on Word's Web toolbar, you can navigate to a specific Web site, search the entire Web, and more. In this activity, you will display the Web toolbar and explore some of the buttons.

1. Start Word, if it is not currently running.

A new (unnamed) document appears. While using the Web toolbar, you may have either an existing or a new document open.

2. Click the **View menu**, point to **Toolbars**, and click **Web**.

If Web has a check mark next to it, the Web toolbar is displayed already. Click outside the menu to leave the toolbar selected and close the menu. The Web toolbar appears as shown in Figure 1.22.

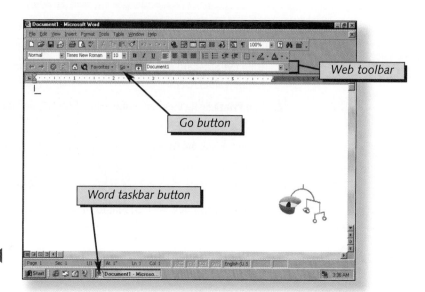

Figure 1.22 ◀
The Web toolbar

Table 1.4 provides a brief description of each button on the Web toolbar.

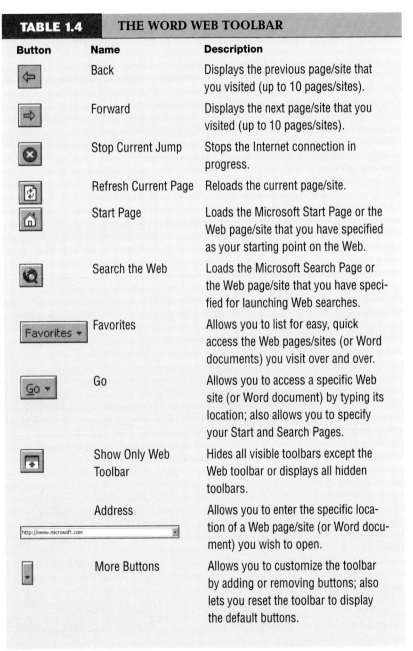

Button	Name	Description
TABLE 1.4	THE WORD WEB TOOLBAR	
	Back	Displays the previous page/site that you visited (up to 10 pages/sites).
	Forward	Displays the next page/site that you visited (up to 10 pages/sites).
	Stop Current Jump	Stops the Internet connection in progress.
	Refresh Current Page	Reloads the current page/site.
	Start Page	Loads the Microsoft Start Page or the Web page/site that you have specified as your starting point on the Web.
	Search the Web	Loads the Microsoft Search Page or the Web page/site that you have specified for launching Web searches.
	Favorites	Allows you to list for easy, quick access the Web pages/sites (or Word documents) you visit over and over.
	Go	Allows you to access a specific Web site (or Word document) by typing its location; also allows you to specify your Start and Search Pages.
	Show Only Web Toolbar	Hides all visible toolbars except the Web toolbar or displays all hidden toolbars.
	Address	Allows you to enter the specific location of a Web page/site (or Word document) you wish to open.
	More Buttons	Allows you to customize the toolbar by adding or removing buttons; also lets you reset the toolbar to display the default buttons.

3. Click the Show Only Web Toolbar button .

The Standard and Formatting toolbars disappear.

4. Click the Show Only Web Toolbar button  again.

The Standard and Formatting toolbars reappear. This button toggles between showing and hiding these toolbars.

5. Connect to the Internet using your *Internet service provider* (ISP). If necessary, type your user name and password.

Note — *If you are not sure how to connect to the Internet or you do not know your user name and password, ask your instructor for assistance.*

6. If the Word window is not active, click the Microsoft Word button on the Windows taskbar.

7. Click the Go button <u>Go ▾</u> and click Open.

The Open Internet Address dialog box appears, as shown in Figure 1.23. You can use this box to go to an Internet site or to open a document on your hard drive or floppy disk.

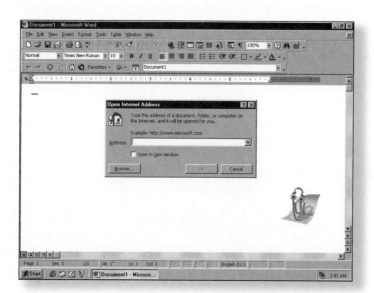

Figure 1.23 ◄
The Open Internet
Address dialog box

8. In the Address box, type www.glencoe.com and then click OK.

Your Web browser launches and connects you to the Glencoe/McGraw-Hill Web home page, as shown in Figure 1.24. The first of several pages at a Web site is commonly called the home page.

ON*the*WEB

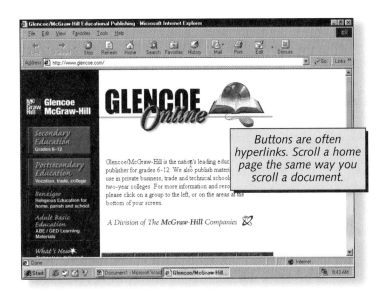

Figure 1.24 ◀
The Glencoe/McGraw-Hill
home page

Buttons are often
hyperlinks. Scroll a home
page the same way you
scroll a document.

9. **Read the main paragraph; then scroll gradually down the page, noting the hypertext and other hyperlinks.**

Not all hypertext is blue, but usually it's a different color than the main text and underlined. Also, remember that buttons, pictures, and even graphic elements, such as bars and bullets, can be hyperlinks. When in doubt, point. If the pointer takes the shape of a hand, you're pointing to a hyperlink.

10. **To return to Word, click the taskbar button.**

11. **Click the Start Page button 🏠 on the Web toolbar.**

Your Web browser reappears and connects you to the Web page designated as your Start Page. Your Internet service provider or your instructor probably designated the Start Page. Start Pages usually provide links to other pages that allow you to explore the Web.

12. **To close each browser window, click the Close button ☒.**

13. **If the Word window is not active, click the Microsoft Word taskbar button.**

14. **Close the current document and exit Word.**

15. **Disconnect from the Internet if your instructor tells you to do so.**

Warning

You may proceed directly to the exercises for this lesson. If, however, you are finished with your computer session, follow the "shut down" procedures for your lab or school environment.

Lesson Summary & Exercises

SUMMARY

More people use computers for word processing than any other task. Word is a powerful word processing application. Lesson 1 introduced basic word processing terms; explained how to start and exit Word; and explored menus, toolbars, and other objects in the Word window. You learned to open, view, navigate, type, edit, name and save, preview, print, and close documents. Also, you learned to get help with Word features from the online Help system. In addition, you learned to connect to the Internet and use Word's Web toolbar for accessing sites on the World Wide Web.

Now that you have completed this lesson, you should be able to do the following:

- Explain word processing. (Word-106)
- Start Microsoft Word and name objects in the document window. (Word-106)
- Provide a brief description of each menu on the Word menu bar. (Word-110)
- Provide a brief description of each button on the Standard toolbar. (Word-112)
- Open a document. (Word-113)
- Use the Office Assistant to obtain help for Word features. (Word-114)
- Search for help with file management tasks. (Word-115)
- Navigate a document using scroll bars. (Word-115)
- Look at documents in four different views. (Word-116)
- Use Insert and Overtype modes to type paragraphs, words, and characters into existing text. (Word-118)
- Find specific pages and text. (Word-119)
- Replace text. (Word-122)
- Use the Undo 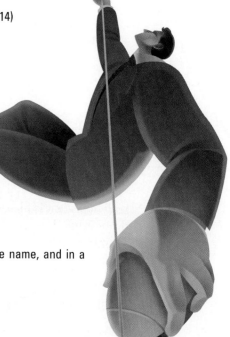, Redo , and Repeat commands to edit text. (Word-124)
- Save a document with the same file name, with a different file name, and in a different folder, and create a folder. (Word-125)
- Insert AutoText. (Word-126)
- Preview a document. (Word-128)
- Print selected pages of a multi-page document. (Word-130)
- Create and send an e-mail message; send an e-mail attachment; and send a Word document via e-mail. (Word-131)
- Close a document and reopen it from the File menu. (Word-132)
- Connect to the Internet. (Word-134)
- Name buttons on the Web toolbar, type a Web address in the Go and Address boxes, and navigate a Web site. (Word-135)
- Disconnect from the Internet. (Word-137)

Lesson Summary & Exercises

CONCEPTS REVIEW

1 TRUE/FALSE

Circle T if the statement is true or F if the statement is false.

T F **1.** Items listed on menus are called commands because they tell the computer what to do.

T F **2.** Only the Formatting toolbar is expandable and customized for individual users.

T F **3.** To display a list of toolbars, click View on the menu bar and point to Toolbars.

T F **4.** The Normal View is the ideal choice for typing and editing text.

T F **5.** Web Layout View, a button on the Web toolbar, is useful for navigating the Web.

T F **6.** To turn on Insert mode, press the Insert key on the keyboard.

T F **7.** The Office Assistant is controlled by a command on the Tools menu.

T F **8.** To scroll rapidly, click a scroll arrow on the vertical scroll bar.

T F **9.** To print all pages of a document, click the Print button on the Standard toolbar.

T F **10.** To exit Microsoft Word, click the Close button or click the Exit command on the File menu.

2 MATCHING

Match each of the terms on the left with the definitions on the right.

TERMS

1. insertion point
2. Edit menu
3. ScreenTip
4. taskbar
5. scroll bar
6. status bar
7. title bar
8. Toolbars submenu
9. Insert menu
10. word processor

DEFINITIONS

a. Flashing vertical bar that indicates where text you type will appear

b. Displays the program name and the current document name

c. Includes the command to find text

d. Controls which Word toolbars display on screen

e. Controls elements that can be added to a document, such as AutoText

f. Part of the Word application window that allows you to move around in a document

g. Contains the Start menu and buttons for all open applications

h. Displays the name of a toolbar button when you point to the button

i. Indicates location within a document and the typing mode

j. Application that allows creation of text-based documents

Lesson Summary & Exercises

3 COMPLETION

Fill in the missing word or phrase for each of the following statements.

1. The _____ menu allows you to change the appearance of text.

2. The animated character that answers specific questions, offers tips, and provides Help for Word features is called the _____.

3. The _____ menu is used to save a document.

4. Use this key to erase errors to the left of the insertion point as you type: _____.

5. The _____ menu allows you to create and arrange text in columns and rows.

6. The _____ menu contains commands that allow you to bring text, pictures, hyperlinks, and special symbols into a document.

7. The _____ menu contains a list of the most recently opened documents.

8. The Print Preview button is on the _____ toolbar.

9. Dragging the _____ displays a text box showing the current page number of a document.

10. To select a word, _____ it.

4 SHORT ANSWER

Write a brief answer to each of the following questions.

1. If the insertion point is at the end of the second line of text, what is a quick way to move the insertion point to the beginning of the first line?

2. Describe how to scroll a document one screen at a time.

3. Describe how to activate the Overtype mode using the mouse and how to deactivate it.

4. On which toolbar is the Open button? the Bold button?

5. Name four document views and describe each view briefly.

6. Name two characters that cannot be used for naming a file in the Save As dialog box.

7. Describe two ways to close Microsoft Word.

8. Describe a way to learn the name and purpose of a button or bar in the Word window.

9. How could you hide the Standard and Formatting toolbars while browsing on the Web?

10. Describe how to start Microsoft Word.

5 IDENTIFICATION

Label each of the elements of the Word window in Figure 1.25.

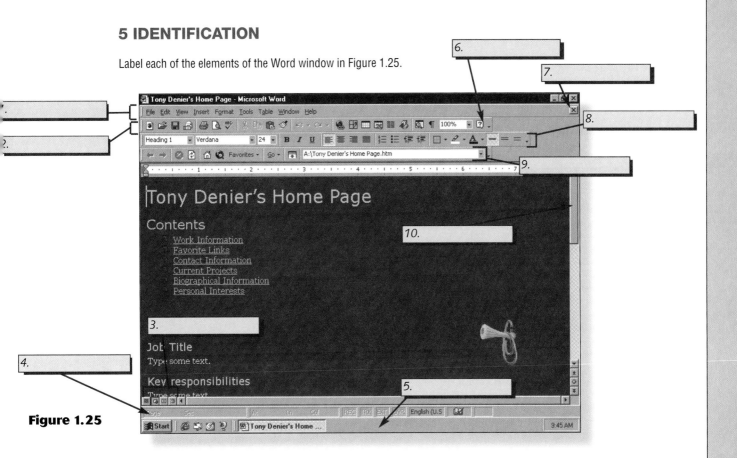

Figure 1.25

SKILLS REVIEW

Complete each of the Skills Review problems in sequential order to review your skills to start Word; identify objects in the document window; open documents; get Help; scroll and view documents; insert, find, and edit text; save, preview, print, and close documents; and exit Word.

1 Starting Word and Opening a File

1. Click the **Start button** 🏁 Start .
2. Point to **Programs**, and click **Microsoft Word**.
3. On the Standard toolbar, click the **Open button** 📂.
4. Click the **Look in arrow**; then click the drive (and folder, if necessary) that contains your Student Data Disk.
5. In the list of files, double-click **Star Gazette Article**.

2 Using Help

1. On the Help menu, click **What's This?**.
2. Click the **Print Preview button** 🔍, and read the ScreenTip.
3. Click anywhere on the screen, and click the **Office Assistant**.
4. In the *What would you like to do?* box, type preview and click **Search**.
5. Click the **Preview a document before printing option**.

Lesson Summary & Exercises

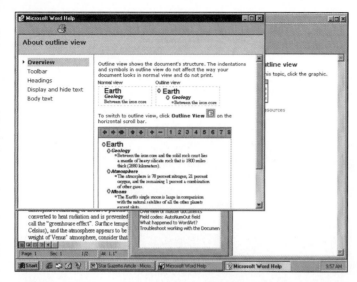

Figure 1.26

6. Read the Help window and explore the **edit text in print preview** link.

7. Click the **Show button** , if necessary.

8. On the Answer Wizard tab in the *What would you like to do?* box, type Outline View and click **Search**.

9. Click the **About outline view topic**.

10. Click the graphic in the Help window, read the information (Figure 1.26), and close this special window.

11. On the Contents tab, open the **Typing, Navigating Documents, and Selecting Text book icon**.

12. Open the **Selecting Text book icon**, and click the **Select text and graphics topic**.

13. Click the **Select text and graphics by using the mouse link**.

14. Read the Help information about selecting a word, line, sentence, and paragraph.

15. Click the **Index tab**, and type print in the *Type keywords* box.

16. Then in the *Type keywords* box, type help topic and click **Search**. Read the Help window.

17. Click the **Hide button** , and close the Help menu.

3 Scrolling and Viewing a Document

1. In *Star Gazette Article*, scroll a line at a time until the *Geology* heading is at the top of the window.

2. Scroll down an entire screen; then scroll rapidly to the top of the document.

3. Click the **horizontal scroll box** and drag it to the right as far as it will go; then drag it all the way to the left.

4. Click the **Print Layout View button** .

5. Scroll to the far left and far right and notice the approximate width of side margins and whether they are even.

6. Click the **Web Layout View button** .

7. Scroll rapidly to the bottom; then press Ctrl + Home to go to the top.

8. Click the **Normal View button** .

4 Inserting a Paragraph

1. With **Star Gazette Article** still open, press [Ctrl] + [End] to go to the end of the document and press [Enter ←].

2. Verify that Insert mode is active and type the following paragraph, erasing errors as you type:

   > The Earth's single moon is large in comparison with the natural satellites of all the other planets except for Pluto. Astronomers actually consider the Earth-Moon system to be a double planet. Its size gives the moon a significant gravitational influence on the Earth, causing our oceans to have tides.

5 Finding Specific Text and Pages

1. Click the **Find button** 🔍 on the Standard toolbar, and type subduction in the Find what box (Figure 1.27).

2. Click the **Find Next button**.

3. Click anywhere in the document.

4. Click after the word *subduction* and type this text with a space before and after it: (one plate sliding under the adjacent plate)

5. Find *the system*; insert the word solar between the two words.

6. Click the **Go To tab**. In the Go to what list box, click **Page** and type 2 in the Enter page number box. Then click the **Go To button**.

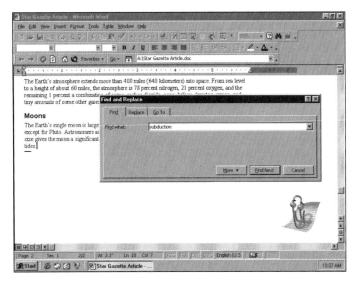

Figure 1.27

7. In the Enter page number box, type -1 and click the **Go To button**.

6 Replacing, Selecting, and Deleting Text

1. Find the word *roman*.

2. Activate **Overtype mode**, and change *r* to *R*.

3. Find the word *sun* and change *S* to *s*.

4. Find *effect* and overtype the punctuation marks to put the period first.

5. Locate *nitrogen*; change the comma after it to a semicolon.

6. In the same sentence, change the comma after *oxygen* to a semicolon, too.

7. Search for *it's* and delete the apostrophe.

8. Click **Find Next** again and delete the apostrophe in the second occurrence.

9. Click **Find Next** once more. The Office Assistant indicates that the search is complete and no more occurrences were found.

10. Find *by far*; then delete the phrase.

11. Click the **Replace tab**. In the Find what box, type Venus's. In the Replace with box, type Venus'. Click **Find Next** and click **Replace**. Continue searching to correct all occurrences.

12. Find the second location of *drift*. Verify that this short sentence appears twice in this paragraph. Drag through the repeated sentence and delete it. Close the Find and Replace dialog box.

7 Undoing, Redoing, and Repeating Actions

1. Find the word *percent*. Select it and replace it with the percent sign (%).

2. Find three other occurrences of the word *percent*. In each instance, use the **Repeat command** to change the word to the percent sign (%).

3. Close the Find and Replace dialog box.

4. Click the **Undo button** until each occurrence of the word *percent* is restored.

5. Click the **Redo button** to restore the percent sign in all four instances; then reverse those actions to restore all four occurrences of *percent*.

8 Naming and Saving a Document

1. With *Star Gazette Article* still open, click **Save As** on the File menu.

2. Be sure the drive that contains your Student Data Disk shows in the *Save in* box and select the *Skills Review* folder.

3. In the File name box, edit the name to be Star Gazette Article - Edited. Click the **Save button**.

9 Inserting AutoText and Saving Changes

1. Press Ctrl + End and press Enter two times.

2. Click the **View menu**, point to **Toolbars**, and click **AutoText**.

3. On the AutoText toolbar, click the **All Entries button**.

4. Point to **Header/Footer** and click **Filename**.

5. Click the **Insert menu** and click **Date and Time**.

6. Click the month-year format and click **OK**.

7. Insert / between the file name and date.

8. Click the **Save button** on the Standard toolbar.

9. Hide the **AutoText toolbar**.

10 Previewing and Printing

1. Open *Long Document - Edited* in the *Tutorial* folder on your Student Data Disk, and click the **Print Preview button**.

2. Click the **Multiple Pages button**, and select **2 x 3 pages**.

3. Click the **scroll arrow** to preview the second set of six pages.

4. Click anywhere in the document, and click anywhere on page 12 (bottom right) to enlarge the text.

5. Click the page again and continue scrolling to the end of the document.

6. Click the **Print Layout View button** ▣.

7. Scroll to page 14 and click anywhere on the page.

8. Click the **File menu** and click **Print**.

9. In the Print Range area, click the **Current page option**.

10. Verify that the Number of copies is set to 1, and click **OK**.

11 Closing and Reopening Files and Exiting Word

1. With *Long Document - Edited* open, click the **Close button** 🖻.

2. Click the **Close button** 🖻 to close *Star Gazette Article - Edited*.

3. Click the **File menu** and click *Star Gazette Article*.

4. Click the **Close button** 🖻 on the Standard toolbar.

5. Click the **Close button** on the title bar ☒ to exit Word.

LESSON APPLICATIONS

1 Opening, Scrolling, and Viewing Documents

Open a document on your Student Data Disk. Navigate and view the document.

1. Start Word, if necessary. Open *Long Document - Edited* in the *Tutorial* folder on your Student Data Disk.

2. Navigate to the end of *Long Document - Edited*.

3. Switch from the current view to Print Layout View.

4. Switch to Outline View and scroll to the far right and back to the far left.

5. Switch to Web Layout View.

6. Compare the page with a Web page you visited recently.

7. On a separate sheet, write three words to represent similarities between this page and the Web page you have in mind. Write three more words to represent differences.

8. Switch to Normal View.

2 Inserting and Editing Text and AutoText

Create a new document. Type and edit the copy; then insert AutoText.

1. In Normal View, click the New Blank Document button.

2. Type a sentence for each of the words noted in step 7 of Lesson Application 1.

3. Type headings for each group of sentences.

4. Revise your text: add and delete or replace words as needed, using the Undo button and the Redo button, if appropriate.

5. Then proofread and edit your text.

6. On the second line below your text, insert Header/Footer AutoText showing Created on.

7. Then, on the next line, insert Header/Footer AutoText showing Last printed.

8. Hide the AutoText toolbar.

3 Previewing and Printing Documents

Word updates the *Printed on* information on your printout as well as in your file. Preview your new document before printing it.

1. Click the Print Preview button.

2. Click the One Page button.

3. Switch to Normal View. Insert enough hard returns at the beginning of the document to put the first heading around two inches from the top of the page.

4. Preview the document again.

5. Verify that you have two hard returns below the first heading and above and below the second heading.

6. Preview once more.

7. Click the Print button on the Standard toolbar.

4 Saving and Closing Documents

Save your document on your Student Data Disk. Close both of the open documents.

1. Click Save As on the File menu and save the document as **Compare** in the **Lesson Applications** folder on your Student Data Disk. Then, close **Compare**.

2. Close **Long Document - Edited** without saving any changes you may have made accidentally.

3. Reopen **Compare** from the File menu and read the updated AutoText at the end of the file. Below the AutoText type By: followed by your name.

4. Click the Save button and close the document.

PROJECTS

1 Two at a Time

Can you open two files with one click of the Open button? Search Help to find out if or how it can be done. In a new, blank document, type a summary of the information you remember. At the same time, open **Step Write Article** and **Write This Way** on your Student Data Disk. Observe the appearance of both documents in Print Layout View and close **Write This Way**. What differences did you notice? Are such differences important? Can you suggest ways to improve the appearance of *both* documents? Type your remarks in the unnamed document. Close the unnamed file without saving changes. Close the **Step Write Article** file.

2 Write This Way

An article you wrote for *The Small Business Journal* needs work before you can fax it to the publisher. Open **Step Write Article** on your Student Data Disk. Save the current document as **Step Write Article Released Version** in the **Projects** folder on your Student Data Disk. Search for *wake?*. Insert the following two paragraphs, starting on the line below the word *wake?*:

Common faults include excess words, which waste time for both writer and readers; impressive-sounding words and jargon, which often block communication; indefinite words, which are colorless and boring; long words and sentences, which raise reading difficulty; and passive voice, which hides meaning by omitting action words.

Use grammar, spelling, and other checker software—but not to replace your editing and proofreading. For extra quality assurance, have documents read by another set of eyes.

Proofread and edit the entire document. Watch for misspelled words, incorrect words, and punctuation errors. In the last paragraph of the document, replace words in parentheses with your name, etc. Insert extra space at the top of the document and AutoText at the end to document the file name and the date the file was created and last printed. Preview the document and print it. Save and close the file.

3 Just the Fax

You need to create a cover page to fax with the article you wrote in Project 2. Open **Fax** on your Student Data Disk. Replace the FROM and DATE information with your name and the current date. Type the number of pages in the Pages information area. Save the revised document as **Fax - Revised** in the **Projects** folder on your Student Data Disk. Close the file.

Reopen **Fax - Revised**, save it as **TSBJ Article** in the **Projects** folder on your Student Data Disk. Add the following message on the second line after the subject. Then, edit, preview, print, and save the document. Close all open documents.

Fritz Kindsvatter approved this article for publication in the next issue. Please let me review typeset copy. My telephone number is *insert your number;* my fax number is *insert your fax number.* If you can, attach it to e-mail *insert your e-mail address.*

4 Writer's Toolbox

You intend to start a business, training people to improve their writing skills and increase their confidence as writers. You realize that Word involves several features that you and the writers you train will find helpful. Display a ScreenTip for the first command on the Tools menu. In a new document window, list these words at the left margin with a hard return after each word: Definition Purpose Location Procedure. Display the Language submenu on the Tools menu. Search extended Help for all you can learn about the Thesaurus feature. What is it? What does it do? How do you use it? Return to your document, recall what you read, and fill in below each word. Don't be concerned about details you may miss. Save the document as **Thesaurus** in the **Projects** folder on your Student Data Disk. Close the document.

5 Background Check

In Lesson Application 4, you created the **Compare** document in which you compared a document in Web Layout View with actual Web sites. Open **Compare** in the **Lesson Applications** folder on your Student Data Disk. Did you note *color* as one of the differences between your documents and Web pages? Display a ScreenTip for the Background command on the Format menu. Ask the Office Assistant for information about it. Jot the procedure on a separate sheet or print the Help window. Apply a background of your choice to the open document. Save the file as **Background** in the **Projects** folder on your Student Data Disk (Figure 1.28). Close the file.

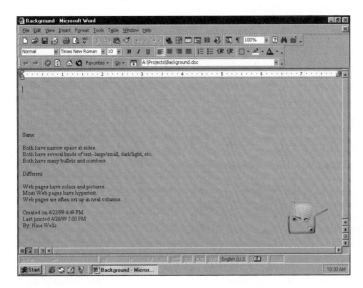

Figure 1.28

6 Out of this World on the Web

You want to explore for information about Venus. With the Web toolbar displayed, connect to the Internet. Visit this site:
solar.cyberworks.net/sb/venus.html

Read the information on the Web page and explore the links for additional information about Venus. Close the browser, disconnect from the Internet, and return to Word.

Project in Progress

7 Now You're in Business

You received state approval to do business under the name *I-Comm*. I-Comm will provide a variety of writing and editing services for small and medium-sized organizations within 75 miles of your office. Today you received a letter from a local high school student, asking if you would present at their annual Writer's Workshop. The letter asked you to propose a topic or to select one of these topics: Writing School Papers, Writing in Business, Writing for Newspapers and Magazines, Writing for the Web. Create a new document with the following information:

Letter address:

Mr. Steven Banks
Young Writers' Society
Anderson High School
1968 Beechmont Ave.
Your City, ST 00000

Body:

Thank you for your invitation to present a workshop for Young Writers' Society at 10:45 on *insert a date three months in the future.* I am happy to accept. Every one of your suggested topics is excellent. I would prefer, though, to tell students of the difference word processing software, such as Word 2000, can make in their writing.

In a week or two, I'll send the exact title of my presentation and my bio. Please arrange an LCD computer and a screen for my PowerPoint slides.

Insert today's date, a salutation, complimentary closing, your name as the sender, and a title such as Writing Consultant. Add, delete, or change any information; for example, you may prefer one of the suggested workshop topics. Then, edit, save, preview, print, and close the document. If time allows, search Help to see if perhaps you could use a letter *template* to save time when typing letters in the future. Save your reply as **AHS Workshop** in the **Projects** folder on your Student Data Disk (Figure 1.29). Send the document as an e-mail message to your instructor. Exit Word.

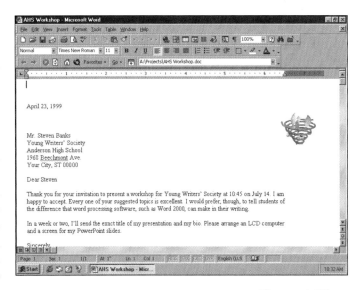

Figure 1.29

LESSON 2

Creating, Editing, and Formatting Documents

CONTENTS

_Creating Documents from Templates

_Assuring Quality

_Selecting and Deleting Sentences, Lines, and Paragraphs

_Moving and Copying Text

_Reformatting Text

_Enhancing the Appearance of Documents

_Inserting and Formatting Graphics

_Sorting Words or Numbers

_Adding Reference Features

_On the Web: Inserting Hyperlinks

OBJECTIVES

After you complete this lesson, you will be able to do the following:

- Open templates and replace variable text to create a new document.
- Check spelling, grammar, and readability.
- Use the Thesaurus feature.
- Use AutoCorrect and AutoText.
- Select and delete sentences, lines, and paragraphs.
- Cut, copy, and paste text.
- Change page and section breaks, margins, alignment, indentations, and character, line, and paragraph spacing; also set tabs.
- Change font style, size, attributes, and color.
- Add special effects to enhance document appearance.
- Use the Format Painter and apply styles.
- Insert symbols and special characters.
- Insert, edit, and format graphics.
- Sort lists and add bullets and numbering.
- Insert and modify page numbers.
- Create and modify headers and footers.
- Create footnotes and a table of contents.
- Create hyperlinks to pages, documents, and Web sites.

This lesson introduces document templates and shows you how to edit, reformat, and enhance documents. You will learn to check spelling and grammar and to move and copy text. You will discover how to add breaks and change margins, alignment, indentations, and spacing. Also, you will learn ways to change text design, size, appearance, and color. You will discover the Clip Gallery as a source of ready-made pictures that you can import into your documents to supplement the text. You will also learn how to sort lists, number pages, insert headers and footers, add footnotes, and create a table of contents.

Organizations that install
Microsoft Word 2000 aim to
minimize input time and
maximize output quality.
Get acquainted with all the
key features of Word 2000,
so that you will know which
features you need in a
given situation. Likewise,
become familiar with var-
ied ways to perform a task
so that you will know which
method(s) you prefer.

CREATING DOCUMENTS FROM TEMPLATES

You have learned that you can create documents by clicking the New Blank Document button. In many situations, though, you do not have to start new documents on a blank screen. Word 2000 has preformatted **template** models that you can follow. A template includes necessary document parts, ordered and formatted. For example, the standard headings (*To:, From:,* and so on) and the current date are already displayed and properly arranged in the memo template. You replace the **variable information**—the text that is different in each memo you create. The template files are in the New dialog box opened by clicking New on the File menu.

Each tab in the New dialog box represents a group of documents, such as Letters & Faxes, Memos, Reports, and Web Pages. To see the templates available in a group, click the tab. When you click the name of a specific template, a Preview box lets you see the template design. When you open the template you want to use, Word opens a *copy* of it. That way, you can change the model document however you want and still have the original template unchanged.

HANDS
On

Opening a Template and Replacing Variable Text

In this activity, you will open a memo template and use it to create a memo.

Warning

If you are storing your files on a floppy disk, be sure to have a blank, formatted disk on hand before proceeding with the following activity. Create new folders on the disk as appropriate prior to saving a file. (To create a new folder from the Save dialog box, select the drive that contains the new disk, click the Create New Folder button, type the folder name, and click OK. You can then save your file in this newly created folder.)

Because all hands-on activities and end-of-lesson activities will not fit on one floppy disk, you may have to check one or more disks to find the files you need for the activities in this tutorial.

1. Start Word; click the **File menu**, and click **New**.

The New dialog box displays, as shown in Figure 2.1. You can access the New dialog box only through the File menu. The New Blank Document button, as you know, opens a new, blank document, rather than the template files.

2. Click the **Memos tab**, if it is not on top.

Templates for creating memos appear.

3. Click the **Contemporary Memo icon**.

A preview of this template is displayed in the Preview window.

4. Click **Document** in the Create New box, if it is not selected, and click **OK**.

Figure 2.1
The New dialog box

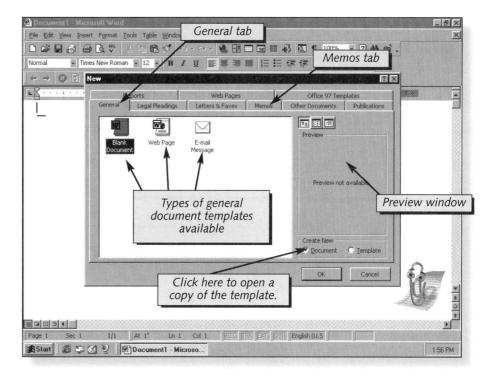

General tab

Memos tab

Types of general document templates available

Preview window

Click here to open a copy of the template.

Note   *If Template was selected when you clicked OK, you would open the actual template, not a copy of it. Then when you type, you would change the template.*

Opening and Using a Template

1. Click New on the File menu.

2. Click the tab for the type of document in the New dialog box.

3. Click the template you want to use.

4. Verify that Document is selected in the Create New box.

5. Click OK.

6. Click anywhere within the brackets.

7. Type the replacement text.

A copy of the **Contemporary Memo** template opens. The title bar indicates *Document* followed by a number, like any other new document, because you opened a copy of the template. If you opened the actual template, the title bar would indicate, *Template1*.

5. Scroll and read the document.

6. After *To:*, click anywhere within the brackets.

You have selected variable text; you need to replace it with your information.

7. Type All Sales Associates **to replace the variable text.**

8. After *CC:* (indicates *copies*), click the variable text and type: Nancy Riberts, Joe DiFillippo.

9. After *From:*, click the words in brackets and type your name.

10. After *Re:* (stands for *in regard*), click the bracketed text and type SALES PARTY.

11. Below the horizontal line, click before the first character and drag to the end of the last paragraph to select all three paragraphs.

When you begin typing, you will replace the selected text.

12. Type the following message exactly as shown. Remember to use `Backspace` **to erase errors as you type, and allow text to wrap at the end of each line. When finished, your memo should look like Figure 2.2.**

Have you heard the good news. Sales for third quarter were way up—37 percent! We'll meet at 4 on Friday afternoon to celebrate our success. Food and drinks will be provided, so come hungry. Those of you—you know who you are—who reached the $200,000 mark for the quarter should be prepared to say a few inspiring words. See you there!

Atrium or Gremban Patio - watch e-mail.

13. Save your document as *Template Memo* in the *Tutorial* folder on your Student Data Disk.

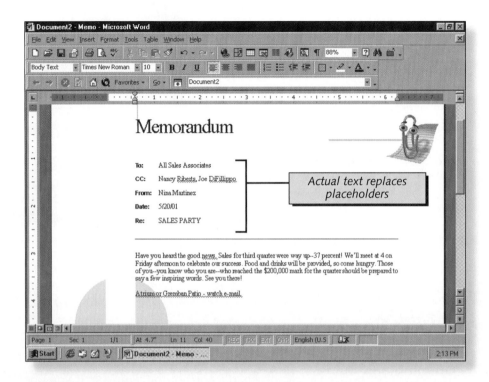

Figure 2.2
Memo created from a template

ASSURING QUALITY

All writers make errors—in spelling, punctuation, subject-verb agreement, word choice, typing, verb tense, and many other things. Good writers ***proof-read*** their documents and correct their mistakes, declaring a document final only when it is free of errors. Editing and proofreading are important for two reasons: communication and image. Errors in documents may cause readers to misunderstand your message, wasting your time and theirs. Besides, the documents you prepare—whether for yourself or an employer—represent you. Their quality and appearance convey a message about your attitude and competence.

No software can edit and proofread for you. Word provides tools to help you check spelling, grammar, and text-difficulty factors. The Spelling and Grammar tools flag potential errors; you can decide if a correction is needed in each instance. When Word detects a potential spelling or grammar error, the Spelling and Grammar Status icon on the status bar displays a red X. Word's AutoCorrect feature helps prevent some spelling, capitalization, and grammar errors by automatically correcting such errors as you type them. To confirm the AutoCorrect settings on the computer you are using, click AutoCorrect on the Tools menu and click the AutoCorrect tab. Then select the options you want Word to automatically correct and click OK. The Copy,

Cut, and Paste features enable you to reword sentences and paragraphs by moving or copying text from one place to another. The thesaurus can find substitutes for words that are overused or used incorrectly in your documents. With the Replace feature you learned about in Lesson 1, you can change occurrences of words used too often and correct repeated errors.

Checking Spelling, Grammar, and Readability

The wavy, red lines in your documents mark words not in the Spelling dictionary. When you right-click one of these words, a ***shortcut menu*** appears. If the menu lists the correct spelling, click the correct word. If the correct spelling is not on the menu, you may correct the spelling manually or click Ignore All. Clicking Ignore All tells Word to disregard all instances of the underlined word in the current document. (Clicking Add would put the underlined word into the Spelling dictionary. You must *not* choose the Add option unless the computer belongs to you.) The wavy, red line disappears when you click one of these options. Another option on the shortcut menu is the Spelling command. Clicking it opens the Spelling dialog box, which is useful for checking spelling in long documents.

Wavy, green lines mark grammatical forms not found in the grammar rules for U.S. English usage. When you right-click this text, a shortcut menu displays. If the menu suggests an improvement to your text, you can click the suggested change if it truly improves your text. If the text is correct as is, you may click Ignore to remove the green underline.

When you click the Spelling and Grammer button ⬛, you can check spelling and grammar simultaneously throughout an entire document. The Spelling and Grammar tool goes automatically to the first potential spelling or grammar error and shows the sentence, with the problem highlighted. A tip displays with grammar problems, providing the related grammar rule and one or more examples. As soon as you choose to change or ignore the highlighted text, Word will move to the next possible error.

The ***readability*** of text refers to how clear and easy it is to read. Word analyzes text, applies a special formula, and rates it with a Reading Ease score. (The length of sentences and the difficulty of words are involved in readability formulas.) Word also assigns a Grade Level score to represent the readability of text. For example, a score of Grade Level 7 indicates that most seventh graders would be able to read and understand the text. Someone with less reading skill may have trouble with it, however. If desired, you can review a readability report after you check the spelling and grammar in a document. Desirable scores for most documents (read by the general public) include a Reading Ease score of 60 to 70 and a Grade Level score of 7 to 8. Technical documents (read by experts in the technical field) often score below 60 and above 8.

Checking Spelling as You Type

In this activity, you will check the spelling of words in your memo underlined with red, wavy lines.

Checking Spelling

1. Right-click a word underlined in red.

2. Click an option on the shortcut menu or correct the spelling manually.

 *If wavy, red or green lines do not show on your screen, the Spelling and Grammar features have been turned off. To activate these tools, click the Tools menu; then click Options. On the Spelling & Grammar tab, click these checkboxes: Check spelling as you type, Always suggest corrections, and Check grammar as you type. Verify that CUSTOM.DIC shows in the Custom dictionary list box and that Standard shows in the Writing style list box.*

1. Point to the underlined name *Riberts* and right-click anywhere in the name.

A shortcut menu opens, showing the suggested word *Roberts* (Figure 2.3). You check a personnel list and see that *Roberts*—not *Riberts*—is the correct name.

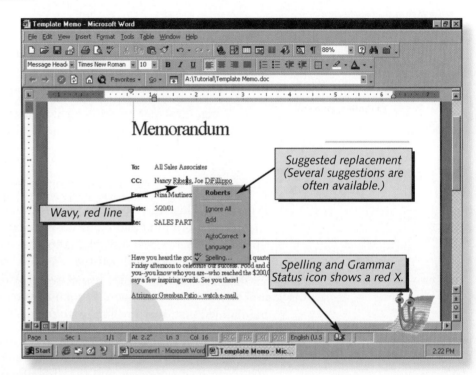

Figure 2.3
Shortcut menu with a suggested word

2. On the shortcut menu, click *Roberts*.

The correct name replaces the incorrect one in your memo, and the red, wavy underline disappears.

3. Now, right-click the name *DiFillippo*.

The shortcut menu offers no suggested replacements since the spelling dictionary does not contain a word similar to this one. You verify that *D-i-F-i-l-l-i-p-p-o* is the correct spelling.

4. On the shortcut menu, click Ignore All.

The wavy, red underline disappears.

5. Right-click the word *Gremban* in the last line, and click Spelling.

The Spelling dialog box appears, as shown in Figure 2.4. The sentence appears in the window, with the specific word highlighted in red.

6. Click the Ignore All button.

To change the Spelling and Grammar options, click Spelling and Grammar on the Tools menu. Click Options and select the items you want Word to check.

Figure 2.4
The Spelling dialog box

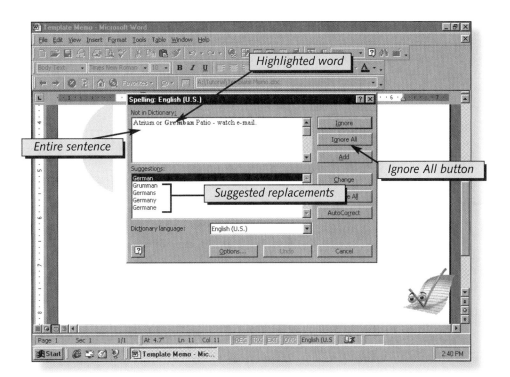

If you insert text later that also contains *Gremban,* the word will not be underlined.

7. Right-click any other word with a red underline, and select either a **suggested word** or **Ignore All**.

If the underlined text is incorrect but the menu does not show the correct spelling, click the text to close the shortcut menu. Make the correction. If the underline remains, right-click the word again and click Ignore All.

Never add words to a dictionary unless you have permission to do so or you own the computer. In any case, always check a word carefully before adding it to the Word dictionary.

8. Save the changes to the document.

Checking Grammar and Readability

In this activity, you will check the grammar of text in your memo underlined with a green, wavy line, and you will check the readability of the document.

1. Right-click anywhere in the last line of text.

The shortcut menu appears, pointing out that you have typed a fragment instead of a complete sentence. You realize that fragments are inappropriate in all but the most casual writing. You choose, however, to go with the text as it is, since your meaning seems clear.

2. On the shortcut menu, click **Ignore**.

The text is unchanged; the green underline disappears.

3. Right-click the period following the word *news* (first sentence), and click **Grammar**.

The Grammar dialog box appears as shown in Figure 2.5, displaying the sentence that contains the word *news*. The Office Assistant explains the grammar rule involved. After reading the rule, you realize that a question mark should replace the period, as suggested in the Grammar dialog box.

Figure 2.5 ◄
The Grammar dialog box
and grammar tip

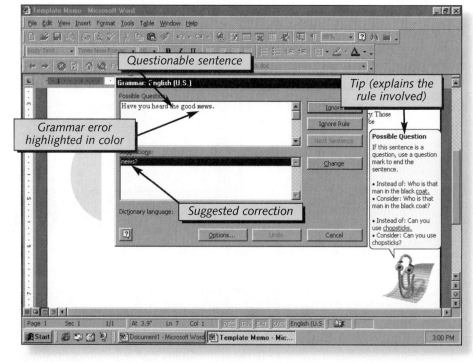

Word
BASICS

Checking Grammar and Readability

To check grammar:

1. Right-click text underlined in green.

2. Click the suggested change, correct the error manually, or click Ignore.

To check readability:

1. Click the Spelling and Grammar button.

2. Click the Options button.

3. Click the Show readability statistics checkbox; click OK.

4. Check the spelling and grammar.

5. Read the readability report; click OK.

Not all suggested grammar changes are improvements. Read the information very carefully before deciding to change your text. Also, Word may not detect some errors.

4. In the Grammar dialog box, click **Change**.

The dialog box and tip close. A question mark replaces the period and the green line disappears.

5. Right-click any other text with a green underline and check it. Click **Ignore** only if you are certain the text is grammatically correct. If you are not sure, click **About this sentence** or **Grammar** and study the rule. Then select the appropriate option.

The Grammar dialog box contains an Ignore All option. This option is useful in editing a long document containing many examples of the same grammatical form. Rather than reviewing each underlined occurrence, you could tell Word once and for all to ignore the rule throughout the document.

6. When finished, save your changes.

7. Navigate to the top of your document, then click the **Spelling and Grammar button** ⌨.

The Spelling and Grammar dialog box opens. You will set the writing style (formality of grammar) and request the reading scores for the text.

8. Click the **Options button**.

The Spelling & Grammar options appear.

9. Under Grammar, click the **Check grammar with spelling option** and click the **Show readability statistics option**, if a check mark doesn't appear. Click the **Writing style arrow** and click **Standard**. Click **OK**.

Word checks the document and jumps to any possible spelling or grammar error.

10. Correct any spelling and grammar errors, if necessary.

When the spelling and grammar check is complete, the Readability Statistics report displays, as shown in Figure 2.6.

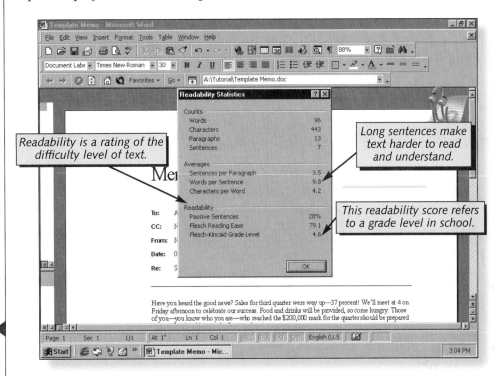

Figure 2.6
The Readability Statistics report

11. Review the readability statistics for the document, noting the word count, the average words per sentence, the Flesch Reading Ease score, and the Flesch-Kincaid Grade Level score.

12. Click **OK** and then save your changes.

HANDS

Using the Thesaurus

If the grade level score for a general document is 8.5 or above, you may want to try replacing some long, uncommon words with short, common words. The ***Thesaurus*** tool—a source of synonyms and anonyms—can help you. If you tend to use the same words repeatedly, the thesaurus can also help you vary your vocabulary. In this activity, you will use the Thesaurus tool to find replacements for several words in the current document.

Using the Thesaurus

1. Select the word in question.

2. Click the Tools menu, point to Language, and click Thesaurus.

3. Click a synonym or type a word in the Replace with Synonym box.

4. Click Replace.

Figure 2.7 ◀
The Thesaurus dialog box

Hints & Tips

To find a synonym quickly, select the word you would like to replace and right-click. On the shortcut menu, point to Synonyms and then, if synonyms are suggested, click the option that fits the context of your sentence.

1. Find and select *good*.

2. Click the **Tools menu**, point to **Language**, and click **Thesaurus**.

Warning

If the Thesaurus command does not appear on the Language submenu, see your instructor. You may need to install the thesaurus.

The Thesaurus dialog box appears, as shown in Figure 2.7.

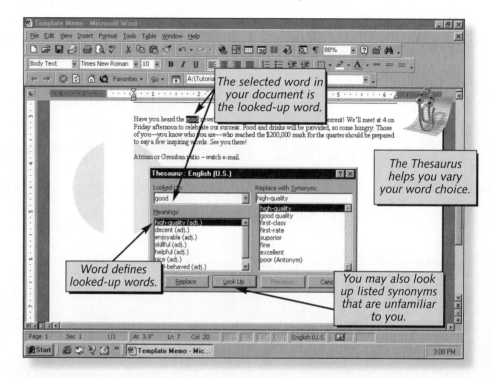

3. In the Replace with Synonym box, click **excellent**. Then click the **Look Up button**.

The word *excellent* now appears in the Looked Up box. As shown in the Meanings box, the word means outstanding—an appropriate replacement for *good*.

4. Click the **Replace button**.

The word *outstanding* replaces *good* in your document.

5. Save your changes and close the file.

SELECTING AND DELETING SENTENCES, LINES, AND PARAGRAPHS

In Lesson 1 you deleted whole words and phrases with one click or by pressing ⌨Delete⌨—if you selected the word or phrase first. For maximum efficiency when editing, you need ways to select bigger chunks of text—sentences, lines, whole paragraphs, or more. You can do many word processing activities, besides deleting, more easily and quickly if you first select the affected text.

Using

Using AutoCorrect and AutoText

In this activity, you will ask the Office Assistant for help using the Word feature called AutoCorrect. (The Spelling Checker must be active.)

(Handwritten notes at top: Tools, Auto Correct — auto correct (c) = © / Add (ac) = (c). space. This lets you do both.)

1. Click the **Office Assistant**, search for information on frequently used text. Explore the **Overview of AutoCorrect topic**, the **Store and insert frequently used text and graphics topic**, and other related links.

2. Click the **Minimize button** 🔲, instead of closing the Help window.

3. In a new document, complete the following thought starters, recalling the Help information. (Type short, complete sentences, without typing the following text.)

    AutoCorrect is a feature that . . .

    Frequently used text may be . . .

    To use AutoCorrect, you must first . . .

    (Handwritten: Ctrl + L + Delete)

    AutoCorrect corrects several kinds of errors; namely, . . .

    AutoCorrect does not correct all spelling and typing errors because . . .

    Individual users can adapt AutoCorrect; for example, . . .

    I often misspell these three words: . . .

4. Explore the same Help screens for information you may have missed previously. Then minimize the Help window, and add any key points to your document that you missed.

(Handwritten left margin: To find a sentence Press control than press click)

Figure 2.8
The AutoCorrect dialog box

5. Click the **Tools menu** and click **AutoCorrect**.

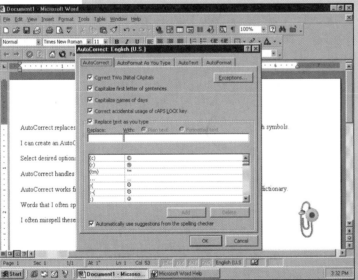

6. Read the five options at the top of the AutoCorrect tab (Figure 2.8), note on a sheet of paper which ones are not selected, and select each option.

7. Scroll the *Replace text as you type* list box to explore the changes that AutoCorrect will make as you type. Verify that the three words you identified are in this list box. Click **OK**.

8. Watch the screen as you type the following sentence three times as fast as you can—so that you will make numerous typing errors: The quick brown fox jumped over the lazy dog. Then delete these sentences.

9. Click **AutoCorrect** on the Tools menu. Refer to your list of AutoCorrect options (step 6). On the dialog box, deselect any options that were deselected previously, and click **OK**.

10. Save the document as *AutoCorrect* in the *Tutorial* folder on your Student Data Disk, close the file, and close Help.

(Handwritten bottom-left notes: Ctrl Z undo / CTRL Y redo / C-C copy / C-X cut / C-V paste / C-F find)

(Handwritten bottom-center notes: C-A = (Highlight all) / If you want to undo continue control then arrow / click any you don't want in the "select all" command)

You can select a word by double-clicking it. You can select a sentence by pressing [Ctrl] and clicking. You can select a line by simply pointing to it in the **selection bar** (the invisible column between the left edge of the document window and the left margin of the page). Selecting an entire paragraph is as easy as triple-clicking anywhere in the paragraph. You can select an entire document by clicking Select All on the Edit menu.

 The Undo button 🔄 *, Redo button* 🔄 *, and Repeat command on the Edit menu reverse actions involving larger units of text as well as individual words. For example, after deleting a sentence or paragraph, you can put it back, if desired.*

Deleting Sentences, Lines, and Paragraphs

In this activity, you will delete a paragraph, a sentence, a line, and a word.

1. **Open the *Home Page Support* file on your Student Data Disk.**

2. **Press [Ctrl] and click anywhere in the last sentence of the first paragraph. Press [Delete] to remove the sentence.**

3. **Move the pointer to the selection bar and point to the second line of text in the second paragraph. When the pointer becomes a right pointer, click the selection bar, as shown in Figure 2.9.**

Figure 2.9
A selected line

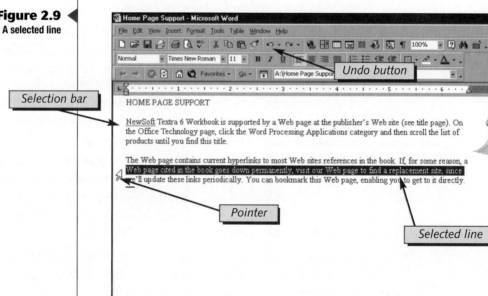

4. **Press [Delete] to erase the entire line.**

5. **Click the Undo button 🔄 to restore the line.**

6. **Triple-click anywhere in the second paragraph.**

The entire paragraph is selected.

Word BASICS

Deleting Text

To select and delete a sentence:

1. Press and hold `Ctrl`.

2. Click anywhere in the sentence.

3. Press `Delete`.

To select and delete a line:

1. In the selection bar, click the line.

2. Press `Delete`.

To select and delete a paragraph:

1. Triple-click anywhere in the paragraph.

2. Press `Delete`.

To copy text using the drag-and-drop method, select the text and then press and hold `Ctrl` while clicking and holding on the selected text. Continue holding `Ctrl` while moving the text to the new location. Then release `Ctrl`.

Edit . Clipboard.
View .

7. Press `Delete` to delete the entire paragraph.

8. Click the **Undo button** to restore the paragraph.

9. Select and delete the second sentence in the second paragraph.

10. On the Edit menu, click **Select All** to select the entire document.

11. Click anywhere in the document window to deselect the text.

12. Save the file as *Select* in the *Tutorial* folder on your Student Data Disk; then close it.

MOVING AND COPYING TEXT

Besides deleting, *cutting* text is another way to remove it from the window. Text that you cut is saved onto the **Office Clipboard,** a temporary holding area for text and graphics. You can then *paste* this cut text into the current document, another one, or to a different Office application, such as Microsoft Excel or Microsoft PowerPoint. Thus, cut-and-paste is a means of moving text. Another way to move text is simply to drag it from its present location and drop it in another place. The drag-and-drop method is handy when you want to move a small amount of text a short distance within the same document.

Cutting and deleting are different procedures. Deleting text is like erasing it; delete text that you know you do not want to use. Cutting is a way to move text; cut text that you know you want to use in another location. If you are unsure, cut the text. If you decide to use it, the text will be on the Office Clipboard, ready to be pasted into your document.

In addition to moving text, you may want to *copy* text in one location and place it in another location. Copying instead of retyping saves time and effort and avoids the risk of typing errors. You can copy text to the Office Clipboard—the original text stays in place—and then paste from it, just like text that you cut. Word also allows you to drag copy to a new location. Again, drag-and-drop works best when you want to copy only a few words and drag them within the same paragraph.

The Paste Special command on the Edit menu allows you to paste items (or *embed*) from the Office Clipboard in a different form. For example, you can cut text from a Word document and paste it as a picture into another Word document or a PowerPoint slide. Similarly, you can cut data from an Excel worksheet and paste it into a Word document.

Cutting, copying, and pasting involve the Clipboard toolbar, which you can display from the View menu like any other toolbar. You can cut or copy a single piece of text and paste it immediately without the Clipboard toolbar; but if you cut a second piece of text without pasting the first, the Clipboard toolbar displays automatically. Then you can paste each text item into a different place or you can paste all the items into one location.

Note   *You can reverse all of these actions—cutting, copying, and pasting—with the Undo and Redo buttons and the Repeat command on the Edit menu.*

Clipbook   Start/Run/clpm

Using the Office Clipboard

In this activity, you will move a sentence to a new location and copy and paste text from one location to another.

1. In the *Tutorial* folder on your Student Data Disk, open *Template Memo.*

2. Display the Clipboard toolbar. Click the **Clear Clipboard button**.

3. Find the words *Food and drinks* and select the sentence.

4. On the Standard toolbar, click the **Cut button**.

The selected sentence disappears from your document and is pasted to the Clipboard. At first, the Clipboard shows four blank areas for holding cut text. If you cut a fifth item from your document, another row of storage areas will open on the Clipboard. If you cut a ninth item without clearing the Clipboard in the meantime, a third row of storage areas will open—12 storage areas in all.

5. Point to the item in the Clipboard toolbar.

A ScreenTip displays the first 50 characters of cut text, as shown in Figure 2.10. You can now paste the cut text wherever you set the insertion point.

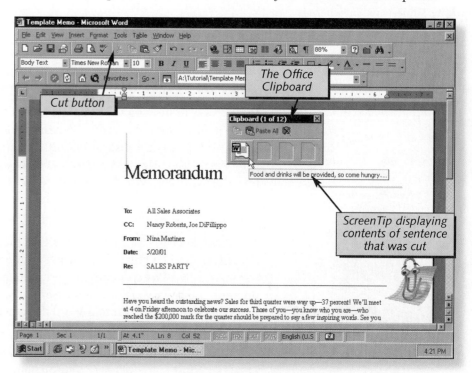

Word BASICS

Using the Office Clipboard

To copy and paste text:

1. Select the text to be copied.

2. Click the Copy button.

3. Click the new location.

4. Click the Paste button.

To cut and paste text:

1. Select the text to be cut.

2. Click the Cut button.

3. Click the new location.

4. Click the Paste button.

Figure 2.10 ◀
Clipboard with one cut item

Another Way

• To open the Toolbars submenu, right-click any displayed toolbar and select the toolbar you want.

• To cut or copy text, select the text to cut or copy and right-click. On the shortcut menu, click Cut or Copy. Right-click the new location to paste the text.

6. Click after *. . . inspiring words.* and click the icon in the Clipboard that represents the cut sentence.

The cut sentence is pasted into this new location.

7. On the Clipboard, click the **Clear Clipboard button**.

The cut text is removed from the Clipboard.

8. After the *From:* heading, select your name, and click the **Copy button** on the Standard toolbar.

The selected text remains in place and is copied to the Clipboard.

9. After the *Date:* heading, select the date, and click the **Copy button** 📋 on the Clipboard toolbar.

The date is copied to the Clipboard. You will paste your name and the date below the circle design on the template.

10. Click below the last line of the memo. Then press ⎋Enter⏎ until the insertion point appears immediately below the circle graphic. Then click the **Paste All button** 📋 Paste All.

Your name and the date are pasted side by side at the insertion point.

11. Insert a space between your name and the date.

12. Save your changes. Clear the Clipboard and close it.

Using Drag-and-Drop) D&D

In this activity, you will drag and drop text in **Template Memo**.

1. Select the phrase *—you know who you are—*.

You will drop this text to appear later in the same sentence.

2. Click and hold the selected text until a box appears below the pointer.

> *Note* — If you see this symbol ⊘ instead of a box below the pointer, the drag-and-drop option is turned off. To turn it on, click the Tools menu and click Options. Click the Edit tab and then select the Drag-and-drop editing option.

⊘ = D&D off)   Tools) Options) Edit > select D&D.

The message *Move to where?* also appears on the status bar.   Drop & Drag

3. Drag the selected text toward the end of the sentence to position the insertion point between *quarter* and *should*.

A faint dotted insertion point shows where the text will be dropped.

4. Click to release the phrase.

The text appears in the new location.

5. Add and delete spaces as necessary in the sentence, and save your changes. Close **Template Memo**.

REFORMATTING TEXT

When you first type text, Word displays every line beginning at the same position on the left side of the screen and on the same line. After you have entered and edited all text, you will want to make sure the *formatting* of your document is professional—especially if the document is for a presentation or a client. The format of a document is the *layout*—the arrangement and spacing of document parts in relation to edges of a *page.* Much reformatting may be done with buttons on the Formatting toolbar. The File menu, Insert menu, Format menu, and horizontal ruler are also involved in reformatting a document.

Formatting is described in terms of printed text. A page usually means a standard-sized sheet (8.5" by 11") on which most documents are printed.

Inserting Page Breaks and Changing Margins

You have not had to think about where one page ends and another begins, though you may have noticed where it occurs. In Normal View, faint, dotted horizontal lines indicate automatic *page breaks.* Page breaks are more obvious in Print Layout View. The blank areas bordering text are called *margins.* So far, you have used the *default* (preset) margins for your documents. In Word, each margin (top, left, right, and bottom) is a conventional width: 1". You can change these margin widths. Narrow margins let you type more text on a page, but wide margins make a page look easier to read.

Page breaks divide text into separate pages. By default, the print area is 9" top to bottom; and Word will fill that area unless you tell it not to. Wherever you want to start a new page you can insert a *manual page break* to override Word's *automatic page breaks*. For example, you might insert page breaks between chapters or main topics of a report. The ones you insert are labeled *Page Break* so that you can tell them from Word's automatic page breaks.

You can also control where automatic page breaks occur. By default, Word will prevent widows and orphans from occurring within a document. A *widow* is the last line of a paragraph printed by itself at the top of a page. An *orphan* is the first line of a paragraph printed by itself at the bottom of a page. If you want to prevent an automatic page break from occurring within certain text (such as a heading and the following paragraph or several paragraphs), select the text that you want to remain together and right-click. Click Paragraph on the shortcut menu and click the Line and Page Breaks tab in the Paragraph dialog box. To avoid an automatic page break within a paragraph, select the *Keep lines together* option in the Paragraph dialog box and click OK; to avoid an automatic page break between two paragraphs, select the *Keep with next* option and click OK.

Margin settings and vertical and horizontal alignment define page setup. In Word, margins may be as narrow as one-quarter inch or as wide as possible for the paper size. Margins of one inch to two inches are typical.

Setting Up Pages

The *vertical alignment*—or relationship of text to the top and bottom edges of a page—is also part of setting up (reformatting) text. Text is *top aligned* by default. The first line of text appears at the top margin, wherever it is. You can change this vertical alignment so that the last line of text prints at the bottom margin *(bottom alignment),* regardless of where the top and bottom margins are set. Another alternative is to place text an equal distance between the top and bottom margin *(centered alignment).*

The *justified* setting distributes *paragraphs* between the top and bottom margins. Justified alignment looks the same as top alignment if the page contains only one paragraph. With two paragraphs on a page, one will be top aligned; the other, bottom aligned. With three paragraphs on a page, one will be aligned at the top, one at the center, and one at the bottom.

Inserting Section Breaks

Varying the margin settings or vertical alignment within a document calls for **section breaks.** Section breaks take the place of page breaks (next page break), or you may use them to divide a page into two or more sections (continuous break), A section break shows up in Normal View as a dotted double line labeled *Section Break* and either *(Next Page)* or *(Continuous).* Section breaks do not show in Print Layout View or a printed page.

HANDS On

Breaking Pages

In this activity, you will insert page breaks and add text in a file on the Student Data Disk.

1. **Open *Astronomy 110* on your Student Data Disk and save it as *Reformatted* in the *Tutorial* folder.**

With the file saved in a different folder with a new name, you can save the changes you make as you go. First, you will add pages by inserting page breaks and type a few words on each new page.

2. **Look at the document in Print Layout View; then switch to Normal View to reformat it.**

3. **Click before the first character; click the Insert menu and click Break.**

The Break dialog box appears, as shown in Figure 2.11.

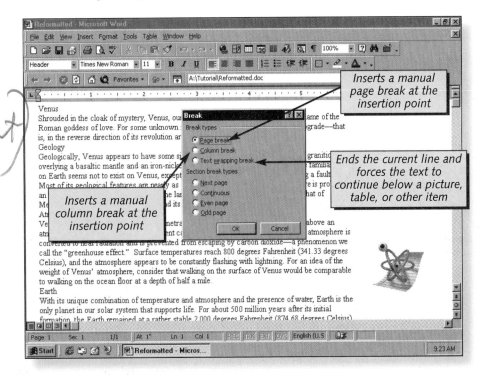

> Inserts a manual page break at the insertion point

> Ends the current line and forces the text to continue below a picture, table, or other item

> Inserts a manual column break at the insertion point

Figure 2.11 ◀
The Break dialog box

4. **Click Page break, if it is not already selected, and click OK.**

You have added a page at the beginning of the document. The text is now on page 2, as shown on the status bar.

5. **Click the Page Break line and type the following text:** Venus: Roman goddess of gardens and fields, of love and beauty

Warning

Do not select the Page Break line. If you do, you will replace the line with the text you type. If this happens, click the Undo button `↶` *and repeat step 5.*

Now you will add a page in the middle of your document and another at the end.

6. **Click before the heading** *Earth.*

7. **Click the Insert menu, Break, Page break, and OK.**

8. **With the insertion point before the heading** *Earth,* **click Repeat Insertion on the Edit menu to insert another page break.**

Your document looks like Figure 2.12. The insertion point is at the top of page 4. Page 3 is represented by the narrow space between the two Page Break lines.

Figure 2.12
Manual page breaks

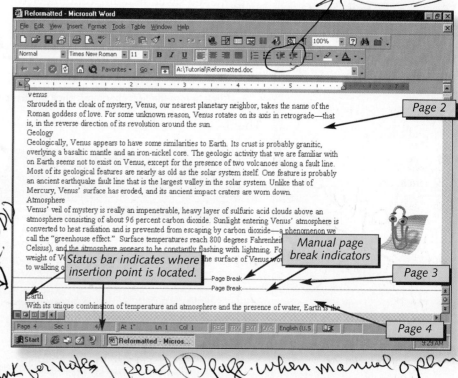

9. **Click the third page break line in the document and press** `Enter←`.

10. **Click between the second and third page break lines and type the following text, with one space before the first dash:** Our roots are in the dark; the earth is our country. --U. LeGuin

11. **Insert a page break below the last line of text at the end of the document, and type** Bibliography **on the new page (5).**

Changing Margins, Breaking Sections, and Aligning Vertically

In this activity, you will change the margins for the document, insert section breaks, and change the vertical alignment.

1. Go to the top of the document and click **File, Page Setup**, and the **Margins tab**, if it is not on top.

The Page Setup dialog box appears, as shown in Figure 2.13.

Figure 2.13
The Page Setup dialog box

Reformatting Pages

To change margins:

1. Click the insertion point where a margin change is desired.

2. Click the File menu, Page Setup, and the Margins tab.

3. Increase or decrease margin width.

4. If necessary, choose an option in the Apply to box.

To change vertical alignment:

1. Click the File menu, Page Setup, and the Layout tab.

2. Select an alignment option.

3. If necessary, choose an option in the Apply to box.

To insert section breaks:

1. Click the Insert menu and click Break.

2. Click Next page to insert a new page as well as a new section, or click Continuous.

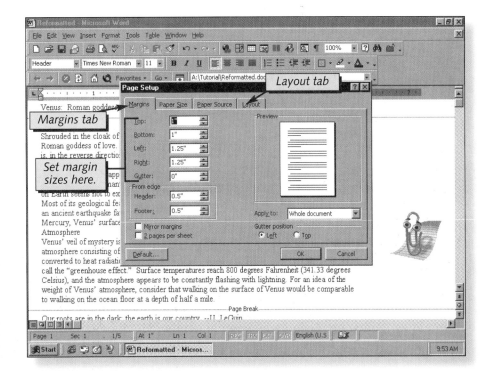

2. Change the top and left margins to 1.5" and the right margin to 1".

3. On the Layout tab, verify that **Top** appears in the Vertical alignment list box and click **OK**.

4. Switch to **Print Layout View**, scroll to view your new margin settings.

The margins are fine, but perhaps the single line on page 1 would look better if it were halfway down the page.

5. Switch to **Normal View** and click at the end of text on page 1. Click **Break** on the Insert menu. Under Section break types, click **Next page** and then click **OK**.

A Next Page section break appears in your document. Page 1 is now a separate section from the rest of the document. You can change the vertical alignment on it, without affecting other pages. You no longer need the manual page break.

6. Delete the Page Break line.

7. At the beginning of page 1, click **Page Setup** on the File menu. On the Layout tab in the Vertical alignment list box, select **Center**. Verify that **This section** shows in the Apply to list box. Then click **OK**.

8. Switch to **Print Layout View** and scroll to see the vertically centered text on page 1. Then scroll to page 2; note that this page is still top aligned.

Figure 2.14 ◀
A Next Page section break

Page 3 is similar to page 1, except that you will need a section break before and after the text to separate it from the preceding and following pages.

9. Switch to **Normal View**, click at the top of page 3, and insert **Next page section breaks** before and after the text on this page. Then, delete the Page Break lines before and after page 3.

Your document should now resemble Figure 2.14.

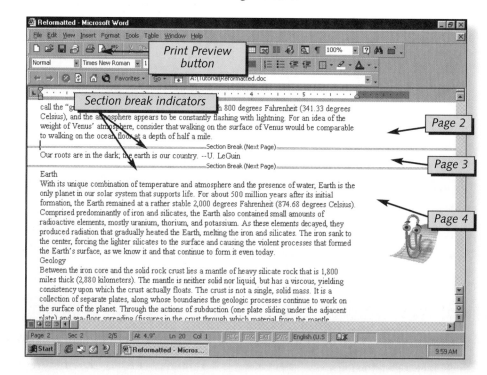

10. Vertically center the text on page 3.

11. To see the overall effect of your changes, click the **Print Preview button** [icon], the **Multiple Pages button** [icon], and the **2 x 3 icon**.

12. Click the **Normal View button** [icon] and save your changes.

Formatting Paragraphs

The *horizontal alignment* of text—how the text lines up with the left and right margins—is a basic formatting element. In the Word window, text is automatically *left aligned.* Every line begins in the same horizontal position on the left, making the left margin perfectly even. You can change this alignment, though. Text may be *right aligned;* that is, every line ending at the same point on the right. Text may be aligned so that *both* margins are perfectly even. This alignment is called *justified.* Also, text may be *center aligned,* or *centered*. With this alignment, short lines of text are placed an equal distance from the left and right margins. The Formatting toolbar provides all four options.

The *indentation style* used for paragraphs is a basic consideration, too. Indentation refers to variations in the side margins of lines in a paragraph and paragraphs on a page. A *first-line indentation* of one-half inch is conventional. *Hanging indentation*—the second and subsequent lines of a paragraph indented one-half inch under the first line—is also common. In Word, a first-line or hanging indentation may be any width; and whole paragraphs may be indented on the left and/or right any amount of space the user desires.

Line spacing—the amount of white space between text lines—is another format consideration. Most business documents use the default line spacing, called single spacing. *Double spacing* (a blank line between each line of text) and *1.5* (one-half blank line between each line of text) are also common. You may insert additional space above and below paragraphs. Adding *paragraph spacing* opens up a page and makes paragraph side headings easy to spot. Paragraph spacing is measured in *points.* With Word, you can also adjust the amount of space between characters, called *character spacing.* If you want to affect the spacing between all selected characters, you can expand or condense the space. If you want to affect the spacing of particular letters, choose the kerning option.

Changing Horizontal Alignment and Indentation Style

In this activity, you will continue reformatting the current document by changing the horizontal alignment and indentation options.

1. Go to the beginning of the document and click the **Center button** 🔳.

2. Click at the beginning of page 2, and click **Repeat Paragraph Alignment** on the Edit menu.

Text on page 1 is centered horizontally, and page 2 has a centered heading.

3. Click anywhere in the first paragraph on page 2, and click the **Justify button** 🔳.

Both the left and right paragraph margins are even, as shown in Figure 2.15.

Changing Horizontal Alignment

1. Select the text to be aligned.

2. Click one of the four align buttons on the Formatting toolbar.

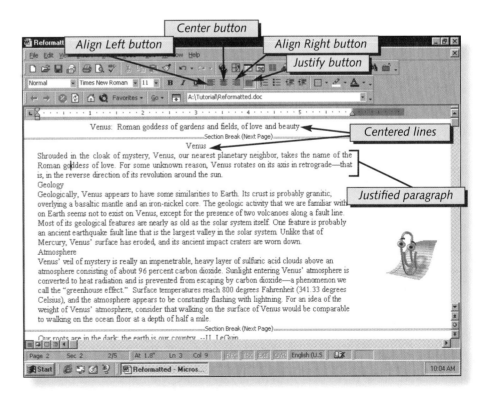

Figure 2.15
Centered and justified text

Changing Indentations

1. Select the paragraph or line to be changed.

2. To move the left paragraph margin to the right or left, click the Increase Indent or Decrease Indent buttons.

Or

Click Paragraph on the Format menu and set the desired Indentation options for the left and right margins.

Or

To move the first line, click the Format menu and Paragraph; in the Special list box, select either First line or Hanging. Select or type the indentation size.

Figure 2.16 ◀
The Paragraph dialog box

Hints & Tips

To indent the first line one-half inch, take advantage of Word's default tab stops: Click in front of the paragraph and press `Tab`.

---

4. Click at the end of page 4, press `Enter⏎` two times, and type the following text, replacing *Your Name* and *Current date.*

Your Name

Submitted to Professor Dowdell

AST 110, Section F3

Current date

5. Select the four lines of text you just typed, and click the **Align Right button** 🔲.

The text aligns on the right margin. Now you will begin changing the indentation style of some paragraphs.

6. On page 5, click after *Bibliography,* press `Enter⏎`, and type the following reference at the left margin: Author, F. M. Venus Overview. [Online] Available: http://solar.cyber works.net/sb/venus.html [February, 1999].

7. Click anywhere in the text you just typed, and click **Paragraph** on the Format menu. On the Indents and Spacing tab in the Special list box, select **Hanging**. Click the **By list box** and type .75. Look at the Preview box, as shown in Figure 2.16, to see how the text now aligns; then click **OK**.

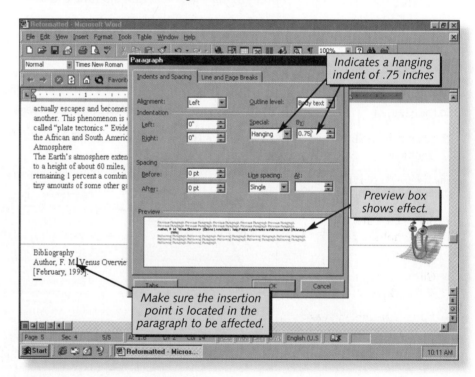

The second line is indented three-quarters of an inch under the first line in hanging indent style.

8. On page 4, click anywhere in the last paragraph. Change the paragraph indent to **First line** and **.75"**. Check the Preview window and then click **OK**.

The first line of the paragraph is indented three-quarters of an inch from the left margin.

Setting Spacing Options

Setting Spacing Options

To change character spacing:

1. Select the characters to be changed.

2. Click Font on the Format menu.

3. On the Character Spacing tab, select the desired options.

To change line spacing:

1. Click anywhere in a paragraph or select consecutive paragraphs to be changed.

2. Click the 1.5 Space or Double Space button.

To change paragraph spacing:

1. Select the paragraph or paragraphs to be changed.

2. Click the Format menu and click Paragraph.

3. Under Spacing, increase or decrease the space above or below the paragraph.

In this activity, you will change character, line, and paragraph spacing in the current document.

1. **Select the *Venus heading* on page 2.**

2. **Click Font on the Format menu, and click the Character Spacing tab. In the Spacing box, click the Expanded option. Verify that the number in the By box is 1 pt and click OK.**

The spacing between the letters in the heading expands slightly.

3. **Select the first paragraph on page 4. On the Formatting toolbar, click the Increase Indent button ⊞ and then, with the paragraph still selected, click the 1.5 Space button ☰.**

 *Note* *If the 1.5 Space button ☰ is not displayed on the Formatting toolbar, click More Buttons ⋮ to add it.*

The paragraph is indented one-half inch from the left margin with 1.5 line spacing, as shown in Figure 2.17.

Now you will change line spacing and paragraph spacing.

4. **Select the second paragraph on page 4. Click Paragraph on the Format menu. In the Spacing box, change the Before spacing to 6 pt and the After spacing to 12 pt. Set the Line spacing to Double. Set the Indentation for the right margin at .5". Look at the Preview box and click OK.**

5. **Select the first paragraph on page 4, and change the paragraph spacing to 6 pt Before and 12 pt After.**

6. **Click anywhere to deselect the text. Switch to Print Layout View.**

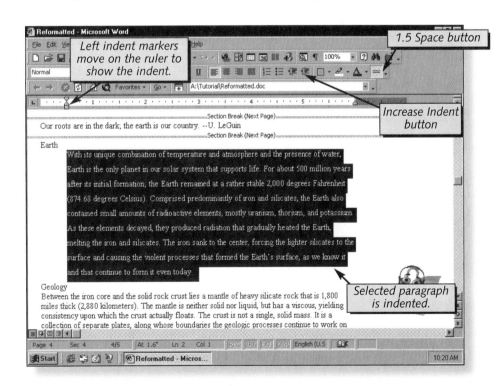

Figure 2.17
Page showing two indentation styles and line spacing

Another Way

To set horizontal alignment, indentation style, line spacing, and paragraph spacing all at once, right-click and click Paragraph.

7. In Normal View, select the first paragraph on page 4. Click the **Decrease Indent button** 📑. Deselect the text and save your changes.

Tabulating Text

Instead of paragraphs, a columns-and-rows arrangement (a tabular form) makes some text easier to read. This format involves **tab stops** that specify where listed items begin in relation to the left margin and the distance between columns of listed items. The default tab stops in Word are *left tabs* at half-inch intervals; they align columns on the left. You may prefer centered tabs for some columns, and columns containing amounts make more sense when aligned at the right or at decimal points. Also, if you have only two or three columns, you do not want the insertion point to stop between them. Therefore, in the Tabs dialog box, you can clear the default tabs and set just the tabs you need.

Setting Tab Stops

In this activity, you will set tab stops and type tabulated text on a separate page of the **Reformatted** document.

1. With *Reformatted* still open, find the phrase *worn down*, click after the end of the sentence, and press ⌷Enter⏎⌷ twice.

2. To open the Tabs dialog box, double-click the white part of the ruler or click **Tabs** on the Format menu.

> *Note* — *If you double-click the shaded area of the ruler, the Page Setup dialog box will appear. If this happens, close the Page Setup dialog box, and repeat step 2.*

3. In the Tabs dialog box, click the **Clear All button** to delete the current tabs.

4. In the Tab stop position box, type .5 and in the Alignment area, click **Left**, if it is not already selected. Click the **Set button**.

As shown in Figure 2.18, the tab position appears in the list box.

5. Now set these tabs: Center tab at 1.75", Left tab at 2.5", Right tab at 5.75".

6. With all four tabs showing in the list box, click **OK**.

The tab stops show on the ruler. Distinctive symbols represent left tabs, center tabs, and right tabs.

7. Press ⌷Tab⌷ and type the first word below, watching the screen as you type. Press ⌷Tab⌷ to move to the next stop and type the column entry. Continue pressing ⌷Tab⌷ and typing alternately; press ⌷Enter⏎⌷ to move to the second line.

Mission	Launch Date	Key Event	Key Event Date
Mariner 2	8/27/62	Passed within 22,000 mi. of Venus	12/14/62
Mariner 5			

Your tabulated text should resemble Figure 2.19.

8. Save your changes.

Word BASICS

Setting Tab Stops

1. Double-click the white part of the ruler or click the Format menu and Tabs.

2. Click the Clear All button to delete existing tabs.

3. Type the Tab stop position and click the desired alignment button.

4. Click the Set button; when all tabs show in the window, click OK.

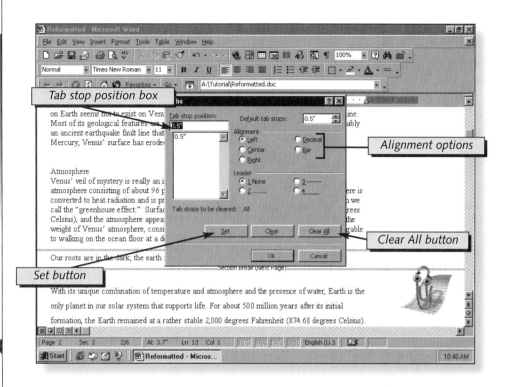

Figure 2.18
The Tabs dialog box

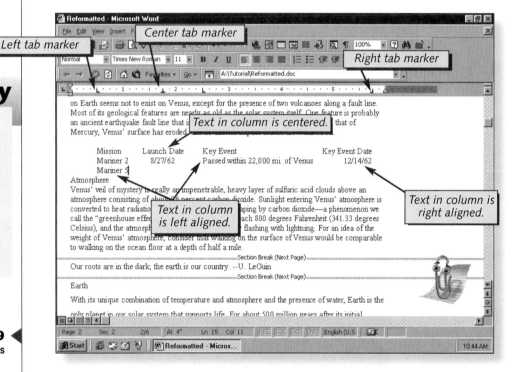

Figure 2.19
Left, centered, and right tab stops

ENHANCING THE APPEARANCE OF DOCUMENTS

When you type, all text in the window looks the same. An effective way to enhance the appearance of documents is to modify some attributes of the characters—selecting new designs; changing the size of text; adding bold, italic, and underline; adding color; and adding borders, shading, and highlighting.

Using HELP

Inserting Symbols and Special Characters

In this activity, you will search Help for information on how to insert symbols and special characters into documents.

1. **Open a new, blank document. Ask the Office Assistant to search for the keyword** *symbols.* **Explore to find answers to these questions: (a) What is the difference between a symbol and a special character? (b) What is a wingding? (c) What are the steps to insert a symbol? Use expanded Help for additional information, if needed. Try out the information.**

2. **Click the Insert menu, click Symbol, and click the Symbols tab.**

3. **Click the Font list box arrow; scroll and click Wingdings. The symbols available in the Wingdings font appear on your screen.**

4. **In the first row, click the open-book icon (sixth from left); watch as an enlarged symbol preview pops up, as shown in Figure 2.20.**

Figure 2.20
The Wingdings font

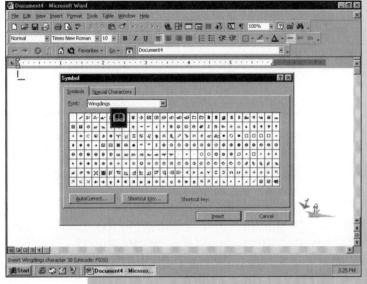

5. **Click the Insert button, and the open-book icon will appear in your unnamed document. Then click after the symbol and press Enter←. (If the Symbol dialog box covers the icon, drag the dialog box out of the way.)**

6. **From the same Wingdings font, find and insert an arrow that points to the right. Then click after the symbol and press Enter←.**

7. **Click the Special Characters tab, and click the AutoCorrect button.**

If any of the five options at the top of the AutoCorrect dialog box *are* selected, AutoCorrect is active on your computer. In the Replace text as you type area, read the information on how to type these symbols: copyright, registered, and trademark. Click OK, close the Symbol dialog box, and go to step 8.

If the five options at the top of the AutoCorrect dialog box are *not* selected, click OK to return to the Special Characters tab. Read the combination of keys *(shortcut keys)* that you can use to insert the copyright, registered, and trademark symbols. Close the Symbol dialog box and go to step 8.

8. **On a separate line, type a symbol for each of these words:** *copyright, registered, trademark.*

9. **Type the following text, inserting the special characters and symbols as you go:**
   Title: Peter Norton's® Introduction to Computers
   Publisher: Copyright © 2000 by the McGraw-Hill Companies, Inc.
   Others: Windows™ 98, Word 2000
   Web page: Click ⊡ to go to our home page. Click the 📖 for the tutorial you want.

10. **Double-click one of the symbols and note that the Symbol dialog box opens. Delete the symbols (and special characters) at the top of the page. Then save your document as** *Symbols* **in the** *Tutorial* **folder and close the file.**

These steps are valuable additions to edited, reformatted documents. Font characteristics help to distinguish *special* copy such as headings, from ordinary paragraphs with characters that contrast in design, size, darkness, and color. The contrast makes documents inviting to readers, and a distinction between special and ordinary text provides clues to how document content is organized.

Changing Font Design

A *font* is a set of characters of one design. In Word, a font named ***Times New Roman*** is the default font. Word offers dozens of other fonts, as you will soon discover. The fonts available to you, though, depend upon the printer you are using. A printer may convert a fancy Word font to less desirable characters—or not print the font at all. Some fonts are ideal for ordinary copy, while others are best suited for headings. A few are special-purpose fonts, designed more for Web pages, posters, and the like, rather than memos, letters, and reports. The Times New Roman font is ideal for paragraphs because it is a ***serif*** font. That is, the characters have *feet* that form a straight line, guiding readers' eyes from left to right. A font without feet—***Arial,*** for example—is best for headings. These fonts are called ***sans serif.***

Changing Font Size

When you start a new document, all text is the same height and width. All characters are the same ***font size*** (sometimes called ***point size***). The default size is 10 point. (Files on your Student Data Disk vary in font size.) The most common font sizes for paragraphs are 10, 11, and 12. Font sizes of 14, 16, and 18 are often used for headings.

Adding Special Effects

Another way to enhance text is to add one or more special effects. You can use ***bold*** to make words stand out from the surrounding copy. Bold helps readers see important points or technical terms at a glance. Another common effect is called ***italic.*** Italic text has thin, delicate characters that slant slightly to the right. A large block of italic text is hard to read, but italic is an attention-getter when used sparingly. Another way to call attention to certain words is to underline them. Besides the standard solid line, Word offers more than a dozen ***underline*** styles—solid, dotted, dashed, and wavy. The key to using bold, italic, and underlines is not using them too much.

Changing Font Color

The default font color is black on a white background. As a Word user, though, you are certainly not limited to black-and-white documents. More than forty basic font colors are provided, along with the tools to create many, many more. (Background colors are equally numerous. Changing the background color, however, switches automatically to Web Layout View—not the best place for editing and formatting tasks.)

If your document happens to be a Web page, the use of various colors is critical to attracting and holding the attention of site visitors. Nowadays, too, many offices are equipped with an ***intranet***—a Web-like network for communicating within an organization. As a result, many documents never make it to paper; they are published on the intranet instead, and read by company employees from their computer screens. In some schools today, students create

documents on the computer and submit them via e-mail or save them to a network drive. These documents, too, never get on paper. Instructors and other students read the documents on their computers. Also, color printers are rapidly becoming standard office equipment. On some black-and-white printers, different font colors appear as various shades of gray.

Adding Borders, Shading, and Highlights

You can also make a paragraph or page stand out by adding a **border** on any or all sides of it or by adding **shading.** If you want a color background to appear over selected text much like a highlighter, add a **highlight.**

HANDS On

Word **BASICS**

Enhancing Text

To change font design:

1. Select the text to be changed.

2. Click the Font arrow; scroll the list.

3. Click the font name.

To change font size:

1. Select the text to be changed.

2. Click the Font Size arrow and scroll the list.

3. Click the desired font size.

To add special effects:

1. Select the text to be changed.

2. Click the button(s) for the desired effect; or for more Underline styles, click the Format menu and Font.

Enhancing Text

In this activity, you will change the font design, size, and color of selected text in your *Reformatted* document. You will apply bold, italic, and underline effects and add a border and highlighting.

1. With *Reformatted* still open, select all the words in the first line of the tabbed text on page 2.

2. On the Formatting toolbar, click the **Font list box arrow** Times New Roman.

The Font list box opens. The font names are listed in alphabetical order. Recently used fonts form a short list at the top of the Font list box.

3. Click **Arial**.

Although the text is still selected, you can see that the selected characters are a different design.

4. Click the **Bold button** B. Click anywhere on the screen to deselect the text.

5. Find the word *roots* and select the entire line of text. Click the **Font Size list box arrow** 10, click **14**, and then click the **Italic button** I.

Since the italic effect should be applied to the quotation only and not the writer's name, you need to reformat part of the line.

6. Select the name and the dash in front of it, and click the **Italic button** I to *remove* the effect. Deselect the text.

After these changes, your screen should appear as shown in Figure 2.21.

7. Find and select your name. Change the font size to 9.

8. Use **Repeat Formatting** to change the next three lines of text to font size 9.

The text shrinks from font size 11 to font size 9.

9. Select your name and the following three lines of text, and click the **Font Color arrow** A. In the Font Color palette, point to the **Sky Blue sample** until the ScreenTip appears, as shown in Figure 2.22 on the following page; then click it. Click anywhere on the screen to deselect the text.

10. Select the *Atmosphere* heading on page 4, and click the **Underline button** U.

A solid, single line appears under the selected word.

11. Change the *Atmosphere* heading to Arial, size 13.

Note *Because 13 point is not listed in the Font Size list, type 13 in the Font Size box and press* Enter⏎.

Word BASICS

Enhancing Text

To change font color:

1. Select the text to be changed.

2. Click the Font Color arrow.

3. Click the desired color sample.

To add borders or shading:

1. Select the text to be bordered or shaded.

2. Click Borders and Shading on the Format menu.

3. Click the Borders or Shading options and click OK.

To highlight text:

1. Select the text to highlight.

2. Click the Highlight button arrow.

3. Click the desired color sample.

4. Click the Highlight button to turn off the feature.

Figure 2.21 ◀
Enhanced text

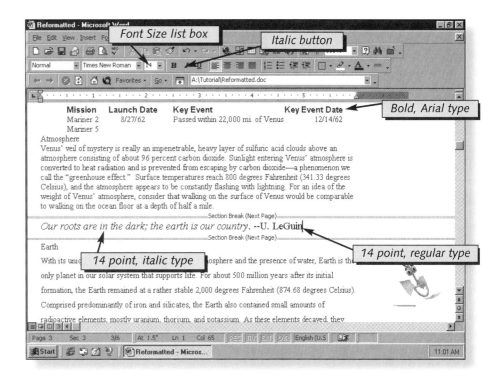

Figure 2.22 ◀
The Font Color palette

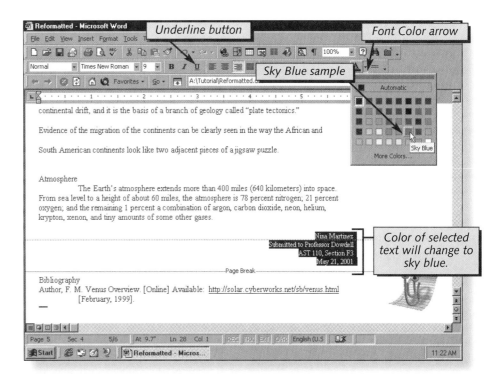

You now want to highlight several terms in this report.

12. Find the word *subduction.* Right-click on the word, and click **Font**.

13. On the Font tab in the Font dialog box, click the **Underline style arrow** and click the wavy line near the bottom of the list box. Click the **Underline color list box arrow** and click the **Gray-40% color sample**. Look at the Preview window and then click **OK**.

14. Select the tabulated text on page 2 and click the **Highlight list box arrow**. Select the **Gray-25% color sample**.

- To choose font style, size, effect, and color at once, right-click and click Font.

- Click the Borders button on the Formatting toolbar if you want a border without shading.

The tabulated text is now highlighted.

15. Save your changes.

Changing Text with the Format Painter

With the reformatting in your current document, you have varied the design, size, and color of the text in some places and added some special effects. It looks good—except the original, unchanged text looks comparatively dull and uninteresting. The Format Painter ✍ is a quick solution to this problem. Select the good-looking text and *brush* over it with the Format Painter; then *paint* the plain paragraphs to look the same—indentations, line spacing, font design, and all. To copy font characteristics with the Format Painter, select text as usual. To copy paragraph formatting (indentations, line spacing, and so on), you need to select the **paragraph mark** along with the paragraph itself. Therefore, you will use the Show/Hide ¶ button ¶ on the Standard toolbar to display (and hide) the **formatting marks** (or nonprinting characters). The Show/Hide feature reveals a paragraph mark wherever you pressed Enter↵, a dot wherever you pressed Spacebar, and an arrow wherever you pressed Tab.

HANDS ON

Word BASICS

Using the Format Painter

1. Select the text that has the formatting you want to copy.

2. Click the Format Painter button.

3. Click the text you want to apply the formatting to.

Using the Format Painter

In this activity, you will use the Format Painter to change the plain text in your document to match the text you have already formatted and enhanced.

1. Find and click the underlined word *subduction*. On the Standard toolbar, click the **Format Painter button** ✍.

A paintbrush appears beside the I-beam.

2. In the same sentence, select the words *sea-floor spreading*. Deselect the text to see the formatting.

The underline effect is copied to this text.

3. Click the underlined *Atmosphere* heading on page 4, and click the **Format Painter button** ✍.

4. Click the *Geology* heading on page 4.

The 13-point Arial font and underline are copied to this heading. Before you copy paragraph formatting, you need to show the paragraph marks.

5. On the Standard toolbar, click the **Show/Hide¶ button** ¶.

Your screen should now resemble Figure 2.23.

6. Triple-click the *Atmosphere* paragraph on page 4 to select the paragraph and the paragraph mark at the end of it.

7. Click the **Format Painter button** ✍. Then click anywhere in the paragraph *above* the *Atmosphere* heading on page 4.

Why not copy this formatting to paragraphs on a preceding page? Since more than one paragraph is involved, you need to double-click the Format Painter button ✍ this time.

8. With the *Geology* paragraph on page 4 (and the paragraph mark) selected, double-click the **Format Painter button** ✍.

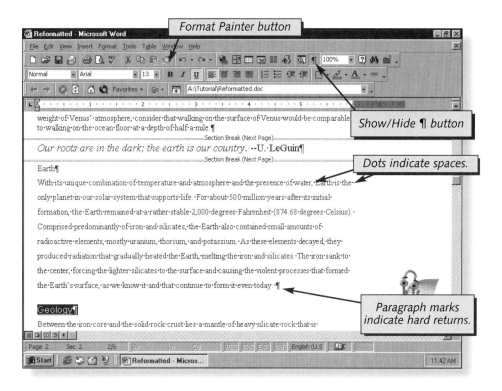

Figure 2.23
Text with paragraph marks

9. Scroll up to a single-spaced paragraph and click anywhere in it.

10. Scroll above the tabulated text on page 2, and click in that single-spaced paragraph.

11. Click the **Format Painter button** to turn off the feature or press `Esc`, and click the **Show/Hide ¶ button** to hide the formatting marks.

12. Select the *Venus* heading at the top of page 2. Change the heading to these attributes: Arial; font size 16, bold, italic, and Green.

13. Use the Format Painter to copy all five attributes of the *Venus* heading to the *Earth* heading on page 4.

14. Select the first paragraph on page 4. Click the **Single Space button** .

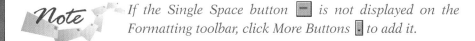

If the Single Space button is not displayed on the Formatting toolbar, click More Buttons to add it.

15. Click the **Print Preview button** and the **One Page button** . If necessary, scroll to page 4.

Your screen should resemble Figure 2.24.

16. In Normal View, press `Enter ←` after the words *jigsaw puzzle.* and after *Mariner 5*. Then save and close the file.

Using the Style Command

Using the Style feature is a quick way to format and enhance documents at the same time. A *style* combines format properties (alignment, indentations, and line spacing) *and* appearance properties (font and font size and bold, italic, or underline effects). Thus, when you choose a style, one click takes care of all these factors at once. In a new blank document, the text you type uses the *Normal style*—the base style for the Normal template in Word.

You can split the Word window horizontally to view two parts of a document at once. This feature is useful when copying or moving text from one page to another page of a long document. Point to the split box at the top of the vertical scroll bar. When the pointer changes to the lines-and-arrows pointer, drag the split bar. (Another way is to click the Window menu and Split.) To restore the single window, double-click the split bar or click Remove Split on the Window menu.

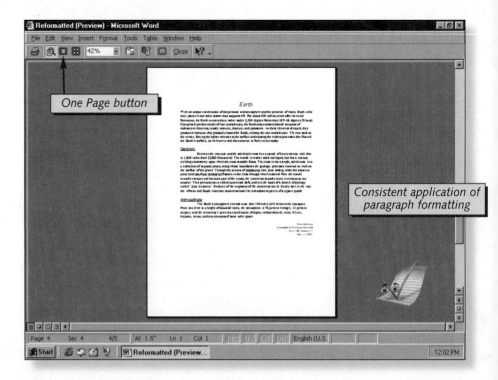

Figure 2.24 ◀
Formatted, enhanced text

Word provides more than one style list. One list is All styles; another is Styles in use. A third option, User-defined styles, would contain only those styles that a Word user created. (Therefore, the User-defined list would vary greatly from one computer to another.) The All styles list—the Word default—is used in the following activity.

Applying Styles

In this activity, you will open *Astronomy 110* on your Student Data Disk. This time you will apply Word styles to reformat and enhance it.

 *The Style button* Normal *displays a list box. The styles listed are not the same for all users; in fact, the styles in your list box may vary from one document to another. Therefore, directions for using the Style button do not specify a style. Instead, a general statement guides your choice of a style in the list box.*

Applying Styles

1. Select the text to be changed.

2. Click the Format menu; click Style.

3. Scroll and click a style; see the preview and the description.

4. Click Apply at the desired style.

1. Open *Astronomy 110* on your Student Data Disk and save it as *Styles* in the *Tutorial* folder.
2. Click the **Show/Hide ¶ button** ¶ to reveal the formatting marks.
3. Select the first word. On the Formatting toolbar, click the **Style list box arrow** Normal ▾.

The Style list box appears. The name of each style tells you its intended use. For example, *heading* indicates a paragraph heading; and *body text* indicates a paragraph itself. Each style also shows how your text will look (font, font color, and alignment or indentation) if you select it. The gray tab indicates whether a style involves paragraph format (paragraph mark) or character appearance (**a**). The tab also shows the font size and, for paragraph styles, the horizontal alignment.

4. Locate and click a heading style that is font size 16 or thereabouts.

The style is applied to the heading.

5. Select the heading *Geology* that appears a few lines below the *Venus* heading. In the Style list, click a heading style that is font size 14 or thereabouts.

6. Select the first paragraph and the paragraph mark. In the Style list, click a body text style that is font size 12 or thereabouts.

The style—which includes font size, indentation, line spacing, and paragraph spacing—is applied to the paragraph.

7. Find and select the heading *Earth*. Click the **Format menu** and click **Style**.

In the List area in the Style dialog box, select **All styles**, if it is not already selected.

8. In the Styles list box, click the **Heading 1 style**.

As shown in Figure 2.25, the Paragraph preview window shows how this heading would look in relation to the surrounding text. The Character preview window shows the font design. The Description includes the font size.

Figure 2.25
The Style dialog box

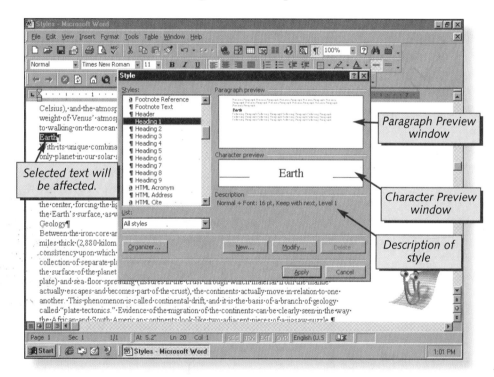

9. Click the **Apply button**.

The heading *Earth* appears as previewed and described.

10. Change the style of the next heading *Geology* to **Heading 9**; notice the paragraph and character previews and read the description. Click the **Apply button**.

 *You can make additional changes to text after a style is applied—add bold, for example.*

11. Change the style of the *Geology* paragraph to **Body Text First Indent**.

The paragraph style is applied.

12. Hide the paragraph marks, save the changes, and close the file.

INSERTING AND FORMATTING GRAPHICS

You may have a hard time getting your points across with text alone. In such cases, you can add a *graphic* (also called an *object* or *image*) to a document. A graphic is any element in a document that is not text. Examples include a drawing object made with lines, curves, or decorative text (called *WordArt*) or pictures (clip art or a photograph). Word has an entire folder called the *Clip Gallery* which includes professionally designed objects (pictures, photographs, sound, and video clips) from which you can choose to complement many different subjects in your documents. The graphics in the Clip Gallery are called *clip art,* or clips. The Drawing toolbar has tools that help you draw geometric shapes and other objects, insert WordArt, and open the Clip Gallery.

Browsing the Clip Gallery

The Insert Clip Art button 🖼 on the Drawing toolbar opens the Clip Gallery. Clips are organized by pictures, sounds, and motion clips and in subject categories, identified by keywords, such as Animals, Buildings, Buttons & Icons, Cartoons, Entertainment, Food & Dining, Office, People, Places, and Travel. You can browse the categories that fit your subject, or you can search for related clips with keywords. Before you insert a clip into your document, you can preview it. When you insert an image from the Clip Gallery, Word switches automatically to Print Layout View.

If the graphic you want to insert into your document is in another location, such as in a program, on the Web, or on a disk, Word will allow you to *import* (or insert) many popular types of graphic files directly into your docu-ment. Click the Insert menu, point to Picture, and then click From File.When you locat the file you want to insert, just double-click it. If you want to import a free image from a web site, you often must copy and save the image to a local drive.

*You can use any Clip Gallery image in the documents you create—as long as you are not selling the documents with the image. Before you add any graphic to a document, be sure to verify the legal restrictions for using it. And, always secure permission from your instructor **before** you add a graphic to the Clip Gallery.*

Inserting an Image

In this activity, you will browse the Clip Gallery and select and insert a picture into a document.

1. Display the Drawing toolbar (if it's hidden).

2. On your Student Data Disk, open *Sandy Reef Island Tour*. Save the file as *Clip Art* in the *Tutorial* folder. Read the document, which describes Sandy Reef Island.

3. On the Drawing toolbar, click the **Insert Clip Art button** 🖼.

The Insert ClipArt dialog box displays, as shown in Figure 2.26.

Figure 2.26
The Insert ClipArt dialog box

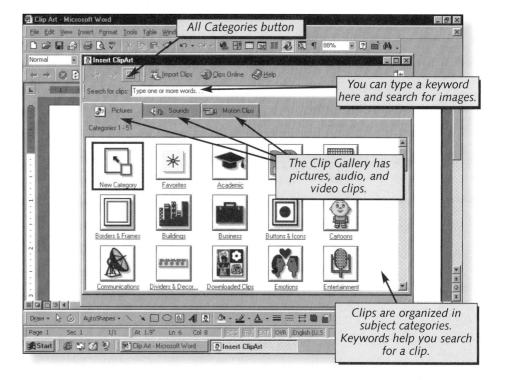

All Categories button

You can type a keyword here and search for images.

The Clip Gallery has pictures, audio, and video clips.

Clips are organized in subject categories. Keywords help you search for a clip.

Inserting an Image

1. Click the Insert Clip Art button on the Drawing toolbar.

2. Click the desired category button.

3. Click a picture and preview it.

4. Click the Insert Clip button and click Close.

Warning *The Clip Gallery graphics must be installed on your computer to view clips from the Clip Gallery. If no pictures, sound files, or motion clips exist in the Clip Gallery, see your instructor. If you have access to the Office 2000 CD and receive a message that additional clips are on the Microsoft Office CD-ROM, click OK to continue. If you receive a message that Word is indexing clips from previous editions, click Postpone.*

4. On the Pictures tab, scroll the list box to view the clip art categories, which are in alphabetical order.

5. Click the **Travel category**; then scroll to view the clips. If you find an appropriate clip for your *Sandy Reef Island Tour* document, go to step 6. If you do not find a clip in the Travel category, click **Keep Looking** or click **Back** to return to the Categories where you can search in another category, such as **Nature, Places,** or **Maps.** Choose a clip and go to step 6.

6. Click the image you have chosen.

The Clip Art toolbar appears.

7. On the Clip Art toolbar, click the **Preview clip icon**.

A larger, more detailed view of the clip displays.

8. Click the **Insert clip button**.

The clip art is inserted into your document, behind the Clip Gallery. The window switched to Print Layout View if you were in a different view option.

9. Close the Clip Gallery.

10. Preview the document and then save the updated document.

If you insert an animated graphic file (*gif* file format) into a document and then save the document as a Web page, you can view the Web page in your browser and play the object.

[Handwritten margin notes:]
Select Precture
B mouse clck go
to Format Picture
Make chace
Layout
If small Tight
Front or Back of Text

HANDS on

Editing and Formatting Graphics

An inserted clip may be the wrong size and in the wrong place. Therefore, you must be able to resize, move, and align the image on the page. You can perform these tasks with resize handles. To move or resize an image, you must first select the image by clicking it. The ***resize handles*** surrounding the image allow you to ***resize*** it. Point to a ***handle*** until a two-way arrow appears. To change only the height of an image, drag a vertical two-way arrow until you see the desired image size. To change only the width of an image, drag a horizontal two-way arrow. To maintain the image proportions while you resize it, drag a corner or diagonal resizing handle. To move an image, click the selected object and drag it to the new location.

Tools on the Picture toolbar allow you to handle images more precisely, however, than using sizing handles. When you select a picture, the Picture toolbar appears with editing tools. You can, for example, change the contrast between light and dark colors, ***crop*** (cut off) unnecessary parts of the picture, and change the size and ***layout*** (how text aligns and wraps in relation to the picture).

Before you change the height and/or width of an image (in the Format Picture dialog box), you need to guard against distortion. If you make a clip wider, for example, without changing the height an equal amount, you change its height-width relationship, or ***aspect.*** Before you change either the height or the width, you need to lock the aspect ratio. Thus, when you change either dimension, Word changes the other dimension proportionately. (If you forget to lock the aspect ratio, or otherwise make a mistake in resizing, you can click the Reset Picture button 🖼 to restore the image to original size.)

Graphics almost always share a page with paragraph copy. Therefore, the ***wrapping style*** becomes an issue. Wrapping, or text wrapping, refers to the visual relationship of the text and the image. You cannot use the buttons for aligning text (on the Formatting toolbar) to align pictures. Instead, you align objects horizontally by clicking the Format Picture (or Object) button 🖼 on the Picture toolbar. In a finished document, text and graphics should complement each other. If they compete for readers' attention, you should change the text appearance or the size, wrapping style, and/or alignment of the graphic.

Editing and Formatting a Graphic

In this activity, you will resize and realign an image.

1. **Click anywhere in the clip to select it.**

A series of small squares appear inside the picture border.

2. **On the Picture toolbar, click the Format Picture button** 🖼**, and click the Size tab, as shown in Figure 2.27.**

3. **Under Scale, select Lock aspect ratio, if a check mark does not appear in the box.**

Figure 2.27
The Size tab in the
Format Picture dialog box

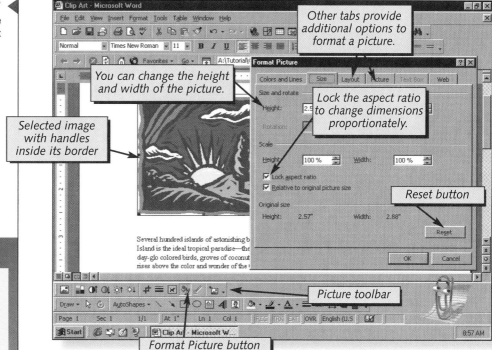

Word
BASICS

Editing and Formatting a Graphic

To resize a graphic:

1. Select the graphic, click the Format Picture button, and click the Size tab.

2. Select Lock aspect ratio, if necessary.

3. Click the Height or Width text box; type the number of inches.

To wrap and align:

1. Select the graphic, click the Format Picture button, and click the Layout tab.

2. Click a wrapping style.

3. Click a horizontal alignment option, or click Other and specify alignment.

4. In the Size and rotate area, click the **Height list box**, and change the number to 2".

The number in the Width text box will change automatically (when you click OK) because you selected lock aspect ratio.

5. On the Layout tab, click the **Square icon** under Wrapping style. Under Horizontal alignment, click **Right**; then click **OK**.

After a few seconds, the image moves to the right of the text. The clip is still selected except now the border is gone and white resize handles surround the image.

6. Click outside the picture to deselect it.

If you want to select another wrapping style to improve the overall appearance of your document, select the clip and click the Text Wrapping button on the Picture toolbar. Then click an option.

7. Move or resize the picture, if desired.

8. Change the text appearance as desired for the text and the picture to complement each other.

9. Save and close the file.

SORTING WORDS OR NUMBERS

Many documents contain lists—sometimes arranged in alphabetical or numerical order. You can *sort* lists manually by cutting and pasting or dragging and dropping. A faster, more accurate way to sort a list is to use the Sort feature on the Table menu. With the Sort feature, you can specify whether you want items sorted in **ascending** or **descending** order. You can sort words, numbers, or dates that appear as text or in tables; the items must be listed vertically, though. Any column in tables can sort items. If you want to sort all lines in a document, just issue the Sort command. If, however, you want to sort particular lines in a document, select the lines and then sort.

Word BASICS

Sorting a List

1. Select text to be sorted.

2. Click the Table menu and click Sort.

3. Click a Sort by option.

4. Click a Type option.

5. Click Ascending or Descending.

6. Click Header Row, if necessary, and click OK.

Sorting a List

In this activity, you will sort a list alphabetically in ascending order.

> **1.** On you Student Data Disk, open *Bookmark* and save the file as *Sort* in the *Tutorial* folder.

Since you want to sort a list of software features near the end of this document, you must select the items to be sorted.

> **2.** Find the phrase *Block Delete* and select the text from *Block Delete* through *Special characters.*
>
> **3.** Click the **Table menu** and click **Sort**.

The Sort Text dialog box appears with the options set to sort text by paragraph in ascending order.

> **4.** Click **OK** to accept the default settings.

Word rearranges the selected items in alphabetical order.

> **5.** Find the phrase *Formula bar* and select the text from *Formula bar* through the last line of text in the document.
>
> **6.** Click **Sort** on the Table menu. Click the options to sort the paragraphs in ascending order and click **OK**.
>
> **7.** Save and close the file.

ADDING REFERENCE FEATURES

You can add reference features to long documents to highlight items, to help readers find information, and to provide supporting facts or sources. Such reference features include bullets or numbers for lists, page numbers, headers and footers, footnotes, and a table of contents.

Using Bullets and Numbers for Items

A **bullet** is a character, typographical symbol, or graphic used as a special effect to highlight an item. Word provides bullet characters, including dots, squares, arrows, and check marks; the Clip Gallery also includes images that you can use as a bullet. You can use bullets to distinguish main items from secondary items when the order of items is not critical. You may add bullets to an existing list or as you type.

If priority is important in a list of items, use numbers to indicate the order of importance in the list. Also, use numbers when you want the reader to know that the items or steps must be completed in sequence. You may add numbers to an existing list or as you type.

You can use an image as a bullet. Click Bullets and Numbering on the Format menu, click the Bulleted tab, and click Picture. Then scroll the Picture Bullet Gallery and select an image.

Word
BASICS

Inserting Bullets and Numbers

To insert bullets:

1. Select the items to be bulleted.

2. Click the Bullets button.

To insert numbers:

1. Select the items to be numbered.

2. Click the Numbering button.

Adding Bullets and Numbers to Lists

In this activity, you will add bullets and numbers to a list of items, change existing bullets, and create a short list with bullets added as you type.

1. On your Student Data Disk, open *Quality Assurance* and save the document as *Bullets & Numbers* in the *Tutorial* folder.

2. Find *Table of Contents.* Select the text from *Table of Contents* through the paragraph with the *Feedback form* heading.

3. On the Formatting toolbar, click the **Bullets button** 📃.

A bullet appears to the left of each selected item, similar to Figure 2.28. The bullet character in your document may differ, depending upon which bullet character is selected in the Bullets and Numbering dialog box.

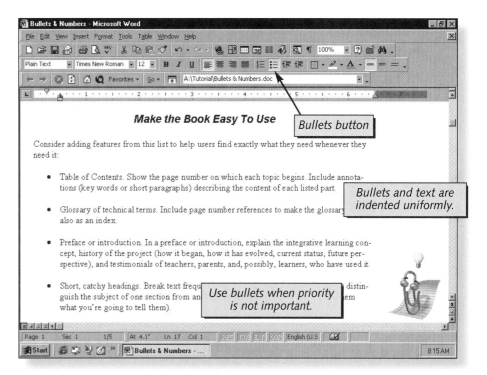

Figure 2.28
A bulleted list

4. With the bulleted items still selected, click the **Format menu** and click **Bullets and Numbering**. Click the **Bulleted tab**.

The Bulleted tab displays seven bullet options.

5. Click a bullet option that differs from what appears in your document and click **OK**.

Word changes the bullet in your document to the bullet character you chose.

6. Find *What WPS Can Do.* Select the bulleted list in this section of the document, and click the **Bullets button** 📃.

The bullets disappear and the text moves to the left margin and remains selected.

7. Click the **Bullets button** 📃 again.

Word inserts the bullet icon you selected in step 5. The bullets and text are uniformly indented from the left margin, 0.25" and 0.5", respectively.

To change bullet and text indentations, first select the items. Then click the Decrease Indent or Increase Indent buttons.

8. Open a new, blank document. Insert an asterisk and press . Then type Bookmark **and press** Enter⏎.

Note

> *If the Office Assistant asks whether you want Word to convert your typing to a Bulleted List item, click Yes. Then, click Cancel to close the Office Assistant and go to step 9.*
>
> *If Word does **not** insert bullet characters automatically, you need to turn on the Automatic bullets feature. Click the Tools menu and click AutoCorrect. Then on the AutoFormat As You Type tab, select the Automatic bulleted lists checkbox and click OK. Delete the asterisk and the word* Bookmark *in your document. Repeat step 8.*

9. **Type the following items and press** Enter⏎ **after each one:** Bullets, Find, Go To, Replace, Sort.

10. **After the last item, press** Enter⏎ **twice to turn off the automatic bullets.**

11. **Save the file as** *Lists* **in the** *Tutorial* **folder. Close the file.**

12. **Go to the beginning of** *Bullets & Numbers*. **Find the word** *incorporate*. **Select this line and the rest of the lines in this section.**

13. **On the Formatting toolbar, click the Numbering button** 📋.

Each selected item is indented and numbered with an Arabic number. The numbers on your screen depend upon which numbering style is selected in the Bullets and Numbering dialog box.

14. **Save and close the file.**

Numbering Pages

Word adds page numbers to documents automatically. If you should add or delete a page, Word renumbers the pages automatically, too. Page numbers are printed in the margin area at the top or bottom of pages and aligned at the left, center, or right, as you choose. Different types of page numbering are available, including lowercase and uppercase letters and Roman numerals or Arabic numbers. By dividing documents into sections, you can use different numbering in each section.

Another Way

To insert numbering automatically as you type, select the Automatic numbered lists option in the AutoCorrect dialog box.

Inserting Page Numbers

In this activity, you will number pages in a document and then modify the original page numbering.

1. **Open** *Ag Ed* **on your Student Data Disk and save as** *Reference Features* **in the** *Tutorial* **folder.**

2. **At the top of the document, click the Insert menu and click Page Numbers.**

The Page Numbers dialog box displays, as shown in Figure 2.29.

3. **Click the Position arrow; click Bottom of page (Footer). Click the Alignment arrow and click Center. Preview the document and then click OK.**

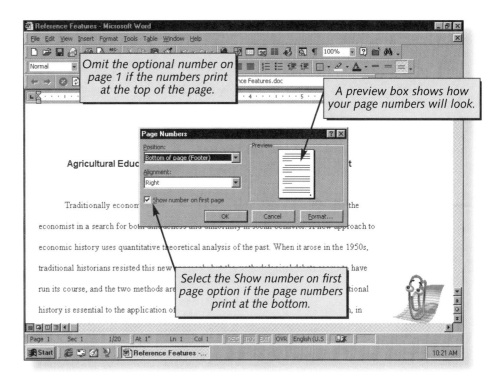

Figure 2.29
The Page Numbers dialog box

Word switches to Print Layout View, if you were not already in that view. A number appears at the bottom center of each page.

4. Scroll to the bottom of the first page; note the page number. Navigate to the end of the document; note the page number.

The page numbers appear dim and you cannot click them. The number is in the Header and Footer View. (You will work with headers and footers in the next section of this tutorial.) You will now divide the document into three sections and use different numbering for each section.

5. Navigate to the top of the document. Insert a Next page section break.

 *Switch to Normal View to see the section break. Switch back to Print Layout View so you will be able to see the page numbers.*

6. Click on page 1. Click the **Insert menu** and click **Page Numbers**. Click the **Alignment arrow** and click **Right**. Then click the **Format button**.

The Page Number Format dialog box appears.

7. Click the **Number format arrow** and click the **i, ii, iii, . . . option**. Click **OK**, preview the page, and click **OK**.

The number *i* appears in the bottom-right corner of the first page. Notice the page number on the status bar also. Now you will number pages in the main part of the document with Arabic numbers, starting with 1.

8. Click the top of the next page. In the Page Numbers dialog box, click the **Format button**.

Under Number format, the Arabic numbers format is already selected; you want to start this numbering at page 1.

Inserting Page Numbers

1. Click Page Numbers on the Insert menu.

2. Click a position option. If the position is Bottom, select Show number on first page.

3. Click an alignment option; click OK.

4. Click Format, set the desired options, and click OK.

5. Click OK.

9. Under Page numbering, type 1 in the Start at box. Then, click **OK**. Click **OK** again to close the Page Numbers dialog box.

Verify the number at the bottom of this page.

10. Go to the *Bibliography* heading. At the bottom of the page, insert a Next page section break and delete the manual page break.

Note — Switch to Normal View to see the breaks. Then switch back to Print Layout View.

11. Go to the *Appendix A* heading. In the Page Numbers dialog box, click the **Format button**.

12. Change the Number format to the **A, B, C, . . . option**. Click the **Start at box**, and type A, if necessary, and click **OK**. Click **OK** again.

The status bar now displays *Page A of Section 3*.

13. Go to the end of the document. Click the **Print Preview button** 🔍 and the **Multiple Pages button** (2 x 2 Pages). Click the page number on the last page.

The page enlarges so that you can see the page number *B* clearly.

14. Click the page number again to reduce this page. Click the top-left page, and click the page number—the Arabic number *18.* Click *18* to reduce the page.

15. Still in the Preview window, scroll to the top of the document. Click the page number on the top-left page—the Roman numeral *i.* Click *i* to reduce the page. Then, click the **Print Layout View button** 🖻 and save your changes.

You used a different page numbering style in each of the three sections of your document.

Adding Headers and Footers

In long documents, other pieces of information are often printed in the top and/or bottom margin, along with the page number, to guide readers who may be looking for a specific topic. On time-sensitive documents, the date and time may appear at the top or bottom of every page. That way, readers know they are reading current information. Information repeated in the top margin is called a *header;* information in the bottom margin is called a *footer.* To specify the information, you will work in the Header/Footer view, where you can insert information by using the ***Click and Type*** feature, by selecting AutoText items, or by clicking buttons on the Header and Footer toolbar. In Print Layout View, the Click and Type feature allows you to double-click a document anywhere and then insert text or an image where the insertion point is located.

Creating and Modifying a Header and a Footer

In this activity, you insert a header to pages in the main section of your current document. The header will contain the title of this document and the date.

1. Click the document title on page 1 of Section 2.

2. Click the **View menu** and click **Header and Footer**.

Word BASICS

Creating a Header or Footer

1. Click the View menu.

2. Click Header and Footer.

3. Type or insert the desired information.

4. Click the Close button.

The Header and Footer View and toolbar appear, as shown in Figure 2.30. Text in the main view becomes dim. You must insert header information (text or graphics) in the dotted Header box.

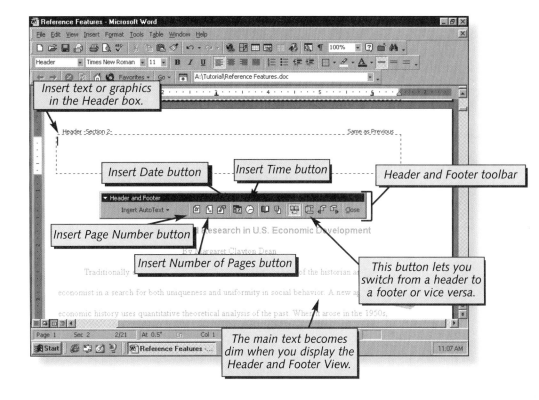

Figure 2.30
The Header and Footer view and tools

Another Way

To insert the current date, click the Insert Date button on the Header and Footer toolbar.

- If you want a footer instead of a header, click the Switch Between Header and Footer button on the Header and Footer toolbar. Then, type the footer information in the Footer box.

- Double-click a header or footer if you want to edit it.

3. With the insertion point at the left margin in the Header box, click the **Insert AutoText button** on the Header and Footer toolbar. Click **Filename** to allow Word to automatically insert the document name.

4. Double-click at the right end of the Header box. Type the current month and year in this style: October 2000.

5. Close the Header and Footer toolbar. Switch to the Print Layout View, if necessary.

The header appears dim, while the main text appears normal.

6. Double-click the header on page i.

The Header and Footer View and toolbar are displayed. Header is displayed in the Styles box.

7. Click the center of the Header box. Click the **Insert Page Number button** on the Header and Footer toolbar.

The page number appears in the designated number format (small Roman numeral).

8. Click the **Switch Between Header and Footer button**.

Word displays the Footer box for the same page.

9. Select and delete the page number (i) and close the Header and Footer View.

10. Select and delete the page number on page 1.

11. Scroll the document, looking at the header in the three sections and noting that the footer is deleted throughout the entire document.

12. Save your changes.

Using Footnotes

Documents often contain **footnotes**—a note at the bottom (or foot) of a page that explains or expands key points on the page or that documents sources. Footnotes invariably refer to a specific word or sentence or paragraph. Labeling the footnote and the text it refers to with the same label—a super-scripted number or symbol—shows this relationship. A documentation footnote typically has four divisions: author name(s), title, publication date, and page reference. The arrangement and punctuation may vary, depending upon the type of publication noted and the style manual followed.

When you type text that requires a footnote, you must use the Footnote command to insert a footnote. You will then verify that you want the footnotes numbered sequentially with Arabic numbers and type the footnote text in Footnote view. Word will automatically number and place the footnotes immediately after a short horizontal line at the left margin between your main text and the footer. The footnote text style is based on the Normal style. When you point to a note reference number, the note text displays above the reference number as a ScreenTip. Later, if you want to delete a footnote, you have only to delete the reference number in the main text. If you want to move a footnote to another location, select the reference number and use the cut and paste method. Word will renumber automatically and move the footnote to the new location. If you need to edit footnote text, double-click the reference number or click Footnotes on the View menu to open the Footnote view and do so. (Some writers use **endnotes** instead of footnotes. Endnotes serve the same purposes as footnotes, but they appear together on a separate page at the end of a document. The same Word feature that inserts footnotes inserts endnotes as well.)

Inserting Footnotes

1. Click Footnote on the Insert menu.

2. Click OK to insert continuously numbered (Arabic) footnotes at the bottom of pages.

3. Type the footnote text; then resume typing body text.

Inserting Footnotes

In this activity, you will insert footnotes in your current document.

1. **Go to the beginning of *Reference Features*.**

2. **Find the second occurrence of the words *economic history*. Click after the period that ends the sentence.**

3. **Click the Insert menu and click Footnote.**

The Footnote and Endnote dialog box displays, as shown in Figure 2.31.

4. **Click OK to insert an Arabic numbered footnote at the bottom of the page.**

Word places the superior number 1 at the insertion point. Then at the bottom of the same page, Word inserts a short horizontal line and the superior number 1. You simply type the footnote text at the insertion point.

5. **Type the following footnote text:** Neimi, A. W., *U.S. Economic History (1975)*, pp. 2-3.

Do not press Enter⏎ *after you type the footnote. Word will automatically adjust the spacing if another footnote appears on the same page.*

Figure 2.31
The Footnote and Endnote
dialog box

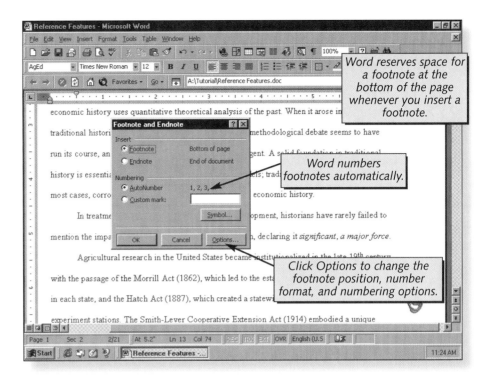

Word reserves space for a footnote at the bottom of the page whenever you insert a footnote.

Word numbers footnotes automatically.

Click Options to change the footnote position, number format, and numbering options.

6. Click the main part of the document.

7. Find the words *major force* and click after the period. Then click the **Insert menu** and click **Footnote**.

8. Click **OK** to accept the footnote settings.

Word inserts the superior number 2 at the insertion point in the text and makes room for the second footnote at the bottom of the page.

9. Type the following footnote text: Ibid., p. 230.

Ibid. is an abbreviation of the Latin word *ibidem,* which means in the same place. In other words, footnote 2 refers to the same publication as footnote 1.

10. Save your changes.

Creating a Table of Contents

A *table of contents* (or *TOC*) is a list of the headings and subheadings and the page numbers on which they are found in the document. A table of contents typically appears at the beginning of a document, before the main section, and provides an overview of the document contents.

Word will create a table of contents on the basis of the heading styles used in your document. Several different arrangements are available, and you will be able to preview the options before you choose one. Word automatically inserts a hyperlink for each heading that appears in a table of contents. Thus, you can click headings in the TOC to jump to the corresponding page in your document. If you add text or headings to your document, you can automatically update the table of contents by selecting it and pressing F9.

Inserting a Table of Contents

In this activity, you will create and modify a table of contents for the *Reference Features* document.

Inserting a TOC

1. Apply a Heading style (All styles list) to all headings.

2. Click the insertion point where the table is to appear.

3. Click the Insert menu, Index and Tables, and the Table of Contents tab.

4. Choose an option in the Formats list box.

5. In the Show levels list box, select the highest heading level to appear in the TOC.

6. Click OK.

1. Click the heading on page 1 of Section 2; then click the **Format menu** and click **Style**. Click **All styles** in the List box, if necessary. Note that in the Styles list, Heading 2 is selected; then close the Style dialog box.

2. Using Go To, go to the next heading in the document. Click the heading and verify that Heading 4 appears in the Style box.

3. Continue verifying the heading styles throughout the document.

4. Navigate to the top of your document; on page i, double-click at the left margin about 0.5" below the insertion point.

5. Click the **Insert menu** and click **Index and Tables**. Then click the **Table of Contents tab**.

The Index and Tables dialog box displays with the Table of Contents tab on top, as shown in Figure 2.32.

6. Click the **Show page numbers option**, if it is not selected. Change the Tab leader to the **solid line option**, if necessary.

7. Click the **Formats arrow**, and click **Distinctive**.

You want to show both Heading 2 and Heading 4 levels in your TOC.

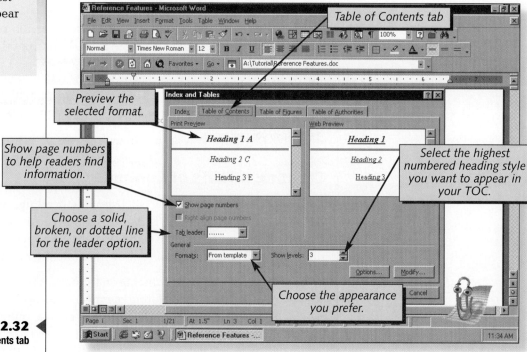

Figure 2.32
The Table of Contents tab

8. Click the **Show levels up arrow** and change the setting to 4. Preview the TOC.

9. Click **OK** to create the table of contents.

Word inserts the table of contents at the insertion point.

10. Click above the table of contents and type Table of Contents. **Then apply the Heading 2 style to create a heading for page i.**

Now you will update the TOC to include the heading you just typed.

11. Select the new heading and the entire TOC. Then press F9.

The Update Table of Contents dialog box appears.

12. Click the **Update entire table option** and click **OK**.

Word adds the *Table of Contents* heading and page number to the TOC.

13. Click *A Quantified View* to jump to the page where the heading appears in the document.

14. Save and close the file.

Test your knowledge by matching the terms on the left with the definitions on the right. See Appendix B to check your answers.

TERMS	DEFINITIONS
___ 1. header	**a.** Distance of text from the left or right page margins
___ 2. Clipboard	**b.** A master document or format model that includes standard text
___ 3. Format Painter	**c.** Feature that copies paragraph format and character appearance
___ 4. indentation	**d.** Information repeated in the top margin
___ 5. template	**e.** Memory in which copies and cuts are stored

ON*the*WEB

INSERTING HYPERLINKS

A hyperlink, you will recall, is a shortcut, or jump, that, when clicked, links you to another page, document, or Web site. In a document, text that contains hyperlinks usually appears in a different color from the main text, often blue, and is underlined. Typically, after you click a hyperlink, the text changes color, generally to purple, to remind you that you followed that link. In this activity, you will insert a hyperlink to another page in the same document, to another Word document, and to a Web site.

1. Open *Atlas Manual* on your Student Data Disk; set the insertion point two lines below the *Contents* heading.

2. Hide the Web toolbar, if it is visible.

3. On the Standard toolbar, click the **Insert Hyperlink button** . In the Insert Hyperlink dialog box, click **Place in This Document** in the *Link to* box. In the *Select a place in this document* box, click **Overview of ATLAS**.

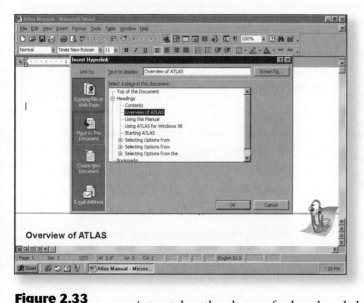

As shown in Figure 2.33, this heading appears in the Text to display window. The display text holds the hyperlink. Now you will set a ScreenTip that contains a short description of what the display text jumps to.

4. Click the **ScreenTip button,** type ATLAS Overview **and click OK. Then click OK** in the Insert Hyperlink dialog box.

A blue, underlined hyperlink displays. When you point to the hyperlink, the pointer takes the shape of a hand and the ScreenTip displays. ScreenTips may be identical to the display text; some are entirely different.

Figure 2.33
The Insert Hyperlink dialog box

5. Click the hyperlink. Watch as the linked page appears and the Web toolbar displays.

6. On the Web toolbar, click the **Back button** .

The Contents page reappears. The hyperlink is now purple.

7. Save the document as *Atlas Manual - Hyperlink* in the *Tutorial* folder on your Student Data Disk and close the file.

8. In the *Tutorial* folder, open *Select* and save it as *Document Link* in the *Tutorial* folder. To insert a hyperlink to another Word document, set the insertion point two lines below the end of the last paragraph.

9. Click the **Insert Hyperlink button** . In the *Link to* box, click **Existing File or Web Page**.

10. Under *Browse for*, click the **File button**. In the Link to File dialog box, navigate to the drive for your Student Data Disk. In the list of files, click *Home Page Support*; then click **OK**.

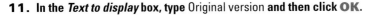

11. In the *Text to display* box, type Original version **and then click OK.**

12. **Point to the hyperlink, read the Screen Tip, and then click. Watch as the** *Home Page Support* **file is opened in the Word window.**

13. **Close** *Home Page Support.* **Save and then close the updated** *Document Link* **file.**

14. **Open** *Star Gazette Article - Edited* **in the** *Skills Review* **folder on your Student Data Disk. (If this file is not available, open the** *Star Gazette Article* **file on your Student Data Disk.)**

15. **Set the insertion point two lines below the end of the document, and type** Click here for Venus on the Web. **Then select this sentence.**

16. **Click the Insert Hyperlink button** 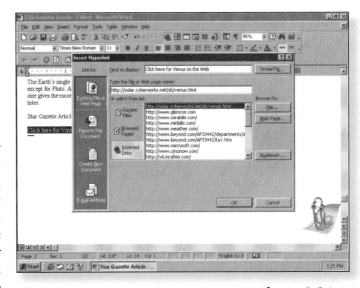. **In the** *Link to* **box, click Existing File or Web Page. Click the Inserted Links button to display a list of Web sites visited recently.**

17. **Scroll the** *Or select from list* **box. If you see the address for the Cyberworks Web site (http://solar.cyberworks.net/sb/venus.html), click it and the address will appear in the** *Type the file or Web page name* **box (Figure 2.34). If you do not see it, type the address in the** *Type the file or Web page name* **box and verify that every character is accurate and no spaces appear between the characters. Click OK.**

18. **Point to the display text, read the ScreenTip, and then click the hyperlink.**

If your connection to the Internet is already active, Word will open your browser and jump directly to the Venus Overview Web site. If your connection to the Internet is *not* active, either the Sign In or Connect To dialog box will appear so that you can connect to the Internet, or you will receive an error message telling you that no connection is established. Sign in or connect to your ISP and then repeat step 18.

Figure 2.34
The Insert Hyperlink
dialog box

19. **Return to your Word document and save it as** *Venus Link* **in the** *Tutorial* **folder on your Student Data Disk. Then close all open files and exit Word.**

20. **Close your browser, and disconnect from the Internet unless your instructor tells you to remain connected.**

Warning

You may proceed directly to the exercises in this lesson. If, however, you are finished with your computer session, follow the "shut down" procedures for your lab or school environment.

Lesson Summary & Exercises

SUMMARY

Word offers a variety of templates that you can adapt to your needs. The Spelling and Grammar and Thesaurus tools and the copy, cut, and paste features help you generate error-free documents. Word provides many features for arranging, or formatting, text. Other options, such as bold, underline, and italic are available for enhancing appearance. The Format Painter and Style features are handy tools for changing format and appearance together. Objects add interest to documents; Word equips users with tools to process objects. Word makes short work of page numbering and the addition of headers and footers, footnotes, and tables of contents. You can add hyperlinks to your pages to link within a document, from one document to another, or to a Web site.

Now that you have completed this lesson, you should be able to do the following:

- Create a new document from a template. (Word-152)
- Use the Spelling tool as you type. (Word-155)
- Use the Grammar tool and check readability. (Word-157)
- Use the Thesaurus tool. (Word-159)
- Use AutoCorrect and AutoText. (Word-161)
- Select and delete blocks of text. (Word-162)
- Use the Office Clipboard to cut, copy, and paste text. (Word-164)
- Use the drag-and-drop method to move and copy text. (Word-165)
- Insert page breaks. (Word-167)
- Change margins, insert section breaks, and change vertical alignment. (Word-169)
- Change horizontal alignment and indentation style. (Word-171)
- Set character, line, and paragraph spacing. (Word-173)
- Use the Tab command and set tabs with leaders. (Word-174)
- Insert symbols and special characters. (Word-176)
- Change font attributes and enhance text. (Word-178)
- Use the Format Painter. (Word-180)
- Apply styles and create sections with various formatting. (Word-182)
- Insert an image. (Word-184)
- Edit and format a graphic. (Word-186)
- Sort lists alphabetically or numerically. (Word-188)
- Add bullets or numbers to lists. (Word-189)
- Insert and modify page numbers. (Word-190)
- Create and modify headers and footers. (Word-192)
- Create footnotes. (Word-194)
- Create a table of contents. (Word-196)
- Create hyperlinks to link pages, documents, and Web sites. (Word-198)

CONCEPTS REVIEW

1 TRUE/FALSE

Circle T if the statement is true or F if the statement is false.

T   F   **1.** A footer is the same as a footnote.

T   F   **2.** The font Times New Roman is often used for paragraph text.

T   F   **3.** Wavy underlines appear only in documents created from a template.

T   F   **4.** For letters and memos a font size of 8 to 10 is recommended.

T   F   **5.** To check the spelling of a word underlined in red, right-click it.

T   F   **6.** The Align Right button makes text even on both side margins.

T   F   **7.** Twelve pieces of text on the Clipboard can be pasted one by one.

T   F   **8.** To link two files with a hyperlink, begin by opening both files.

T   F   **9.** Open the Paragraph dialog box to choose hanging indentation style.

T   F   **10.** Handles around an object show that a copy is on the Clipboard.

2 MATCHING

Match each of the terms on the left with the definitions on the right.

TERMS

1. align
2. bold
3. cut
4. drag-and-drop
5. font
6. clip
7. line spacing
8. paste
9. styles
10. Ignore

DEFINITIONS

a. To line up text at a side page margin

b. Group of characters that share a common design

c. Distance between lines of text within paragraphs

d. Text that looks thick and dark

e. Way to move text without the Clipboard

f. A ready-made image

g. Menu option when checking spelling or grammar

h. Way to remove text from the document window

i. Sets of text characteristics with names like Body or Title

j. To use text stored on the Clipboard

Lesson Summary & Exercises

3 COMPLETION

Fill in the missing word or phrase for each of the following statements.

1. Two ways that hypertext looks different from ordinary text are _____ and _____ .

2. You can place repeating information on each page of your document using the _____ and _____ command.

3. To change margins or vertical alignment, select the _____ command on the File menu.

4. Word temporarily stores information that you have cut or copied from your document in the _____.

5. To align all lines of a paragraph on both the right and left, use the _____ button.

6. Use _____ to highlight listed items when all items have the same priority.

7. To prepare a document by following a preset pattern, open a _____.

8. The _____ dialog box has Set, Clear, and Clear All buttons.

9. Use the _____ menu to start a new document from a template.

10. The _____ button removes text from your document and places the text on the Clipboard.

4 SHORT ANSWER

Write a brief answer to each of the following questions.

1. Briefly describe how to copy double spacing and italic from one paragraph to another.

2. Explain the usefulness of a template.

3. Define paragraph spacing and explain how it differs from line spacing.

4. How many available paragraph alignments exist on the Formatting toolbar?

5. Describe the Clip Gallery.

6. Describe the use and purpose of the Style button on the Formatting toolbar.

7. Explain how to find all formatting marks in a document.

8. Name the steps for inserting a hyperlink to jump from one document to another.

9. Explain the purpose of section breaks and name the two kinds.

10. Besides font and indents, what factors should you consider in creating a paragraph style?

5 IDENTIFICATION

Label each of the buttons on the Formatting toolbar in Figure 2.35.

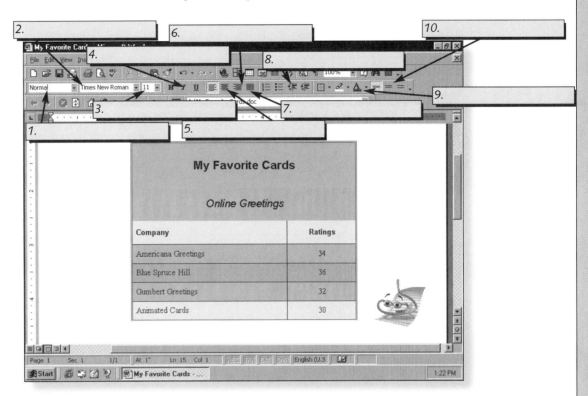

Figure 2.35

SKILLS REVIEW

If you are storing your files on a floppy disk, insert a blank, formatted disk before proceeding with this activity. Create new folders on the disk, as appropriate. Complete each of the Skills Review problems in sequential order to review your Word skills to create a document from a template; check spelling, grammar, and readability; use the thesaurus; select, delete, copy, and move text; reformat pages and paragraphs; enhance the appearance of documents; insert, edit, and format an image; and add reference features.

1 Open a Template and Replace Variable Text

1. Click **New** on the File menu. On the Letters & Faxes tab, click the **Professional Fax template**.

2. Verify that **Document** is selected in the Create New box and click **OK**. Save the document as *Template Fax* in the *Skills Review* folder on your Student Data Disk.

3. In the fax header area, replace the variable text using this information: This 3-page fax (you will have attachments) is to your instructor from you. Create a fax and phone number. The subject is Word 2000. Delete the Copy variable information.

4. The information you're sending is For Review. The message is: The Word feature that I use most is (*finish the sentence*).

5. Save and close the file.

Lesson Summary & Exercises

2 Check Accuracy and Reading Ease

1. Open *Reference Features* in the *Tutorial* folder and save it as *SGR Check* in the *Skills Review* folder on your Student Data Disk.

2. At the top of the document, click **Spelling and Grammar** on the Tools menu.

3. In the Spelling and Grammar dialog box, click the **Options button**.

4. In the Spelling & Grammar tab, verify that the **Check grammar with spelling** and the **Show readability statistics options** are selected. Click **OK**.

5. Study each spelling and grammar question presented before choosing an option. Do not add words to the spelling dictionary. Change the word *disemination* to *dissemination*.

6. Change the word *mathamatics* to *mathematics*.

7. The word *Hise's* is spelled correctly and is the correct possessive form; click **Ignore All**.

8. Continue checking the spelling and grammar in the document. Click **Ignore** if you are unsure of the correction.

9. Note the word count and the average words per sentence. Note the Reading Ease score and Grade Level score.

3 Use the Thesaurus

1. Go to page 1. Find and select the word *cogent*.

2. Click the **Tools menu**, point to **Language**, and click **Thesaurus**.

3. In the Replace with Synonym box, click **sound**; then click **Replace**.

4. Find and select *empirical* and replace it with a synonym.

5. Find *expenditure;* look up the synonym *disbursement*. Replace the original word with a synonym of *disbursement*.

6. Navigate to the top of page 1 and click.

TABLE 2.1	FIND AND REPLACE SUGGESTIONS
Occurrence	**Replace?**
expenditures of the stations	No
work and expenditures	Yes
public expenditure	Yes
a government expenditure	Yes
of government expenditure	No
all expenditures	Yes
by these expenditures	No
early government expenditure	No
Work and Expenditures	No

7. On the Replace tab, type expenditure in the Find what box and payout in the Replace with box. Click **Find Next**. Table 2.1 indicates the occurrences to replace in the document.

8. Change all occurrences of *regarding* with *about*.

9. Save and close the document.

4 Delete Sentences, Lines, and Paragraphs

1. Open **Write This Way** on your Student Data Disk and save it as **Select** in the **Skills Review** folder on your Student Data Disk.

2. Select and delete the first paragraph.

3. Find *1-3*; select and delete the line.

4. At the end of the document, select and delete the last sentence.

5. Save your changes; remember to save changes often as you work.

5 Use the Office Clipboard

1. Display and clear the Clipboard.

2. Select the next-to-last paragraph; click **Cut** ✂.

3. At the end of the document, paste the cut text from the Clipboard.

4. Then, type: Which of these titles do you like best? and press Enter⏎.

5. Display and clear the Clipboard toolbar.

6. Copy the document title and subtitle as separate items.

7. Using the Clipboard, paste these items on separate lines below the question at the end of the document.

6 Use Drag-and-Drop

1. Find the word *positive*; select the entire sentence.

2. Drag the sentence to the right and drop it before *Does the text. . .*

3. Save the updated file.

7 Reformat Pages

1. Save **Select** as **Reformat** in the **Skills Review** folder on your Student Data Disk.

2. Find the word *stopping*. After the end of this sentence, click **Insert menu**, **Break**, **Page break**, and **OK** to insert a page break.

3. At the beginning of the document, click **Page Setup** on the File menu. Change the margins as follows: Top: 2", Bottom: 1.25", Left: 1.25", Right: 1.25".

4. Check the results in **Print Preview** and click **Close**.

5. Insert a **Next page section break** after the last word on page 1, and delete the page break there.

6. Delete any extra space at the top of page 2. In the Page Setup dialog box, change the top margin on page 2 to 1.25".

7. On page 1, change the top margin to match the bottom margin. On the Layout tab, change the vertical alignment to **Center**. Delete any extra space at the top of the page.

8. Click **Print Preview** 🔍 and view your pages. Save your changes.

Lesson Summary & Exercises

8 Reformat Paragraphs

1. In *Reformat*, select the title and subtitle and click **Align Right** 📃.

2. On page 1, align the paragraph headings (*Plan*, *Draft*) to match the main titles.

3. Select the first paragraph after *Five Steps Up and to the Right*, and click **Increase Indent** 📄. Change the selected paragraph to 1.5 spacing.

4. Under the *Plan* heading, select the first paragraph, right-click, and click **Paragraph**. Use justified alignment. Indent text 0.5" on both the left and right margin, but do not use a special first-line indentation. Also, add paragraph spacing (12 pt.) before and after the paragraph.

5. The other three paragraphs under *Plan* should have a first-line indentation of 0.5". Also, double-space these paragraphs and retain the paragraph spacing (6 pt.) before and after the paragraph.

6. Save your changes.

9 Set Tab Stops

1. Open a new document and save it as *Decimal Tabs* in the *Skills Review* folder on your Student Data Disk.

2. Open the Tabs dialog box (double-click the ruler) and clear all default tabs. Then set Left tabs at each of these positions: 2", 3", 3.75", and 4.75".

3. Tab to the first stop, and begin typing the following words as column headings, pressing Tab between each word: Actual, Budget, Variance, Total Budget.

4. Press Enter⏎, clear all tabs, and set these new tabs: Left tab at 1", Decimal tab at 2.25", Decimal tab at 3.25", Decimal tab at 4", and Right tab at 5.5".

5. Tab to the first stop and begin typing the entries below, pressing Tab between each entry and Enter⏎ at the end of each line. (When figures are later available, you can overtype the *0's* in this tabulated text.) Note that decimal points line up in some of the columns. Save your file.

| Income | 0,000.00 | 00,000.00 | 000.00 | 000,000.00 |
| Expenses | 00,000.00 | 0,000.00 | 0.00 | 000,000.00 |

10 Enhance Text

1. In the *Decimal Tabs* file, select all headings and click **Bold** ⒷB. Add italic to the *Total Budget* heading. Underline each amount in the *Expenses* row.

2. Save these changes and close this file.

3. In the *Reformat* document, select the title and change it to these attributes: a sans serif option, font size 18, bold, and red.

4. Select the subtitle and change it to the same sans serif font as the title. Use these attributes: font size 16, italic, and gray-50%.

5. Change the opening paragraph to font size 14 and red.

6. Change the *Plan* heading to the same sans serif font as the title. Make it red, too; add bold; and change the font size to 16.

7. Select the first two *Plan* paragraphs and change the font size to 12.

8. Save your changes.

11 Use the Format Painter

1. Select the *Plan* heading, double-click the **Format Painter button** 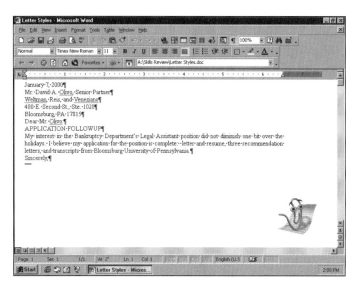, and paint the *Draft* heading.

2. Scroll to the *Revise* heading and copy the font attributes to it; then do the same with the *Edit* heading and the *Publish* heading.

3. Turn off the **Format Painter**.

4. Click the **Show/Hide ¶ button** . Copy the paragraph formatting of the first paragraph under *Plan* (on page 1) to the first paragraph under *Draft*.

5. Copy the paragraph formatting of the second paragraph under *Plan* to the second paragraph under *Draft*.

6. Preview the document in **One Page view**. Click the **Zoom arrow** , and select **50%**.

7. Hide the formatting marks and save your changes. Close the document.

12 Apply Styles

1. Open *Application Followup* on your Student Data Disk and save it as *Letter Styles* in your *Skills Review* folder.

2. Show the formatting marks (Figure 2.36).

3. Select the date. Click **Style** on the Format menu. Each time you open this dialog box, verify that you are selecting from the **All styles list**.

4. In the Styles list box, select the **Date style**, verify the format and appearance in the preview boxes, and click the **Apply button**.

5. Select the name and address. Click the **Style arrow** and apply the **Inside Address style**.

6. Apply the **Salutation style** to the next line.

7. Apply the **Subject Line style** to the all-cap text.

8. Apply the **Body Text style** to the message.

9. Apply the **Closing style** to the next line.

10. Press and type your name.

11. Hide the paragraph marks. Save and close the document.

Figure 2.36

Lesson Summary & Exercises

13 Insert, Edit, and Format an Image

1. Open **Write This Way** on your Student Data Disk and save it as **Insert Clip** in the **Skills Review** folder.

2. Switch to Print Layout View.

3. Click the **Insert Clip Art button** 📷.

4. Click the **Metaphors icon**. Look for and choose a clip that suggests stairs or footsteps. (If none is available here, look in Business, Office, and People categories.)

5. Click the **Preview clip button** 🔍. Then click **Insert clip** 📷 to insert the image into your document. Close the Clip Gallery.

6. Select the first two paragraphs and set the alignment to justify.

7. Select the image.

8. Point to the lower-right corner. Click when the resize handle appears, and drag up and to the left to align the image at about 1" on both rulers. If you make a mistake, undo it and try again.

10. Drag the clip to the first line of the first paragraph at the right margin.

11. Click the **Text Wrapping button** ▦ and click **Square**.

12. Save and close the file.

14 Sort a List

1. Open **Sort** in the **Tutorial** folder and save it with the same file name in the **Skills Review** folder.

2. Navigate to the *Master List of Suite Features* heading and select from *AutoText 4* through *Zoom 4*.

3. Click the **Table menu** and click **Sort**.

4. In the Type list box; select **Number**. Verify that **Ascending** is selected, and then click **OK**. The items are in alphabetical order within three numbered groups—2, 4, and 6.

5. Edit the list as follows: Envelope & Bar Code 4, Horizontal Line 4, Insert & Delete Rows (Table) 2, Mail Merge 6, Shading 6, Split Cells (Tables) 2. Delete these entries: Outline 6 and Equation box 6. Then select and re-sort the list in numerical order.

6. In the Spreadsheet list, type **5** in front of these entries: AVERAGE, COUNT, IF, MAX, MIN, NOW, SUM, TODAY.

7. Select beginning from *Absolute and relative cell references* to the end of the list of spreadsheet items. Sort the items in numerical order by Field 1. (The numbered items form a separate alphabetized list.)

15 Add Bullets and Numbers to Lists

1. Select all items in the 2 group and click the **Bullets button** ▤. Decrease the indentation.

2. Select all items in the 4 group and add bullets.

3. Insert bullets in the items in the 6 group and increase the indentation. (A different bullet character is applied to bullets at this level.)

4. Select the alphabetized Spreadsheet list except the items starting with *5*.

5. Click the **Numbering button** .

6. With the numbered items still selected, right-click and click **Bullets and Numbering**. Click the **Customize button**. Under Number position, change the Aligned at position to 0". Under Text position, change the Indent at position to .25". Click **OK**.

7. Insert a blank line below Item 29. (If 30 appears automatically, backspace to delete it.)

8. Select all the items that start with a *5* and number the items 1 through 8. (Hint: In the Bullets and Numbering dialog box, click Restart Numbering.)

9. Save the file.

16 Insert Page Numbers and Add a Header/Footer

1. Navigate to the top of the document and click.

2. Click **Page Numbers** on the Insert menu.

3. In the Position box, click **Top of page (Header)**. In the Alignment box, click **Right**. Deselect **Show number on first page**. Click **OK**.

4. Navigate to page 2 to verify the page number.

5. Navigate to the top of the document. Click the **View menu**, and click **Header and Footer**. Click the **Switch Between Header and Footer button** .

6. In the Footer area, use AutoText to insert the filename. At the center, insert the date, using the **Insert Date button** . At the right, insert the page number (**Insert Page Number button**), followed by /. Then insert the total pages (**Insert Number of Pages button**).

7. Close the Header/Footer view. Save and close the file.

17 Insert Footnotes

1. Open *SGR Check* in the *Skills Review* folder and save it as *Footnotes* in the same folder.

2. Using the Go To tab, navigate to the first footnote. Note the footnote style in the document.

3. Find *thoroughly scientific institutions* in the document. Click after the quotation mark at the end of the sentence.

4. Click **Footnote** on the Insert menu. Under Numbering, verify that **AutoNumber** is selected and click **OK**.

5. Type the following as the footnote text: True, A. C., *A History of Agricultural Education in the United States,* p. 101.

6. Find *unjust, and unconstitutional* in the document. Insert this footnote after the sentence: Ibid., p. 103.

7. Save and close the file.

Lesson Summary & Exercises

18 Insert a Table of Contents

1. Open **Nonprinting** on your Student Data Disk and save it as **TOContents** in the **Skills Review** folder.

2. At the top of the document, insert a page break.

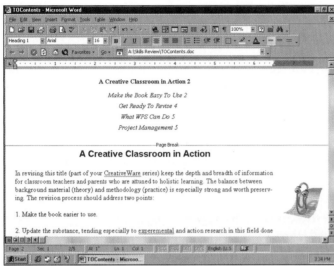

Figure 2.37

3. Using Go To, confirm the level of headings in your document.

4. Go to page 1. Click the **Insert menu**, click **Index and Tables**, and click the **Table of Contents tab**.

5. Under Formats, click **Simple**. Click the **Show page numbers option**, if it is not already selected. Change the Show levels setting to 2. Click **OK**.

6. Center the TOC horizontally (Figure 2.37).

7. Save the file.

LESSON APPLICATIONS

1 Edit and Enhance a Brochure

Using a file on your Student Data Disk, you will edit and enhance a brochure for a travel agency.

1. Open **Sandy Reef Island Tour** on the Student Data Disk. Save it as **Sandy Reef Island Tour Brochure** in the **Lesson Applications** folder on your Student Data Disk.

2. Find the phrase *Several hundred islands* and change it to *Almost a thousand islands*.

3. Move the first sentence of the second paragraph to the beginning of the document.

4. Copy the words *Sandy Reef Island* and place them at the top of the document to make a heading. Center and bold this heading. Change it to Arial, size 14, and a color of your choice.

5. Delete the words *color and* in the last sentence of the second paragraph.

6. Save your changes and close the file.

2 Reformat and Enhance a New Document

Create an announcement for a workshop scheduled in your area.

1. Open a new, blank document and save it as **Workshop Announcement** in the **Lesson Applications** folder on your Student Data Disk. Your finished document will resemble Figure 2.38.

2. Change all the margins to 2"; change the vertical alignment to Center.

3. Set two tabs: Left tab at 1.5",
Center tab at 4".

4. Type City and Date at the tabs;
underline and change the words
to a larger font.

5. Beneath the headings, type three
cities in your state and three
dates.

6. Above the headings, type: We're
Coming to Your Area this Year!

7. Look at the document in a different view; add enhancements of
your choice.

8. Save your document and close
the file.

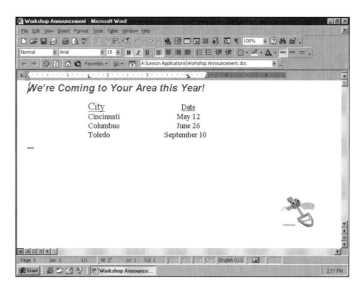

Figure 2.38

3 Insert a Clip

Insert a picture into a document on your Student Data Disk.

1. Open **Textra 6** on your Student Data Disk and save it as **Picture This** in the
Lesson Applications folder. This document describes a book similar to this
tutorial.

2. Insert a page break at the end of the document.

3. Open the Clip Gallery and browse the categories. Insert any clip that you
might expect to see in the book described.

4. Resize the clip to approximately 3" wide and 3" tall.

5. Save and close the file.

4 Watch More than Your P's and Q's

Check spelling and grammar for an entire document and evaluate reading difficulty.

1. Open the **Woodsy View News** file on your Student Data Disk and save it as
Woodsy View News Readability in the **Lesson Applications** folder.

2. Check spelling and grammar for the entire document and ask to see readability statistics at the end of the check. Assume that all names are spelled
correctly as you respond to the spelling and grammar problems.

3. Note the word count for future reference.

4. Decide if the document is appropriate for a general audience on the basis of
sentence length, reading ease, and grade level. Consider it acceptable if two of
the following statements are true: (a) Average words per sentence are less
than 18; (b) The Reading Ease score is above 50; (c) The Grade Level score is
8.0 or lower.

5. Save and close the file.

Lesson Summary & Exercises

5 A Different Sort

Find synonyms in the Thesaurus. Replace a nickname with a proper name. Sort paragraphs alphabetically and add bullets and numbering.

1. Open **Woodsy View News Readability** in the **Lesson Applications** folder and save it as **Woodsy View News Sort** in the same folder.

2. Find a synonym to replace *vigilance.* Find a synonym to replace *capacity.*

3. Change *Kay Gradison* to *Kathryn Gradison* throughout the document.

4. Under *Memory Joggers,* type a heading (and a period) at the beginning of each paragraph as follows: Water., Carports., Repairs., Gutters., Trash., Trash., Pets., Repairs.

5. Sort the paragraphs in the *Memory Joggers* section alphabetically and insert bullets. Sort the *Thank You* paragraphs in descending order; insert bullets.

6. Number the list under *Summer Summary:* Use the Numbered tab in the Bullets and Numbering dialog box; select the style with a parenthesis after the number.

7. Save and close the file.

6 Cut it Out

Cut a paragraph; paste it into a footnote. Number the pages and insert a footer.

1. Open **Step Write Article** on your Student Data Disk. Save it as **Footnote** in the **Lesson Applications** folder.

2. Near the end of the document, delete the dividing line and the extra paragraph marks. Cut the last two sentences to use as footnote text. Insert a footnote after the main heading; use a custom mark, such as *. Paste the paragraph you cut as the footnote text. Change the font color of the footnote to black.

3. Number the pages—except the first—at the top center. Change the line spacing to Double.

4. Create a footer showing the title of the article, the date, and your initials (all caps).

5. Check the spelling and grammar and correct the errors.

6. Save and close the file.

PROJECTS

1 My Bio from a Template

Since you often give presentations to people in your field, you need to write your *bio* (biography, a brief account of your life). Then you can give a copy to program planners, who may print the information in their program and/or prepare to introduce you to meeting participants. A sample bio appears on your Student Data Disk: ***Tony Denier's Bio***. Use the ***Report*** template that you prefer to create your own bio. You may copy part or all of Tony's bio and then delete and replace text to create your unique document. (Hint: Navigate between the two files using taskbar buttons or use Arrange All on the Window menu.)

Your bio should have at least two short paragraphs and should mention your education, career achievements and/or goals, hobbies, and special interests. Edit your document carefully, checking spelling and grammar so that no wavy underlines appear on your screen. Reformat and enhance your bio to project an image in keeping with your personality. Save the document as ***My Bio*** in the ***Projects*** folder on your Student Data Disk. Send the document as an e-mail message to your instructor. Close the file.

2 By Design

Open a new, blank document and save it as ***Personal*** in the ***Projects*** folder in your Student Data Disk. Design a letterhead for yourself, using fonts, font sizes, font colors, and special effects of your choice. Before adopting a particular font, verify that the printer you use can print the font. In addition to your name and address, include a telephone number and an e-mail address. Include additional information, such as a favorite quotation, if you wish. (Hint: You will want to use a very narrow top margin so that the design is as close to the edge of the page as possible when the letterhead is printed.) Save the file. When finished, create a brief message to your instructor on the letterhead. In the message, name the fonts, font sizes, and effects used in the letterhead. Omit your typed name below the message since it appears in the letterhead (Figure 2.39). Save the message as ***By Design*** in the ***Projects*** folder on your Student Data Disk. Save and close the file.

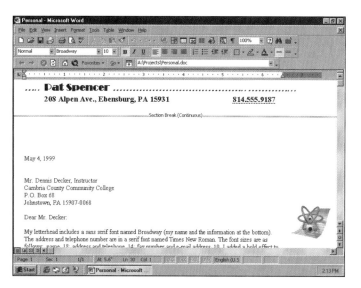

Figure 2.39

Lesson Summary & Exercises

3 What's a Wizard?

Open a new, blank document and save it as **Wizard** in the **Projects** folder on your Student Data Disk. Look up the definition of *Wizard* in the glossary of this tutorial; then search Help for more information. (Hint: Ask the Office Assistant for help on installing wizards and explore the wizard topics.) In the New dialog box, you will determine the types and number of Wizards available on each tab (omit the Office 97 tab). Create tabulated text to summarize the information you gather. Your text should contain two columns similar to Table 2.2.

TABLE 2.2	DATA FOR PROJECT 3
Category (Tab)	**Number of Wizards**
General	
Legal Pleadings	
Letters & Faxes	
Memos	
Other Documents	
Publications	
Reports	
Web Pages	

In the New dialog box, count the files on each tab that contain the name *Wizard* and complete the second column of information, omitting any category that contains no Wizard. Above the tabulated text, type a heading and a statement to introduce the text. Edit, format, and enhance the document. Add shading to the introductory paragraph. Change the character spacing of the heading; change the line spacing of the text. Save and close the file.

4 Hot Button

In a new, blank document, quickly create a list of five toolbar buttons you use often (with each button name on a separate line). Beneath it, list five buttons that you rarely or never use. Finally, list five buttons not on the first two lists. Using the Office Clipboard or dragging and dropping, combine the lists in alphabetical order. Use bold, italic, and underline to distinguish most-used, rarely used, and other. Add a heading and a note explaining the significance of the special effects. Add a border around the text. Edit, format, and enhance the document as desired. Save the document as **Buttons** in the **Projects** folder on your Student Data Disk.

5 Under Cover

In your office, pictures prepared as book covers have been stored in the Clip Gallery. As a member of the Textra team, you are to select three possible images for *Textra 6 Workbook* for the team to consider at its next meeting. Open **Picture This** in the **Lesson Applications** folder on your Student Data Disk and save it as **Textra Graphic** in the **Projects** folder. Decide if the picture inserted in this document is one you would recommend as a cover option. If not, delete it. Your finished document should contain three graphics (clip art, photograph, image, drawing, or other object), each on a separate page. Resize each graphic to a height of 3". Ask the Office Assistant about inserting a text box and label, as well as enhancing graphics. Then, add a text box near the bottom of each graphic and label each object in 8-point type with a number (*No. 1*) and a name that you create to describe the image (Figure 2.40). Then change the fill, line, and font colors so the text box blends with the background, more or less, while the text stands out. Save and close the file.

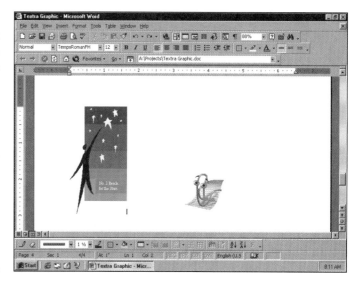

Figure 2.40

6 Tip of the Day

You already knew Word 2000 features when you were hired at Rainmaker Associates. Some other assistants, though, are still not up to speed, according to a recent survey conducted by human resources. The H.R. department will implement small, simple solutions before investing in Word training. For starters, they will circulate *Tip of the Day*, a how-to sheet that also will encourage use of Help (an example appears in Figure 2.41). Soon they will be able to e-mail a tip each morning, and eventually such information will be standard fare on Rainmaker's intranet.

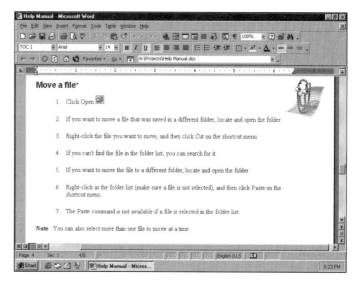

Figure 2.41

Ask the Office Assistant about removing a hyperlink and deleting display text. Compile several tips for H.R. by copying Microsoft Word Help screens for copying, deleting, moving, and renaming files. Delete all hyperlinks and unnecessary display text. Check readability scores. Create a table of contents. Insert a footnote on each page to document the information source and encourage users to search Help for more information. Save the document as **Help Manual** in the **Projects** folder and close the file.

7 Write This Way on the World Wide Web

Open **Reformat** in your **Skills Review** folder and save it as **Web Link** in the **Projects** folder on your Student Data Disk. At the end of the document, type a heading Links and then copy the formatting of the *Publish* heading. Delete the previous three lines in the document that refer to titles. After the *Links* heading, insert a hyperlink to **Step Write Article** on your Student Data Disk. Insert hyperlinks to the following Web sites; change the display text as desired for each hyperlink:

Online Writing Lab	http://owl.english.purdue.edu/Files/32.html
Ten Proofreading Tips	http://www.ascs.org/10tips.html
Successful Proofreading Strategies	http://www.temple.edu/writingctr/cw06005.htm

Follow the link to all three sites and decide which two provide information that you can use. Delete the link to the site not chosen. Consult the Help system, if necessary. Arrange the links in the desired order in your document. Save and close the document.

Project in Progress

8 Following Through

As the founder-owner of I-Comm, you provide a variety of writing and editing services for small and medium-sized organizations in your area. Besides the business writing workshops that you present to clients, you also maintain a relationship with local high schools. Recently you accepted an invitation to present a workshop at Anderson High School. In replying to the invitation, you promised to send your bio in the near future.

Open a letter template of your choice. Save the document as ***Bio Letter*** in the ***Projects*** folder on your Student Data Disk. Create a letter to the student at Anderson High School who invited you to give a presentation at the school in the near future. If the ***Projects*** folder contains ***AHS Workshop***, open that file, copy the delivery address and salutation, read the letter to refresh your memory, and then close the file. (If the file is not available, type the delivery address in Project 7 of Lesson 1, and read those directions to get the gist of the *Project in Progress*.) Paste or type the delivery address to your new document. Include these document parts: your company name (I-Comm) and address (create one), current date, salutation, complimentary closing, your name as the writer/sender, your title (Writing Consultant), and enclosure notation (Figure 2.42).

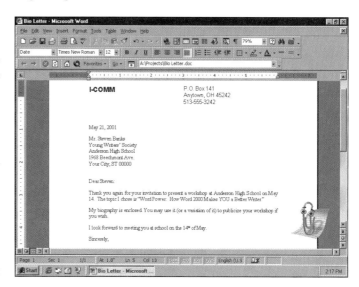

Figure 2.42

Your message should remind the receiver that you will present a workshop at the school. State that your bio is enclosed and that it is okay to print it as is or to shorten it in promotional materials. Check spelling and grammar, edit, reformat, and enhance your letter until you are completely satisfied. Then save the changes and close the file.

Now it's time to organize the handouts you will take to the workshop. List five Word features to emphasize at the workshop. For each feature, write a sentence describing what it does and give an example of when the high school students might use it. Include two or three keywords for finding information about the feature in Help. Create a table of contents and add a footnote, giving copyright information for Microsoft Word 2000. (Hint: For details, see About Microsoft Word on the Help menu.) You decided that you want an attractive cover sheet for your handouts. Set up the cover sheet as a separate section at the beginning of the file. On the cover sheet, insert a piece of clip art that relates to writing. Size and position the image as desired. Include the title of your presentation, your name, and the date of the presentation. Reformat and enhance the cover as desired. Save the document as ***Word Power*** in the ***Projects*** folder and close the file.

Case Study

Overview: Congratulations! You have completed the lessons in the Word tutorial and now have the opportunity in this capstone project to apply the Word skills you have learned. Your biennial family reunion is set for next August in your hometown, and you will be preparing the invitations, sign-up forms, and family newsletter, and putting together the family cookbook. As you create the case study documents, try to incorporate the following skills:

- Create and save various kinds of documents—letters, forms, graphics, among others.
- Proofread and edit text. Use the Spelling and Grammar and Thesaurus features; use the Undo, Redo, Repeat, and Find and Replace commands.
- Ask the Office Assistant for help as needed.
- Navigate efficiently within and among documents.
- Use templates and wizards as desired to create documents.
- Search the Internet.
- Manage the files you create.
- Use the Office Clipboard to cut, copy, and paste text.

- Change page orientation, page and section breaks, margins, horizontal and vertical alignment, indentations, and character, line, and paragraph spacing; also set tabs.
- Add bullets and numbering to lists.
- Change font style, size, attributes, and color.
- Create headers and footers, footnotes, and table of contents.
- Add special effects to enhance document appearance, including highlighting, shading, and borders.
- Use the Format Painter and apply styles.
- Create hyperlinks to pages, documents, and Web sites.
- Insert, edit, and format graphics.
- Use Print Preview; print all documents.

Instructions: Read all directions and plan your work before you begin. You will be evaluated on these factors: (1) the number of skills involved in completing the case; (2) creativity; (3) practical applications for the task; (4) appropriate use of word processing features; (5) quality of the documents produced, including mechanical accuracy, format, and writing style; and (6) oral presentation of the case.

1. *Manage the Files and Research the Data*—Create a *Reunion* folder in the *Projects* folder on your Student Data Disk in which to save all your Case Study documents. Search the Web, using keywords such as *reunions, genealogy, family ties,* and *entertaining,* for family reunion ideas that you can use. You may also want to search magazine sites, such as Family PC on the Web at www.zdnet.com/familypc, for additional ideas on how to use technology to plan a family reunion.

2. *Design a Family Graphic*—Design a family emblem to represent your family or this year's reunion. You may use this emblem on the letterhead, t-shirts, caps, sun visors, and so on. Using the family emblem, design a letterhead that you will use as a multipurpose document (e.g., heading for forms, newsletter banner). (Hint: You may want to ask the Office Assistant about drawing an object.)

3. *Prepare the Invitation Letter*—Develop an invitation letter, using the letterhead you created. Cover what, when, where, and whom to contact; announce the family Web page address; ask to have a sign-up form returned to you by a certain date; request favorite recipes for the family cookbook; request pictures of individuals and families; announce that an all-family picture will be taken at the reunion; announce that a donation will be collected (as usual) to cover expenses.

4. *Create the Sign-up Form*—Create a sign-up form to include with the invitation letter; you may want to use the letterhead with a table inserted. On the form, gather this information from family members: the number of persons who will attend the reunion; the full name, birth date, and birthplace of each one; news items for the family newsletter; a list of general menu preferences for each person (e.g., poultry, red meat, seafood, vegetarian). (Hint: You may want to ask the Office Assistant about creating a table.)

5. *Create a Newsletter*—Create a newsletter sharing family reunion information. Limit the newsletter to two pages. Insert clip art, a poem, and a brainteaser. Secure feedback from others and edit as desired. (Hint: You may want to ask the Office Assistant about creating a newsletter.)

6. *Create the Cookbook*—Set up the sections of your cookbook. Type section headings on separate pages and apply a Headings style: (for example, Desserts; Eggs & Cheese; Meat, Fish & Poultry; Pasta, Rice & Other Grains; Salads & Dressings; Soups & Stews; Vegetables). Type a recipe in any two sections, searching the Web for recipes, if necessary. Add a header and/or footer and a table of contents. Create a cover page for the cookbook; you may want to add a border and shading to the cover.

Excel 2000

Reaching Higher

Technology advances raise the bar for business communication

Yesterday's standard business documents have become today's splashy multimedia presentations. In the modern business world, it is no longer possible to compose even the most routine report or presentation with only text. Corporate communications are dressed in spiffier business attire than ever before. Worksheets have found their way into word-processed reports, and graphics pop up in worksheets to engage the readers and focus their attention on important points.

Worksheets are used to manipulate numeric data for accounting, engineering, scientific research, and all sorts of everyday business and home-related tasks. Sometimes a table of numeric results is exactly what customers, employees, bosses, or colleagues need to see. However, most presentations are more informative and persuasive when you translate the numbers into images, such as charts. Information conveyed in charts is often understood more easily—charts make it easy for users to see comparisons, patterns, and trends in data.

Because charts are so important, you can use Microsoft® Excel 2000 to automatically convert numbers in your worksheets to charts that you can include as part of your presentation. You can present a chart on a separate chart sheet as a summary of the important trends or conclusions you are making, or as an embedded illustration within your worksheet to guide readers to a particular focal point in the worksheet. You can also publish a chart on a Web page.

You can enhance your chart with colors, borders, text formats, special symbols, pictures, freehand drawing, and hyperlinks. You can also add illustrations to better convey a point you want to make that may otherwise be buried within a large array of information. You can even enhance a chart with a sound clip that automatically plays when the reader opens the worksheet or clicks a speaker icon in the worksheet. Or, how about inserting a video clip? All of these enhancements are possible; all you need is a computer equipped with multimedia capabilities, which is often a standard feature on newer computers.

Although at first it may seem difficult to build charts, Excel 2000 offers a Chart Wizard to guide you through the process to create a chart almost painlessly, even the first time. The most difficult decisions you must make before you begin building a chart are when to use a chart and what kind to use. Consider these guidelines when building a chart:

1. You can use charts effectively in any worksheet. Most people notice visual patterns much more readily than patterns in a set of numbers.

2. Choose a chart type appropriate for the information you are presenting:

   ■ Use pie charts to show the relative fractions of a whole, such as the relative portions of a company's total income produced by each of the major departments.

   ■ Use bar charts to compare sizes of related items, such as the comparative amounts of the different inventory items in a warehouse.

   ■ Use line charts to show changing totals over time, such as how profits for a company have varied over the past ten years.

3. Include limited, relevant information in a chart. Too many items, such as too many bars or too many slices in the pie, obscure your point.

4. Use a scale in your chart that reflects the point you want to make.

5. Include a title, a legend, source information, and a date on your chart; and be sure to label the elements of the chart, such as the axes and data elements.

6. Choose enhancements carefully to make your chart more effective.

Advances in computer technology—both hardware advances, such as multimedia capabilities, and software advances, such as the Microsoft Excel 2000 program—have "raised the bar" in terms of communicating with and persuading your audience. By understanding and using the full capability of the Excel 2000 program, you can easily engage your audience and communicate your message more effectively than ever before.

Excel Basics

CONTENTS

OBJECTIVES

After you complete this lesson, you will be able to do the following:

- Explain worksheets and demonstrate their use.
- Start and exit Microsoft Excel.
- Name the main features of the Excel window.
- Understand the menu bar and toolbar.
- Open and close workbook files.
- Explore the worksheet.
- Get help from Excel's Office Assistant.
- Print a worksheet.
- Troubleshoot printing problems.
- Enter data, including text and numbers.
- Edit the contents of single cells.
- Use the AutoCorrect feature to correct common mistakes.
- Use the Spelling tool to verify spelling of text entries.
- Use the Find and Replace commands to review and edit data.
- Save workbooks.
- Create hyperlinks to another sheet in the same workbook, to another workbook, or to a Web site.

Lesson 1 teaches you basic worksheet terms, shows you how to launch Microsoft Excel, and introduces the Excel window. You will learn how to open, close, and print worksheets—essential skills that you'll use whenever you work with Excel. In addition, you will develop the skills you need to create simple worksheets. You will learn the basics of entering data and correcting errors. You will also learn how to save a workbook so you can reopen the file later.

INTRODUCING MICROSOFT EXCEL

Microsoft Excel is a powerful worksheet program that enables you to organize and analyze sets of numbers, perform calculations, graph data, develop reports, and convert Excel files for use on the Web. Excel does much of the work automatically and offers help with more complex tasks. A *worksheet* is a grid of columns and rows for entering, viewing, and editing data. A worksheet is like a computerized ledger in which you can type text and numbers and then perform calculations.

Worksheets are useful any time you have to organize a set of numbers. You can use worksheets to track sales data, generate expense reports, calculate loan payments, create budgets, and record and analyze research data, among other things. As an example, the worksheet in Figure 1.1 contains first quarter sales figures for Pet Paradise, a pet food and supply store.

Figure 1.1
A simple worksheet

Pet Paradise--Pet Food and Pet Supplies				Column
First Quarter Sales				
	January	February	March	1st Quarter
Cat Food	112712	114229	111842	338783
Dog Food	113243	101459	115378	330080
Flea Spray	17391	21037	36457	74885
Bones and Treats	43753	34087	44429	122269
Toys	31738	41973	37763	111474
Totals	318837	312785	345869	977491

The sales information in Figure 1.1 is arranged in well-marked columns and rows. Column headings indicate in which months the sales occurred, and row headings tell you which items were sold. Monthly totals appear at the bottom of each column, and first quarter totals are in the far-right column. Excel calculates these totals automatically, so you don't have to add everything yourself. This simple worksheet can help you determine which items are selling the most and the least, determine the fluctuations of monthly sales, and see at a glance how well Pet Paradise did this quarter.

Although worksheets can include text, their main purpose is to organize and analyze sets of numbers. In a way, worksheet programs are like calculators that can operate on groups of numbers. For instance, Excel can add sales figures, as you saw in Figure 1.1. But unlike calculators, worksheet programs automatically recalculate the results when any of your numbers change.

Excel provides easy methods for improving the appearance of your worksheets—by adding italics, lines, shading, and more. Figure 1.1 is unformatted and plain. Figure 1.2, a formatted version of Figure 1.1, gives you an idea of the possibilities available with Excel. Formatted worksheets are easier to read and look more professional.

Figure 1.2
A formatted worksheet

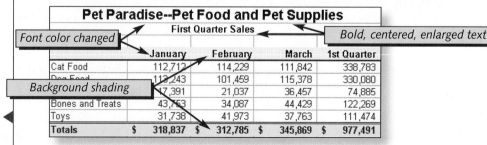

Like most worksheet programs, Excel can do several things at once. You can use Excel to enter and format text and numbers and to perform calculations involving those numbers. You can also use Excel to build chart sheets, or graphs, based on your data. ***Charts*** display your worksheet data in the form of circles, lines, or bars. You can also display charts independently in a ***chart sheet,*** a separate worksheet that shows only your chart, not the worksheet data. Figure 1.3 shows a chart sheet of January sales for Pet Paradise. As you can see, this graph conveys information more effectively than numbers alone.

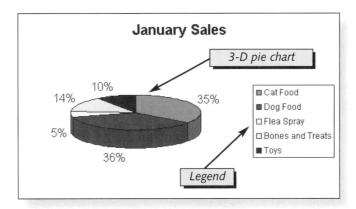

Figure 1.3
A chart illustrating January sales

Once you have entered data into a worksheet, you can use Excel as a database. A ***database*** is an organized collection of data about similar entities—such as employees, customers, or inventory items. When you work with Excel, you'll notice the term ***workbook*** is used often. This is a specialized name for a file that contains a group of related worksheets and chart sheets. (In some worksheet programs, these workbook files are called ***spreadsheets.***) Excel workbooks may consist of one or more ***workbook pages.*** Each workbook page is a worksheet (also called simply a sheet) or a chart sheet, and the workbook file is like a binder holding all the pages. This arrangement allows you to group several sheets in the same file. For example, Pet Paradise could have a series or ***group*** of revenue statements—one for every month—and could store each on a separate workbook page within the same workbook file. Using the Pet Paradise group, you could analyze the data for any single month and make calculations based on data from several months or all 12 months.

Web support, another feature of Excel, lets you save entire Excel workbooks or parts of a workbook in ***Hypertext Markup Language (HTML)*** format. HTML is a system for tagging a document so that you can publish the document and allow others to view it on the Web. With Web support, you can view and manipulate workbooks using your Web browser, as well as access real-time data using Web queries.

STARTING MICROSOFT EXCEL

Before you can start Microsoft Excel, both Microsoft Excel and Windows 95 (or higher version) must be installed on the computer you're using. The figures in this tutorial use Windows 98; if you are using a different version of Windows, the information appearing on your screen may vary slightly.

Note *You must create the Student Data Disk for this tutorial from the Data CD located on the inside back cover of this tutorial. If you have not created the Student Data Disk, ask your instructor for help.*

Excel
BASICS

**Launching
Microsoft Excel**

1. Turn on the computer.

2. Click the Start button
and point to Programs.

3. Click Microsoft Excel.

Launching Microsoft Excel

In this activity, you'll learn how to start Microsoft Excel.

1. Turn on your computer.

 *If you are prompted for a user name and/or password, enter the information at this time. If you do not know your user name and/or password, ask your instructor for help.*

The Windows operating system boots the computer. Your screen should resemble Figure 1.4. If the Welcome to Windows screen appears, click its Close button ☒ to close the window.

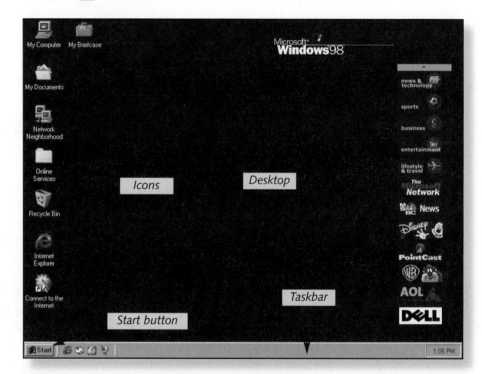

Figure 1.4 ◀
The Windows desktop

2. Click the Start button 🏁Start **on the Windows taskbar.**

3. Point to Programs.

The Programs menu appears, as shown in Figure 1.5. (Depending on the applications installed on your computer, your Programs menu may be different than Figure 1.5.)

4. Click Microsoft Excel.

The Excel program starts and a new, blank worksheet appears, as shown in Figure 1.6.

EXPLORING THE EXCEL WINDOW

In the next few activities, you will learn how to identify and use the components of the Excel window. As you can see in Figure 1.6, the Excel window contains many standard Windows elements, including a title bar; the Minimize, Restore, and Close buttons; a menu bar; and the scroll bars. These items should seem familiar if you've used Windows 95, Windows 98, or any other Windows 95 or Windows 98 application.

The mouse pointer will change shape depending on where it appears on the screen. In the worksheet area, it will appear as a block plus sign. Outside the worksheet area, it will appear as a block arrow.

Hints & Tips

The menu bar will change to other menu names when you work with various areas of Excel. If you work with a chart sheet instead of a worksheet, for example, the Chart menu bar will display.

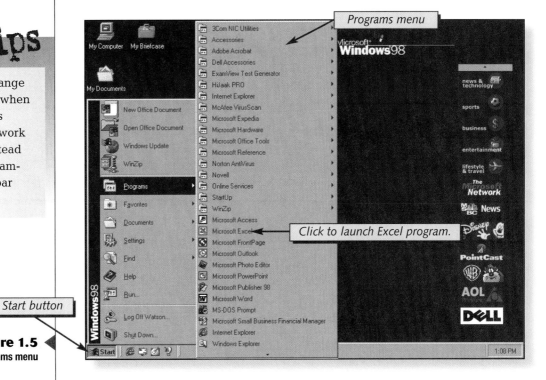

Programs menu

Click to launch Excel program.

Start button

Figure 1.5
The Programs menu

Minimize button

Title bar

Menu bar

Standard toolbar

Close button

Formatting toolbar

Restore button

Scroll bars

Microsoft Excel taskbar button

Windows taskbar

Figure 1.6
The Excel window

Note   *When this tutorial mentions a toolbar button, a picture of the button is displayed within the text. For instance, when a step instructs you to click the Bold button* **B** *, the button will be illustrated as shown here.*

Understanding the Menu Bar

As shown in Figure 1.6, the Excel *menu bar* appears below the title bar. The menu bar displays some of the menu names found in most Windows applications, such as File, Edit, and Help. Excel also includes several menus that contain commands specific to worksheets, such as Format and Data.

The menus list the commands available in Excel. You can display the list in several different ways. The most common way is to click the menu name to display the commands. If you prefer to use the keyboard, you can press [Alt] on your keyboard and then press the underlined letter in the menu name to display that menu. For example, to display the File menu, you would press [Alt] and then the letter F ([Alt] + F).

When you click a menu in the Excel window, the *short menu,* a list of the most commonly used commands, appears. If you keep your pointer on the menu for a few seconds or if you click the double arrow at the bottom of the menu, an *expanded menu* appears. This expanded menu shows all of the commands available on the menu; this includes commands that are used less frequently as well as the common commands. Figure 1.7 shows both versions of Excel's Insert menu—as a short menu and an expanded menu.

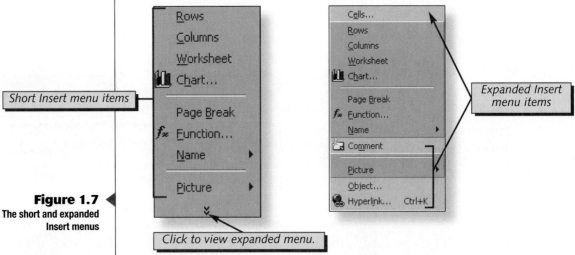

Short Insert menu items

Expanded Insert menu items

Figure 1.7
The short and expanded Insert menus

Click to view expanded menu.

As you can see in Figure 1.7, eight commands appear on the initial Insert menu. These eight commands are considered to be the commands that users issue most often from this menu. The expanded menu shows four additional commands—Cells, Comment, Object, and Hyperlink—which are not used as frequently. The backgrounds of the additional commands are shaded with a lighter shade of gray. After you issue one of these additional commands, this command is added to the short menu. For instance, assume you choose Object from the Insert menu; the next time you click the Insert menu, the Object command will be shown on the short menu with a darker gray background. This *adaptive menu* feature allows menus to be customized for each user.

After you display a menu, you can choose a command using either the mouse or the keyboard. To choose a command using the mouse, click the command you want. To choose a command using the keyboard, press the underlined letter of the command. For example, to choose the Open command from the File menu, press the letter O while the File menu is displayed.

Table 1.1 provides a brief description of the menus available on the Excel menu bar.

TABLE 1.1	THE EXCEL MENU BAR
Menu	**Contains Commands that Let You...**
File	Control your workbook files by opening, saving, and printing them.
Edit	Rearrange the elements within your workbook by copying, moving, and deleting them.
View	Change the appearance of your screen display, such as by displaying or hiding toolbars and magnifying or reducing the appearance of the worksheet area.
Insert	Insert various elements into your workbook, such as pictures or additional rows and columns.
Format	Change the appearance of the numbers and text within your workbook, such as the number of decimal places in a number or the alignment of text in a cell.
Tools	Access some of Excel's specialized tools, such as the spelling checker or macro recorder.
Data	Change the information that appears on your screen by sorting or filtering the data.
Window	Split your worksheet area into several smaller windows that contain different parts of one workbook or several workbooks.
Help	Access Excel's online Help system and the Microsoft Office Home Page on the Internet for worksheet assistance and support.

Working with Toolbars

Below the menu bar is Excel's Standard toolbar, as shown in Figure 1.6 on page 9. A **_toolbar_** contains buttons for many of the most frequently used commands, such as opening or printing a file. Although you can access these commands by clicking the command on one of the menus, using the buttons on the toolbar as a shortcut is often more convenient. You can quickly identify any command button by pointing to the button and reading the short description that appears. Table 1.2 shows the commands that are available on the Excel Standard toolbar.

The Formatting toolbar appears directly below the Standard toolbar. This toolbar contains buttons that change the appearance of your worksheet. For instance, using the Formatting toolbar, you can modify the font, text size, text style, alignment, color, and other features of the data that appears in your worksheet. You will learn more about formatting your worksheets in Lesson 2.

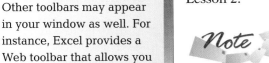

Note   _If your Standard and Formatting toolbars share one row below the menu bar, you can display them as two separate toolbars by clicking Customize on the Tools menu. On the Options tab, deselect the_ Standard and Formatting toolbars share one row _option._

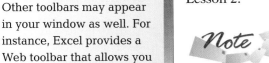

Other toolbars may appear in your window as well. For instance, Excel provides a Web toolbar that allows you to access Internet sites directly from Excel.

TABLE 1.2	THE EXCEL STANDARD TOOLBAR	
Button	**Name**	**Action**
	New	Creates a new workbook.
	Open	Opens a workbook you have already created and saved.
	Save	Makes a permanent copy of a workbook to a file on disk.
	E-mail (or Mail Recipient)	Sends the current worksheet as the body of an e-mail message.
	Print	Prints a worksheet or workbook.
	Print Preview	Allows you to preview how your worksheet or workbook will look on the printed page.
	Spelling	Checks the spelling in your workbook.
	Cut	Moves the selection from the cell(s) chosen to the Clipboard—a temporary storage place for information that is used by all Windows applications.
	Copy	Copies the selected element from the cell(s) chosen and places this copy on the Clipboard.
	Paste	Pastes an element from the Clipboard into the current location in your worksheet.
	Format Painter	Copies the formatting of one block of text or numbers to another block of text or numbers.
	Undo	Reverses the last action you performed that changed your workbook.
	Redo	Reverses the last Undo action.
	Insert Hyperlink	Inserts a link from the current cell to another cell, workbook, document, or an Internet site.
	AutoSum	Selects the adjacent range of cells and totals the numbers in them.
	Paste Function	Allows you to use a predetermined calculation such as sum or average.
	Sort Ascending	Allows you to sort a range of data either alphabetically or numerically from lowest to highest.
	Sort Descending	Allows you to sort a range of data either alphabetically or numerically from highest to lowest.

TABLE 1.2	THE EXCEL STANDARD TOOLBAR—cont.	
Button	**Name**	**Action**
	Chart Wizard	Guides you with step-by-step instructions to create a chart that illustrates the data in a worksheet.
	Drawing	Displays or hides the Drawing toolbar.
100%	Zoom	Increases or decreases the displayed size of the worksheet.
	Microsoft Excel Help	Displays the Office Assistant—an animated character that can answer your specific questions, offer helpful tips, and provide help for an Excel feature.
	PivotTable and PivotChart Report	Start the PivotTable and PivotChart Wizard.
	New Comment	Insert a comment.
	AutoFilter	Allows you to find and work with a subset of data in a list.
	More Buttons	Allows you to customize the toolbar by adding additional buttons or removing existing buttons. Also lets you reset the toolbar to display the default button.

Identifying the Name Box, Formula Bar, and Worksheet Area

Just below the toolbars are the Name Box and the formula bar, as shown in Figure 1.8. The *formula bar* displays the contents of the active cell. You can enter and edit data in the formula bar. You can determine your position in the worksheet by looking in the *Name Box* to the left of the formula bar.

Below the formula bar is the worksheet area. The *worksheet area,* which occupies most of the screen, is where your data appears. You can enter and edit data here, as well as in the formula bar. The gray area at the top of the worksheet area contains the *column headings,* which are the letters that identify the columns running down the worksheet. The gray area on the left side of the worksheet area contains the *row headings,* which are the numbers that identify the rows running across the worksheet.

The worksheet area consists of *cells*—rectangles formed by the intersection of columns and rows. Each cell can hold a single value or a text entry. A cell is identified by its *cell address,* which is the letter of the column and the number of the row where the column and row intersects to form the cell. For example, the cell address of the upper-left cell in a workbook is called cell A1 because it is located in column A, row 1. The cell directly below cell A1 has a cell address of A2, and so forth.

WEB NOTE

All Web addresses begin with the protocol *http://*, which identifies the address as a Web address to your browser (as opposed to an FTP site or a Gopher site). However, depending upon your Web browser, you may not have to type *http://* when entering a Web address—many of the newer browsers assume the address you enter is a Web address.

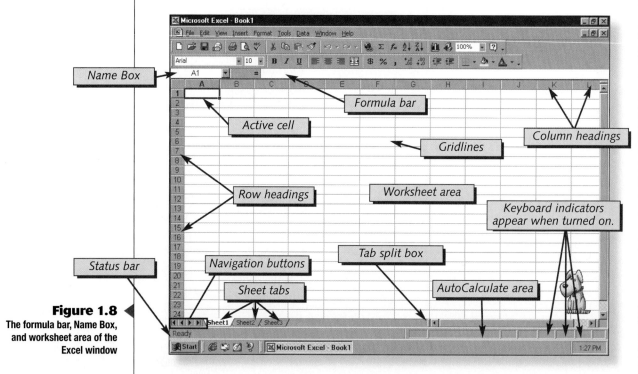

Figure 1.8 ◄
The formula bar, Name Box, and worksheet area of the Excel window

At the bottom of the worksheet area are the sheet tabs. Sheet tabs are numbered by default, but you can use descriptive names to identify the information the worksheets contain. To rename a sheet tab, double-click the sheet tab, type the new name, and press Enter←. The sheet tabs, and the navigation buttons to their left, allow you to move among different sheets in your workbook. To increase or decrease the view of the sheet tabs, drag the *tab split box,* which is located to the right of the sheet tabs. Finally, at the bottom of the Excel window is the *status bar,* which displays what's going on with the program. The status bar may display keyboard indicators, such as showing that Caps Lock is on, or it may show that Excel is ready for you to enter data. You can use the *AutoCalculate area* in the middle of the status bar instead of a calculator to display the sum, average, or other values of a range of cells.

OPENING WORKBOOK FILES

Any time you want to use a workbook that you or someone else created earlier, you need to *open* the workbook. Opening a file means copying that file from disk into the memory of your computer so that you can update or view the file. To open any Excel workbook, you can either click the Open button 🗁 or issue the Open command on the File menu. If you've used a workbook recently, you may also open a workbook by choosing the file name from the list of recently opened files that appears near the bottom of the File menu. You can have several workbook files open at the same time. To move between open files, click the appropriate button on the Windows taskbar.

Opening a File

Before you can view or modify a workbook, you must open the file. In this activity, you'll learn how to open a file on your Student Data Disk.

Another Way

To open a workbook file, click Open on the File menu.

1. Click the **Open button** 📂.

Excel displays the Open dialog box, as shown in Figure 1.9.

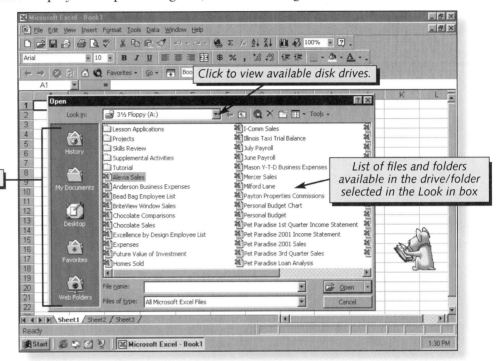

Figure 1.9 ◀
The Open dialog box

Warning *If you're sharing a computer with one or more users in a lab or school environment, the list of files displayed in the Open dialog box may not contain the file you wish to open. Continue with steps 2 and 3 to properly navigate to your files.*

2. Verify that the Files of type is set to **All Microsoft Excel Files**.

3. Click the **Look in box arrow**.

A list displays the available drives.

4. Click the drive that contains your Student Data Disk. If necessary, click the folder in which the Student Data Disk files are stored.

A list of the files on the Student Data Disk appears in the Open dialog box.

Note *If you copied the Student Data Disk files for this tutorial onto a Zip disk or a floppy disk, you must insert the disk into the drive.*

5. Double-click *Pet Paradise 2001 Income Statement* in the list of file names.

Excel opens the *Pet Paradise 2001 Income Statement* workbook file, as shown in Figure 1.10.

Opening a File

1. Click the Open button.

2. Select the appropriate drive from the Look in box.

3. Select the appropriate folder, if necessary.

4. Double-click the file name.

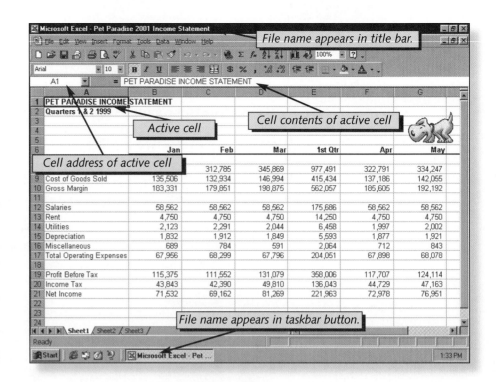

Keep the workbook open; you will work with this file again in this lesson.

EXPLORING THE WORKSHEET AREA

Although you can see many cells at once in the worksheet area, you can only enter data into a single cell at a time. The cell you're entering data into is known as the *active cell,* as indicated by the *cell cursor,* a black box surrounding a single cell. The address of the active cell appears in the Name Box, and the contents of the active cell appears in the formula bar. In Figure 1.10, for example, A1 is the active cell, and you can see its address in the Name Box and its contents in the formula bar.

When you are navigating a workbook, remember that the worksheet area shows only a small portion of the entire worksheet, which actually contains 256 columns and more than 65,000 rows! Since letters are used to indicate column headings, and there are only 26 letters in the alphabet, how are columns 27-256 identified? After column Z (the 26th column), the column headings consist of two letters. For example, column 27 has a column heading of AA, column 28 has a heading of AB, and so forth. After column AZ, the column headings increment to BA – BZ, then CA – CZ, followed by DA – DZ, and so on. The last column in a worksheet is column IV. Always remember that more data may exist in a worksheet than you can see on the screen at the moment, and you are not limited to just entering data in the visible screen area!

Sometimes you may want to see more cells displayed in the worksheet area, or perhaps you would like to magnify the cells displayed in the worksheet area. You can easily reduce or magnify the worksheet area displayed on screen by changing the Zoom setting.

HANDS On

Navigating Cells and Changing the Zoom Setting

When viewing, entering, and editing data, you'll often explore the entire worksheet area. You can easily navigate the worksheet area using either the keyboard or the mouse. In this activity, you'll compare the sales figures for March and June in the Pet Paradise Income Statement workbook. Then you'll look at March and June net income figures. You will enlarge and reduce the worksheet area, and then return it to its original size.

1. Click cell D8, the cell containing March sales figures.

The cell address and the cell contents appear in the Name Box and formula bar, as shown in Figure 1.11. The column heading D and the row heading 8 appear in bold to indicate the active cell.

Figure 1.11
The Name Box and formula bar show the address and contents of active cell D8

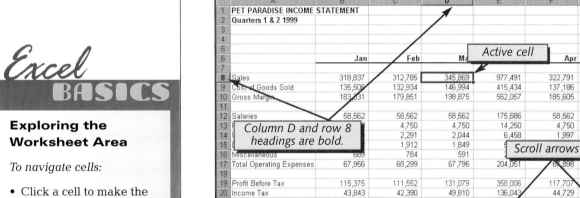

Excel
BASICS

Exploring the Worksheet Area

To navigate cells:

• Click a cell to make the cell the active cell.

• Press a keyboard arrow key to move the cell cursor.

• Press Ctrl + Home to move to cell A1.

• Press Ctrl + End to move to the last cell that contains data.

To change the Zoom setting:

1. Click the Zoom arrow on the Standard toolbar.

2. Click a magnification or reduction option or enter the percentage of magnification or reduction.

2. Press → four times.

Excel scrolls the display to activate cell H8, displaying the address and contents in the Name Box and formula bar. As you can see, March sales (345,869) were higher than June sales (336,883).

3. Press → two times.

Excel moves to cell J8. Notice that the first few columns have scrolled off the screen (unless you have a large monitor that still displays them).

4. Click and hold the left horizontal scroll arrow to scroll to the left as far as you can.

When you stop scrolling, column A reappears. The Name Box and the formula bar still contain the cell address and data for cell J8. Using the scroll bars to move around the window changes the data you see but does **not** change the active cell.

Another Way

- To move one cell to the right, press `Tab`.

- To move one cell to the left, press `Shift` + `Tab`.

- To move to a specific cell address, click the Name Box, type the cell address, and press Enter.

5. Click **cell D21**.

The cell cursor moves to cell D21 and it becomes the active cell.

6. Move the cell cursor to **cell H21**.

Cell H21 (net income for June) contains a lower value than cell D21 (net income for March).

7. Press `Ctrl` + `Home`.

The cell cursor moves back to cell A1.

Notice the number of columns and rows you can see in the worksheet area. Now let's change the Zoom setting to first enlarge and then reduce the appearance of the worksheet area.

8. Click **View** on the menu bar, and click the **Zoom option**.

Note *If the Zoom option does not appear on your View short menu, click the double arrow at the bottom of the menu to reveal the View expanded menu.*

The Zoom dialog box appears.

9. Click the **200% option** and click **OK**.

Excel enlarges the appearance of the worksheet area and displays it at twice its actual size.

10. Click **Zoom** on the View menu again.

11. Now click the **Custom option**, type 70, and click **OK**.

Excel reduces the appearance of the worksheet area and displays it at 70% of its actual size. Notice that you can now view more columns and rows in the worksheet area.

12. Click the **Zoom arrow**  on the Standard toolbar, and click the **100% option**.

Excel returns the worksheet area to its actual size.

GETTING HELP WITH EXCEL

While you are using Excel, you may need to reference the online Help system. Excel provides several different Help tools: ScreenTips, the Office Assistant, the Contents tab, the Index tab, and a tool called the Answer Wizard. You can activate the Office Assistant by clicking the animated character on your screen, by clicking the Microsoft Excel Help button 🔲, by clicking Microsoft Excel Help on the Help menu, or by pressing `F1`. For more detailed Help instructions, review pages 91-97 in *Lesson 3: Introducing Office 2000.*

It's easy to change the Office Assistant character—click the Office Assistant, click the Options button, click the Gallery tab, and select the character you want to display. You can also change the way the Office Assistant works and specify the types of tips you see—click the Office Assistant, click the Options button, click the Options tab, and select or deselect the appropriate options.

PRINTING A WORKSHEET

Now that you've explored the Excel window and know how to access the Help features, you are ready to learn another Excel fundamental—printing a worksheet. You'll need printouts to submit assignments to your instructor, to deliver reports to your boss, to mail information to a client, and much more. Although Excel offers several advanced printing features, for now you'll generate a basic printout of your worksheet. To print a worksheet, click the Print button or click Print on the File menu, verify the printing options, and click OK. In Lesson 2, you will learn that you can also print selected portions of your workbook, including a selected range of cells, the current workbook page, or the entire workbook.

Obtaining a Printout

In this activity, you'll print the *Pet Paradise 2001 Income Statement* workbook you opened earlier.

1. Turn on the printer, if necessary.

2. Click Print on the File menu.

You'll see the Print dialog box shown in Figure 1.12.

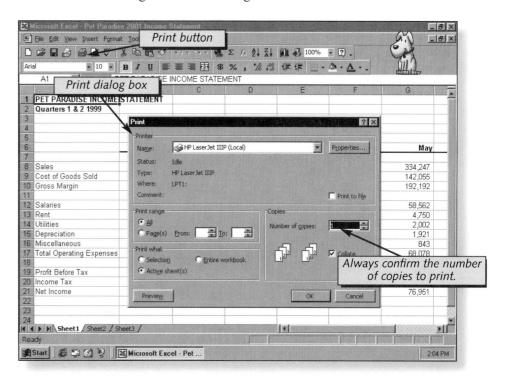

Figure 1.12
Print dialog box

3. Change the Number of copies option to 1, if necessary.

4. Click the OK button.

You may have to wait a moment, but Excel will generate a printout of the workbook.

HELP

Using

Troubleshooting Printing Problems

You can use Microsoft Excel Help to troubleshoot printing problems. For example, you can explore Help to determine why Excel printed the wrong data or why your printout doesn't look the way you thought it would.

1. Click the Office Assistant.

Note — If the Office Assistant is not displayed, select Show the Office Assistant on the Help menu.

2. Type print **in the** *What would you like to do?* **box and click the Search button.**

3. Find and click the Troubleshoot printing option to open the Troubleshoot printing Help window (Figure 1.13).

Figure 1.13
Troubleshoot printing Help window

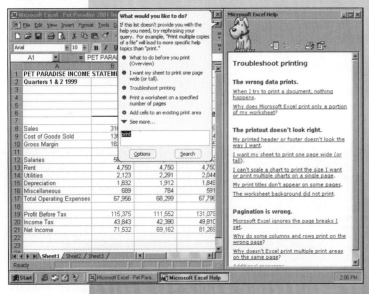

4. Read the text in the window and click the When I try to print a document, nothing happens. link.

5. Read the new text.

6. Click the Back button ⬅ **in the Help window.**

7. Click the I want my sheet to print one page wide (or tall). link.

8. Read the new text.

9. Explore other links in which you have interest. When you are finished exploring, click the Close button ⊠ **to close the Help window.**

10. If necessary, click anywhere on the screen to remove the *What would you like to do?* **box.**

CLOSING WORKBOOK FILES

When you're finished with a workbook file, you should *close* the file. Closing a file removes the file from memory, but leaves Excel running. Remember that you don't need to close one workbook to open another; Excel lets you open several files at once. However, to have more free memory, you should close files that you're no longer using.

To close a workbook file, click the Close button ⊠ on the far right side of the menu bar. When you close a file using the Close button, be sure to click the correct Close button! Clicking the Close button ⊠ at the far right corner of the *menu bar* in the open worksheet window will close the worksheet, but will keep Excel running. Clicking the Close button ⊠ at the top-right corner of the *title bar* in the Excel window will close both the worksheet file and the Excel program. Figure 1.14 indicates each of the Close buttons.

Closes Excel program

Closes workbook file

Figure 1.14
The Close buttons

Closing a File

1. Click Close on the File menu.

Or

Click the Close button on the far right side of the menu bar.

2. Click the appropriate answer, if Excel asks if you want to save changes.

Closing a File

In this activity, you'll close the ***Pet Paradise 2001 Income Statement*** workbook.

1. Click Close on the File menu.

2. Click No if Excel asks whether you want to save changes to the file.

Excel closes the workbook file, clearing the screen completely—except for the Office Assistant. Since you just closed the only open file, your screen will be blank and will not contain a worksheet area.

ENTERING DATA

Now that you are familiar with the worksheet area, you're ready to enter data. Entering data requires three steps: (1) move the cell cursor to the desired cell; (2) type your data; and (3) finalize the data entry.

Excel recognizes two basic types of data. You can enter *text,* such as worksheet titles and column and row labels. You cannot perform calculations on text data. You can also enter *values,* such as numbers, dates, times, and formulas on which you can perform calculations.

You can let the Excel program know in several ways that you want it to accept your data. Depending on the method you choose, Excel will accept the data and move the cursor to another cell. Table 1.3 lists the common methods you can use to finalize your data.

TABLE 1.3	COMMON METHODS FOR FINALIZING DATA
Keyboard or Mouse Action	**Result**
Enter↵ or ↓	Finalizes your data entry and moves the cell cursor down one row.
Tab or →	Finalizes your data entry and moves the cell cursor to the right one column.
⇧ Shift + Enter↵ or ↑	Finalizes your data entry and moves the cell cursor up one row.
⇧ Shift + Tab or ←	Finalizes your data entry and moves the cell cursor to the left one column.
✓	Finalizes your data entry without moving the cell cursor.

HANDS On

Adding Data to a Worksheet

In this activity, you'll enter some text and numbers to create a sales worksheet for Pet Paradise, a pet food and supply company.

1. Click the New button ▯ **on the Standard toolbar.**

You should see a blank worksheet area with the cell cursor in cell A1.

2. Press Caps Lock **to turn on capital letters and type** PET PARADISE.

Notice that the text appears both in cell A1 and in the formula bar. Also, buttons for canceling or finalizing your data entry appear on the formula bar, as shown in Figure 1.15. The status bar displays *Enter,* indicating you are entering data. The keyboard indicator displays *CAPS,* indicating that Caps Lock is turned on.

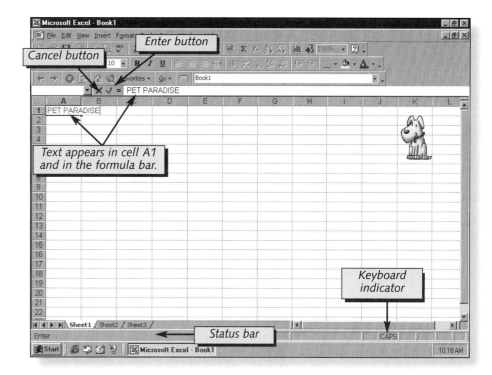

Figure 1.15
Entering data

Entering Data

1. Navigate to the cell where you want to enter data.

2. Type the data.

3. Press Enter⏎ .

3. Press Enter⏎ .

Excel finalizes the entry, removes the extra buttons from the formula bar, and displays the word *Ready* on the status bar, indicating that you may enter some more data. The cell cursor moves to the next row and is in cell A2.

4. Type REVENUE **in cell A2.**

5. Press ↓ .

Excel finalizes your entry and moves down to cell A3.

6. Press Caps Lock **again to turn off capital letters. Type** Third Quarter 2000 **and press** Enter⏎ **.**

Notice that Excel accepts numbers in a text entry.

As you can see, all the text you entered is displayed. Although the text in some of the cells is too wide for the column, the text displays in the adjacent blank cells. However, if cell B1, B2, or B3 contained data, the text from column A would not display in column B. Instead, the text in column A would only display to the width of column A. Later in this lesson you'll learn to widen columns so the data will fit in one column.

7. Press Enter⏎ **again to leave row 4 blank.**

The cell cursor moves to cell A5.

8. Type July **and press** Enter⏎ **.**

9. Type 122378 **and press** Enter⏎ **.**

Do not type commas or spaces in your numbers. You'll learn how to format numbers—adding commas, dollar signs, and so on—in Lesson 2.

As shown in Figure 1.16, the number you entered is aligned on the right edge of the cell, while all the text entries are aligned on the left edge. This is how Excel positions data by default.

If you leave blank space between your titles and your data, your worksheets will be easier to read.

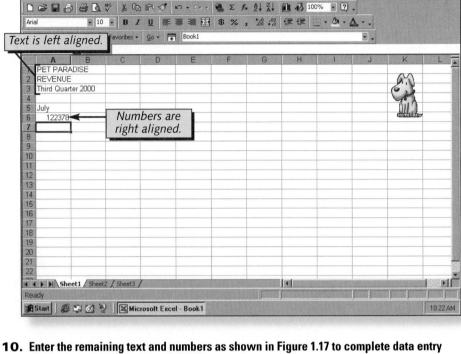

Figure 1.16
Default alignment of text and numbers

10. Enter the remaining text and numbers as shown in Figure 1.17 to complete data entry of the third quarter sales information.

Don't worry about making mistakes; you'll learn how to correct errors in the next activity.

After you type data in cells, you can create hyperlinks to jump from one cell to another cell, a workbook, or a Web page. You'll learn more about creating hyperlinks in the *On the Web* activity at the end of this lesson.

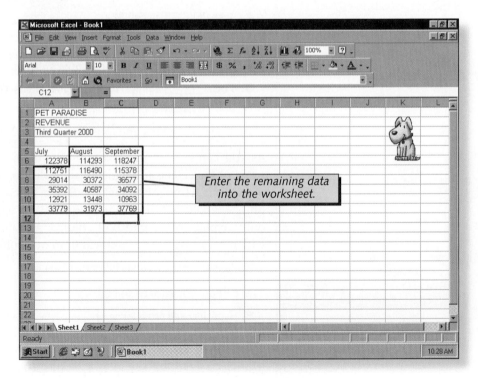

Figure 1.17
Third quarter sales

EDITING SINGLE CELLS

Since you may make mistakes as you enter data or you may want to update a file, you'll need to learn how to edit. ***Insert mode*** is the default mode in Excel. In Insert mode, typed text is inserted into existing text, pushing the characters after it to the right. Pressing `Delete` deletes characters to the right of the insertion point; pressing `Backspace` deletes characters to the left of the insertion point; and pressing the arrow keys moves the insertion point. If you recognize your mistake before you press `Enter←`, you can press `Backspace` to delete one character at a time. You can also press `Esc` to cancel the entire entry, deleting everything you've typed and returning the cell to its previous state. ***Overtype mode*** is another mode you can use. In Overtype mode, text replaces existing text as you type.

You may also use the AutoCorrect feature of Excel to correct common mistakes when you finalize a text entry in a cell. To verify whether the AutoCorrect features are turned on, or to change the selected features, click AutoCorrect on the Tools menu. AutoCorrect makes these types of corrections *as you type:*

- Corrects two initial capital letters by changing the second letter to lowercase.
- Capitalizes the first letter of a sentence.
- Capitalizes the names of days.
- Corrects accidental use of `Caps Lock` by changing the letters to lowercase except for the first letter of a word that starts a sentence or the names of days.
- Replaces commonly misspelled words with their correct spelling. You can also add misspelled words and their corresponding corrections to the AutoCorrect list.

If you've already finalized your entry by pressing `Enter←`, you must return to the cell containing the mistake and either edit or overwrite the contents completely. To edit existing data, you can use the Edit mode. Double-click in the cell you want to edit; then drag to select characters (or double-click to select entire words); and type new data to replace the selected characters. Sometimes you want to change the contents of a cell completely without salvaging any existing data. In that case, you can easily overwrite existing data by moving to the cell you want to overwrite and then simply typing new data.

You can also use the Spelling tool to check the spelling of text entries in a cell, a range of cells, a worksheet, or the entire workbook. Click the Spelling button ![ABC] on the Standard toolbar or click Spelling on the Tools menu. As Excel checks the cells, you can ignore highlighted words if the spelling is correct, or you can change the spelling by selecting or typing the correct spelling.

HANDS On

Correcting Errors in a Worksheet

In this activity, you will introduce several errors into the worksheet you just created and then correct intentional errors. You will also use the Auto-Correct and Spelling tools.

Editing Data

To edit data before pressing [Enter←]:

- Press [Esc] to cancel the entry and restore the previous cell contents.

- Press [Delete] or [Backspace] to delete characters.

To edit data after pressing [Enter←]:

1. Move to the cell you want to edit.

2. Double-click in the cell, drag to select the characters to be replaced, and type new data to replace a portion of the cell contents.

Or

Begin typing new data to overwrite the entire cell contents.

To use AutoCorrect:

1. Click AutoCorrect on the Tools menu.

2. Select the desired features.

3. Click OK and enter data.

To use the Spelling tool:

1. Click the Spelling button.

2. Correct highlighted errors.

Figure 1.18 ◀
Overwriting the contents of a cell

1. Click AutoCorrect on the Tools menu.

If the AutoCorrect option does not appear on your Tools short menu, click the double arrow at the bottom of the menu to display the expanded menu.

2. Verify that each AutoCorrect option is selected and click OK.

As you type, the AutoCorrect feature will automatically fix common errors.

3. Move to cell D5 and type October, **but do not press** [Enter←].

While reviewing the worksheet, you decide to include a column for quarterly sales after each three-month period (quarter). Since September is the last month of the third quarter, you should enter a column for third quarter sales totals before you create the October sales column.

4. Press [Esc].

Excel cancels the entry, deleting what you just typed. Pressing [Esc] doesn't actually delete the contents of a cell but just cancels your current entry, restoring the cell to its previous state.

5. Type Quarter 3 **and press** [Enter←].

Don't worry if the columns are not wide enough for your labels. You'll learn how to widen columns in Lesson 2.

6. Move to cell A2, the one that reads *REVENUE*.

7. Type Sales **and press** [Enter←].

As shown in Figure 1.18, the newly typed text overwrites the previous contents of the cell. When an entry is short and/or you want to replace rather than revise data, you can easily overwrite the existing text rather than edit it.

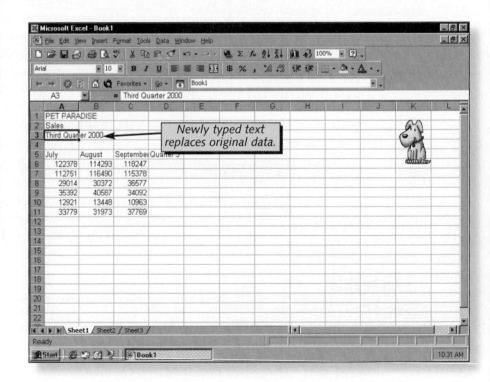

Now you decide to edit the contents of cell A3, because you remembered that these are 2001 sales rather than 2000 sales. In this case, you want to modify rather than replace the text, since you want to make a minor change to the existing text entry. Usually editing rather than overwriting cells is the best method when you want to change a little, especially if the existing entry is fairly long.

 Warning *Make sure the cell cursor is in cell A3, not cell B3. Even though the text appears to be in both cells, the text is actually in A3 only. You can check this by looking at the formula bar. If you place the cell cursor in cell B3, no text appears in the formula bar; if you place the cell cursor in cell A3, the entire text appears in the formula bar.*

Another Way

To prepare a cell for editing, move to the cell you wish to edit and click the text in the formula bar.

8. Double-click cell A3.

An insertion point appears in the cell, and the status bar reads *Edit.* This tells you that you're in Edit mode, ready to edit your data.

9. Press the arrow keys until the insertion point is immediately to the left of the last *0* in *2000*, as shown in Figure 1.19.

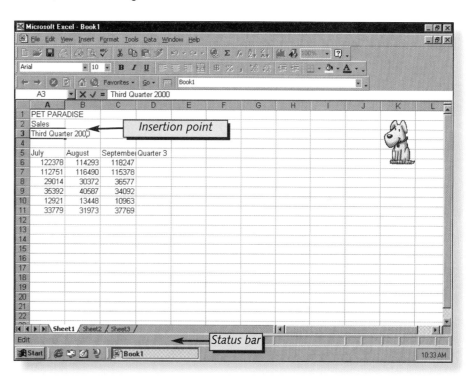

Figure 1.19
Positioning the insertion point

Hints & Tips

When you're in Edit mode, you must press Enter↵ or click the Enter button ✓ on the formula bar to finalize your entry.

10. Press Delete .

11. Type 1 and press Enter↵ .

The character you type appears at the insertion point. Note how much easier this is than retyping the entire text. Your screen should now look like the one shown in Figure 1.20.

Figure 1.20 ◄
The modified worksheet

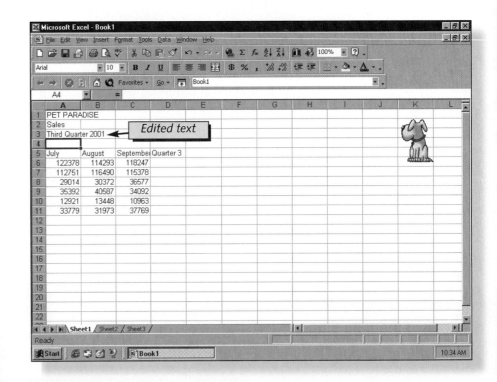

To find data:

1. Click Find on the Edit
menu.

2. In the Find what box,
type the data you want
to locate.

3. Click Find Next.

4. Review or edit each
occurrence and close
the Find dialog box.

To replace data:

1. In the Find dialog box,
click the Replace button.

2. In the Replace with box,
type the replacement
data (or leave the box
blank).

3. Click Replace to replace
the occurrence or click
Replace all to replace all
occurrences of the data.

12. Click cell A1.

13. Click the Spelling button  **on the Standard toolbar.**

Excel will check the spelling of all text entries in the worksheet.

Note

> *If Excel finds any words that do not match its dictionary,
> the Spelling dialog box will highlight the word and offer
> suggestions to correct the spelling. Click Ignore if the word
> is spelled correctly. To change the spelling of a word, select
> the correctly spelled word from the list of suggestions or
> type the correction in the Change to box. Then click
> Change. The Office Assistant will inform you when the
> spelling check is complete; click OK.*

FINDING AND REPLACING DATA

Occasionally you may want to review or change specific text or value entries
without knowing exactly where the data is located within a worksheet. You
can search for data easily with Excel's Find command. You may also automatically replace data that you find.

To find data, click Find on the Edit menu. In the Find what box, type the text
or numbers you want to locate. Then click Find Next. Excel will move
through the worksheet searching for the data and highlighting each occurrence. You can review or edit each instance.

If you want to edit or replace data you have searched for, click the Replace button in the Find dialog box. In the Replace with box, type the replacement data or leave the box blank if you want to delete the data. Click Replace to replace the data. Then click Find Next to review the next occurrence. Click Replace All to replace all occurrences of the data.

SAVING YOUR WORK

After you've entered and edited your data, you should **save** your file. Saving a file transfers all of the data from the memory of your computer to disk for you to retrieve later. Saving your work frequently is important in case something goes wrong with the computer. For example, if you haven't saved your workbook and your computer malfunctions or someone kicks the power cord, all your work is lost.

When you're working on a new workbook that you have not yet saved, Excel names the file *Book1* as the default file name. When you save the file, you should give it a more meaningful name, so you can see at a glance what information the file contains. In addition to naming a file, you must also specify the drive and path of where to store the file.

HANDS On

Excel **BASICS**

Saving a File

1. Click the Save button on the Standard toolbar.

Or

Click Save on the File menu.

2. Type a file name in the File name box of the Save As dialog box.

3. Click a drive and folder.

4. Click the Save button in the Save As dialog box.

Saving the Sales Workbook

In this activity, you'll save the file on which you've been working.

1. Click the Save button 🖫 **on the Standard toolbar.**

Excel displays the Save As dialog box. Notice that the default file name *Book1* is highlighted in the File name box.

2. Type Third Quarter Sales **in the File name box.**

The text you type will overwrite the *Book1* file name. After naming the file, you must tell Excel where you want to store the file. Most of the time, Excel will default to a folder on your hard drive. For this activity, you will want to save the file to your Student Data Disk.

3. Click the Save in: triangle button to display the folder list, and click the drive that contains your Student Data Disk from the folder list.

4. Double-click the *Tutorial* **folder to open it.**

The Save As dialog box should look like the one shown in Figure 1.21.

5. Verify that the Save as type box is set to Microsoft Excel Workbook.

6. Click the Save button in the lower-right corner of the Save As dialog box.

Excel saves your file in the designated drive and folder and displays the new file name in the title bar. Depending on your computer settings, Excel may automatically add an extension of *.xls* to the end of your file name. This extension identifies the file as an Excel file.

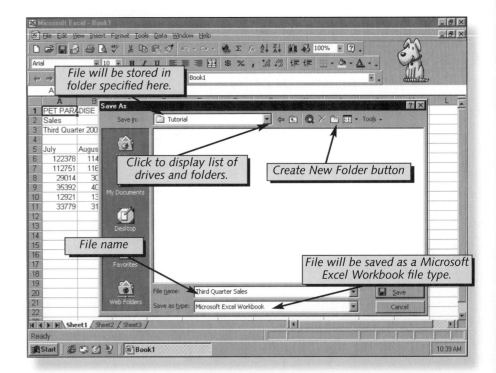

Figure 1.21 ◀
The Save As dialog box

After you've named and saved a file, issuing the Save command on the File menu or clicking the Save button 🖫 replaces the file on disk with the version currently in memory without displaying the Save As dialog box.

If you want to save the file in a different place or under a new name, you must click the Save As command on the File menu. The Save As dialog box appears, and you can enter a new file name and/or location. Note that when you use the Save As command, you are not renaming a file. Instead, you're saving a copy of the file under a different name or in a different place. The original file with the original name will not be deleted. You can also create a new folder in which to save the file. To do so, select the drive (and folder, if appropriate) for the location of the new folder. Then click the Create New Folder button 📂, as shown in Figure 1.21. Type the folder name and click OK. You can then save the file in this newly created folder.

You should save your files often—especially after adding or editing data. Even if you've already saved a file once, you'll lose any added but unsaved data if your computer malfunctions or a power outage occurs.

EXITING EXCEL

When you're finished working with the Excel program, you should exit the program properly. Exiting the program closes any open Excel files and removes Excel from the memory of your computer.

Exiting Excel

1. Click Exit on the File menu.

Or

Click the Close button on the far right side of the title bar.

2. Click the appropriate answer, if Excel asks if you want to save changes.

Closing a File and Exiting Excel

In this activity, you'll close the *Third Quarter Sales* workbook and exit Excel.

1. Click **Close** on the File menu.

Excel closes the workbook file, clearing the screen completely—except for the Office Assistant. Since you just closed the only open file, your screen will be blank and will not contain a worksheet area.

2. Click **Exit** on the File menu, or click the **Close button** ⊠ at the right end of the Excel title bar.

If you have not opened any other application, your screen will return to your Windows desktop.

Test your knowledge by answering the following questions. See Appendix B to check your answers.

1. To jump quickly to cell A1, press _____.

2. Name two ways to identify the active cell.

_____

_____

3. The column letter and row number combination used to identify a specific cell is known as the _____.

4. When you enter data, pressing _____ finalizes the data you type and moves the cell cursor one cell to the right.

5. To restore the contents of a cell in which you began to replace the text, press _____.

ON*the*WEB

ADDING HYPERLINKS TO A WORKSHEET

In a previous On the Web activity (in Lesson 2 of the Word tutorial), you learned how to insert hyperlinks in a document. In this activity, you will insert hyperlinks in a worksheet. You can use hyperlinks to jump quickly from one cell to another. This is useful when you have a large worksheet or a workbook with several pages. You can also link to another workbook. If the workbook to which you are linking is not open, Excel automatically opens the document. In addition, you can insert a hyperlink to a Web site. The process for creating a Web hyperlink is similar to that of creating a hyperlink for a file. When you click the hyperlink, Excel will jump to the site located at the specified URL. As you're working through this activity, refer to Exploring the Web Toolbar (pages 134–137) and Inserting Hyperlinks (pages 198–199).

1. **Launch Excel and open the *Surfside Income Statement & Sales* workbook on your Student Data Disk. Display the Web toolbar, if it is not already displayed.**

2. **Click the Sales sheet tab (Figure 1.22).**

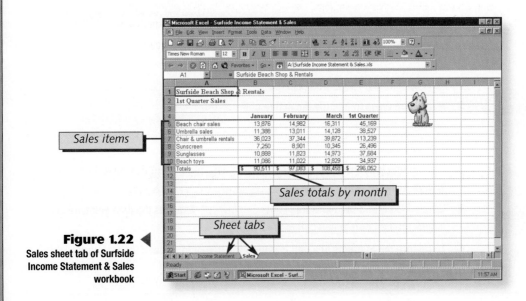

Figure 1.22 ◀
Sales sheet tab of Surfside
Income Statement & Sales
workbook

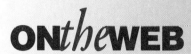
Notice that the Sales worksheet shows how individual items contributed to each month's sales.

3. Click the **Income Statement sheet tab** to view the Surfside income statement. Then click **cell B6**.

This cell contains the sales total for January. You will link this cell to the cells that contain the January sales items on the Sales worksheet.

4. Click the **Insert Hyperlink** button  on the Standard toolbar.

The Insert Hyperlink dialog box appears.

5. Click the **Recent Files button** in the *Or select from list* box, and click the *Surfside Income Statement & Sales* workbook.

The workbook name appears in the *Type the file or Web page name* box.

6. Click the **Bookmark button** located in the Insert Hyperlink dialog box.

The Select Place in Document dialog box appears.

7. Type B5:B10 in the *Type in the cell reference* box.

8. In the *Or select a place in this document* box, click **Sales**.

Clicking *Sales* tells Excel to link to the worksheet entitled Sales. Since the reference is listed as B5:B10, Excel will highlight that range in the Sales worksheet; cells B5:B10 contain the January sales figures for individual items sold.

9. Click **OK** to return to the Insert Hyperlink dialog box. Then click **OK** to return to the worksheet.

10. Move to **cell A1** so that you can see the hyperlink in cell B6.

11. Click the hyperlink.

Excel jumps to the Sales sheet and highlights cells B5:B10, the range you specified when you created the hyperlink.

12. Return to the Income Statement worksheet and create hyperlinks for the February and March sales totals in cells C6 and D6. Link these totals to the corresponding sales data in cells C5:C10 and cells D5:D10 of the Sales sheet, respectively.

Note

To return to the Income Statement worksheet, you can click the Back button ⇐ on the Web toolbar or you can click the Income Statement sheet tab.

13. Click the hyperlinks to test them.

14. Click **Save As** on the File menu and save the revised workbook as *Surfside Income Statement & Sales with Hyperlinks* in the *Tutorial* folder on your Student Data Disk.

15. Click **cell A10** and click the **Insert Hyperlink button**.

16. Click the **File button** in the *Browse for* section in the dialog box. Navigate to your Student Data Disk files, click the *Surfside Employee List* workbook, and click **OK**.

You will not set a bookmark since you want to review the entire worksheet instead of highlighting a specific area.

17. Click **OK** in the Insert Hyperlink dialog box.

18. Click the new hyperlink in cell A10.

Excel opens the ***Surfside Employee List*** workbook so that you can review the information about the employees.

19. To return to the income statement, click the **Back button** on the Web toolbar or click the **Excel taskbar button** for this file. Click **cell A1** and click the **Save button** to save the revised workbook.

Excel also allows you to create hyperlinks to other types of documents, such as Microsoft Word or PowerPoint files.

20. Click the **Forward button** on the Web toolbar to move to the *Surfside Employee List* workbook.

21. Select **cell H4** and click the **Insert Hyperlink button**.

22. In the *Type the file or Web page name* box, type www.usps.gov and click **OK**.

23. Click your new hyperlink.

If your connection to the Internet is already active, Excel will open your browser and jump directly to the Web site for the U.S. Postal Service.

ON*the*WEB

If your connection to the Internet is not active, either the Sign In or Connect To dialog box will appear so that you can connect to the Internet, or you will receive an error message telling you that no connection is established. Sign in or connect to your Internet service provider and then repeat step 23.

24. Click the **ZIP Codes** link.

Many Web sites are frequently updated and their links may change. If the links are not exactly as specified in this tutorial, click a link that you think will lead you to the appropriate information.

25. Follow the instructions on the Web page to find the missing ZIP Codes for your *Surfside Employee List* workbook. The addresses for which you are trying to locate ZIP Codes are as follows:

> 1901 N. Atlantic Blvd., Apt. 14A   10640 Indian Trail
> Fort Lauderdale, FL   Cooper City, FL

26. After you find the ZIP Codes, return to your worksheet and enter them in the appropriate cells.

27. Click **cell A1** and save the revised workbook as *Surfside Employee List with ZIP Codes* in the *Tutorial* folder on your Student Data Disk.

28. Close all open workbooks and exit Excel. Close your browser.

29. Disconnect from the Internet unless your instructor tells you to remain connected.

You may proceed directly to the exercises for this lesson. If, however, you are finished with your computer session, follow the "shut down" procedures for your lab or school environment.

Lesson Summary & Exercises

SUMMARY

Worksheets allow you to present data in an organized form and to perform calculations on that data. Lesson 1 introduced basic worksheet terms and taught you how to open a workbook, navigate the Excel window, print a worksheet, close a workbook, and exit Excel. You learned how to create a new worksheet. When you create a new worksheet, you enter two basic types of data—text and values. You can use several ways to finalize your data entry, including keyboard methods and mouse actions. You can edit data in your worksheet and save the worksheet for future viewing and modification. You also learned how to create hyperlinks in a worksheet.

Now that you have completed this lesson, you should be able to do the following:

- Identify columns and rows in a worksheet. (Excel-226)
- Explain the differences between a workbook and a worksheet. (Excel-227)
- Start Excel and identify the screen elements. (Excel-228)
- Provide a brief description of each menu on the Excel menu bar. (Excel-230)
- Provide a brief description of each button on the Standard toolbar. (Excel-231)
- Open a workbook file. (Excel-235)
- Move around the worksheet area using the mouse, arrow keys, and keyboard combinations. (Excel-237)
- Use the Office Assistant to obtain help for Excel features. (Excel-238)
- Print a worksheet. (Excel-239)
- Troubleshoot printing problems. (Excel-240)
- Close a workbook. (Excel-241)
- Enter data, including text and values. (Excel-242)
- Use `Enter←`, `Tab`, `⇧ Shift` + `Tab`, `⇧ Shift` + `Enter←`, and the arrow keys to finalize data and move to a desired cell. (Excel-242)
- Edit the contents of a cell before finalizing the entry. (Excel-245)
- Edit the contents of a cell by modifying existing text. (Excel-245)
- Overwrite the contents of a cell with new data. (Excel-246)
- Use the AutoCorrect feature to correct common mistakes. (Excel-246)
- Use the Spelling tool to verify the spelling of text entries. (Excel-248)
- Use the Find and Replace commands to review and edit data. (Excel-248)
- Save workbooks, specifying an appropriate file name and location. (Excel-249)
- Exit Excel. (Excel-250)
- Create hyperlinks to a range of cells on a different sheet in the same workbook, to another workbook, and to a Web site. (Excel-252)

Lesson Summary & Exercises

CONCEPTS REVIEW

1 TRUE/FALSE

Circle T if the statement is true or F if the statement is false.

T   F   **1.** The sheet tab displays the cell address of the active cell.

T   F   **2.** By default, each worksheet contains three workbooks.

T   F   **3.** You cannot mix text and numbers in a cell entry.

T   F   **4.** You can finalize data that you enter in a cell by pressing an arrow key.

T   F   **5.** You could use a worksheet to track and calculate your personal budget.

T   F   **6.** If you want to save a file in a different place or under a new name, you must click the Save As command on the File menu.

T   F   **7.** Saving a file may avoid loss of data due to a computer malfunction.

T   F   **8.** You can use [Backspace] to move one cell to the left.

T   F   **9.** You can display an expanded menu by clicking the double arrow at the bottom of the menu.

T   F   **10.** To move to the last cell that contains data, press [Ctrl] + [Home].

2 MATCHING

Match each of the terms on the left with the definitions on the right.

TERMS

1. cell address
2. cell cursor
3. workbook
4. toolbar
5. active cell
6. formula bar
7. values
8. text
9. Overtype mode
10. column headings

DEFINITIONS

a. Specialized name for a group of related Excel worksheets

b. Bar below the toolbars that displays the cell contents of the active cell

c. Data that can be used in calculations

d. Data used for descriptive purposes

e. Text replaces existing text as you type

f. Box surrounding the active cell

g. The letters that identify the columns in a worksheet

h. A row of buttons that you can click for quick access to commonly used commands

i. Cell into which any data you type is entered

j. Cell identifier formed by a column letter and a row number

Lesson Summary & Exercises

3 COMPLETION

Fill in the missing word or phrase for each of the following statements.

1. Press the _____ and _____ keys to move to cell A1 of the current workbook page.

2. An easy way to determine your position in the worksheet area is to glance at the _____.

3. The intersection of a column and a row is a _____.

4. The _____ menu allows you to rearrange the elements within your document by copying, moving, or deleting them.

5. Transferring a file into your computer's memory is called _____ that file.

6. Use the _____ command on the _____ menu to print your workbook.

7. Use the _____ to change which part of the workbook is displayed without changing the active cell.

8. When you need an answer to a specific question, you can ask the _____ for help.

9. When you're finished using a workbook, you should _____ the file.

10. A label that isn't displayed in full in the cell because data is in the cell to the right still appears in its entirety in the _____ .

4 SHORT ANSWER

Write a brief answer to each of the following questions.

1. Suppose you typed *scarlet* in a cell, pressed [Enter↵], and decided to change the text to *red*. What would be an efficient way to change the entry and why?

2. What's the difference between closing a workbook file and exiting from Excel? Describe briefly when you would do each.

3. Approximately how large is the worksheet area, in terms of columns and rows? Name one reason why you should remember this.

4. In which two places can you enter and edit data?

5. What is the difference between the Save and the Save As commands?

6. What is the relationship between workbook pages, worksheets, and workbooks?

7. When would you use the scroll bars while working on a worksheet?

8. Describe at least three different ways to make cell A1 the active cell.

9. What steps would you take to open a workbook called *2001 Expenses* from a disk in Drive B:?

10. What is the relationship between a short menu and an expanded menu? What is the adaptive menu feature?

Lesson Summary & Exercises

5 IDENTIFICATION

Label each of the elements of the Excel window in Figure 1.23.

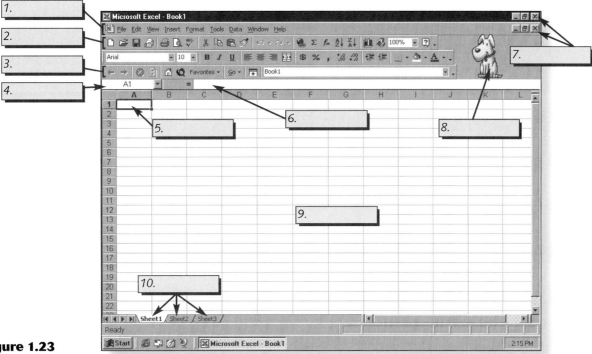

Figure 1.23

SKILLS REVIEW

Complete each of the Skills Review problems in sequential order to review your Excel skills to open, navigate, and print a workbook; use the Excel Help system; close a workbook; enter and edit data in a workbook; save a file; and close the Excel program.

1 Launch Excel

1. Click the **Start button** [Start].
2. Point to **Programs**.
3. Click **Microsoft Excel**.

2 Open a Workbook

1. Click the **Open button** [icon].
2. Click the drop-down arrow next to the Look in box and click the drive (and folder, if necessary) that contains your Student Data Disk.
3. Double-click *Pet Paradise Personnel Records* in the list of file names.
4. Review the worksheet data in the opened file (Figure 1.24).

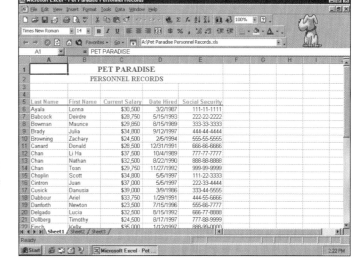

Figure 1.24

Lesson Summary & Exercises

3 Explore the Worksheet and Change the Zoom Setting

1. With the *Pet Paradise Personnel Records* workbook still open, click **cell D10** and note the hire date for Zachary Browning.

2. Press ⬇ until the cell cursor surrounds a cell that contains a date of hire after 1998.

3. Press ⬅ three times to select the cell that contains the last name of the employee hired after 1998.

4. Use the scroll bar to scroll up and down the worksheet. Count the number of employees earning more than $40,000.

5. Press `Ctrl` + `Home` to move to cell A1. Note the number of columns and rows that appear in the worksheet area.

6. Click **Zoom** on the View menu.

7. Click the **75% option** and click **OK**. Note the number of columns and rows that now appear in the worksheet area.

8. Click the **Zoom arrow** `100% ▼` on the Standard toolbar.

9. Click the **100% option** to return the worksheet area to its actual size.

4 Use the Office Assistant

1. Click the **Office Assistant** to activate it.

2. Type sorting numbers in a column and click the **Search button**.

3. When the results of your search are displayed, click the **Sort a list option**.

4. When the Help window appears, click the **Sort rows in descending order based on the contents of one column link**.

5. Read the text that appears in the new Help window.

6. Click the **Close button** ☒ of the Help window to close Help.

5 Print a Worksheet

1. With the *Pet Paradise Personnel Records* workbook still open, click the **File menu** and click **Print**.

2. Change the number of copies to 1, if necessary.

3. In the Print dialog box, click **OK**.

6 Close a Workbook

1. Click the **File menu** and click **Close**.

2. If Excel asks if you want to save the changes, click **No**.

7 Enter Data

1. Click the **Open button** 🖼.

2. Click the **Look in box arrow**.

3. Click the drive that contains your Student Data Disk, and double-click the *Tutorial* folder.

4. In the *Tutorial* folder, double-click ***Surfside Employee List with ZIP Codes*** in the list of file names.

5. Click cell **A10**.

6. Type Wakui and press [Enter←].

7. Press [→] and then press [↑] to move to cell B10.

8. Type Toshi and press [Tab].

9. Type the data contained in Table 1.4 in cells C10 through H10.

TABLE 1.4	DATA FOR SKILLS REVIEW #7
Cell	Data
C10	6.85
D10	3/15/2000
E10	21 N. Ocean Blvd.
F10	Fort Lauderdale
G10	FL
H10	33308-2352

8 Edit Data and Insert a Hyperlink

1. Move the cell cursor to **cell A10**.

2. Type Whitman but do not press [Enter←].

3. Since you realize that you want to enter the employee name in cell A11, not cell A10, press [Esc] to restore the previous contents of cell A10.

4. Move the cell cursor to **cell A11**.

5. Type Whitman and press [Tab].

6. In cell B11, type Charlie but do not press [Enter←].

7. Press [Backspace] twice to delete the *ie*.

8. Type es to change the name to *Charles* and press [Tab].

9. Enter the data contained in Table 1.5 in cells C11 through H11.

10. Double-click **cell E10**.

11. Press the arrow keys until the insertion point moves before the *2* in the address.

12. Press [Delete] to delete the *2*.

13. Type 3 and press [Enter←] to change the address to *31 N. Ocean Blvd.*

14. Move the cell cursor to **cell A1** and click [icon].

TABLE 1.5	DATA FOR SKILLS REVIEW #8
Cell	Data
C11	6.85
D11	3/15/2000
E11	2767 Washington Drive
F11	Fort Lauderdale
G11	FL
H11	33311-6659

15. Browse to find the ***Surfside Income Statement & Sales with Hyperlinks*** workbook in the *Tutorial* folder on your Student Data Disk and click **OK**.

16. Click **OK** in the Insert Hyperlink dialog box.

17. Test the new hyperlink in cell A1 and then close the ***Surfside Income Statement & Sales with Hyperlinks*** workbook.

9 Save and Close the Workbook and Exit Excel

1. In the ***Surfside Employee List with ZIP Codes*** workbook, click the **File menu** and click **Save As**.

Lesson Summary & Exercises

2. When the Save As dialog box appears, type Updated Surfside Employee List with Hyperlink in the File name box. (Edit the existing file name instead of typing a new one.)

3. If necessary, select **A:** (or another appropriate drive) from the Save in list.

4. Double-click the *Skills Review* folder.

5. Click the **Save button** in the Save As dialog box.

6. Click the **File menu** and click **Close**.

7. Click the **File menu** and click **Exit**.

LESSON APPLICATIONS

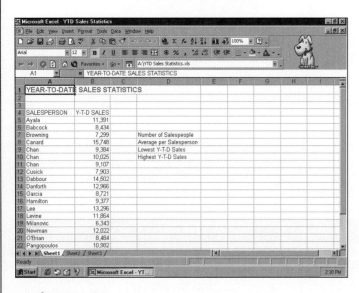

Figure 1.25

1 Start Excel and Open a Workbook

Launch the Excel program and open a workbook stored on your Student Data Disk.

1. Using the Start button ![Start] and the Programs menu, launch Excel.

2. Click the Open button ![open].

3. Open the *YTD Sales Statistics* workbook on your Student Data Disk (Figure 1.25).

2 Navigate the Worksheet

Use various methods to navigate a worksheet to find specific information.

1. If the *YTD Sales Statistics* workbook is not open, open it on your Student Data Disk.

2. Use the scroll bar to find the cell that contains the employee named Weaver.

3. Click the cell to activate it.

4. Activate the cell that contains Weaver's year-to-date sales.

5. Return to cell A1.

6. Click cell E7; this cell will eventually contain a number referring to the number of salespeople.

7. Close the file without saving it.

3 Create a New Workbook and Enter Data

Create a worksheet that tracks signatures obtained by participants in a signature drive.

1. Create a new workbook and type SIGNATURE DRIVE in cell A1.

2. Starting in cell A3, type the information in Table 1.6.

Lesson Summary & Exercises

TABLE 1.6	SIGNATURE DRIVE DATA	
Name	**Signatures**	**Hours**
Alvarez	273	21.5
Burns, A.	481	33
Burns, D.	332	24.5
Goldsmith	109	11.5
Haskell	520	44
Lee	227	17
Minceberg	425	31.5
Stoll	217	15
Weinmiller	375	29
Yamaguchi	399	29

3. Save the file as *Signature Drive* in the *Lesson Applications* folder on your Student Data Disk.

4. Click the File menu and click Print.

5. Change the number of copies to 1, if necessary.

6. In the Print dialog box, click OK.

7. Close the *Signature Drive* workbook.

PROJECTS

1 How Can You Use a Worksheet?

Think of something you do in your personal, academic, or business life for which you might use a worksheet. Draw a rough sketch to show how your worksheet might be organized, remembering to arrange the data in columns and rows. A sample sketch of a worksheet is shown in Figure 1.26; be sure to use a different topic for your worksheet.

BOOK EXPENSES
First Quarter

Class	Textbook Needed	Cost
Psychology	Basic Psychology	45.95
Accounting	Managerial Accounting, 8th Edition	38
Geography	World Geography, 2nd Edition	29.95
Economics	Macro Economics	29.95
Total		143.85

Figure 1.26

2 Make It Look Good!

Describe some ways of formatting a worksheet to make it look more professional. Apply your ideas to the worksheet you created in Project 1. Again, draw a rough sketch to show the types of changes you would make. A sample worksheet is shown in Figure 1.27.

BOOK EXPENSES
First Quarter

Class	Textbook Needed	Cost
Psychology	Basic Psychology	$45.95
Accounting	Managerial Accounting, 8th Edition	$38.00
Geography	World Geography, 2nd Edition	$29.95
Economics	Macro Economics	$29.95
Total		$143.85

Figure 1.27

3 What's Available on the Toolbars?

Review the buttons on the Excel Standard toolbar and determine what each one does. If you're not sure, point to the button to see a description or use ScreenTips. Using Word, list the buttons on the Standard toolbar and what they do.

Use the same procedure to investigate the buttons on the Formatting toolbar.

4 How Do You Open Two Files?

Use the Office Assistant to find help for opening two files at once. Follow the steps to open any two workbooks on your Student Data Disk. When you're finished, use Word to write as much as you can remember about what you just learned. Don't worry about mentioning every detail. Close each workbook.

5 Compare and Contrast These Worksheets

Open the *Sales Quarter 2* workbook on the Student Data Disk and print it. On the printout, write a sentence or two explaining the use of this worksheet. Compare and contrast this worksheet with the one you worked with in this lesson *(Pet Paradise 2001 Income Statement)* and write your answers on the printout. (If necessary, open the *Pet Paradise 2001 Income Statement* workbook to review it.)

Open the *Pet Paradise 2001 Sales* workbook on the Student Data Disk and print it. On the printout, write a sentence or two explaining the use of this worksheet. Compare and contrast this worksheet with the *Sales Quarter 2* workbook you just opened. Write your answers on the printout. Close each workbook.

6 Link to the Web!

Assume that you need to make travel arrangements to fly to Boston for business. Create a new workbook and type FLIGHTS TO BOSTON in cell A1. In cell A1, insert a hyperlink to http://www.delta-air.com. Connect to the Internet and click the hyperlink. Read the information on the Web page. What do you think you would need to do to find a flight to Boston? Close the browser and return to Excel. Save the file as *Boston Flights* in the *Projects* folder on your Student Data Disk. Close any open workbooks.

Project in Progress

7 Check Out These Sales!

Assume you own a small business called I-Comm that provides a variety of writing, editing, and training services to other business owners. You facilitate training seminars; write materials such as brochures, training manuals, annual reports, employee handbooks, and newspaper and magazine articles; and create Web pages for small businesses.

Think of ways you could use worksheets in your business. Then start Excel and open the *I-Comm Sales* workbook on your Student Data Disk (Figure 1.28).

When you created this workbook, you itemized the sales of promotional materials and employee literature in separate worksheets, as shown on Sheet2 and Sheet3. Rename the first sheet tab as Total Sales. Then rename the second sheet tab as Employee Literature Sales and the third sheet tab as Promotional Materials Sales. On the Total Sales worksheet, insert a hyperlink from the Employee literature label to the Employee Literature Sales worksheet.

Reduce the appearance of the worksheet area to see the data for the last few months of the year. Return the worksheet area to its actual size. What other information would you add to this workbook to make it more useful? What would you do to make the workbook look more professional? Explore Help for information on formatting a worksheet. Print the workbook. What would you do to make your printout more attractive? Write your responses to these questions on the printout. Save the workbook as *Updated I-Comm Sales* in the *Projects* folder on your Student Data Disk. Close the workbook and exit Excel.

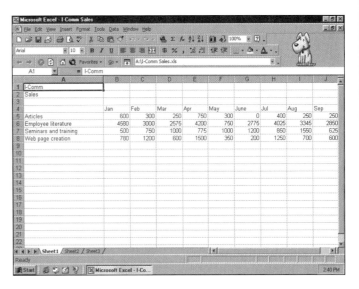

Figure 1.28

Customizing Worksheets

CONTENTS

OBJECTIVES

After you complete this lesson, you will be able to do the following:

■ Select single cells, ranges of cells, rows, columns, the entire workbook page, or noncontiguous ranges.

■ Erase the contents of one or more cells.

■ Undo and redo changes.

■ Insert and delete cells, rows, and columns.

■ Move and copy the contents of one or more cells.

■ Adjust column widths and row heights.

■ Fill ranges with values automatically.

■ Create, revise, and copy formulas.

■ Understand the precedence of mathematical operators.

■ Use functions and the AutoSum button.

■ Display and print formulas.

■ Change the page setup options.

■ Align and rotate data and apply numeric formats.

■ Modify font characteristics.

■ Add borders and shading.

■ Use AutoFormat and conditional formatting.

■ Copy and clear cell formats.

■ Identify the elements of a chart.

■ Create a chart using the Chart Wizard.

■ Move and resize charts.

■ Create a Web page from an Excel workbook.

This lesson continues to develop the skills you need to create simple worksheets. You will learn more about editing to correct errors and update files. You will see the real benefits of using formulas and functions to perform your calculations. You will learn to copy and display formulas.

Excel lets you improve the appearance of your worksheet in many ways. You can modify font characteristics and format numbers. You will also master printing options that result in professional outputs that are easy to interpret. Lastly, you will learn how to create a chart in Excel so that you can display your data in another form.

SELECTING GROUPS OF CELLS

In Lesson 1, you learned how to edit data in a single cell. Sometimes you'll want to change not just one, but many, cells. In this case, you need to *select* the cells you want to modify before you start editing or issuing commands. Selecting means highlighting one or more cells; then, when you issue a command, Excel performs the desired action on those selected cells.

You can select any single cell or one or more ranges of cells; a *range* is a group of adjacent cells. When you select one cell, it is surrounded by the cell cursor. When you select multiple cells, they become highlighted (their backgrounds change color), except for the active cell, which remains white.

As you know, each cell has an address to help you locate the cell in the worksheet. Similarly, ranges have *range addresses* so you can tell where they are in the worksheet. A range address consists of any two cells in opposite corners of the range, separated by a colon (:). A range can span part of a column, part of a row, or several columns and several rows. You can select ranges using several methods, including *shift-clicking,* which is clicking the first cell in the range, pressing and holding [⇧ Shift], and clicking the last cell in the range. Figure 2.1 shows some examples of various ranges.

Figure 2.1 ◄
Examples of ranges

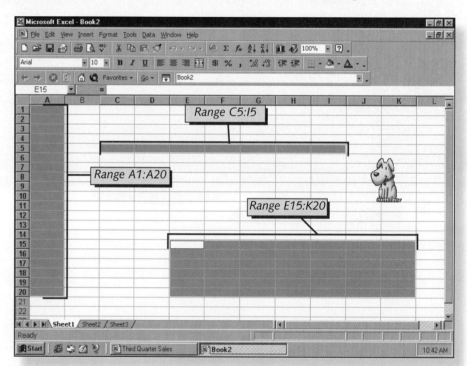

Selecting Ranges of Cells

You may select ranges of cells in several ways. An intuitive method is to drag across the cells—that is, you click one corner of the range, hold down the mouse button, and then drag to the opposite corner of the range.

Sometimes you may want to print only a selected range of data instead of an entire worksheet. You can do this easily through the Print Dialog box, or you can set a print area. To set a print area, select the range to be printed, point to Print Area on the File menu, and click Set Print Area. To clear a print area, point to Print Area on the File menu and click Clear Print Area.

HANDS On

Selecting a Range

1. Click the first cell of the range you want to select. (Make sure the pointer looks like this: ⊕.)

2. Drag to the last cell you want to select.

3. Release the mouse button.

Figure 2.2 ◄
Selected range A5:C11

Another Way

You can also use mouse and/or keyboard methods to enter the cell addresses for a range. Using both the mouse and the keyboard, you can click the Name Box, type the range, and press Enter←. Remember to separate the opposite corners with a colon, as in A5:C11. Using only the keyboard, you can use the arrow keys to position the cell cursor in the upper-left corner of the range, press and hold ⇧Shift, and then repeatedly press the arrow keys to highlight the desired range.

Selecting and Printing Ranges

In this activity, you will select and print the sales data and month text in the *Third Quarter Sales* workbook you created in Lesson 1.

1. Start Excel and open the *Third Quarter Sales* workbook in the *Tutorial* folder on your Student Data Disk.

2. Click cell A5, hold down the mouse button, and drag diagonally to cell C11. Then release the mouse button.

Warning

Before you begin to drag, make sure the pointer looks like this: ⊕, not like an arrow ▢ or a black crosshair symbol ✚. Since Excel uses different pointer symbols to invoke different actions, you must be certain to use the correct cursor when selecting a range.

The cells in this range are highlighted to indicate that they're selected, as shown in Figure 2.2.

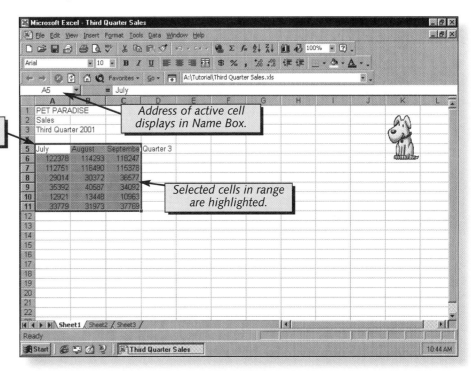

If you have trouble dragging accurately, you can click one corner of the range, press and hold ⇧Shift, and click the opposite corner of the range.

3. Click File on the menu bar and click Print.

The Print dialog box appears.

4. Click Selection in the *Print what* box and click OK.

Note

Verify that the Number of copies option in the Print dialog box is set to 1.

Compare your printout to Figure 2.2. Notice that only the highlighted range printed, not the entire worksheet.

5. **Click cell A1, press and hold** ⇧ Shift **, and click cell D11.**

Excel selects all the cells that appear between the two cells you clicked—the range A1:D11.

6. **Point to Print Area on the File menu and then click Set Print Area.**

You will see a dashed line around the range on the worksheet.

7. **Click the Print button.**

Notice that only cells A1 through D11 printed.

8. **Point to Print Area on the File menu and then click Clear Print Area.**

Selecting Rows, Columns, or the Entire Worksheet

You can also select whole rows or columns by clicking the appropriate row or column heading, and you can select several rows or columns at one time by dragging across their row or column headings. In some cases, you may want to select the entire worksheet—it's easy to do using the Select All button.

Selecting Rows and Columns of Sales Data

In this activity, you'll select one or more rows or columns in the ***Third Quarter Sales*** workbook.

1. **Click row heading 5 on the left side of the worksheet area.**

Row 5 is highlighted, as shown in Figure 2.3. You can scroll to check that you have selected every cell in the row. Incidentally, notice that the new selection automatically replaces the old selection you made in the previous Hands On activity.

2. **Click column heading A and drag to column heading D.**

Before you begin to drag, make sure the pointer looks like this: ⊕*, not like an arrow pointer* ⇗ *or a black crosshair symbol* ⊞*.*

Excel selects all the designated columns. You can also select an entire workbook page by clicking the Select All button in the upper-left corner of the worksheet area (to the left of column A and above row 1).

3. **Click the Select All button.**

Excel highlights the entire worksheet.

4. **Click the Sheet2 sheet tab at the bottom of the worksheet area.**

Notice that none of the cells are highlighted in Sheet2. The Select All button highlights all cells in the worksheet in which it is issued; it does not select all cells in the entire workbook.

Selecting Entire Rows, Columns, or Worksheets

- To select a row, click the row heading.

- To select a column, click the column heading.

- To select multiple, adjacent rows, drag across row headings.

- To select multiple, adjacent columns, drag across column headings.

- To select the entire worksheet, click the Select All button.

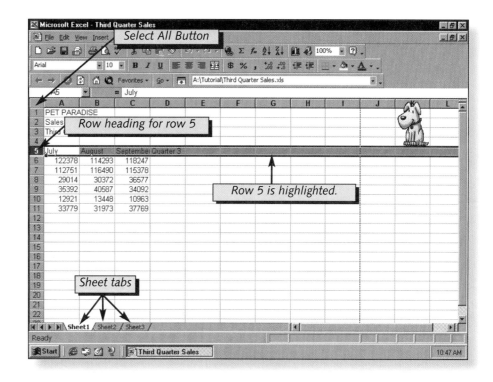

Figure 2.3
Selected row

5. **Click the Sheet1 sheet tab to return to the first sheet in your workbook.**

Selecting Noncontiguous Ranges

Oftentimes you will need to select several noncontiguous, or nonadjacent, ranges at once. To do this, select the first range as usual. Then press and hold `Ctrl` while selecting additional ranges. If you don't press and hold `Ctrl`, selecting a new range automatically deselects any previously selected ranges. In fact, you can deselect a range not only by selecting a new range but also by clicking anywhere within the worksheet or by pressing any of the arrow keys.

Selecting Noncontiguous Ranges

1. Select the first range.

2. Press and hold `Ctrl` and select the second range.

3. Repeat step 2 until all desired ranges are selected.

Highlighting Noncontiguous Ranges

In this activity, you'll select two noncontiguous ranges in the **Third Quarter Sales** workbook.

1. **Click row heading 1.**

2. **Press and hold `Ctrl` and click row heading 5.**

Both rows 1 and 5 should be selected, as shown in Figure 2.4.

3. **Click any cell.**

Excel deselects all the selected ranges and the cell you clicked becomes active.

Rows 1 and 5 are selected.

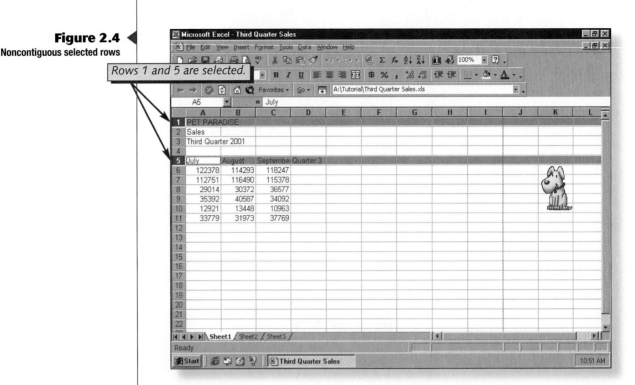

ERASING DATA

One important way of editing your worksheet is to simply erase data that you've entered. For example, suppose you need to enter revised sales data for August in the **Third Quarter Sales** workbook. You can start by deleting the old values before you enter the new ones.

HANDS On

Deleting the Contents of a Range

In this activity, you'll erase the August data in **Third Quarter Sales** and update this range with the correct data.

1. **Select the range B6:B11.**

2. **Press** Delete.

The numbers in the highlighted cells are removed from the worksheet, as shown in Figure 2.5. Using this method, you delete the contents of the cells but not the cells themselves.

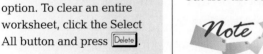
Note *Do not save your file at this time.*

UNDOING AND REDOING CHANGES

After you start editing and erasing data with any frequency, you'll need to know how to restore data and edits. For example, in the previous activity you erased the August data, but suppose you should have erased the July data instead. When you make errors like this, you can use the **Undo** command to reverse your most recent action.

Another Way

To clear cell contents, right-click the cell or the range and click the Clear Contents option. To clear an entire worksheet, click the Select All button and press Delete.

Deleting the Contents of a Cell or Range

1. Select the cell or range whose contents you wish to delete.

2. Press [Delete].

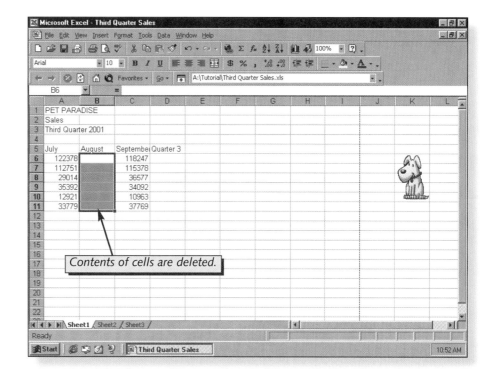

Figure 2.5 ◀
Erasing a range

Contents of cells are deleted.

Many application programs provide the Undo command. For instance, Microsoft Word, PowerPoint, and Access all provide this option. However, not all of these programs provide the Redo command.

The Undo command is invaluable and can reverse as many as 16 of your most recent actions. However, remember that you can undo *many*, but not *all*, actions. For example, you can't deselect a range you just selected by issuing the Undo command, and you can't press an arrow key and then move back to your previous location by choosing Undo.

Sometimes you'll undo something and then change your mind again. You may decide that you do need to keep the sales data you just deleted. Immediately after you issue the Undo command, you can issue the ***Redo*** command—which lets you reverse the most recent Undo command. Using the Redo command, you are able to restore the data once again.

Both the Undo and Redo commands are options on the Edit menu. The exact names of these commands change depending on your previous action. For example, if you erased some data that you now wish to restore, the command name will be Undo Clear. If you typed some data that you now wish to delete, the command name will be Undo Typing. The Redo command is not used as often as the Undo command and may not appear on the Edit short menu. If the Redo command does not appear, expand the menu by clicking the double arrow at the bottom of the menu or by pointing to the menu for a few seconds.

The Undo button [↶] and the Redo button [↷] also appear on the Standard toolbar. Notice the triangle buttons that appear to the right of the Undo and Redo buttons. When you click the triangle button, a drop-down list appears, listing the 16 most recent actions you can undo (or redo).

Reversing Changes

In this activity, you will use the Undo command to restore the data that you just erased. Then you will reverse the Undo action by using the Redo command. Lastly, you'll learn how to undo several changes at once.

1. Click the Undo button ↶.

Excel restores the August sales data that you erased in the last activity.

2. Click the Redo button ↷.

Your Undo command is reversed, and the August data is deleted again.

3. Click cell B6 to deselect the range.

4. Type the new August data as listed in Table 2.1.

TABLE 2.1	NEW DATA FOR AUGUST
Cell	**Data**
B6	117944
B7	118213
B8	31749
B9	39857
B10	14384
B11	32991
B12	84327
B13	78249
B14	32195

Looking at your worksheet, you can see that you entered too much data.

5. To clear the last three cells, click the Undo triangle button. (Don't click the Undo button itself.)

6. Highlight the three most recent actions as shown in Figure 2.6 and click the mouse button again.

The values in cells B12, B13, and B14 are deleted.

7. Click the Save button 🖫 **to save this revised version of the *Third Quarter Sales* workbook.**

REARRANGING YOUR WORKSHEET

The editing you've done so far involves adding, modifying, or deleting the contents of one or more cells. Often, however, you'll want to rearrange your worksheet—insert and delete cells, rows, and columns or move and copy data. To perform some of these tasks, you can use the ***shortcut menu,*** a context-sensitive menu that appears when you right-click certain screen elements.

Hints & Tips

The best approach to take when creating a new workbook is to plan in advance. Planning decreases the need for major changes in the structure of a workbook.

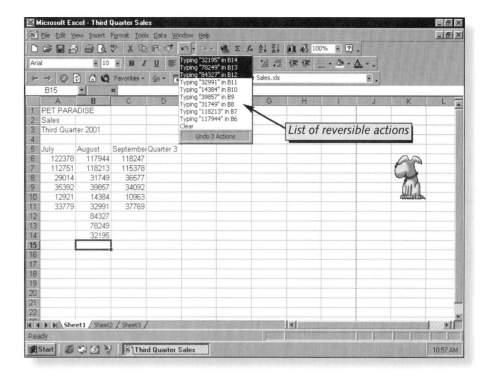

List of reversible actions

Figure 2.6
Actions that can be reversed

Inserting and Deleting Cells, Columns, and Rows

Sometimes you have to insert cells, columns, and rows into your workbook to make room for new data. When you add new cells, rows, or columns, Excel automatically moves your existing data. Excel inserts new cells either to the right of or below the cell cursor. Excel inserts new rows above the cell cursor and new columns to the left of the cell cursor.

Likewise, you may need to delete cells, rows, or columns you no longer need. Deleting a cell, row, or column is not the same as deleting (or clearing) the *contents* of a cell, row, or column. When you delete a cell, row, or column, Excel totally removes the cell, row, or column, including its contents, and moves up or over the remaining cells, moves up the remaining rows, or moves over the remaining columns.

HANDS On

Adding a Column, Removing a Row, and Inserting and Deleting Cells

In this activity, you'll insert a new column into the *Third Quarter Sales* workbook so you can add labels for the Pet Paradise sales items. You will then delete a row that is no longer needed. Finally, you will insert and delete a cell.

1. **Click any cell in column A.**
2. **Click the Insert menu and click Columns.**

Excel adds a new column to your workbook, moving the existing columns to the right, as shown in Figure 2.7. Notice that the cell cursor is positioned in the new column.

Figure 2.7 ◄
Inserting a column moves the
existing columns to the right

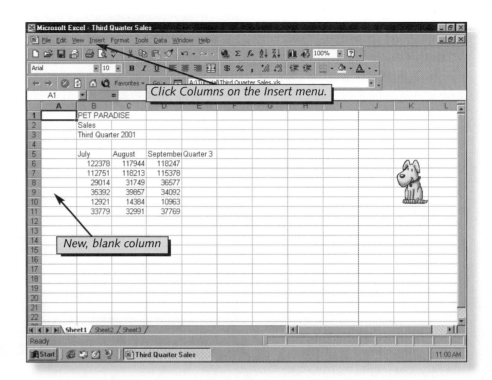

Inserting and Deleting Columns and Rows

To insert a column:

1. Position the cell cursor anywhere in the column to the right of where you want to insert the new column.

2. Click Columns on the Insert menu.

To delete a column:

1. Click the column heading.

2. Click Delete on the Edit menu.

To insert a row:

1. Position the cell cursor anywhere in the row below where you want to insert the new row.

2. Click Rows on the Insert menu.

To delete a row:

1. Click the row heading.

2. Click Delete on the Edit menu.

3. In column A beginning in row 6 and ending in row 11, type Cat Food, Dog Food, Flea Spray, Bones and Treats, Bedding, **and** Toys.

Don't worry that you can't see all of the text in cell A9; you'll fix that later in this lesson. If you make cell A9 the active cell, you will see that its text still appears in full in the formula bar.

Next you'll delete the contents of row 10, since the store is eliminating the Bedding sales category.

4. Click row heading 10 to select the entire row.

5. Press Delete .

This action deletes the data, but leaves the row intact.

6. With the row still selected, click Delete on the Edit menu.

Excel removes the row and moves the data from row 11 to row 10, as you can see in Figure 2.8. A row does not have to be blank to be deleted; any data in a row will be erased when you delete the row.

7. Click the Save button 🖫 .

8. Click cell B10 to select it.

9. Click the Insert menu and click Cells.

If the Cells option does not appear on your Insert short menu, click the double arrow at the bottom of the menu to display the expanded menu.

10. In the Insert dialog box, click the Shift cells right option and click OK.

Notice what happens—the data in cells B10:D10 shift to the right and now occupy cells C10:E10.

11. With the cursor still in cell B10, click the Edit menu and click Delete.

Figure 2.8

Deleting a row

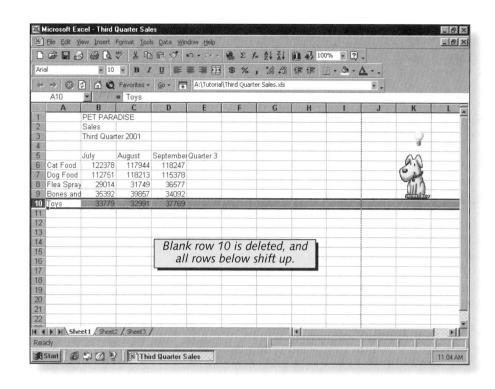

Inserting and Deleting Cells

To insert a cell:

1. Select the cell where you want to insert the new cell.

2. Click Cells on the Insert menu.

3. Select the direction to move the remaining cells.

To delete a cell:

1. Select the cell you want to delete.

2. Click Delete on the Edit menu.

3. Select the direction to move the remaining cells.

12. **In the Delete dialog box, click the Shift cells left option (if necessary) and click OK.**

The data is restored in cells B10:D10. (You could have clicked the Undo button to restore the data.)

Warning *Be very careful when inserting or deleting cells—it is very easy to misalign your data and totally ruin your worksheet! As a general rule, it is best to insert or delete entire rows or columns, not individual cells.*

13. **Click the Save button.**

Copying and Moving Cell Contents

If you've already typed some data that you need to use elsewhere, you can copy the data rather than type it again. And if some of your data is in the wrong location, you don't have to delete your data from one place and retype the information in another. Instead, you can move the data. Excel provides two ways to move and copy data. You can use the drag-and-drop method or the Cut or Copy commands in conjunction with the Paste command. Regardless of which method you use, the data you move or copy will replace any existing data in the new location.

The drag-and-drop method is very intuitive. To move data, first select the cell(s) you want to move and point to the cell border—the pointer changes to an arrow. Then click and drag the selection to the upper-left cell of the new location. To copy data, press and hold Ctrl while dragging the selection to the new location.

The pointer must be in the shape of an arrow before you begin a move or copy action. If it is in the shape of a plus sign (used to select a range) or a black crosshair symbol (used to fill a range), you will not achieve the desired result.

You're probably familiar with the Cut, Copy, and Paste commands if you have used other Windows programs. These commands make use of the **Clipboard,** a temporary storage area for information that is used by all Windows applications. Clicking Cut ✂ moves the selected data from the workbook to the Clipboard; clicking Copy 🖹 copies the selected data to the Clipboard, without removing that data from the workbook. The Paste command 🖺 places a copy of the Clipboard data in the workbook at the position of the cell cursor.

HANDS On

Copying and Moving Data using Toolbar Buttons and Drag-and-Drop

In this activity, you'll copy text from one cell and paste to another cell, replacing the existing text. Then you'll use two methods to move the three headings at the top of the **Third Quarter Sales** workbook into column A.

1. Click **cell B3**.

2. Click the **Copy button** 🖹.

Cell B3 is surrounded by a moving border, as shown in Figure 2.9. The contents of the cell have now been copied to the Clipboard.

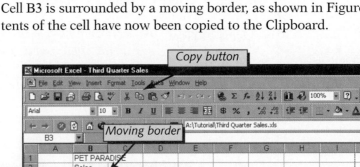

Figure 2.9 ◀
Using the Copy command

Moving Data

1. Select the cell or range you want to move.

2. Click the Cut button.

3. Click the cell to which you wish to move the data; or, if pasting a range of data, click the upper-left cell of the range to which you wish to paste data.

4. Click the Paste button or press `Enter←`.

 *If the Clipboard contains other sets of data, the Clipboard may appear on your screen at this time.*

3. Click **cell E5**.

4. Click the **Paste button** 🖺.

The text from the Clipboard, *Third Quarter 2001,* is copied into cell E5. Notice that the moving border still appears around cell B3. If desired, you could paste these Clipboard contents again (without issuing the Copy command again).

5. Double-click in **cell E5** and delete *2001.*

6. Click **cell B1**.

7. Click the **Cut button** ✂.

Cell B1 is surrounded by a moving border and the contents of the cell are copied to the Clipboard. The status bar reads *Select destination and press ENTER or choose Paste*. The Clipboard may also appear on the screen, displaying icons that represent sets of data that have been cut or copied. If you point to an icon on the Clipboard, the contents (or a portion of the text) appears in a small box. You can paste data to the active cell by clicking the appropriate Clipboard icon.

8. Click **cell A1**.

9. Click the **Paste button** 🖺 or press `Enter←`. **(You can also paste the PET PARADISE text to the active cell by clicking the appropriate Clipboard icon.)**

As shown in Figure 2.10, Excel moves the text *PET PARADISE* from cell B1 to cell A1.

Figure 2.10
Cutting and pasting text using toolbar buttons

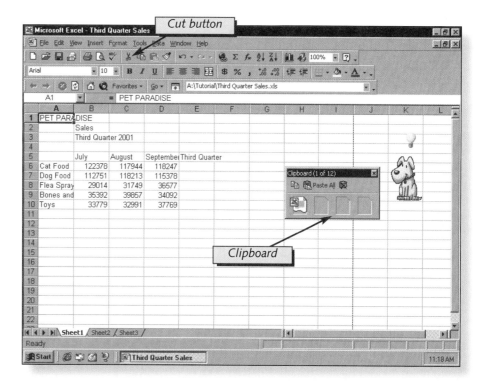

Resizing Columns and Rows

To resize automatically:

1. Click the column heading of the column to be resized.

2. Click Column on the Format menu.

3. Click AutoFit Selection from the submenu.

To resize manually:

1. Select the column(s) or row(s) to resize.

2. Point to the border between the column or row headings.

3. Drag to the desired width or height.

10. Select the range **B2:B3**.

11. Point to the border of the selected range.

The pointer now appears as an arrow ⬉.

12. Click and drag to enclose cells A2 and A3. Then release the mouse button.

Excel drops the selected text into cells A2 and A3.

13. Click the **Save button** 🖫.

MANIPULATING COLUMNS AND ROWS

To improve the appearance of your worksheet, you'll often need to change column widths and row heights, depending on the data. You don't want to leave too much white space in a column, nor do you want to make a column so narrow that critical data is not visible. Excel allows you to resize columns and rows manually and also provides a feature that allows you to resize columns and rows to automatically fit the data. You can also *hide* columns and rows to remove them from view. Just right-click the selected column or row and click Hide on the shortcut menu. To redisplay a hidden column or row, select the surrounding columns or rows, right-click the selection, and click Unhide on the shortcut menu.

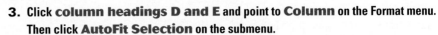

Resizing Columns and Rows

You may have noticed that you can't see all the text contained in column A. To see the text, you must widen the column. In this activity, you'll widen columns A and D automatically and increase the height of row 5 manually.

1. Click **column heading A**.

2. Click **Format** on the menu bar and point to **Column**. Then click **AutoFit Selection** on the submenu.

Excel widens column A so you can see the longest entry. You can use the AutoFit Selection command to widen or narrow columns to better fit your data.

3. Click **column headings D and E** and point to **Column** on the Format menu. Then click **AutoFit Selection** on the submenu.

Excel widens columns D and E slightly. As Figure 2.11 shows, the headings *September* and *Third Quarter* fit in their columns.

4. Point to the border between row headings 5 and 6.

When you see the double-headed arrow, you can drag up to decrease the row height or down to increase the row height. This change affects the row above the arrow.

5. Drag down to increase the row height.

As you drag, notice the value of the row height is displayed in a small box next to the pointer.

6. When the number in the box reaches 21.00, release the mouse button.

Excel increased the height of row 5. You can change the height of rows individually using this method, or you can select numerous rows and change the height of all at once.

7. Click the **Undo button** 🗠 to reverse the row height.

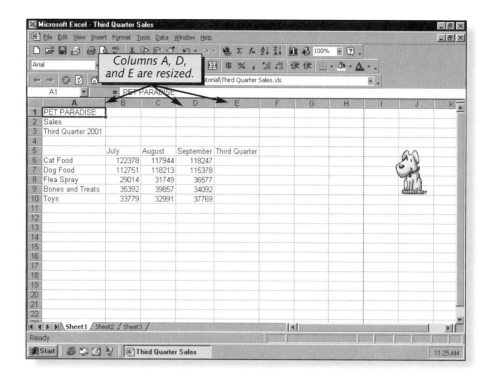

Columns A, D, and E are resized.

Figure 2.11
Columns are resized to the appropriate width

8. Press `Ctrl` + `Home` to move to cell A1.
9. If the Clipboard is open, click its **Close button**.
10. Click the **Save button** 🖫 to save the revised version of *Third Quarter Sales*.
11. Click the **Print button** 🖨.

Excel prints your *Third Quarter Sales* workbook.

12. Close the *Third Quarter Sales* workbook.

FILLING RANGES WITH VALUES

Excel provides time-saving techniques for entering certain kinds of data. For example, if your workbook includes days of the week, months of the year, or numbers incremented at regular intervals, you can use the AutoFill feature to generate the data automatically.

Entering Data in a New Worksheet

In this activity, imagine that you want to create an exercise schedule to help prepare you for an upcoming walkathon.

1. Click the **New button** 🗋.

Excel displays a new, blank workbook.

2. Type EXERCISE SCHEDULE in cell A1 and press `Enter⏎`.
3. In row 3, type Week in cell A3, Date in cell B3, and Miles in cell C3.
4. Type 1 in cell A4 and type 2 in cell A5.

Entering Data with the AutoFill Feature

This exercise schedule starts with week 1 in cell A4, followed by week 2 in cell A5. Cell A6 should contain 3, and so on. Instead of typing all these numbers manually, you can use the AutoFill feature to have Excel enter them for you. Just select the two initial values and drag the *fill handle* down to select the range to be filled. The fill handle is the small square at the bottom-right corner of the cell cursor.

Entering Data in a Series

In this activity, you will use the AutoFill feature to fill (or extend) a series of numbers and a series of dates. To complete a series, you usually must provide at least two numbers; the difference between the two numbers tells Excel the increment to use when completing the rest of the series. (However, if you want a series of dates to increase by one day, you need to provide only one date.)

1. Select cells A4 and A5.

Notice the fill handle located at the bottom-right corner of the selection, as shown in Figure 2.12.

Figure 2.12 ◄
The fill handle

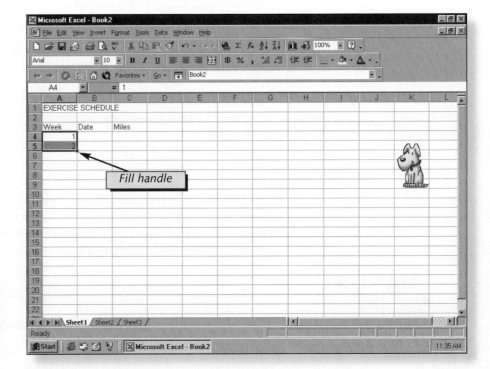

Completing a Series

1. Enter two or more values of a series.

2. Select the two values.

3. Drag the fill handle to the last cell to be filled and release the mouse button.

2. Point to the fill handle.

Your pointer changes to a black crosshair symbol ⊞.

3. Click and hold.

The status bar will display this message: *Drag outside selection to extend series or fill; drag inside to clear.*

4. Drag to **cell A18** and release the mouse button.

Excel automatically fills the selected cells with the additional values 3, 4, and so on to 15. You can use the same strategy to enter dates.

5. Type 1/1/2001 **in cell B4 and type** 1/8/2001 **in cell B5**.

Depending on the default settings used on your computer, the dates may display as MM/DD/YY or some other date format. You can customize the appearance of dates in your worksheet by clicking Cells on the Format menu and choosing Date in the Number tab. Then select the date format you wish to use.

6. Select **cells B4 and B5**.

7. Click the **fill handle** for the selection. Make sure the pointer is the shape of a crosshair symbol ⊞.

8. Drag to **cell B18** and release.

Excel fills the selected range with the dates 1/15/2001, 1/22/2001, and so on.

9. Click the **Save button** 🖫.

Since you haven't yet named this workbook, Excel displays the Save As dialog box.

10. Type the file name Exercise Schedule **and save the file in the** *Tutorial* **folder of your Student Data Disk**.

Entering Data with the Fill, Series Command

The Fill, Series command on the Edit menu provides another way to fill a range of cells. You can increase the number in each cell by a specific amount (such as increments of 3) or by a certain percentage (such as 20 percent). For example, suppose each week you want to walk .5 miles more than the previous week. Your first cell might contain 1 mile. The next cell, increased by .5 miles, would be 1.5 miles.

The number used to begin the fill is called the ***start value***. The ***step value*** is the number by which to increment each value, and the ***stop value*** is the ending number or entry. When you enter numbers, you can choose between Linear (to add the step value to the previous value) or Growth (to multiply the step value by the previous value). When you enter dates, you can choose a unit increment of Day, Weekday, Month, or Year.

Increasing Numbers in a Series by a Specific Value

In this activity, you'll learn how to increase each number in a series by a specific amount. Specifically, you will assume that each week you will walk .5 miles more than the previous week. You will use the Fill, Series command to instruct Excel how to complete the series of numbers.

1. In cell C4, type the number 1 as the number of miles you plan to walk for the first week and press Enter↵.

2. Select the range **C4:C18**.

**Increasing Numbers
in a Series by a
Specific Value**

1. Type the first value in a
series in the desired cell.

2. Select the range to be
filled.

3. Click the Edit menu,
point to Fill, and click
Series.

4. Type the desired step
value and click OK.

 Warning

Select the range by clicking cell C4 and then dragging from within cell C4 to cell C18. Do not drag the fill handle, as this will fill all *of the cells with the value of 1.*

3. Click **Edit** on the menu bar, point to **Fill**, and click **Series** in the submenu.

4. In the Series dialog box, enter .5 in the Step value box and click **OK**.

Excel fills the selected range with values starting at 1.5 in cell C5 and incrementing by .5, as you can see in Figure 2.13.

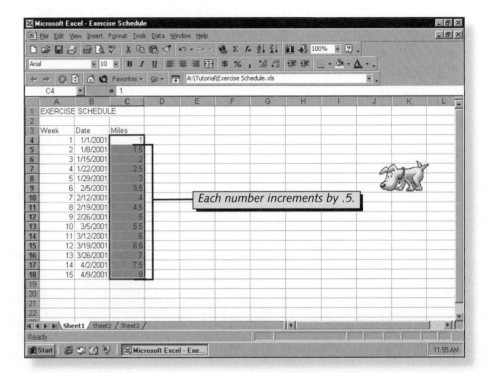

Figure 2.13 ◀
Series filled with values

5. Click **cell A1**.

When you open a workbook, the cell cursor appears in the location it was in when you last saved the file. For that reason, you should develop the habit of moving the cell cursor to cell A1 before saving and closing a workbook.

6. Click the **Save button** 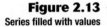.

7. Close the file.

UNDERSTANDING FORMULAS

In Lesson 1, you learned that Excel can calculate your arithmetic for you. For example, if you have columns listing January, February, and March sales, you can have Excel generate monthly sales totals, as well as totals for the quarter. To perform these and other types of calculations, you need to know how to build formulas.

Learning about Obtaining External Data

In previous activities, you learned about entering data in a worksheet. Excel also allows you to obtain external data. If you have Internet access, you can run a **Web query** to retrieve data from a Web site.

1. Click the **Office Assistant**.

2. Type retrieve external data **in the *What would you like to do?* box.**

3. Click the **Search button**.

Figure 2.14
Web query topic in Help window

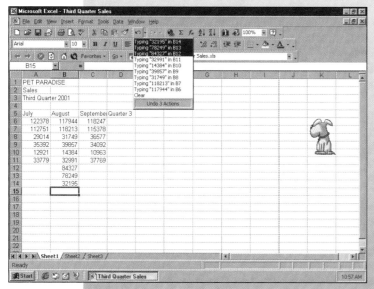

4. Click the **Retrieve data from a Web page option**.

5. Read the text that appears in the Help window (Figure 2.14).

6. Click the **create your own Web queries link** and then read the Help information.

7. Click the **retrieving data from a Web page link** and read the Help information.

8. Consider instances when you might want to obtain data from a Web page.

9. Close the Help window.

10. If time allows, experiment with Web queries in a worksheet.

A **formula** is a group of instructions that tells Excel to perform a calculation and display the results. Formulas consist of values, such as numbers and cell references, and calculation operators, such as plus and minus signs. The operators tell Excel what to do with the values on either side of them. Table 2.2 shows some of the arithmetic operators available in Excel.

TABLE 2.2	ARITHMETIC OPERATORS	
Symbol	**Function**	**Example**
+	Addition	2+3=5
-	Subtraction	5-2=3
*	Multiplication	2*3=6
/	Division	6/3=2
^	Exponentiation	2^3=8
%	Percent	10*10%=1

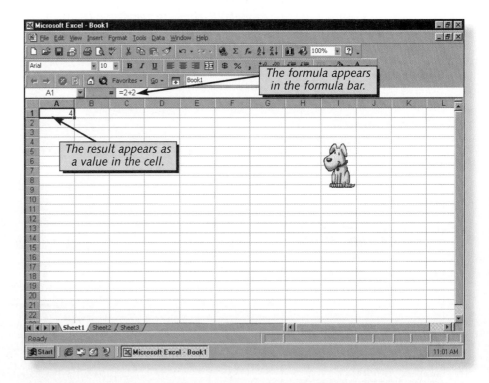
Creating, Editing, and Copying Formulas

A formula can be as simple as =2+2. In Excel, formulas start with an equal sign (=), which is a signal to Excel that you are entering a formula. If you were to type =2+2 in cell A1, Excel would display the result *4* in that cell and would show the formula in the formula bar, as you can see in Figure 2.15.

Figure 2.15
A simple formula

Based on the preceding example, you may think that entering a formula in a cell instead of simply entering the desired result is time consuming and of little value. However, the power of using formulas becomes apparent when you use cell references instead of numbers in your formulas. ***Cell references*** are cell addresses in a formula that tell Excel to perform calculations using whatever value is currently contained in the designated cell. For example, if you entered =B1+B2 in cell B3, cell B3 would display the sum of the values in cells B1 and B2, as shown in Figure 2.16. By using cell references in formulas, you can perform all sorts of calculations involving data you've already entered in other cells. And, when you revise some or all of the data in those other cells, the formula will automatically calculate new results based on the changed data.

To edit a formula, select the cell in which the formula appears. Click the formula bar, edit as appropriate, and press ⌷Enter⏎⌷. You can also double-click the cell in which the formula appears and edit the formula directly in the cell.

You will often use formulas that are very similar. Excel allows you to copy formulas, so you don't have to enter them multiple times. In addition, Excel automatically adjusts the cell references in a copied formula to reflect the formula's new location.

Excel interprets cell references (cell or range addresses) within a formula based on their position *relative to* the cell that contains the formula. Rather than reading a formula literally, Excel reads it as a set of general instructions based upon the position of the cell that contains the formula. For example,

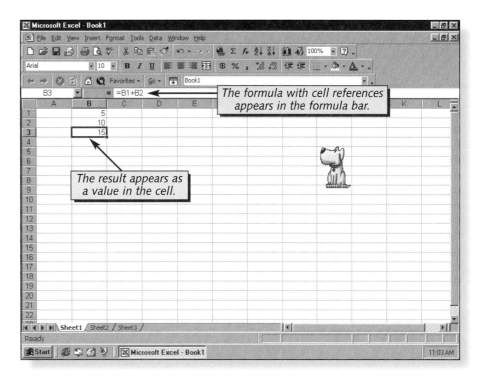

Figure 2.16
A formula with cell references

Excel would interpret the formula = *D14+D15* in cell D16 as "add together the two cells above this one." If you were to copy that formula in cell D16 to cell E16, Excel would change the cell references in the formula to correspond to the formula's new location, interpreting those cell references as the two cells above cell E16. Thus, the formula in cell E16 would be = E14+E15. Cell references within formulas are known as ***relative references***, since they change to correspond to their new location when copied. By default, Excel interprets all cell references as relative references.

The process of copying formulas is much like the process of copying a cell that contains any other type of data. You can use the Copy ⧉ and Paste ⧉ buttons, the drag-and-drop method, the keyboard shortcuts, or the fill handle.

Calculating Gross Margin

In this activity, you'll open the first quarter income statement for Pet Paradise that contains sales and expenses data, but no formulas. You will use two methods (typing and pointing) to enter formulas to determine the gross margin for each month.

1. Open the *Pet Paradise 1st Quarter Income Statement* workbook on the Student Data Disk.

This file contains financial data for the first quarter, but as yet does not include formulas.

2. Move to cell B10, type =B8-B9 and press `Tab`.

Excel subtracts 135,506 (the cost of goods sold for January) from 318,837 (the sales for January) and displays the result of 183,331 (gross margin) in cell B10.

3. Type = (equal sign) in cell C10.

4. Click cell C8.

If you make a mistake, you can edit the formula just as you would edit any other cell. You can select the cell and type changes or type over the current contents.

Excel enters the cell reference C8 into your formula. As shown in Figure 2.17, a moving border surrounds cell C8, and the status bar reads *Point*.

Figure 2.17 ◀
Click cells to include references to them in formulas

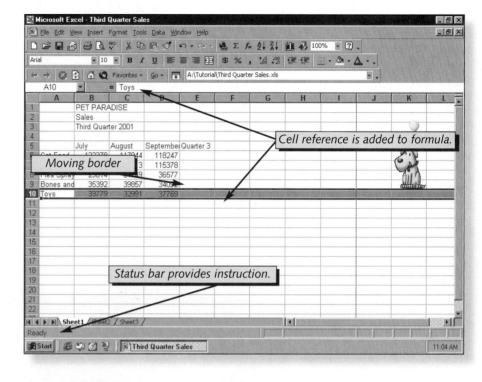

1. Move to the cell in which you want the result of the formula to appear.

2. Type the formula, beginning with an equal sign. Include values and calculation operators in the formula.

3. Press Enter←.

4. To edit a formula, select the cell in which the formula appears. Click the formula bar, edit, and press Enter←.

Or

Double-click the cell in which the formula appears and edit in the cell.

5. Type - (minus sign).

6. Click **cell C9**.

Now cell C9 is surrounded by a moving border, and Excel enters the cell reference for C9 into your formula, which now reads =*C8-C9*.

7. Press Tab to finalize the formula.

The result of 179,851 appears in cell C10.

8. Copy cell C10 to cell D10, using any method you choose.

The result of 198,875 appears in cell D10. Notice that the cell references in cell D10 changed to correspond to their new location.

Operators and Operator Precedence

When formulas have a single operator, such as +, you don't need to worry about how the mathematical expression is evaluated. But when formulas include more than one operator, the various operations are performed in a particular order. Excel doesn't automatically perform operations from left to right. Instead, Excel uses a standard order of ***precedence,*** a set of rules that determines the order in which mathematical expressions are calculated.

Here is the standard order of operator precedence:

■ The exponentiation operator (^) has the highest precedence, so two numbers separated by a ^ are evaluated first.

■ The multiplication (*) and division (/) operators are evaluated next.

■ The addition (+) and subtraction (-) operators are evaluated last.

Note *When operators have the same precedence, they are evaluated from left to right.*

Let's analyze the formula =3+4*5. You might think the result of this formula would be 35 (3+4=7; 7*5=35). Actually, 4 is first multiplied by 5, since multiplication has a higher level of precedence than addition. Then 3 is added to 20 (4*5), for a final result of 23. Similarly, the formula =2*2^3 is equal to 16 (2^3 which is equal to 8, multiplied by 2).

When necessary, you can use parentheses to modify the order in which operators are evaluated. Operations within parentheses are always evaluated first. So, for example, =(3+4)*5 is equal to 35. First 3 is added to 4 and then that result, 7, is multiplied by 5.

You can even use parentheses within parentheses, or **nested parentheses,** to regulate the order in which Excel performs calculations. In such cases, Excel performs the operations in the innermost sets of parentheses first. For example, in the formula =5*((4+4)/2), the first operation is addition (4+4), the second operation is division (8/2), and the last operation is multiplication (5*4).

When entering complicated formulas, carefully check the order in which operations will be calculated. If you're getting strange or unanticipated results, review the operator precedence. To get the results you need, you may have to use parentheses to modify the precedence.

USING FUNCTIONS

You can build highly complex formulas using only the operators mentioned earlier (+, -, *, /, ^, and %); however, these formulas can become quite lengthy and time consuming to enter. Oftentimes, it is more efficient to use **functions.** Functions are predefined formulas that perform specialized calculations. For example, functions exist to obtain the average of a set of numbers, for totaling a group of numbers, and much more. Excel offers over 200 functions.

Suppose you want to total the values in cells B1 through B10. You can do so with the addition operator, and your formula will look like this: =B1+B2+B3+B4+B5+B6+B7+B8+B9+B10. On the other hand, you can use the SUM function to enter this lengthy calculation quickly. When using functions, you refer to range addresses instead of individual cells. So, to add the numbers in the range B1:B10, you use the function =SUM(B1:B10). Any rows or columns that you insert or delete within or at the bottom of the range address of the function will be automatically reflected in the result.

Functions consist of two parts: the name of the function (in this case SUM) and the **arguments** of the function (in this case B1:B10). The arguments of a function must be contained within parentheses. The function operates on the arguments to determine the results. Most functions require at least one argument, and some require more. You can type a function and its arguments in the formula bar, or you can "build" a function using either the Paste Function button *f* or the Formula Palette.

When you click the Paste Function button *f*, Excel displays the Paste Function dialog box. All the Excel functions are listed in the Paste Function dialog box, grouped by category—such as, all functions, statistical functions, financial functions, and so on. When you highlight a category and a function within the category, Excel displays a description of the function. After you select the desired function to use in a particular cell, the function's dialog box appears. In the function's dialog box, you can enter or edit cell references or values for each argument in the function.

You can also use the Formula Palette to build functions. To display the Formula Palette, click the Edit Formula button [=] in the formula bar, click the Function box arrow to display a list of most recently used functions, and select a function from the list. The function's dialog box appears in which you can enter or edit the function's arguments. If the function you want to use is not displayed on the list of most recently used functions, you can click More Functions to view all Excel functions in the Paste Function dialog box.

Statistical functions perform statistical analysis on ranges of data. The AVERAGE function computes the average value for a group of cells. The COUNT function counts the number of cells that contain numbers in a designated range. The MAX function picks a maximum value, and the MIN function determines a minimum value.

Using the SUM Function

Typing the range address:

1. Type =SUM(

2. Type the address of the range to be summed.

3. Type)

4. Press [Enter←].

Dragging to select the range:

1. Type =SUM(

2. Drag to select the range to be summed.

3. Type)

4. Press [Enter←].

Using AutoSum:

1. Select the range to be summed.

2. Click the AutoSum button.

Totaling Operating Expenses

In this activity, you'll use the SUM and AVERAGE functions in the ***Pet Paradise 1st Quarter Income Statement*** workbook.

1. Go to **cell B16** in the ***Pet Paradise 1st Quarter Income Statement*** workbook.

You want to display a total for cells B12 through B15 in this cell.

2. Type =SUM(B12:B15) and press [Tab].

Excel totals the specified range and displays 67,267 in cell B16. Notice also, that when the cell cursor is in the cell, the function =SUM(B12:B15) appears in the formula bar, as shown in Figure 2.18.

3. Type =SUM(in cell C16, but do not press [Enter←].

4. Drag to select the range C12:C15 and release the mouse button.

Excel surrounds the designated cells with a moving border and places the range address in your formula, which should now read =*SUM(C12:C15*. Dragging is an efficient way to place range addresses in formulas.

5. Type) and press [Enter←].

Excel totals the specified range, displaying 67,515 in cell C16. As a general rule, you should always include a closing parenthesis ")" after the function arguments. But in this case, even if you forget to type the closing parenthesis, Excel understands what you mean and totals the designated values.

6. Select the range **D12:D15**.

7. Click the **AutoSum button** [Σ].

You'll see the March operating expense total—67,205—in cell D16. When you're totaling values in a range, selecting the range and clicking the AutoSum button [Σ] is the fastest method. Excel automatically places the total in the cell immediately below the selected range when you use the AutoSum button [Σ] to total a column of numbers.

Figure 2.18 ◄
The SUM function

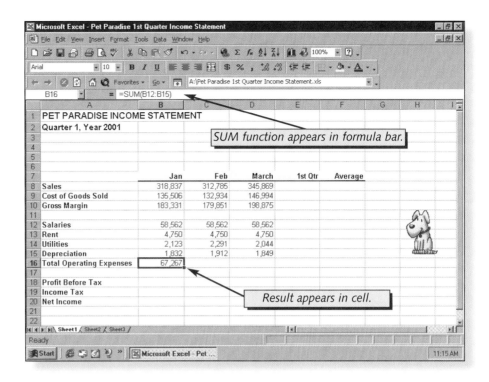

Figure 2.18 ◄
The SUM function

Calculating Statistics

- Enter the function =AVERAGE*(range address of cells)* to calculate the average of the values in a range.

- Enter the function =COUNT*(range address of cells)* to count the number of cells that contain numbers in a range.

- Enter the function =MIN*(range address of cells)* to find the lowest value in a range.

- Enter the function =MAX*(range address of cells)* to find the highest value in a range.

8. Click cell D16 and look at the formula bar.

Notice that Excel has placed the formula =SUM(D12:D15) in this cell.

9. In cell F16, click the Paste Function button f_x.

The Paste Function dialog box appears.

10. Click Statistical in the *Function category* box and then click AVERAGE in the *Function name* box.

Your dialog box should now look like the one shown in Figure 2.19.

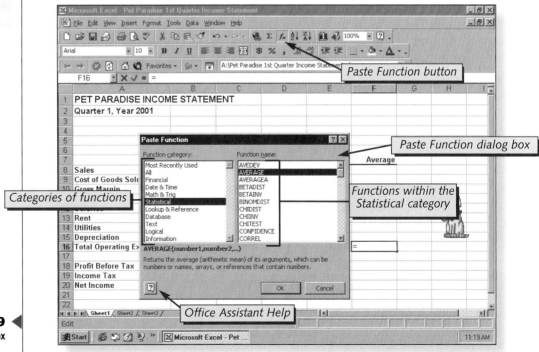

Figure 2.19 ◄
Paste Function dialog box

11. Click **OK**.

The Average dialog box appears.

12. In the Average dialog box, type B16:E16 in the Number1 box, if necessary, and click **OK**.

You should see the result 67,329 in cell F16. This is the average monthly operating expense for the quarter. The function =*AVERAGE (B16:E16)* appears in the formula bar.

13. Click the **File menu**, click **Save As**, and save the revised workbook as *Pet Paradise 1st Quarter Income Statement with Totals* in the *Tutorial* folder on your Student Data Disk.

DISPLAYING AND PRINTING FORMULAS

As you know, when you select a cell that contains a formula, the formula bar displays the formula itself and the result appears in the cell in the worksheet. With this method, you can view only one formula at a time. However, you can choose an option to display all of the formulas directly in the cells of the worksheet. This is a useful tool that allows you to check consistency among cells or to look for the source of an error in your worksheet. (Excel offers various ways to verify formulas in your worksheets. When your time allows, ask the Office Assistant for help on verifying formulas.)

You can even print a copy of your worksheet while the formulas are displayed. To display formulas, Excel enlarges the columns; thus, when you print, the worksheet may no longer fit onto a single sheet of paper. However, you can change the page orientation and/or adjust the print scaling to fit the worksheet onto a single page.

Changing Page Orientation, Using Print Scaling, and Previewing Your Document

Changing the page orientation simply means choosing whether data is printed vertically or horizontally on the page. *Portrait orientation* is the Excel default—in portrait orientation, data is printed vertically on the page (whereby the height of the page is greater than the width). In *landscape orientation,* data is printed horizontally on the page (across the long edge of the paper). Oftentimes, it is better to use landscape orientation when you want to print a worksheet that contains wide columns or several narrow columns.

Even after you change the page orientation, a worksheet may still not fit on a page. In those instances, you can use print scaling to "shrink" the worksheet or use the Fit to option to print a worksheet on one page. *Print scaling* lets you alter the size of printed text by a specified percentage without changing the actual font size. To access the Fit to option, click Page Setup on the File menu and click the Page tab.

Get into the habit of previewing your worksheets before you print. A *print preview* provides an accurate on-screen image of your printout. Regularly previewing your worksheets before you print can save valuable time and paper, giving you the opportunity to correct many mistakes before you go to the trouble of generating a hard copy. To access print preview, click Print Preview on the File menu or click the Print Preview button on the Standard toolbar.

Switching between Formulas and Values and Previewing and Changing the Page Setup

In this activity, you will display the formulas in the **Pet Paradise 1st Quarter Income Statement with Totals** workbook. Then you will change the page setup. After previewing and printing a copy of the formulas, you'll redisplay values.

1. Click the **Tools menu** and click **Options**.

The Options dialog box appears.

2. If necessary, click the **View tab**.

 *If other users have changed the default settings, the selected options may vary.*

3. In the Window options area, click **Formulas** to insert a check mark in the Formulas option box.

4. Click **OK**.

The worksheet now displays the formulas, as shown in Figure 2.20. Notice that the contents of the cells that contain text and numbers remain unchanged. In the cells that contain formulas, the formulas are displayed in place of the results. The columns are widened to accommodate the length of the formulas, and the formulas and values in the cells are positioned flush left.

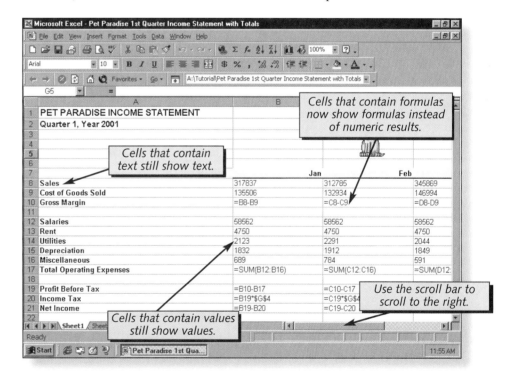

5. Scroll to view the entire worksheet.

6. Click the **Print Preview button** 🔍.

Excel displays a print preview of the worksheet. Although you can't read the contents of the worksheet in this preview, you gain a good sense of what the overall printed page will look like. Notice also that the entire worksheet no longer fits on one page.

Excel
BASICS

Displaying Formulas

1. Click the Tools menu, click Options, and click View.

2. Click Formulas so that a check mark appears in the box.

3. Click OK to view formulas.

4. Click the Tools menu, click Options, and deselect Formulas in the View tab to return to display values.

Or

1. Press ⎈Ctrl + ⌐ to display formulas.

2. Press ⎈Ctrl + ⌐ again to redisplay values.

Figure 2.20 ◄
Viewing formulas

Working with Printouts

To preview a printout:

1. Click the Print Preview button.

2. Click the Zoom button to zoom in or out.

3. Click the Next button to preview other pages.

4. Click the Previous button to preview previous pages.

5. Click the Close button to return to the worksheet area.

To print formulas:

1. Display the formulas.

2. Click Print Preview.

3. Change Setup options, if desired.

4. Click Print.

To change page setup:

1. Click the File menu, click Page Setup, and click the Page tab.

2. Click the desired orientation.

3. Set the Scaling option.

4. Click Print Preview to verify selected options.

5. Click Setup to change page setup or click Print to print the worksheet.

---

7. Click the **Zoom button** [Zoom].

Excel enlarges the display; now you can see the worksheet text.

8. Click the **Zoom button** [Zoom] again to return the display to the full-page view.

Notice that the status bar reads Preview: Page 1 of 3—meaning that the worksheet will be printed on three pages.

9. Click the **Next button** two times.

Excel displays the next pages of the worksheet.

10. Click the **Close button** on the Print Preview toolbar to close the Preview window.

Excel closes the preview screen, returning you to the worksheet area. Since the worksheet is too wide to fit on one page, you will need to change the page orientation.

11. Click **File** and click **Page Setup**.

The Page Setup dialog box appears.

12. If necessary, click the **Page tab**. In the Orientation section, click **Landscape**.

Now the worksheet will be positioned horizontally across the page.

13. In the Scaling section, click the **Fit to option** and verify that this option is set to 1 page(s) wide by 1 tall.

You have instructed Excel to fit all data in this worksheet onto one page.

14. Now click the **Print Preview button** in the Page Setup dialog box.

Now all of the worksheet appears on one page.

15. Click the **Print button** at the top of the Preview window.

16. Click **OK** in the Print dialog box.

A copy of the worksheet is printed. The printout will show formulas. Notice that Excel automatically reduces (scales) the type to fit the entire worksheet on one page.

17. To redisplay values, click the **Tools menu** and click **Options**.

18. On the View tab, click **Formulas** to remove the check mark and then click **OK**.

The worksheet returns to the original state.

19. Click **cell A1** and save and close the revised workbook.

ALIGNING DATA

As you've seen, text is automatically aligned on the left side of the cells, while numbers are aligned on the right. Changing this default alignment is easy. For example, you can center or right align a text label to align better with a column of numbers below. You can also center text or numbers across several cells. This feature works especially well when you want to center titles above your worksheet data.

Excel allows you to align data quickly with the click of a toolbar button or menu option. You can align one cell at a time or a range of cells. To add interest to your worksheet, you can also rotate data in a cell or range.

Aligning and Rotating Data

- To right align data, select the cell(s) and click the Align Right button.

- To left align data, select the cell(s) and click the Align Left button.

- To center data in a cell, select the cell(s) and click the Center button.

- To rotate data, select the cell(s), click Cells on the Format menu, click and hold the Degrees up or down arrow until the desired degree of rotation is displayed, and click OK.

Figure 2.21 ◀
Alignment tab of the Format Cells dialog box

You can use the rotation option in conjunction with any alignment styles except Fill and Center Across Selection.

Right Aligning, Rotating, Merging Cells, and Centering Text

In this activity, you'll improve the **Pet Paradise 3rd Quarter Sales** workbook by right aligning and rotating column labels, centering row labels, merging cells, and centering text across columns.

1. Open the **Pet Paradise 3rd Quarter Sales** workbook on your Student Data Disk.

Notice that all the text in this workbook file is left aligned in their cells, and all the numbers are right aligned in their cells.

2. Select the range **B5:F5**, the cells containing the column labels.

3. Click the **Align Right** button ▤ on the Formatting toolbar.

Excel right aligns the selected text. The labels now align with the numbers below them.

4. With range B5:F5 still selected, click **Cells** on the Format menu.

The Format Cells dialog box appears.

5. Click the **Alignment tab**.

The Alignment tab of the Format Cells dialog box is divided into three sections, as shown in Figure 2.21. The *Text alignment* section allows you to specify the horizontal and vertical placement of data in cells; the *Orientation* section allows you to specify the degree to which data can be rotated in cells; and the *Text control* section allows you to choose more specialized alignment features, such as wrapping text in cells and shrinking text to fit a cell.

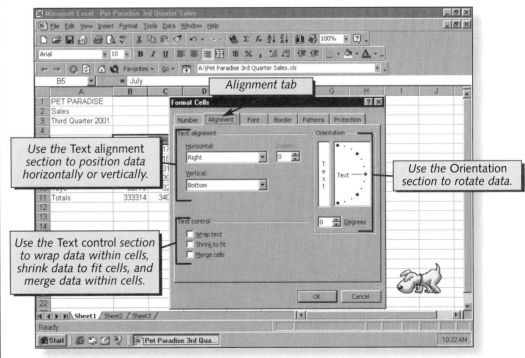

6. Click and hold the **Degrees up arrow** in the *Orientation* section of the dialog box until the angle of rotation reaches 30 degrees. Then release the mouse button.

7. Click **OK**.

Excel rotates the text in cells B5:F5 upward, placing it on a 30-degree angle.

Centering Data Across Columns

- To center data over two or more columns and merge the cells together, select the cells over which the data should be centered (including the cell that contains the data) and click the Merge and Center button.

- To center data over two or more columns without merging the cells together, select the cells over which the data should be centered (including the cell that contains the data), click Cells on the Format menu, click the Horizontal drop-down arrow in the Alignment tab, click Center Across Selection, and click OK.

Figure 2.22 ◀
Worksheet titles centered
across columns

To start text with one of the special characters usually associated with values (+, -, ., or =), first type an apostrophe (') and then the text.

8. Select cells **A6:A11**.

9. Click the **Center button** ▦.

Excel centers the selected text within each cell.

10. To merge and center the label in cell A1 across columns A through F, select the range **A1:F1**.

11. Click the **Merge and Center button** ▦.

12. To center the labels in cells A2:A3 across the columns, select the range **A2:F3**.

13. Click **Cells** on the Format menu.

The Format Cells dialog box appears.

14. If necessary, click the **Alignment tab**.

15. Click the **Horizontal drop-down arrow** and then click **Center Across Selection**.

16. Click **OK**.

Excel centers your text across the selected range, as shown in Figure 2.22.

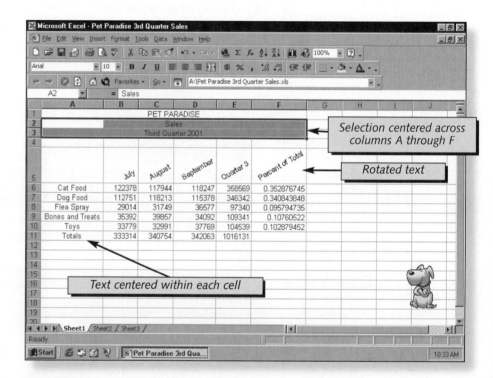

Warning

Use the Merge and Center button ▦ to center the contents of only one cell at a time. If you use the Merge and Center button ▦ to center more than one cell, you may lose some of your data.

Note

When you're using the Cells command on the Format menu to center text across a range, the text must be in the leftmost cell of the selected range. For example, you can't have text in cell B1 and center it across A1:D1. However, if you're using the Merge and Center button, the text can be in any of the selected cells because the cells are merged (or combined) into one cell.

17. Click **cell A1**.

The text *PET PARADISE* appears in the formula bar. This text is actually in cell A1.

18. Save your revised workbook as *Formatted Pet Paradise 3rd Quarter Sales* in the *Tutorial* folder on your Student Data Disk.

FORMATTING NUMBERS

The numbers you've entered in new worksheets so far have been displayed exactly as you have entered them, without commas or formatting of any type. You can, however, use ***numeric formats*** to change the way Excel displays numbers without changing the way Excel stores the numbers. Excel has many available numeric formats, including formats to add commas as thousands separators, to add dollar signs, and to display numbers as percentages. Several numeric formats also let you specify exactly how many decimal places are displayed. Formatting changes the appearance of the data; it does not change the data itself.

You can apply numeric formats in two ways. If you have simple needs, you can click a predefined ***style***—a combination of formats that has a specific name. An example of a style is Currency, which formats a value using a dollar sign, commas as thousands separators, and two decimal places, among other things. If you want to create a less common numeric format, you can specify it using the Format Cells dialog box.

Applying Numeric Formats

The Formatting toolbar contains several predefined numeric formats that you can apply with the click of a button. These predefined styles of numeric formats are shown in Table 2.3.

TABLE 2.3	PREDEFINED STYLES OF NUMERIC FORMATS	
Name	**Button**	**Function**
Currency Style	$	Applies the currency format to the selected cell(s).
Percent Style	%	Applies the percent format to the selected cell(s).
Comma Style	,	Applies the comma format to the selected cell(s).
Increase Decimal		Increases the decimal places displayed in the selected cell(s).
Decrease Decimal		Decreases the decimal places displayed in the selected cell(s).

The **Comma Style** displays numbers with commas and two decimal places. In **Currency Style,** Excel adds fixed dollar signs at the left side of the cell, and commas and two decimal places appear. In the **Percent Style,** Excel displays the selected numbers as percentages with no decimal places. To display more or fewer digits after a decimal point, click the Increase Decimal button 🔢 or the Decrease Decimal button 🔢. In most cases, when you apply any of these styles, Excel automatically increases the column width to accommodate the extra digits and symbols.

HANDS On

Applying Numeric Formats

1. Select the cells to which you want to apply a numeric format.
2. Click the appropriate numeric style button(s).

Hints & Tips

Text that is too wide to fit in a cell either spills into the adjacent cell (if it's empty) or is truncated (cut off). In contrast, *values* that are too wide for their cells are displayed either as # or in scientific notation. Numbers are not truncated because you're more likely to misread a truncated number. To display the number, you must widen the column.

Using Numeric Formats to Clarify Your Worksheet

In this activity, you'll apply predefined numeric formats to the **Formatted Pet Paradise 3rd Quarter Sales** workbook to improve readability and appearance.

1. Select the range **B6:E10**.
2. Click the **Comma Style button** 🔢.

Excel inserts commas as thousands separators and adds two decimal places in the selected range.

3. Click the **Decrease Decimal button** 🔢 two times.

Each number is displayed with commas but no decimal places.

4. Click **cell B6** and look at the formula bar.

Notice that a comma is displayed in the cell but not in the formula bar. The stored number (rather than the displayed number) is shown on the formula bar when a cell is active. Remember, formatting only affects the appearance of the data, not the data itself.

5. Select the range **B11:E11**.
6. Click the **Currency Style button** 🔢.

Most of the cells in range B11:E11 now contain dollar signs, thousands separators, and two decimal places. Cell D11, however, contains # signs as shown in Figure 2.23. These # signs indicate that the column is not wide enough to hold the number of digits, the comma, the dollar sign, and the two decimal places.

7. Click the **Decrease Decimal button** 🔢 two times.

By eliminating the two decimal places, you can now see all of the numbers in the range B11:E11.

8. Select cells **F6:F10**.
9. Click the **Percent Style button** 🔢.
10. Click the **Increase Decimal button** 🔢 once.

Even though Excel displays the numbers as percentages with one decimal place, it remembers the exact number and will display additional decimal places when you tell it to do so.

11. Click **cell A1** and save the revised workbook.

Figure 2.23
Numbers formatted as currency

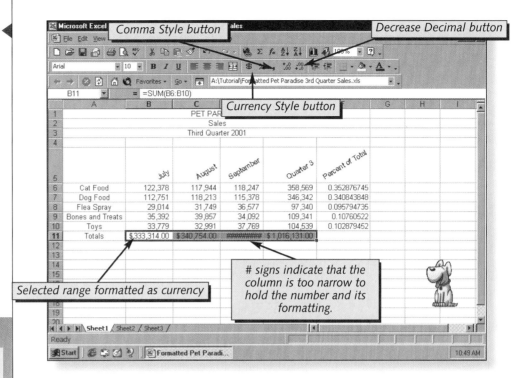

Selected range formatted as currency

 # signs indicate that the column is too narrow to hold the number and its formatting.

To make the Format Cells dialog box instantly accessible, you can add the Format Cells button to your Formatting toolbar. Click More Buttons at the right end of your Formatting toolbar, click Add or Remove Buttons, and click Cells. Click anywhere on your worksheet to close the button list. The Format Cells button 🖼 will appear on your Formatting toolbar.

FORMATTING YOUR WORKBOOK

After you've entered all your data, you'll want to spend some time formatting your workbook to make it look more professional. You can do this in several ways. You can modify font characteristics by selecting new typefaces; changing the size of text; and adding bold, italic, and underline styles. You can also add borders around cells, change the color of the background of cells, and change the color of the text within cells. The common font-enhancing options are available on the Formatting toolbar. If you want to make several formatting changes at once, use the Format Cells dialog box. As an example, in the Format Cells dialog box, you can choose a new typeface, a new font size, bold style, and a different color—all in one operation.

HANDS On

Modifying Your Workbook

In this activity, you'll format the **Formatted Pet Paradise 3rd Quarter Sales** workbook to improve the appearance.

1. Select the range B5:F5 and click the Bold button B.

Excel changes the text in the selected cells to bold type.

2. Click cell A1.

Remember, even though this text appears to be in cells C1 and D1, the text is actually in cell A1. You can check by looking at the formula bar.

3. Click the Font Size drop-down arrow [10].

Excel displays the Font Size list.

Changing Font Characteristics

1. Select the cell(s).

2. Click the appropriate toolbar button(s) to apply the formatting.

4. Click 14.

Excel changes the font size of the text in the selected cell.

5. Select cell A2 and click the Italic button ⊞.

Excel changes the text in the selected cell to italic type.

6. Click cell A11 and click the Bold button ⊞.

7. Click the Select All button above row heading 1 to select all of the cells in the workbook.

8. Click the Font drop-down arrow [Arial ▾].

9. Scroll the list of available fonts and click Times New Roman.

The selected text changes to Times New Roman. (The available fonts may vary depending upon your printer and installed fonts. If Times New Roman is not displayed in your list of available fonts, choose another font that is not Arial.)

10. Select cells A1:A3, and change the font to Arial.

The worksheet titles are changed back to the Arial typeface. Since you selected Times New Roman as the font for the rest of the worksheet, any new text you enter will be shown in Times New Roman.

11. Click any cell in the worksheet to deselect the range, and then right-click cell A3 and click Format Cells on the shortcut menu.

Excel displays the Format Cells dialog box.

12. Click the Font tab. Under Font style, click Italic. Click the Underline drop-down arrow and click Single.

Your dialog box should look like the one in Figure 2.24. Notice that the Preview window shows sample text as Arial, italic, 10 point, and underlined. (You can use bold, italic, underline, and strikethrough in any combination.)

Figure 2.24 ◀
Font tab of the Format Cells dialog box

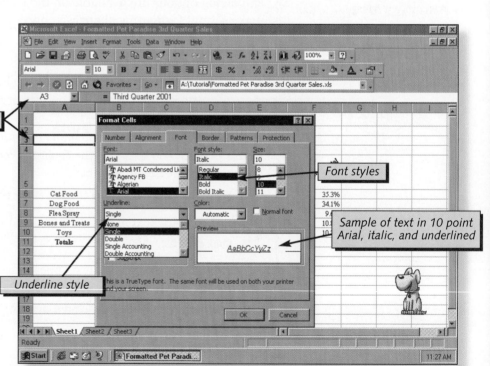

Cell A3 is selected.

Font styles

Sample of text in 10 point Arial, italic, and underlined

Underline style

You can apply formatting to empty cells. When you type data in those cells, Excel will format the data as you previously specified.

13. Click **OK** and then save your revised worksheet.

 *Changing the appearance of text in your worksheet may result in truncation if the column is not wide enough. For example, bold text takes up more horizontal space than regular text. When necessary, widen the columns appropriately.*

14. Select the range **B5:F5**. Click the **Borders drop-down arrow** on the Formatting toolbar. Click the **All Borders option**, as shown in Figure 2.25.

Figure 2.25
Selecting a border

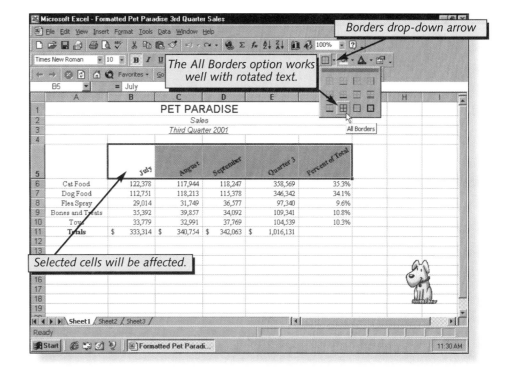

Excel
BASICS

Adding Borders and Background Colors

1. Select the range to which you want to add a border.

2. Click the Borders drop-down arrow.

3. Click the desired line style option.

4. Select the range whose background color you wish to change.

5. Click the Fill Color drop-down arrow.

6. Click the desired color square.

The All Borders option works well with rotated text. Note how the entire width of each cell is bordered—forming a continuous line. (You can see the border better if you deselect the range.) If you had used the text underlining feature instead, Excel would have underlined the text only, not the entire cell.

 *Remember that the type of border discussed here is a property of the cell rather than a property of the cell contents. In other words, if you delete underlined text, you delete both the text and the underline. But if you delete the contents of a bordered cell, you remove only the contents; the border remains. To remove a border, you must select the bordered cells, click the Borders drop-down arrow, and click the No Border option.*

15. Select **A10:F10** and click the **Borders drop-down arrow**. Click the **Bottom Double Border option**.

A continuous double underline appears at the bottom of cells A10:F10.

16. Select the range **A6:A10**. Click the **Fill Color drop-down arrow**. Click the **Light Yellow color square**, as shown in Figure 2.26.

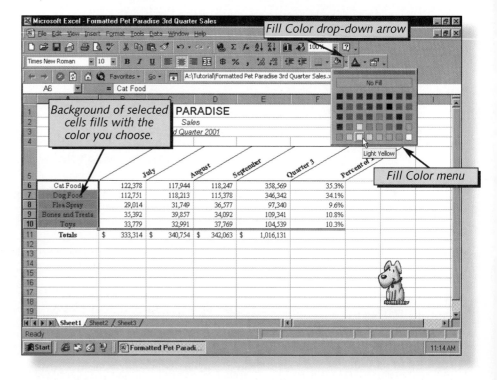

Figure 2.26 ◀
Shading a range with a
background color

Excel applies the background color (shading) you chose to the selected cells.

17. Click anywhere in the workbook to deselect the range. Save the revised workbook.

Clearing Cell Formats

Sometimes you may decide that you don't like the way portions of a worksheet look. If you want to change the formatting, there are several ways in which you can return the cell (or range) to its unformatted state. Select the cell(s) whose formatting you want to undo, point to Clear on the Edit menu, and then click Formats on the submenu. Or, you can click Style on the Format menu and then click Normal in the Style name box. The cell or range that is selected will be returned to "normal"—that is, Excel will remove all formatting. You can also clear cell formats on a worksheet by selecting None from the AutoFormats samples. If you want to remove only the most recent formatting changes, click the Undo button [↶] to restore the cell to its original state.

USING AUTOFORMATS AND CONDITIONAL FORMATTING

Applying shading, font characteristics, colors, and borders to your workbook one by one can take a lot of effort. Also, you may have trouble deciding just what combination of formatting characteristics to use. To make formatting easier and create professional-looking worksheets, you can use one of Excel's ready-made worksheet designs, which are called **AutoFormats.**

If you use AutoFormats a lot, you can add an AutoFormats button [AutoFormat...] to your Formatting toolbar. Select the range to be formatted and click the AutoFormats button on the Formatting toolbar to display the AutoFormats dialog box. Then select the AutoFormats sample you wish to use.

AutoFormats override any existing formatting. For example, if the selected text is bold, but you apply an AutoFormat that doesn't call for bold text, Excel removes the bold style.

You can also use *conditional formatting* to apply a specified format to cells that meet certain requirements. For instance, if operating expenses exceeded a certain amount, you could instruct Excel to bold the data. Conditional formatting overrides AutoFormats. Both Conditional Formatting and AutoFormat are options on the Format menu.

Applying an AutoFormat and Conditional Formatting

In this activity, you'll use the AutoFormat feature and conditional formatting in a workbook.

1. **Open the *Pet Paradise 2001 Sales* workbook on your Student Data Disk.**

2. **Save the file as *Pet Paradise 2001 Sales with AutoFormatting* in the *Tutorial* folder on your Student Data Disk.**

3. **Select the range A4:F10.**

4. **Click AutoFormat on the Format menu.**

Excel displays the AutoFormat dialog box, as shown in Figure 2.27. A sample of each format is displayed.

Using the AutoFormat Feature

1. Select the range to be formatted.

2. Click AutoFormat on the Format menu.

3. Click the sample of the format you wish to use.

4. Click OK to apply the format.

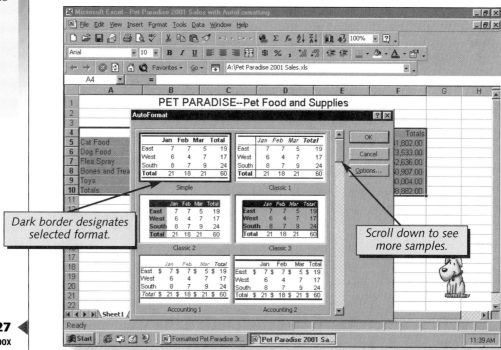

Figure 2.27
AutoFormat dialog box

Using Conditional Formatting

1. Select the range to be formatted if it meets the specified criteria.

2. Click Conditional Formatting on the Format menu.

3. Click the appropriate comparison operator in the second entry box.

4. Type the condition in the third box.

5. Click the Format button.

6. Click the options to be applied to the cells that meet the criteria.

7. Click OK to close the Format Cells dialog box.

8. Click OK to close the Conditional Formatting dialog box.

5. Click the **Classic 2 sample**.

A dark border surrounds the Classic 2 sample. If you click the Options button, you can deselect such formats as number, border, font, patterns, alignment, and width and height. Deselecting a format omits the designated feature from the AutoFormats. You'll be able to see the change in the samples.

6. Click **OK** to apply the format, and then click anywhere to deselect the range A4:F10.

Excel applies the selected format to your workbook

7. Select the range **B10:E10**.

8. Click **Conditional Formatting** on the Format menu.

The Conditional Formatting dialog box appears.

9. Click the **drop-down arrow in the second entry box**, and click **less than** to specify the comparison operator.

10. Press `Tab` and type 995000 in the third box.

11. Click the **Format button**. When the Format Cells dialog box appears, set the color as red and the font style as bold. Then click **OK**.

The Conditional Formatting dialog box reappears, displaying a preview of how the text will appear when the condition you specified (value is less than 995,000) is met.

12. Click **OK** in the Conditional Formatting dialog box.

As shown in Figure 2.28, two of the cells are shown with the special formatting to alert you of total sales below $995,000. (Deselect the cells to get a better look at them.)

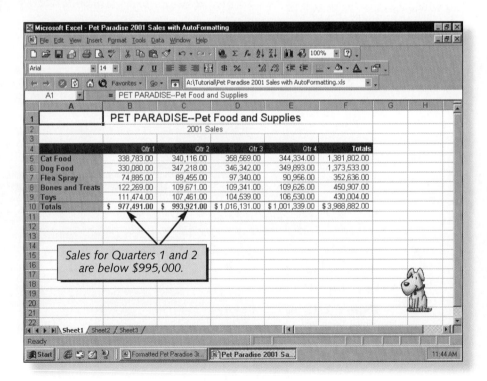

Figure 2.28
Formatting applied to cells that meet the condition

13. Change the amount of Flea Spray sales for Quarter 2 to 91455.

Since sales for the second quarter now exceed $995,000, the conditional formatting is removed from cell C10.

14. Click **cell A1** and save the revised workbook.

15. Print the workbook. Close all workbooks.

USING CHARTS IN EXCEL

Excel lets you display and work with charts in several ways. You can create charts right on your worksheet; these types of charts are called ***embedded charts.*** Embedded charts are displayed on the same workbook page that contains the numeric data on which the chart is based. In this lesson, you'll work primarily with embedded charts.

Elements of an Excel Chart

Figure 2.29 illustrates the elements that comprise a typical Excel chart. When you create an embedded chart, Excel automatically surrounds the chart with a border. Any area within this border that is "empty" is referred to as the chart area. An Excel chart has several elements: the chart title, the plot area, the data markers, the data labels, the legend, the x-axis (or category axis), and the y-axis (or value axis). Some of these elements are optional, such as the chart title, the legend, and the data labels. You can manipulate each element within a chart independently of the others—that is, you can resize, move, format, or even delete any element. Ask the Office Assistant for help with manipulating the elements of a typical chart.

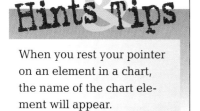

When you rest your pointer on an element in a chart, the name of the chart element will appear.

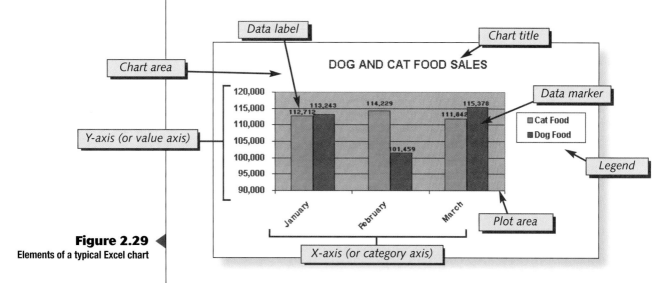

Figure 2.29
Elements of a typical Excel chart

HANDS On

CREATING CHARTS WITH THE CHART WIZARD

To create an Excel chart, you must first identify the worksheet data on which to base the chart. The ***data series*** is the set of related values you want to chart. A ***data point*** is one value in a data series. One of the easiest ways to create charts in Excel is to use the ***Chart Wizard.*** This tool asks a series of questions about the type of chart you want to create and builds a chart based upon your responses. When using this technique, you simply choose the data to be charted (the data series), start the Chart Wizard, and follow the instructions on screen. You can think of the Chart Wizard as a computerized questionnaire you complete for Excel to create the type of chart you want. If you have questions or run into trouble along the way, you can turn to the Office Assistant for help.

Creating a Pie Chart

In this activity, you'll build a pie chart based upon the January sales data in the ***Pet Paradise 1st Quarter Sales*** workbook.

1. Open the ***Pet Paradise 1st Quarter Sales*** workbook on the Student Data Disk.

2. Select cells **A5:B9** (the data series).

When selecting the data series to be charted, you can select cells that include descriptive text that you want to display on the chart, as well as cells that contain numbers.

3. Click the **Chart Wizard button** ⊞ on the Standard toolbar.

The Chart Wizard - Step 1 of 4 - Chart Type dialog box appears. This is the first of a series of four dialog boxes that gives you options from which to choose to create a chart. In this dialog box, you will select the type of chart to create.

4. In the Chart type box, click **Pie**.

The selections available in the Chart sub-type box change, and you can select from the variety of pie charts displayed. Pie charts are helpful for showing how various components contribute to the whole.

5. In the Chart sub-type box, click the **3-D pie chart** (the second option in row 1).

6. To preview your chart, click and hold the **Press and Hold to View Sample button**. Then release the mouse button.

7. Click the **Next button**.

The Chart Wizard - Step 2 of 4 - Chart Source Data dialog box appears, as shown in Figure 2.30. The data range that you selected on the worksheet (A5:B9) appears in the Data Range box. If you change your mind about which data to chart, you can change the range here.

Figure 2.30
Chart Wizard Step 2
dialog box

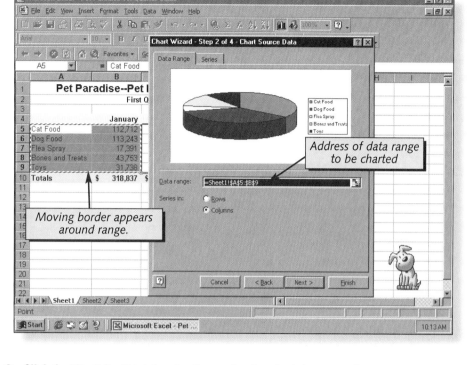

Excel BASICS

Using the Chart Wizard

1. Select the cells that contain the data to be charted (the data series).

2. Click the Chart Wizard button.

3. Click the type of chart you wish to create and click Next.

4. If necessary, change the range to be charted and then click Next.

5. Click the appropriate options in the Data Labels and Show Legend tabs.

6. Type a title in the Titles tab if desired and click Next.

7. Click the appropriate option to indicate where to store the chart.

8. Click Finish.

8. Click the **Next button**, leaving the previously selected range active.

The Chart Wizard - Step 3 of 4 - Chart Options dialog box appears. This dialog box allows you to add or change several features of the chart, including the title, the data labels, and the placement of the legend. (To return to a previous step in the Chart Wizard, click the Back button.)

9. Click the **Data Labels tab**, if it is not already selected.

10. Click **Show label and percent** in the Data labels box.

Labels and percentages for each slice of the pie appear in the preview window of the dialog box.

11. Click the **Legend tab** and deselect **Show legend**.

The legend disappears and the size of the chart increases.

12. Click the **Titles tab** and type Pet Paradise January Sales **in the Chart title box.**

After a moment, the title appears in the preview window.

13. Click the **Next button**.

The Chart Wizard - Step 4 of 4 - Chart Location dialog box appears. This dialog box allows you to insert the chart into the current worksheet or create a new sheet to hold the chart.

14. Click the **As object in option**, if it is not already selected, and click **Finish**.

Excel generates your pie chart and places it in the worksheet. The entire pie chart represents one data series—that is, sales of all items during the month of January—and is the charted version of the data range you specified in step 2 (cells A5:B9). One slice of the pie chart represents one data point, for example, cat food sales for January.

If the chart is covering the worksheet area, you can move it. Notice that the chart is selected—as indicated by the square *selection handles* that appear on the border of the chart. Thus, any commands or actions you issue will affect only this chart. (If the Chart toolbar appears, close it by clicking its Close button.)

15. **Click and hold the mouse button within the chart area, and drag the chart so that the top chart border is in row 13 and the left side starts in the middle of column A.**

To drag the entire chart and not just an object within the chart, be sure to click in the chart area, not any of the chart elements.

When you scroll down, your screen should resemble the one in Figure 2.31.

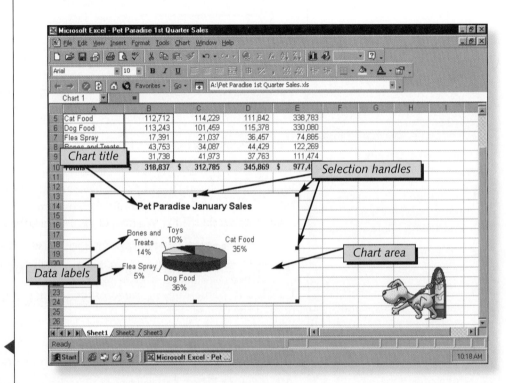

Figure 2.31
Moving the chart

16. **Rest your pointer on various elements of the chart.**

Notice the names of the chart elements appear.

17. **Click each chart element.**

Notice that selection handles surround each element. When selection handles appear around an element, you can manipulate that element independently of the other chart elements.

18. Click **cell A1** and save the workbook as *Pet Paradise 1st Quarter Sales Pie Chart* in the *Tutorial* folder on your Student Data Disk.

Excel saves the workbook file, along with the chart you just created. Saving a workbook automatically saves any charts within the workbook.

19. Close the workbook.

Test your knowledge by answering the following questions. See Appendix B to check your answers.

1. You must supply at least _____ numbers to use the AutoFill feature to complete a series of numbers.

2. The formula *=30-5*9+(3+17)* results in _____.

3. Functions consist of two parts: the name of the function, such as SUM, and the _____ of the function.

4. Cell references within copied formulas are known as _____ if they change to correspond to their new location.

5. _____ is a tool that asks a series of questions about the type of chart you want to create and builds a chart based upon your responses.

CREATING A WEB PAGE FROM AN EXCEL WORKBOOK

Assume you are the marketing manager for Chocolate Mania, a company that sells chocolates through catalogs. In this activity, you will create a Web page for Chocolate Mania that introduces their new line of reduced-calorie and reduced-fat items.

1. Open the *Chocolate Comparisons* workbook on the Student Data Disk.

A worksheet that shows comparisons between the regular and Lite items appears. Note that the page contains two charts that emphasize the differences.

2. Click **Web Page Preview** on the File menu. If necessary, click the **Maximize button** 🔲 in the upper-right corner of the preview window. Scroll to view the entire page.

Excel launches your Web browser and displays a preview of the page. This option allows you to preview how your page will appear in the browser before you save the file as a Web page. Note that both the worksheet data and the charts appear on the page and the formatting is carried over from Excel.

As you view the Web page, you decide to revise the workbook.

Variations of fonts, font sizes, and colors will catch the user's eye, so consider adding these enhancements to any worksheet that you will publish as a Web page.

3. Return to the *Chocolate Comparisons* workbook by clicking its Windows taskbar button.

4. Click **cell C5** and type 120 to replace the 100.

Notice that the first column in the first chart is automatically updated to reflect your change.

5. Click the column representing the Lite chocolate bar in the first chart.

All of the columns are selected, as indicated by the selection handles that appear.

6. Click the column representing the Lite chocolate bar in the first chart again.

Excel changes the selection handles so that only the column you click is selected.

7. Double-click the selected column.

The Format Data Point dialog box appears. Any changes you make in this dialog box will affect only the selected column.

8. On the Patterns tab, click the pale blue color square (row 5, column 6) and click **OK**.

The color of the selected column changes to pale blue.

9. **Click the column representing the Lite brownies in the first chart.**

10. **Click the Fill Color arrow**  **on the toolbar and click the pale blue color square.**

The color of the selected column changes to pale blue.

11. **Use the method used in steps 7-8 or in step 10 to change the rest of the columns in both charts that represent Lite products to pale blue.**

12. **Type your e-mail address in cell A36 and press** [Enter←].

If you do not have an e-mail address, ask your instructor what address you should type in this cell.

13. **Click Web Page Preview on the File menu.**

Excel switches to your Web browser and displays a preview of the page. The changes you made to the worksheet and the charts are reflected in the new page preview.

14. **While viewing the preview, click the hyperlink to your e-mail address.**

Your e-mail program launches, creating a new message addressed to you. Users of your Web page will be able to send e-mail to you using this link.

15. **Close the New Message window without sending a message.**

16. **Click the Chocolate Comparisons Windows taskbar button to return to the worksheet. Click cell A1 and click Save as Web Page on the File menu. (You may need to expand the File menu to view this option.)**

The Save As dialog box appears. Notice that the Save as type box indicates that the file will be saved in the Web Page (*htm* or *html*) format.

17. **Save the workbook as *Chocolate Comparisons Web Page* in the *Tutorial* folder on your Student Data Disk.**

Note *Excel automatically creates a Web page folder for all files associated with any Web page you create and save. You can view the folders and files in a Web page folder in Windows Explorer. Or, click Open on the File menu. In the Open dialog box, you must change the Files of type to All Files.*

Now that you've saved your workbook as a Web page, you can use your Web browser, in Excel or in any program that can read HTML files, to open the file.

18. **Click the Print Preview button** **to preview your printout. Make any necessary adjustments to fit your document on one page and then print your Web page.**

19. **Resave and close the Web page. Close your browser and exit Excel.**

Warning *You may proceed directly to the exercises for this lesson. If, however, you are finished with your computer session, follow the "shut down" procedures for your lab or school environment.*

Lesson Summary & Exercises

SUMMARY

After you've created a worksheet, you can make changes to that worksheet. You can rearrange your worksheet by inserting and deleting columns and rows, copying and moving data, and resizing columns and rows. You can use formulas and functions to perform calculations. Excel automatically recalculates the results of formulas that reference cells in which data has been changed. You can format your worksheet to make it look more professional. You can also use charts to display your data more efficiently. In addition, you can create a Web page from an Excel workbook.

Now that you have completed this lesson, you should be able to do the following:

- Select single cells and ranges of cells—including rows, columns, and the entire workbook page. (Excel-269)
- Select two or more noncontiguous ranges. (Excel-271)
- Erase the contents of one of more cells. (Excel-272)
- Cancel and restore changes. (Excel-274)
- Insert and delete cells, rows, and columns. (Excel-275)
- Move and copy the contents of one or more cells using toolbar buttons. (Excel-278)
- Move and copy the contents of one or more cells using the drag-and-drop method. (Excel-278)
- Change column widths and row heights. (Excel-280)
- Fill ranges with values using the AutoFill feature and the Fill, Series command. (Excel-282)
- Understand when to use formulas. (Excel-284)
- Use the arithmetic operators in formulas and understand operator precedence. (Excel-285)
- Create, revise, and copy formulas that contain values as well as cell references. (Excel-286)
- Use functions. (Excel-289)
- Display and print formulas in a worksheet. (Excel-292)
- Change the page setup options. (Excel-292)
- Align and rotate data. (Excel-295)
- Merge cells. (Excel-295)
- Apply various numeric formats. (Excel-298)
- Modify font characteristics such as sizes, styles, and typefaces. (Excel-299)
- Add borders. (Excel-301)
- Change the background color of a cell and the color of a cell's contents. (Excel-301)
- Copy and clear cell formats. (Excel-302)
- Apply predefined formatting to your worksheets using the AutoFormat command. (Excel-303)
- Use conditional formatting to automatically apply formatting to cells that meet specified criteria. (Excel-303)
- Identify the elements of a chart. (Excel-305)
- Create a chart using the Chart Wizard. (Excel-306)
- Create a Web page from an Excel workbook. (Excel-310)

CONCEPTS REVIEW

1 TRUE/FALSE

Circle T if the statement is true or F if the statement is false.

T F **1.** If you issue a command while a group of cells is selected, the command affects the entire group.

T F **2.** A range address contains four cell references—each representing a corner of the range.

T F **3.** You can drag selected cells to move their contents to other cells.

T F **4.** If you click a hyperlink to jump to a workbook that is not open, Excel automatically opens the workbook for you.

T F **5.** The Undo command can cancel up to 22 actions.

T F **6.** You can select a range of cells by clicking the first cell, holding Ctrl, and clicking the last cell.

T F **7.** Addition and subtraction operators are evaluated last in formulas.

T F **8.** A formula contains predefined commands; you simply fill in the cell references or values.

T F **9.** Functions usually refer to a range of cells, using the range address.

T F **10.** When you copy a formula from one cell to another, the relative cell references within the formula change to reflect the new position.

2 MATCHING

Match each of the terms on the left with the definitions on the right.

TERMS

1. select
2. hide
3. step value
4. start value
5. range address
6. range
7. AutoFormat
8. landscape orientation
9. AutoFill
10. Undo

DEFINITIONS

a. To temporarily remove a column or row from a worksheet

b. Value that tells Excel by how much to increment when filling a selected range of cells

c. Feature that enables you to automatically fill a group of selected cells with data

d. To highlight one or more cells so they will be affected by the following action

e. A predefined format provided by Excel

f. Feature you can use to change your mind about the last action you performed

g. Option that you choose to print a page horizontally on the paper

h. Value that tells Excel the initial value to use in a selected group of cells to be filled with data

i. A group of adjacent cells

j. Set of two cell references, separated by a colon, that identifies a group of cells

Lesson Summary & Exercises

3 COMPLETION

Fill in the missing word or phrase for each of the following statements.

1. To select noncontiguous ranges, select the first range and then press and hold _____ while clicking to select additional ranges.

2. When operators have the same level of precedence, they are evaluated from _____ to _____.

3. You can use the _____ command to reverse the effects of your most recent action.

4. You press _____ while dragging to copy rather than to move data.

5. If you type letters and numbers, Excel considers the entry to be _____; if you type only digits, Excel considers the entry to be a(n) _____.

6. By default, numbers are aligned on the _____, and text is aligned on the _____.

7. If you want to insert a row, select the row below where you want the new row and then click the _____ command on the _____ menu.

8. To delete the contents of a column but not the column itself, click the column heading and press _____.

9. If you move to a cell and type *1*, Excel assumes you are entering a(n) _____. If you go on to type *1st Quarter*, Excel treats this entry as _____.

10. To display formulas instead of results, click _____ on the menu bar, click _____, and then click _____ in the View tab.

4 SHORT ANSWER

Write a brief answer to each of the following questions.

1. Suppose you have a document that doesn't quite fit on a single page. Describe at least two ways you could try to fit it on a single page.

2. What is one primary difference between text and values?

3. Describe one situation in which you would press Delete and another in which you would use the Delete option on the Edit menu.

4. What is the quickest way to enter the text Monday, Tuesday, Wednesday, Thursday, Friday, Saturday, Sunday?

5. Write the number 6591.73 in at least three different numeric formats.

6. Name at least two keys you can use to finalize data entry.

7. Describe at least two different ways you could change the word *aligator* to *alligator* after you typed the word in a cell and pressed Enter ↵ .

8. Briefly describe the Copy, Cut, and Paste commands. List three ways of executing each command.

9. What technique could you use to select the range A5:B10? Columns A through D? Rows 3 and 7?

10. What is the difference between the AutoFill feature and the Fill, Series command on the Edit menu? When is it better to use one rather than the other?

Lesson Summary & Exercises

5 IDENTIFICATION

Label each of the elements in the Excel window in Figure 2.32.

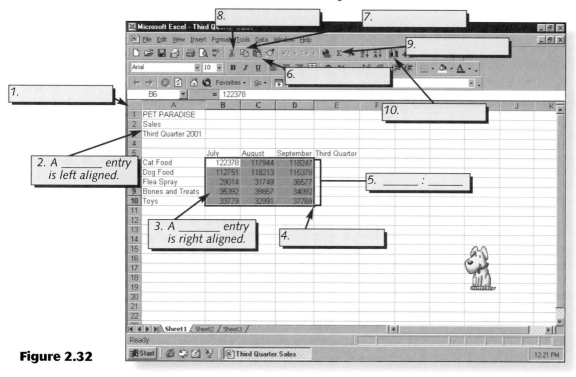

Figure 2.32

SKILLS REVIEW

Complete each of the Skills Review problems in sequential order to review the Excel skills to select ranges of cells, erase data, undo and redo changes, rearrange your worksheet, fill ranges, create and copy formulas and functions, display and print formulas, format data, and create a chart.

1 Select a Range of Cells

1. Open the **Updated Surfside Employee List** workbook on your Student Data Disk.

2. Click **cell A5**.

3. Drag to select through **cell C11**. The cells containing the employees' names and pay rates are now selected.

4. Click **cell A5** again.

5. Press and hold ⇧ Shift ; then click **cell D11**. The cells containing the employees' names, pay rates, and hire dates are now selected (Figure 2.33).

Figure 2.33

Lesson Summary & Exercises

2 Select Rows, Columns, and the Entire Worksheet

1. To highlight information about Daniel Longworth, click **row heading 6**. The entire row is highlighted.

2. To highlight the list of cities in which the employees live, click **column heading F**. The entire column is highlighted.

3. To select the entire worksheet, click the **Select All button** (located above row heading 1 and to the left of column heading A).

4. Click any cell to remove the highlighting from the worksheet.

3 Select Multiple Ranges

1. Select range **A7:D7**, the cells that contain some of the data for the employee hired in 1992.

2. Press and hold Ctrl and select cells **A10:D11**. Both ranges are selected so that you can easily compare the pay rates of those employees most recently hired to the rate of the employee who has been with the company the longest.

3. Click any cell to remove the highlighting.

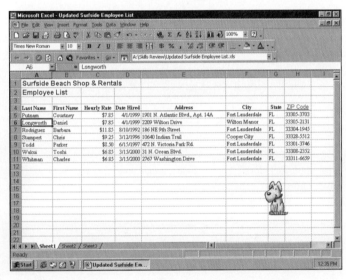

Figure 2.34

4 Erasing Data

1. Click **cell A5**.

2. Press Delete to erase the data in the cell.

3. Since Courtney Adams has changed her name, type Putnam in cell A5 and press Enter← (Figure 2.34).

4. Save the workbook as **_Revised Surfside Employee List_** in your **_Skills Review_** folder.

5 Reverse Changes

1. Click **cell C8**.

2. Type 9.45 to change Chris Stampert's pay rate; press Enter← to finalize the change.

3. Since you just realized that Chris Stampert's raise should not go into effect until next month, click the **Undo button** to change the pay rate back to 9.25.

4. After you cancel this change, your manager informs you that she is raising Chris's pay rate early. Redo the change by clicking the **Redo button**.

5. Add the information contained in Table 2.4 for an employee who will start working next week.

Lesson Summary & Exercises

6. After typing the information for the new employee, you learn that he has decided to take a position with another company. To quickly undo the typing you just entered, click the **triangle button next to the Undo button**, highlight the most recent actions that affect row 12, and click.

7. Click the **Save button** to save your changes.

TABLE 2.4	DATA FOR SKILLS REVIEW #5
Cell	**Data**
A12	Birch
B12	Owen
C12	6.85
D12	4/15/2000
E12	21 SE 8th Street
F12	Fort Lauderdale
G12	FL
H12	33316-1033

6 Insert and Delete Cells, Rows, and Columns

1. Click **row heading 9** to select the row that contains data for Parker Todd.

2. Since Parker has quit, click **Delete** on the Edit menu.

3. Click the **Save button** to save the change.

4. You need to rearrange your worksheet for some upcoming changes. First, click **row heading 7** to select the row that contains data for Barbara Rodriguez.

5. Click **Rows** on the Insert menu to insert a blank row.

6. Click **row heading 9** to select that row.

7. Click **Rows** on the Insert menu to insert another blank row.

8. Click **column heading A** to select the first column.

9. Click **Columns** on the Insert menu to insert a blank column.

10. Save the workbook.

7 Copy and Move Data

1. Select the range **B8:I8**.

2. Click the **Copy button**.

3. Click **cell B9**.

4. Press Enter.

5. You need to change the data in row 9 to reflect information for Barbara's daughter, who has just been hired. First click **cell C9**, type Mary, and press Tab.

6. Change Mary's hourly rate to **6.85** and her date of hire to **4/15/2000**.

7. Save the workbook.

8. Click **cell F11** to select it.

9. Click **Cells** on the Insert menu, click **Shift cells down** (if necessary), and click **OK**.

10. With the cell cursor still in cell F11 (which is now blank), click **Delete** on the Edit menu, click **Shift cells up** (if necessary), and click **OK**.

Lesson Summary & Exercises

11. Select range **B1:B2**, the cells that contain the worksheet titles.

12. Click the **Cut button** ✂.

13. Click **cell A1**.

14. Press ⌨Enter↵.

15. Select range **B5:I5**.

16. Point to the border of the selected range.

17. When the pointer takes the shape of an arrow, click and drag the selection to range **B7:I7**, and release the mouse button.

18. To delete the blank row, click **row heading 5** and then click **Delete** on the Edit menu.

19. Save the workbook.

8 Resize a Column and a Row

1. Select **column F**.

2. Point to **Column** on the Format menu.

3. From the submenu, click **AutoFit Selection**.

4. Point to the border between row headings 4 and 5.

5. Drag down to increase the row height to 18.00.

6. Save the workbook.

9 Use AutoFill and Fill, Series

1. Type 100 in cell A5 and press ⌨Enter↵.

2. Type 101 in cell A6 and press ⌨Enter↵.

3. Select **cells A5:A6**.

4. Drag the **fill handle** to cell A11 to automatically enter the other employee numbers. (Make sure the pointer changes to a black crosshair symbol.)

5. Since you have decided to assign employee numbers spaced in increments of 10, click the **Edit menu**, point to **Fill**, and click **Series** in the submenu.

6. Type 10 in the Step value box and click **OK**.

7. Click **cell A1** to remove the highlighting.

8. Save and close the workbook.

10 Use Formulas and Automatic Recalculation

1. Open the **Petty Cash** workbook on the Student Data Disk.

2. Click **cell E4**, type =D4, and press ⌨Enter↵.

3. In cell E5, type =E4-C5+D5 and press ⌨Enter↵.

4. Verify that you typed the formulas correctly in cells E4 and E5. Edit these cells, if necessary.

5. Click **cell E5** and click the **Copy button** 📋.

6. Select the range **E6:E17**.

7. Press [Enter ◄─┘] to paste the formula.

8. Click **cell C5** and change the amount in cell C5 to 11.50.

9. Press [Enter ◄─┘] and notice the recalculation of the result in cell E5.

10. Save the workbook as **Petty Cash Register** in the **Skills Review** folder on your Student Data Disk.

11. Print and close the revised workbook.

11 Use Functions

1. Open the **Personal Budget** workbook on your Student Data Disk.

2. Click **cell B6**.

3. To calculate the total monthly income, type =SUM(B4:B5) and press [Enter ◄─┘].

4. Select **cells E4:E19**.

5. Click the **AutoSum button** [Σ] to total the monthly expenses.

6. Click **cell E21** and click the **Paste Function button** [*fx*].

7. Click **Statistical** in the *Function category* box, click **AVERAGE** in the *Function name* box, and click **OK**.

8. In the Average dialog box, type E4:E19 in the Number1 box and click **OK**.

9. Notice that the average monthly expense is calculated (Figure 2.35).

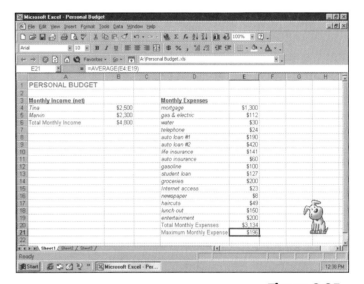

Figure 2.35

10. Click **cell A1** and save the revised workbook as **Sample Personal Budget** in the **Skills Review** folder on your Student Data Disk.

11. Print the workbook.

12 Display and Print Formulas and Change the Page Setup

1. With the **Sample Personal Budget** workbook still open, click the **Tools menu** and click **Options**.

2. Click the **View tab**, if necessary.

3. Click the **Formulas option** so that a check mark appears.

4. Click **OK**.

5. Click the **File menu** and click **Page Setup**.

6. Click **Landscape** in the Orientation section and click **Fit to** in the Scaling section.

7. Click the **Print Preview button** in the Page Setup dialog box.

8. Click the **Zoom button** to adjust the view.

9. Click the **Print button** and click **OK**.

10. Press `Ctrl` + `~` to deselect the Formulas option.

11. Close the workbook without saving it.

13 Format a Worksheet

1. Open the *Mercer Sales* workbook on your Student Data Disk.

2. Select cells **B5:C5** and click the **Align Right button** ▤.

3. Select **cell E5** and click the **Center button** ▤.

4. Select cells **A1:F1** and click the **Merge and Center button** ▦.

5. Select cells **A2:F3**. Click **Cells** on the Format menu, click the **Alignment tab**, and click **Center Across Selection** in the Horizontal box. Then click **OK**.

6. Save the workbook as *Formatted Mercer Sales* in the *Skills Review* folder on your Student Data Disk.

7. Select cells **B6:B16** and click the **Comma Style button** ▣.

8. Click **cell B17** and click the **Currency Style button** ▣.

9. Select cells **C6:C16** and click the **Percent Style button** ▣. Click the **Increase Decimal button** ▣ three times.

10. You decide you only want two decimal places shown for the percentages, so click the **Decrease Decimal button** ▣ once.

11. Select cells **F7:F9** and click the **Currency Style button** ▣.

12. Select cells **A5:E5** and click the **Bold button** ▣.

13. Click **cell E5** and click the **Underline button** ▣.

14. Click **cell A3** and click the **Italic button** ▣.

15. Click cells **A17:B17**. Click **Cells** on the Format menu, click the **Font tab**, click **Bold Italic** in the Font Style box, and click **OK**.

16. Click **cell A1** and click the **Font Size drop-down arrow** `10 ▾`. Click **14** to change the font size.

17. Select cells **A1:A3** and click the **Bold button** ▣.

18. Select cells **E5:F9**. Click the **Font drop-down arrow** `Arial ▾` and click **Times New Roman** from the list.

19. Select cells **A5:C5**. Click the **Borders drop-down arrow** ▣ and click the **Thick Bottom Border option**.

20. Select cells **A17:B17**. Click the **Borders drop-down arrow** ▣ and click the **Top and Double Bottom Border option**.

21. Select cells **E5:F9**. Click the **Fill Color drop-down arrow** ▣ and click the **Light Turquoise color square**.

22. With cells E5:F9 still selected, click the **Borders drop-down arrow** ▣ and click the **Thick Box Border option**.

23. Right-click **cell A1** and click **Format Cells** on the shortcut menu. Click the **Patterns tab** and click the aqua color square (in the third row, fifth column of the color palette).

24. Click the **Font tab**, click the **Color drop-down arrow**, and click the **White color square**. Then click **OK**.

25. Select cells **A2:A3**. Click the **Font Color drop-down arrow** 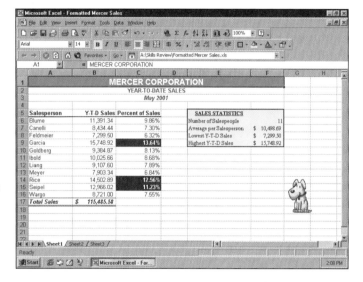 and click the **Teal color square**.

26. Save the revised workbook.

14 Apply Conditional Formatting

1. With the *Formatted Mercer Sales* workbook still open, select cells **C6:C16**.

2. Click **Conditional Formatting** on the Format menu.

3. Click the **drop-down arrow on the second entry box** and click **greater than**.

4. Type .10 in the third entry box.

5. Click the **Format button**.

6. In the Format Cells dialog box, click **Bold** in the Font style box. Click the **Color drop-down arrow** and click the **White option**.

7. Click the **Patterns tab** and click the violet color square (in the third row, seventh column of the color palette). Click **OK** to close the Format Cells dialog box.

8. Click **OK** to close the Conditional Formatting dialog box. Click **cell A1** to deselect the range. The conditional formatting affects the cells that contain a value greater than 10 percent (Figure 2.36).

9. Save the revised workbook.

10. Print and close the workbook.

Figure 2.36

15 Apply AutoFormats

1. Open the *Sales by Department* workbook on your Student Data Disk.

2. Select cells **A4:E11**.

3. Click **AutoFormat** on the Format menu.

4. Click the **Accounting 2 sample** and click **OK**.

5. Deselect the range to see the formatting.

6. Save the revised workbook as *Sales by Department with AutoFormatting* in the *Skills Review* folder on your Student Data Disk.

7. Print and close the workbook.

16 Use the Chart Wizard

1. Open the *Mason Y-T-D Business Expenses* workbook on your Student Data Disk.

2. Select cells **A5:A9**. Then press and hold Ctrl and select cells **H5:H9**.

Lesson Summary & Exercises

3. Click the **Chart Wizard button** 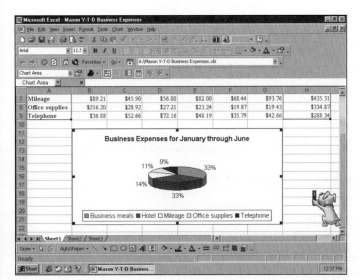.

4. In the Chart type box, click **Pie**.

5. In the Chart sub-type box, click **3-D pie** (the second option in row 1).

6. Click the **Press and Hold to View Sample button** to see a preview of your chart.

7. Click **Next**.

8. Leave the data range setting as is and click **Next**.

9. Click the **Titles tab**, if necessary, and type Business Expenses for January through June in the Chart title box.

10. Click the **Data Labels tab** and click the **Show percent option**.

11. Click the **Legend tab** and click **Bottom** in the Placement box.

12. Click **Next**.

13. Click the **As object in option** in the last dialog box, if necessary, and click **Finish**.

14. Drag the bottom-right corner selection handle down and to the right to enlarge the chart a bit.

15. Drag the middle-right selection handle to the right to widen the chart so that the chart title fits on one line.

16. Drag the chart to center it below the workbook data (Figure 2.37).

Figure 2.37

17. Click **cell A1**, and save the workbook as *Mason Expenses Pie Chart* in the *Skills Review* folder on your Student Data Disk.

18. Close the workbook.

LESSON APPLICATIONS

1 Change the Data, Rearrange the Worksheet, Highlight Ranges, and Format the Worksheet

Using an existing worksheet, correct errors, add a row and a column, select ranges to analyze top performers, resize a row and column, and apply formatting.

1. Open the *Signature Drive* file in the *Lesson Applications* folder on your Student Data Disk.

2. Change the number of signatures obtained by Goldsmith to 112 and the number of hours worked to 12.

3. Insert a row before the row that contains the data for Stoll.

4. Type data for a participant named Siegel in the new row. Siegel collected 187 signatures and worked 12 hours.

5. Between the Signatures and Hours columns add a new column called *Days*. In the Days column, enter 8, 15, 11, 6, 17, 7, 12, 5, 8, 13, and 14 to represent the total number of days each person has worked.

6. In cell A1, make the text bold and the font size 14.

7. Select A1:D1 and merge and center the title.

8. With that range still selected, change the background color to Turquoise.

9. Select A3:D3 and underline the titles.

10. Center the title in cell A3.

11. Right align the titles in cells B3:D3.

12. Use the AutoFit feature to increase the width of column 1.

13. Drag to increase the row height of row 4 to add space below the titles.

14. Click cell A15 and type Total.

15. In cell A16, type Average.

16. Click cell A1 and save the workbook as ***Formatted Signature Drive*** in the ***Lesson Applications*** folder on your Student Data Disk.

2 Use Formulas and Functions, Copy Formulas, and Apply Formatting

Use the worksheet from Lesson Application 1 to create and copy formulas, insert functions, and add borders and background colors.

1. With the ***Formatted Signature Drive*** workbook still open, click cell B15. Use the SUM function to total cells B4:B14.

2. Using the Copy and Paste method, copy the formula in cell B15 to cell C15.

3. Use the AutoSum feature to total cells D4:D14.

4. In cell B16, enter a function that determines the average for cells B4:B14.

5. Drag the fill handle to copy the average formula to cells C16 and D16.

6. Apply a Bottom Double Border to cells A14:D14.

7. Apply a Lavender background color to cells A15:D16, as shown in Figure 2.38.

8. Save your file.

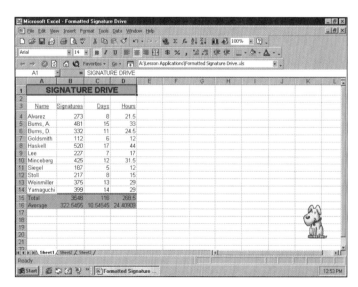

Figure 2.38

Lesson Summary & Exercises

3 Apply AutoFormatting and Conditional Formatting

Quickly format a workbook by applying a predesigned AutoFormat. Then add conditional formatting to alert you to a low number of signatures.

1. With the **Formatted Signature Drive** workbook still open, select cells A3:D16 and apply the Classic 2 AutoFormat style. Deselect the range to view the formatting.

2. Apply conditional formatting to indicate signatures less than 200. Select cells B4:B14, type the criteria in the Conditional Formatting dialog box, and specify formatting of pink, bold italic text if the cell meets the condition.

3. Save the revised workbook as **Signature Drive with Conditional Formatting** in the **Lesson Applications** folder on your Student Data Disk and close the file.

4 Apply Numeric Formatting

Format the **Homes Sold** workbook by applying comma, currency, and percentage numeric formats.

1. Open the **Homes Sold** workbook on your Student Data Disk.

2. Format cells D6:D29 with commas and no decimal places.

3. Format cells G6:H29 as currency with no decimal places.

4. Format cells I6:I29 as percentages with one decimal place.

5. Deselect the range and save the workbook as **Formatted Homes Sold** in the **Lesson Applications** folder on your Student Data Disk. Close the workbook.

5 Display Formulas, Change Page Orientation, and Create a Bar Chart with the Chart Wizard

View the formulas in a workbook and change page orientation so the formulas will print on one page. Use the Chart Wizard to create a 3-D bar chart from the sales data in the workbook.

1. Open the **Chocolate Sales** workbook on your Student Data Disk.

2. Use the Options command on the Tools menu to display formulas.

3. Change the page orientation and scaling so the worksheet fits on one page. Preview and print the worksheet while the formulas are displayed.

4. Display the values again.

5. Select the cells that contain the month names, product names, and sales data.

6. Use the Chart Wizard to create a 3-D clustered bar chart with the title *First Quarter Sales*.

7. Place the chart as an object in the worksheet.

8. Drag the chart below the worksheet data and enlarge it.

9. Click cell A1 and save the revised workbook as **Chocolate Sales Bar Chart** in the **Lesson Applications** folder on your Student Data Disk.

10. Close the workbook.

PROJECTS

1 A Burst of Sales

You would like to track sales of your home-based business—selling and decorating with balloons. Create a new workbook. Enter the title BALLOON SALES in the upper-left corner of your worksheet.

Skip a row and enter the data shown in Table 2.5, using the AutoFill technique or the Fill, Series command whenever possible. Check the spelling of text entries in the worksheet. Print one copy of the worksheet. Save the file as **Balloon Sales** in the **Projects** folder on your Student Data Disk. Send the workbook in an e-mail to your instructor.

TABLE 2.5	BALLOON SALES					
Jan	Feb	Mar	Apr	May	Jun	Jul
202	212	222	232	242	252	262
204	214	224	234	244	254	264
206	216	226	236	246	256	266
208	218	228	238	248	258	268
210	220	230	240	250	260	270

2 Identify the Colors

Open the **Balloon Sales** file in the **Projects** folder on your Student Data Disk, if it is not already open. Insert a new column to the left of the Jan column. Type the following text into the new column, beginning in cell A4: Red, Green, Blue, Yellow, Purple.

Change the number of red balloons sold in June to 253, and change the number of purple balloons sold in January to 347. Add rows for Orange and Polka-Dotted balloons to the worksheet, placing these two rows directly below the row for red balloons. Fill the Orange row with the values 123, 234, 345, 456, 567, 678, and 789 from left to right. Since the same number of yellow balloons and polka-dotted balloons were sold, copy the numbers from the Yellow row to the Polka-Dotted row. Widen column A so you can see the Polka-Dotted label in full. Increase the height of row 4. Undo your last step. Move the BALLOON SALES heading in cell B1 to cell A1.

Since you've decided to show only sales of balloons for the first half of the year, delete all of the data in the Jul column. Lastly, move the row containing data for Polka-Dotted balloons to appear as the last row, immediately following the data for the purple balloons. Delete the blank row. Remember to verify the spelling of all text entries in the worksheet. Print one copy of the revised **Balloon Sales** file. Move the cursor to cell A1. Save and close the file.

3 Setting Goals

You are the national sales manager for Good Life Insurance Company. Your manager has asked you to analyze the sales made over the past year and set realistic goals for each region for the next three years. Create a new workbook

Lesson Summary & Exercises

that contains the information provided in Table 2.6. Enter an appropriate title for the worksheet. (Do not enter commas in any numbers.)

TABLE 2.6	GOOD LIFE INSURANCE COMPANY		
ANNUAL SALES, YEAR 2001			
Region	No. Of Agents	No. Of Sales	Amount Of Sales
East	15	1500	750000
Southeast	12	1650	891000
Midwest	33	3600	1674000
Central	12	1300	517400
West	37	3900	1786200
Southwest	24	2400	1231200

Save the workbook as **Good Life Sales** in the **Projects** folder on your Student Data Disk. Adjust the sizes of columns B, C, and D to fit the data in them.

Copy the data in range A4:A10 and paste it below the worksheet data, starting in cell A14. In cell B14, enter a label of **2001 Sales** and copy the appropriate data for each region.

In cells C14, D14, and E14 enter labels of **2002 Goals**, **2003 Goals**, and **2004 Goals**. Select cells B15:E20. Issue the Fill, Series command and enter a step value of 1.05. In the Series dialog box, click the Rows option and the Growth option. This combination of selections will increase each value by five percent per year. Click OK to see the results. Remember to verify the spelling of all text entries in the worksheet. Print the **Good Life Sales** workbook. Move the cursor to cell A1 and save the workbook.

Select cells A4:B10. Use the Chart Wizard to create a 3-D pie chart. Accept all defaults and place the chart as an object in the worksheet. Move and resize the chart below the data. Save the revised file as **Good Life Sales Pie Chart** in the **Projects** folder on your Student Data Disk. Close the workbook.

4 Tracking Inventory

You work as the office manager at USA Computer Center. You have been asked to create a worksheet to track inventory of the computers, printers, and monitors in stock. Create a new workbook. Enter the company name in cell A1 and Inventory in cell A2. Starting in cell A4, enter the information in Table 2.7. Use the techniques you have learned. Edit the cells as necessary for accuracy.

After the existing columns, add a column called Profit. In the Profit column, enter a formula that subtracts the cost of each item from its price; copy the formula to all appropriate cells. Save the workbook as **USA Computer Inventory** in the **Projects** folder on your Student Data Disk.

In column A of the row directly below the last product (probably cell A16), type Total Profit. In column F of that same row, type a SUM function that totals the profit of all of the products.

TABLE 2.7	TYPES OF PRODUCTS SOLD			
Type	**Stock No.**	**Quantity**	**Cost**	**Price**
Computer	C250	22	800	999
Computer	C350	13	1040	1299
Computer	C450	15	1520	1899
Computer	C550	19	2070	2599
Monitor	M100	20	210	259
Monitor	M200	6	385	479
Monitor	M300	18	425	529
Printer	P60	10	320	399
Printer	P70	12	560	699
Printer	P80	17	720	899
Printer	P90	3	1120	1399

Below the existing rows, type the labels Average Computer Price, Average Monitor Price, and Average Printer Price. Next to each label, create a function that computes the average price of each type of product. Verify your formulas. Explore Help, if necessary. Print the workbook on one sheet of paper. Click cell A1, and then save and close the workbook.

5 How Many Items Did You Sell?

Create a new workbook. In cell A1, type Bead Bag Sales and in cell A2, type Sales by Product. Using the data in Table 2.8, enter the column labels in row 4 and enter the actual data items beginning in cell A5.

TABLE 2.8	BEAD BAG SALES DATA		
Product	**Quantity Sold**	**Sales Amount**	**Percent Of Sales**
Necklaces	1587	47690.19	.3924
Earrings	2302	46045.90	.3789
Bracelets	644	14148.17	.1164
Anklets	310	4030.67	.0332
Pins	299	4485.34	.0369
Watches	79	5135.22	.0423
Total Sales			

Adjust the column widths so you can see all the data. Create a formula to total the sales amount of each product. Center the worksheet titles across the columns of data. Format the numbers in the Quantity Sold column with commas and no decimal places; format the numbers in the Sales Amount column as currency; and format the numbers in the Percent of Sales column as percentages with one decimal place. Center the numbers in the Percent of Sales column.

Use bold type for the worksheet titles and column labels, and use italic type for each product name. Enlarge the text in cell A1 to 16 point and change it to violet (dark purple) text in the Times New Roman font; change the text in cell A2 to 14 point, underlined, Times New Roman. Add a thick bottom border under the column labels. Format the Total Sales label and amount as bold italic.

Resize column A to an appropriate width, and size columns B, C, and D so that they are all the same width. Align each column label appropriately over its data. Preview the workbook and center it horizontally on the page. Click cell A1 and save the workbook as *Bead Bag Sales* in the *Projects* folder on your Student Data Disk. Print the workbook.

Select the cells that contain the column and row labels, the numeric data, and the totals. Format this portion of the workbook using the 3D Effects 1 AutoFormat. Use conditional formatting to warn of sales amounts less than $10,000 by changing the font color to red and the font style to bold. Display the formulas. Change the page orientation to landscape and preview the worksheet. Verify the worksheet will fit on one page. Print the workbook. Display the values again and then save the worksheet.

Select cells A4:B10. Create a 3-D pie chart to display the quantity of each product sold. Place the chart as an object in the worksheet and move the chart as necessary. Click cell A1 and save the workbook as *Bead Bag Sales Pie Chart* in the *Projects* folder on your Student Data Disk.

6 How Will It Look on the Web?

As a real estate agent for Payton Properties, Inc., you've proposed the idea of publishing a Web site to advertise homes. Your supervisor isn't very familiar with the Internet and wants you to create a prototype of what a Web page would look like. To create a sample, first open the *Milford Lane* workbook on your Student Data Disk. Add the company's name above the data for the house and remove the selling price data. Change the color and size of the text and make any other formatting changes that you think will improve the appearance of the worksheet. Import a photo of the property to the right of the worksheet data—the photo is stored in the *House Photo* file on the Student Data Disk. Resize and move the photo as necessary to enhance the appearance of your worksheet. Use the Web Page Preview command on the File menu to view the worksheet as a Web page. Return to the worksheet to make any additional changes; then preview the Web page again. When you are satisfied with the page, use the Save as Web Page command and save the workbook as *Milford Lane Web Page* in the *Projects* folder on your Student Data Disk. Print preview the Web page and scale it to fit on one page, if necessary. Print the Web page. Close the file and the browser.

Now reopen the *Milford Lane Web Page* and click Web Page Preview on the File menu. Click Open on the File menu of your browser. Browse and locate the *Milford Lane Web Page* folder on your Student Data Disk. View the list of Web page files in the folder. (Hint: Change the Files of type to All Files.) Open one of the image files. Close the browser and all open files.

Project in Progress

7 Adding Sales Data and Formatting Your Workbook

As the owner of a small business that provides writing, editing, and training services, you track your sales in a workbook. Open the **_Updated I-Comm Sales_** workbook in the **_Projects_** folder on your Student Data Disk. Insert a row above row 8. In the new row, type the data provided in Table 2.9.

TABLE 2.9	SALES DATA
Cell	**Data**
A7	Promotional materials
B7	3500
C7	2405
D7	1760
E7	3190
F7	2580
G7	1600
H7	2000
I7	2450
J7	3040
K7	1780
L7	2075
M7	1700

Change the text in cell A5 to News articles and change the amount in cell G9 to 250. Adjust the width of column A so that its data fits in it nicely. Remember to verify the spelling of all text entries in the worksheet.

You want to calculate total sales per month as well as total sales per category. Type Totals in cell A10 and create and copy a formula to calculate total sales for each month. Then type Totals in cell N4 and calculate total sales for each category of sales. Be sure to calculate the total of all the monthly sales as well. In cells A13:A15, type the labels Average Monthly Sales, Highest Monthly Sales, and Lowest Monthly Sales. In cells B13:B15, use the AVERAGE, MAX, and MIN functions to calculate the appropriate value for each of these labels. Calculate total fees on the second and third worksheets. Click cell A1 on the Total Sales worksheet. Save the revised workbook as **_Formatted I-Comm Sales_** in the **_Projects_** folder on your Student Data Disk.

Format the Total Sales worksheet as desired to improve the appearance of the worksheet. Format all cells that contain dollar amounts as currency with no decimal places. Use conditional formatting to highlight the cells that contain monthly totals below $6,000. Align column labels and the title as desired. Change column widths, if necessary, and make any other formatting adjustments to improve the appearance of the Total Sales worksheet. Change the orientation of the Total Sales worksheet to fit onto one page. Print all three worksheets. Use the Chart Wizard to create a clustered column chart to show the sales for each category for all 12 months. Save and close the revised workbook.

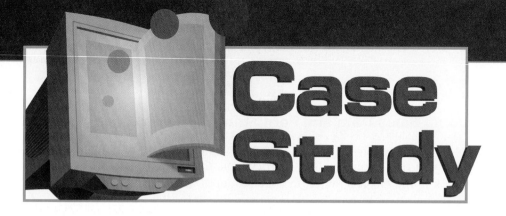

Overview: Congratulations! You have completed the lessons in the Excel tutorial and now have the opportunity in this capstone project to apply the Excel skills you have learned. You will plan and create a workbook that acts as an electronic check register. As you create the check register, try to incorporate the following skills:

- Create and save a workbook.
- Enter and edit data.
- Fill ranges with values.
- Insert columns and rows.
- Adjust column widths and row heights.
- Create and copy formulas.
- Format numbers and text.
- Move among worksheets.
- Rename worksheets.

- Affect several worksheets in a group.
- Add borders and shading.
- Search the Internet.
- Create hyperlinks to a Web site.
- Use functions.
- Chart data.
- Preview and print a workbook.
- Use Excel Help

Instructions: Follow these instructions to create your workbook for this case study.

1. Create a new workbook and save it as *Check Register Case Study* in the *Projects* folder on your Student Data Disk.

2. Record the entries provided in Table CS.1.

3. Create a formula in a new column to calculate the checkbook balance. Copy this formula to the appropriate cells to show the new balance each time an entry is recorded.

TABLE CS.1	FEBRUARY WORKBOOK DATA			
DATE	CHECK NO.	DESCRIPTION	AMOUNT OF CHECK	AMOUNT OF DEPOSIT
2/1/2001		Initial deposit		900.00
2/5/2001	501	Century Rentals - rent pmt.	450.00	
2/7/2001	502	Hilltop Grocery	62.87	
2/15/2001	503	Mt. Hollister Bank - car pmt.	219.25	
2/20/2001	504	Michelle Ramos - concert tickets	52.75	
2/23/2001	505	JQ Loan Corp. - student loan pmt.	125.15	

4. Your employer directly deposits your paycheck (in the amount of $790.00 for each paycheck) to your account on the 15th and 28th of each month. Insert rows to reflect the deposits for February.

5. On another sheet of your workbook, record entries for your rent, car, and student loan payments for the month of March using check numbers 506, 508, and 509. All of these payments are constant from month to month. Also record your direct deposits. Insert the ending balance from February as your first entry. (Hint: Use Copy and Paste or explore Help to find a formula to reference a cell on another worksheet.)

6. On a third sheet of your workbook, record the ending balance from March as your first entry, and record entries for your rent, car, and student loan payments using check numbers 511, 512, and 514. Also record your direct deposits.

7. Rename each sheet with an appropriate name.

8. Record the entries provided in Table CS.2.

TABLE CS.2	MARCH AND APRIL WORKBOOK DATA			
DATE	CHECK NO.	DESCRIPTION	AMOUNT OF CHECK	AMOUNT OF DEPOSIT
3/8/2001	507	The Book Stop	18.97	
3/13/2001		Deposit - birthday gift		45.00
3/26/2001	510	Harris Bike Shop	10.18	
4/18/2001	513	Hilltop Grocery	56.90	
4/23/2001	515	Pizza Castle	9.99	
4/27/2001	516	Rollins Insurance Co. - auto ins.	432.18	

9. Format the numbers and text in all three worksheets appropriately. (Hint: To ensure consistency, group the worksheets first.) Ask the Office Assistant for help on affecting several worksheets at one time. Use at least two fonts and two sizes. Add borders and shading to the check register, and include a title on each sheet.

10. You are thinking about buying a new car. Create a fourth worksheet and search the Web to find bank sites and car loan interest rates. Insert a hyperlink on the fourth sheet that links to at least one Web site that proves to be useful.

11. Create a fifth worksheet that contains the totals of the various expenditures during the months of February through April. Include categories for rent, car payment, groceries, student loan payment, auto insurance, and miscellaneous. Then create a 3-D pie chart that illustrates the percentage of your money spent on these expenses.

12. Rename the fourth and fifth worksheets appropriately. Review your workbook and make any changes that will improve its appearance or accuracy.

13. Preview the workbook, make any necessary adjustments, and print the entire workbook.

14. Save and close the workbook.

Access 2000

Managing the "Infoglut"

Data warehousing and data mining offer a new approach

For many corporations, data is their lifeblood. For years, companies have collected, sorted, stored, and spit out vast amounts of data about their customers, products, inventories, employees, sales, and stores. They also store external data about their competitors and their industry. This data is crucial for managers, employees, and executives to better understand their organization and industry.

All this collected data—this *infoglut*—raises two major issues that affect companies all around the world: Where's the best place to store all this data? And once we have it stored, how can we access it efficiently? The usual approach to managing infoglut is to maintain well-designed databases. At some point, however, the law of diminishing returns comes into play—there is just too much information, and it simply is not practical to create a new database or a new database management system (DBMS) for each new situation that comes along.

The newest approach to solving the problem of infoglut is to build a *data warehouse* and then *data mine* the warehouse for critical information. A data warehouse is a massive collection of corporate information, often stored in gigabytes or terabytes of data. It can include any and all data that is relevant to running a company. All this data is stored in databases spread among many storage devices on computers running tens or even hundreds of central processing units. However, setting up a data warehouse is much more complicated than simply dumping all kinds of data into one storage place. You should consider the following factors when setting up a data warehouse:

Photo: Don Smetzer/Tony Stone Images

What type of processing scheme will be used? Generally, two types of technologies, Symmetrical Multiprocessing (SMP) or Massively Parallel Processing (MPP), are used. For smaller storage needs, such as between 50 GB to 300 GB, companies use SMP. For data warehouses larger than 300 GB, many companies opt for MPP because of the ability to scale (or add) additional processors as their storage needs grow.

How much storage space is needed and what type of backup plan is needed? One of the most popular storage schemes is RAID (Redundant Array of Independent Disks). RAID is a storage system that links any number of disk drives to act as a single disk. In this system, information is written to two or more disks simultaneously to improve speed and reliability and to ensure that data is available to users at all times. RAID's capabilities are based on three techniques: (1) mirroring, (2) striping, and (3) striping-with-parity:

- In a *mirrored* system, data is written to two or more disks simultaneously, providing a complete copy of all the information on a drive, should one drive fail.

- *Striping* provides the user with speedy response by spreading data across several disks. Striping alone, however, does not provide backup if one of the disks in an array fails.

- *Striping-with-parity* provides the speed of striping with the reliability of parity. Should a drive in such an array fail, the system administrator can use the disk that stores the parity information to reconstruct the data from the damaged drive. Some arrays using the striping-with-parity technique also offer a technique known as *hot swapping,* which enables a system administrator to remove a damaged drive while the array remains in operation.

What type of data scrubbing will be set up? Whenever a lot of data is collected, it will, no doubt, contain some errors. *Data scrubbing* means sifting through data and performing such tedious tasks as eliminating duplications and incomplete records and making sure that similar fields in different tables are defined in exactly the same ways.

After a data warehouse has been set up, a company can perform targeted data mining to solve complex business problems, such as determining better ways to serve the needs of customers, outsmarting the competition, discovering trends in the market, and developing new products. To be successful, a company must mine its vast storehouse of information effectively to find out exactly what it knows, how to get to it, and what to do with it. By understanding and using the full capability of the Microsoft® Access 2000 program, you will be well on your way to building effective databases to manage the infoglut!

Photo: Richard Morrell/The Stock Market

Access Basics

CONTENTS

OBJECTIVES

After you complete this lesson, you will be able to do the following:

- Understand databases and how they work.
- Start and exit Microsoft Access.
- Open an existing database.
- Name the main features of the Database window.
- Select an object using the Objects bar and switch between object views.
- Identify the basic components of an Access database.
- Navigate a table and edit a record in a table.
- Enter records using a form.
- Find specific records using a query.
- Preview and print database objects.
- Use the Office Assistant to get online help.
- Compact and close a database.
- Plan your database.
- Create a database.
- Create tables by using the Table Wizard or Design view.
- Set primary keys.
- Modify field properties.
- Use multiple data types.
- Modify tables in Design view.
- Use a search engine.

Access is a powerful database program that enables you to organize and manipulate data, perform selection queries, develop reports, and convert files for use on the Web. Access does much of the work automatically and offers help with more complex tasks.

The first part of Lesson 1 teaches you basic database terms, shows you how to launch Microsoft Access, and introduces the Database window. You will open and close a database, become familiar with the various objects in a database, and print a report—essential skills that you will use whenever you work with Access. In the latter part of the lesson, you will learn the value of planning ahead when creating a database to avoid duplication of data, eliminate unnecessary data entry, and increase the effectiveness of the database. Then you will create a new database and learn various ways to create tables in the database.

INTRODUCING MICROSOFT ACCESS

This tutorial teaches you how to use the database program Microsoft Access. A **database** is an organized collection of data about similar things—such as employees, customers, or inventory items. A database is like a computerized Rolodex, paper filing system, or telephone book. As you begin to work with databases, you may encounter the term **DBMS,** for **database management system.** A DBMS is a system for storing and manipulating the data in a database.

Databases are useful any time you have to store, retrieve, and manipulate information. You can use databases to store massive amounts of data in a very small space; to manipulate data with ease, sorting to the desired order; and to extract required information. As an example, the database table in Figure 1.1 contains customer information.

Last Name	First Name	Address	City	State	ZIP Code
Kenber	Fra~~Field~~	1777 Lois Ln.	Rock Creek	NC	28333-1234
Reid	Alyson	7374 Backwoods Rd.	Sebastopol	CA	97777-1111
Turlow	Will	1 Oak Place	Providence	RI	02900-2338
Zheng	Anne	25 Forest Knoll	Santa Rosa	CA	99887-2355
O'Hara	Joan	2234 Hanley Place	Baltimore	MD	21122-5634
Quinonez	James	32123 Overlook Ave.	Portland	OR	99876-2389
Bechdel	Mason	75 Grizzly Peak Blvd.	Orinda	CA	94700-5412
Isherwood	Emma	1314 23rd Ave.	Biddeford	ME	57432-6034
Smith	Christine	5457 Park Pl.	New York	NY	10001-8763
Jackson	Jacqueline	6633 Dallas Way	Houston	TX	47532-7843
Everett	Richard	1310 Arch St.	Berkeley	CA	98765-3368
Wintergreen	Shelly	21 Barbary Ln.	Omaha	NE	66332-9004
Menendez	Erica	303 Hollywood St. #15	Los Angeles	CA	99887-3489
Zheng	Alicia	32 B St.	Ashland	OR	97998-5098
Ng	Patrick	1112 Spruce St.	Shaker Heights	OH	45678-7842
Apfelbaum	Bob	81 Hacienda Blvd.	Santa Fe	NM	55554-3449
Hatfield	James	15A Vine St.	Ashland	OR	97998-6907
Marais	Jean-Luc	1379 Montgomery Ave. #3	Boston	MA	02101-3930
Savallis	Jordi	100 Riverside Dr. #10B	New York	NY	10025-8035
Yates	Lily	999 35th Ave.	Oakland	CA	94602-8532
Criton	Molly	71 Panoramic Way	Seattle	WA	99981-9532

(Callouts in figure: "Field" pointing to First Name column; "Record" pointing to the Zheng/Alicia row.)

Figure 1.1
Sample table from a database

The customer information in Figure 1.1 is arranged in well-marked columns and rows and is easy to read. In Access, data is stored in **tables.** Tables organize information into a series of **fields** (columns) that contain categories of data and **records** (rows) that contain the set of fields for one particular entity. The table shown in Figure 1.1 includes fields for each customer's last name, first name, address, city, state, and ZIP Code. In this case, a record consists of all fields that apply to a single customer.

Most Access databases will actually contain one or more tables that you can use together when the need arises. If you have more than one general category of information—such as customer addresses and customer orders—you should place the data in separate tables. While you work, you may require data from multiple tables; for example, you might want to list both customer addresses and orders on an invoice form. You can do this easily in Access, provided that the tables include common fields by which they can be linked.

To use two tables together, you must first define the relationship between them. For instance, Access lets you link two tables that contain a common field. For example, if both your customer address and order tables include a field that contains customer ID numbers, Access can find each customer's orders by scanning the order table for records with the matching customer ID number. This arrangement saves you from having to store copies of the customer name and address data in several places, streamlining your database by eliminating the duplication of data and at the same time reducing the risk of data entry error. (If you enter a name only once, you are less likely to make a mistake.) Database programs that let you link, or relate, two tables in this manner are known as ***relational databases.*** You will learn more about working with multiple tables in Lesson 2.

STARTING MICROSOFT ACCESS

Before you can start Microsoft Access, both Microsoft Access and Windows 95 (or higher version) must be installed on the computer you're using. The figures in this tutorial use Windows 98; if you are using a different version of Windows, the information appearing on your screen may vary slightly.

 You must create the Student Data Disk for this tutorial from the Data CD located on the inside back cover of this tutorial. If you have not created the Student Data Disk, ask your instructor for help.

Launching Microsoft Access

In this activity, you will start Microsoft Access.

1. Turn on your computer.

 *If you are prompted for a user name and/or password, enter the information at this time. If you do not know your user name and/or password, ask your instructor for help.*

The Windows operating system boots the computer. If the Welcome to Windows screen appears, click its Close button ☒ to close the window.

2. Click the Start button 🔳 Start **on the Windows taskbar.**

3. Point to Programs.

The Programs menu appears, as shown in Figure 1.2. (Depending on the applications installed on your computer, your Programs menu may be different than Figure 1.2.)

4. Click Microsoft Access.

The Access program starts and the initial Microsoft Access dialog box appears, as shown in Figure 1.3. This dialog box lets you create a new database or work with an existing one.

Launching Microsoft Access

1. Turn on the computer.

2. Click the Start button and point to Programs.

3. Click Microsoft Access.

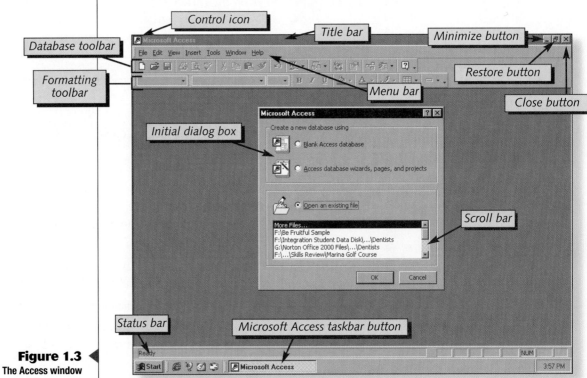

Figure 1.2 ◀
The Programs menu

Figure 1.3 ◀
The Access window

5. **For the moment, click the Cancel button to close the dialog box.**

You will see the Microsoft Access application window. In the application window, many features are not yet available because you haven't opened a database. For example, note that if you click Edit on the menu bar, all the options beneath are grayed (meaning that they're currently disabled). As you will soon find out, the available Access options change depending on what you're doing at the moment.

EXPLORING ACCESS

The Access **application window** on your computer may look slightly different than the one shown in Figure 1.3, because Access allows users to **customize,** or alter, the Access window to suit their individual needs. The Access window contains many standard Windows elements, including a title bar; the Minimize, Restore, and Close buttons; a menu bar; and the status bar.

As shown in Figure 1.3, the Access **menu bar** appears below the title bar. The menu bar displays some of the menu names found in most Windows applications, such as File, Edit, and Help.

Menus list the **commands** available in Access. To display a menu's commands, click a menu name on the menu bar. The menu will display a **short menu,** a list of the most-used commands, with a double arrow at the bottom. If you keep your pointer on the menu for a few seconds or if you click the double arrow at the bottom of the menu, an **expanded menu** appears. This expanded menu shows all of the commands available on the menu. The most-used commands appear when a menu opens; when the list expands, less common commands appear. Figure 1.4 shows both versions of Access' Insert menu—as a short menu and an expanded menu.

- To display a menu, press
  [Alt] and then press the
  letter in the menu name
  that is underlined.
- To choose a menu command, press the underlined letter of the
  command.

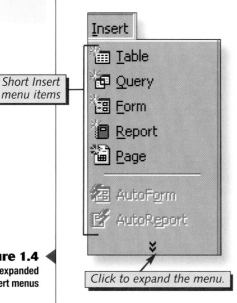

Short Insert
menu items

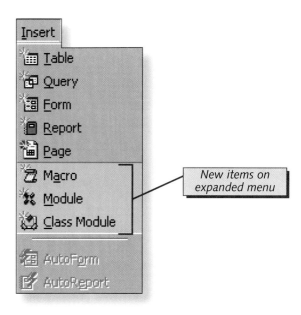

New items on
expanded menu

Figure 1.4
The short and expanded
Insert menus

Click to expand the menu.

If you prefer to always see
the expanded menus, you
can click Tools on the menu
bar and click Customize.
On the Options tab of the
Customize dialog box,
deselect the *Menus show
recently used commands
first* option.

As shown in Figure 1.4, five active commands and two inactive commands appear on the initial Insert menu. These seven commands are considered to be the commands that users issue most often from this menu. The expanded menu shows three additional commands—Macro, Module, and Class Module—which are not used as frequently. The backgrounds of the additional commands are shaded with a lighter shade of gray. After you issue one of these additional commands, the command is added to the short menu. For instance, assume you choose Macro from the Insert menu; the next time you click the Insert menu, the Macro command will be shown on the short menu with a darker gray background. This **adaptive menu** feature allows menus to be customized for each user.

Hints & Tips

• To display a toolbar, click View, point to Toolbars, and click Customize. On the Toolbars tab, click the toolbar name to place a check mark in the selection box and click Close.

• To move a toolbar left or right, point to the handle on the left end. When the four-way arrow appears, drag the toolbar.

After you display a menu, you can choose a command using either the mouse or the keyboard. To choose a command using the mouse, click the command you want. To choose a command using the keyboard, press the underlined letter of the command. For example, to choose the Open command on the File menu, press the letter **O** while the File menu is displayed.

Working with Toolbars

Below the menu bar is the Database toolbar, as shown in Figure 1.3 on page 340. A **toolbar** contains buttons for many of the most frequently used commands, such as opening or printing a file. Although you can access these commands by clicking the command on one of the menus, using the buttons on the toolbar as a shortcut is often more convenient.

You may be wondering how you will remember the purpose of each button. The icons themselves often provide a clue—for instance, the button for opening a file features a picture of an open file folder. If you can't guess the button's purpose from the picture, point to the button. Access displays the button name in a small box immediately below the button; this is called a **ScreenTip**. ScreenTips are handy reminders when you can't recall the function of a particular button.

If it has been activated on your system, the Formatting toolbar appears directly below the Database toolbar, as shown in Figure 1.3. The buttons on the Formatting toolbar are used to control the appearance of text. Different Formatting toolbars are available, depending on whether you are formatting text in a table, form, report, or other Access object. In addition to the Database and Formatting toolbars, Access also includes a Web toolbar that you will use in the On the Web section at the end of this lesson. The View menu includes the Toolbars command. The Toolbars submenu allows you to control which toolbars are displayed as you work. A check mark next to a toolbar name indicates that the toolbar is displayed. Clicking a check mark will **deselect**, or hide, that toolbar.

OPENING DATABASES

Any time you want to use a database that you or someone else created earlier, you need to **open** the database. Opening a database means copying that file from disk into the memory of your computer so that you can update or view the file. To open any Access database, you can either click the Open button or click File on the menu bar and click the Open command. If you've used a file recently, you may also open a file by choosing the file name from the list of recently opened files that appears near the bottom of the File menu. In Access, you can have only one database open at a time. If you open a second database when another database is already open, Access will automatically save and close the first database and then open the second database.

Note *It is possible to have two databases open at the same time; however, you must open Access twice and open a database within each Access program. Then you can use the taskbar buttons to move between the open databases.*

HANDS

Another Way

To open a file, click Open
on the File menu or press
`Ctrl` + O.

Opening a Database

Before you can modify a database, you must open the database. In this
activity, you will open a database on your Student Data Disk.

1. Click the Open button **on the Database toolbar.**

Access displays the Open dialog box, as shown in Figure 1.5. The Look in
box shows the current folder or drive or the last folder used to open a document on your computer.

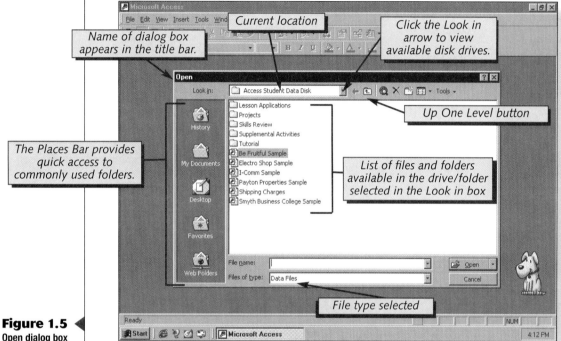

Figure 1.5
The Open dialog box

Warning   *If you're sharing a computer with one or more users in a lab
or school environment, the list of files displayed in the Open
dialog box may not contain the file you wish to open.
Continue with steps 2 and 3 to properly navigate to your files.*

The Places Bar in various dialog boxes gives you quick access to commonly
used folders. For instance, in the Open dialog box, you can click the Favorites
folder to see a list of the files stored in this folder. You can access files of different formats by changing the Files of type setting in the Open dialog box.

**2. Verify that the Files of type is set to Data Files (for any database file) or
Microsoft Access Databases (for only Access database files).**

3. Click the Look in box arrow to display a list of the available drives.

If you click the hard drive icon, all of the folders directly under the drive C:
root folder appear in the list box. The *root folder* is the main folder on a
disk. Within the root folder may be files and other folders—themselves containing files and folders. You can double-click folders in the list box, use the
Look in box, or click the Up One Level button to find the folder and database file you want to open.

Opening a Database

1. Click the Open button.

2. Select the appropriate drive from the Look in box.

3. Select the appropriate folder, if necessary.

4. Double-click the file name.

4. Click the drive that contains your Student Data Disk for this tutorial. If necessary, click the folder in which the Student Data Disk files are stored.

A list of files on the Student Data Disk appears in the Open dialog box.

 *If you copied the Student Data Disk files for this tutorial onto a Zip disk, be sure to insert the disk into the drive.*

5. Click *Be Fruitful Sample* in the list of file names and click the **Open button**.

Access opens the *Be Fruitful Sample* database and displays the Database window, as shown in Figure 1.6. The *Be Fruitful Sample* database is a sample database for a fruit-of-the-month club. Notice that many more menu and toolbar options become available.

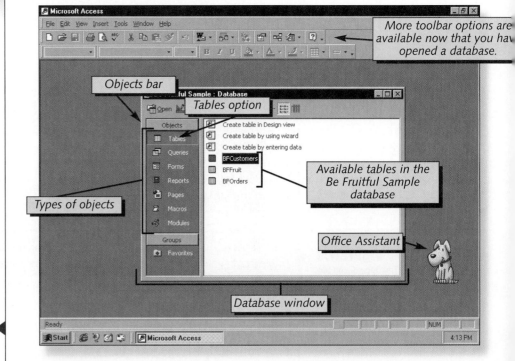

Figure 1.6
The Database window

The Database Window

The *Database window* enables you to gain access to all the tables in your database, as well as to a number of other database objects (or components), such as forms and reports. The Objects bar along the left side of the Database window represents the types of objects available in Access. When you click an object type in the Objects bar, a list of the objects of that type appears in the right side of the Database window. The first two or three items in the list are options that allow you to create a new object. The remaining items are an alphabetical listing of existing objects. For example, in Figure 1.6, the Tables option in the Objects bar is selected, and the first three options allow you to create new tables. The last three allow you to

open existing tables. The Tables option in the Objects bar is selected by default; unless you choose another, you will see a list of the tables in the **Be Fruitful Sample** database. Clicking the Reports option would display any reports in the **Be Fruitful Sample** database, and so on.

When you're finished working with a particular database, you can close the Database window by clicking File on the menu bar and clicking Close, or by clicking the Close button ☒ in the upper-right corner of the Database window. For now, leave the **Be Fruitful Sample** database open so you can explore the various components of Access in the next section.

OBJECTS: THE COMPONENTS OF ACCESS

In Access, the term database means not just the raw data stored in tables, but a collection of **objects.** These objects are the various components of Access—the data, reports, requests, actions, and forms that you use to enter, display, print, and find exactly the information you need in the database. An Access database can contain seven types of objects—tables, queries, forms, reports, pages, macros, and modules.

Tables

You've already learned a little about one Access object: the table, which is the holding area for all of your data. The table is like a large sheet of paper divided into columns and rows, which contain the information central to the database. In addition to the information it contains, a table also has a *structure*. The structure controls the kind of information that can be entered into the table. You can work with a table in two different views—*Design view* and *Datasheet view*. You use Design view to create and modify the structure of a table. You use Datasheet view to view, add, delete, and edit the actual information in a table.

Navigating a Table, Editing Data, and Viewing Table Design

In this activity, you will look at the contents of one of the tables in the **Be Fruitful Sample** database. Then you will change the contents of one of the records.

1. With the **Be Fruitful Sample** database open, click the **Tables option** in the Objects bar of the Database window, if necessary.

You should see the **Be Fruitful Sample** Database window on the screen, as previously shown in Figure 1.6. Notice that the names of the three tables in the **Be Fruitful Sample** database are displayed as the last three items in the list of table objects.

2. Click the **BFCustomers table**, if it is not already selected, and then click the **Open button** directly below the title bar of the Database window.

The data in the BFCustomers table appears, arranged in a grid of columns (fields) and rows (records), as shown in Figure 1.7. Because you have opened a table, different toolbar buttons—ones used when working with tables—appear on the Database toolbar. Also, a set of navigation buttons appears at the bottom of the window to help you move efficiently among records in the table.

Figure 1.7 ◄
The BFCustomers table

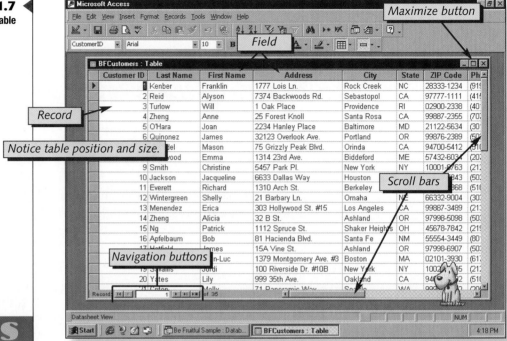

Access
BASICS

Working with Tables

To open a table and edit data:

1. Open the database that contains the table you want to open.

2. Click the Tables option in the Objects bar.

3. Click the name of the table you want to open.

4. Click the Open button.

5. To edit data in a table, type text in a column and row.

To view table structure:

1. Click the View button while viewing a table.

2. Click the View button again to return.

3. Click the Maximize button 🔲 **on the right side of the BFCustomers title bar.**

You should see a full screen display of the table.

4. Click and use the *scroll bars*—the shaded bars along the bottom and right side of a window—to view portions of the table not visible on the screen.

5. Press Ctrl + End **to move to the end of the table.**

6. Press Ctrl + Home **to move to the beginning of the table.**

7. Press Tab **twice.**

This action selects the word *Franklin.* Pressing Tab moves the insertion point to the next column (field).

8. Press ↓.

This action selects the word *Alyson.* Pressing ↓ moves the insertion point down one record (row) at a time.

9. With *Alyson* selected, type Alice, as shown in Figure 1.8.

The word *Alice* replaces the selected word *Alyson.* (If all capital letters appeared when you typed the name, press CapsLock to turn off capital letters. Then press Backspace until you remove the capital letters, and type Alice.)

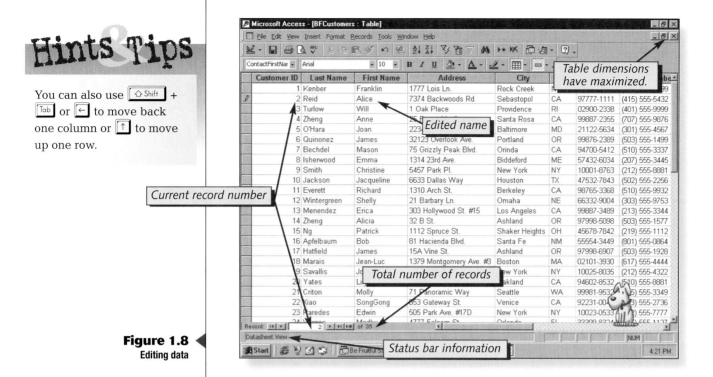

Figure 1.8
Editing data

10. Click the **View button** 🗷 on the **Database toolbar**.

You now see the BFCustomers table in Design view, as shown in Figure 1.9. As you will learn later in this lesson, you can set up and modify the layout of a table in Design view.

The Design view is split into two panes. The upper pane shows the names and other information about the fields (columns) used in the table. The lower pane further defines the properties used for the field currently selected.

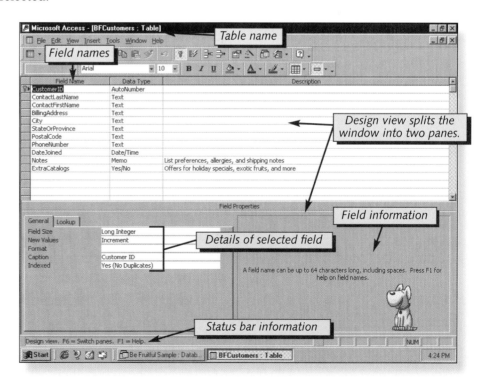

Figure 1.9
Design view of the BFCustomers table

To edit information, click the appropriate pane.

11. Press $\boxed{\text{F6}}$.

Your insertion point moves into the lower pane.

12. Click the Field Size arrow.

You see the options for the size of the field. Later in this lesson, you will learn about these options.

13. Click File on the menu bar and then click Close.

 Do not click the Close button ☒ *on the Access title bar; this will close the Access program.*

Access removes the BFCustomers table from the screen, returning you to the Database window for the **Be Fruitful Sample** database. Since you maximized the table in step 3, the Database window is now maximized as well. Also, the change you made in step 9 is automatically saved.

Queries

A *query* is just what the name implies: a question to the database, generally asking for a set of records from one or more tables that meets specific criteria. For example, you might ask the database to display all the customers in Hawaii or any customers whose bills are past due. Access responds to such queries by displaying the requested data. Because a query is a stored question, rather than the stored response to a question, the results of the query will remain up to date even if the data in your tables changes. Queries are particularly valuable because they enable you both to view and operate on selected subsets of your data. Just as with tables, you can view a query using different views. You use Datasheet view to display the query results and use Design view to display and modify the underlying structure of the query. (Access also provides another view for queries called SQL view, which allows you to view the query as equivalent SQL statements. SQL view is beyond the scope of this tutorial.)

Viewing Queries

Queries are stored in the Queries option of the Database window. In this activity, you will first display the results of a query that asks for customers who joined the fruit club after 1997. Then you will display and view the query design.

1. Click the Queries option in the Objects bar in the Database window.

You will see two options that allow you to create new queries, followed by the names of the two existing queries in the **Be Fruitful Sample** database.

2. Click the Post 97 Customers query, if it is not already selected, and then click the Open button 🖉 Open **in the Database window.**

Access displays the Post 97 Customer query results, as you can see in Figure 1.10. Notice that this query displays selected data from the BFCustomers table that you saw earlier. As you may have figured out, the query asks to display the customers who joined after 1997.

Opening a Query

1. Click the Queries option in the Database window.

2. Click the query you want to open.

3. Click the Open button.

4. To view the query design, click the query name and then click the Design button in the Database window.

Figure 1.10 ◀
Query results

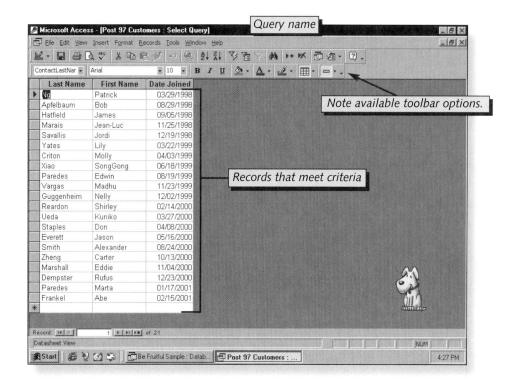

Query name

Note available toolbar options.

Records that meet criteria

---

3. Click the Close button ☒ **at the right end of the menu bar.**

Access closes the query results, returning you to the Database window.

Another Way

To display the query in Design view, click the View button on the toolbar while you are looking at the query results.

4. With the Post 97 Customers query still selected, click the Design button 🖉 Design .

Access displays the *Select Query window*, shown in Figure 1.11. This window shows the structure of the query and lets you choose the fields to be displayed, the order in which they will appear, and the criteria to be used to select records.

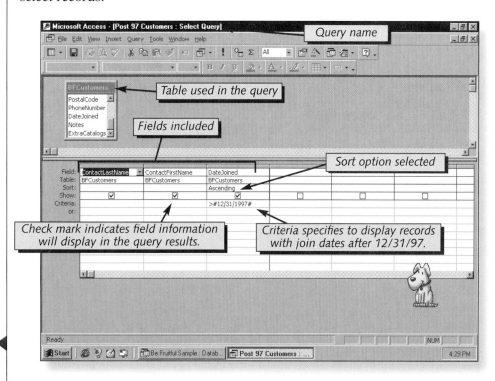

Query name

Table used in the query

Fields included

Sort option selected

Check mark indicates field information will display in the query results.

Criteria specifies to display records with join dates after 12/31/97.

Figure 1.11 ◀
Design view of a query

5. Click the **Close button**  at the right end of the menu bar.

Once again, you return to the Database window.

Forms

You can view, enter, and edit data in tables (where data is laid out in a series of rows and columns). Often, however, you can more easily use custom forms for this purpose. Access *forms* are the electronic equivalent of paper forms, but electronic forms enable you to create a custom layout for your data—determining how the data from your tables is presented. For example, you could create a form that presents a single record at a time for data entry or editing, or one that displays only certain fields from a particular table. Forms are especially useful when you want to create a more friendly or visually manageable environment for data entry or when you need to control which data is displayed.

Forms have three views: Datasheet view, Design view, and Form view. As you may have guessed, you use Design view to create a new form or change the structure of an existing form. To view, enter, and edit data in forms, you can use either Datasheet view or Form view. In Datasheet view, you see several records at one time, and it is very similar to viewing a table in Datasheet view. In *Form view,* however, you can view only one record at a time, if you wish, and display only pertinent fields in a record. Thus, Form view is often used as a means to enter records into a table.

Adding a Record in Form View

In this activity, you will open a form that displays all of the fields for one record in the BFCustomers table in a clear format. Then you will add data in a new record.

1. Click the **Forms option** in the Objects bar in the Database window.

You will see two options that you can use to create new forms and one option that opens a form that has already been created.

2. Click the **Columnar Form with All Fields form**, if it is not already selected, and then click the **Open button** .

Access reveals the Columnar Form with All Fields form. Notice that this form displays the first record from the BFCustomers table you saw earlier.

3. Click the **New Record button** on the Database toolbar.

A new blank record is displayed.

4. Press Tab.

The insertion point moves into the second entry, *Last Name.*

Note *When you start typing data in the Last Name field, Access will automatically insert a number in the Customer ID field.*

Displaying a Form and Adding Data

1. Click the Forms option in the Database window.

2. Double-click the form you want to view.

3. Click the New Record button to add a record.

4. Type data into each field of the new record.

Another Way

To create a new record, click the New Record button at the bottom of the form.

5. Type each of the following entries into the form, pressing  after each item. The new record should look like the one in Figure 1.12.

Last Name: Rodriguez
First Name: Francisco
Address: 6312 Ogden Dr.
City: Los Angeles
State: CA
ZIP Code: 900268623
Phone Number: 2139344420
Date Joined: 3/3/2001

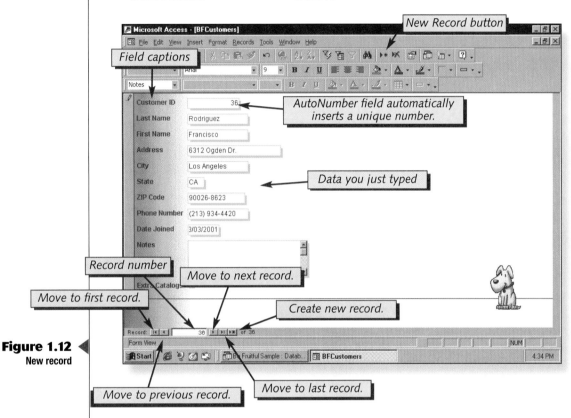

Figure 1.12
New record

6. Click the **Close button** ☒ to close the form.

Access closes the form, returning you to the Database window. The new record is added. If you opened the BFCustomers table, the new record would be displayed at the bottom of the table.

Reports

Often, you will want not only a set of data on the screen but also some type of printed output. You can print forms, as well as data from tables and queries, but *reports* enable you to produce presentation-quality output with ease. You can base your reports on data from tables or queries. You can also create reports that show totals and grand totals of the values in a particular field, such as salary or sales.

Hints & Tips

When you enter the ZIP Code and phone number, Access fills in the punctuation marks normally used in these items. Also, a new blank form appears when you press Tab after entering data in the last field of the form.

You can use three different views to work with reports: Design view, Print Preview, and Layout Preview. You use Design view to create a new report or change the structure of an existing report. (You will use Design view to create a report in Lesson 2.) You use Print Preview to display a *WYSIWYG* (what you see is what you get) preview of all the data in a report, which gives you a good idea of what a report will look like when it is actually printed. You use Layout Preview to view the layout of a report with only a sample of the data contained in the report.

Previewing a Report

Before you print a database report, you can preview the report on the screen. In this activity, you will display a database report using Print Preview.

1. Click the Reports option in the Objects bar in the Database window.

Access displays two options that help you create reports and one report in the *Be Fruitful Sample* database.

2. Click the Fruit Type Summaries report, if it is not already selected, and then click the Preview button ![Preview] **.**

In a moment, Access reveals the Fruit Type Summaries report, as shown in Figure 1.13. You can scroll the report to see more.

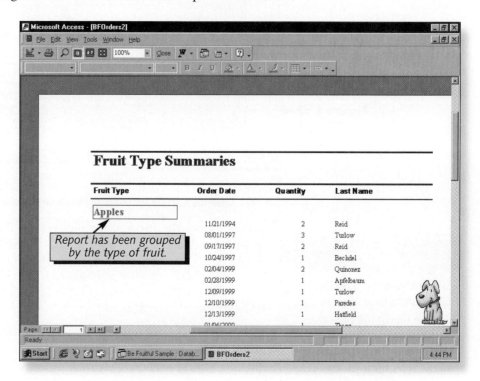

Figure 1.13
Fruit Type Summaries report

3. Click File on the menu bar and then click Close.

Access closes the report, returning you to the Database window.

Data Access Pages

Access allows you to post your database data on Web pages. To do so, you can create **data access pages.** Data access pages are directly connected to a database and are designed to be viewed in a Web browser—a tool used to navigate the World Wide Web. Using data access pages, you can view data stored in an Access database, and also add and edit records in a database, from a remote location via the Internet.

Macros and Modules

A **macro** is an Access object that is composed of a command or series of commands that you can use to automate a task. Each command within a macro is called an **action.** Macros are often created to automate tasks that you repeat frequently. Then, instead of issuing several separate actions manually, you can run the macro and the set of actions will be performed automatically. Macros are designed to save time and effort.

Macros are best used for relatively simple tasks, such as opening forms or running reports. For more complex tasks, a module can be programmed. **Modules** are sets of programmed statements that are stored together as a unit.

GETTING HELP WITH ACCESS

While you are using Access, you may need to reference the online Help system. Access provides several different Help tools: ScreenTips, the Office Assistant, the Contents tab, the Index tab, and a tool called the Answer Wizard. You can activate the Office Assistant by clicking the animated character on your screen, by clicking the Microsoft Access Help button 🔲, by clicking Microsoft Access Help on the Help menu, or by pressing 🔲. For more detailed Help instructions, review pages 91-97 in *Lesson 3: Introducing Office 2000.*

PRINTING OBJECTS

Now that you've explored the Database window and various Access objects, you are ready to learn another Access fundamental—printing Access objects. You will need printouts to submit assignments to your instructor, to deliver reports to your boss, to mail information to a client, and much more. You can easily print objects by clicking the database object and clicking the Print button 🖨. Tables will print all the information that has been entered in a column and row format. Forms print the information using the layout and design of the selected form, but once again print all the data. Queries can limit the data you print, but a printed query will be in the column and row format. By using reports, you can access the information in the tables and select the layout and design of the information.

Printing an Object

1. Click the database object.

2. Click the File menu and click Print.

3. Verify the printing options.

4. Click OK.

Printing a Report

In this activity, you'll print the Fruit Type Summaries report that you previewed earlier.

1. **Turn on the printer, if necessary.**

2. **Click the Reports object and click the Fruit Type Summaries report**, if it is not already selected.

3. **Click the File menu and click Print.**

You'll see the Print dialog box, as shown in Figure 1.14.

Figure 1.14 ◀
Print dialog box

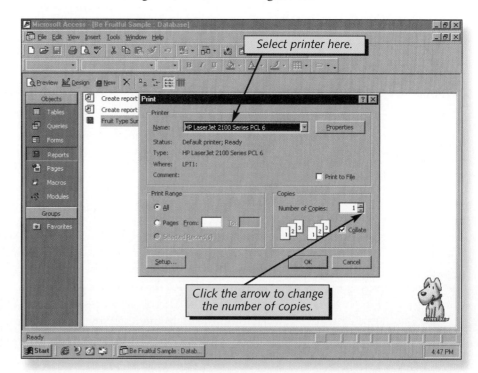

4. **Change the Number of Copies option to 1, if necessary, and click OK.**

You may have to wait a moment, but Access will generate your report.

COMPACTING AND CLOSING DATABASES

As you add, edit, and delete objects, a database changes in size. To minimize the size of a database and to improve performance, you should compact your databases on a regular basis. *Compacting* a database rearranges how a fragmented database is stored on disk. You can use two methods to compact a database. First, you can set Access to compact each database as you close. Second, you can issue a menu command to compact and repair a database at any time.

When you're finished working with a database, you should *close* the file. Closing the file removes the file from memory, but leaves Access running. When you close a database using the Close button, be sure to click the correct Close button! Clicking the Close button **✕** at the right end of the *menu bar* in the Database window or clicking the File menu and clicking Close will close the database but will keep Access running. Clicking the Close button  at the right end of the *title bar* in the Access window will close both the database and the Access program.

Databases (or other documents) that you have opened recently are added to a list near the bottom of the File menu. If you need to reopen a database you just closed, you can select the database quickly from that list. By default, Access lists the last four files; a user may choose to list up to nine files on the File menu.

HANDS On

Compacting a Database Upon Closing

In this activity, you will instruct Access to compact a database when you close. Then you will close the *Be Fruitful Sample* database.

1. If any objects are open in the *Be Fruitful Sample* database, close them.

2. Click the **Tools menu**, click **Options**, and then click the **General tab** of the Options dialog box, as shown in Figure 1.15.

Figure 1.15
The Options dialog box

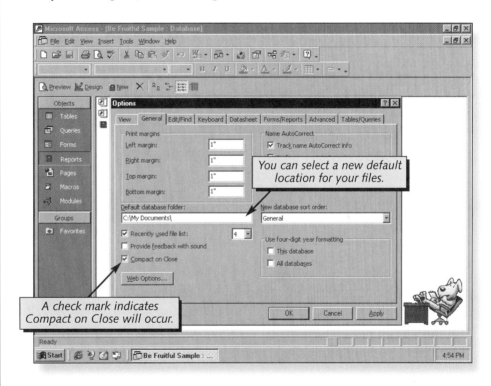

3. Verify that a check mark appears before the **Compact on Close** option and then click the **OK button**.

The dialog box closes and you return to the Database window.

4. Click the **Close button**  on the Database window.

The *Be Fruitful Sample* database closes. If you watch the left side of the status bar, you may see a brief message indicating that the database is being compacted. Access closes the file, clearing the screen completely—except for the Office Assistant. Since you just closed the only open file, the Access window on your screen will be blank and will not contain a Database window.

PLANNING AHEAD

Now that you are familiar with the various objects that comprise a database, you are ready to create a new database. Creating a database requires careful thought. Although you can certainly make changes to a database, making those changes is a bit more complex than when using some programs, such as a word processor. Advanced planning alleviates the problems you can experience from quickly creating a database without preparation. After you design your database, creating an Access database and building a few tables will be remarkably easy. Before beginning to build a database, you should answer several questions:

- What is the database for and what should the database do?

- What categories of information (or fields) do you need to achieve the desired results?

- How should these fields be divided into separate tables?

- How might these tables relate to each other to use information from two or more of them simultaneously?

Determining the Purpose of the Database

The first step in determining how to configure your database is to decide how you will use the database. If you have an existing manual database system, investigate that system; review any reports and forms that you'll need to duplicate and note the items of information they must include. Also be sure to talk to people who actually use the database; check to see what they use the system for and what they need.

If you're not working with an existing system, think very carefully about what you want the new system to do; jot down the items of information the system should track and sketch any forms and reports you think you'll need. Throughout the planning process, remember that as you determine what you want your database to do, you are learning what data you must have in your database. For example, if you need to be able to print salary reports according to department, your database must list the department for each employee. Also, consider how you want to sort or extract data. For instance, if you'll want to sort customers by last name, you'll need to include separate fields for a first name and a last name, rather than a single field to contain both names. At this stage in planning, you can make just one large list of all the information you need. You'll then learn how to organize this information into more manageable chunks.

In the planning stage, you can ask users of the current system to supply you with a wish list of things they'd like to be able to do. Remember that you aren't confined to duplicating a current manual system; often you can improve on the existing system while computerizing.

Determining the Categories of Information You Need

The second step in creating a database is to determine all of the categories of information you need. At this point, you do not need to list the categories in any particular order. For instance, the sample application in this tutorial is

the database for a fruit-of-the-month club called Be Fruitful. Members of this club can choose whether to order the fruit offered for a particular month, and they can also decide how much fruit to order. Some of the information categories needed in this database include:

- The name, address, and phone number of each customer, as well as notes about shipping

- The date the customer joined the club

- The types of fruit, their prices, and the units offered (3 pints strawberries, 2 dozen kiwis, and so forth)

- The number of units of fruit each member orders in a month

- The date an order was placed and when and how the customer paid

Determining How Many Tables You Need

All but the simplest of databases will contain multiple tables so that Access can use your data more efficiently. In other words, your task is not only to determine what categories of information (or fields) your database should contain but also how that information should be broken down logically into several tables.

The first thing to consider is that each table should contain information on a single subject. In the database for Be Fruitful, for example, you will have one table that contains customer information, a second table that includes information about available fruits, and a third one with order information. You wouldn't include customer names and addresses in the Orders table, because these fields describe the customer, not the order. This way of breaking down your database avoids duplication of data, or *redundancy*. You want to avoid entering the customer's name and address in each order, for example, because this wastes storage space, requires extra typing, and increases the likelihood of data-entry errors. In addition, if you store the customer name and address information in a single customer record rather than in multiple order records, you can more easily update your data later. At first, you may believe dividing the data among multiple tables in this way is inefficient—for example, you may want to use information about both customers and orders in an invoice form—but remember that Access enables you to combine data from many sources as you create forms and reports.

Tables also should avoid multiple instances of the same field or a similar set of fields. For example, suppose you had a mail-order business and your customers often ordered multiple items at once. To record all of those orders in the Orders table, you could have one long record with fields for each item ordered. A better solution would be to have a separate Items table where each item being ordered is in a separate record.

Finally, as a general rule, do not include fields in your table that will contain data that you can calculate from other fields. For instance, if you have one field for price and one for quantity, you can calculate the total by multiplying these two values together—you don't need to create a separate field for the total. Figure 1.16 shows a tentative list of fields for the three tables in Be Fruitful's database.

BE FRUITFUL FIELDS

BFCustomers	**BFFruit**	**BFOrders**
Customer ID	Fruit Type	Order Number
Contact Last Name	Price	Customer ID
Contact First Name	Descriptive Units	Order Date
Billing Address		Fruit Type
City		Quantity
State or Province		Price
ZIP Code		Shipping Amount
Phone Number		Payment Date
Date Joined		Payment Amount
Notes		Payment Type
Extra Catalogs		Reference

Figure 1.16
Lists of fields in each table

Determining How Tables Will Work Together

After you've decided how to divide the database information into multiple tables, you have a corresponding task—to determine how to set up those tables to combine the information they contain into single forms or reports. For instance, if you have separate tables for orders and customers, you clearly need a way to pull the data from both tables to create an invoice that includes corresponding customer and order information.

For you to be able to use two tables in combination, they must include a ***common field.*** For example, to ensure that you can relate the fruit-of-the-month club's Customers and Orders tables, you could include a Customer ID field in both tables. This field would enable Access to match the order with the customer who placed the order. When determining the ***relationships*** (how tables are related) among tables, you must also consider the concept of primary keys: A ***primary key*** is a field or set of fields that uniquely identifies each record in the table. Assigning a primary key is particularly important if you must link data in two tables. In the fruit-of-the-month club's database, for instance, you need a primary key in the Customers table—some way to uniquely identify each customer so that you can tell which orders belong to which customers. A Customer ID field can serve this purpose. (You wouldn't want to use the name fields as the primary key, in case you had two customers with the same name.) When you set a primary key, Access sorts records in order according to the values in that key. Because the primary key must uniquely identify each record, Access won't permit you to enter duplicate values in the primary key field(s).

Although determining how to link your tables can be more complex, at this stage of the game you'll just include common fields in the tables you need to use together and set some primary keys. In Lesson 2, you'll learn how to create queries that pull data from multiple tables.

CREATING A DATABASE

As you may remember from earlier in this lesson, in Access, the term database means not just a collection of data, but a set of related tables, forms, reports, queries, and more. Before you begin to create tables in which to store your data, you need to create a database.

HANDS On

Another Way

To create a database, you can click File on the menu bar and click New. Then, click the Database option on the General tab and click OK.

Opening and Naming a New Database

In this activity, you will create a database to hold your tables, as well as all the related queries, forms, and reports you'll create in Lesson 2. Then you'll assign a name to identify the database.

1. Click the New button 🗋 on the Database toolbar.

The New dialog box appears with the General tab active.

2. On the General tab, click Database, if it is not already selected, and click OK.

You should see the File New Database dialog box, as shown in Figure 1.17. Notice that this dialog box is very similar to the Open dialog box you saw earlier in this lesson.

Figure 1.17 ◄
File New Database dialog box

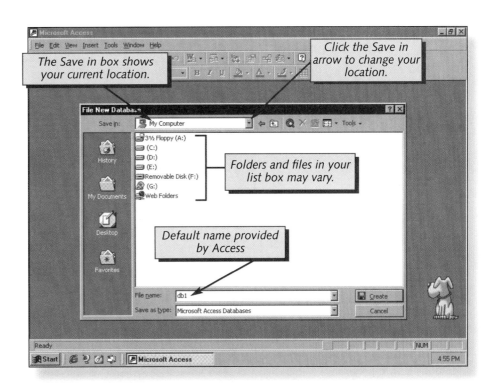

The Save in box shows your current location.

Click the Save in arrow to change your location.

Folders and files in your list box may vary.

Default name provided by Access

Hints & Tips

If you want to create a database when you start the Access program, you can click the Blank Access database option in the initial dialog box that appears immediately after the Access program loads. (See Figure 1.3 on page 340.)

3. Click the Save in arrow.

4. Select the location that contains your Student Data Disk files.

Note
Your instructor may direct you to save your files on a Zip disk, the hard drive of your computer, or a network folder. If you are not sure where to save your database, ask your instructor for direction.

Creating a New Database

1. Click New on the Database toolbar.

2. On the General tab of the New dialog box, click Database and click OK.

3. Choose the drive and folder in which you want to save the database.

4. Type a name in the File name box and click Create.

Figure 1.18 ◀
The Database window

You can use the Database Wizard provided by Access to automatically create databases with preconfigured tables, forms, reports, and other objects. Click the New button on the Database toolbar, click the Databases tab, and double-click the icon that best represents the type of database you'd like to create.

---

5. **Click the *Tutorial* folder in the window below the Save in box; click the Open button**.

The *Tutorial* folder opens and appears in the Save in box.

6. **Double-click the default file name *db1* in the File name text box.**

7. **Type** Be Fruitful, Lesson 1 **to replace the existing name.**

Depending upon how your computer is set up, Access may automatically add an extension of *.mdb* to the file name. The extension identifies the file as an Access database.

8. **Click the Create button**.

After a pause, Access displays the Database window for the ***Be Fruitful, Lesson 1*** database, as shown in Figure 1.18.

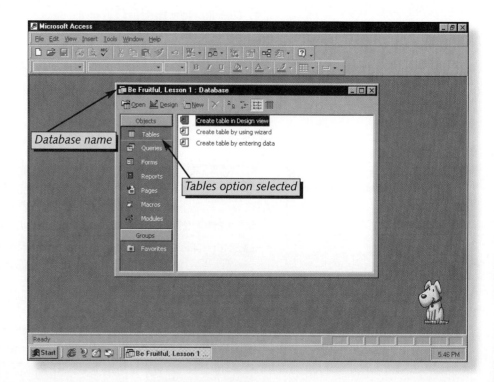

When you create a new database, it doesn't contain any objects—you must create the objects that will be stored in the database. Notice that the Tables option in the Objects bar is selected. Three options appear to help you create tables, but no actual tables exist yet. If you selected any of the other object options, you would see that they also contain no queries, forms, reports, or other objects—only options to create new objects.

CREATING TABLES

Now that you've created a database, the next step is to create some tables so that you can enter your data. You'll be creating the table structure—you'll spell out the fields that the table needs and select various properties for them. In the next lesson, you'll enter and edit data in the tables you've created. These are the first two essential steps for building a database.

Three ways exist to create tables in Access: First, you can use the Table Wizard, described next. Second, you can work in Design view, described later in this lesson. Lastly, you can create a table by entering data; using this method, you must later revise your table to create field names.

Creating a Table with the Table Wizard

During the following activities, you'll use the Table Wizard to design Be Fruitful's Customers table, which will include the names and addresses of the Be Fruitful customers. When you use a *wizard,* Access prompts you for the needed information each step of the way. The Table Wizard is a tool provided by Access used specifically to create tables. The Table Wizard gathers information through a series of dialog boxes. At any point in the table-creation process, you can click the Back button to move back one step. You'll use the wizard to select fields to be included in the database, deselect and rename fields, name the table, and select a primary key.

HANDS On

Access BASICS

Using the Table Wizard

1. Double-click the *Create table by using wizard* option in the Database window.

2. Click the table you want to use in the Sample Tables box.

3. Click the field(s) you want to use in the Sample Fields box and click the Add Field button.

4. Click the Next button.

Selecting Fields

The first step in creating a table is to select the fields to be included. In this activity, you'll start the Table Wizard and select fields from the samples provided.

1. With the *Be Fruitful, Lesson 1* Database window still open, click the **Tables option** in the Objects bar, if necessary.

2. Double-click the **Create table by using wizard option** in the Database window.

The Table Wizard dialog box appears. Don't be overwhelmed by the number of options. This is simply a long selection of sample tables—and their accompanying fields—from which you can choose.

3. Click **Customers** in the *Sample Tables* list box.

Notice that the list of field names in the *Sample Fields* list box changes; this list box now includes sample fields appropriate for a table of customers. (If you want to see a list of sample tables that are targeted to personal use, click the Personal option button.)

4. Click the **CustomerID field name**, if it is not selected.

5. Click the **Add Field button** > .

This button permits you to add one field at a time to your new table. As shown in Figure 1.19, Access lists the CustomerID field in the *Fields in my new table* list box on the right side of the Table Wizard dialog box. The CustomerID field will be used to link customers and orders.

6. Click the **ContactFirstName sample field** and click the **Add Field button** > .

The ContactFirstName field should appear directly under CustomerID in the *Fields in my new table* list box. Notice that Access places the added field below the CustomerID field. Note that the ContactLastName field in the *Sample Fields* list box is now selected.

When you select fields, the
fields appear in your table
in the order that they are
listed in the *Fields in my
new table* list box. You can
easily change the order of
fields later.

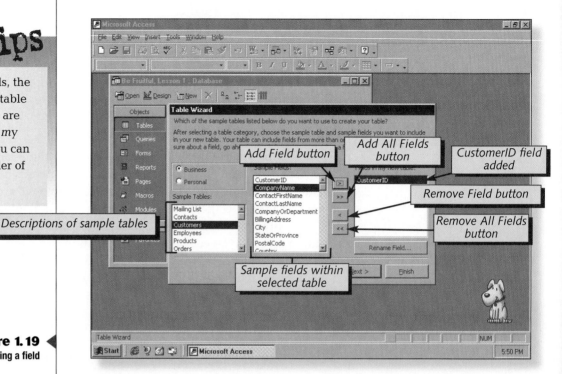

Figure 1.19
Adding a field

7. Click the Add Field button [>].

Access adds the ContactLastName field to the *Fields in my new table* list box.

8. Double-click the BillingAddress field in the *Sample Fields* list box.

Access adds the BillingAddress field to the list on the right; double-clicking one of the sample fields is a shortcut for adding a field name to a table.

9. Add the fields City, StateOrProvince, PostalCode, PhoneNumber, FaxNumber, and Notes, in that order.

You may have to scroll down in the *Sample Fields* list box to find all of these fields. Access lists all the selected fields in the *Fields in my new table* list box.

Changing Fields in the Field List

At times, you may decide against including a particular field in your table. Fortunately, this kind of change to the field list is relatively simple to make. In this activity, you will remove a field from the field list and rename another field.

1. Click FaxNumber in the *Fields in my new table* list box.

2. Click the Remove Field button [<].

Access promptly removes the FaxNumber field from the list. You can change field names with ease, too.

3. Click the PostalCode field in the *Fields in my new table* list box.

4. Click the Rename Field button.

The Rename field dialog box appears with the current field name selected.

5. Type ZIPCode, as shown in Figure 1.20.

**Removing and
Renaming Fields**

1. Click the field you wish
to remove and click the
Remove Field button.

2. Click the field you wish
to rename, click the
Rename Field button,
type the new name, and
click OK.

Hints&Tips

- You can click the Remove All Fields button or Add All Fields button to remove or add all of the fields at once.

- Typing new text will replace the selected text. Using keys such as `Delete`, `Backspace`, `Home`, and `End` work the same in text boxes as they do in word processing programs.

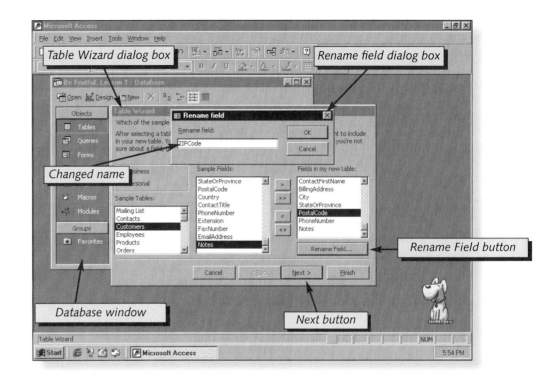

Figure 1.20
Rename field dialog box

6. Click OK.

ZIPCode appears in the *Fields in my new table* list box.

HANDS On

Access BASICS

Naming the Table and Selecting a Primary Key

1. Type a name for the table.

2. Click the *No, I'll set the primary key.* option and click Next.

3. Select the field to be used as the primary key and click Next.

Naming the Table and Selecting a Primary Key

You have now selected the desired fields for your table and are ready to choose a name for the table. In this activity, you provide a name when the Table Wizard prompts you to enter one. Then you will choose a field to act as the primary key.

1. Click the Next button near the lower-right corner of the Table Wizard dialog box.

You'll see the next Table Wizard dialog box, which lets you name your table and set the primary key.

Access suggests the name *Customers*—the name of the sample table you selected—for your new table. Object names such as table names, as well as field names, can be up to 64 characters long. Access allows any combination of letters, numbers, spaces, and many punctuation characters. Access does not permit any of the following: period, exclamation mark, grave accent, square brackets, or double quotation marks. Also, object names cannot begin with a space or an equal sign.

2. Click to the left of the letter *C*. (The table name will be deselected and the insertion point will move to the left of the letter *C*.) Then type BF before the word *Customers*.

The entire table name should read *BFCustomers,* indicating that this table will contain information about the customers of the Be Fruitful fruit-of-the-month club.

3. Click the No, I'll set the primary key. option and then click Next.

Access displays the next Table Wizard dialog box, as shown in Figure 1.21.

Figure 1.21
Selecting a primary key

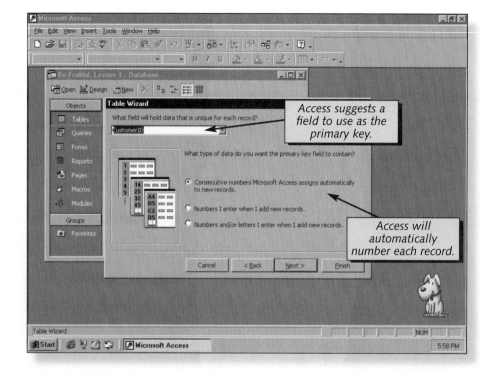

Notice that Access suggests the CustomerID field as the primary key field. You could change this by selecting another field from the drop-down list; however, since each customer will have a unique ID number, this field is an appropriate one to set as the primary key.

Also notice that the *Consecutive numbers Microsoft Access assigns automatically to new records.* button is selected. When you choose this option, Access automatically provides the CustomerID numbers, ensuring that you don't enter duplicate values in any CustomerID field.

4. Click the **Next button** to accept the selections.

Access displays the final Table Wizard dialog box.

5. Choose the **Modify the table design.** option and click the **Finish button**.

Access displays the BFCustomers table in Design view, as shown in Figure 1.22.

6. Click the **BFCustomers: Table Close button** ☒.

Access returns you to the *Be Fruitful, Lesson 1* Database window, which now includes the BFCustomers table.

Creating Tables in Design View

The Table Wizard makes creating a table a straightforward process, but allows you little flexibility. Fortunately, you can also create tables in Design view, which gives you much more control over field characteristics, including their size and the type of data they'll contain. You can use Design view both to create new tables and to modify existing tables—whether you created them in Design view or with the Table Wizard.

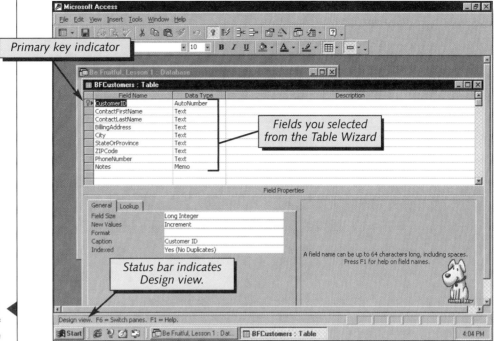

Primary key indicator

Fields you selected from the Table Wizard

Status bar indicates Design view.

Figure 1.22
Design view of
BFCustomers table

Using Design View to Create a Table

In this activity, you'll create a new table in Design view, which is slightly more involved than the Table Wizard. You'll create two fields in the Orders table for Be Fruitful's database to get a feel for the process. After that, you'll learn more about the various aspects of fields before you complete the table.

1. Click the **Tables option** in the *Be Fruitful, Lesson 1* Database window, if it is not already selected.

2. Double-click the **Create table in Design view option**.

Access opens an empty table in Design view. Notice that the ***insertion point***—the flashing vertical line—is in the Field Name column. Read the information in the lower-right corner of the window, which describes field names.

3. Click the **Maximize button** ▢.

The screen fills with the Design view of the table you are creating.

4. Enter the field name OrderNumber in the Field Name column.

5. Press [Tab] to move to the Data Type column.

Access activates the Data Type column, displaying the default data type (Text) as well as a drop-down list arrow that provides you with access to other choices. Notice that the information in the lower-right corner of the window now describes data types.

6. Click the **Data Type drop-down list arrow**.

Access reveals a drop-down list box displaying the available data types, as shown in Figure 1.23.

Access
BASICS

Creating a Table in Design View

1. Double-click the Create table in Design view option.

2. Type the first field name and press [Tab].

3. Click the desired data type and press [Tab].

4. If desired, type a description for the field and press [Tab].

5. Repeat steps 2–4 for each field.

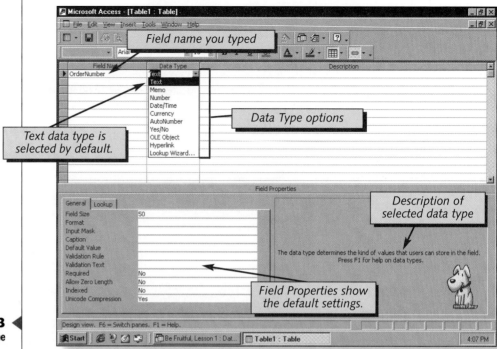

Figure 1.23
Selecting a data type

7. Click the AutoNumber data type. Then press [Tab].

Your insertion point moves to the Description field. You can enter a description of up to 255 characters for each field. Access displays some information about field descriptions in the lower-right corner of the window.

8. Press [Tab] again to move to the second row in the Field Name column.

9. Type CustomerID and press [Tab].

The insertion point moves to the Data Type column.

10. Click the Data Type drop-down arrow and click the Number data type. Then press [Tab].

11. Type the text Enter same Customer ID used in the BFCustomers table.

The Field Properties pane in the lower half of the Design view window lists the default settings for the field size and other characteristics of the current field.

12. Press [F6] to move to the Field Properties pane of the window; then press [F6] again.

Note that pressing [F6] a second time moves your insertion point back to the upper pane of the Design view window.

13. Press [Tab].

Access moves the insertion point down to the next row; now you can enter the specifications for another field. You'll enter additional fields later, after you learn more of the details about some of the field characteristics you've just encountered.

Another Way

To select the data type more quickly, type the first letter while the insertion point is in the Data Type column; for example, type n to choose number, c to choose currency, and so on.

Calculations can be performed more easily if your field names don't include spaces.

Selecting Data Types

When you work in Design view, you need to decide what data type to use. A **data type** controls the kind of data that can be entered into a field. For example, if you assign the Number data type to a field, you can't enter letters into that field. (Note that when you choose fields using the Table Wizard, Access automatically assigns the data types.) The ten available data types are described in Table 1.1.

TABLE 1.1	DATA TYPES
Data Type - Field	**Description**
Text	Holds up to 255 characters, including letters, numbers, and punctuation marks. Use this data type for fields with (1) numbers that won't be used to perform calculations and (2) both numbers and some type of punctuation characters (such as phone numbers or Social Security numbers).
Memo	Holds up to 65,535 letters, numbers, and punctuation marks. Use this data type for fields with longer amounts of text (such as free-form comments or fairly lengthy descriptions).
Number	Holds only digits, the decimal point, and the minus (negative) sign. Use this data type (7 options) for fields with numbers only and for numbers to be used to perform calculations—for example, quantity or discount fields.
Date/Time	Holds dates and times. When you use this data type for dates and times, Access prevents you from entering invalid dates or times (such as 2/31/98 or 34:35). Access provides different display formats for dates and times and lets you sort dates and times into chronological order. You can also perform date arithmetic—subtracting one date from another to determine the number of days between them or adding or subtracting a specified number of days to or from a date to calculate a later or an earlier date.
Currency	Holds numeric values (such as salaries or prices) that you want to display with a currency symbol, a decimal point, and separators (usually commas) for every three digits.
AutoNumber	Holds numbers that Access increments by 1 automatically as each new record is added to the table. You cannot edit the values in these fields. AutoNumber fields can be used as primary keys because a unique value for each record will be created automatically.

TABLE 1.1	DATA TYPES—cont.
Data Type - Field	**Description**
Yes/No	Can accept only one of two logical values. Usually the responses are shown as either Yes or No, but they can also be displayed as True or False or as On or Off.
OLE Object	Holds objects—such as Microsoft Word documents, pictures, graphs, and sounds—that have been created in other programs using the OLE protocol.
Hyperlink	Allows you to store text or graphics that links to a file or an Internet site.
Lookup Wizard	Lets you choose values from another table or create a list of values to be used. Choosing this option starts the Lookup Wizard.

Adding Field Names and Data Types

In this activity, you will add more field names and data types to the table you are creating.

1. **If necessary, click in the row below the CustomerID field name.**

The insertion point is positioned in the third row in the Field Name column.

2. **Type** OrderDate **and press** `Tab`.

Access moves you to the Data Type column, automatically selecting Text as the data type.

3. **Click the Data Type arrow and click Date/Time.**

4. **Click directly below the OrderDate field.**

5. **Type** FruitType **as the field name and press** `Tab`. **Accept Text as the data type and press** `Tab` **twice to move to the next row.**

6. **Enter the remaining field names and data types as shown in Table 1.2.**

TABLE 1.2	FIELDS AND DATA TYPE INFORMATION
Field Name	**Data Type**
Quantity	Number
Price	Currency
ShippingAmount	Currency
PaymentDate	Date/Time
PaymentAmount	Currency
PaymentType	Text
Reference	Text

Access BASICS

Adding Fields in Design View

1. Click below the last field name.

2. Type the new field name and press `Tab`.

3. Click the desired data type and press `Tab`.

4. Type a description for the field, if desired. Press `Tab`.

5. Repeat steps 2–4 for each new field.

Setting Field Properties

After assigning a data type to a field, you may have noticed that Access automatically sets default (preset) values in the text boxes in the Field Properties
pane of the Design view window. These text boxes vary depending on the data
type of the selected field, and they enable you to change a range of properties,
or characteristics, associated with the current field. These *field properties*
control the way a field looks and behaves.

Even though Access assigns default values to field properties, you can modify
the field property settings. For example, fields specified as Text data types can
be anywhere from 0 to 255 characters, and Access automatically sets the
default field size to 50 characters. However, you can determine the size of the
field simply by clicking the Field Size text box in the Field Properties pane
and entering the desired value. The number you enter determines the maximum number of characters that will fit in the field.

You'll usually want to decrease the sizes of Text fields, using only as many characters as you need. Among other reasons, decreasing field sizes helps ensure
that correct values are entered. As an example, you would set the field size of
a field to hold state abbreviations to two characters. Limiting this field size will
prevent users from unintentionally entering three-character state codes.

For Number fields, you modify the field size by specifying the *type* of number
the field will contain—the number type restricts the size of the number, usually
by limiting the number of digits to the right and the left of the decimal point.
There are seven number types; however, in this lesson you will only work with
the more common number types.

Modifying Field Properties

Now that you have additional knowledge of some of the basic field properties, you're ready to complete Be Fruitful's Orders table in Design view. In this
activity, you'll change the properties of some of the fields.

1. **Click the FruitType field name.**

2. **Press** F6.

Access moves to the Field Size text box in the Field Properties pane. Note the
default size for the FruitType field is 50.

3. **Type** 20 **in the Field Size text box.**

The value you type replaces the default, as shown in Figure 1.24.

4. **Click the PaymentType field name and then press** F6.

5. **Type** 15 **in the Field Size text box.**

6. **Click the Reference field name and press** F6. **Change the field size to 25.**

The field sizes are now smaller, more accurately reflecting the amount of data
they will contain.

7. **Click the CustomerID field name, press** F6, **and read the description in the
lower-right corner of the Field Properties pane.**

The Field Size text box says *Long Integer.*

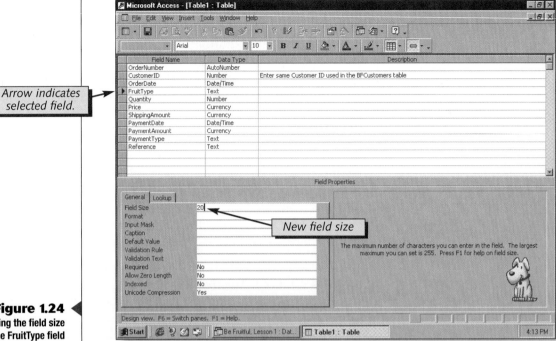

Arrow indicates selected field.

New field size

Figure 1.24 ◀
Changing the field size of the FruitType field

This field must be set to *Long Integer* to match the CustomerID field in the BFCustomers table, which is an AutoNumber field.

8. Click the Quantity field name and press F6.

The Field Size is displayed as Long Integer. You can save storage space by making this field smaller.

9. Click the Field Size arrow.

The list of number type options appears.

10. Click Integer.

11. With the Quantity field still selected, double-click the Default Value text box.

The 0 in the box is highlighted.

12. Type 1 in the Default Value text box.

Now when an order is completed, Access will assume the quantity ordered is one.

13. Type Enter check or credit card number in the Description column of the Reference field.

The default settings set by Access have been modified now to meet your needs.

Choosing a Primary Key

When creating a table with the Table Wizard, you set the primary key in the Table Wizard dialog box or you allow Access to set one. When you create a table in Design view, you must set the primary key yourself. To set the primary key, you first select a field with the row selector. The *row selector* is the small box to the left of a field.

If you're curious about some of the other field properties, select the field property and read the description.

Setting the Primary Key

In this activity, you will designate the OrderNumber field as the primary key.

1. Click the row selector to the left of the OrderNumber field.

The entire OrderNumber row is highlighted.

2. Click the Primary Key button  on the Database toolbar.

Note *To assign the primary key, you can also click Primary Key on the Edit menu or right-click the highlighted row and click Primary Key on the shortcut menu that appears.*

Access places a small key-shaped icon in the row selector for the OrderNumber field, as shown in Figure 1.25.

Figure 1.25
Setting the primary key

Key icon indicates that this field is set as the primary key.

Row selectors

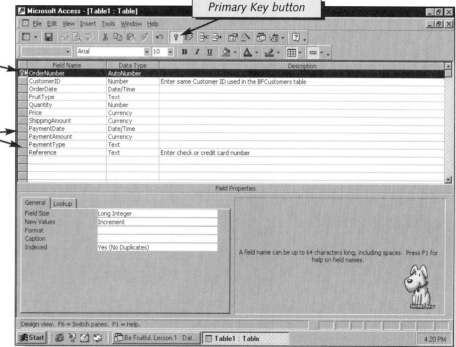

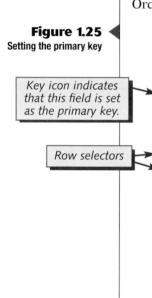

Designating a Primary Field

1. In Design view, click the row selector of the field you wish to designate as the primary key.

2. Click the Primary Key button.

Some tables require you to set a combination of two or more fields as the primary key. For instance, if the Orders table didn't contain the OrderNumber field, no other single field could be used as a primary key since none uniquely identifies each record. For instance, if you picked the CustomerID field as the primary key, you would not be able to distinguish between different orders made by the same customer. In this case, you could select the CustomerID, OrderDate, and FruitType fields and then issue the Primary Key command. The combination of these three fields would be considered the primary key.

You've completed the structure for the Orders table, but you need to complete one more step; you need to save this table for future use.

SAVING THE TABLE

As you may know, to *save* is the process of taking information from your computer's memory and storing it on a more permanent medium—usually a hard drive or a removable disk. When you create tables with the Table Wizard, Access automatically saves them, using the table name you supply. When you create or modify tables in Design view, in contrast, you need to tell Access to save the table, much as you need to save documents you create with a word processing program. You'll want to save frequently as you work, in case of a power outage or other event that can cause you to lose data that hasn't been saved.

When you use the Save command to save a table for the first time, Access requests a table name. When you update your table design and save again, the modified table is simply saved under the same name, so Access has no need to prompt you for a new name. If for some reason you want to save a copy of the table under a new name, however, you can do so by clicking Save As on the File menu.

Saving the Orders Table

In this activity, you'll save Be Fruitful's Orders table so you can change the design later if necessary, and, equally important, so you can enter data in the next lesson.

1. Click the Save button 🖫 **on the Database toolbar.**

Access displays the Save As dialog box, as shown in Figure 1.26; you will enter a name for your table in this dialog box.

Another ◆Way

To save a table, click File on the menu bar and click save.

Figure 1.26 ◀
Save As dialog box

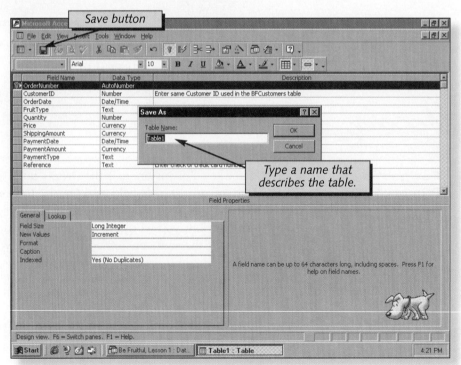

Saving a Table

1. Click the Save button.

2. Type a descriptive name and click OK.

2. Type BFOrders **in the Table Name text box and click** OK.

Access returns you to Design view, with your table design still visible. Note, however, that the table name BFOrders now shows in the title bar. This indicates that the table has been saved.

3. Click the **Close button** ☒ **at the right end of the menu bar.**

Access closes the BFOrders table and returns you to the Database window for the *Be Fruitful, Lesson 1* database.

If you attempt to close a table that includes unsaved design changes, Access displays a dialog box asking whether you want to save your changes. You would choose *Yes* if you want to save the changes, *No* to discard them, or *Cancel* to cancel the operation and return to Design view.

Understanding Relationships Among Tables

Now that you've created two tables, use Help to learn more about how the tables can be related to each other.

1. Click the **Office Assistant**.

2. Type relationships among tables **in the *What would you like to do?* box.**

3. Click the **Search button**.

4. Click the **Create or modify relationships option** to open the associated Help window. Maximize the Help window, if necessary.

Figure 1.27
The Access Help window

5. Click the **Learn about relationships in a database link** (Figure 1.27).

6. Scroll and read all of the information in the Help window to learn about the different types of relationships that you can assign to fields in tables.

7. Find and click the glossary term *relationships* to view the definition.

8. Click the button or link that leads you to more information on how to define a relationship.

9. Read the new text and explore other links.

10. When you are finished exploring, click the **Close button** ☒ to close the Help window.

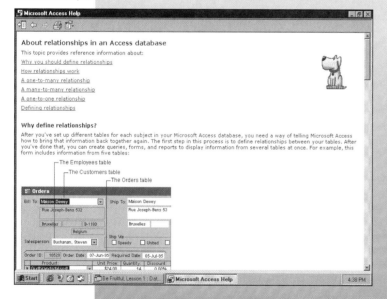

Adding Captions

1. In Design view, click the field to which you want to add a caption.

2. Type a caption in the Caption box in the Field Properties pane of the window.

MODIFYING TABLES IN DESIGN VIEW

Whether you've created a table with the Table Wizard or in Design view, at some point you may need to make changes to the structure of your table. You might need to change field names or data types, to add a field you left out, to eliminate a field you no longer need, or to reorder your fields to better suit your needs or your sense of order. All of these changes can be made in Design view.

Warning *You can change the table structure after you've entered data into the table, but proceed with caution if you do. You run the risk of losing or unintentionally modifying your data.*

Adding Captions to Fields

Captions are the words and phrases you type to either abbreviate or clarify field names. Captions are used as labels in forms, reports, tables, and other objects. In this activity, you will add a field to the end of a table and create captions for fields. The captions you create will clarify field names that you will later use in reports and other objects. For example, rather than a report heading of *ExtraCatalogs* (one word), you can change the caption so the heading will appear as *Extra Catalogs* (two words).

1. **In the** *Be Fruitful, Lesson 1* **Database window, click the BFCustomers table and then click the Design button ⬛ Design .**

You'll see the BFCustomers table in Design view.

2. **Click directly below the field name Notes.**

To add a new field at the end of the table structure, you go to the bottom of the display and enter the information for the new field.

3. **Type ExtraCatalogs and press [Tab] to move to the Data Type column.**

4. **Type y to select the Yes/No data type and press [Tab] .**

5. **Type Offers for holiday specials, exotic fruits, and more in the Description field.**

6. **Type Extra Catalogs in the Caption text box in the Field Properties pane.**

Your new field should look like Figure 1.28.

7. **Click the BillingAddress field in the top portion of the window.**

Notice that the Caption box contains the text *Billing Address*. When a field name is selected from the Table Wizard—as this one was—a caption is automatically assigned to a field name that contains two or more words. However, when you create fields in Design view, captions are not automatically created. For consistent spacing within labels (which will appear on reports and forms), add captions to those field names that you create in Design view.

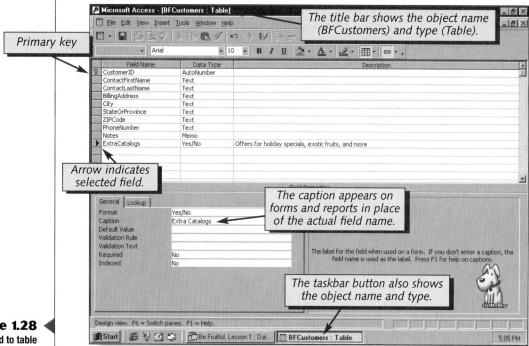

The title bar shows the object name (BFCustomers) and type (Table).

Primary key

Arrow indicates selected field.

The caption appears on forms and reports in place of the actual field name.

The taskbar button also shows the object name and type.

Figure 1.28
New field added to table

8. Click the **ZIPCode field** in the top portion of the window.

Earlier in this lesson, you created this field using the Table Wizard. So why didn't Access automatically create a caption? If you'll recall, you changed the name of the field from PostalCode to ZIPCode. When you change a field name, Access does not automatically create a caption.

9. Type ZIP Code **in the Caption text box.**

During data entry and the display of the table, your fields will now appear with easier-to-read labels.

Adding and Removing Fields

Although you should always plan ahead regarding fields to be included in your database, sometimes you'll discover that you need to make changes. Access allows you to add and remove fields within Design view. You can add a field (row) to the end of a table, as you previously learned, but you can also insert field names between other fields. You can also delete fields that become unnecessary. There are several ways to insert a row: click Rows on the Insert menu; right-click the field and click Insert Rows on the shortcut menu; or click the Insert Rows button [icon]. There are also several ways to delete a field: click Delete Rows on the Edit menu; right-click the field and click Delete Rows on the shortcut menu; or click the Delete Rows button [icon].

Access also provides an Undo feature that lets you reverse the last action you completed. You'll learn how to add and remove fields and use the Undo feature in the following activity.

Clicking the row selector highlights the entire field. You can select multiple adjacent fields by dragging over their row selectors. You can select nonadjacent fields by pressing Ctrl and clicking the row selector of each field to be selected.

Inserting and Deleting Fields

In this activity, you will add a new field between existing fields. Then you'll learn how to remove a field. Lastly, you'll undo a change.

1. **Click anywhere within the Notes row in the top pane of the Design view window.**

2. **Click the Insert Rows button** ⅊.

As shown in Figure 1.29, Access adds a blank row above the Notes field and places the insertion point within this row. You use this technique to insert new rows between existing ones rather than after the last row.

Figure 1.29 ◄
Inserting a row

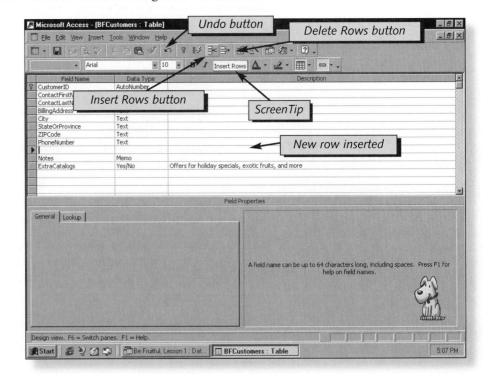

Adding and Removing Fields

To add a field:

1. In Design view, click in the field to appear below the new field.

2. Click the Insert Rows button.

3. Type the field name, data type, and description in the new row.

To delete a field:

1. Click the field that you wish to delete.

2. Click the Delete Rows button.

To undo a change:

Click the Undo button.

3. **Type** DateJoined **in the Field Name column and press** ⎄.

4. **Choose the Date/Time data type.**

5. **Type the caption** Date Joined **in the Caption box.**

6. **Click anywhere within the Notes field.**

7. **Click the Delete Rows button** ⅊.

Access deletes the active row—in this case, the Notes field. Now you realize that you actually need to retain the Notes field.

8. **Click the Undo Delete button** ↺.

Access restores the Notes field.

Warning *You can take advantage of the Undo command only if you act quickly enough. Choosing Undo generally undoes your most recent action only, whether you deleted a row, moved a row, typed some text, or chose a new data type. If you've done something else in the interim, however, such as deleting another field or typing some text, you won't be able to undo your earlier action with this command.*

Moving a Field

At times, you'll include all of the correct fields in your database but later notice that the order in which they appear could be improved. Instead of using the methods to add and delete fields, Access allows you to change the order of fields by dragging them to their new locations in Design view.

HANDS

Reorganizing Fields and Improving Table Design

After looking at your database, you decide to display each customer's last name before the customer's first name. In this activity, you will switch the order of these two fields. Then you will make additional modifications to the two tables you've created to improve their appearance and efficiency.

1. Click the row selector for the ContactFirstName field.

Access highlights the entire row.

2. Point to the row selector for the selected row; click and hold the mouse button to drag downward until the dark horizontal line appears just below the ContactLastName field, as shown in Figure 1.30. Release the mouse button.

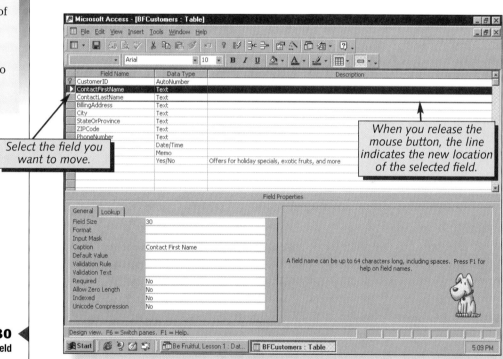

Select the field you want to move.

When you release the mouse button, the line indicates the new location of the selected field.

Figure 1.30
Moving a field

Access attaches a small grayed rectangle to the bottom of the pointer and also displays a dark horizontal line; the selected field will move to just below the horizontal line when you release the mouse button. Access moves the field to the new location in the table, below the last name field. You can even move several adjacent fields at once using this method.

3. Change the field size of the ContactLastName field to 30.

4. Change the size of the BillingAddress field to 50.

Access
BASICS

Moving a Field

1. Click the row selector of the field you wish to move.

2. Drag the row selector to the new position.

---

5. **Change the size of the City field to** 30.

6. **Change the size of the StateOrProvince field to** 2.

7. **Type** List preferences, allergies, and shipping notes **in the Description for the Notes field.**

Now that you're through modifying the BFCustomers table, you need to save again to preserve your changes.

8. **Click the Save button** 🖫.

Since you named and saved this table earlier, Access saves the updated table without first prompting you for a table name.

9. **Close the BFCustomers table.**

10. **Select the BFOrders table in the Database window and click the Design button** 🖾 Design .

11. **Create captions for each of the fields shown in Table 1.3.**

TABLE 1.3	CAPTIONS FOR BFORDERS TABLE
Field	**Caption**
OrderNumber	Order No.
CustomerID	Customer ID
OrderDate	Order Date
FruitType	Fruit Type
ShippingAmount	Shipping Amt.
PaymentDate	Payment Date
PaymentAmount	Payment Amt.
PaymentType	Payment Type

12. **Save and close the BFOrders table.**

13. **Click Options on the Tools menu, click the General tab, and select the Compact on Close option, if necessary.**

A check mark appears in the Compact on Close box. Remember, choosing this option minimizes the size of a database and improves performance.

14. **Click OK.**

15. **Close the Be Fruitful, Lesson 1 database.**

EXITING ACCESS

When you close a database, you remove the specific database from memory but leave Access operating. When you're finished working with the Access program, you should exit the program properly. Exiting the program closes any open Access databases and removes Access from the memory of your computer. You can exit Access by clicking the title bar Close button ☒ or by clicking the Exit command on the File menu. After exiting Access, you will see the desktop if you have no other programs running. From there, you may choose to shut down your computer.

Exiting the Access Program

In this activity, you will exit the Access program and return to the Windows desktop.

1. Click **Exit** on the File menu or click the **Close button** ☒ on the Access title bar.

If you have not opened any other application, the Office Assistant will close and your screen will return to the Windows desktop.

2. Remove your Student Data Disk from the drive, if you are finished with your computer session.

Exiting Access

Click Exit on the File menu.

Or

Click the Close button on the Access title bar.

Test your knowledge by answering the following questions. See Appendix B to check your answers.

1. A table organizes information into a series of columns called _____ that contain categories of data and rows called _____ that contain all the categories for one particular entity.

2. _____ are the various components of Access that you use to enter, display, print, and manipulate the information in a database.

3. To create or modify the structure of a table, you must use _____ view.

4. A _____ is a field or set of fields that uniquely identifies each record in a table.

5. _____ replace field names as labels in forms, reports, and other objects.

ON*the*WEB

ACCESSING THE SEARCH PAGE

In previous lessons, you've learned how to access Web pages by typing their addresses. However, often you'll want to use the Internet to find information on a specific topic, but you won't know the address of a specific site. In these cases, you can use the Search page.

In this activity, you act as the marketing manager for Be Fruitful. Lately, you've been considering creating a Web site for the company in hopes of increasing sales. One link on the Web page would provide customers with recipes that contain fresh fruit. In this activity, you will use the Search the Web button 🔍 in Access to navigate to the Search page of your browser; then you'll search for Web sites that contain fruit recipes.

1. **Connect to the Internet.**

2. **Start Access. Close the initial dialog box.**

3. **Click the Search the Web button 🔍 on the Web toolbar.**

 *To display the Web toolbar, right-click either the Database toolbar or the Formatting toolbar and click Web on the list that appears.*

Access launches your browser, and the page that is specified as your Search page appears. A ***Search page*** allows you to type keywords that describe material for which you are looking and then searches the Web for documents that contain those keywords.

4. **If necessary, maximize the browser window and then click a search engine option. (You may use the default if one is already selected or if you do not have a choice of search engines.)**

A ***search engine*** allows you to search for information on a particular topic. Some search engines search every word of every document they find on the Internet; others search only portions of documents they find.

5. **When your Search page appears, type** recipes **in the Search text box.**

6. **Click the button to process your search request.**

The button that processes your search request is often labeled *Search* or *Find*.

7. **When the results of your search appear, scroll down to see the numerous sites to which you can connect.**

The results of your search appear in the form of links that you can click to navigate to the page described. The results that you get from typing the keyword *recipes* will vary depending on the search engine you use. They will lead to a variety of topics including recipes of all sorts using many types of foods and for many different meals. The top of the page may tell

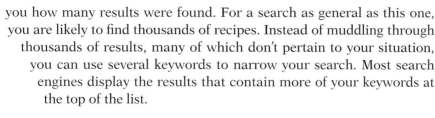

you how many results were found. For a search as general as this one, you are likely to find thousands of recipes. Instead of muddling through thousands of results, many of which don't pertain to your situation, you can use several keywords to narrow your search. Most search engines display the results that contain more of your keywords at the top of the list.

Many search engines allow you to use special symbols to narrow your results even further. For instance, most search engines allow you to use quotation marks around words that should always be found together. Some search engines, such as one called *AltaVista,* allow the use of a plus symbol (+) to specify that the keyword must be found in the result and a minus sign (-) to indicate a word that should not be found in the resulting pages. For instance, the keywords + *fruit company "mail order" - balloons* will result in pages that contain the word *fruit,* may contain the word *company,* may contain the words *mail order* together but will exclude those pages that contain just the word *mail* and just the word *order,* and do not include the word *balloons.* To find out if your search engine allows the use of special symbols, look for a Help or an Advanced Search button that describes them.

8. **Return to the top of the Search page (click the Back button on your browser toolbar, if necessary) and type the keywords "fresh fruit" recipes in the Search text box.**

9. **Choose a search engine, if necessary, and click the button to process your search request.**

When the results appear, scroll down to see them. As you can see, the results using several keywords usually suggest sites that are more targeted to the information you are seeking.

10. **From your results, click one of the links that you think will lead you to a Web page that contains one or more fresh fruit recipes. Explore the site.**

11. **Using Word 2000, describe what you do and do not like about the site and list any suggestions to improve the site. Then click the Back button on your browser toolbar to return to the list of results.**

12. **Explore a link to another site. Using Word 2000, describe your reactions to this site and list any suggestions to improve the site. If time allows, explore other related sites.**

13. **Close your browser, disconnect from the Internet (unless your instructor tells you to remain connected), and exit Access.**

You may proceed directly to the exercises for this lesson. If, however, you are finished with your computer session, follow the "shut down" procedures for your lab or school environment.

Lesson Summary & Exercises

SUMMARY

Databases are used every day, both for business and personal applications. They allow you to present data in an organized form and to maintain and retrieve information electronically. Lesson 1 introduced basic database terms and taught you how to open a database. You learned about the various objects that comprise a database, and you used the Database window to access four database objects—a table, a query, a form, and a report. You also learned how to print a database object and compact and close a database. To build an effective database, you must plan ahead to avoid redundancy. In the latter part of Lesson 1, you created a new database, and then you created two tables—one using the Table Wizard and one using Design view. You modified the tables by changing the field properties, saved the tables, and exited Access. Finally, you learned to search the Internet for information by using the Search page.

Now that you have completed this lesson, you should be able to do the following:

- Describe what a database is, explain the use, and give examples of data you can enter. (Access-338)
- Describe the difference between a record and a field. (Access-338)
- Start Microsoft Access and identify parts of the Database window. (Access-339)
- Identify the Database and Formatting toolbars. (Access-342)
- Open a database. (Access-343)
- Explain the purpose of the database objects in Access—tables, queries, forms, reports, pages, macros, and modules. (Access-345)

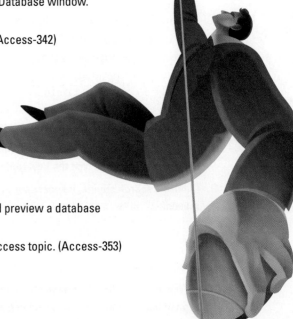

- View and edit tables in Datasheet view and switch between Datasheet and Design views. (Access-345)
- View queries, use Form view to add records, and preview a database object. (Access-348)
- Use the online Help system to get help on any Access topic. (Access-353)
- Print a database object. (Access-354)
- Compact and close a database. (Access-355)
- Plan a database. (Access-356)
- Create a new database. (Access-359)
- Create a table using the Table Wizard. (Access-361)
- Create a table using Design view. (Access-365)
- Select data types. (Access-367)
- Add field names and data types. (Access-368)
- Set and modify field properties. (Access-369)
- Choose a primary key. (Access-370)
- Save a table. (Access-372)
- Understand relationships among tables. (Access-373)
- Modify tables using Design view. (Access-374)
- Exit Access. (Access-379)
- Use a search engine to find information. (Access-380)

Lesson Summary & Exercises

CONCEPTS REVIEW

1 TRUE/FALSE

Circle T if the statement is true or F if the statement is false.

T   F   **1.** You can modify the structure of an object in Design view.

T   F   **2.** The Database window always first displays the reports in a database by default.

T   F   **3.** A telephone book is an example of a manual database.

T   F   **4.** You can move to the beginning of a table by pressing ⟨⇧ Shift⟩ + ⟨Home⟩.

T   F   **5.** A field in a database contains the set of data for one entity, such as the name, address, and phone number for one customer.

T   F   **6.** Creating a table in Design view allows you more flexibility than when you create one with the Table Wizard.

T   F   **7.** Text, Number, and Currency are examples of data types.

T   F   **8.** You should always create at least two tables that contain redundant data to help you check for data-entry errors.

T   F   **9.** In Design view, the small box to the left of each field is called the row selector.

T   F   **10.** Captions are automatically created when you type field names in Design view.

2 MATCHING

Match each of the terms on the left with the definitions on the right.

TERMS	DEFINITIONS
1. query	**a.** Database programs that allow you to link tables
2. objects	**b.** Screen display showing things much as they will be printed
3. record	**c.** Questions requesting specific information from the database
4. relational databases	**d.** Name for various components of Access
5. WYSIWYG	**e.** Group of fields related to a particular entity
6. primary key	**f.** Value that Access enters into fields automatically
7. AutoNumber	**g.** Field of same name in two tables that enables you to link those tables
8. Date/Time	**h.** Data type that enables you to perform date arithmetic
9. default value	**i.** Field or fields that uniquely identify each record in a table
10. common field	**j.** Field that Access increments by 1 for each new record

Lesson Summary & Exercises

3 COMPLETION

Fill in the missing word or phrase for each of the following statements.

1. You can use the _____ object to automatically perform a set of actions.

2. When you want presentation-quality hard copy, you should print a _____.

3. A(n) _____ is a set of programmed statements that are stored together as a unit.

4. In Access, the term _____ means a set of related tables, forms, reports, queries, pages, macros, and modules.

5. When you've finished using Access for the day, you should _____ the program.

6. The _____ guides you through each step of creating a table, prompting you for the needed information.

7. When a field name is long or difficult to identify, you can use a(n) _____ to abbreviate or clarify.

8. In the top pane of the Design view window, you specify the _____, _____, and _____ for each field in a table.

9. To reverse your previous action, click the _____ button.

10. A(n) _____ controls the kind of information that can be entered into a field.

4 SHORT ANSWER

Write a brief answer to each of the following questions.

1. Name the seven types of Access objects.

2. When would you use forms rather than tables for data entry?

3. From within a Database window, how would you open a table to change the layout?

4. Describe the relationship between tables, records, and fields.

5. Why is it important to compact a database on a regular basis?

6. List at least two reasons to divide your data into multiple tables instead of placing all the information in one large table.

7. Identify one advantage and one disadvantage of creating tables using the Table Wizard.

8. Explain why you can't enter duplicate values in primary key fields.

9. List the steps you would perform to add a new field between the DatePurchased and Amount fields in a table.

10. How would you make a field called AccountNumber the primary key in a table when in the Design view?

5 IDENTIFICATION

Label each of the elements of the Access window in Figure 1.31.

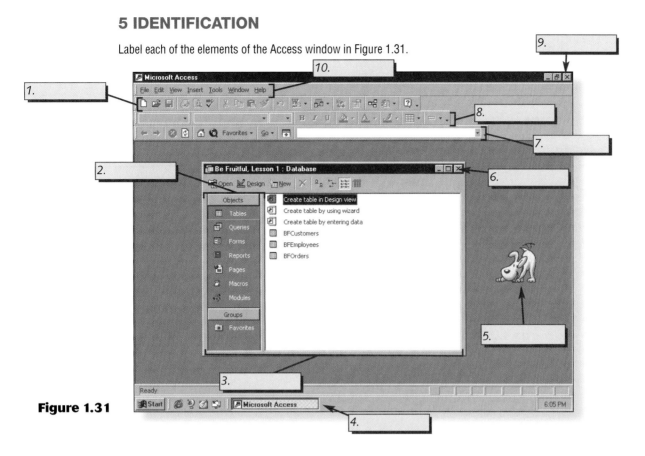

Figure 1.31

SKILLS REVIEW

Complete each of the Skills Review problems in sequential order to review your Access skills to open an existing database; display various views of database objects; edit data in a database; use the Help system; create a new database; and create and modify tables.

1 Launch Access, Open a Database, and Edit a Table

1. Click the **Start button** 🏁Start on the Windows taskbar, point to **Programs**, and click **Microsoft Access**.

2. Click the **Cancel button** to remove the initial Access dialog box.

3. Click the **Open button** 📂 on the Database toolbar.

4. Click the **Look in arrow** in the Open dialog box, and click the drive and folder that contains your Student Data Disk.

5. Double-click *Smyth Business College Sample*. Click **Tables**, if necessary (Figure 1.32).

6. Click the **Student Information table** and click the **Open button** 📂Open in the Database window.

Lesson Summary & Exercises

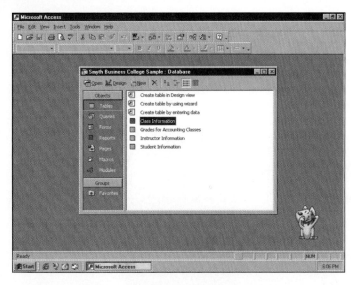

Figure 1.32

7. Click the **Maximize button** 🔲.

8. Press `Tab` three times to move to the Address field for George Robinson.

9. Type 1765 Lyle Ave. and press `Tab`.

10. In the City field, type Atlanta and press `Tab` twice.

11. In the ZIP Code field, type 303371202 and press `Tab`.

12. In the Phone Number field, type 4045552969 and press `Tab`.

13. Click the **Close button** ❎ on the menu bar to close the table.

2 View a Table Design

1. Click the **Class Information table** and click the **Design button** 🔲 Design.

2. Press `F6` to move to the lower pane.

3. Click the **View button** 🔲▾ on the Database toolbar to display the table in Datasheet view.

4. Click the **Close button** ❎ on the menu bar to close the table.

3 Open, Edit, and Print Objects

1. Open the **Student Grades for Basic Accounting Classes query**.

2. Click the **View button** 🔲▾ on the Database toolbar to view the query in Design view.

3. Click the query window's **Close button** ❎.

4. Open the **Student Information form**.

5. Click the **New Record button** ▸⁎ and press `Tab`.

6. Type each of the following entries into the form, pressing `Tab` after each item:

Last Name:	Pittinger
First Name:	Rose
Address:	2575 Delk Rd.
City:	Marietta
State:	GA
ZIP Code:	300676584
Phone Number:	7705550737
Major:	Management

7. Click the **Close button** ❎ on the menu bar.

8. Select (but do not open) the **Students Listed by Major report**.

Lesson Summary & Exercises

9. Click the **Preview button** [🔍 Preview] in the Database window.

10. Click the **Print button**.

11. Click the **Close button** [✕] on the menu bar.

4 Use Help

1. Click the **Office Assistant**. Type group data in a report and click the **Search button**.

2. Click the **Group records in a report option** from the results that appear.

3. Maximize the Help window, if necessary, and read the text that appears.

4. Click the **Sorting And Grouping button** in the Help window and read the definition. Then click to remove the definition from the screen.

5. Click the **How? link** in the Help window and read the new text that appears.

6. With the Help window still open, click the **Show button** [◀] to display the Contents, Answer Wizard, and Index tabs.

7. Click the **Answer Wizard tab**. Type input mask and click the **Search button**.

8. In the *Select topic to display* pane, click **Examples of input masks**.

9. Read the text that appears in the right pane of the Help window.

10. Click the **Close button** [✕] on the Help window.

5 Compact and Close a Database

1. Click **Tools** on the menu bar and click **Options**.

2. On the General tab, click the **Compact on Close option**, if it is not already selected.

3. Click **OK**.

4. Click the **Close button** [✕] on the *Smyth Business College Sample* Database window.

6 Create a New Database and Use the Table Wizard

1. Click the **New button** [🗋]. If necessary, click **Database** on the General tab of the New dialog box; then click **OK**.

2. In the Save in box, navigate to the *Skills Review* folder on your Student Data Disk.

3. Type Smyth Business College, Lesson 1 in the File name box. Click the **Create button**.

4. In the Database window, double-click the **Create table by using wizard option**.

5. In the *Sample Tables* box, click **Students**.

6. Click the **StudentID field name** and click the **Add Field button** [▷].

7. Double-click the **FirstName field** to add it to the *Fields in my new table* box.

8. Add the following fields to the *Fields in my new table* box: MiddleName, LastName, ParentsNames, Address, City, StateOrProvince, PostalCode, PhoneNumber, and Major.

9. Click the **ParentsNames field** in the *Fields in my new table* box and click the **Remove Field button** <.

10. Click the **StateOrProvince field** in the *Fields in my new table* box. Click the **Rename Field button** and type State in the Rename field dialog box. Then click **OK**.

11. Click **Next** in the Table Wizard dialog box.

12. Edit the suggested name *Students* to be Student Information.

13. Click the **No, I'll set the primary key. option** and click **Next**.

14. Select the **StudentID field** from the drop-down list, if it is not already selected.

15. Click the **Consecutive numbers Microsoft Access assigns automatically to new records. option**, if it is not already selected. Then, click **Next**.

16. Click **Modify the table design. option** and click **Finish**.

17. Close the table by clicking the **Close button** ✕.

7 Create a Table in Design View, Change Field Properties, and Save a Table

1. Double-click the **Create table in Design view option**. Type StudentID in the first row of the Field Name column; then press `Tab`.

2. Click the **Data type arrow**, click **Number**, and press `Tab`.

3. Type Enter same Student ID used in the Student Information table in the Description column and press `Tab`.

4. Type ClassCode as the second field name. Press `Tab` twice to accept Text as the data type and to move to the Description column.

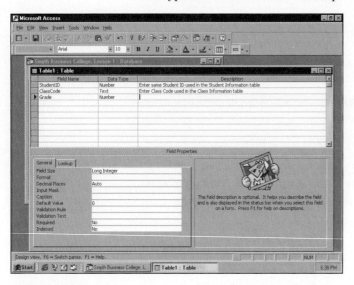

5. Type Enter Class Code used in the Class Information table in the Description column and press `Tab`.

6. Type Grade as the third field name and press `Tab`.

7. Click the **Data type arrow** and click **Number** (Figure 1.33).

8. Click the **ClassCode field**, press `F6`, and type 7 in the Field Size text box.

9. Click the **Grade field** and press `F6`. In the Field Size box, click **Byte**.

Figure 1.33

10. Click the **ClassCode field**, press ⬚, and click the **Input Mask text box**. Type LLL000 (three Ls and three zeros). This input mask will require three letters and three numbers to be typed when you add data to this field.

11. Click and hold the mouse button on the **row selector** to the left of the StudentID field to select the entire field and drag to include the ClassCode field. Both rows will be highlighted.

12. Click the **Primary Key button** ⬚.

13. Click **Save** ⬚, type Grades for Accounting Classes in the Table Name box, and click **OK**.

14. Close the Design window by clicking the **Close button** ⬚.

8 Modify Tables

1. In the Database window, click the **Student Information table** and click the **Design button** ⬚.

2. Click the **PostalCode field**, press ⬚, click the **Caption box**, double-click the word **Postal**, and type ZIP.

3. Press ⬚ and click in the next blank row below the Major field. Type FullTime in the Field Name column and press ⬚.

4. Click **Yes/No** in the Data Type column.

5. Type Full Time in the Caption text box.

6. Click anywhere within the Major field in the top pane of the Design window.

7. Click the **Insert Rows button** ⬚.

8. Type GradePointAverage in the Field Name column and press ⬚.

9. Type n to select the Number data type and press ⬚.

10. Type the caption GPA in the Caption text box.

11. Click anywhere in the FirstName field.

12. Click the **Delete Rows button** ⬚.

13. Since you realize you meant to delete the MiddleName field instead, click the **Undo Delete button** ⬚.

14. Click the **MiddleName field** and click the **Delete Rows button** ⬚.

15. Click the **row selector** in front of the FirstName field.

16. Drag the row selector down so that the dark horizontal line appears directly below the LastName field and release.

9 Improve Table Design and Exit Access

1. In the Student Information table, change the field size of the LastName field to 30, the FirstName field to 30, the Address field to 50, the City field to 30, the State field to 2, and the Major field to 20.

2. Click **Save** ⬚ and then close the Student Information table.

3. Click the **Grades for Accounting Classes table** and click the **Design button** ⬚.

4. Create these captions: Student ID for the StudentID field and Class Code for the ClassCode field.

5. Click **Save** 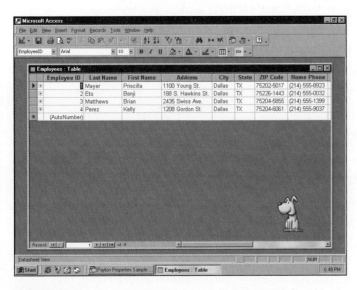 and then close the Grades for Accounting Classes table.

6. Click **Options** on the Tools menu. On the General tab, click the **Compact on Close option** and click **OK**.

7. Close the *Smyth Business College, Lesson 1* database.

8. Click **Exit** on the File menu to close the Access program.

LESSON APPLICATIONS

1 View and Edit Tables

As a new employee of Payton Properties, Inc., you need to familiarize yourself with the database that the agency uses to track employee information and data on homes available for sale. Start by opening and editing some tables.

Figure 1.34

1. Start Access and open the *Payton Properties Sample* database stored on your Student Data Disk.

2. Click the Tables option in the Database window, select the Employees table, and use the Open button to display the data in Datasheet view.

3. Read the data. Then change Brian Matthews' phone number to (214) 555-1399, press [Tab], and press [Ctrl] + [Home] (Figure 1.34). Close the Employees table.

4. Use the Design button to view the design of the Homes for Sale table.

5. Close the Homes for Sale table.

2 Work with a Query

One of your clients is looking for a home with four bedrooms. Display the results of a query that asks to view four-bedroom homes available. Then view the design of the query.

1. Open the *Payton Properties Sample* database stored on your Student Data Disk, if it is not already open.

2. Click the Queries option in the Database window, select the Homes with Four Bedrooms query, and use the Open button to display the query results in Datasheet view.

3. Read the data and then close the Homes with Four Bedrooms query.

4. Use the Design button to view the design of the Homes with Four Bedrooms query.

5. Close the query.

Lesson Summary & Exercises

3 Add a Record Using a Form

As an employee of Payton Properties, you also need to know how to add records to their database. First, display the homes that Payton Properties has for sale using a form. Then, add a new listing.

1. Open the **Payton Properties Sample** database stored on your Student Data Disk, if it is not already open.

2. Click the Forms option in the Database window and use the Open button to display the first record in the Homes for Sale form.

3. Use the New Record button to add a new, blank record. Type the following data into the new record:

Address:	18 Milikin Dr.
Bedrooms:	3
Baths:	2
Square Feet:	1690
Rooms:	7
Year Built:	1989
Price:	120900
Employee ID:	3

4. Close the Homes for Sale form.

4 Preview and Print a Report and Compact and Close a Database

Your manager has asked you to print a report that shows the basic facts of newly listed homes. Open a report that provides this information and then print a copy for your manager.

1. Open the **Payton Properties Sample** database stored on your Student Data Disk, if it is not already open.

2. Click the Reports option in the Database window and use the Preview button to display the data in the New Listings by Agent report.

3. Scroll through and read the report.

4. Click the Print button and then close the report.

5. Click Tools on the menu bar, point to Database Utilities, and click Compact and Repair Database. Watch the status bar for an immediate message that the database is being compacted.

6. Close the **Payton Properties Sample** Database window.

5 Create a Database and Use the Table Wizard

Create a new database and use the Table Wizard to create a table, add fields, remove and rename fields, name the table, and assign a primary key.

1. Create a new database named Payton Properties, Lesson 1 and save it in the **Lesson Applications** folder.

2. Create a table using the Table Wizard. Use the Employees sample table to add the following fields: DepartmentName, EmployeeID, FirstName, LastName, Address, City, StateOrProvince, PostalCode, HomePhone, Birthdate, and DateHired.

Lesson Summary & Exercises

3. While using the Wizard, remove the Birthdate field from the *Fields in my new table* box.

4. Rename the EmployeeID field to AgentID.

5. Name the table Employees and select the AgentID field as the primary key. Indicate that you want Access to automatically assign consecutive numbers to new records in the primary key field. Also indicate that you want to modify the table design after the wizard creates the table. Close the table.

6 Create a Table in Design View

Create a table in Design view and add field names, data types, and descriptions.

1. Open the **Payton Properties, Lesson 1** database in the **Lesson Applications** folder on your Student Data Disk, if it is not already open. In the Database window, create a new table in Design view.

2. Enter the field names, data types, and descriptions found in Table 1.4.

TABLE 1.4	INFORMATION TO ADD	
Field Name	**Data Type**	**Description**
Address	Text	Enter street address of home for sale
Bedrooms	Number	
Baths	Number	
Rooms	Number	
YearBuilt	Number	
Price	Currency	
SellingPrice	Currency	
AgentID	Number	Enter Agent ID from Employees table

3. Assign the Address field as the primary key.

4. Save the table as Homes for Sale.

7 Change Field Properties, Add Captions, and Insert and Remove Fields

Change field sizes and other properties in the Homes for Sale table and add captions to a few of the fields. Then add and delete fields and undo a change.

1. In the **Payton Properties, Lesson 1** database in the **Lesson Applications** folder on your Student Data Disk, open the Homes for Sale table in Design view, if necessary.

2. Change the field size of the Address field to 40.

3. Click the Price field and change the Decimal Places box in the Field Properties pane to 0 (zero).

4. Click the SellingPrice field and change the Decimal Places box in the Field Properties pane to 0 (zero).

5. Click the Baths field. Change the Field Size to Decimal, change the Format to General Number, change the Precision to 4, and change the Scale to 1.

6. Add appropriate captions to the YearBuilt, SellingPrice, and AgentID fields.

7. Use the Insert Rows button to add a field between the Baths and Rooms fields. In the new field, type **SquareFeet** as the field name and assign Number as the data type.

8. In the Field Properties pane for the SquareFeet field, type **Sq. Feet** as the caption, assign a format of **Standard**, and enter **0** (zero) in the Decimal Places box.

9. Insert another field between the Rooms and YearBuilt fields.

10. Since you decide that you don't want to add another field, use the Undo command to reverse the change.

11. Delete the SellingPrice field, since this table will only list homes currently for sale.

12. Save and close the table.

8 Move Fields and Change Field Properties

Edit the Employees table to change field sizes and modify the order of fields.

1. Open the ***Payton Properties, Lesson 1*** database in the ***Lesson Applications*** folder on your Student Data Disk, if it is not already open. Open the Employees table in Design view.

2. Create a caption for the AgentID field.

3. Change the field size of the DepartmentName field to 20 and type **Sales** in the Default Value box.

4. Change the field size of the FirstName field to 20, the LastName field to 30, the Address field to 50, the City field to 30, and the StateOrProvince field to 2.

5. Click the DateHired field and notice the input mask that the Wizard entered.

6. Reverse the order of the FirstName and LastName fields.

7. Move the DepartmentName field to appear as the last field (Figure 1.35).

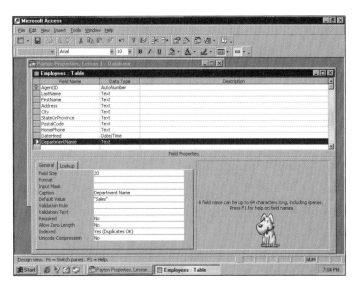

Figure 1.35

8. Save and close the table.

9. Open the Options dialog box on the Tools menu. On the General tab, select the Compact on Close command.

10. Close the ***Payton Properties, Lesson 1*** database and exit Access.

Lesson Summary & Exercises

PROJECTS

1 Working with Database Objects

You work as the retail manager at Electro Shop—a store that sells stereos, televisions, and other electronics. You have created a database to track employee data as well as product data. Start Access and open the database called **Electro Shop Sample** on your Student Data Disk. Open the Products table. Change the availability date of the RML VCR Model 1200 to 12/3 in the Notes field. Then view the table in Design view. Write down the name and data type of each field in the table, and then close the table.

Open the Stereos Sold query. View the query in Design view and notice how the query is structured (Figure 1.36). Can you tell in Design view which field contains criteria to be met? Close the query.

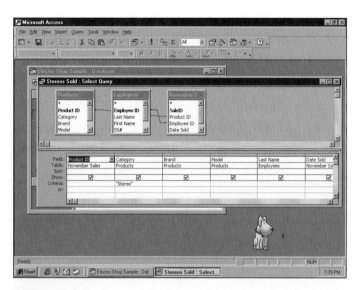

Figure 1.36

Open the Employees form. Add the following record in Form view.

Employee ID:	*allow the AutoNumber feature to assign a number*
Last Name:	Richards
First Name:	Susan
SS#:	121-21-2121
Hourly Rate:	$7.75
FT/PT:	PT

Close the form and use the Contents tab of the Help system to learn more about previewing and printing forms.

Open the Sales by Employee report and maximize the window. Print one copy of the report and then close the report. Use the Office Assistant to learn more about creating a report with a wizard.

Use either of the methods learned in this lesson to compact the **Electro Shop Sample** database. If you share your computer with others and plan to compact the database upon closing it, make sure that the Compact on Close option has not been deselected. If you prefer to compact the database immediately, issue the command from the Database Utilities option. Close the database.

2 Calling All Be Fruitful Employees

As an employee of the Be Fruitful fruit-of-the-month club, you've already created tables to hold customer information and order information. Your supervisor has requested that you develop a third table to hold employee data. Open the **Be Fruitful, Lesson 1** database in the **Tutorial** folder. Create a table with the Table Wizard. Base your new table on the Employees sample table. Add the following fields: EmployeeID, SocialSecurityNumber, LastName, FirstName, MiddleName, Address, City, StateOrProvince, PostalCode, and Salary. Rename the Postal Code field to ZIPCode and the StateOrProvince field to State. Remove the MiddleName and Salary fields. Name the table BFEmployees and

let Access create the primary key for you. Since other tables exist, the wizard will ask if the new table is related to any of the existing tables in the **Be Fruitful, Lesson 1** database (Figure 1.37). Click Next to indicate that this new table is not related.

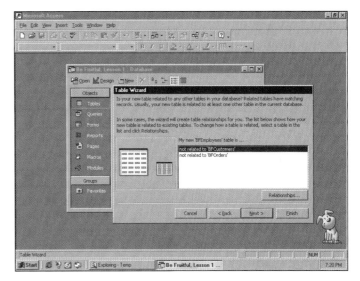

In the final Table Wizard dialog box, choose the *Modify the table design.* option and click Finish to view the newly created table in Design view. Notice the primary key. On a separate sheet of paper, state the field that was selected as the primary key and explain why you think Access chose this field as the primary key.

Figure 1.37

To improve the efficiency of your database, you decide to reduce the size of some of your fields and add some captions. Make the changes described in Table 1.5. Then, save and close the table. Make sure the Compact on Close option is selected and close the **Be Fruitful, Lesson 1** database.

TABLE 1.5	CHANGES TO BFEMPLOYEES TABLE	
Field Name	**Property**	**Change to**
SocialSecurityNumber	Caption	SS#
ZIPCode	Caption	ZIP Code
LastName	Field Size	30
FirstName	Field Size	20
Address	Field Size	50
City	Field Size	30
State	Field Size	2

Lesson Summary & Exercises

3 When Does that Class Start?

You work in the Administration building at Smyth Business College and are in charge of maintaining student records and class schedules. In the Skills Review activities, you created tables to hold student information and grades. Now you need to create a table to hold class-scheduling information. Open the **Smyth Business College, Lesson 1** database in the **Skills Review** folder. Create a table in Design view called Class Schedules. Include the fields and assign the properties found in Table 1.6. Assign the ClassCode field as the primary key and save the table.

TABLE 1.6	INFORMATION FOR CLASS SCHEDULES TABLE			
Field	**Data Type**	**Field Size**	**Caption**	**Input Mask**
ClassCode	Text	6	Class Code	LLL000 (three Ls and three zeros)
ClassName	Text	30	Class Name	
Time	Text	20		
Days	Text	5		

You decide that the Class Schedules table could be improved by adding a field so that students know which instructor teaches each course. You also decide to change some other elements of the table. Add a field between the ClassName and Time fields called Instructor. Assign a data type of Text and a field size of 30. Switch the order of the Time and Days fields. Save and close the table. Make sure the Compact on Close option is selected and close the **Smyth Business College, Lesson 1** database.

4 Tracking Your Agents

At Payton Properties, you have been tracking the homes sold. Your manager has asked you to provide a table in the existing database that tracks the number of homes sold, the number of new listings, and the commissions earned by each sales agent. Open the **Payton Properties, Lesson 1** database in the **Lesson Applications** folder. Create a table in Design view called Agent Statistics. Include the fields and assign the properties found in Table 1.7. Assign the AgentID field as the primary key and save the table.

TABLE 1.7	INFORMATION FOR AGENT STATISTICS TABLE		
Field	**Data Type**	**Field Size**	**Caption**
AgentID	Number	Long Integer	Agent ID
AgentLastName	Text	30	Last Name
Y-T-DHomesSold	Number		Homes Sold
Y-T-DListings	Number		Listings
Y-T-DCommissions	Currency		Commissions

Since each sales agent's name is provided in the Employees table, you realize that repeating this information in the table you just created could cause potential problems. Delete the AgentLastName field. Change the data type of the Y-T-DListings to Text. Then, since you realize this change was made in error, undo the change. Save and close the table. Make sure the Compact on Close option is selected and close the **Payton Properties, Lesson 1** database.

5 Making Sense Out of a Lot of Data

Electro Shop, the retail store that sells televisions, stereos, and other electronics, has asked you to set up a database for them. After interviewing several employees who will use the database, you've discovered that they want to include the following information in the database:

- Employee names and ID numbers
- Employee Social Security numbers
- The hourly rate earned by each employee
- The employee's working status (full time or part time)
- A product number that identifies each product Electro Shop carries
- The general category (TV, stereo, VCR, etc.) for each product
- The brand of each product
- The price of each product
- Notes about each product
- A sale number for each sale made in December and which salesperson made the sale
- The product ID for each item sold in December and the quantity sold in each individual sale
- The date of each sale

On paper, sketch how you would set up tables to contain the information to be included in the database. Provide a name for each table. (Hint: Use at least two or three tables of logical categories.) Under each table name, list the fields to be included and the data type of each field.

Create and name a new database **Electro Shop, Lesson 1** in the **Projects** folder. Use the wizard or Design view to create two or three new tables that contain the fields that you listed on paper. Assign appropriate data types, field sizes, captions, and other field properties to each field. Set a primary key for each table. After saving and closing each table, choose the Compact on Close option and close the **Electro Shop, Lesson 1** database.

6 Higher Education on the Web

Assume you work at Smyth Business College as the assistant to the dean. Students often ask the dean about continuing their education after they graduate from Smyth. She would like you to use the Internet to research other schools in Georgia that offer graduate programs. Connect to the Internet and use a search engine to find information on graduate schools in Georgia. Click several links to results and generate a list of at least three schools that meet the dean's needs, listing their locations and the types of graduate degrees offered.

Lesson Summary & Exercises

Project in Progress

7 Building a Database for a Communications Business

You own a small business called I-Comm that provides a variety of writing, editing, and training services to other business owners. You facilitate training seminars; write materials such as brochures, training manuals, annual reports, employee handbooks, and newspaper and magazine articles; and create Web pages for small businesses. Think of ways you could use a database in your business. Now open the *I-Comm Sample* database on your Student Data Disk. Open each of the three tables in the database and examine the information in them. Open the Writers query and determine the purpose of the query. Open the Projects AutoForm form and add the following information in Form view:

Project ID:	(AutoNumber)
Customer ID:	28
Item Developed:	Web site
Services Performed:	Web page creation
Project Manager:	11
Total Hours:	160
Fee:	$9,600

Open and scroll through the Projects report. Print the report. Close all objects. Click Tools on the menu bar and click Options, then click the General tab. Click Compact on Close, if it is not already selected, and then click OK. Close the database.

Now that you've examined a sample database for your company, you are ready to begin building your own database. Create and name a new database *I-Comm* in the *Projects* folder. Use the Table Wizard to create a table called Customers and use Design view to create a table called Projects. Create and modify the two tables so that they contain the fields and field properties listed in Table 1.8. After saving and closing each table, choose the Compact on Close option and close the *I-Comm* database. Exit Access.

TABLE 1.8	INFORMATION FOR TABLES			
Field Name	**Data Type**	**Field Size**	**Caption**	**Other**
Table Name: Customers				
*CustomerID	AutoNumber	Long Integer	Customer ID	
CompanyName	Text	50	Company Name	
ContactLastName	Text	30	Contact Last Name	
ContactFirstName	Text	20	Contact First Name	
ContactTitle	Text	30	Contact Title	
BillingAddress	Text	50	Billing Address	
City	Text	30		
State	Text	2		
ZIPCode	Text	20	ZIP Code	
PhoneNumber	Text	30	Phone Number	
Table Name: Projects				
*ProjectID	AutoNumber	Long Integer	Project ID	
CustomerID	Number	Long Integer	Customer ID	
ItemDeveloped	Text	30	Item Developed	
ServicesPerformed	Memo		Services Performed	
I-CommProjectManager	Number	Long Integer	I-Comm Project Mgr.	
TotalHours	Number	Long Integer	Total Hours	
Fee	Currency			Zero decimal places

* Set as primary key.

Maintaining Records and Creating Queries, Forms, and Reports

OBJECTIVES

After you complete this lesson, you will be able to do the following:

- Add data to your tables in Datasheet view.
- Copy and paste data from another database and import data from another database.
- Navigate the datasheet and edit records.
- Understand the types of relationships that can exist between two tables.
- Create a relationship between two tables.
- Open and close a subdatasheet.
- Sort records.
- Specify criteria in a query.
- Edit the data in the recordset of a query.
- Save queries.
- Create and modify a multi-table query.
- Use expressions, calculated fields, and statistical functions in a query.
- Create an AutoForm.
- Add and edit data with forms and subforms.
- Use the Report Wizard to create a columnar report, a tabular report, and a report with totals.
- Group and sort records in a report.
- Preview and print reports.
- Create a hyperlink to another object, another database, and a Web site.

Now that you have created a database with tables, you need to learn how to enter data quickly and efficiently into a database. In the first part of Lesson 2, you will learn to enter and update records and establish relationships between the tables in a database. Later in the lesson, you will manipulate data using sort commands and queries, including queries that use comparison operators, calculated fields, and statistical functions. Finally, you will create forms to facilitate data entry and reports to effectively present the information contained in your database.

Another Way

To open a table, double-click the table name in the Database window.

ENTERING RECORDS USING A DATASHEET

In Lesson 1, you learned how to create tables. You built table structures—choosing the fields that your tables would include and their properties. Now that these structures are in place, you're ready to actually enter data into them. You can add data to your tables by using forms, which you'll learn more about later in this lesson. However, Access also provides the *datasheet,* a layout of rows and columns that permits you to add, edit, and view all the data in a table. Even if you devise custom forms for data entry, the datasheet remains useful for browsing a large number of records at once and making minor additions and modifications as you go along. As you may have guessed, you use Datasheet view to work with a datasheet.

Adding Data to the BFCustomers Table

In this activity, you'll type the information for several records into the BFCustomers table.

1. **If necessary, turn on your computer. Then start Access.**

2. **When the initial Microsoft Access dialog box appears, double-click More Files in the list box at the bottom of the dialog box. Navigate to the *Tutorial* folder on your Student Data Disk and double-click *Be Fruitful, Lesson 2.***

Access displays the *Be Fruitful, Lesson 2* Database window.

3. **Maximize the Database window. Click the Tables option in the Database window and click the BFCustomers table, if it is not already selected.**

4. **Click the Open button [⊞ Open] in the Database window.**

Access opens the BFCustomers table in Datasheet view, as shown in Figure 2.1. You can see some of the *field selectors* (field names or captions at the top of each column), but the table is empty; that is, it contains no data. A single blank row appears, waiting for your input.

The triangle to the left of the record indicates the *current record,* sometimes called the record with the *focus.* The box to the left of each record in Datasheet view is called the *record selector.*

5. **Press [Tab] or click the blank box under the Contact Last Name field.**

Access moves the insertion point into the Contact Last Name field.

6. **Type Kenber in the Contact Last Name field and press [Tab].**

As soon as you start typing, Access automatically enters a value into the Customer ID field for this first customer. When you press [Tab], the insertion point moves into the Contact First Name field. Note that Access has created a second blank record with an asterisk (*) in the record selector. An asterisk indicates a new record in which you can type data. The record in which you are typing has a pencil icon in the record selector. The pencil icon indicates that you are currently editing the record and the edits have not yet been saved.

7. **Type Franklin in the Contact First Name field and press [Tab].**

Access moves the insertion point into the Billing Address field.

8. **Type 1777 Lois Ln. in the Billing Address field and press [Tab].**

Adding Records

1. Type data in a field.

2. Press `Tab` to move between fields.

3. Press `Tab` after the last field of a record to create a new record, or press the New Record button to move to a new record.

Figure 2.1 ◀
BFCustomers table

To move to the next field in the datasheet, press `Enter⏎`.

A computer virus is a harmful human-made program or code that copies itself into files. A virus can damage your computer by causing crashes or erasing data. To avoid viruses, you should use anti-virus software to check files, especially those you receive from an outside source.

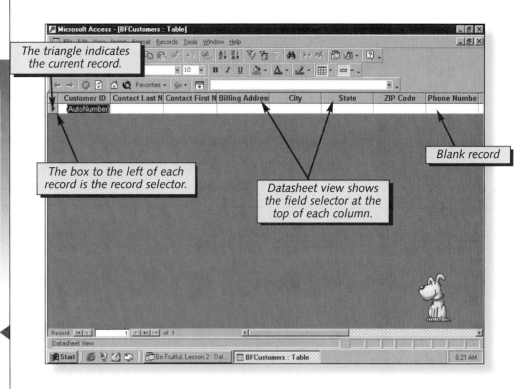

The triangle indicates the current record.

The box to the left of each record is the record selector.

Datasheet view shows the field selector at the top of each column.

Blank record

9. Type Rock Creek **in the City field and press** `Tab`.

10. Type NC **in the State field and press** `Tab`.

11. **In the ZIP Code field, type** 28333 **and then type** 1234.

Note that you don't have to enter the hyphen; because of the input mask, Access automatically formats the ZIP Code as 28333-1234.

12. **Press** `Tab` **to move to the Phone Number field, type** 919, **type** 555, **and finally type** 9999 **and press** `Tab`.

Notice that Access once again enters the punctuation because of the input mask associated with the Phone Number field. Access scrolls the display so you can see the Date Joined field in full. Only some of the fields of a large table show in Datasheet view at once. Pressing `Tab` automatically scrolls the display to bring any additional fields into view.

13. **Type** 4/15/94 **in the Date Joined field and press** `Tab`.

If you enter an invalid date, such as 13/15/92, you will see a warning box about your error. If you enter 13/5/92, Access will assume that you intend to enter the 13th day of the 5th month and will translate the date to 5/13/1992.

Notice that a description of the Notes field appears on the status bar. As you may recall, you entered this description when you modified the table design in Lesson 1.

14. **Press** `Tab` **to leave the Notes field blank.**

You should now see a box in the Extra Catalogs field. Clicking this box adds a check mark to the box, meaning Yes. Leaving the box blank means No. Also, since you entered a description for this field, the description appears in the status bar.

If you want to move back to a previous field, you can click the field or press ⬅.

15. Press ⭾ to accept the default value of *No.*

16. Press ⭾ and type Reid in the Contact Last Name field. Then press ⭾ again.

As before, Access automatically increments the value in the Customer ID field and creates a new blank record at the end of the table.

17. Type Alice in the Contact First Name field and press ⭾.

18. Type 7374 Kennedy Heights Ave. in the Billing Address field and press ⭾.

As you typed, some of the address scrolled out of view. When you pressed ⭾ to move to the next field, only the beginning of the address appeared. The information is still there, even though you cannot see everything in the datasheet display.

19. Point to the right boundary of the field selector for the Billing Address field.

The pointer changes into a vertical bar with a horizontal double-headed arrow attached, as shown in Figure 2.2. This pointer indicates that you can drag to the left to narrow the column or drag to the right to widen the column.

Figure 2.2 ◀
Adding records and
resizing a column

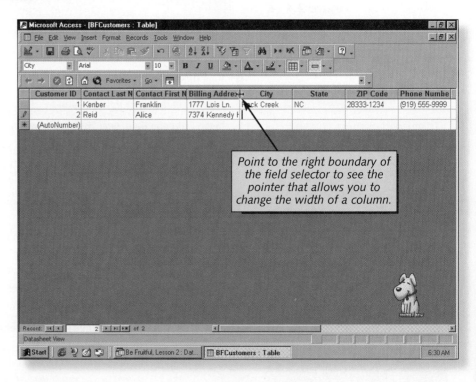

Point to the right boundary of the field selector to see the pointer that allows you to change the width of a column.

To automatically resize a column so you can see all of the data in the longest records (or the entire field name if it's longer than the data), double-click the right boundary of the field selector.

20. Drag to the right to widen the Billing Address field until the entire address for Alice Reid is visible.

21. Type Sebastopol in the City field and press ⭾, then type CA in the State field and press ⭾ .

22. Type 97777-1111 in the ZIP Code field, press ⭾, and type (415) 555-5432 in the Phone Number field. (Remember, you do not need to type the punctuation.)

23. Press ⭾ and type 11/21/94 in the Date Joined field.

You have now entered all of the data for the second record. The remaining fields will be left blank or take on their default value.

24. Click the New Record button  **on the Database toolbar.**

Access moves down to the next row (the new blank record) into which you can enter data.

25. Enter the names and addresses listed in Table 2.1. Leave all Notes fields blank and retain the default setting of *No* for all the Extra Catalog fields.

TABLE 2.1	NAMES AND ADDRESSES TO ENTER		
Field	**Record 3**	**Record 4**	**Record 5**
Contact Last Name	Turlow	Zheng	O'Hara
Contact First Name	Will	Anne	Joan
Billing Address	1 Oak Pl.	25 Forest Knoll	2234 Hanley Pl.
City	Providence	Santa Rosa	Baltimore
State	RI	CA	MD
ZIP Code	02900-2338	99887-2355	21122-5634
Phone Number	(401) 555-9972	(707) 555-9876	(301) 555-4567
Date Joined	1/5/95	7/15/95	2/5/96

If you're used to word processing and spreadsheet programs, you may be wondering when to save your data. Access automatically saves your data when you move to a new record. If you want to save before that point, however—perhaps you're entering a long memo field—click Records on the menu bar and then click Save Record or press ⇧ Shift + Enter↵.

26. Close the table. Click Yes in response to the message to save changes to the layout of the BFCustomers table.

Note

Even though Access automatically saves changes to data *(when you move to a new record), you must still instruct Access to save changes to the table* design. *By changing the width of the Billing Address field in step 20, you changed the design of the table.*

RETRIEVING DATA FROM ANOTHER TABLE

So that you can work with a more realistic amount of material, you'll now retrieve some records from another database on the Student Data Disk. As you know, however, if you open another database, the current database will automatically close. Instead, you can copy data to the Office ***Clipboard***—a temporary storage space in the memory of your computer—and then paste the data to another location in the same database or another database. A few words of caution when using the copy and paste technique—this technique enables you to retrieve data only from Access, not from other programs; also, for this technique to work smoothly, you must be copying data from a table with the same structure as the one into which you're pasting the data.

Another method you can use to add data from another database is to *import*—the process of bringing data from one file into another. When you import data, however, you copy an entire table into your database, including both the records and the structure of the table.

HANDS On

Copying and Pasting Records Between Tables

In this activity, you will copy records from a table in the *Be Fruitful Sample* database to the Office Clipboard. Then you will paste the records into the BFCustomers table in the *Be Fruitful, Lesson 2* database.

1. **Click File** on the menu bar and click **Open.** Navigate to your Student Data Disk files.

2. **Double-click the *Be Fruitful Sample* database. Click the Tables option,** if necessary.

You should see the *Be Fruitful Sample* Database window. The BFCustomers, BFFruit, and BFOrders tables appear in the list of table objects.

3. **Open the BFCustomers table in Datasheet view.**

4. **Click the record selector in front of record 6, scroll down to record 35, press** **, and click the record selector for record 35.**

Access highlights records 6 through 35 in the table, as shown in Figure 2.3.

Figure 2.3
Selecting records

Selected records are highlighted.

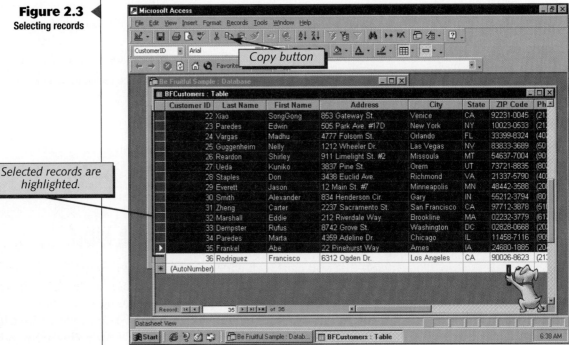

Another Way

To copy, click Edit on the menu bar and click Copy.

5. **Click the Copy button** 📋 **on the Database toolbar.**

Although you can't see any change to the screen, Access has copied all of these records to the Clipboard.

6. **Click the Close button** ☒ **to close the BFCustomers table.**

Access displays a warning box about the data on the Clipboard.

7. Read the text in the warning box and click **Yes** to save the data on the Clipboard.

Access closes the BFCustomers table and returns you to the *Be Fruitful Sample* Database window.

8. Click the **Open button** 📂 on the Database toolbar. Navigate to and open the *Be Fruitful, Lesson 2* database in the *Tutorial* folder on your Student Data Disk.

9. Double-click the **BFCustomers table**.

You will see the BFCustomers table with the records that you entered earlier.

10. Click **Edit** on the menu bar and click **Paste Append**.

 *If the Paste Append command doesn't appear, click the double arrow at the bottom of the Edit menu to display the expanded menu.*

The Paste Append option lets you add records to the end of your table. Before the option adds the records, however, Access displays a message asking if you're sure you want to paste the records. In this box, you can click *Yes* to add the records or *No* to cancel the operation.

Warning *You can't use the normal Paste button 📋 on the Database toolbar to paste these records from the Clipboard; you must use the Paste Append command on the Edit menu.*

11. Read the text in the dialog box and click **Yes** to add the records from the Clipboard to the BFCustomers table.

12. Click anywhere within the table to remove the highlighting. Then click the **Maximize button** 🗖.

The display at the bottom of the table window indicates that the table now contains 35 records.

13. Close the BFCustomers table.

Copying and Pasting Data to the BFOrders Table

Now that you've copied and pasted data from one table to another, you can reopen the first database and copy data from another table. In this activity, you will copy the records from a table on the Student Data Disk into your BFOrders table, using the same technique you used in the previous activity.

1. Open the *Be Fruitful Sample* database on your Student Data Disk. Open the BFOrders table in Datasheet view.

 The names of the most recently used databases appear at the bottom of the File menu. You can click File on the menu bar and then click the ***Be Fruitful Sample*** *file name to open the database.*

2. Press Ctrl + A to select all records.

All of the records in the BFOrders table are selected (or highlighted), as shown in Figure 2.4.

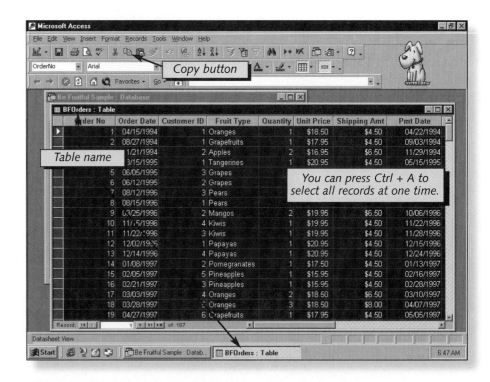

Figure 2.4

Selecting all records

3. **Click the Copy button**  **and then close the BFOrders table.**

The warning box asks if you want to save the data you copied on the Clipboard.

4. **Click Yes.**

5. **Open the *Be Fruitful, Lesson 2* database in the *Tutorial* folder on your Student Data Disk. Open the BFOrders table.**

Notice that no data has been entered into the table yet.

6. **Click Edit on the menu bar and click Paste Append.**

A warning box asks if you want to paste 187 records into the table.

7. **Click Yes.**

You now have a table with 187 records. Imagine how much time you saved by pasting the data rather than entering each record one at a time!

8. **Close the BFOrders table.**

Importing a Table from Another Database

In this activity, you will use the Import feature to bring an entire table into your ***Be Fruitful, Lesson 2*** database.

1. **With the *Be Fruitful, Lesson 2* Database window open, click File on the menu bar, point to Get External Data on the expanded menu, and then click Import on the submenu.**

The Import dialog box appears.

2. **Navigate to and double-click the *Be Fruitful Sample* database on your Student Data Disk.**

Hints & Tips

Remember that you can copy and paste between tables with the same structure. If Access identifies a problem, Access creates a Paste Error table to hold the data that could not be pasted.

Importing a Table

1. Click File on the menu bar, point to Get External Data, and click Import.

2. Double-click the database name in the Import dialog box.

3. Click the table name you wish to import in the Import Objects dialog box and click OK.

Figure 2.5
The Import Objects dialog box

The Import Objects dialog box appears, as shown in Figure 2.5. This dialog box lets you select the objects that you want to copy from the **Be Fruitful Sample** database into the **Be Fruitful, Lesson 2** database.

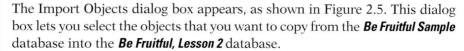
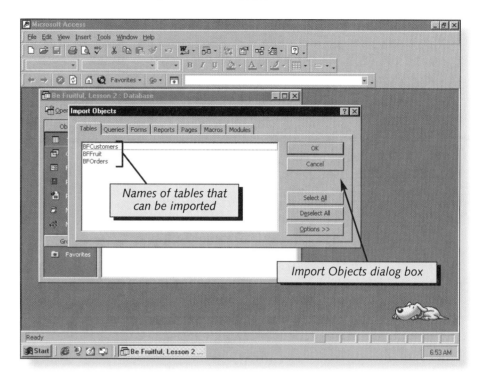

3. **Click the Tables tab**, if necessary, and click **BFFruit**. Then click **OK**.

After a short pause, the BFFruit table—including all of the records in the table and the table structure—are copied into the **Be Fruitful, Lesson 2** database. You should see the BFFruit table in the **Be Fruitful, Lesson 2** Database window.

NAVIGATING THE DATASHEET AND EDITING RECORDS

After you've entered a substantial amount of data into your table, you need to know how to move around in the datasheet. When you have only a few records, you can always move the focus to another record just by clicking. When you have larger amounts of data, you need a few additional strategies to find the records you want and select the fields you want to work on. You'll learn both keyboard and mouse techniques for navigating the datasheet while you move through the records that you just entered into the BFCustomers table. Remember, the record with the focus is simply the one you're editing at the moment. This record usually has a triangle in the record selector, but will have a pencil if you've made any changes that you haven't yet saved.

After you've located the records in which you're interested, you're ready to begin editing. You can delete or replace the contents of a particular field, and you can add to or change the contents of a field easily. You can delete one or more entire records as well. The Undo feature is useful when you need to reverse your previous action.

Although many people use the terms *Internet* and *World Wide Web* synonymously, they are separate entities. The World Wide Web (or Web) is just one tool used to access the Internet. The Web organizes information into easy-to-use pages, called Web pages.

HANDS On

Moving Among Records and Editing Data

In this activity, you will navigate the datasheet and edit records.

1. With the *Be Fruitful, Lesson 2* database in the *Tutorial* folder open, double-click the BFCustomers table. Click the Maximize button ☐.

Notice the navigation buttons at the bottom of the window, as shown in Figure 2.6. You use these buttons to move from record to record. Note that the text box reads "1" and the gray area to the right reads "of 35." This tells you that the table has 35 records and the focus is on the first record.

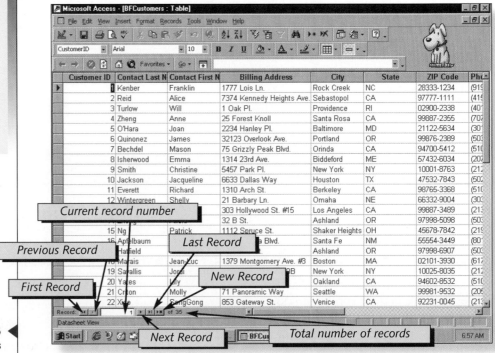

Figure 2.6
Navigation buttons

2. Click the Last Record button ▶|.

Access moves the focus to the last record in the table, placing a triangle in the record selector and highlighting the data in the Customer ID field. The current record is now listed as record 35.

 *When you use any of the navigation buttons, Access moves the focus to a new record but leaves the same field high-lighted. For instance, if the Contact First Name field is selected, clicking the Last Record button* ▶| *moves the focus to the last record in the table and highlights that record's Contact First Name field.*

3. Click the First Record button |◀.

Access moves the focus to the first record in the table—the record for Franklin Kenber. Once again, the data in the Customer ID field is selected.

4. Double-click the Next Record button ▶.

Access moves the focus to the record for Will Turlow, the third record.

Navigating a Table

To navigate records:

- Use the navigation buttons to move to the first, last, previous, or next record.

- To move to a specific record, type the number of the record to which you want to move in the text box at the bottom of the datasheet, and press `Enter←`.

- Press `↓` or `↑` to move to an adjacent record.

To navigate fields:

- Press `Tab` to move one field to the right.

- Press `⇧ Shift` + `Tab` to move one field to the left.

- Press `End` to move to the last field of a record.

- Press `Home` to move to the first field of a record.

- Press `Ctrl` + `Home` to move to the first field of the first record.

- Press `Ctrl` + `End` to move to the last field of the last record.

---

5. Click the Previous Record button ◄.

The focus moves to the record for Alice Reid, the second record.

6. Double-click the current record number in the text box at the bottom of the screen.

7. Type 25 and press `Enter←`.

The focus moves to record 25—that of Nelly Guggenheim.

8. Press `F5`, type 5, and press `Enter←` to move to the record for Joan O'Hara.

9. Press `Tab` until you get to the Contact First Name field for Joan O'Hara.

Access selects the first name *Joan*. Note that the entire field is highlighted. ***Select*** means to choose an item to indicate to Access that you want to operate on that particular item. You now see the field in ***reverse video,*** with white text against a dark background.

 Warning *If you press `Delete` when any field is selected, you will delete the contents of the field, and anything you type will replace that content.*

10. Click after the *n* in Joan or press `F2`.

Notice that the highlighting disappears and is replaced by a blinking insertion point immediately after the *n* in Joan. As you probably know, the insertion point indicates where the text you type will appear, as well as where any deletions will occur.

11. Type ne to change the name to *Joanne.*

12. Press `←`.

This action does not move you to the previous field but instead moves the insertion point one character to the left.

13. Press `F2` to select the contents of the Contact First Name field.

14. Press `←` again.

This time, pressing `←` selects the Contact Last Name field for Joanne O'Hara's record.

15. Type Elias.

Access automatically deletes the last name *O'Hara,* replacing it with the name *Elias.*

Undoing Editing Mistakes and Deleting Records

When you're making changes to a table, you can make changes to the wrong field or the wrong record. Fortunately, the Undo feature that you used in the previous lesson works here, too. In this activity, you will use the Undo feature to reverse changes. Then you will remove one of the records from the table.

1. Click the arrow at the bottom of the scroll bar on the right side of the window until you can see record 28.

2. Double-click the last name *Staples* in record 28.

Undoing Mistakes and Deleting Records

To reverse a change:

Click the Undo button or press ⌐Esc⌐ to reverse a change.

To delete a record:

1. Click the record selector of the record you wish to delete.

2. Click the Delete Record button.

3. Click Yes when the warning box appears.

To delete a record, select the record and press ⌐Delete⌐.

Figure 2.7 ◄
Deleting a record

3. Press ⌐Delete⌐ to delete the entire name.

4. Click the **Undo button** ⌐↺⌐.

Access reverses the change, bringing back the last name you just deleted.

5. Double-click the last name *Isherwood* in record 8.

6. Type Hernandez and press ⌐Tab⌐ to move to the Contact First Name field.

Access replaces the old last name with the new one.

7. Type Rosa and press ⌐Tab⌐ again.

8. Type 204 Panoramic Way in the Billing Address field, but do not press ⌐Tab⌐ or ⌐Enter⌐.

9. Press ⌐Esc⌐ or click the **Undo button** ⌐↺⌐.

The address changes from *204 Panoramic Way* back to *1314 23rd Ave*.

10. Press ⌐Esc⌐ again or click the **Undo button** ⌐↺⌐ two more times.

Access reverses the rest of the changes to the current record all at once, restoring the name *Emma Isherwood*.

Note

Depending on the last action you performed, the Undo button's name changes. For instance, if you just typed text and want to undo it, the ToolTip for the Undo button reads Undo Typing. If you want to undo a deletion you just made, the name changes to Undo Delete.

11. Click the **record selector** for Richard Everett's record (record number 11).

The entire record is selected.

12. Click the **Delete Record button** ⌐✗⌐.

Access displays the warning box shown in Figure 2.7, warning you that you're about to delete a record and giving you a chance to stop the change.

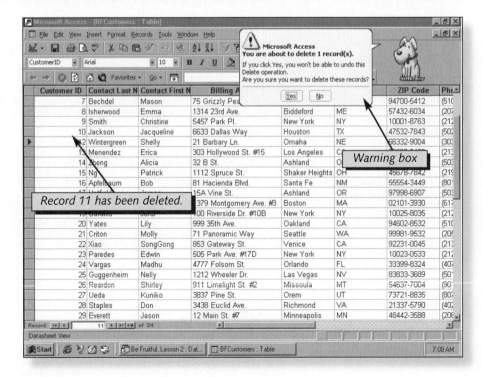

Hints & Tips

If [Home], [End], [Ctrl] + [Home], and [Ctrl] + [End] aren't working as anticipated, first press [F2] to highlight the current field and then try again. The [F2] key lets you switch between editing and navigating your data.

Undoing Changes to a Saved Record

1. Click Edit on the menu bar.

2. Click Undo Saved Record.

13. Read the text in the box and click **Yes**.

When you delete one or more records, you cannot undo the operation with the Undo command. Your only way out is to click No to cancel the operation when Access displays the warning box.

Access deletes the selected record and moves the subsequent records up. Note, however, that the values in the Customer ID field have not changed. As you'd expect, customers retain the same ID numbers even if other customers are removed from the database.

You can also delete entire fields in Datasheet view by clicking Edit on the menu bar and clicking Delete Column. However, be extremely sure that you want to delete the field and all of the contents before issuing this command. This action cannot be reversed with the Undo command, so if you change your mind, you must add the field and retype all of the data in it.

Undoing Changes to a Saved Record

Thus far, you have learned how to undo changes to the current field or undo multiple changes to the current record. When you complete the edits in a record and move to another record, your changes are saved automatically. You might think that the regular Undo keys will not reverse these changes. Fortunately, the Undo option will fix the changes if you catch them in time. In this activity, you will use the Undo option to reverse unwanted or accidental changes.

1. Move the insertion point to the Notes field for record number 4, Anne Zheng.

2. Type Loves kiwis and press [Tab] to move to the Extra Catalogs field.

3. Press [Spacebar].

Pressing [Spacebar] puts a check mark in this Yes/No field.

4. Press [Tab].

Access automatically saves the changes to Anne Zheng's record when you move to the next record.

5. Click **Edit** on the menu bar and click **Undo Saved Record**.

Access reverses the changes to the Zheng record, even though the record had been saved. This Undo command reverses only the most recent action; if you've done anything else since then, you can't undo the changes to a saved record in this way.

Editing in the Zoom Window

When you have a lot of text in a field such as a large text or memo field, editing can be difficult. In this activity, you work with the fields more easily using the Zoom window.

1. Navigate to the Notes field for Shelly Wintergreen's record.

2. Press ⇧Shift + F2.

Access opens the Zoom window shown in Figure 2.8; you can use this window to enter longer amounts of text or to edit fields that have a lot of text.

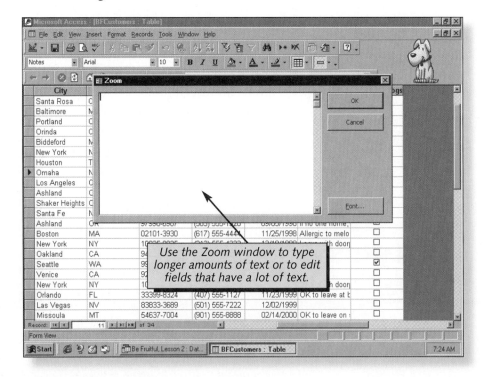

Use the Zoom window to type longer amounts of text or to edit fields that have a lot of text.

Access BASICS

Editing in the Zoom Window

1. Move to the field you wish to edit.

2. Press ⇧Shift + F2.

3. Type the text and click OK.

Figure 2.8 ◄
The Zoom window

3. Type the following text:

Mrs. Wintergreen is an elderly woman. If she is home and you have a moment, try to knock (loudly) on the door and chat for a minute. She is allergic to pomegranates but loves all other fruits we currently offer. OK to leave packages at the back door if she is not home.

4. Click OK.

You return to the Datasheet window, where you see only a tiny amount of the text you just typed.

5. Press Home **and then press** → **to scroll the text in Mrs. Wintergreen's Notes field.**

Notice how much more difficult this is than viewing the text in the Zoom window.

6. Click the Close button X **to close the BFCustomers table.**

ESTABLISHING AND DEFINING TABLE RELATIONSHIPS

Now that you've created several tables in your database, you can establish permanent relationships among them. This way, Access will always be certain which records match up and also will understand precisely the type of relationship the two tables have. Defining a relationship allows you to create reports and other objects that combine data from two or more tables. Defining formal relationships between tables involves only a few simple steps. First, however, you need to know more about the various types of relationships that can exist between tables.

Hints & Tips

F2 is a toggle key. Pressing once removes the highlighting from a selected field and lets you edit the field's contents. Pressing again highlights the field's contents.

Identifying Relationships Between Tables

Any two tables can have one of three types of relationships: one-to-one, one-to-many, and many-to-many. If two tables have a *one-to-one relationship,* every record in a table can have either no matching records or only a single matching record in the other table. This situation might arise, for example, if you want to keep track of mailing addresses as well as regular addresses. You could include the mailing addresses in a separate table; each person would have at most one mailing address in this table, and many people would have none, because their mailing addresses would be the same as their regular addresses.

When you have a *one-to-many relationship,* one of the tables is called the primary table, while the other is called the related table. The *primary table* holds a primary key that is unique. In your BFCustomers table, the Customer ID field is the primary key. You ensured that the Customer ID field would be unique by defining it as an AutoNumber field. In that way, no two customer records have the same Customer ID.

The second table in a one-to-many relationship is called the related table. The *related table* has a field that links it to the primary table. This field is called the *foreign key.* It need not be unique. In the BFOrders table, the foreign key is the Customer ID. This field was not defined as an AutoNumber field, because one customer can place many orders. Two tables have a one-to-many relationship when each record in the primary table can have no records, one record, or many matching records in the other table, but every record in the related table has exactly one associated record in the primary table—no more and no less.

In a *many-to-many relationship,* a record in either table can relate to many records in the other table. While you will not create such a relationship in the *Be Fruitful, Lesson 2* database, they are quite common.

Referential integrity refers to certain rules that Access enforces to safeguard your data, ensuring that it makes sense and does not violate the relationship that you have defined for the tables. In the *Be Fruitful, Lesson 2* database, every orders record must have an associated customer record but cannot have more than one related customer record. For instance, when referential integrity is enforced, Access won't let you delete a customer record if there are matching order records. After you have established the relationships, you can print this information for your reference while continuing to build and modify your database.

HANDS On

Creating and Printing Database Relationships

In this activity, you will create a one-to-many relationship between the BFCustomers table (the primary table) and the BFOrders table (the related table); you will also create a one-to-many relationship between the BFFruit table (the primary table) and the BFOrders table (the related table). Then you will print these database relationships.

1. Click the **Relationships button** ⊞.

The Show Table dialog box appears, which lets you choose the tables you want to relate.

2. Click **BFCustomers**, if necessary, and click **Add**.

A Field list appears for the BFCustomers table in the Relationships window.

3. Double-click **BFOrders** and then double-click **BFFruit**.

4. Click the **Close button** in the Show Table dialog box.

The BFCustomers, BFOrders, and BFFruit Field lists are displayed in the Relationships window.

5. Click the **CustomerID field** in the BFCustomers Field list.

6. Drag and drop the CustomerID field from the BFCustomers Field list onto the CustomerID field on the BFOrders Field list.

The Edit Relationships dialog box appears, as shown in Figure 2.9.

Figure 2.9
The Edit Relationships dialog box

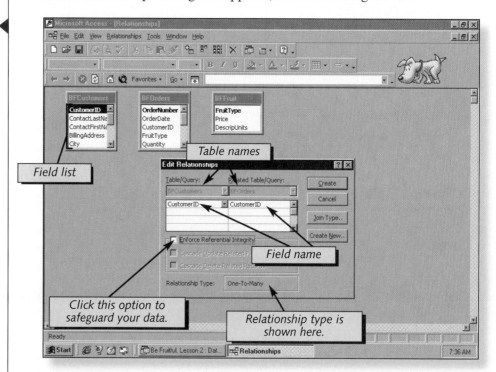

7. Click the **Enforce Referential Integrity box** so that a check mark appears in it and then click **Create**.

Access creates the relationship, the dialog box closes, and a line now appears between the CustomerID fields in the two tables.

8. Drag and drop the FruitType field from the BFFruit Field list to the FruitType field in the BFOrders Field list.

9. When the Edit Relationships dialog box appears, click the **Enforce Referential Integrity box** and click **Create**.

Lines like the ones in Figure 2.10 join the related fields. The small 1 on the line indicates the one side of the relationship, while the ∞ on the line shows the many sides of the relationship.

10. Click the **Close button** ☒ of the Relationships window.

A warning box asks if you want to save these relationships.

Figure 2.10
Assigning relationships

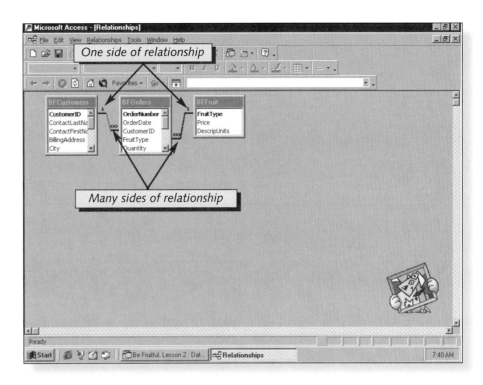

Working with Relationships

To create a relationship:

1. Click the Relationships button.

2. Double-click the tables you wish to work with in the Show Table dialog box and then close the dialog box.

3. Drag a field name from one field list to the same field name on another field list.

4. If desired, click the Enforce Referential Integrity option and click the Create button.

5. Close the Relationships window.

To print database relationships:

1. Click Tools on the menu bar.

2. Click Relationships.

3. Click File on the menu bar and click Print Relationships.

4. Click the Print button.

11. Click **Yes**.

The relationships are saved and you return to the Database window.

12. Click **Tools** on the menu bar and click **Relationships**.

The Relationships window appears, displaying the assigned relationships between the three tables.

13. Click **File** on the menu bar and click **Print Relationships**.

After a few moments, the database relationships report opens in Print Preview.

14. Click the **Print button** 🖨 to print the report.

15. Close the Print Preview.

A warning box appears and asks if you want to save changes to the design of the report.

16. Click **No** and then close the Relationships window.

Access closes the window and returns you to the *Be Fruitful, Lesson 2* Database window.

Displaying Related Records in a Subdatasheet

When you create relationships between tables, Access automatically creates subdatasheets. *Subdatasheets* allow you to view and edit data in a related table, query, or form. For instance, since the BFCustomers table has a one-to-many relationship with the BFOrders table, you can view and edit the related rows of the BFOrders table in a subdatasheet. You can bring subdatasheets into view by clicking the plus sign in front of any record in a table.

Opening and Closing a Subdatasheet

1. Click the plus sign in front of any record to open the subdatasheet.

2. Click the minus sign in front of any record to close the subdatasheet.

Opening a Subdatasheet

In this activity, you'll open a subdatasheet for the first customer listed in the BFCustomers table.

1. **Open the BFCustomers table.**

A plus sign now appears before each record in the BFCustomers table.

2. **Click the plus sign in front of the record for Franklin Kenber.**

The subdatasheet for Franklin Kenber appears, as shown in Figure 2.11, showing the fields in the BFOrders table. All of the orders that Franklin Kenber has placed are listed in the subdatasheet. You can edit data in the subdatasheet here, if desired.

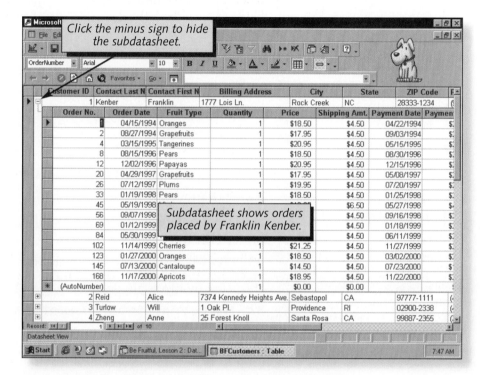

Figure 2.11
A subdatasheet

3. **Click the minus sign in front of the record for Franklin Kenber.**

Access hides the subdatasheet.

4. **Close the BFCustomers table.**

USING THE SORT COMMANDS

Access automatically arranges the data in your tables according to the value in the primary key. In the BFCustomers table, for instance, the customers are arranged by customer ID, with customer 1 appearing before customer 2, and so on. Undoubtedly, however, at times you'll want to view your data in some other sequence—maybe in order by last name or by ZIP Code.

You can *sort* records on any field except for Memo, Hyperlink, and OLE Object fields. Access sorts Text fields into alphabetical order, considers lowercase and uppercase letters to be the same, and lists digits before letters. An *ascending sort* arranges data from A to Z, and a *descending sort*

Did you know?

Access will sort up to 255 characters, in one or more fields.

arranges data from Z to A. Access sorts Number or Currency fields into numerical order—from lower to higher values in an ascending sort and from higher to lower values in a descending sort. Finally, Access sorts Date/Time fields into chronological order. An ascending sort places the earliest dates first, while a descending sort places the most recent dates first.

The field on which you sort the records is called the *sort key*. When you sort records on multiple fields, such as alphabetically by customer last name and also alphabetically by customer first name, the more important field (in this case, the customer last name) is called the *primary sort key* or *major key*. The less important field (customer first name) is called the *secondary sort key* or *minor key*. (Be careful not to confuse these terms with the *primary key*, which is the field that uniquely identifies each record.) When you sort records in a datasheet using multiple fields, Access sorts first by the leftmost field, then by the field to the right, and so on. To override this default, you can sort records using a query, which will be discussed later in this lesson.

HANDS On

Sorting a Table

In this activity, you'll experiment with the Sort commands to rearrange the records in the BFCustomers table in a variety of ways.

1. Open the BFCustomers table and click anywhere within the Contact Last Name field.

Another Way

To sort, click Records on the menu bar, point to Sort, and then click Sort Ascending on the submenu.

2. Click the Sort Ascending button 🔼.

Access rearranges the records in the table to display them in ascending order by last name, as shown in Figure 2.12. Notice, for instance, that the record for the customer named Jason Everett is placed after the record for Joanne Elias.

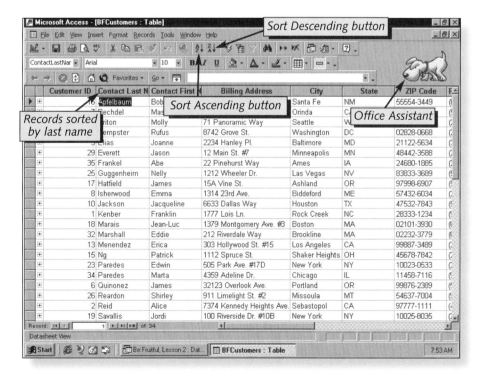

Figure 2.12
Records sorted in ascending order by last name

Sorting a Table

1. Click within the field you wish to sort by.

Or

Drag over the field selectors to choose more than one field.

2. Click the Sort Ascending or Sort Descending button.

When you close the table, the sort orders established by the Sort commands are only saved if you instruct Access to do so. So, you don't need to worry about returning your data to the original state.

3. Scroll down the records and notice that when there are duplicate last names, such as Smith and Zheng, the first names are not in any kind of order.

4. Click and hold the mouse button on the Contact Last Name field selector and drag to select the Contact First Name field selector so that both fields are highlighted. Then click the **Sort Ascending button** 🔼.

Access sorts the records in order by last name, and then, where there are duplicate last names, sorts the records in order by first name. The Smiths and the Zhengs are now in alphabetical order by first as well as last names. As stated earlier, when you sort on more than one field, Access sorts first by the leftmost field, then by the field to the right, and so on.

5. Now click anywhere within the ZIP Code field and click the **Sort Descending button** 🔽.

Access rearranges the records in order by ZIP Code, with larger numbers first and smaller numbers last.

6. Click anywhere within the Date Joined field and click the **Sort Descending button** 🔽.

Access arranges the records in order by date joined. Notice that the most recent dates are displayed first. To see the earliest dates first, you would instead choose an ascending sort.

Access interprets the dates 1/1/30 through 12/31/99 as 1/1/1930 through 12/31/1999. The dates 1/1/00 through 12/31/29 are interpreted by Access as 1/1/2000 through 12/31/2029. To override these interpretations, you can enter dates with four-digit years such as 5/12/2032.

7. Click anywhere in the Customer ID field and click the **Sort Ascending button** 🔼.

Access returns the records to their original sort order—in ascending order by the primary key field, Customer ID. You can also return a table to its original state just by closing the table and not saving the changes.

8. Close the BFCustomers table. When you are asked if you want to save changes to the design of your table, click **No**.

DESIGNING BASIC QUERIES

Queries allow you to sort your data in a variety of ways and to extract the data you need by using all types of selection criteria. *Selection criteria* are instructions that tell Access exactly which records to gather from the database. You can use queries to perform calculations and to work with data

Numbers stored in Text fields are sorted as strings of characters, not numeric values. Therefore, to sort them in numeric order, all text strings must be the same length with shorter numbers padded with leading zeros.

from multiple tables. You can also use the results of queries in forms and reports. You can even save your queries so you can use them in the future—getting up-to-the-minute responses to questions about the data in your database.

Access allows you to create several different kinds of queries. This lesson concentrates on the most often-used query type, select queries. You can use *select queries* to sort, select, and view records from one or more tables. When you run a query, the result is called a recordset. A *recordset* is the portion of your data sorted and selected as spelled out in the query. This portion of data changes to reflect modifications to the data in your tables, so the data in the recordset is always up-to-date. Recordsets are also dynamic in that you often can make changes to them and have those changes reflected in the underlying table(s).

Creating a Simple Query

You create queries in Design view, which is similar to using Design view to create tables. As you may recall from Lesson 1, the Select Query window appears when you create (or open) queries in Design view. The Select Query window has an upper pane that includes lists of fields from one or more tables (or queries) on which the query will be based. The lower pane consists of a grid—called the *query design grid,* which you use to make decisions about how to sort and select your data and also about the fields to include in the recordset.

Creating a Query in Design View

In this activity, you'll create a simple query in Design view.

1. **In the *Be Fruitful, Lesson 2* Database window, click the Queries option in the Objects bar.**

No queries exist in the *Be Fruitful, Lesson 2* database.

2. **Double-click Create query in Design view.**

Access displays the Show Table dialog box, which lists all tables in the open database. You must choose the tables and/or queries on which to base your new query in this dialog box.

3. **Double-click BFCustomers.**

Access adds a Field list for BFCustomers to the upper pane of the Select Query window. You will be able to select fields to include in the query from the Field list of the BFCustomers table.

4. **Close the Show Table dialog box.**

The Show Table dialog box doesn't close automatically, in case you want to create a query that includes multiple tables, as discussed later in this lesson. Access removes the Show Table dialog box from view, leaving you in the query design grid at the bottom of the Select Query window.

Creating a Simple Query

1. Click the Queries option in the Objects bar of the Database window.

2. Double-click Create query in Design view.

3. Double-click the table(s) you wish to use in the Show Table dialog box and then close the dialog box.

4. Add the desired fields to the query design grid.

5. Choose the desired options in the *Sort* and *Criteria* rows.

6. Click the Run button.

Figure 2.13 ◀
The completed Select Query window

Hints & Tips

If you make mistakes while creating a query, you can simply click Clear Grid on the Edit menu to clear the query design grid and start over.

5. **Double-click the ContactLastName field in the Field list.**

Access adds the field name to the query design grid. Notice that the check box in the *Show* row is selected automatically, indicating that Access will display the ContactLastName field in the recordset.

6. **Double-click the ContactFirstName field in the Field list.**

7. **Scroll down the Field list and double-click the State field and then the PhoneNumber field to place them in the next boxes of the *Field* row in the query design grid.**

8. **Click in the *Sort* row for the ContactLastName field and select Ascending from the drop-down list.**

9. **Click in the *Sort* row for the ContactFirstName field and select Ascending from the drop-down list.**

The query will display records alphabetically by the last name. If two or more records have the same last name, the records will be alphabetized by the first names.

10. **Type CA in the *Criteria* row under the State field.**

Only those records within California will be included in the query. Your Select Query window should look like that in Figure 2.13.

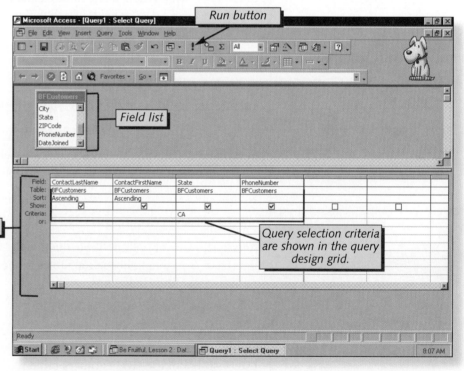

11. **Click the Run button** ![!].

Access displays the recordset; notice that you see only the selected fields, rather than all of the fields in the table. Also note that the fields are displayed in the order in which you arranged them in the query design grid.

Modifying and Saving a Query

You can create, modify, and save queries. Remember, when you create a query, the criteria you specified in the query design grid are saved, not the data in the recordset. If your data changes and you run a query again, the appropriate updated data will appear in the recordset.

Hiding the State Field and Naming the Query

In this activity, you'll make a change to the query you just created. Then you'll save the query so you can view the recordset at any time in the future.

1. Click the View button  **on the Database toolbar.**

Clicking the View button switches to display Design view. Notice that after you click the button, the icon changes to indicate that clicking again will switch back to Datasheet view. To check the available views, click the arrow next to the View button or click View on the menu bar. Then make a choice from the available options.

2. Click the Show check box under the State field in the query design grid.

Clicking deselects this box. This lets you select records based on state without displaying the State field in the recordset.

3. Click the Run button !.

Access displays the new recordset shown in Figure 2.14; all customers in California are displayed as before, but this time the State field does not appear.

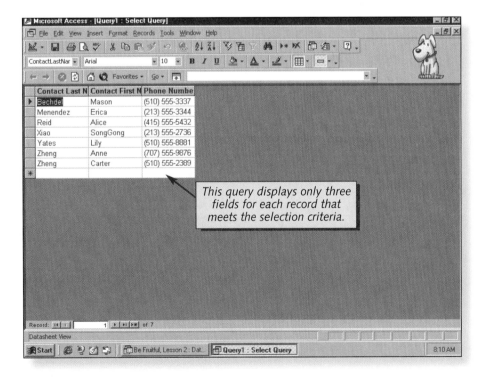

This query displays only three fields for each record that meets the selection criteria.

Modifying and Saving a Query

1. Open the query you wish to modify in Design view.

2. Modify the query as desired.

3. Click the Run button.

4. Click File on the menu bar and click Save As.

5. Type a query name and click OK.

Figure 2.14
Recordset with State field hidden

Access BASICS

Adding and Deleting Fields in a Query

1. Open the query you wish to change in Design view.

2. To delete one or more fields, select their column selectors and press Delete.

3. To add a field, drag the field from the Field list to the desired location in the query design grid.

4. Set the sort and criteria options for the new field.

5. Click the View button to view the new results.

---

4. Click **File** on the menu bar and then click **Save As**.

Remember, saving a query doesn't save the data you currently see in the recordset but instead saves the query design—the set of instructions for sorting and extracting a particular set of data. Access displays a Save As dialog box much like the one you saw when you saved your table structure. This time, however, Access requests a query name rather than a table name.

5. Type California Phone Numbers **as the query name and click OK**.

The new query name appears in the title bar and in the taskbar button.

6. Click the **View button** to switch to Design view.

Adding and Deleting Fields in a Query

After you save a query, you can still make changes. For instance, you can easily add new fields in Design view and remove them as well. The changes are reflected in the resulting recordset. In this activity, you will delete the Phone Number and State fields and add the DateJoined field in the query design grid. You will also move a field to a new location and give the revised query a new name.

1. In the query design grid, point to the **State column selector**—the small, blank, gray box above the *Field* row. The pointer will change to a down arrow. Hold down the mouse button and drag to also select the **PhoneNumber column selector**. Both columns should be highlighted. Release the mouse button and press Delete.

Access deletes the State and PhoneNumber fields from the query design grid.

2. Drag the DateJoined field in the Field list so the field is directly over the ContactLastName field in the query design grid, and then release.

Access adds the DateJoined field to the query design grid, placing the DateJoined field in the ContactLastName field's former position and pushing all other fields to the right.

3. In the *Sort* row of the DateJoined column, click **Ascending**. Type >12/31/1998 in the *Criteria* row of the DateJoined column.

4. Click the **View button**.

Access runs the query, displaying the names of customers who joined after 12/31/1998, as shown in Figure 2.15.

5. Click the **View button** to switch to Design view.

6. Click the **column selector** for the DateJoined field to select the field.

7. With the pointer still over the column selector, drag to the right until the heavy vertical line is just to the right of the ContactFirstName field, and then release.

Access moves the DateJoined field to the right end of the query design grid. Remember, this will change the arrangement of data in the recordset, as well as affect the sort order.

8. Click the **Run button**.

Access displays the revised recordset. The same records are included, but now last names are displayed first and the records are then sorted by last name.

You can define sorting and selection instructions based on a field without displaying that field in the recordset.

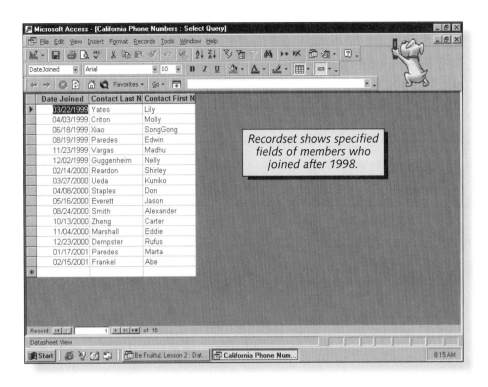

Figure 2.15
Revised query results

Recordset shows specified fields of members who joined after 1998.

9. Click **File** on the menu bar and click **Save As**.

You see the Save As dialog box. This dialog box lets you save your query in the database with a new name. You want to save this new query without overwriting the California Phone Numbers query.

10. In the first text box, type Joined After 1998 **and click OK**.

Access returns you to Datasheet view and displays the new query name in the title bar and the taskbar button.

11. Close the query window.

Access returns you to the *Be Fruitful, Lesson 2* Database window, which now includes the two queries—California Phone Numbers and Joined After 1998.

Editing Data in a Query

1. Open the query that contains the data you wish to edit.

2. Edit the desired data and close the query.

Editing Data in a Query

Being able to save the query to view the recordset at a later date is one of the great benefits of a query. Even when the data in a table changes, the changes are reflected when you reopen a query. In this activity, you will open one of your saved queries and make changes to the data.

1. Double-click the **California Phone Numbers query**.

Access displays the results of the California Phone Numbers query in Datasheet view. (You can run your queries from the Database window, either by double-clicking the name or by selecting the query name and clicking the Open button .) Now you'll change data in the recordset, noting that your changes are reflected in the underlying table.

2. Change the phone number for Alice Reid to (415) 555-6543. **Then close the recordset.**

3. In the *Be Fruitful, Lesson 2* Database window, click the **Tables option** in the Objects bar and open the BFCustomers table.

4. **Scroll to the right until you can see the phone number for Alice Reid.**

As you can see, the new number that you just entered through the recordset is reflected in the BFCustomers table.

5. **Close the table.**

QUERYING MULTIPLE TABLES

You've just learned how to build queries based on a single table. Now you will create queries that display data from more than one table. Essentially, you add the Field lists for the desired tables to the top of the Select Query window and then choose fields and specify the sort and selection instructions as you do for a single-table query. However, you must also *join* the tables—that is, you must tell Access how to match up records from one table with the appropriate records from any other tables. Otherwise, Access wouldn't know which orders corresponded with which customers, for example.

You can join tables by means of their common fields. In some cases, Access joins the tables for you automatically. This happens if one table has a field of the same name and the same data type as the primary key in the other or if you've already defined a formal relationship between the tables.

Displaying Field Lists from Two Tables

1. In the Database window, click the name of one of the tables you wish to use in the query.

2. Click the New Object drop-down arrow and click Query.

3. Click the Design View option and click OK.

4. Click the Show Table button and double-click the name(s) of one or more tables you wish to use in the query.

Building a Multi-Table Query

Now you'll build a query that draws data from both the BFCustomers and BFOrders tables. Before you can enter your selection criteria, you need to display Field lists from both tables. Then you can select the fields and values upon which to extract and/or sort your data. In this activity, you'll tell Access to display Field lists from both tables.

1. **Select the BFCustomers table in the *Be Fruitful, Lesson 2* Database window, if it is not already selected, and click the drop-down arrow beside the New Object button** 🔲 **on the far right side of the Database toolbar.**

2. **Click Query from the drop-down list.**

Access displays the New Query dialog box, as shown in Figure 2.16.

3. **Click the Design View option and click OK.**

Access opens the Select Query window. Since the BFCustomers table was selected when you chose to create the query, its Field list is already displayed; you must add the second Field list.

4. **Click the Show Table button** 🔲 **to display the Show Table dialog box.**

5. **Double-click the BFOrders table and then close the Show Table dialog box.**

The Field list for the BFOrders table has been added to the upper pane of the Select Query window. Since a one-to-many relationship was previously assigned to these tables, Access inserts a line showing the joined fields.

Hints & Tips

If the tables are not related or if Access can't guess where to place the join, you can establish one. To join two tables, drag from one field in the first Field list to the corresponding field in the second Field list.

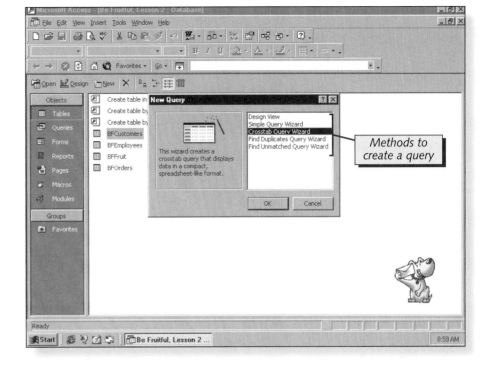

Methods to create a query

Figure 2.16
New Query dialog box

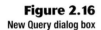

Creating Selection Criteria and Omitting Duplicates

Now that you have Field lists from both tables in the window and they are joined, you are ready to set up your selection criteria. In this activity, you will create your selection criteria from two tables.

1. In the BFCustomers Field list, double-click the **ContactLastName field** and then double-click the **ContactFirstName field**.

Access adds both of these field names to the query design grid.

2. Choose a sort order of **Ascending** for the ContactLastName field and for the ContactFirstName field.

3. Add the **FruitType field** in the BFOrders Field list to the query design grid and type Apples in the *Criteria* row for the FruitType field.

4. Click the **Run button** !.

Access displays the recordset, which lists records for customers who have ordered apples. Notice that customers who ordered apples more than once are listed more than once.

5. Click the **View button** to return to Design view.

6. Click anywhere in the Select Query window outside the query design grid and the Field lists. Then click **Properties** on the toolbar.

The Query Properties window opens.

7. Click in the **Unique Values property box**; then click the drop-down arrow and click **Yes**.

When the Unique Values property is set to Yes, only unique values—that is, no duplicates—will appear in the recordset.

Choosing Selection Criteria from Two Tables

1. Add one or more fields from each Field list to the query design grid.

2. Assign sort orders and criteria to each field.

3. Click the Run button.

4. Save the query with a new name.

8. Click the **Close button** ☒ in the Query Properties window.

9. Click the **Run button** ❗.

Access displays the recordset shown in Figure 2.17. As you can see, each customer who ordered apples is listed only once.

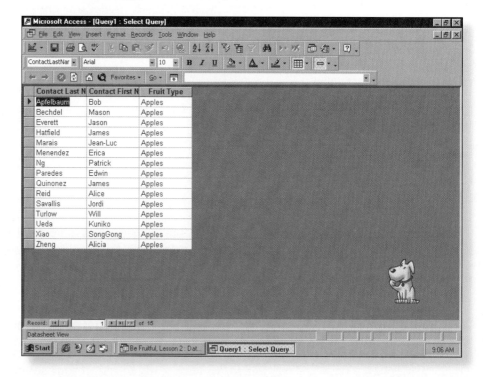

Figure 2.17 ◀
Recordset of customers who
have ordered apples with
duplicates omitted

10. Click **File** on the menu bar and click **Save As**. Type Apple Orders as the query name. Then click **OK** and close the recordset.

You are back to the **Be Fruitful, Lesson 2** Database window. Even though you created the new query from the Tables option, you do not see the new query in the Tables list. The query is listed under the Queries option.

11. Click the **Queries option** in the Objects bar to see the Apple Orders query.

BUILDING COMPLEX QUERIES

In Access, you can easily build complex queries to extract specific information from a database by using wildcard characters, expressions, calculated fields, and statistical functions. The criteria specified in a query can range from simple text or numeric data to complex calculations and expressions. For example, in the California Phone Numbers query you created earlier, you entered simple text criterion *(CA)* in the *Criteria* row of the State field to narrow the information to include only those records with CA in the State field.

If you need to locate specific records, but you're not sure of the spelling of the data, you can use a **wildcard character** in the *Criteria* row to search for unknown characters. Access offers two wildcard characters: the asterisk (*) and the question mark (?). You can use the asterisk to represent any number of characters—for example, if you specify *S** as the criterion in the ContactLastName field, the query would return all records for contacts whose last names begin with *S*, such as Savallis, Smith, and Staples. You can use the question mark to represent a specific character—for example, if you specify *?ill* as the criterion in the ContactFirstName field, the query would return all records containing any character followed by *ill*, such as Bill, Jill, and Will. When using wildcard characters, you must precede the criteria with the word *like*.

Using Expressions as Criteria in a Query

In the Joined After 1998 query you created earlier, you used the expression *12/31/1998* as criterion in the query. An **expression** is a combination of field names, values, and comparison operators that Access can evaluate. You can use expressions as criteria in many instances. You may have a situation, for instance, in which you need to show records within a range of values—for example, you might want to find only those customers who joined between 1997 and 1999. In contrast, you might want to exclude particular records, such as when you want to display all records except those of customers in California. An essential part of most expressions is the comparison operator. A **comparison operator** is a symbol that is used to compare a value or text in the database to characters that you enter. Table 2.2 describes the common comparison operators used in Access.

TABLE 2.2	**COMPARISON OPERATORS**
Operator	**Description**
=	Equal to
<>	Not equal to
>	Greater than
<	Less than
>=	Greater than or equal to
<=	Less than or equal to
Between...And	Between two specified values

You can create compound expressions using *AND* or *OR*. In an *AND* expression, all conditions in the expression must be true in order for the compound expression to be true. For example, to display the records for customers who joined between 1997 and 1999, you would enter the compound expression *>12/31/1996 and <=12/31/1999* in the *Criteria* row. In an *OR* expression, if just one condition is true, the compound expression is true. For example, to display the records for customers who live in Washington, Oregon, or California, you would enter the compound expression *WA or OR or CA*. When you create an *AND* expression, you place the entire compound expression on the same line in the *Criteria* row in the query design grid.

However, when you create an *OR* expression, you can either place the entire expression in the *Criteria* row or place each *OR* condition in a separate *or* row in the query design grid. (After you save the query, Access will automatically place all the *OR* conditions on one line in the *Criteria* row.)

Using Calculated Fields in a Query

As you may recall from the discussion on planning a database in Lesson 1, you should not include fields in your database that contain data you can calculate from other fields. For instance, if you have one field for price and one for quantity, you can calculate the total cost by entering an expression to multiply the values in these two fields together in a ***calculated field.*** You can create a calculated field in a query (or a table) by typing the name of the calculated field, followed by a colon, and then the expression, directly into the *Field* row of the query design grid. Any field names used in the expression must be enclosed in square brackets ([ ]). For example, to calculate the total mentioned above, you could enter the expression *Total:[Price]*[Quantity].* However, instead of entering an expression manually, you can use the ***Expression Builder*** to choose the fields on which you want to perform calculations and the operators you want to use in those calculations.

HANDS On

Creating a Calculated Field

In this activity, you will create a query that contains a calculated field to determine the total price of a customer order.

1. Double-click **Create query in Design view** in the Database window.

2. In the Show Table dialog box, add the BFCustomers and the BFOrders tables to display their Field lists. Then close the Show Table dialog box.

The BFCustomers and BFOrders Field lists appear in the Select Query window. As before, Access displays a join line between the two CustomerID fields.

3. From the BFCustomers Field list, add the ContactLastName and ContactFirstName fields to the query design grid.

4. Click **Ascending** from the drop-down lists in the *Sort* row of the ContactLastName field and the ContactFirstName field.

5. Add the OrderNumber, OrderDate, Price, and Quantity fields from the BFOrders Field list to the query design grid, in that order.

6. Click the **Run button** ! and view the query results.

7. Save the query as Orders Placed.

8. Click the **View button** to return to Design view.

9. Scroll to the first blank field (after Quantity) in the query design grid and click in the *Field* row.

10. Click the **Build button** on the toolbar.

Hints & Tips

To rename a field in a query, right-click anywhere in the column of the field whose name you want to change and click Properties on the shortcut menu that appears. In the Caption text box of the Field Properties window, type the new caption for the field.

The Expression Builder dialog box opens with the **Orders Placed** folder open and the fields available displayed in the second column, as shown in Figure 2.18.

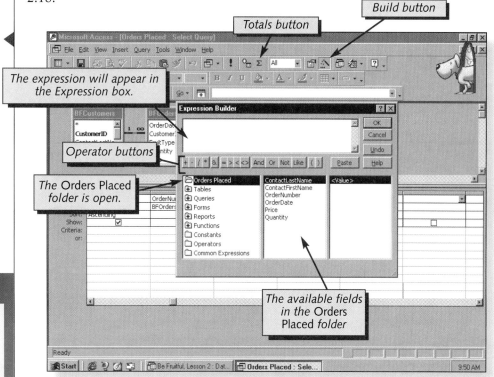

Access
BASICS

Creating a Calculated Field

1. Open an existing query in Design view or create a new query.

2. Scroll to the first blank field in the query design grid, click in the *Field* row, and click the Build button on the toolbar.

3. In the Expression Builder dialog box, select the fields and operators you wish to include in the expression. Then click OK to close the dialog box.

4. Right-click anywhere in the calculated field column and select Properties from the shortcut menu.

5. Type a caption for the calculated field and close the Field Properties window.

6. Run and save the query.

11. Double-click the **Price field** in the second column.

Access inserts the *Price* field in the Expression box at the top of the Expression Builder dialog box.

12. Click the **asterisk button** in the row of operator buttons directly beneath the Expression box.

An asterisk (multiplication symbol) appears in the Expression box.

13. Double-click the **Quantity field** in the second column.

Access inserts the *Quantity* field in the Expression box. This calculation will allow you to obtain the total cost (Price × Quantity).

14. Click **OK**.

The Expression Builder dialog box closes, and the expression you just created is inserted in the field. You can press [⇧ Shift] + [F2] to view the entire expression in the Zoom window.

15. Right-click anywhere in the calculated field column and click **Properties** on the shortcut menu.

The Field Properties window opens.

 *If the Query Properties window opens instead of the Field Properties window, close the Query Properties window, click in the field, then right-click again, and select Properties from the shortcut menu.*

16. Type Total Order **in the Caption text box of the Field Properties window. Then close the Field Properties window.**

When you run the query, the *Total Order* caption will appear as the field name instead of the name *Expr1* assigned by Access to the calculated field.

17. **Click the Run button** ! **and view the query results.**

18. **Save and close the Orders Placed query.**

Using Built-in Statistics in a Query

With Access, you can use built-in statistical functions to perform a variety of calculations. The most common statistical functions are AVG (average), COUNT, MAX (largest value), MIN (smallest value), SUM, and STDEV (standard deviation). To use these functions in a query, you click the Totals button ∑ on the toolbar while in Design view. Access then adds a *Total* row in the query design grid. For each field in the query design grid, you specify the function to be performed on that field. When you apply a function to a field, Access creates a new field name by combining the function and the field name. For example, if you apply the SUM function to the Quantity field, Access would rename the field *SumOfQuantity*.

HANDS On

Creating a Query that Includes a Statistical Function

In this activity, you will create a query that calculates the total payments made by each customer of the Be Fruitful fruit-of-the-month club.

1. **Double-click Create query in Design view in the Database window.**

2. **In the Show Table dialog box, add the BFCustomers and BFOrders tables to display their Field lists. Then close the Show Table dialog box.**

3. **From the BFCustomers Field list, add the ContactLastName and ContactFirstName fields to the query design grid.**

4. **From the BFOrders Field list, add the PaymentAmount field to the query design grid.**

5. **Click Descending from the drop-down list in the *Sort* row of the PaymentAmount field.**

6. **Click the Totals button** ∑ **on the toolbar.**

Access inserts the *Total* row in the query design grid and the Group By function (default) appears in each field in the *Total* row.

7. **Click in the *Total* row of the PaymentAmount field and click the drop-down arrow.**

The list of available functions appears.

8. **Click Sum from the drop-down list, as shown in Figure 2.19.**

9. **Click the Run button** ! **.**

Access runs the query, displaying the sum of each customer's payment amounts.

Did you know?

You can calculate statistics for records that meet specific criteria by choosing the *Where* function in the *Total* row for the field and entering the criterion in the *Criteria* row.

Figure 2.19
Entering a statistical function in
the query design grid

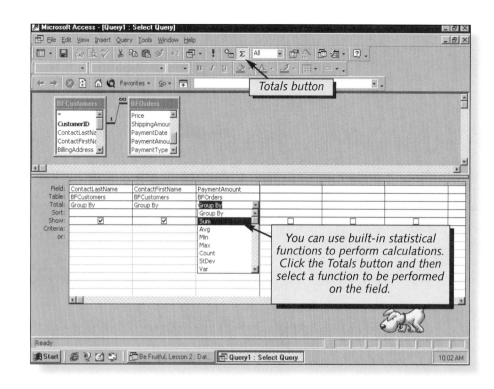

Using Statistical Functions in a Query

1. Open an existing query in Design view or create a new query.

2. Click the Totals button on the toolbar.

3. In the query design grid, click in the *Total* row of the field on which you wish to apply a statistical function.

4. Click the drop-down arrow and click the desired statistical function from the drop-down list.

5. Run and save the query.

You can instruct Access to check the spelling of your data in a form, table, or query. Open the object you wish to check and click Spelling on the Tools menu.

10. Click the **Contact Last Name field selector** and drag to highlight all three fields. Position the pointer on the right border of any field selector; when the pointer changes into the shape of a vertical bar with a horizontal double-headed arrow attached, double-click the **right field selector border**.

Access automatically resizes the three columns so you can see the entire field names. Notice that Access renamed the PaymentAmount field to *SumOfPaymentAmount*.

11. Click anywhere in the recordset to remove the highlighting. Save the query as Sum of Payments **and close the query.**

CREATING AND WORKING WITH FORMS

As you probably remember from Lesson 1, Access forms are electronic versions of paper forms. You can use forms to view, edit, and enter data into your tables. For the most part, you've only used the datasheet to work with your data. Although this setting provides a fine overview, generally it doesn't permit you to see all fields at once—making assessing or editing your data awkward. To create a more comfortable working environment, you can create a custom form and determine how the form will present the data from a table or query. Among other things, you can build forms that display a single record at a time as well as forms that reveal only selected fields from the chosen table or query. Forms are particularly helpful when you want to simplify data entry or when you need to control which data is displayed.

You can create a basic form easily with an AutoForm or with the many Form Wizards. To create an AutoForm, you must choose the table or query on which you want to base the form and then click a single button. An *AutoForm* is actually a specialized type of Form Wizard that doesn't request

any special choices on your part but instead gathers the information it needs by examining the selected table or query. The wizard builds a basic form that includes every field from the table or query arranged in columns. The field names (or captions) appear on the left side of the form to identify the fields, and the name of the table or query appears at the top as a heading. Most fields are displayed as text boxes; Memo fields are displayed as slightly larger text boxes, and Yes/No fields appear as check boxes that you can click to either select or deselect.

Most of the time, you use Form view to enter and edit records in a form. In Form view, you move through fields and records much as you do in Datasheet view. In fact, you can switch any time to the form's Datasheet view to see multiple records at once. (This view is identical to the Datasheet view of the table but displays only the information that you would see in the form.) And, since you already know how to add, edit, delete, sort, and select data in the datasheet, you'll soon learn that the procedures are much the same for forms.

Creating an AutoForm

In this activity, you'll create an AutoForm based on the BFCustomers table, and you'll view and move through your data using the form. Since the records in the BFCustomers table contain subdatasheets, Access will automatically create a subform for each record. A *subform* is a form within a form that displays related records.

1. Click the **Tables option** in the Objects bar of the Database window and select the BFCustomers table, if it's not already selected.

2. Click the **New Object drop-down arrow** 📇 ▾ on the Database toolbar and click **AutoForm**.

Access automatically creates a form based on the BFCustomers table. Notice that the form displays the data for the first record in the BFCustomers table. The form will include all of the fields for a single record. The subform created by Access is displayed at the bottom of the form.

3. Click the **Last Record navigation button** ▶️.

Access displays the information for the last record in the table, as shown in Figure 2.20. All the navigation buttons at the bottom of the form work as they do in the datasheet.

4. Click twice on the **Previous Record button** ◀.

Access moves up two records in the table. The Notes field has a larger text box because it's a Memo field, and the Extra Catalogs field is displayed as a check box because it's a Yes/No field. You can click this check box to turn it on or off.

5. Click the **View drop-down arrow** 📄 ▾ and click **Datasheet View**.

Access displays the form in Datasheet view. You'll see the portion of the data that you were viewing in Form view. In Datasheet view, the data appears in columns and rows. If you like, you can also scroll your data up and down (and left and right), as you can when working on a table in Datasheet view.

Figure 2.20
The last record

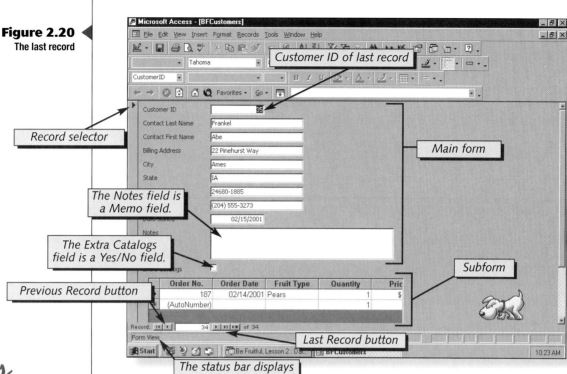

Customer ID of last record

Record selector

Main form

The Notes field is a Memo field.

The Extra Catalogs field is a Yes/No field.

Subform

Previous Record button

Last Record button

The status bar displays the current view.

Creating and Exploring an AutoForm

1. Select the table you want to base the form on, click the New Object drop-down arrow, and click AutoForm.

2. Click the navigation buttons to move from record to record.

3. Click the View drop-down arrow and click the appropriate option to change views.

Did you know?

A form can contain more than one subform.

6. Click the **View drop-down arrow** and click **Form View**.

Access returns you to Form view. In Form view, the data appears like a paper form.

7. Click the form's **Close button**.

Because you haven't saved the form, Access displays a warning box.

8. Click **Yes**.

9. In the Save As dialog box, type BFCustomers AutoForm **as the form name and click OK.**

Access saves and then closes the form, returning you to the *Be Fruitful, Lesson 2* Database window. The form you just created becomes one of the objects under the Forms option in the Objects bar.

Adding and Editing Data by Using Forms and Subforms

Sometimes you may want to use forms to browse your data. The real purpose of forms, however, is to facilitate the entering and editing of data. In forms, as in the datasheet, you need to know how to find the records that you want to edit. Once you're there, you need to know a few editing strategies. Fortunately, the techniques for navigating in forms are basically the same as those for moving around in the datasheet.

Modifying Records Using a Form and Subform

When you add, edit, or delete records in a form or subform, the change is automatically reflected in the appropriate table. The data you add to the main form affects one table, while the data you add to the subform may affect a different table. In this activity, you'll use the BFCustomers AutoForm to add records for a new customer and order, edit a record, and delete a record.

1. Click the **Forms option** in the Objects bar of the Database window and then double-click **BFCustomers AutoForm**.

Access displays the selected form and shows the first record for the underlying table.

2. Click the **New Record button** ▶*.

Access presents you with a new, blank record.

3. Press `Tab` **to move to the Contact Last Name field. Type** Myrianthopoulos **and press** `Tab`.

Notice that Access automatically enters the next record number in the Customer ID field. (If you're confused about why there are more customer IDs than customers, don't forget that you deleted a record earlier.)

4. Type Zoe **in the Contact First Name field. Pressing** `Tab` **to move from field to field, type** 1357 Birch St. #7 **in the Billing Address field,** Woodstock **in the City field,** NY **in the State field,** 11223-4432 **in the ZIP Code field,** (917) 555-1234 **in the Phone Number field, and** 4/22/2001 **in the Date Joined field. Leave the Notes field blank for now, and leave the Extra Catalogs field deselected (the default).**

You now have a new record in the table. This new customer placed an order. Rather than entering the order data in the BFOrders table, you can enter it in the subform currently displayed. Access will automatically change the BFOrders table to reflect the new order.

5. Press `Tab` **until you get to the Order Date field of the subform.**

6. Type 4/22/2001 and press `Tab`.

As shown in Figure 2.21, once you start typing in the Order Date field, the Order Number is automatically assigned.

7. Pressing `Tab` **to move among fields, type** Pears **in the Fruit Type field, (a 1 should already appear in the Quantity field),** 18.50 **in the Price field, and** 4.50 **in the Shipping Amt. field. Leave the remaining fields blank.**

8. Type 7 **in the record indicator of the main form and press** `Enter◄┘`.

Access moves you to the seventh record in the table—the record for Mason Bechdel.

9. Click the **Notes field text box.**

Although there's no text, Access places the insertion point within the field and adds a vertical scroll bar.

10. Type the following text:

7/15/2001: Mr. Bechdel reported not receiving his order of pears, although the fruit was delivered to his front door. Please send him a replacement box, rush delivery,

Modifying Records with a Form and a Subform

1. To add a record, click the New Record button and type the data.

2. Press `Tab` to move to the subform and type data, if appropriate.

3. To edit data, move to the record to be edited and delete and/or type the new data.

4. To delete a record, click the record selector and press `Delete`. When the warning box appears, click Yes.

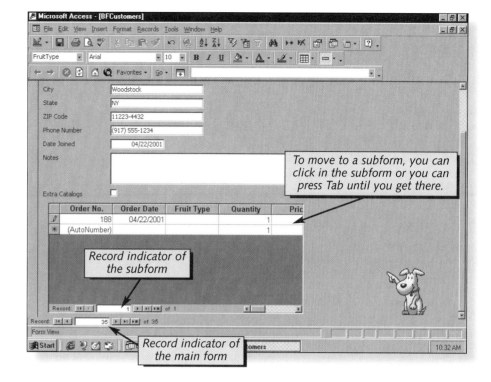

Figure 2.21
Entering data in a subform

and include a half dozen extra pears. Leave all packages at the back door in the future.

11. **Move to record 31—the record for Eddie Marshall.**

12. **Click the record selector—the long vertical bar on the left side of the window.**

The record selector should turn a darker shade of gray, which indicates that this entire record is selected.

13. **Press** ⌨Delete **to remove the record.**

Because you asked Access to enforce referential integrity when you defined the relationship between the BFCustomers and BFOrders tables, Access displays a warning stating that the record cannot be deleted. You cannot delete a customer from the BFCustomers table unless there are no related orders in the BFOrders table. Therefore, Mr. Marshall's order record must be deleted before his customer record can be deleted. Let's assume that Mr. Marshall canceled both his fruit order and his membership in the Be Fruitful fruit-of-the-month club.

14. **Click OK to remove the warning message and click the record selector for Mr. Marshall's fruit order in the BFOrders subform.**

The entire record is highlighted.

15. **Press** ⌨Delete **to remove the order record.**

Access displays a warning to verify that you want to delete the record.

16. **Click Yes in the warning dialog box and click the record selector for Mr. Marshall's customer record in the main form.**

17. **Press** ⌨Delete **to remove the customer record.**

- To view a form in Datasheet view, click Datasheet View on the View menu.

- To create an AutoForm, click Insert on the menu bar and click AutoForm. You can also create an AutoForm within Datasheet view.

- To save an AutoForm, click Save As on the File menu.

Many reports contain facts and figures that originate in business and other periodicals. You can find interesting information at Web sites published by resources such as *Business Week* (www.businessweek.com) and *USA Today* (www.usatoday.com).

Once again, Access displays a warning to verify that you want to delete the record.

18. Click Yes to delete the record. Then close the form.

The BFCustomers AutoForm closes, and you return to the Database window.

CREATING AND WORKING WITH REPORTS

You generally use reports when you need professional-looking printed output. You might have to provide handouts for a presentation. Or, perhaps you need to share information with someone who isn't familiar with Access, doesn't have access to a computer, or prefers to spread pages out on a desk rather than view them on a computer screen. Although you can print datasheets and forms, reports look more polished and provide much more control over how your data is presented. In addition, from reports you can automatically generate summary data, such as totals and grand totals.

Just as with forms, you can create a report in two ways—by using either AutoReport or the Report Wizard. *AutoReports* are basic reports generated automatically by Access. To create an AutoReport, you choose the table or query on which to base your report and then click the New Object drop-down arrow and click Report. Like the AutoForm, the AutoReport tracks the required information by examining the selected table or query—without asking you for any input. Access builds a basic report that includes every field from the table or query arranged in columns. The field names (or captions) appear on the left, to identify the fields. You can also create a second type of AutoReport that contains a header and a footer. In this type of report, the name of the table or query appears as a report header. A *header* is text information printed at the top of *every page* of the report; a *report header* appears at the top of the *first page* only. A report *footer* appears at the bottom of every page and includes the date on which the report is printed, the page number, and the number of pages in the entire report.

If you need a basic report, an AutoReport might do the job. If, however, you want to choose the layout, decide the fields to include and their order, determine the text layout on the page (columnar, tabular, or justified), and more, then you should use the Report Wizard. Using the Report Wizard is similar to using the Table Wizard: Access prompts you for information and then constructs a report based on your replies. As with any other wizard, you can click the Back button any time you want to move back one step.

Creating a Columnar Report

The Report Wizard allows you to choose the layout and orientation of the report. The columnar layout displays the records one after another. The tabular layout shows the fields of each record in rows. The justified layout displays each record in its own small box. In *portrait orientation,* pages print down the long side of the page. In *landscape orientation,* pages print across the wide side of the paper. If you want a *columnar report*, all of the

Using the Report Wizard

1. Click the table or query name on which you want to base the report.

2. Click the New Object drop-down arrow and click Report.

3. Double-click Report Wizard.

4. Select the table or query name in the Tables/Queries box.

5. Select the fields to include in the report and click Next.

6. Click Next twice if you don't want to group or sort the records.

7. Click the desired layout and orientation options and click Next.

8. Click the style and click Next.

9. Type a name for the report and click Finish.

fields for a record are displayed vertically on the page. In this activity, you will use the Report Wizard to create a columnar report.

1. Click **Tables** in the Objects bar of the Database window, select the **BFCustomers table**, and click the **New Object drop-down arrow** . Click **Report** and then double-click **Report Wizard**.

Access displays the first Report Wizard dialog box. The selected table name appears in the Tables/Queries text box.

2. Click the **Add All Fields button** ⌗.

Access moves all of the field names to the *Selected Fields* list box.

3. Click the **CustomerID field** in the *Selected Fields* list and click the **Remove Field button** ⌗.

Access removes the CustomerID field from the list of fields.

4. Select the **DateJoined field** and click the **Remove Field button** ⌗. Click the **Remove Field button** ⌗ two more times.

Access removes the DateJoined, Notes, and ExtraCatalogs fields from the list of fields to include in the report.

5. Click **Next** to move to the dialog box that allows you to group the records. (You will learn more about grouping for reports later in this lesson.)

6. Click **Next** to move to the dialog box that allows you to sort records by up to four fields. (You will learn more about sorting for reports later in this lesson.)

7. Click **Next** to move to the dialog box that allows you to choose the report layout and the orientation.

8. Click the **Columnar** and **Portrait option buttons**. Then, click **Next** to move to the dialog box that allows you to choose a style for your report.

9. Click **Corporate** and click **Next**.

In the final Report Wizard dialog box, you enter the title of the report and tell Access what you want to do next.

10. Type Customer Names and Addresses **in the title text box and click the Preview the report. option**. Then click **Finish**.

In a moment, Access displays the first page of the report you just created, as shown in Figure 2.22. The report contains data from the selected BFCustomers table. Note that the report displays only designated fields from the underlying table.

You can rename your report later by selecting it in the Database window. Click the name again. When you see the insertion point, press ⌷Backspace⌷ *or* ⌷Delete⌷ *to delete the existing name and type a new one. If you want to create a copy of the same report using a different name, open the report, click Save As on the File menu, and type a name for the copy of the report.*

11. Click the **Last Page navigation button** ⌗.

Access shows the last page in the report. Note that the report header appears on the first page only.

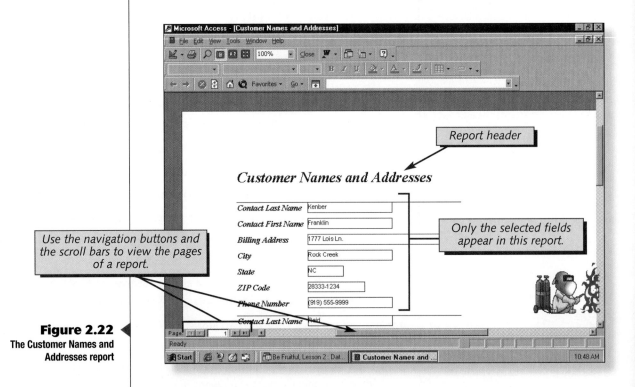

Report header

Customer Names and Addresses

Contact Last Name	Kenber
Contact First Name	Franklin
Billing Address	1777 Lois Ln.
City	Rock Creek
State	NC
ZIP Code	28333-1234
Phone Number	(919) 555-9999
Contact Last Name	Reid

Only the selected fields appear in this report.

Use the navigation buttons and the scroll bars to view the pages of a report.

Figure 2.22
The Customer Names and Addresses report

12. **Scroll to the bottom of the page.**

The date and page number appear as a report footer.

13. **Click the report's Close button ☒ to close the report.**

Access closes the report and returns you to the Database window. The report you just created becomes one of the objects under the Reports option in the Objects bar.

Creating a Tabular Report

If you have a large amount of data to display in a relatively small amount of space, use a tabular report. A *tabular report* displays the fields for a single record in one row and presents multiple records at once. Field names or captions appear near the top of the report as column headings. Realize that tabular reports don't work well with long Text or Memo fields or with too many fields to fit on a single page.

HANDS On

Creating a Tabular Report Based on a Query

In this activity, you will create a query to display all the fruit orders for the year 2000. Then you will begin building a report using the Report Wizard.

1. **Click the BFOrders table in the *Be Fruitful, Lesson 2* Database window. Click Query on the New Object drop-down list.**

Access displays the New Query dialog box.

Access BASICS

Creating a Report Based on a Query

1. Click the table on which to base the query.

2. Click the New Object drop-down arrow and click Query.

3. Click Design View and click OK.

4. Add the desired fields to the query design window.

5. Add any desired sort orders and criteria and click the Run button.

6. Click Save As on the File menu, name the query, and click OK.

7. Click Reports in the Objects bar.

8. Double-click Create report by using wizard.

9. Select the query or table on which to base the report in the Tables/Queries box.

10. Add the desired fields and click Next.

Figure 2.23 ◄

Choosing all of the fields in the BFOrders Field list

---

2. Click Design View and click OK.

Access displays the Select Query window.

3. Double-click the title bar of the BFOrders Field list.

As shown in Figure 2.23, Access selects all of the fields in the Field list.

4. Drag the selected list of fields to the first column in the query design grid.

Access inserts all fields into the query design grid.

5. In the *Sort* row of the OrderDate field, click Ascending.

6. Type >12/31/1999 and <= 12/31/2000 in the *Criteria* row of the OrderDate field.

This compound expression using *AND* instructs Access to display all orders after 12/31/1999 and on or before 12/31/2000—that is, all orders in the year 2000.

7. Click the Run button ▮.

Access displays a recordset that includes only the orders from 2000.

8. Save the query as 2000 Orders. Then close the query.

9. In the Reports option, double-click Create report by using wizard.

Access displays the initial Report Wizard dialog box, where you can choose the fields to include in the report.

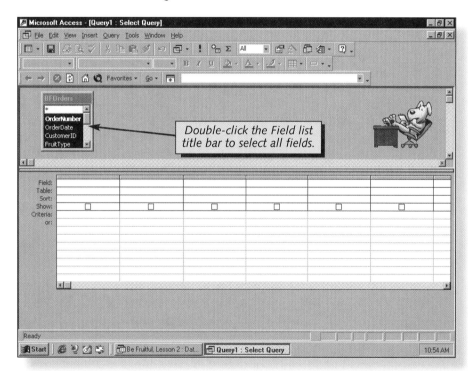

10. Click Query: 2000 Orders from the Tables/Queries box, if it is not already selected.

11. Add the OrderDate, FruitType, Quantity, Price, ShippingAmount, and PaymentAmount fields to the *Selected Fields* list, in that order. Then click Next.

The second dialog box should look like the one in Figure 2.24. As shown in the sample report area, Access assumes you want the records grouped by fruit type.

Figure 2.24 ◄
The Report Wizard dialog box
with grouping settings

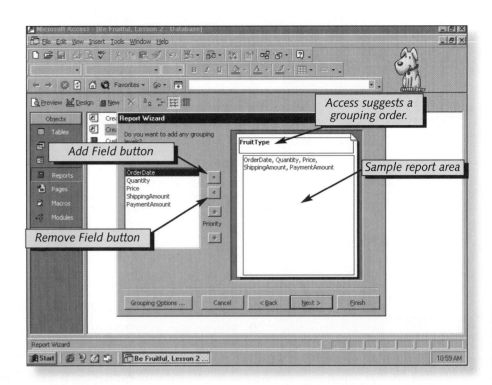

Grouping and Sorting Records in a Report and Previewing a Report

Groups, as the name implies, are collections of records with like information. Examples of groups include records with a city field of Philadelphia or records with the same order date. You can group records by any field in the report. In this activity, you will finish building the report, in which the orders are grouped by month and the records are sorted chronologically within each group (month). Then you will preview the report.

1. Since you don't want to group records by fruit type, click the **Remove Field button** ◄.

Access removes the FruitType heading from the sample area.

2. Click **OrderDate** and click the **Add Field button** ►.

The sample area now shows *OrderDate by Month.*

3. Click **Next** to move to the dialog box that allows you to control the order in which records appear within each group.

In this case, you want the records to be in chronological order within each month.

4. Click the **drop-down arrow** beside the number 1 field and click the **OrderDate field**.

The OrderDate field will determine the sequence of the records within each group. The Sort button [↕] beside each field is a toggle button that allows you to sort in ascending or descending order. Ascending order is the default.

5. Click **Next** to move to the dialog box to choose the layout for the tabular report.

Grouping and Sorting Records

1. If you want to change a grouping level, click the Remove Field button.

2. Click the field on which you want to group and click the Add Field button. Click Next.

3. Click the first field's drop-down arrow and click the field on which you want to sort.

4. Click the Sort button beside the field name to change the sort order, if desired. Then click Next.

5. Click the desired layout and orientation options and click Next.

6. Click the desired style and click Next.

7. Type a report name and click Finish.

As you can see, when you create a report that groups and sorts the records, a tabular report is selected automatically. The preview box inside the dialog box illustrates what the Stepped layout looks like.

6. Click the **Align Left 1 option button** and look at the layout in the preview box.

7. Click **Landscape** in the Orientation box and click **Next** to move to the dialog box to choose a style.

8. Click **Soft Gray** as the style and then click the **Next button** to move to the final Report Wizard dialog box.

9. Type Be Fruitful 2000 Orders as the title and click **Finish**.

In a moment, Access displays the tabular report, which shows the data from your 2000 Orders query in a tabular layout.

10. Scroll the report.

Access has grouped the records by month and sorted each month's records by order date, as shown in Figure 2.25.

Notice that some of the report's column headings don't line up that well with the data and the columns could be spaced better. You can fix these problems easily in Design view, as you'll learn in the Using Help section of this lesson. Although you'll frequently want to revise tabular reports in Design view, using the Report Wizard is the quickest way to create the basic report.

11. Click anywhere on the page to zoom out. Use the navigation buttons to preview each page of the report.

Although much of the text is not readable, you can use this view to preview the layout of an entire report.

12. Close the report and return to the *Be Fruitful, Lesson 2* Database window.

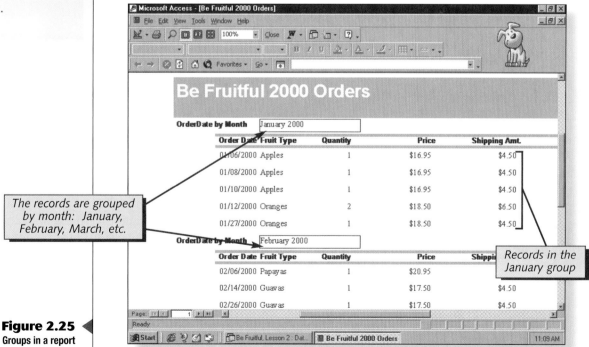

Figure 2.25
Groups in a report

Modifying Reports and Forms

The spacing and alignment of data in reports and forms doesn't always look perfect. And, depending on the page layout, some column labels may not be entirely visible. Use Help to learn how you can modify a report or form in Design view.

1. Click the **Office Assistant**.

2. Type resize a control **in the *What would you like to do?* box and click Search.**

3. Click **Move, size, align, and format text boxes or controls in a form or report**.

4. Maximize the Help window, if necessary, and click **Move a control and its label**. Read the Help information to learn how to work with controls in Design view (Figure 2.26).

Figure 2.26
Learning about moving controls

5. Explore for answers to these questions: What is a control? What view do you use to move a text box or other control? What shape does the pointer have when you are dragging the control? How do you maintain vertical or horizontal alignment with other controls?

6. Click the **Show button** on the Help window and then click the **Contents tab**.

7. Scroll and click the **plus sign** before the **Working with Controls on Forms, Reports, and Data Access Pages topic**.

8. Open the **Creating, Manipulating, and Formatting Controls topic**. Explore for information on aligning controls.

9. Close the Help window.

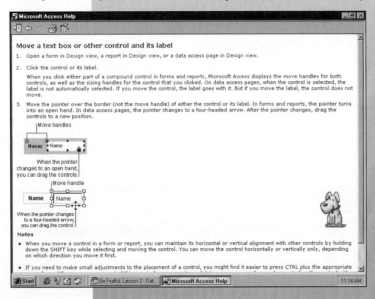

Did you know?

Just as a form can contain a subform, a report can contain a subreport that provides details of the main report.

Creating Totals in Reports

Access can easily group records in tabular reports. Sometimes, however, you may want to include totals of the numeric fields in the report as well. In the Be Fruitful 2000 Orders report, you might want subtotals for each month's orders and a grand total for all of the records in the query or table. You might also like to see the total sales per year rather than only the entire sales over the life of the company. In such cases, you can add totals to a report.

HANDS On

Figure 2.27 ◀
Adding groups and subgroups
to a report

Building and Printing a Report with Totals and Subtotals

In this activity, you will use the Report Wizard to create a report that groups records by year and, within each year, groups the records by fruit type. Then you will add totals and subtotals for the numeric fields in the report. Finally, you will calculate a grand total at the end of the report.

1. Double-click Create report by using wizard in the Reports option of the Database window.

In the first Report Wizard dialog box, you will choose the tables, queries, and fields you want to include in the report.

2. Click Query: 2000 Orders in the Tables/Queries box, if necessary.

3. Use the Add Field button > **to include the OrderDate, FruitType, Quantity, Price, ShippingAmount, and PaymentAmount fields, in that order. Then click Next.**

In this dialog box you will choose up to four fields to use as the basis for grouping data in your report. Access sorts on the first designated field first and then on each designated field in the order you choose them.

4. Click the Remove Field button < **to remove the FruitType heading as the grouping level.**

5. Click OrderDate and click the Add Field button > **.**

6. Click FruitType and again click the Add Field button > **.**

Both fields are added to the list box on the right as shown in Figure 2.27, indicating that you want the records in the table grouped by OrderDate. Then, within each group, you want the orders grouped by FruitType.

7. Click the Grouping Options button.

8. In the Grouping Intervals dialog box, click Year for the Grouping intervals of the OrderDate field.

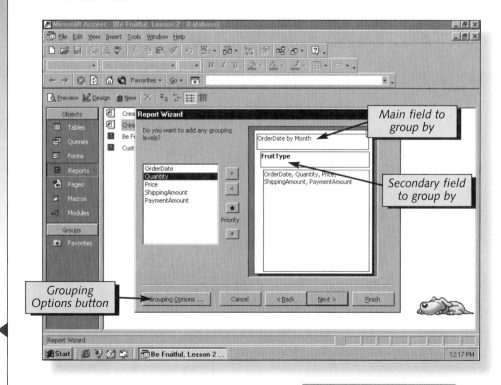

9. Click **OK** to group the records by the year in which the orders were placed. Then click **Next** to move to the dialog box to choose the fields to sort by.

10. Click the drop-down arrow in the Field 1 box and click **Quantity**.

Access will use the Quantity field to sort records that have the same order year and type of fruit.

11. Click the **Summary Options button**.

In the Summary Options dialog box, you can select from four different types of summary information—totals (Sum), average (Avg), minimum value (Min), and maximum value (Max)—for each numeric field. The option buttons on the right allow you to choose between *Detail and Summary* or *Summary Only*. If you choose *Detail and Summary*, you will see the data for each record as well as summary information for each group, subgroup, and final totals. If you choose *Summary Only*, you will see the summary information for each group, subgroup, and final totals, but you will not see the data for individual records.

12. Click the **Sum check boxes** for the Quantity, ShippingAmount, and PaymentAmount fields. Verify that the *Detail and Summary* option is selected.

13. Click **OK**; then click **Next** to choose the layout and orientation for the report.

14. Click the **Outline 1 layout** and **Landscape orientation**. Then click **Next**.

15. Click **Compact style** and click **Next**.

16. Type Orders by Year and Fruit Type as the title of the report and click **Finish**.

After a few moments, the Report Wizard displays a preview of your report.

17. Navigate the report to see the totals and subtotals, as shown in a portion of the report in Figure 2.28.

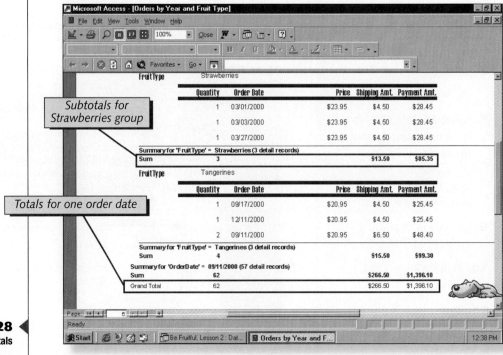

Figure 2.28
A report with totals and subtotals

Access BASICS

Printing a Report

1. Open the report you wish to print.

2. Click Print on the File menu.

3. Change the settings in the Print dialog box, if desired, and then click OK.

18. Click Print on the File menu.

Note that you can print while viewing the report in Print Preview mode, or you can select the report name in the Database window and print from there. In the Print dialog box, you can choose to print only selected pages of the report; you also can choose to print multiple copies of the pages or the full report.

19. Click Pages in the Print Range box and type 1 in the *From* and *To* boxes. Verify that the Number of Copies is set to 1. Click OK.

Access will display a message to tell you that it is printing the first page of your report.

20. Close the report.

21. Click the Compact on Close option, if necessary, and close the *Be Fruitful, Lesson 2* database.

Test your knowledge by answering the following questions. See Appendix B to check your answers.

1. To view and edit a field that contains a large amount of data, you can open the _____ window.

2. A set of rules that Access can enforce to preserve the defined relationship between tables is called _____.

3. When you run a query, the result is called a _____.

4. A(n) _____ is a specialized type of Form Wizard that doesn't request any special choices on your part, but instead gathers the information it needs by examining the table or query on which it is based.

5. In a report that contains student information, all of the students who chose Finance as a major could be considered a _____.

CREATING HYPERLINKS IN AN ACCESS DATABASE

I n previous On the Web activities, you learned how to insert hyperlinks in a Word document and an Excel worksheet. In Access, you can create hyperlinks that link you to another object, database, or Web site. If the database is not open, Access automatically opens the file. In forms, you can create hyperlinks that appear as text, graphics, button, or other shapes. In a database, text that contains hyperlinks usually appears in a different color than other items, often blue, and is underlined. Typically, after you click a hyperlink, the text changes color, generally to purple, to remind you that you followed the link. In this activity, you will create hyperlinks to another object in the same database, to another database, and to a Web site.

1. Open the *Be Fruitful, Lesson 2* database in the *Tutorial* folder on your Student Data Disk. Open the California Phone Numbers query in Design view.

2. Replace the text *"CA"* in the *Criteria* row of the State field with "NC" to find all of the phone numbers for North Carolina customers.

3. Save the new query as North Carolina Phone Numbers **and close the Select Query window.**

4. Open the BFCustomers table, maximize the window, and click the **ZIP Code field selector** to highlight the entire column. Then click **Insert** on the menu bar and click **Hyperlink Column**.

A new column appears between the State and ZIP Code fields and the insertion point moves to the first record within that column. Since the state in the first record is North Carolina, you will create a hyperlink to jump to the query that displays the phone numbers for all of the customers in North Carolina.

5. Click the **Insert Hyperlink button** .

The Insert Hyperlink dialog box appears. When you are linking to an object within the current database, filling in the *Type the file or Web page name* box is optional. If you leave this blank, Access assumes that you want to link to an object within the active database.

6. Click the **Bookmark button**.

7. In the *Select Place in Document* dialog box, click the **plus sign** in front of **Queries**, and click the **North Carolina Phone Numbers query**. Then click **OK**.

Access returns to the completed Insert Hyperlink dialog box, as shown in Figure 2.29.

8. Click **OK** to return to the BFCustomers table. Press to move the cursor to the next record.

ON*the*WEB

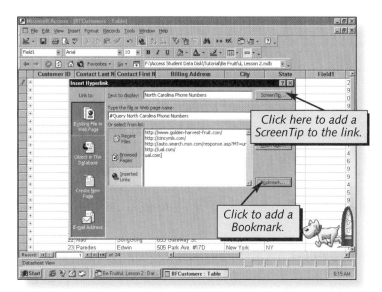

Figure 2.29 ◀
The Insert Hyperlink
dialog box

Note that the hyperlink is now visible in the column labeled *Field1*. The text, which displays the name of the linked object, appears in blue and is underlined to indicate that a hyperlink exists.

9. Point to the hyperlink and notice that the pointer changes to the shape of a hand and a ScreenTip displays for the North Carolina Phone Numbers query. Then click the hyperlink.

Access opens the North Carolina Phone Numbers query. Notice the query name appears in the title bar.

10. Click the **Back button** ⬅ on the Web toolbar to return to the BFCustomers table.

To return to the previously viewed object, you can click the Back button ⬅ on the Web toolbar or you can click the object's taskbar button.

11. Move to the second record and place the insertion point in the Field1 hyperlink column.

You can also type the name of an object in the active database to create a hyperlink. This method will only work if the field (column) has already been designated as a hyperlink field.

12. In Field1 of the second record, type California Phone Numbers and press [Enter←]. Then test the hyperlink.

13. Close the California Phone Numbers and North Carolina Phone Numbers queries and then close the BFCustomers table.

14. Open the BFOrders table and add this new record: Order No.: press [Tab], Order Date: 2/15/2001, **Customer ID**: 4, **Fruit Type**: Apricots, **Quantity**: 2, **Price**: 18.95.

Now you need to find the shipping amount charged to a customer who orders two items. To do so, you can create a hyperlink to another database that contains shipping charges.

15. Click the **Shipping Amt. field**. Then click **Insert** on the menu bar and click **Hyperlink Column**.

A new column appears to the left of the Shipping Amt. field and the insertion point moves to that column.

16. Click the **Insert Hyperlink button** 🌐.

17. In the Insert Hyperlink dialog box, click the **File button** and navigate to the database named *Shipping Charges* on your Student Data Disk. Click the name and then click **OK** to return to the Insert Hyperlink dialog box.

18. In the Insert Hyperlink dialog box, click the **Bookmark button**, click the **plus sign** in front of **Tables**, select the **Shipping Charges table**, and click **OK**. Click **OK** again to close the Insert Hyperlink dialog box.

A hyperlink to the ***Shipping Charges*** database now appears in the column labeled *Field1*.

19. Point to the hyperlink; the pointer changes to the shape of a hand. Click the hyperlink.

Another copy of Access opens and the Shipping Charges table in the ***Shipping Charges*** database opens. (Remember, to have two databases open at the same time, you must open another copy of Access.) You can now see that the charge to send two items is $6.50.

20. Click the **Back button** ⬅ or click the **BFOrders taskbar button** to return to the BFOrders table. Type 6.50 in the Shipping Amt. field. Complete the record by entering the following information: **Payment Date:** 2/23/2001, **Payment Amount:** 44.40, **Payment Type:** Credit Card, **Reference:** 2222-2222-2222.

21. Close the Shipping Charges table and database and the second copy of Access. Then close the BFOrders table.

22. Open the BFCustomers AutoForm form in Design view and click the **Insert Hyperlink button** 🌐. In the *Type the file or Web page name* box, type www.golden-harvest-fruit.com and click **OK**.

Access inserts the hyperlink toward the top of the form, but it is not in a very good location. Notice that selection handles appear around the hyperlink.

23. Move the pointer over the hyperlink until the pointer changes into the shape of a hand. (Do not position the pointer on a selection handle.) When the pointer takes the shape of a hand, click and drag the hyperlink to the right of the *Extra Catalogs* check box, as shown in Figure 2.30. Then release the mouse button.

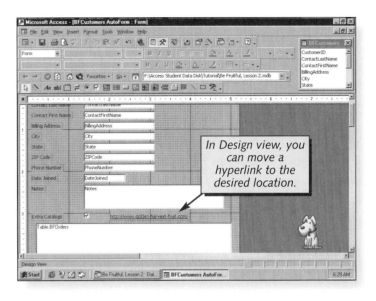

In Design view, you can move a hyperlink to the desired location.

Figure 2.30 ◀
Hyperlink inserted in the
BFCustomers AutoForm

24. Click the **View button** to switch to Form view.

The label *http://www.golden-harvest-fruit.com/* becomes a hyperlink. When you click the hyperlink, Access will jump to the site located at the specified URL. A ***URL (Uniform Resource Locator)*** is the address of a Web site. A URL can be made up of letters, numbers, and special symbols that are understood by the Internet.

25. Test your new hyperlink. (Connect to the Internet, if necessary.)

26. When the Web page for the Golden Harvest Fruit Company appears, explore the link regarding the products the company offers. Click the **Back button** to return to the previous page. Explore the fundraising tips that Golden Harvest offers to users.

27. Disconnect from the Internet unless your instructor tells you to remain connected. Close your Web browser. Close your database, saving all changes, and exit Access.

 Warning

You may proceed directly to the exercises for this lesson. If, however, you are finished with your computer session, follow the "shut down" procedures for your lab or school environment.

Lesson Summary & Exercises

SUMMARY

Working in Datasheet view is an important part of working with tables—the building blocks of databases. You learned in this lesson that you can add, edit, and delete records in Datasheet view. You learned how to assign relationships between tables and work with subdatasheets. While the data contained in tables can be useful in its raw format, the ability to quickly sort records provides great advantages over a manual system. You first performed a simple sort of all of your data. Then you created queries to select and sort specific records and fields from one or more tables. You also created, modified, and saved forms and reports. Forms are useful for entering and editing data, as well as viewing data. You can calculate totals and subtotals in reports, and you can print them. Finally, you added hyperlinks to a database to link to other objects within a database, to another database, and to a Web site.

Now that you have completed this lesson, you should be able to do the following:

- Add new records and type data in Datasheet view. (Access-402)
- Use the Office Clipboard to copy and paste data between tables. (Access-406)
- Import an entire table from another database. (Access-408)
- Edit data in records, undo a change, and delete records. (Access-410)
- Undo changes you have made to a saved record. (Access-413)
- Open a Zoom window to look at and edit text. (Access-413)
- Understand the types of relationships that can exist between two tables. (Access-415)
- Create and print database relationships. (Access-415)
- Open and close a subdatasheet. (Access-418)
- Use the Sort Ascending and Sort Descending buttons to sort one or more fields in alphabetical, numerical, or chronological order. (Access-419)
- Use the query design grid to specify the sort order, criteria, and fields to appear in a query. (Access-421)
- Hide, add, and remove fields in a query. (Access-423)
- Save a query with a name. (Access-423)
- Edit data in a query. (Access-425)
- Create a query that uses multiple tables and omit duplicates from a query. (Access-426)
- Use expressions as criteria in a query, create a calculated field in a query, and use statistical functions in a query. (Access-429)
- Explain the purposes and uses of forms and create an AutoForm. (Access-433)
- Add and edit data in forms and subforms. (Access-436)
- Explain the purposes and uses of reports and use the Report Wizard to create a columnar report. (Access-438)
- Create a query and use it as the basis for a report. (Access-440)
- Group and sort records in a report and preview a report. (Access-442)
- Use Help to modify reports and forms. (Access-444)
- Create and print a report with totals and subtotals. (Access-445)
- Create hyperlinks to another object, database, or Web site. (Access-448)

Lesson Summary & Exercises

CONCEPTS REVIEW

1 TRUE/FALSE

Circle T if the statement is true or F if the statement is false.

T F **1.** The record with the focus is the same thing as the current record.

T F **2.** The < > comparison operator can be translated as not equal to.

T F **3.** Using the Sort Ascending or Sort Descending button to sort data is somewhat limited as you can only sort on one field at a time.

T F **4.** The set of results of a query is known as a recordset.

T F **5.** In a one-to-many relationship, the related table contains a foreign key that relates it to the primary table.

T F **6.** Calculated fields can be created in queries or tables.

T F **7.** The Report Wizard generates reports, but does not allow customization.

T F **8.** Subforms can be used to add and edit data.

T F **9.** You can create reports that generate totals.

T F **10.** Forms are often used to simplify data entry.

2 MATCHING

Match each of the terms on the left with the definitions on the right.

TERMS	DEFINITIONS
1. datasheet	**a.** To rearrange records into alphabetical, numerical, or chronological order
2. referential integrity	
3. Clipboard	**b.** Area of Select Query window in which you enter sorting and selection criteria
4. sort	
5. query design grid	**c.** Area of the query design grid that enables you to choose whether fields are displayed in the recordset
6. Show check box	
7. groups	**d.** Printing setup in which report text is printed horizontally across a page
8. landscape orientation	
9. portrait orientation	**e.** An Access tool that creates a database object based on your responses to a series of questions
10. wizard	
	f. Collections of records with similar information
	g. Printing setup in which report text is printed vertically across a page
	h. Temporary storage area in your computer's memory
	i. Column-and-row layout you can use to enter, edit, and view data
	j. Rules that Access enforces to safeguard data

Lesson Summary & Exercises

3 COMPLETION

Fill in the missing word or phrase for each of the following statements.

1. In a _____ relationship, every record in a table can have either no matching records or only a single matching record in the other table.

2. To copy an entire table into your database, you can _____ it.

3. Plus signs before the records in a datasheet indicate that a _____ exists for each record.

4. The _____ button lets you reverse your most recent changes.

5. The _____ window makes editing large text or memo fields easier.

6. When you want to extract records and sort them into some order that you can use again in the future, you should use a(n) _____.

7. To select Field lists for tables in the Select Query window, click the _____ button.

8. Click the _____ Options button in the Report Wizard dialog box to change the way records are collected.

9. The _____ option on the New Object drop-down list automatically creates a form.

10. Before you print a hard copy of a form, you should display it on the screen using the _____ button.

4 SHORT ANSWER

Write a brief answer to each of the following questions.

1. Identify the three types of relationships and explain the differences between them.

2. What command do you use to reverse all changes you have made to the current record? What command would you use to reverse the changes to a record that has already been saved?

3. Describe the steps you would take to copy some of the records from a table called Unpaid to a table called Payables.

4. Describe the steps you would take to copy a table from a database called Inventory into a database called Assets.

5. Describe the purpose of the *Show* row in the query design grid.

6. Describe how you would create a query to display the last and first names of customers who have a ZIP Code lower than 45000.

7. Describe how you would create and save a query using both the BFCustomers and BFOrders tables to show all customers who did not order apples, grapefruit, or pears. The query should show the first and last names, in that order.

8. Describe briefly what Access does for you when you click the AutoForm button. What type of form does it create? What fields are included? What is used as the form title?

9. Describe the benefit of creating a form for data entry. What are the advantages over working on the table in the Datasheet view?

10. What must you do to display totals in a report? What option would you choose if you want individual records displayed as well?

Lesson Summary & Exercises

5 IDENTIFICATION

Label and briefly describe each of the elements of the Select Query window in Figure 2.31.

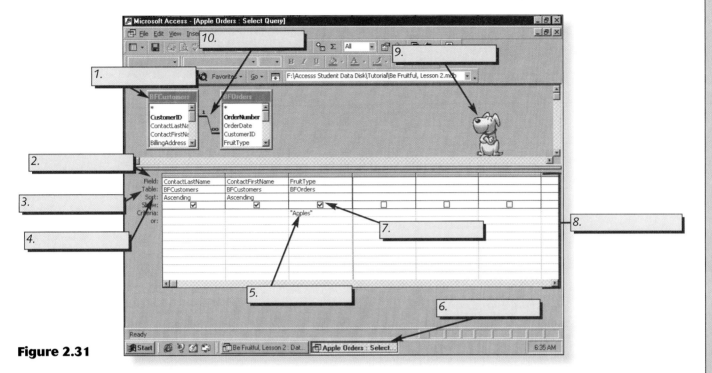

Figure 2.31

SKILLS REVIEW

Complete each of the Skills Review problems in sequential order to review your skills to add, copy and paste, import, and edit data in a table; sort and query data; create and use forms; and create and print reports.

1 Open a Table and Add Data

1. Start Access and open the **Smyth Business College, Lesson 2** database in the **Skills Review** folder on your Student Data Disk.

2. Click the **Class Schedules table** and click the **Open button** [Open] in the Database window.

3. Type AC101 in the first row of the Class Code field and press [Tab].

4. Type Accounting 1 in the Class Name field and press [Tab].

5. Type Berbarg in the Instructor Name field and press [Tab].

6. Type MWF in the Days field and press [Tab].

7. Type 8:00-8:50 am in the Time field and press [Tab] to move to the second record.

8. Type the data in Table 2.3 into the table. Then close the table.

Lesson Summary & Exercises

TABLE 2.3   CLASS SCHEDULES TABLE DATA

Field	Record 2	Record 3	Record 4	Record 5
Class Code	AC102	AC201	AC202	AC203
Class Name	Accounting 2	Financial Accounting	Managerial Accounting	Cost Accounting
Instructor Name	Abner	Nieves	Way	Crawford
Days	MWF	TR	TR	MWF
Time	10:00-10:50 am	10:00-11:30 am	4:00-5:30 pm	12:00-12:50 pm

2 Copy and Paste Data from a Table and Import Tables

1. Open the **Smyth Business College Sample** database and open the Class Information table.

2. Click the **record selector** in front of the record for AC301 and drag down to select the records through MK202.

3. Click the **Copy button** 🖺 on the Database toolbar.

4. Close the table and click **Yes** if a warning box asks you if you want to save the data to the Clipboard. (Since you are copying only 18 records, the message may not appear.)

5. Reopen the **Smyth Business College, Lesson 2** database in the **Skills Review** folder and open the Class Schedules table.

6. Click **Edit** on the menu bar and click **Paste Append**.

7. When the message appears asking if you want to paste the records, click **Yes**.

8. Click anywhere in the table to remove the highlighting and click the **Maximize button** 🔲. Then close the table.

9. Reopen the **Smyth Business College Sample** database and open the Student Information table.

10. Press Ctrl + A to select all of the records in the table, click the **Copy button** 🖺, and close the table. Click **Yes** to save the data to the Clipboard.

11. Reopen the **Smyth Business College, Lesson 2** database in the **Skills Review** folder.

12. Open the Student Information table, click **Edit** on the menu bar, and click **Paste Append**. Click **Yes** to paste the records. Then close the table.

13. Click **File** on the menu bar, point to **Get External Data**, and click **Import** on the submenu.

14. Navigate to your Student Data Disk files and open the **Smyth Business College Sample** database.

15. On the **Tables tab**, click **Grades for Accounting Classes**. Then click **OK** to import the table.

16. Click **File**, point to **Get External Data**, and click **Import**.

17. Open the **Smyth Business College Sample** database, click the **Tables tab**, and click **Instructor Information**. Then click **OK** to import the table.

Lesson Summary & Exercises

3 Move Among Rows and Columns

1. Open the Student Information table and maximize your view.

2. Click the **Next Record navigation button** ▶ five times. Note which record is current.

3. Click the **Last Record button** ▶❘.

4. Double-click the **Previous Record button** ◀.

5. Click the **First Record button** ❘◀.

6. Double-click the current record number in the text box at the bottom of the datasheet.

7. Type 46 and press Enter↵. The focus moves to the record for Owen Shrimp.

8. Press ↑ four times. The focus moves to the record for Donald Brewer.

9. Press ↓ twice. The focus moves to the record for Glenn Comrey.

10. Press Tab four times.

11. Press ⇧ Shift + Tab to move back one column.

12. Press Ctrl + Home to move to the first field of the first record.

13. Press Ctrl + End to move to the last field of the last record.

4 Edit Records and Undo Changes

1. In the Expected Graduation field of the last record, type 12/15/2003, press ⇧ Shift + Tab, and type 3.50 in the GradePointAverage field.

2. Press F5, type 29, and press Enter↵ to move to the record for Casey Bridges.

3. Navigate to the Major field. Type Accounting and press Tab.

4. Move to the Address field for Susan Ozinga (record 30). Click after the word *Spring* and type Grove so that the address reads *2475 Spring Grove Rd. SE.* Then press F2 to select the contents of the field.

5. Double-click the **City field** for Utamaro Isobe (record 12) and press Delete to delete the city name.

6. Click the **Undo button** ↺ to reverse the change.

7. Move to the first record (for George Robinson) and change the Phone Number field to (770) 555-3536. Press Tab and change the major to Marketing. Click the **Undo button** ↺ to change the major back to Finance.

8. Double-click the **Undo button** ↺ to change the phone number back to (404) 555-2969.

9. In record 9, change the text in the Last Name field to Dorsey and press Tab.

10. Change the text in the First Name field to Mitchell and press Tab.

11. Press ↓ to move to record 10.

12. Click **Edit** on the menu bar and click **Undo Saved Record**.

13. Click the **record selector** for Stephen Carrington (record 23). Click the **Delete Record button** ⊠. When the warning box appears asking if you want to delete the record, click **Yes**.

14. Move to the Address field for Marietta Jolly (record 2).

15. Press `⇧ Shift` + `F2` to open the Zoom window. Change the apartment number to #310. Click **OK**.

16. Point to the right boundary of the field selector for the Address field. Drag to the right to widen the Address column so that you can see the entire address in record 2.

17. Drag the right boundary of the field selector for the Student ID field to the left to narrow the Student ID column so that it is about three or four characters wide.

18. Click the **Close button** ☒.

19. When the message box appears asking if you want to save the changes, click **Yes**.

5 Create and Print Relationships and Open a Subdatasheet

1. Click the **Relationships button** ⊞. When the Show Table dialog box appears, double-click the **Student Information table**, the **Class Schedules table**, the **Grades for Accounting Classes table**, and the **Instructor Information table**. Close the Show Table dialog box.

2. Click the **StudentID field** in the Student Information Field list and drag it to the StudentID field in the Grades for Accounting Classes Field list.

3. When the Edit Relationships dialog box appears, click the **Create button**.

4. Click the **ClassCode field** in the Class Schedules Field list and drag it to the ClassCode field in the Grades for Accounting Classes Field list.

5. When the Edit Relationships dialog box appears, click the **Enforce Referential Integrity option** and click the **Create button**.

6. Click the **InstructorName field** in the Instructor Information Field list and drag it to the InstructorName field in the Class Schedules Field list.

7. When the Edit Relationships dialog box appears, click the **Create button**.

8. Close the Relationships window.

9. When the warning box asks if you want to save the relationship, click **Yes**.

10. Click **Tools** on the menu bar and click **Relationships**.

11. Click **File** on the menu bar and click **Print Relationships**. Then click the **Print button** 🖨.

12. Close the Print Preview window, saving your changes with the default report name, and close the Relationships window.

13. Open the Class Schedules table.

14. Click the **plus sign** in front of the record for AC203.

15. Look at the subdatasheet that appears listing the grades earned by students enrolled in this class.

16. Close the subdatasheet by clicking the **minus sign** in front of the record for AC203.

17. Close the Class Schedules table.

6 Sort a Table

1. Open the Grades for Accounting Classes table.

2. Click anywhere in the Class Code field and click the **Sort Ascending button** .

3. Drag over the Class Code and Grade field selectors to highlight both fields. Then click the **Sort Ascending button** .

4. Click anywhere within the Grade field and click the **Sort Descending button** .

5. Click the **Close button** and close the table without saving the changes.

7 Create, Modify, and Save Queries

1. Click the **Queries option** in the *Smyth Business College, Lesson 2* Database window and double-click the **Create query in Design view option**.

2. In the Show Table dialog box, double-click **Class Schedules** and close the Show Table dialog box.

3. Double-click **ClassName** on the Field list to add the field to the query design grid.

4. Add the **InstructorName**, **Days**, and **Time** fields to the query design grid.

5. Choose **Ascending** order in the *Sort* row for ClassName and type Kellinghaus in the *Criteria* row under InstructorName.

6. Click the **Run button** to view the classes taught by Kellinghaus.

7. Click the **View button** and click the **Show check box** under the InstructorName field.

8. Click the **Run button** to rerun the query.

9. Click **File** on the menu bar, click **Save As**, and type Classes Taught by Kellinghaus as the query name. Then click **OK**.

10. Click the **View button** to switch to Design view.

11. Drag across the Days and Time column selectors and press Delete to delete the fields from the query.

12. Drag the ClassCode field from the Field list to the box in the query design grid where the ClassName field currently appears.

13. In the *Sort* row of the ClassCode field, click **Ascending**.

14. Type AC* in the *Criteria* row for the ClassCode field.

15. Delete "Kellinghaus" in the *Criteria* row of the InstructorName field.

16. Click the **Run button** .

17. Save the query as Accounting Classes and click **OK**. Then close the query.

Lesson Summary & Exercises

8 Use Queries

1. Open the Classes Taught by Kellinghaus query and change the Class Name of Advertising to Principles of Advertising. Then close the query.

2. Open the Class Schedules table and verify that the class name change is reflected in the table; then close the Class Schedules table.

3. Click the **Class Schedules table** in the Database window, if it's not already selected, click the **New Object drop-down arrow** 🗔, and click **Query** from the drop-down list.

4. Click the **Design View option** and click **OK**.

5. Click the **Show Table button** 🗔.

6. Add the Student Information table and then add the Grades for Accounting Classes table. Close the Show Table dialog box.

7. In the Class Schedules Field list, double-click **ClassName**.

8. In the Student Information Field list, double-click **LastName**.

9. In the Grades for Accounting Classes Field list, double-click **Grade**.

10. Type Accounting 1 in the *Criteria* row under ClassName.

11. Click **Descending** in the *Sort* row under Grade.

12. Click the **Run button** 🗔.

13. Save the query as Grades for Accounting 1 and click **OK**. Then click the **Close button** ☒.

9 Use a Statistical Function in a Query

1. Click the **Queries option** in the Database window and double-click **Create query in Design view**.

2. Click the **Queries tab**, click **Grades for Accounting 1**, and click **Add**. Close the Show Table dialog box.

3. Double-click **Grade** in the Field list.

4. Click the **Totals button** 🗔.

5. In the *Total* row for the Grade field, click **Avg** from the drop-down list.

6. Click the **Run button** 🗔 to view the query results.

7. Save the query as Class Average for Accounting 1 and close the query.

10 Create a Form and Add and Edit Data

1. Click the **Tables option** in the Database window and click the **Instructor Information table**.

2. Click the **New Object drop-down arrow** 🗔 and click **AutoForm**. Maximize the form, if necessary.

3. Click the **Next Record button** ▶ several times to move through the records. (Be sure to use the navigation buttons for the main form, not the subform.)

4. Click the **View drop-down arrow** [icon] and click **Datasheet view**.

5. Return to **Form view** and close the form.

6. Click **Yes** to save the form; type Instructor Information AutoForm as the form name. Then click **OK**.

7. Click the **Forms option** in the Database window, open the Instructor Information AutoForm, and click the **New Record button** [icon].

8. Type Little in the Instructor Name field.

9. Press [Tab] to move through the remaining fields, typing General Business in the Department field, 8/15/1999 in the Start Date field, General Business in the Undergraduate Degree field, Education in the Graduate Degree field, and PT in the FT/PT field.

10. In the Class Code field of the subform, type BU202; type Business Ethics in the Class Name field; type TR in the Days field; and type 10:00-11:30 am in the Time field. Access will automatically add the new class data to the Class Schedules table.

11. With the Instructor Information AutoForm still open, navigate to the record for the instructor named Kellinghaus.

12. Since the time for the marketing class taught by Kellinghaus has been changed, replace the 2:00-2:50 pm time currently indicated for the MK201 class with 3:00-3:50 pm.

13. Navigate to the record for the instructor named Franklin, click the **record selector** for the record, and press [Delete].

14. Click **Yes** to delete this record. Then click **Close** on the File menu.

11 Create a Query and a Tabular Report

1. Click the **Tables option** in the Database window and click the **Instructor Information table**, if necessary. Click the **New Object drop-down arrow** [icon] and click **Query**.

2. Click **Design View** and click **OK**.

3. Double-click the **title bar** of the Instructor Information Field list to select all of the fields, and then drag the selected fields to the first column in the query design grid.

4. In the *Sort* row of the InstructorName field, select **Ascending**.

5. Type FT in the *Criteria* row of the FullTime/PartTime field, and click the **Show check box** to hide the field.

6. Click the **Run button** [icon].

7. Save the query as Full Time Instructors and click **OK**. Then close the query.

8. Click the **Reports option** and double-click **Create report by using wizard**.

9. Click **Query: Full Time Instructors** in the Tables/Queries box.

10. Add the InstructorName, Department, UndergraduateDegree, GraduateDegree, and StartDate fields, in that order. Then click **Next**.

Lesson Summary & Exercises

12 Group and Sort Records and Preview the Report

1. In the dialog box that requests a grouping field, click **Department** and click the **Add Field button** [>]. Then click **Next**.

2. Click the **drop-down arrow** beside the first field in the Sorting dialog box and click **InstructorName**. Click **Next**.

3. Click the **Align Left 1 option** and then click **Portrait**, if necessary. Click **Next**.

4. Click **Bold** as the style and click **Next**.

5. Type Full Time Instructors by Department and click **Finish**.

6. Scroll the first page of the report.

7. Click anywhere on the page to zoom out.

8. Close the report.

13 Build and Print a Report with Totals

1. Double-click **Create report by using wizard** in the Database window.

2. Click **Table: Student Information** in the Tables/Queries box and add the LastName, FirstName, Major, GradePointAverage, and EstimatedGraduationDate fields to the Selected Fields list. Then click **Next**.

3. Select **Major** as the grouping field.

4. Click the **Grouping Options button** and select **Normal** in the Grouping Intervals box, if it is not already selected. Click **OK**.

5. Click **Next** and click **GradePointAverage** in the Field 1 box.

6. Click the **Summary Options button** and click the **Avg check box** for the GradePointAverage field.

7. Click **OK**, click **Next**, and click the **Outline 1 layout** and **Portrait orientation**. Then click **Next**.

8. Click the **Formal style** and click **Next**.

9. Type GPAs of Students by Major and click **Finish**.

10. Scroll the report to see the subtotals for the majors.

11. Click **Print** on the File menu. Set the print range to print only one copy of the last page of the report.

12. Close the report.

13. Click the **Compact on Close option**, if necessary, and close the *Smyth Business College, Lesson 2* database.

LESSON APPLICATIONS

1 Enter and Edit Records

As an employee of Payton Properties, Inc., you need to add data to the tables in the **Payton Properties, Lesson 2** database and add records to an existing table. You will also copy and paste records into the database.

1. Open the **Payton Properties, Lesson 2** database in the **Lesson Applications** folder of your Student Data Disk. Open the Homes for Sale table.

2. Type the data in Table 2.4 into records 1 through 4.

TABLE 2.4	HOMES FOR SALE TABLE DATA			
Field	**Record 1**	**Record 2**	**Record 3**	**Record 4**
Address	1010 Springfield Pike	117 Pinehurst Dr.	121 Pleasant Ridge Ave.	1316 Morten Ct.
Bedrooms	4	2	4	3
Baths	2.5	2	1.5	1.5
Sq. Feet	2200	1560	1850	1250
Rooms	8	6	7	6
Year Built	1998	2001	1994	1967
Price	$176,000	$130,700	$134,000	$89,000
Agent ID	2	3	4	1
Lot Size	2.20	.60	.68	.25
School District	Kings	Kings	Milfort	West Avon
Pool	Yes	Yes	No	No
Occupancy	60 days	30 days	30 days	30 days

3. Click File on the menu bar, click Open, and open the **Payton Properties Sample** database on your Student Data Disk.

4. Open the Homes for Sale table and highlight records 5 through 19 (addresses from *16 Van Buren Ave.* through *861 Ridgedale Dr.*).

5. Click the Copy button. Then close the table.

6. Reopen the Homes for Sale table in the **Payton Properties, Lesson 2** database in the **Lesson Applications** folder on your Student Data Disk. Paste the records into the table using the Paste Append command.

7. Change the price of the house at 2600 Alexandria St. to $160,500.

8. You realize that you changed the price of the wrong home; reverse the change and then change the price of the house at 3237 Sugar Tree Rd. to $160,500.

9. The house at 69 Shayler Ct. has just sold. Delete the record for this house.

10. You realize some data is missing in one of the records—the house at 18 Miliken Dr. is in the Milfort school district, does not have a pool, and has a 30-day occupancy.

11. Adjust the size of each column in the table to better fit the data contained in it.

12. Close the table. When the Office Assistant asks if you want to save the changes, click Yes.

13. Open the *Payton Properties Sample* database, open the Employee Statistics table, and copy all of the records. Close the table.

14. Open *Payton Properties, Lesson 2* in the *Lesson Applications* folder on your Student Data Disk. Open the Agent Statistics table.

15. Paste the copied records into the table. Then, close the Agent Statistics table.

2 Import a Table and Edit the Data

Use the Import command to create a new table in the *Payton Properties, Lesson 2* database. Then edit some of the data in the new table.

1. Open *Payton Properties, Lesson 2* in the *Lesson Applications* folder on your Student Data Disk, if necessary.

2. Click File on the menu bar, point to Get External Data, and click Import.

3. Select *Payton Properties Sample* in the Import dialog box. Then, select the Employees table in the Import Objects dialog box. Click OK to import the Employees table.

4. Open the Employees table and read the data in it. Move to the field that contains the hire dates for each employee.

5. Move to the field that contains the address for Kelly Perez and change it to 1288 Gordon St.

6. Click the View button to view the Employees table in Design view. Change the name of the first field to AgentID and change the caption to Agent ID.

7. Save and close the table.

3 Create a New Record and Undo Changes to a Saved Record

Enter data for a new record. Then when you discover the sellers have changed their minds, undo the changes to the saved record.

1. Open the Homes for Sale table in the *Payton Properties, Lesson 2* database in the *Lesson Applications* folder, and click the New Record button.

2. Type 804 Sycamore Dr. in the Address field and press ⌨Tab.

3. Enter the following data, pressing ⌨Tab to move from field to field: Bedrooms, 4; Baths, 1.5; Sq. Feet, 1950; Rooms, 7; Year Built, 1997; Price, 140,000; Agent ID, 1; Lot Size, 1; School District, West Maple; Pool, Yes; Occupancy, 60 days.

4. Press ⌨Tab to save the record.

5. You just found out that the sellers have decided to wait to sell their home. Use the Undo Saved Record command to remove the entire record you just created.

6. Close the table.

4 Define Relationships and View Subdatasheets

Join fields in all four tables in the *Payton Properties, Lesson 2* database to form relationships. Then, you will view two subdatasheets in two tables.

1. Open the *Payton Properties, Lesson 2* database in the *Lesson Applications* folder, if necessary.

2. Click the Relationships button ▦ to display the Relationships window. When the Show Tables dialog box appears, double-click each table to display it and then close the dialog box.

3. Create a relationship between the Agent Statistics and Employees tables by joining the AgentID fields. Do not choose the option to enforce referential integrity.

4. Create a relationship between the Employees and Homes for Sale tables by joining the AgentID fields. Choose the option to enforce referential integrity.

5. Create a relationship between the Employees and Homes Sold tables by joining the AgentID fields. Choose the option to enforce referential integrity.

6. Close the Relationships window, saving the relationships.

7. Open the Agent Statistics table and view the subdatasheet for the first record. Close the subdatasheet and then close the table.

8. Open the Employees table and click the plus sign in front of the record for Brian Matthews (record 3).

9. Since the Employees table is related to more than one other table, the Insert Subdatasheet dialog box appears. Click Homes for Sale and then click OK. The list of homes for sale by this agent appears in the subdatasheet.

10. Close the table and save the layout changes.

5 Use the Sort Buttons

As an employee of Payton Properties, you need to analyze the variety of homes you have for sale. Use the Sort buttons to sort the data in a table in various orders.

1. Open the *Payton Properties, Lesson 2* database in the *Lesson Applications* folder on your Student Data Disk, if necessary, and open the Homes for Sale table.

2. Use one of the Sort buttons to sort the records by lot size from the largest lot size to the smallest.

3. Use one of the Sort buttons to sort the records in alphabetical order by school district.

4. Use one of the Sort buttons to sort the records by number of bedrooms and bathrooms. The homes with the fewest bedrooms should appear first. Homes with the same number of bedrooms should be sorted with those with the fewest number of bathrooms as a secondary sort. Close the table without saving changes.

Lesson Summary & Exercises

6 Create, Modify, and Run a Query

Your manager would like you to generate some facts about homes that have been sold through Payton Properties.

1. Open the **Payton Properties, Lesson 2** database in the **Lesson Applications** folder on your Student Data Disk, if necessary. Click Queries on the Objects bar.

2. Create a new query in Design view.

3. Add the Homes Sold Field list and close the Show Table dialog box.

4. Add the following fields in the order shown to your query design grid: AgentID, PropertyAddress, ListingPrice, SellingPrice, and YearBuilt.

5. Type an appropriate criteria in the AgentID field to show only those homes listed by Brian Matthews, agent 3.

6. Sort the records in descending order by SellingPrice and run the query.

7. View the query in Design view again and choose the option to hide the AgentID field. Run the query again.

8. Save the query as Homes Sold by Matthews.

9. Switch to Design view and add the PercentofListingPrice field to the query before the YearBuilt field.

10. Delete the YearBuilt field from the query. Then run the query.

11. Edit the address of the home on Sagamore Rd. to 1702 Sagamore Rd.

12. Close the query, saving the changes, and open the Homes Sold table to verify that the address change is reflected. Then close the Homes Sold table.

7 Query Two Tables

Your manager has asked you to generate a list of homes for sale priced over $120,000. Your list should only include homes that do not have swimming pools and be sorted by the sales agents' last names.

1. Open the **Payton Properties, Lesson 2** database in the **Lesson Applications** folder on your Student Data Disk, if necessary.

2. Create a new query and add Field lists for the Homes for Sale and Employees tables.

3. Add the following fields to the query design grid: LastName, Address (from the Homes for Sale Field list), Bedrooms, Baths, Price, and Pool.

4. Sort the records in alphabetical order by LastName.

5. Issue a secondary sort by Price in descending order.

6. Type criteria that will limit the query to homes priced over $120,000.

7. Type No in the Pool Criteria box to eliminate homes with swimming pools. Hide the Pools field. Then run the query.

8. Save the query as Homes over $120,000 without Pools and close the query.

8 Calculate Sales Totals and Commissions

Your manager has requested a list of sales agents and a total, by agent, of the actual selling price of the homes each has sold. In addition, your manager asks you to calculate a 3 percent commission on the total for each agent.

1. In the ***Payton Properties, Lesson 2*** database, create a new query and add Field lists for the Homes Sold and Employees tables.

2. Add the LastName and SellingPrice fields to the query design grid and sort the records alphabetically by LastName.

3. Click the Totals button and select Sum in the *Total* row for the SellingPrice field. Run the query.

4. Save the query as Agent Totals and Commissions.

5. In Design view, click in the *Field* row of the first empty field in the query design grid and click the Build button. Create the expression *SumOfSellingPrice*0.03* in the Expression Builder dialog box. Close the dialog box.

6. Right-click anywhere in the calculated field column and click Properties on the shortcut menu.

7. In the Field Properties window, select Currency in the Format text box and type Commissions in the Caption text box. Close the Field Properties window.

8. In the query design grid, select Expression from the drop-down list in the *Total* row for the calculated field. Then run the query.

9. Save and close the query.

9 Create Forms

As a manager at Payton Properties, Inc., you decide to create some Access forms to ease data entry for all employees. You will create an AutoForm that displays employee addresses and other information.

1. Open the ***Payton Properties, Lesson 2*** database in the ***Lesson Applications*** folder on your Student Data Disk, if necessary.

2. Click the Employees table and click the New Object drop-down arrow 🗗▾ to create an AutoForm. Maximize the form and navigate all of the records.

3. View the form in Datasheet view; then return to Form view and close the form, saving the form as Employees AutoForm.

4. Open the Employees AutoForm and add two new records that contain the data in Table 2.5.

Lesson Summary & Exercises

TABLE 2.5	EMPLOYEES AUTOFORM DATA	
Field	**1st New Record**	**2nd New Record**
Last Name	Kaplin	Sallinger
First Name	Robert	Pat
Address	29 Mainview Rd.	18 Blossom Dr.
City	Dallas	Dallas
State	TX	TX
ZIP Code	75226-4993	75226-1872
Home Phone	(214) 555-2567	(214) 555-1334
Date Hired	09/01/2000	09/01/2000

5. In the subform for Pat Sallinger, add the following homes for sale, as listed in Table 2.6.

TABLE 2.6	PAT SALLINGER SUBFORM DATA	
Field	**1st Home for Sale**	**2nd Home for Sale**
Address	1800 Twiggs Ln.	20398 Sycamore St.
Bedrooms	5	3
Baths	3	1.5
Sq. Feet	2,095	1,700
Rooms	8	6
Year Built	1999	1999
Price	$172,000	$105,500
Lot Size	1.3	1.0
School District	West Avon	Milfort
Pool	No	No
Occupancy	30 days	30 days

6. Robert Kaplin has changed his mind and decides to take a job with a different company. Delete his record while in Form view.

7. Move to the record for Benji Eto and change his telephone number to (214) 555-0053.

8. Save and then close the form.

10 Create and Navigate Reports

Now that you've created a form in the database, you want to generate some reports for your agents. You'd like to practice using the Report Wizard to create a simple report based on the Homes Sold table and a tabular report based on a query.

1. Open the *Payton Properties, Lesson 2* database in the *Lesson Applications* folder, if necessary. Start the Report Wizard. In the first dialog box, tell the wizard to base your report on the Homes Sold table and to include the PropertyAddress, Bedrooms, Baths, SquareFeet, Rooms, YearBuilt, SellingPrice, and AgentID fields.

2. Do not change the default grouping, and do not add any grouping or sorting levels. Choose the Align Left 1 layout, portrait orientation, and the Corporate style. Save the report as Homes Sold Columnar Report.

3. Navigate the pages and then close the report.

4. Create a query based on the Homes for Sale table. In the query, include the Address, Bedrooms, Baths, SquareFeet, Rooms, YearBuilt, Price, LotSize, and Pool fields. Sort the recordset in ascending order by square feet and only include homes that measure 2,000 or more square feet. Save the query as Homes with 2,000+ Square Feet.

5. Create a tabular report based on the query you just created. Include the Address, SquareFeet, Bedrooms, Baths, LotSize, and Price fields, in that order.

6. Group the records in the report by number of bedrooms. Within each group, sort the records in ascending order by price.

7. Assign the Align Left 1 layout, portrait orientation, and the Casual style. Save the report as Homes with 2,000+ Square Feet. Zoom in to see a full page of the report. Then print and close.

11 Create and Print a Report that Calculates Totals

You'd like to create a report that shows how your agents are doing as a team. Create a report that sums the total listings, homes sold, and commissions earned by your agents.

1. In the *Payton Properties, Lesson 2* database in the *Lesson Applications* folder, use the Report Wizard to create a report based on the Agent Statistics table. Include all of the fields in the table in the report.

2. Group the records by Agent ID. In the Summary Options dialog box, choose to sum the HomesSold, Listings, and Commissions fields. Choose the *Summary Only* and the *Calculate percent of total for sums* options. Then click OK.

3. Choose the Stepped layout, portrait orientation, and the Bold style.

4. Save the report as Combined Sales, Listings, and Commissions.

5. Preview, print, and close the report.

12 Create and Print a Report that Calculates Averages

Your last activity for the day requires you to generate a report about the homes that have been sold through Payton Properties. Your report should list all of the homes that were sold, grouping them by the number of bedrooms in each. Within each group, the records should be sorted by selling price, and the list and selling prices should be averaged within each group.

1. In the *Payton Properties, Lesson 2* database in the *Lesson Applications* folder, use the Report Wizard to create a columnar report based on the Homes Sold table. Include the PropertyAddress, Bedrooms, Baths, ListingPrice, SellingPrice, and AgentID fields in the report.

2. Group the records by the number of bedrooms in each home. Sort the records in each group in descending order by selling price.

Lesson Summary & Exercises

3. In the Summary Options dialog box, choose to average the ListingPrice and SellingPrice fields. Choose the *Detail and Summary* option.

4. Choose the Align Left 1 layout, landscape orientation, and the Corporate style.

5. Save the report as Average Listing and Selling Prices and view the report.

6. Print and then close the report.

7. Click the Compact on Close option, if necessary, and close the **Payton Properties, Lesson 2** database

PROJECTS

1 Making Product Changes

You work as a manager for Electro Shop, a retail store that sells home electronics. A few prices and features of some of your products have changed, so you need to edit the table that contains them. Open the Products table in the **Electro Shop, Lesson 2** database in the **Projects** folder on your Student Data Disk. Change the price of the RML 900 video camera (record 13) to $399.95 and change the price of the Keiko VCR (record 16) to $549.95. Reverse the last change (the price change to record 16) and change the price of the Wiley/Markle video camera to $549.95 instead. Open the Zoom window for the Notes field of the Keiko VCR (record 16) and type Manufacturer is offering a $50 rebate on VCRs sold between 12/1/2001 and 12/15/2001. Close the table.

2 Connecting the Tables

Since you'd like to view subdatasheets, assign relationships among the tables in the **Electro Shop, Lesson 2** database in the **Projects** folder on your Student Data Disk. Create a one-to-many relationship, enforcing referential integrity, between the Employees and December Sales tables by joining the EmployeeID fields. Then create a one-to-many relationship, enforcing referential integrity, between the Products and December Sales tables by joining the ProductID fields. Then open the Products table. Open the subdatasheet for record 17 and see how many RML VCRs have been sold so far this month. Lastly, open the Employees table and use a subdatasheet to view the sales by David Trimble. Close all open tables.

3 The Effects of Merging Stores

Two of your stores recently merged and you need to familiarize yourself with the new employee data. Open the **Electro Shop, Lesson 2** database in the **Projects** folder, if necessary. Open the Employees table. Sort the employees by last name in ascending order. Then sort the records in descending order by hourly rate. How much do the highest and lowest paid employees earn? Lastly, sort the records by last name again; however, this time, use the first names as a secondary sort. Close the table without saving changes.

4 Should We Keep This Product?

Open the **Electro Shop, Lesson 2** database in the **Projects** folder on your Student Data Disk, if necessary. As manager, you like to track sales of each product sold to analyze whether you should continue stocking. In the past few months, two products—products 5 and 18—have not been selling well. Create a query using the December Sales table that lists the sales for the ClearPict television (product 5). Include the ProductID, SaleID, EmployeeID, and DateSold fields. Sort the records by DateSold and hide the ProductID field. Name the query ClearPict TVs Sold. Create another query with the same information except use this query to analyze the Wiley/Markle VCR (product 18). Name the second query Wiley/Markle VCRs Sold. How many of each product were sold this month? Do you think you should consider removing either item from your product list?

Open each of the queries you just created and add the QuantitySold field. Remove the Employee ID field from each. In the Wiley/Markle VCRs Sold query, edit the quantity sold to 2 for sale number 75. Close the queries, saving the changes, and open the December Sales table. Was your edit incorporated? Close the December Sales table.

5 Recognizing the Best

Create a new query that uses the December Sales, Products, and Employees tables in the **Electro Shop, Lesson 2** database in the **Projects** folder on your Student Data Disk. Include the following fields in the order given: DateSold, LastName, ProductType, Brand, Model, Price, and QuantitySold. Sort the records in ascending order by DateSold. Set the criteria to show only sales made by Marta Fuentes, one of your past sales leaders, and hide the LastName field. Run the query and save the query as Sales by Fuentes. Print the recordset and close the query.

6 New Products and New Sales

As the sales manager at Electro Shop, you are using Access to create several forms to better input and review data on your employees, sales, and products. Create an AutoForm based on the Products table. Add two new records to the AutoForm to represent new products your store is carrying. Include the information in Table 2.7 in the main forms for the records.

Lesson Summary & Exercises

TABLE 2.7	RECORD DATA TO ADD	
Field	**1st New Record**	**2nd New Record**
Product ID	(AutoNumber)	(AutoNumber)
Product Type	TV	VCR
Brand	Keiko	Keiko
Model	KS650	KS6100
Price	$1,299.95	$359.95
In Stock	5	5
Notes	52" screen	

So far, your sales associates have sold two of the new TVs and three of the new VCRs. Record the data in Table 2.8 in the subform for each of the products. Close the AutoForm, saving it as Products AutoForm.

TABLE 2.8	SUBFORM DATA TO ADD	
Keiko KS650 TV		
Sale ID	(AutoNumber)	(AutoNumber)
Date Sold	12/19/2001	12/20/2001
Employee ID	3	23
Quantity Sold	1	1
Keiko KS6100 VCR		
Sale ID	(AutoNumber)	(AutoNumber)
Date Sold	12/20/2001	12/20/2001
Employee ID	7	16
Quantity Sold	2	1

7 Submitting a Printout of Employee Updates

You need to submit an updated copy of employee information to your payroll department. In the *Electro Shop, Lesson 2* database in the *Projects* folder, use the Report Wizard to create a columnar report that contains the HireDate, First Name, Last Name, Hourly Rate, and Position fields from the Employees table. Sort the report in descending order by hire date. Choose portrait orientation and a style of your choice. Save the report as Employees by Hire Date. Preview, print, and close the report.

8 Analyzing Big Ticket Items

You are analyzing the prices of some of your products, specifically those priced over $350 in the *Electro Shop, Lesson 2* database in the *Projects* folder. To generate a list of products that meet the criteria, first create a query based on the Products table. Include all of the fields in the query and sort the records in the query in ascending order by price; include only those that sell for more than $350. Name the query Products Priced Over $350.

Create a tabular report based on the query you just created. In the report, include only the ProductType, Brand, Model, and Price fields. Group the records by product type and sort the records within each group by price. Choose landscape orientation, Align Left 2 layout, and a style of your choice. Name the report Products Over $350 Grouped by Product Type. Preview, print, and close the report.

9 Totaling the Sales

Your district manager wants you to provide a report that lists and totals sales so far this month by product. In the **Electro Shop, Lesson 2** database in the **Projects** folder, create a report that includes all of the fields from the December Sales table except for the Sale ID field. Group the records by Product ID and sort the records within each group by the date sold. Calculate totals for the QuantitySold field as well as a grand total for the month. Choose the Align Left 1 layout, portrait orientation, and the Corporate style. Name the report December Sales by Product. Preview, print, and then close the report.

10 Linking Your Data

Some of the new employees at Electro Shop haven't yet memorized all of the product codes, making it difficult for them to use the December Sales table in the company database. They find themselves switching back and forth between the Sales table and the Products table to look up product IDs. To help them out, open the **Electro Shop, Lesson 2** database in the **Projects** folder and open December Sales AutoForm. Add a hyperlink next to the Product ID field that links to the Products table. Test the hyperlink to verify it opens the Products table.

Also, you've been talking with a representative from Sony, a manufacturer of electronics, about selling their products. To learn more about Sony, add a hyperlink to the bottom of the December Sales AutoForm that links to Sony's Web site at www.sony.com. Test the hyperlink. Close the **Electro Shop, Lesson 2** database. Then close your browser and disconnect from the Internet unless your instructor tells you to remain connected.

Project in Progress

11 Adding and Manipulating Data in the I-Comm Database

Open the **I-Comm** database in the **Projects** folder that you created in Lesson 1. Open the Customers table and add the records listed in Table 2.9. Use Help to find out how to use the Input Mask Wizard to create input masks for the ZIP Code and Phone Number fields.

Copy records 4 through 32 from the Customers table of the **I-Comm Sample** database on your Student Data Disk to the new Customers table. Reopen the **I-Comm Sample** database and copy all of the records in the Projects table. Paste those records to your new, blank Projects table in the **I-Comm** database.

Lesson Summary & Exercises

TABLE 2.9	RECORDS TO ADD TO CUSTOMERS TABLE		
Fields	**Record 1**	**Record 2**	**Record 3**
Customer ID	(AutoNumber)	(AutoNumber)	(AutoNumber)
Company Name	Liette Lawn Care	Eastwood Insurance Agency	Little Tots Daycare
Contact Last Name	Liette	Saini	Bess
Contact First Name	Alec	Reeta	Samuel
Contact Title	Owner	Human Resources Manager	Owner
Billing Address	34 Mitchell Ave.	1799 Northwest Blvd.	2020 Hopkins Rd.
City	Memphis	Bartlett	Memphis
State	TN	TN	TN
ZIP Code	38119-8324	38133-7444	38101-7233
Phone Number	(901) 555-2839	(901) 555-0034	(901) 555-7632

Import the Employees table from the *I-Comm Sample* database to your new *I-Comm* database. Adjust the column sizes of each of the tables appropriately. With the *I-Comm* database open, make the following changes to your tables:

TABLE 2.10	REVISIONS TO TABLES
Table Name	**Revision**
Projects	Change the hours in record 11 to 26; change the fee for this record to $1,440.
Customers	Change the phone number in record 24 to (901) 555-7500.
Customers	Change the company name in record 29 to Kirsten Weinberg-Mertz, CPA and change the last name for this record to Weinberg-Mertz.

Open the Relationships window for the database and create a one-to-many relationship, enforcing referential integrity, between the Customers and Projects tables by joining the CustomerID fields. Then create a one-to-many relationship, enforcing referential integrity, between the Employees and Projects tables by joining the EmployeeID field to the I-CommProjectManager field. Save and print your database relationships.

Since you'd like to sort your customers by the area in which they live, open the Customers table, select the City, State, and ZIP Code fields, and sort them all at once in descending order. Then sort the customers again in ascending order by company name.

Create a query that uses all three tables. Include the CompanyName (Customers table), ItemDeveloped (Projects table), ServicesPerformed (Projects table), I-CommProjectManager (Projects table), and LastName (Employees table) fields. In your query, include only brochures, advertisements, and Web sites developed. Sort the recordset by company name and print it. Save the query as **Brochures, Ads, and Web Sites**. Close the query.

As an employee of I-Comm, you use forms and reports to input and edit data and generate printouts of information. First, you'd like to generate a form to enter data for customers. Create an AutoForm named **Customers and Projects** based on the Customers table. Add the new customer and the new project information in Table 2.11.

TABLE 2.11	NEW CUSTOMER INFORMATION
Main Form	
Customer ID	(AutoNumber)
Customer Name	The Door Store
Contact Last Name	Rivera
Contact First Name	Carmen
Contact Title	Owner
Billing Address	1800 Lakeside Dr.
City	Memphis
State	TN
ZIP Code	38112-8344
Phone Number	(901) 555-1000
Subform	
Project ID	(AutoNumber)
Item Developed	brochure
Services Provided	writing, editing, design
I-Comm Project Mgr.	14
Total Hours	83
Fee	$4,980
Lock-All Security Systems (customer 19) Subform	
Project ID	(AutoNumber)
Item Developed	project proposal
Services Provided	writing, editing, design
I-Comm Project Mgr.	8
Total Hours	139
Fee	$8,340

Next, your manager has asked you to generate a report that displays all of the projects completed so far this year, grouped by the employee who acted as project manager on each. Use the Report Wizard to generate a tabular report using all of the fields in the Projects table. Group the records by the project manager and sum the hours and fees for each group. Use landscape orientation and a layout and style of your choice. Save the report as **Projects by Manager**. Print the report and then close. Click the Compact on Close option, if necessary, and close the *I-Comm* database. Exit Access.

Overview: **Congratulations!** You have completed the lessons in the Access tutorial and now have the opportunity in this capstone project to apply the Access skills you have learned. You have opened a daycare and want to use a database to track employees, students, and classes. As you create and use the database, try to incorporate the following skills:

- Plan and create a new database.
- Create tables and add data to them.
- Assign appropriate data types to fields.
- Determine the primary keys.
- Establish relationships among tables and enforce referential integrity.
- Change column widths in a datasheet.
- View data in subdatasheets.

- Sort data.
- Create a multi-table query.
- Create an AutoForm.
- Add data to a form.
- Create a report with groups and totals.
- Preview and print a report.
- Search the Web and create a hyperlink.
- Compact and close a database.

Instructions: Follow these instructions to create your database for this project.

1. Create a new database and save it as *Tiny Tots Daycare* in the *Projects* folder on your Student Data Disk.

2. Create three new tables, assigning appropriate primary keys, data types, field sizes, captions, and other field properties.

   - Name the first table *Employees* and create fields to include the following information: employee ID number, employee last name, employee first name, Social Security number, hourly pay rate, and full-time or part-time status. Enter the data in Table CS.1 in the Employees table.

   - Name the second table *Classes* and create fields to include the following information: class ID, class name, room number, head teacher, age range of students, teacher-to-student ratio, and weekly fee. Enter the data in Table CS.2 in the Classes table.

   - Name the third table *Students* and create fields to include the following information: student ID number, student last name, student first name, birth date, class ID, guardian name, guardian phone number, and allergies/special needs. Enter the data in Table CS.3 in the Students table.

TABLE CS.1 — DATA FOR EMPLOYEES TABLE

Employee ID	Employee Name	SS#	Hourly Rate	FT/PT
1	Betty Strickley	111-11-1111	$9.50	FT
2	Robert McVey	222-22-2222	$9.25	FT
3	Lorna Williams	333-33-3333	$7.75	PT
4	Mario Delgado	444-44-4444	$8.75	FT
5	Eric Huffman	555-55-5555	$8.00	FT
6	Arthur Hughes	666-66-6666	$8.00	FT
7	Maria Dugan	777-77-7777	$8.25	FT
8	Stacey Renning	888-88-8888	$8.25	FT
9	Tatsu Iwasaki	999-99-9999	$8.75	PT
10	Matthew Milton	101-01-0101	$7.75	FT
11	Donna Wolfe	110-11-0011	$7.50	FT
12	Mary Levine	121-21-2121	$7.75	FT
13	Dale Shepherd	131-31-3131	$7.50	FT
14	Gordon Crofts	141-41-4141	$7.50	PT
15	Chris Gregg	151-51-5151	$7.25	FT

TABLE CS.2 — DATA FOR CLASSES TABLE

Class ID	Class Name	Room Number	Head Teacher	Age Range	Ratio	Fee
1	Infants	1	13	2 to 18 months	1:4	$165
2	Toddler 1	2	11	19 to 28 months	1:6	$155
3	Toddler 2	5	6	29 to 36 months	1:7	$145
4	Young Threes	7	8	37 to 42 months	1:7	$140
5	Old Threes	8	14	43 to 48 months	1:7	$135
6	Four Year Olds	4	4	49 to 60 months	1:7	$130
7	Five Year Olds	9	7	61 to 72 months	1:7	$125

TABLE CS.3 — DATA FOR STUDENTS TABLE

Student ID	Student Name	Birth Date	Class ID	Guardian	Guardian Phone	Allergies/ Special Needs
1	Lauren Johnson	8/2/95	7	Gary Johnson	(402) 555-3111	
2	Marie Rappold	5/28/97	6	Sylvia Rappold	(402) 555-4893	
3	Roger Stephenson	7/28/97	5	Mia Stephenson	(402) 555-2093	
4	Michael Kroger	12/13/95	7	Doug Kroger	(402) 555-8026	
5	Michelle Goodwin	3/23/97	6	Cary Goodwin	(402) 555-6339	allergic to penicillin

Student ID	Student Name	Birth Date	Class ID	Guardian	Guardian Phone	Allergies/ Special Needs
6	Chi-luan Kuo	5/19/99	2	Yu-lan Kuo	(402) 555-8349	
7	Joey Buhr	8/3/97	5	Marti Buhr	(402) 555-3902	
8	Morgan Adams	5/27/98	4	Samantha Rye	(402) 555-4456	
9	Ashley Sohngen	3/3/96	7	Sarah Sohngen	(402) 555-7987	
10	Kenneth Feingold	8/18/98	3	Kenneth Feingold	(402) 555-1902	
11	James Danson	3/2/99	2	Marianne Danson	(402) 555-5893	prone to ear infections
12	Mitchell Tepe	12/24/96	6	Mark Tepe	(402) 555-6592	vegetarian diet
13	Violeta Torres	6/1/98	4	Vincente Torres	(402) 555-2569	
14	Courtney Morris	7/9/99	2	Drew Morris	(402) 555-7670	
15	Carl Carson	6/23/96	6	Angela Carson	(402) 555-4023	
16	Abby Simms	1/10/99	3	Ginny Simms	(402) 555-9833	
17	Allison Kuhlman	4/23/96	7	Jennifer Kuhlman	(402) 555-3990	
18	Marcus Matracia	10/31/99	2	Andrew Matracia	(402) 555-6847	
19	Aaron Potter	10/3/97	5	Bert Potter	(402) 555-5389	
20	Anna Hartlaub	3/16/98	4	Amy Hartlaub	(402) 555-7227	
21	David Yeager	9/30/97	5	Bob Yeager	(402) 555-1455	
22	Alan Bockenstette	11/3/98	3	Sue Bockenstette	(402) 555-8600	
23	Stephanie Roberts	10/7/00	1	Sharon Roberts	(402) 555-2784	allergic to milk
24	Kathy Zerkle	6/26/01	1	Patrick Zerkle	(402) 555-9324	
25	Mason Jasper	1/5/98	4	Anne Jasper	(402) 555-5203	
26	Elizabeth Finke	2/1/99	3	Martin Finke	(402) 555-1288	

3. Assign relationships among the tables, relating the Employees table to the Classes table by joining the Employee ID field to the Head Teacher field. Then relate the Classes and Students tables by joining the Class ID fields. Establish referential integrity in both relationships.

4. Adjust the widths of columns of each table, if necessary.

5. Open the Classes table and use the subdatasheets to view the names of the students enrolled in each class. How many students are enrolled in the Toddler 2 class? How many students are enrolled in the Five Year Olds class?

6. Sort the Employees table in ascending order by the employees' last names. Then, sort the employees in descending order by their pay rate.

7. Your supervisor would like to know how many full-time employees earn over $7.75 per hour. Create a query to generate a list of employees who meet these criteria, sorting them so that the highest paid employees appear at the top of the list. Save the query as *Employee Top Pay Rate*.

8. Two new students have just enrolled in the daycare. Create an AutoForm named *Students* and enter the new records shown in Table CS.4.

TABLE CS.4	DATA FOR STUDENTS FORM						
Student ID	Student Name	Birth Date	Class ID	Guardian	Guardian Phone	Allergies/ Special Needs
27	Gabrielle March	1/30/00	1	Sally March	(402) 555-4002	
28	Darren Finch	6/2/99	2	Ron Finch	(402) 555-9977	

9. The daycare is considering the startup of a field trip program for some of the older students. Create a query that lists students born before June 15, 1997. For each student, include the student's name, birth date, class name, room number, and teacher's last name. Save the query as *Students Eligible for Field Trips*.

10. The daycare director would like a list of students, grouped by the classes in which they are enrolled. Generate a report that includes each student's name, birth date, class name, and weekly fee. Group the report by classes and sum the fee field. Save the report as *Class Lists*. Preview and print it. Look at the report to determine the total weekly fees generated by the Toddler 2 class. What are the total fees generated by all classes?

11. Search the Web for information on early childhood and preschool education. Insert a hyperlink in the Classes table to one of the Web sites you find.

12. Compact the database and then close it.

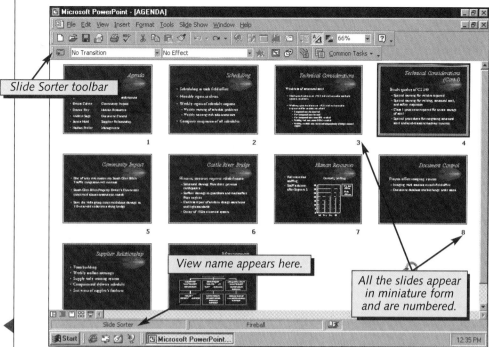

Figure 1.11
Slide Sorter View

GETTING HELP WITH POWERPOINT

While you are using PowerPoint, you may need to reference the online Help system. PowerPoint provides several different Help tools: ScreenTips, the Office Assistant, the Contents tab, the Index tab, and a tool called the Answer Wizard. You can activate the Office Assistant by clicking the animated character on your screen, by clicking the Microsoft PowerPoint Help button ⏹, by clicking Microsoft PowerPoint Help on the Help menu, or by pressing ⏹. For more detailed Help instructions review pages 91-97 in *Lesson 3: Introducing Office 2000*.

NAVIGATING SLIDES

When working in a presentation, you must be able to navigate the slides quickly and easily. Use the vertical scroll bars on the panes in Normal, Outline, and Slide Views to scroll from the first to last slide or to move one slide at a time. You can adjust the magnification in Normal, Outline, and Slide Views. The default magnification may be suitable for general use, allowing you to zoom in or zoom out as needed.

PowerPoint lets you adjust the magnification of slides for more accurate editing and viewing. The view scale in the Zoom list box controls the magnification of outline and slide panes. Magnification measurements are in percentages. The Zoom box lists magnification rates ranging from 25% to 100% for outline panes. Magnification rates for slide panes range from 25% to 400%. When you select a low magnification, you zoom out. You will see more of the outline text or slide, but the information may be too small to read. When you select a high magnification, you zoom in. You will see only a small portion of the outline text or slide. Horizontal scroll bars allow you to scroll the width of the pane to see all areas. The view scale for slide panes includes Fit, in addition to the percentages. Choosing Fit ensures seeing the entire slide at whatever magnification rate is necessary to make that possible.

Navigating Presentations

At the right of the application panes, a scroll bar lets you move up and down through the slides of a presentation. In Outline and Slide Sorter Views, clicking the scroll arrows at each end of the bar, dragging the scroll box within the bar, and clicking between the scroll box and a scroll arrow result in moving a document at varying speed. The horizontal scroll bar moves the outline or slide from side to side. In Slide View, clicking the scroll box displays a Slide Indicator box. The Slide Indicator box shows the number and title of the slide in the view and the number of slides in the presentation. Also in Slide View, clicking the scroll bar, scroll arrows, or the double arrows at the bottom of the scroll bar moves to the next or previous slide.

HANDS On

PowerPoint

Scrolling Presentations

1. To see a specific slide, click the scroll box.

2. To see the previous or next slide, click the Previous Slide or Next Slide button.

Scrolling the Agenda Presentation

In this activity, you will navigate the *Agenda* presentation using the scroll bars.

1. Open the *Agenda* file on your Student Data Disk.

The Agenda presentation opens.

2. If necessary, click the Outline View button ▤ to switch views. Adjust the pane sizes, as shown in Figure 1.12.

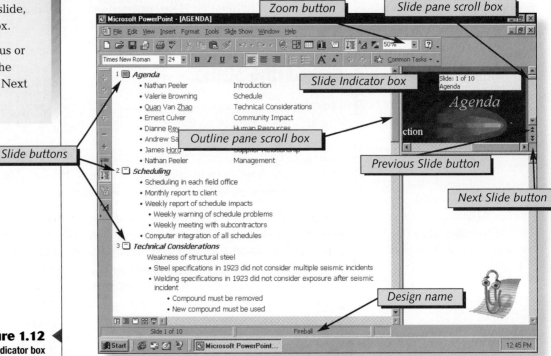

Figure 1.12 ◀
Slide Indicator box

3. Drag the scroll box in the outline pane to the bottom of the scroll bar.

4. Click the **Slide button** next to the *Management* slide title.

5. On the slide pane, drag the vertical scroll box as far to the top as possible.

The Slide Indicator box, as shown in Figure 1.12, tells that the *Agenda* slide is the first of ten in this presentation. The slide number also appears in the status area.

6. Click the **down scroll arrow** in the slide pane until the Slide Indicator box shows that you are viewing slide 2.

7. Click the **Next Slide button**.

PowerPoint navigates directly to slide 3.

8. Click the **Zoom drop-down arrow** and click **Fit**.

PowerPoint adjusts the magnification of the slide so that the entire slide appears in the small slide pane.

9. Click the **Previous Slide button** 📇.

PowerPoint moves back to slide 2.

EDITING TEXT

Sometimes you will need to insert a single word or a missing character within a word, which you can do in ***Insert mode.*** Occasionally, you will need to replace incorrect characters with correct ones by overtyping them. You can replace text in ***Overtype mode.*** While editing, you will often need to delete characters, words, or phrases. Deleting text is a two-step procedure. First, you must select the text you want to delete. Dragging across a single letter selects the letter, and dragging over words or phrases selects them. You can select a word by double-clicking the word. After you select a word, character, or phrase, press Delete to remove; or type to replace the text with the appropriate information. As you edit presentations, you may also use the Undo button 🖘, the Redo button 🖙, and the Repeat command on the Edit menu.

You can also edit text while you are typing. If you notice a mistake before you press Enter←, press Backspace to delete all characters to the left of the insertion point. If you've already pressed Enter← and your insertion point is on a new line, press Backspace to move the insertion point to the end of the previous line of text.

Promoting and Demoting Subtitles and Bullets

Every slide contains a title; most contain a title and several subtitles. A ***title*** is the main topic of a slide. A ***subtitle*** explains the main topic. In PowerPoint, a subtitle is any text under the title (except text appearing in an object). Each subtitle has an ***indent level***—a number that describes the position of the subtitle in relation to the title. A level 1 subtitle communicates a more important point than a level 2 subtitle; therefore, the level 1 subtitle has larger text and a larger bullet than a level 2 subtitle. When you move a subtitle to the next highest indent level, you ***promote*** it (a level 2 subtitle becomes a level 1, and so on). You ***demote*** a subtitle when you move it to the next lower indent level (a level 1 subtitle becomes a level 2, and so on).

Slides may also contain bulleted lists. Just as subtitles have indent levels, each bullet in a bulleted text list is also assigned a *level,* a number that describes the position of the bullet. A slide that contains more than one level of bulleted text is called a *multi-level bulleted list slide.* You can promote and demote bullets in the same way that you promote and demote subtitles.

Promoting and Demoting Subtitles in Agenda

In this activity, you will promote and demote subtitles in Outline View and Slide View.

1. Display the text for slide 8 in the Outline View pane.

Slide 8 has a level 1 subtitle and two level 2 subtitles.

2. Select both level 2 subtitles.

PowerPoint highlights both bulleted items.

3. On the Formatting toolbar, click the Promote button ◄ **twice.**

If the Promote button ◄ does not show on your Formatting toolbar, click the More Buttons button ∙. As shown in Figure 1.13, the level 2 subtitles become titles and the number of slides has increased to twelve.

Figure 1.13 ◄
Text promoted to titles

Another ◆ Way

To promote or demote a title, click the appropriate button on the Outlining toolbar.

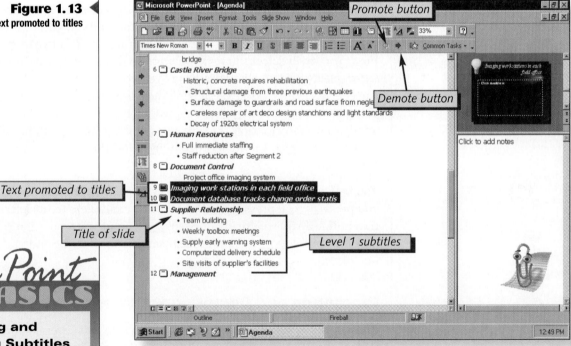

Promoting and Demoting Subtitles

1. Select the subtitle to promote or demote.

2. Click the Promote or Demote button.

4. With the text still selected, click the Demote button ➤ **once.**

The selected subtitles become level 1 subtitles.

5. Click the Demote button ➤ **again to return the subtitles to level 2.**

Figure 2.20
The last record

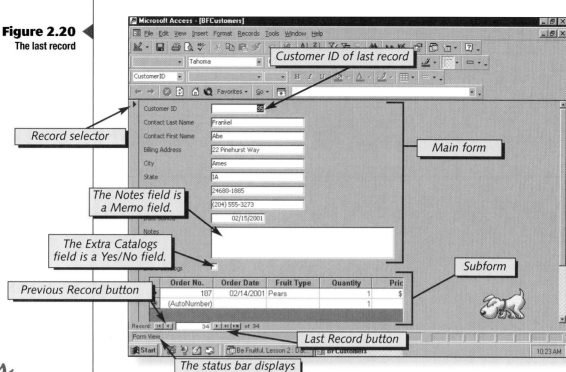

Customer ID of last record

Record selector

Main form

The Notes field is
a Memo field.

The Extra Catalogs
field is a Yes/No field.

Subform

Previous Record button

Last Record button

The status bar displays
the current view.

Creating and Exploring an AutoForm

1. Select the table you want to base the form on, click the New Object drop-down arrow, and click AutoForm.

2. Click the navigation buttons to move from record to record.

3. Click the View drop-down arrow and click the appropriate option to change views.

A form can contain more than one subform.

6. Click the View drop-down arrow ![icon] **and click Form View.**

Access returns you to Form view. In Form view, the data appears like a paper form.

7. Click the form's Close button ![X]**.**

Because you haven't saved the form, Access displays a warning box.

8. Click Yes.

9. In the Save As dialog box, type BFCustomers AutoForm **as the form name and click OK.**

Access saves and then closes the form, returning you to the *Be Fruitful, Lesson 2* Database window. The form you just created becomes one of the objects under the Forms option in the Objects bar.

Adding and Editing Data by Using Forms and Subforms

Sometimes you may want to use forms to browse your data. The real purpose of forms, however, is to facilitate the entering and editing of data. In forms, as in the datasheet, you need to know how to find the records that you want to edit. Once you're there, you need to know a few editing strategies. Fortunately, the techniques for navigating in forms are basically the same as those for moving around in the datasheet.

HANDS On

Modifying Records Using a Form and Subform

When you add, edit, or delete records in a form or subform, the change is automatically reflected in the appropriate table. The data you add to the main form affects one table, while the data you add to the subform may affect a different table. In this activity, you'll use the BFCustomers AutoForm to add records for a new customer and order, edit a record, and delete a record.

1. Click the **Forms option** in the Objects bar of the Database window and then double-click **BFCustomers AutoForm**.

Access displays the selected form and shows the first record for the underlying table.

2. Click the **New Record button** ▶*.

Access presents you with a new, blank record.

3. Press [Tab] to move to the Contact Last Name field. Type Myrianthopoulos **and press** [Tab].

Notice that Access automatically enters the next record number in the Customer ID field. (If you're confused about why there are more customer IDs than customers, don't forget that you deleted a record earlier.)

4. Type Zoe **in the Contact First Name field. Pressing** [Tab] **to move from field to field, type** 1357 Birch St. #7 **in the Billing Address field,** Woodstock **in the City field,** NY **in the State field,** 11223-4432 **in the ZIP Code field,** (917) 555-1234 **in the Phone Number field, and** 4/22/2001 **in the Date Joined field. Leave the Notes field blank for now, and leave the Extra Catalogs field deselected (the default).**

You now have a new record in the table. This new customer placed an order. Rather than entering the order data in the BFOrders table, you can enter it in the subform currently displayed. Access will automatically change the BFOrders table to reflect the new order.

5. Press [Tab] **until you get to the Order Date field of the subform.**

6. Type 4/22/2001 **and press** [Tab].

As shown in Figure 2.21, once you start typing in the Order Date field, the Order Number is automatically assigned.

7. Pressing [Tab] **to move among fields, type** Pears **in the Fruit Type field, (a 1 should already appear in the Quantity field),** 18.50 **in the Price field, and** 4.50 **in the Shipping Amt. field. Leave the remaining fields blank.**

8. Type 7 **in the record indicator of the main form and press** [Enter⏎].

Access moves you to the seventh record in the table—the record for Mason Bechdel.

9. Click the **Notes field text box**.

Although there's no text, Access places the insertion point within the field and adds a vertical scroll bar.

10. Type the following text:

7/15/2001: Mr. Bechdel reported not receiving his order of pears, although the fruit was delivered to his front door. Please send him a replacement box, rush delivery,

6. **Enlarge the slide pane and display slide 9.**

7. **Demote the last three subtitles.**

These subtitles indent to the second level.

8. **With the three subtitles selected, click the Promote button** [image].

The subtitles return to their original position.

Using Tools to Check Spelling

A well-designed and effective presentation is not only one where you have presented the information in the best possible way, but one that is error free. Always carefully proofread all presentations as well as all text documents, such as letters and reports. PowerPoint helps you spot potential spelling errors by placing a red, wavy line under the questionable word. These questionable words do not appear in the PowerPoint spelling dictionary.

If you right-click a flagged word, a shortcut menu appears. This menu may contain a list of suggested replacement words and contains the Ignore All and Add commands. You can eliminate the wavy lines by correcting the word or by telling PowerPoint to ignore the word, often the name of a person or place. PowerPoint also allows users to add words to the dictionary. You should not add words to the dictionary unless you own the computer, however. PowerPoint users can also check spelling for an entire presentation without looking for red, wavy lines. This feature is available through the Spelling button [image] on the Standard toolbar.

HANDS On

Checking Spelling

In this activity, you will check spelling in the **Agenda** presentation, starting with the name *Hord* on slide 1. You will work in the outline pane, although you can check spelling in the slide pane as well.

1. **On the outline pane, click anywhere in slide 1. Right-click the name *Hord* to see the spelling options provided.**

Note   *If* Hord *does not have a red, wavy underline on your screen, the spelling feature may not be active. To turn on the spelling feature, click Tools on the menu bar and click Options. On the Spelling and Style tab, select the* Check spelling as you type *check box.*

Hints & Tips

You can check for style consistency by clicking a light bulb that appears on a slide and viewing the tips offered by the Office Assistant.

The shortcut menu suggests five words to replace *Hord* and also offers Add and Ignore All options. In fact, *H-o-r-d* is the correct spelling.

2. **On the shortcut menu, click Ignore All.**

By selecting Ignore All, you erase the flag from this word—and any other occurrences of *Hord* in this presentation.

Checking Spelling

To check spelling as you type:

1. Right-click words that have a red, wavy underline.

2. Click an option to correct the error or to ignore the word.

To check spelling any time:

1. Click the Spelling button.

2. Click an option to correct the error or to ignore the word.

3. Right-click the name *Rey.* This name should actually be spelled *Reye.* Click the appropriate suggested word.

The name changes to *Reye* and the red, wavy underline disappears.

4. If any other name on slide 1 is flagged, right-click the word and click **Ignore All**.

Now you will use the Spelling dialog box to check spelling throughout the entire presentation.

5. On the Standard toolbar, click the **Spelling button** 🧹 .

The Spelling dialog box appears, as shown in Figure 1.14. The abbreviation *Contd* appears in the Not in Dictionary box. The word *coned* appears in the Change to box. A number of possible replacements appear in the Suggestions list box. *Contd* is the correct abbreviation for Continued; however, you need to add a period.

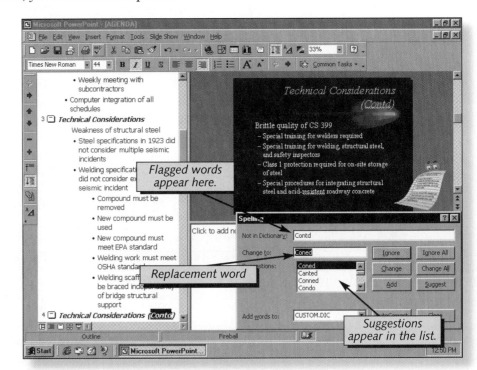

Figure 1.14
The Spelling dialog box

6. Scroll the Suggestions list box to see if *Contd.* appears on the list.

Since *Contd.* is not suggested as a replacement, you should make the change manually.

7. Double-click the word in the Change to box. Type Contd. Then click the **Change All button**.

PowerPoint makes this change and proceeds to the next word.

8. Correct three misspelled words in this presentation. Change *resistent* to *resistant*; change *noside* to *noise*; and change *statis* to *status*. If the correction appears in the Suggestions list box, click it and then click the **Change button**.

The Office Assistant announces completion of the spell check.

9. Close the Spelling dialog box, if it does not close automatically.

Hints & Tips

- To undo two or more actions, click the Undo button two or more times.

- To redo two or more actions, click the Redo button and select two or more actions.

Editing Text with Undo and Redo

When you point to the text area of a slide or an outline, the pointer changes to the I-beam pointer. If you click when the pointer is shaped like an I-beam, a blinking vertical line, called the insertion point, appears. The **insertion point** indicates where text will appear when typing begins.

As you add or delete text or change a presentation any other way, you may be indecisive about a particular word choice, the position of a graph, or whether a deleted slide should be returned to the sequence. These moments of indecision call for the Undo button and the Redo button . As the name implies, the Undo button reverses mouse and keyboard actions. The ScreenTip on the Undo button changes to Can't Undo if you cannot reverse the last action. The Redo button reverses an action that you undo. For example, after you select and delete a slide, you can restore the slide by clicking the Undo button. However, after restoring, you can click the Redo button to delete the slide again. The ScreenTip changes to Can't Redo if you cannot repeat the previous action. You can also use the Repeat command on the Edit menu to repeat an action.

Undoing and Redoing Actions

In this activity, you will select and delete text. Then you will use Undo and Redo. The outline pane or Outline View is the best place to enter and edit text because you enter and edit the text all on one screen. Since you will be working with the level 3 subtitles, you will increase the magnification rate.

Using Undo and Redo

1. Click the Undo button to delete the last action. Click the Undo arrow to undo a series of actions.

2. Click the Redo button to reverse an undone action.

1. In the outline pane, scroll to slide 3. Then, click the **Zoom list box** and select **33%**. Move the pane border to the right, if necessary, to see all of the level 3 subtitle text.

2. In the first level 3 subtitle, double-click the word *removed* and type replaced.

Now you will select the next subtitle and delete it.

3. Point to the bullet in front of *New compound must be used.*

The pointer changes to a four-way arrow.

4. Click the screen to select the subtitle text and then press Delete.

The subtitle disappears.

5. After EPA in the next subtitle, change the word *standard* to *specs.* After OSHA in the following subtitle, change *standard* to *specs.,* as shown in Figure 1.15.

Now you will undo the latter changes.

6. On the Standard toolbar, click the **Undo button drop-down arrow** and select the top two actions (Typing).

The list box indicates Undo 2 actions. The Undo command restores the word *standard* on both lines.

7. On the Standard toolbar, click the **Redo button** twice.

Using the Redo command, you now have changed the word *standard* back to the word *specs.*

8. Move the pane border to the left and click the **slide pane**. Change the magnification rate to 66%.

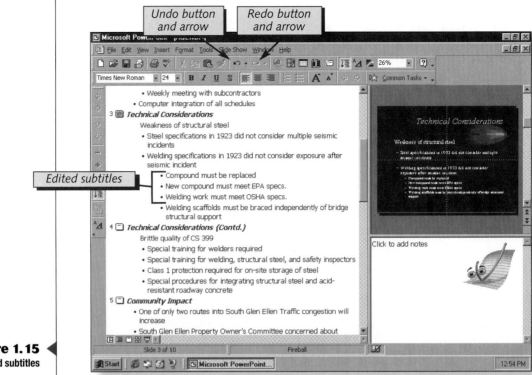

Figure 1.15
Slide 3 with edited subtitles

MOVING AND DELETING SLIDES

You can move slides in several ways. In Outline View or the outline pane of Normal View, you can move a slide with the click of Move Up ▲ or Move Down ▼. However, you should collapse the outline first. If the outline is expanded (all subtitles show), the title only will move up in response to the Move Up button ▲; and it will move above the last subtitle on the previous slide.

The Slide Sorter View lets you move a slide by cutting and then pasting it into a new location. Cut slides are stored on the Clipboard. Once stored on the Clipboard, you can paste the item to another location. You can also drag and drop slides. The slide icon pointer shows the position of the slide as you drag the slide. Either way you move a slide, you must first select the slide. A black border surrounds a selected slide. Once selected, you may move slides easily. You can also delete selected slides by pressing ⬚Delete.

HANDS
On

Rearranging Agenda Slides

In this activity, you will change the order of slides using various methods. You will also delete two of the **Agenda** slides.

1. **In the outline pane, scroll to slide 9 and click the slide title.**

2. **On the Standard toolbar, click Expand All ⬚.**

Only the slide titles are displayed as the subtitles are hidden.

Moving a Slide

To move up or down (Outline):

1. Click the Expand All (or Collapse All) button.

2. Click a slide title, and then click the Move Up or Move Down button.

3. Click the Expand All button.

To cut and paste (Slide Sorter):

1. Select the slide and click the Cut button.

2. Click the new location and click the Paste button.

To drag and drop (Slide Sorter):

1. Select the slide.

2. Drag and drop in the new location.

3. On the Outlining toolbar, click **Move Up** ⬆.

Slide 9 moves up and becomes slide 8, and PowerPoint renumbers the slides.

4. Scroll to slide 3, click the **title** and click **Move Down** ⬇.

Slide 3 changes places with slide 4, and PowerPoint renumbers the slides.

5. On the Standard toolbar, click the **Expand All button** 🔢.

The subtitles reappear in the outline pane. Now you will switch to Slide Sorter View and move other slides.

6. On the View toolbar, click the **Slide Sorter View button** ⊞.

7. Scroll to the bottom of the screen; click **slide 10**.

A border surrounds slide 10, as shown in Figure 1.16.

Figure 1.16 ◀
Slide Sorter View with a slide selected

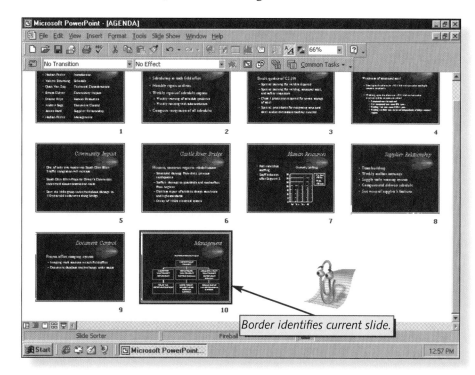

Border identifies current slide.

8. On the Standard toolbar, click the **Cut button** ✂.

PowerPoint moves slide 10 from the presentation to the Clipboard. A line after slide 9 marks the spot where slide 10 used to be.

9. Click the area between slide 1 and slide 2 to paste slide 10 from the Clipboard.

A line now appears between slides 1 and 2.

10. On the Standard toolbar, click the **Paste button** 📋.

Slide 10 is pasted after slide 1. Slide 10 is now numbered slide 2, and PowerPoint has renumbered the other slides. The border still surrounds slide 2.

11. Drag and drop slide 6 to a position immediately before slide 3.

Slide 6 drops into place and becomes slide 3. PowerPoint renumbers the other slides.

Deleting a Slide

1. Select the slide.

2. Press Delete.

12. Click slide 5, press and hold ⇧ Shift, and click slide 6.

A border surrounds both slides.

13. Press Delete.

PowerPoint deletes these slides and renumbers the others.

PREVIEWING PRESENTATIONS

Creating effective individual slides is not enough. The slides together must create an effective presentation. Using the Slide Show view, you can preview your presentation manually or automatically, from beginning to end. In doing so, you may notice gaps in the information or overlapping information. You may see that some text is too large or too small or that some slides are crowded. Now is the time to detect and correct errors in your presentation.

You can preview a Slide Show manually in three ways. You can click once to move to the next slide, you can right-click and use the shortcut menu to move to a new slide or to end the slide show, or you can use the *Slide Navigator dialog box*, which allows you to move to any slide in the presentation.

Presenters often print slides to distribute to the audience before, during, or after a presentation. In addition, all or part of a presentation may be incorporated into a written report. For these reasons, PowerPoint allows users to see what the printouts would look like when printed in black and white. Furthermore, PowerPoint lets you change the appearance of the black-and-white printouts.

In a slide show, the default PowerPoint setting is to end the show with a black slide. To verify that this setting is activated, click Options on the Tools menu. In the Options dialog box, click the View tab and make sure a check mark appears in the *End with black slide* box. Or, if you prefer to make your last slide one with a more powerful message that will remain on the screen for your audience, click to remove the check mark in the *End with black slide* box.

Previewing a Slide Show

In this activity, you will view the entire presentation manually to verify that your changes have created an effective presentation.

1. While in Slide Sorter View, click slide 1.

2. On the View toolbar, click the Slide Show button 🖥.

3. Click anywhere on the screen to move to the next slide.

Slide 2 appears on the screen.

4. Click anywhere on the screen again.

Slide 3 appears on the screen.

Figure 1.17 ◄
Shortcut menu

5. Right-click the screen to display the shortcut menu and click **Previous**, as shown in Figure 1.17.

Slide 2 reappears.

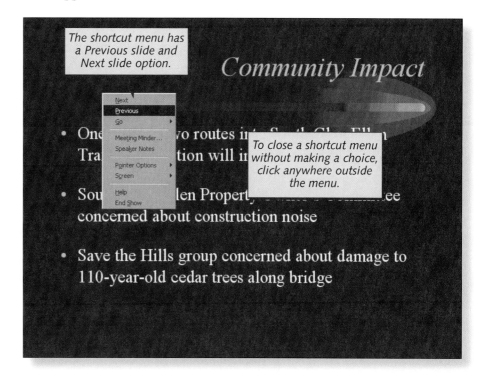

6. Click the screen seven more times, pausing briefly to view each slide.

7. When the End message appears, click the screen.

 *If your presentation did not end in a black screen, click Options on the Tools menu. On the View tab, place a check mark in the* End with black screen *box.*

8. Click the **Slide Show button** 🖵 again.

9. Right-click, click **Go**, and then click **Slide Navigator** on the shortcut menu.

10. In the Slide Navigator dialog box, double-click **Community Impact**.

PowerPoint navigates directly to slide 5.

11. Right-click and click **End Show**.

PowerPoint returns to Slide Sorter View.

PRINTING PRESENTATIONS

While many presentations are shown and never printed, some presentations are printed—entirely or partly, in color or black and white—as notes pages or handouts for the audience or included as illustrations in a written report. Printing an outline or slides is a way to prepare a presentation for review—an alternative to routing the presentation electronically. Others in your organization may review printouts of your outline, key slides, or an entire presentation; write comments on them; and return them to you.

You likely have seen acetate sheets called ***overhead transparencies*** used to project images on a screen via an overhead projector. You may print PowerPoint slides as overhead transparencies if you use special transparency film in your printer or in a photocopier. You can emphasize key points by writing directly on the transparencies with a felt tip pen.

Before printing a presentation, you should click Page Setup on the File menu and select either ***portrait*** (vertical, like a portrait painting) or ***landscape*** (horizontal, sideways) orientation. If you are printing slides as overhead transparencies, open the Page Setup dialog box again, click the *Slides sized for* drop-down arrow, and select Overhead.

When you click the Print button 🖨 on the Standard toolbar, PowerPoint prints one copy of each slide in the default ***grayscale*** mode. PowerPoint adjusts the color scheme and uses grays to suggest contrasting colors. When you click File on the menu bar and click Print, a dialog box displays in which you can specify the number of copies, certain slides, and a more efficient mode, called ***Pure black and white.*** Pure black and white saves printer memory and time by ignoring colors, printing all slides in black and white only.

In the Print dialog box, you can choose to print only the current slide (slide holding the insertion point), current selection, several slides, or all slides. To print a few slides of a presentation, type slide numbers with a hyphen or comma between two numbers to tell PowerPoint which slides to print. For example, typing 1,3,5-8 would result in printing slides 1 and 3, and 5 through 8.

Printing Slides, Notes, and Handouts

In this activity, you will print selected slides and a slide outline in the ***Agenda*** presentation.

1. Click **slide 6**.

You will print this slide in grayscale mode.

2. Click **File** on the menu bar and click **Print**.

The Print dialog box opens, as shown in Figure 1.18.

3. Under Print range, click the **Current slide button**.

PowerPoint will print the slide you selected.

4. Under Copies, verify that **1** shows in the Number of copies list box. Under Print what, verify that **Slides** appears in the list box. Click the **Grayscale** check box.

5. Click **OK**.

While you wait for that slide to print, you will send slides 2 and 8 to the printer.

6. Click **File** on the menu bar and click **Print**. Under Print range, click the **Slides button**. Type **2,8** in the text box.

Figure 1.18 ◀

The Print dialog box

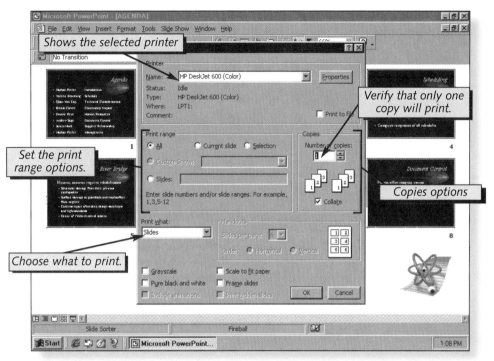

Printing Slides

To print all slides in grayscale (one copy):

Click the Print button to print a presentation in grayscale.

To print selectively:

1. Click File on the menu bar and click Print.

2. Select the desired Print range option.

3. Select the desired Print what: option.

4. Select the Number of copies option.

5. Click OK.

7. Verify that the **Number of copies** is set to **1** and **Print what** is set to **Slides**. Click the **Pure black and white check box**. Click **OK**.

One copy of slides 2 and 8 will be printed.

8. Click **File** on the menu bar and click **Print**. Under Print range, click the **Slides button**. Type 3 in the text box.

9. Under Print what, click the drop-down arrow and select **Outline View**. Click **OK**.

One copy of slide 3 will be printed in Outline View.

 *The text prints exactly as it was last displayed in Outline View. If you want to print the outline in a larger type size, return to Outline View, click Zoom on the View menu, and adjust the Zoom setting.*

SAVING PRESENTATIONS

After changing a presentation, you should save your work. Saving a presentation transfers the information from computer memory to your disk, and you can open the presentation later. Saving your work often is important in case something goes wrong with the computer. For example, if you have not saved your presentation and your computer malfunctions or someone kicks the power cord, all your work may be lost.

You can send a slide or presentation as an e-mail message directly from PowerPoint. You can also send the slide or entire presentation as an attachment to an e-mail message. Explore Microsoft PowerPoint Help to learn more about this feature.

When you create a new presentation, the presentation is unnamed until you save it. In the meantime, PowerPoint names the file *Presentation1* as the default file name. When you save the file, you should give the file a more meaningful name, so you can see at a glance what information the file contains. Besides naming a file, you also must specify where to store the file (the drive and folders/path). The file name may not include any of the following characters: \ / < > * ? " ; : or |

After you name and save a file, clicking the Save button ⊟ replaces the file on disk with the version currently in memory, without displaying the Save As dialog box. If you want to save the file in a different place or under a new name, you must click File on the menu bar and click Save As. The Save As dialog box appears, and you can type a new file name and/or location. When you use the Save As command, you are not renaming a file. Instead you are saving a copy of the file under a different name or in a different place. The original file with the original name will not be deleted.

You can also create a new folder in which to save a file. To do so, select the drive (and folder, if appropriate) for the location of the new folder. Then click the Create New folder button ⌹. Type the folder name and click OK. You can then save the file in this newly created folder.

If you want to run a presentation on another computer, you can pack the presentation and all elements associated with the file by using the *Pack and Go Wizard.* If you are not sure whether PowerPoint is installed on the computer you will be using, you can include the *PowerPoint Viewer,* a program that will allow you to run a slide show without PowerPoint being installed on the computer. Simply click Pack and Go on the File menu and follow the instructions. When you want to unpack the presentation, open Windows Explorer, locate the presentation files, double-click Pngsetup, and enter the location to copy the presentation to. You can then run the show.

Naming and Saving a File

1. Click File on the menu bar and click Save As.

2. Select the drive (and folder if appropriate) in the Save in box.

3. Type a name for the document in the File name box.

4. Click the Save button.

Naming and Saving a File

In this activity, you will use the Save As command to save the *Agenda* presentation in the *Tutorial* folder on your Student Data Disk.

1. Click **File** on the menu bar and click **Save As**.

The Save As dialog box appears, as shown in Figure 1.19.

2. If the location of your Student Data Disk files does not appear in the Save in box, click the **Save in drop-down arrow** and click the drive or folder.

3. Click the *Tutorial* folder in the window below the Save in box and click the **Open button**.

4. In the File name box, edit the file name to *Agenda Revised* and click the **Save button**.

PowerPoint saves the file as you specified, and your open file remains in the window. The title bar and the taskbar button show the new file name.

You should save your files often—especially after making any changes. Even if you have saved a file, unsaved changes will be lost if your computer malfunctions or a power outage occurs.

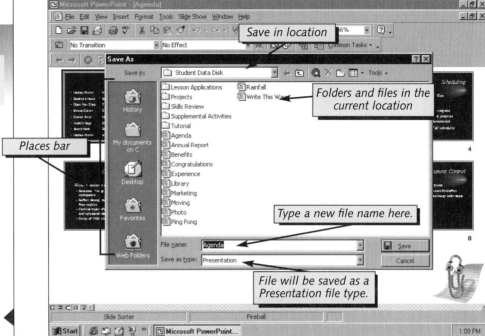

Places bar

Save in location

Folders and files in the current location

Type a new file name here.

File will be saved as a Presentation file type.

Figure 1.19
The Save As dialog box

CLOSING FILES AND EXITING POWERPOINT

When you are finished working with a presentation, you should *close* the file. Closing a file removes the file from memory but leaves PowerPoint running. You do not need to close your file to open another PowerPoint presentation, however. PowerPoint lets you open several files at once. To have more free memory, though, you should close files that you are no longer using.

When only one presentation is open, two Close buttons ☒ are present: one for the presentation on the *menu bar* and one for PowerPoint on the *title bar*. Clicking the Close button on the menu bar will close the file. Clicking the Close button on the title bar will close PowerPoint—so be careful! When more than one presentation is open, click the menu bar Close button to close the displayed presentation. PowerPoint also has a Close button 📋 on the Standard toolbar. Using this button avoids the problem of accidentally closing PowerPoint when you intend to close a file.

Presentations that you have opened recently are added to a list near the bottom of the File menu. If you need to reopen a file you just closed, you can select the presentation quickly from that list. By default, PowerPoint lists the last four files; a user may choose to list up to nine files on the File menu.

Before turning off your computer, you should exit PowerPoint and return to the Windows desktop. Windows may take longer to shut down if PowerPoint is open. Also, Windows will take longer to start the next time if not shut down properly.

Finding and Replacing Text

In this activity, you will search Help for information about PowerPoint's Find and Replace features. Then you will apply the Help information to an existing presentation.

1. **Click the Office Assistant and type** find text **in the *What would you like to do?* box. Click Search. Then, click the Find text option and read the Help information that appears.**

2. **Ask the Office Assistant for information on** replace text. **Click the appropriate option and read the Help information. Close the Help window.**

Now you will open a presentation and use Find and Replace.

3. **Open *Ping Pong* on your Student Data Disk and save the file as *Find & Replace* in the *Tutorial* folder. Switch to Slide View.**

4. **Click the Edit menu and click Find.**

Figure 1.20
The Find dialog box

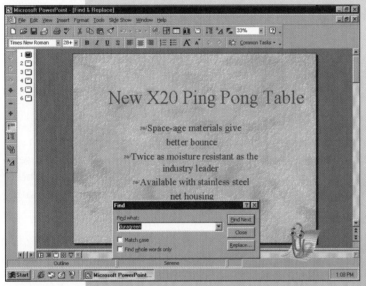

5. **In the Find what text box of the Find dialog box, type** duragreen, **as shown in Figure 1.20. Then, click the Find Next button.**

PowerPoint jumps to the first occurrence of *Duragreen* following the insertion point. You will add a special effect (italic) to the word. If you had checked the Match case checkbox in the Find dialog box, PowerPoint would have skipped this occurrence because it begins with a capital letter.

6. **With *Duragreen* selected, click the Italic button [*I*] on the Formatting toolbar. Then click the Find Next button again to find the next occurrence of *duragreen*.**

The Office Assistant indicates that no additional occurrences are located in the presentation.

7. **Click OK; then click the Replace button on the Find dialog box.**

8. **In the Replace dialog box, type** percent **in the Find what box, and type** % **in the Replace with box.**

9. **Click the Replace All button.**

The Office Assistant indicates the number of replacements made. If you are not sure you want to replace all occurrences, click the Find Next button repeatedly until you find an occurrence that you do want to replace. Then click the Replace button and resume clicking the Find Next button, until the Office Assistant announces that the search is over.

10. **Click OK and close the Replace dialog box. Click the Save button [🖫]. Click the Close button [X].**

Closing Agenda and Exiting PowerPoint

In this activity, you will close the **Agenda Revised** file. Then you will exit PowerPoint and return to the Windows desktop. First, though, you will make a change on one of the slides.

1. Scroll to slide 1 and select the name *Valerie Browning*.

2. Type your name to replace the selected text.

Your name replaces *Valerie Browning*. Now you will close the file.

3. Click **File** on the menu bar and click **Close**.

The Office Assistant asks whether you want to save the changes you made to this file.

4. Click **Yes** in the Office Assistant dialog box.

The **Agenda Revised** presentation disappears from the PowerPoint window.

5. Click **File** on the menu bar.

The bottom of the File menu shows a list of recently used files, including **Agenda Revised**. If you needed to open this file now, you could simply click the file name in this list.

6. Click **Exit**.

PowerPoint disappears from the screen; the Windows desktop appears if you have no other programs running.

7. Remove your Student Data Disk from the disk drive, if necessary.

Test your knowledge by answering the following questions. See Appendix B to check your answers.

T F 1. The Standard, Formatting, and Drawing toolbars are expandable and customized for individual users.

T F 2. The Slide View (or pane) is the ideal choice for entering and editing text.

T F 3. Text in titles and subtitles is the same size but indented differently.

T F 4. To see the number of the displayed slide in Slide View (or pane), click the scroll box.

T F 5. To exit PowerPoint, click File on the menu bar and click Close.

CREATING HYPERLINKS

A hyperlink is text or a graphic that serves as a shortcut, or jump, to another slide, presentation, or Web page. A text hyperlink is shown in color, often blue, and is underlined. Once you *jump* using a text hyperlink, the text changes color, usually to purple, to let you know that you have used the hyperlink. (Objects used as hyperlinks do not change color.) You must use the Slide View to create hyperlinks, but they work (jump) only in Slide Show. When showing large presentations, you may want to use a hyperlink to jump quickly from one slide to another, to another presentation, or to a Web address (***URL*** or ***Uniform Resource Locator***). In this activity, you will open a presentation and link an item on one slide to another slide in the presentation and to a Web site.

1. Open *Benefits* on your Student Data Disk and save the file as *Benefits with Hyperlinks* in the *Tutorial* folder.

2. Switch to Slide View and go to slide 2. Select *Health care.* On the Standard toolbar, click the **Insert Hyperlink button** .

3. In the Link to panel, click **Place in This Document**. A list of all slides in this presentation appears in the *Select a place in this document* list box. Click **slide 3** to insert a hyperlink to the Health Care slide, as shown in Figure 1.21.

4. Click **OK**.

PowerPoint inserts the hyperlink and closes the Insert Hyperlink dialog box.

5. Deselect the text by clicking outside the text box.

Health care is underlined and a different color, two indications of hypertext. When you point to the hyperlink, though, the pointer does not take the shape of a hand. That happens only in Slide Show.

6. Switch to Slide Show, point to Health care, and click the hyperlink.

The pointer changes to the shape of a hand and then jumps to the Health Care slide.

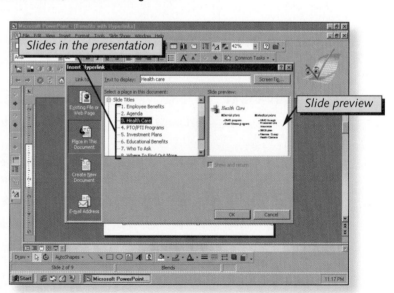

Figure 1.21 ◀
The Insert Hyperlink dialog box

7. Press [Esc], navigate to slide 2, and note that the display text (Health care) has changed color to indicate that you followed the link. Save the updated file.

8. Navigate to slide 8, select the slide title, *Where To Find Out More,* and click the **Insert Hyperlink button** to insert a hyperlink to a Web page.

The Insert Hyperlink dialog box appears.

9. Click **Existing File or Web Page** in the Link to panel of the Insert Hyperlink dialog box.

Another option now appears in the Insert Hyperlink dialog box—*Type the file or Web page name* box.

10. In the *Type the file or Web page name* box, type www.prusec.com **(Prudential Securities Web site), as shown in Figure 1.22.**

To insert a link to another presentation, you would click File under Browse for. Then, in the Look in box, navigate to the file you want to link to and click the name. The file name would appear in the *Type file or Web page name* box.

You should specify an easy-to-read ScreenTip. Otherwise, the Web address will appear as the ScreenTip when you point to the hyperlink.

11. Click the **ScreenTip button** and type Prudential Securities **in the text box. Then click OK.**

The Set Hyperlink ScreenTip dialog box closes, and you return to the Insert Hyperlink dialog box.

12. Click **OK.**

The Insert Hyperlink dialog box closes, and you return to slide 8, with the title text still selected.

13. Deselect the title; click the **Slide Show button** 🖵.

The slide displays in Slide Show view with the title text in a different color and underlined.

14. Click the title text.

If your connection to the Internet is already active, PowerPoint will jump directly to the Prudential Securities site. When you click a Web page hyperlink, you may have to manually switch to your browser, depending on your computer setup.

15. When the home page appears, navigate the Web site.

16. Click the **Back button** ◀ until your slide displays, or switch to your presentation.

17. Save your changes, close the file, and exit PowerPoint. Close your browser and disconnect from the Internet unless your instructor tells you to remain connected.

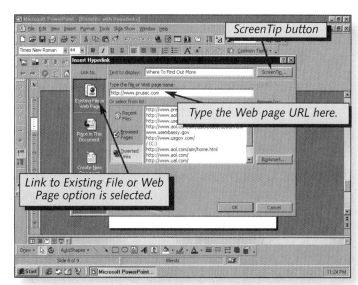

Figure 1.22 ◀
The Insert Hyperlink dialog box
with a link to a Web page

Warning
You may proceed directly to the exercises for this lesson. If, however, you are finished with your computer session, follow the "shut down" procedures for your lab or school environment.

Lesson Summary & Exercises

SUMMARY

Using PowerPoint, you can create a presentation and relay information to an audience in an efficient, effective way. The PowerPoint window contains menus, tool-bars, and scroll bars for working with and navigating presentations. The View toolbar contains buttons for PowerPoint's five views, each suited for specific tasks. Working with slides entails a variety of PowerPoint features such as Promote and Demote for changing the level of subtitles, Undo and Redo for reversing mouse and keyboard actions, Slide Show for previewing a presentation, and Grayscale Preview for viewing slides in black and white. Frequently, you will want to print slides and outlines to review. The Pure black and white mode is more efficient than the default grayscale mode. The Save As command enables you to save an existing presentation with a different file name and/or in a different folder. Close all files before exiting PowerPoint, and exit PowerPoint before shutting down your computer. You can add hyperlinks to your presentations to link within a presentation, from one presentation to another, or to a Web site.

Now that you have completed this lesson, you should be able to do the following:

- Define a presentation program; give examples of how you can use presentations. (PowerPoint-486)
- Start PowerPoint and identify the parts of the PowerPoint window. (PowerPoint-488)
- Provide a description of each menu on the menu bar and use a menu. (PowerPoint-490)
- Explain the dialog box features and enter choices in dialog boxes. (PowerPoint-491)
- Provide a brief description of each button on the Standard and Formatting toolbars. (PowerPoint-493)
- Issue a PowerPoint command using a toolbar button. (PowerPoint-493)
- Open a presentation. (PowerPoint-495)
- Navigate among the five PowerPoint views. (PowerPoint-496)
- Use the Office Assistant to get help with PowerPoint. (PowerPoint-499)
- Navigate a presentation using the scroll bars, arrows, and boxes. (PowerPoint-500)
- Edit text using Insert mode and Overtype mode. (PowerPoint-501)
- Promote and demote subtitles and bullets. (PowerPoint-502)
- Check spelling as you type and in the entire presentation. (PowerPoint-503)
- Use the Undo, Redo, and Repeat commands. (PowerPoint-505)
- Move and delete slides in various views. (PowerPoint-506)
- Preview a slide show manually and automatically. (PowerPoint-508)
- Print outlines, slides, notes, and handouts. (PowerPoint-510)
- Name and save a file as a new presentation. (PowerPoint-512)
- Use the Find and Replace features. (PowerPoint-514)
- Close a file and exit PowerPoint. (PowerPoint-515)
- Create a hyperlink to a slide within a presentation and to a Web page. (PowerPoint-516)

Lesson Summary & Exercises

CONCEPTS REVIEW

1 TRUE/FALSE

Circle T if the statement is true or F if the statement is false.

T F **1.** The Normal View combines the outline, slide, and notes panes.

T F **2.** Changing the view scale in Normal View changes the size of text in all panes.

T F **3.** Changing the view scale in Outline View from 25% to 33% enables you to see more text.

T F **4.** In Slide Sorter View, a border around a slide shows that the slide is selected.

T F **5.** Hyperlinks work only in Slide Show.

T F **6.** Grayscale is a more efficient print mode than pure black and white.

T F **7.** The best way to check the flow of a presentation is to see it in Slide Show.

T F **8.** A PowerPoint presentation, while less effective than a written report, saves paper.

T F **9.** Toolbar buttons are quick ways to issue software commands.

T F **10.** In Slide View you can see the title and number of a slide by clicking the Help button.

2 MATCHING

Match each of the terms on the left with the definitions on the right.

TERMS

1. Normal View

2. Office Assistant

3. Outline View

4. Slide Navigator dialog box

5. Slide Show

6. Slide Sorter View

7. Slide View

8. subtitle

9. title

10. toolbar button

DEFINITIONS

a. An animated character representing the PowerPoint Help system

b. Indented text on a slide

c. First line of text on a slide

d. An icon representing a software command

e. Dialog box available in Slide Show that allows you to move to any slide in a presentation

f. The best view for copying, deleting, and moving slides

g. A means of previewing a presentation, as an audience would see it

h. The best way to see the graphics on a slide

i. The best place to work on text, graphics, and speaker notes at the same time

j. The best place to create a presentation (type text)

Lesson Summary & Exercises

3 COMPLETION

Fill in the missing word or phrase for each of the following statements.

1. Use the _____ command to save an existing file with a different name or to a different location.

2. If you want to see how a slide will look during a real presentation, click the _____ button.

3. When the PowerPoint window is maximized, the name of the application and the name of the file appear in the _____.

4. To increase or decrease the size of text in an outline or a slide, adjust the _____.

5. Click the _____ button to access all Windows programs, including PowerPoint.

6. To exit PowerPoint, click the _____ button on the title bar or click File on the menu bar and click _____.

7. This method of moving a slide does not involve the Clipboard: _____.

8. The address of a Web site is called a(n) _____.

9. Hyperlinks can be attached to text or _____.

10. The _____ button will change a level 2 subtitle to a level 1 subtitle.

4 SHORT ANSWER

Write a brief answer to each of the following questions.

1. Name five things a presentation may incorporate to present information to an audience.

2. Explain how to edit text if you discover your mistake as you are typing.

3. How do you display the next slide in Slide Show view?

4. Name two ways you can tell whether a slide displayed in Slide View is the fifth or sixth in order.

5. If the magnification of outline text is too small to read, how do you enlarge it?

6. If you do not want your slide show to end with a black slide, explain how to deactivate this option.

7. You have just moved slide 3 to follow slide 9. How do you renumber slide 3?

8. Describe how to ask the Office Assistant to find a Help topic for you.

9. Describe the procedure to print an entire presentation in grayscale mode.

10. What is the advantage of looking at a presentation in Slide Sorter View?

5 IDENTIFICATION

Label each of the items of the PowerPoint window in Figure 1.23.

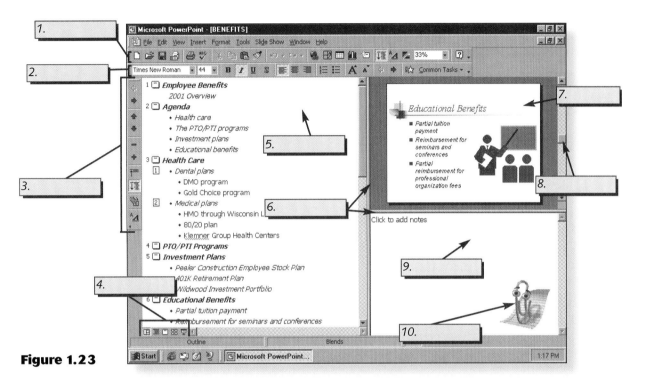

Figure 1.23

SKILLS REVIEW

Complete each of the Skills Review problems in sequential order so that you will review your PowerPoint skills to start PowerPoint, open a file, switch views, use the Help system, work with a presentation, preview and print slides, save and close a file, and exit PowerPoint.

1 Start PowerPoint and Open a Presentation

1. Click the **Start button** 🔎Start, point to **Programs**, and click **Microsoft PowerPoint**.

2. When the initial PowerPoint dialog box appears, click **Cancel**.

3. Click the **Open button** 📂 on the Standard toolbar.

4. Click the **Look in box drop-down arrow** and click the drive (and folder, if necessary) that contains your Student Data Disk files.

5. In the list of files, double-click **_Moving_**.

6. Review the presentation.

Lesson Summary & Exercises

2 Work in Various Views

1. On the View toolbar, click **Outline View** 📃.

2. Drag the vertical pane border to the left and drag the horizontal pane border to display the notes pane at about 2 inches high.

3. Click in the notes pane.

4. Click **Slide View** 🔲. Drag the vertical pane border about an inch to the right.

5. Drag the horizontal border up just enough to see *Click to add notes*.

6. Switch to Slide Sorter View.

7. Select **slide 13**.

8. Click **Slide Show** 🖳 and click anywhere on the screen.

9. Advance to the End screen. Click to end the slide show.

10. Click **Normal View** 🔳.

11. Adjust borders so the outline pane fills half the window and the slide and notes panes each fill one-fourth of the window.

3 Use the Help System

1. Click the **Office Assistant**.

2. In the *What do you want to do?* box, type find a word and click **Search**.

3. Look at the complete list of options and click the **Find text option**.

4. Read the Help screen; then click the **Close button**.

4 Scroll a Presentation and Change Magnification

1. In Normal View, click the outline pane. Drag the scroll box to the end of the presentation.

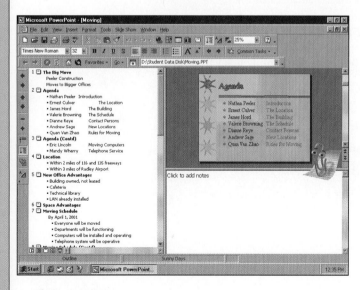

Figure 1.24

2. Click the scroll bar above the scroll box.

3. In the slide pane, scroll rapidly to the beginning of the presentation.

4. Click the scroll bar below the scroll box.

5. Click the down scroll arrow, then the **Next Slide button** 🔽. Click the **Previous Slide button** 🔼.

6. Verify the number of the current slide.

7. On the Standard toolbar, click the **Zoom button** 66% ▼ and set a magnification rate of 66%.

8. Switch to Slide View and change the magnification rate to Fit.

9. In the tri-pane view, change magnification in the outline pane to 25% (Figure 1.24).

10. Switch to Slide Show.

11. Right-click, click **Go**, and then click **Slide Navigator** on the shortcut menu.

12. In the Slide Navigator dialog box, double-click **Location**.

13. Right-click and click **End Show**.

5 Promote and Demote Subtitles

1. In the outline pane, navigate to slide 14.

2. Select the two subtitles that begin with *Same* and demote them.

3. On slide 7, select the level 4 subtitles (bulleted) and promote them.

4. In the slide pane, select the subtitles again and demote them one level.

6 Check Spelling

1. On the Standard toolbar, click the **Spelling button** 🔤.

2. For each highlighted word, take the appropriate action: Select or type the correct word in the Change to box and click the Change button, or click the Ignore All button. Assume that all names have been spelled correctly. Do not add words to the PowerPoint dictionary.

7 Undo and Redo Actions

1. On slide 4, in the outline pane, change the second subtitle as follows:
   . . . Greater Radley International Airport.

2. Look at the slide pane. Since the subtitle is too close to the map, undo your typing by clicking the **Undo button** 🔙.

3. In the first subtitle, type I- (for Interstate) in front of *116* and *135*. Check the slide pane and undo the changes.

4. Click the **Redo button** ↪ to restore *I-116* and *I-135*. Then select and delete *freeways*.

8 Rearrange and Delete Slides

1. Click the **Expand All button** 📑 to hide the subtitles. In the outline pane, select **slide 13** and click the **Move Up button** ⬆ to place the slide above slide 12. Click the **Expand All button** 📑 again.

2. Switch to Slide Sorter View. Select **slide 9** and cut it to the Clipboard; then paste it at the end of the presentation.

3. Drag **slide 12** and drop it between slides 9 and 10.

4. Select **slide 1** and the **Telephone Service slide** and delete them.

Lesson Summary & Exercises

9 Preview a Presentation and Print

1. While still in Slide Sorter View, click **slide 7**. Then switch to Slide Show.

2. Advance to **slide 8**; click five more times, pausing briefly to view each slide.

3. When the End message appears, click to exit the slide show.

4. Preview the slides in Pure black and white by pressing and holding ⬆ Shift as you click the **Grayscale Preview button** 🖼.

5. Select **slide 5** and switch to Slide View. Right-click the middle of the graph and select **Black and White** on the shortcut menu. On the submenu, click **Light Grayscale**.

6. On slide 4, right-click the picture. Change to Light Grayscale.

7. Click **File** on the menu bar and click **Page Setup**. Verify that the Slides Orientation is set to **Landscape**.

8. Click **slide 8**.

9. Click **File** on the menu bar and click **Print**.

10. Print one copy of the current slide in Pure black and white mode.

10 Name, Save, and Close a File and Exit PowerPoint

1. Click **File** on the menu bar and click **Save As**. In the Save in list box, navigate to the *Skills Review* folder on your Student Data Disk.

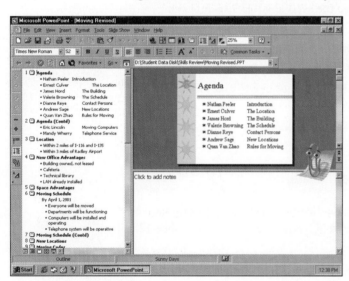

Figure 1.25

2. Name the file *Moving Revised* and click **Save**.

3. Switch to Outline View and navigate to slide 1 (Figure 1.25).

4. Delete the first subtitle *(Nathan Peeler)*. Move the fourth subtitle *(Dianne Reye)* below Eric Lincoln (on slide 2).

5. On slide 2, delete the third subtitle *(Mandy Wherry)*. Select the two remaining subtitles on slide 2 and move them to the end of slide 1. Look at the slide pane to be sure they fit properly.

6. Delete slide 2: In the outline pane, point to the slide number and click. When the slide title is selected, press Delete.

7. Save these changes, then click the **Close button** ⊠ on the menu bar to close the file.

8. Click the **Close button** ⊠ on the title bar to exit PowerPoint.

Lesson Summary & Exercises

LESSON APPLICATIONS

1 Chasing a Rainbow

Start PowerPoint and open a presentation. Make changes and check spelling. Save the changes and close the file.

1. Start PowerPoint and open **Rainfall** on your Student Data Disk. Save the file as **Rainfall Revised** in the **Lesson Applications** folder.

2. On slide 4, change *five* to *5* in the first subtitle. Then undo the change and then redo it. On slide 6, demote the second and fourth subtitles.

3. Check spelling. (*T-o-r-b-o-r-g* is correct). In *aquaduct,* the second *a* should be an *e*.

4. Preview the entire presentation in Slide Show.

5. Save your changes and close the file.

2 At the Library

Open a presentation, save the file in the **Lesson Applications** folder, and move slides. Preview in black-and-white and print selectively before closing.

1. Open the **Library** presentation on your Student Data Disk. Save the file as **Library Revised** in the **Lesson Applications** folder.

2. Delete slide 1 and then move slide 4 so it becomes slide 1.

3. Print preview the slides in grayscale mode. On slide 3, change the graph to Light Grayscale.

4. Print the slide titled *Lessons Learned* in grayscale mode.

5. Save your changes and close the file.

3 Ping Pong Player

Open an existing presentation. Rearrange the slides. Preview the slide show and print a key slide.

1. Open **Ping Pong** on your Student Data Disk. Save the file as **Ping Pong Revised** in the **Lesson Applications** folder.

2. On slide 2, eliminate the red, wavy line under *Duragreen,* which is spelled correctly. Change *20 percent* to *20%*.

3. On slide 5, change *25 percent* to *25%*. On slide 6, promote all level 2 subtitles. Then undo this change. In each level 2 subtitle, delete *the* and add *s* to *player.*

Lesson Summary & Exercises

4. Change the order of slides as shown in Table 1.5.

5. Print preview the presentation in Pure black and white. Print slide 3 in Pure black and white mode.

6. Save all changes and close the file.

TABLE 1.5	ORDER OF PING PONG SLIDES	
Current Slide Number	**Title**	**Revised Slide Number**
4	Title slide	1
6	Three Winning Model Lines	2
1	New X20 Ping Pong Table	3
2	The X20 is Clearly Superior	4
5	The X15 is a True Bargain	5
3	Sales Potential	6

PROJECTS

1 Rainfall Revisited

Your job title at Stand and Deliver is presentation specialist. Your employer offers a range of services related to creating and presenting slide shows. A few Fortune 500 companies are among your clients, though most clients are local businesses, such as Peeler Construction Inc. and the Liberty County Environmental Services Department (ESD). Right now, you have a presentation (2001 Rainfall Totals) from Liberty County ESD on your desk. Open *Rainfall* on your Student Data Disk.

Yesterday you noted that slide 8 is too wordy. Now you will rewrite it. On a separate sheet of paper, write the subtitles (2 or 3 levels) to replace the client's paragraphs. Edit the subtitles; delete all words not needed. Start a new slide in Outline View below the slide to be rewritten. Type the text on a new slide from your sheet. Cut the original slide from the presentation. Preview the presentation to ensure smooth flow. If you need to refer to the original slide to improve or correct the new slide, undo the cut.

Increase the actual text size (explore Help for information on font size) on the new slide. Make other changes to the presentation as desired. Save your file as *Rainfall* in the *Projects* folder on your Student Data Disk.

2 Designer Backgrounds

As designers of many varied presentations for Stand and Deliver clients, you and your coworkers are interested in the different looks available in PowerPoint and other presentation programs. For example, the *Rainfall* presentation you worked on recently seemed different, with its plain gray panels for text and the waves that seemed to splash as you scrolled. You have agreed to prepare a catalog of presentation designs, containing the information shown in Table 1.6.

TABLE 1.6	CATALOG OF PRESENTATION DESIGNS				
Design	**File Name**	**Main Color**	**Other Color(s)**	**Object(s)**	**Description**
Fireball	Agenda				
High Voltage	Library				
Japanese Waves	Rainfall				
Serene	Ping Pong				
Sunny Days	Moving				

Re-create Table 1.6 on a separate sheet of paper. Open each file in the File Name column and verify the design name in the status bar. Then fill in the color and object columns. In the description column, write one to four words to describe the mood of the design. Examples: Lively! Somber. Autumn Leaves.

Explore PowerPoint Help to determine if you can change the background design. If so, choose one of the five presentations shown in Table 1.6 and select a different design for it. Save the updated presentation as *New Design* in the *Projects* folder on your Student Data Disk. Close the presentation when you finish with it. Update the catalog table to include the information for the new design.

3 Making a Model

When presentation specialists interview clients about new presentations, they like to show models. Showing other clients' presentations to a new client is not a good idea, since the slides may contain confidential information. Ideally, each specialist will have a model that gives presentation advantages, etc.

Open *Congratulations* on your Student Data Disk and save the presentation as *Slide Shows* in the *Projects* folder. Add four slides to the title slide (in the outline pane, press Enter↵ four times). Type a title on each slide and a subtitle on slide 1, as shown in Table 1.7. Click and type as indicated in the slide pane.

TABLE 1.7	SLIDE TITLES	
Slide No.	**Slide Title**	**Subtitle**
1	Stand & Deliver Presentations	Your Name, Presentation Specialist
2	Description of a Presentation	Supply two or more to fit the title
3	Advantages of Presentations	Supply two or more to fit the title
4	Purposes of Presentations	Supply two or more to fit the title
5	Features of Presentations	Supply two or more to fit the title

Then add subtitles to slides 2–5 as indicated. For at least three of the slides, type a sentence in the notes pane—a comment you would make while projecting the current slide. Save the changes to your modified presentation.

4 Just the Basics

Sometimes you are the presenter. That is, you conduct workshops for Stand and Deliver clients. A common workshop objective is to enable clients' employees to use certain software features properly. Soon you will present such a workshop at MKL Meetings and Tours.

Open **Congratulations** on your Student Data Disk and save the presentation as **Basics** in the **Projects** folder. Create a series of slides to present the View toolbar and the five PowerPoint views. Give the name of the view and the purpose of it. (See Table 1.4 on page 496.) In the notes pane, type the remark(s) you will make when projecting the slide. Preview the slides and print one or more of them.

5 In-depth Analysis

After working with Peeler Construction's **Moving** presentation, you realize that this presentation would be useful in training sessions. This presentation includes slides with a variety of features and methods to present information. However, before you can use the presentation for training, you must first analyze the entire presentation. Open **Moving** on your Student Data Disk. As you review the slides, look for these features in the presentation: level 2 subtitles, text in two columns, a table (data arranged in columns and rows), a graph, a shape (e.g., circle), and a picture. Close the **Moving** presentation without saving.

6 Links

You're busy—job, college courses, home, family. You're always looking for ways to get organized. A little trick you read about recently is to have a PowerPoint or Word file that contains links to files you use often and Web sites you especially like or need to visit frequently. Explore Help for information on creating a new presentation. Create a new two-slide presentation. Use the Blank Presentation (on the General tab) or click a template design that especially appeals to you. One slide should contain hyperlinks to any two (or more) presentations in the **Projects** folder—the ones that show your best work. The other slide should contain links to two or more Web sites. If you do not have personal favorites, see the Web Note in this lesson. Create links to Web sites listed in the note. Use the name of the Web site, not the URL, as the display text. Test all hyperlinks. Save the presentation as **Links** in the **Projects** folder on your Student Data Disk.

Project in Progress

7 Now You're in Business

You received state approval to do business under the name *I-Comm.* Your business, I-Comm, will provide a variety of writing and editing services for small and medium-sized organizations within 75 miles of your office. Create a title slide for the business, including your name and (real or fictional) e-mail address as subtitles. Open **Congratulations** on your Student Data Disk and save the presentation as **I-Comm Title** in the **Projects** folder. Use PowerPoint Help to change the design to suit your preference. Print a sample (Figure 1.26). Ask the Office Assistant for help on sending a copy of the title slide in this presentation as an e-mail message. Then, send this title slide to your instructor.

Figure 1.26

LESSON 2

Customizing a Presentation

CONTENTS

OBJECTIVES

After you complete this lesson, you will be able to do the following:

- Create a presentation from a template.
- Create a specific type of slide.
- Apply a design template.
- Enter text in tri-pane view.
- Add speaker notes.
- Import text from Word.
- Apply formatting to text.
- Use the Slide Master to change fonts for an entire presentation.
- Add header and footer information.
- Insert, resize, and move clip art and WordArt.
- Change a presentation design and slide layout.
- Apply and preview animation effects.
- Save presentations as Web pages and preview them in your browser.

PowerPoint provides many tools to help you prepare an effective presentation. Using PowerPoint features, you can design and create a presentation that will help you communicate effectively. In this lesson, you will create a presentation from a design template, add new slides, and type and format text. You will also import text from a Microsoft Word file. In addition, you will insert, resize, and move clip art, and learn about the Slide Master. You will add a footer to slides and a header and footer to outline pages. You will learn to change designs and layouts, add animations, and run an animated slide show.

BEGINNING WITH A TEMPLATE

A *design template* is a collection of designs that you can apply to a presentation. In the initial PowerPoint dialog box, you can choose to begin a presentation with a design template. You can also view the list of presentation designs by clicking File on the menu bar and then clicking the New command.

PowerPoint offers more than forty design templates. Before selecting a design template, plan your presentation. Think about the material you are presenting, the audience who will see and hear the presentation, and the style desired for your presentation. Also, consider how many slides you will need and which slides will include a picture, graph, or table. You should plan the words and carefully edit the text for conciseness and accuracy. After you have planned your presentation, you will select the design template and the specific type of slide layout that you want for the first slide. This choice is generally the easiest, since the Title slide layout is usually the most appropriate choice.

HANDS On

PowerPoint **BASICS**

Creating Presentations

To create a presentation at start-up:

1. Click Design Template in the PowerPoint dialog box; click OK.

2. Click a template; click OK.

3. Select a layout (slide 1); click OK.

To create a presentation in PowerPoint:

1. Click the File menu and New.

2. Click the Design Templates tab.

3. Select a template; click OK.

4. Select a layout; click OK.

Opening a Template and Adding a Slide

In this activity, you will open the New Presentation dialog box, choose a design template, and add the first slide. Eventually you will add more slides to the presentation.

Warning

If you are storing your files on a floppy disk, be sure to have a blank, formatted disk on hand before proceeding with the following activity. Create new folders on the disk as appropriate prior to saving a file. (To create a new folder from the Save As dialog box, select the drive that contains the new disk, click the Create New Folder button 📁*, type the folder name, and click OK.) You can then save your file in this newly created folder.*

Because all hands-on activities and end-of-lesson activities will not fit on one floppy disk, you may have to check one or more disks to find the files you need for the activities in this tutorial.

1. Start PowerPoint.

The initial PowerPoint dialog box appears. If PowerPoint is already open, click File on the menu bar and click New to open the New Presentation dialog box. Click the Design Templates tab and skip to step 3.

2. In the *Create a new presentation using* section, click Design Template and click OK.

The New Presentation dialog box opens with the Design Templates information displayed, as shown in Figure 2.1. If you opened the New Presentation dialog box by clicking New on the File menu, you may need to click the Design Templates tab.

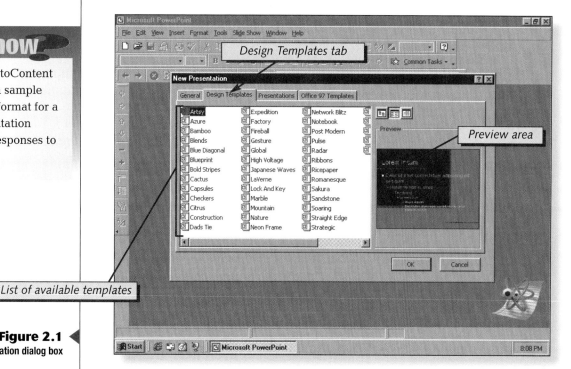

Design Templates tab

Preview area

List of available templates

Figure 2.1
The New Presentation dialog box

3. Click **Capsules** in the Design Templates list box.

A preview of the Capsules template displays. If a preview does not display, you may need to ask your instructor about installing the templates component.

4. Click each of these templates to preview them: **High Voltage, Marble, Sumi Painting**.

As you click each template, a sample displays in the Preview section of the New Presentation dialog box.

5. Click **High Voltage** again and click **OK**.

Note   *If High Voltage is not available and you do not have the Office 2000 CD-ROM to install the template, click another design template, such as Capsules.*

The New Slide dialog box appears. The first AutoLayout, Title Slide, is selected.

6. Click **OK** to accept the Title slide as the first slide in your presentation.

The New Slide dialog box closes and a one-slide presentation displays in Normal View.

7. Click the **Slide View button** [icon] to change the view.

8. Click the **Save button** [icon]. In the Save As dialog box, save the file as *Transportation Projects* in the *Tutorial* folder on your Student Data Disk.

ADDING SLIDES, TEXT, AND NOTES

Adding a new slide requires you to select a layout. PowerPoint offers over twenty layouts for slides. The title slide you just selected is one example. Different kinds of information—text, pictures, graphs, tables—require different layouts. Areas for typing are clearly marked. Adding text to a presentation is usually a simple click-and-type procedure. You can type notes for the speaker and/or the audience in the notes pane as you work in Normal, Outline, or Slide View. Printed notes pages for an audience include a small image of the slide. Ideally, notes pages to be printed and distributed are prepared in Notes Page View, available from the View menu.

 *If the Office Assistant offers capitalization, punctuation, and other tips, you can stop the tips without hiding the Office Assistant. Click the Office Assistant character; then click the Options button. On the Options tab, clear the Guess Help topics check box.*

Adding New Slides and Inserting Text

Each time you add a new slide, you have a choice of 24 slide types, called AutoLayouts. An **AutoLayout** obtains a name by the kind of material the layout design contains. In the New Slide dialog box, you also will find AutoLayouts with these names: Bulleted List, Chart, Large Object, and Table, to name a few. The choice of a layout for each slide is easy—when you have planned your presentation. Your plan shows whether the slide you are adding is to contain text, graphics, or both.

Areas surrounded by dotted lines are reserved for typing or copying text from another PowerPoint file or importing text from another application, such as Microsoft Word. The reserved spaces are called **placeholders.** A placeholder may reserve space for a graph, a picture, or another object, as well as text. When you click a placeholder, a box surrounds the area and small squares appear in the corners of the box. To deselect a placeholder, click the area surrounding the slide.

A placeholder is an **object**, which is a single element on your PowerPoint slide. A placeholder that contains text or graphics is referred to as a **filled object**. A **text object** is a filled object that contains text. An empty placeholder is referred to as an **unfilled object**.

The dotted line area labeled *Click to add title* is the **title area**. It is the location of the text placeholder where you will type the main title of the slide. PowerPoint assumes that all slides have a title. The dotted line area below the title area labeled *Click to add text* is the **object area**. It can also be a placeholder for graphics or charts.

If you are entering more text than will fit in an Object Area placeholder, PowerPoint will automatically use its Auto-Fit feature to reduce the point size of text when you reach the bottom of the placeholder. To deactivate this feature, click Options on the Tools menu. On the Edit tab, click the *Auto-fit text to text placeholder* box to remove the check mark, and click OK.

PowerPoint BASICS

Adding Slides and Text

To add slides:

1. Click the New Slide button.

2. Select an AutoLayout and click OK.

To add slides with the same layout:

Press `⇧ Shift` and click the New Slide button.

To add text:

1. Click the placeholder and type the text.

2. Click the area around the slide to deselect the placeholder.

Figure 2.2 ◀
New Slide dialog box

Microsoft PowerPoint, Word, Excel, and Access provide the Undo command. However, not all of these programs provide the Redo command.

Adding a Slide and Typing Text

In this activity, you will add a slide to *Transportation Projects*. You will replace the text placeholders on the slides and type a multi-level bulleted list. Then you will add a new slide with the same AutoLayout.

1. On the Standard toolbar, click the **New Slide button** 🗔.

The New Slide dialog box opens and displays the AutoLayout options.

2. Click the **AutoLayout icon** for 2 Column Text.

The name of the AutoLayout icon, 2 Column Text, appears in the New Slide dialog box, as shown in Figure 2.2.

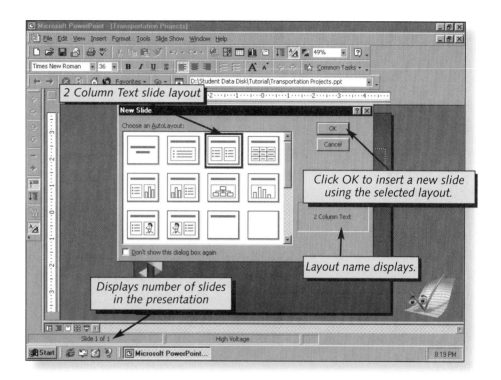

3. Click **OK**.

The slide is added. Notice that the status bar shows the number of the current slide and the total number of slides in the presentation. In this case, slide 2 of 2.

4. Switch to Normal View. In the slide pane, scroll to slide 1 and click the **title placeholder**.

Notice that a box surrounds the title area and small squares appear in the corners of the box. The sample text disappears and the insertion point blinks inside the box, where you will add text.

5. Type Peeler Construction Co. **as the slide title, and then click the subtitle placeholder. In this box, type** Transportation Projects.

Your typed text has now replaced both placeholders on the slide.

6. Scroll to slide 2, click the **slide title placeholder**, and type Transportation Projects.

7. **Click the text placeholder in the first column. Type** McNair Airport parking structure **and press** Enter⏎.

A new bullet appears.

8. **Click the Demote button** ▶.

Notice that a different bullet appears in a smaller font size. This is a level 2 bullet.

9. **Type** parking garage **and press** Enter⏎.

10. **Next, type** parking lot **and press** Enter⏎.

11. **Click the Promote button** ◀.

The new bullet becomes a level 1 bullet.

12. **Type** Hadley Airport luggage claim area. **Then click the text placeholder in the second column.**

13. **Type** Petersburg bus station **and press** Enter⏎.

14. **Next, type** Westchester Expressway overpass. **Then click the area surrounding the slide to deselect the placeholder.**

15. **If wavy, red lines show under any words, check spelling by right-clicking the word. Check and correct the entire document.**

16. **Save these changes to the presentation; then close the file.**

Creating and Printing Notes

While you are working on a presentation, you can create notes in the notes pane. Notes help you as the speaker to remember the key points to present. You can also print notes for a live audience. Such notes are most effective when distributed after a presentation to reinforce your message. If you distribute notes beforehand, the audience may pay more attention to the papers than to you or your slide show. You can use either the notes pane or the Notes Page View to prepare notes for an audience. Notes Page View is not included on the View toolbar. To use this view, click the View menu and Notes Page.

Preparing Notes

In this activity, you will open a presentation, prepare notes on two slides, and print a notes page.

1. **Open** *Moving* **on your Student Data Disk and save the file as** *Notes Pages* **in the** *Tutorial* **folder.**

2. **Scroll to slide 5. In Normal View, drag the horizontal pane border up a couple of inches to enlarge the notes pane. Click the notes pane. If the magnification rate (on the view scale) is less than 100%, click the Zoom arrow** 66% ▾ **and click 100%.**

3. **Type the following text and check spelling as you type:**

   Will have designed landscape with mature trees immediately.

   Will have accessible patio and rock garden outside the cafeteria.

   Will have multimedia conference/presentation room, with LCD computer.

Working with Notes

To create speaker (only) notes:

1. Click the notes pane.

2. Type the notes to accompany the current slide.

To create a notes page:

1. Click the View menu and Notes Page.

2. Click the notes place-holder and adjust the magnification rate as needed.

3. Type the notes.

Figure 2.3 ◄
The Notes Page View

Now you will switch to Notes Page View to see how the slide and notes would look on a printed (audience) notes page.

4. Click **View** on the menu bar, click **Notes Page**, and change magnification to the Fit option, if necessary.

Your screen should now look similar to Figure 2.3.

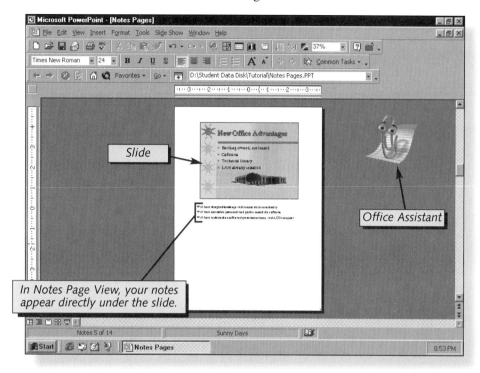

5. Switch to Normal View and navigate to slide 4. Click the **notes pane** and type the following text:

Will have 50% more parking space than we have now.

Will fully comply with ADA guidelines for handicapped parking.

Will have entirely separate entrances for personal autos and company fleets.

6. Switch to Notes Page View.

PowerPoint switches the view, and the notes display on the page directly below the image of the slide.

7. Click **File** on the menu bar and click **Print**.

8. In the Print range section of the Print dialog box, click **Current slide** and verify that in the Copies section, *Number of copies* is set to 1. Click the **Print what drop-down arrow** and click **Notes Pages**. Then click the **Pure black and white check box**.

9. Click **OK**.

PowerPoint closes the Print dialog box and sends the document to the printer.

10. Switch to Normal View.

PowerPoint returns to the standard tri-pane view.

11. Save these changes; then close the file.

CREATING A PRESENTATION AND FORMATTING SLIDES

In addition to creating a presentation by typing text into placeholders in Slide View, you also can create a presentation by typing in Outline View. When you type in Outline View, you type all of the text at one time, just as you would if you typed an outline on a piece of paper. You can also use text created in other programs to make a new presentation or to add slides to an existing presentation. With a few clicks, you can insert that text into the presentation, instead of retyping the material in PowerPoint.

Additionally, PowerPoint offers many special text formatting features. Text format involves the appearance of the characters (design, size, and color) and special effects, such as underlines, used to emphasize certain words. Formatting also includes the position of text in relation to the left and right edges of a slide. Text often aligns on the left side—subtitle text almost always does. Sometimes slide titles may align on the right side or midway between the two sides. Once you format a piece of text—a subtitle, for example—you can copy the appearance to other text, using the Format Painter button .

Importing or Inserting Text from Word

With PowerPoint 2000, you can create a new presentation using the data from a Microsoft Word file. You can also add slides to a presentation by inserting a Word document or an outline. Text created in Word's Outline View works best because this text automatically contains *styles,* or sets of character and paragraph attributes. (Of course, a Word user can add styles to ordinary text.) When you import a Word document, PowerPoint uses the outline structure from the styles in the document. A Heading 1 style becomes a slide title; a Heading 2 style becomes a first-level subtitle, and so on. If the Word document contains no styles, PowerPoint uses the paragraph indentations or tabs at the beginning of paragraphs to create an outline.

Suppose you want to create a presentation from a report. Instead of importing or inserting the entire document to PowerPoint, you should edit the report in Word. Condensing the paragraphs in outline form gives you ready-made titles and subtitles for your slides.

 *You can export a PowerPoint presentation to Microsoft Word. Click the File menu and Send To; then click Microsoft Word on the submenu. While working in Word, you can send a document to PowerPoint using the same procedure.*

Inserting a Word Outline

In this activity, you will insert a Word outline from your Student Data Disk into a presentation.

1. Open *Write This Way* on your Student Data Disk. Save the presentation as *Import Word Outline* in the *Tutorial* folder.

PowerPoint displays the new file name in the title bar and in the Web toolbar.

2. Click the Outline View button .

Slide 1 should appear highlighted in the outline pane. If the slide is not selected, click slide 1.

3. Click Insert on the menu bar and click Slides from Outline.

The Insert Outline dialog box appears, as shown in Figure 2.4.

Figure 2.4 ◀
The Insert Outline dialog box

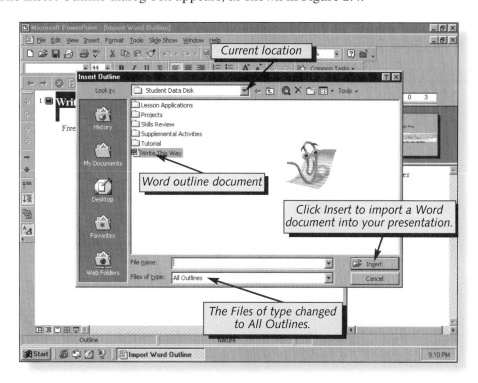

Using Word Text in PowerPoint

To import a Word document:

1. Click the Open button.

2. Click the Files of type drop-down arrow and select All Files.

3. Locate the desired Word file and click the Open button.

To insert a Word outline:

1. Click the slide (in the outline pane) that the Word outline is to follow.

2. Click the Insert menu and click Slides from Outline.

3. Locate the desired Word outline and click the Insert button.

4. Navigate to your Student Data Disk files, if necessary.

The Word outline, also named ***Write This Way***, is selected. Your presentation files do not show because the Files of type option automatically changed from All PowerPoint Presentations to All Outlines when you clicked Slides from Outline on the Insert menu.

5. Click the Insert button.

The Word file opens into PowerPoint, adding five slides to your presentation.

 If the import feature is not available, see your instructor.

6. Navigate the presentation in Slide View beginning with slide 1.

7. Save the changes to your presentation.

Formatting Text

When formatting text, three main attributes are involved: the font, the font size, and the font color. A ***font*** is a set of named characters of one design. In the open presentation, for example, text on slide 1 is a font named Times New Roman, while another is a font named Arial. PowerPoint offers dozens of other fonts. The fonts available to you, though, depend upon the printer you are using. Some fonts—like Times New Roman—are ideal for subtitles. Times New Roman is also ideal for paragraphs because this font is a *serif* font. That is, the characters have *feet* that form a straight line, guiding readers' eyes from left to right. A font *without feet*—Arial, for example—is better for titles and labels. These fonts are called *sans serif.*

In PowerPoint, characters vary in *font size* (sometimes called point size) according to the outline levels. Titles are largest—44 points is a common title size. Level 1 subtitles are larger than level 2 subtitles and so on. If first-level subtitles are 32 points, for example, second-level subtitles may be 28 points, and third-level subtitles may be 24 points. As a general rule, no subtitles should be smaller than 18 points. (Special text, such as footers and labels on pictures and charts, may be much smaller.)

The automatic font color depends on the template design. Font colors are chosen to contrast with the background color. Sometimes you may want to vary from the template by using a different font color on one slide. When you create a blank presentation, the automatic font color is black on a white background. In that case, you would need to apply a background color. If you choose a dark background, you would change the font color for adequate contrast.

After formatting some text in a presentation, you can use the Format Painter to change other text to match. Select the changed text and click the Format Painter; then brush over the other, unchanged text to match.

Formatting also involves special effects and alignment. Special effects include bold, italic, underline, and text shadow. *Bold* is a thick, heavy effect applied to text for emphasis. *Italic* is a thin, right-slanted effect—also applied for emphasis. *Underline,* a line under an occasional word or phrase, is another way to emphasize text. Text *shadow* is a decorative effect—a way to add appeal. The key to using bold, italic, and underline is not using them too much—so they continue to be special. Use the text shadow only on slide titles with very large characters.

Changing the Font and Adding Special Effects

In this activity, you will format text in the current presentation and apply italic, bold, and underline.

1. Switch to Normal View and select the slide title on slide 1 in the outline pane.

You now see the presentation in tri-pane view with the slide title highlighted in the outline pane.

2. On the Formatting toolbar, click the Font drop-down arrow `Times New Roman ▾`.

The Font list box displays, as shown in Figure 2.5. The recently used fonts display at the top of the list. The additional fonts appear below the recently used fonts, in alphabetical order.

3. Click the Arial font located at the top of the list.

PowerPoint applies the Arial font to the slide title, and the text remains selected.

Figure 2.5
The Font list box

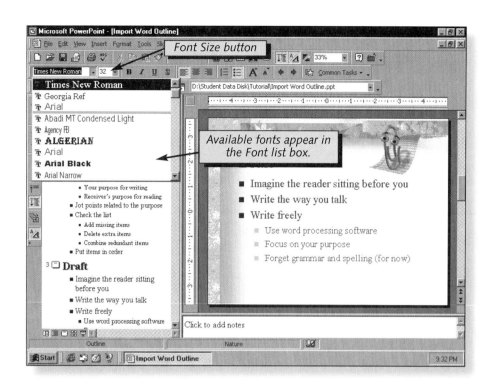

Changing Font Attributes

To change font style:

1. Select the text to change.

2. Click the Font drop-down arrow.

3. Select the desired font.

To change font size:

1. Select the text to change.

2. Click the Increase Font Size button or Decrease Font Size button.

Or

Click the Font Size drop-down arrow and click the desired font.

To change font color:

1. Select the text to change.

2. Click the Font Color button.

To use the Format Painter:

1. Select the formatted text.

2. Click the Format Painter button.

3. Select the text to change.

4. Deselect the changed text.

4. Select the subtitle on slide 1 and change the font to Arial. Then navigate to slide 2 and change the slide title to Arial.

The text changes to Arial and remains selected.

5. On the Standard toolbar, click the Format Painter button ☑. Then scroll to slide 3 and select the slide title.

PowerPoint copies the font information from the slide 2 title text and paints the slide 3 title text to match.

6. Select the slide 3 title and double-click the Format Painter button ☑. Scroll to slide 4 and select the slide title. Then scroll to slide 5 and select the slide title. Change the slide 6 title to match the others. Finally, click the Format Painter button ☑ to turn off the feature.

Now, each of the titles in your presentation uses the Arial font. By double-clicking the Format Painter button ☑, you were able to copy the font information from the slide 3 selected title to the titles on slides 4, 5, and 6.

7. Scroll to slide 5, on which the last line of text is below the edge of the slide.

8. Select the first group of level 2 subtitles. On the Formatting toolbar, click the Decrease Font Size button ☑.

The 24-point subtitles become 20-point subtitles. Clicking the Decrease Font Size button ☑ reduced the selected text to the next lowest size shown in the Font Size list box.

9. Select the second group of level 2 subtitles. Click the Font Size drop-down arrow 24 ☑ and click 20.

These subtitles are reduced from 24 points to 20 points—and now fit the text placeholder.

10. Scroll to slide 1 and select the title.

The number 44 shows in the Font Size list box.

11. Click the **Font Size drop-down arrow** 24 ▾, click the **list box**, and type 50. Then press Enter⏎.

The font size 50 does not automatically appear in the Font Size list box. However, PowerPoint accepts manual entry and changed the font from 44 to 50 points.

12. Select the subtitle. On the Formatting toolbar, click the **Increase Font Size button** A̅.

The subtitle changes from 32 points to 36 points, and may cause a word to wrap to the next line, as shown in Figure 2.6.

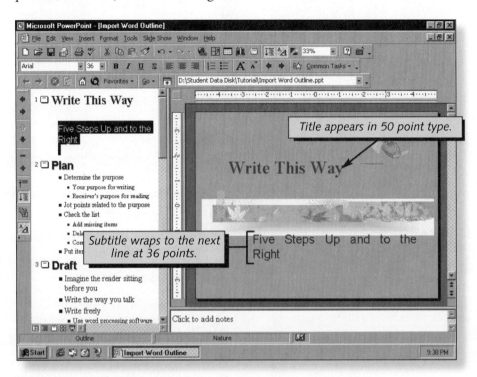

Figure 2.6
Text wrapping

13. With the subtitle still selected, click in the **Font Size box** 24 ▾ and type 34. Then press Enter⏎.

Once again, PowerPoint accepts the manual entry and changes the font size. The subtitle now fits on one line.

14. Click **View** on the menu bar, point to **Toolbars**, and click **Drawing** if a check mark does not appear before the toolbar name.

The Drawing toolbar displays across the bottom of the PowerPoint window.

15. Navigate to slide 3 and select the slide title. On the Drawing toolbar, click the **Font Color drop-down arrow** A̲ ▾.

The Font Color toolbar appears. The colors of the Nature template are shown. More colors are available by clicking More Font Colors.

16. Click the **gold sample**.

The font color changes from black to gold.

17. Scroll to slide 3. Right-click the slide in the lower-right corner, outside the text placeholders. On the shortcut menu, click **Background**.

The Background dialog box appears, as shown in Figure 2.7.

Figure 2.7
The Background dialog box

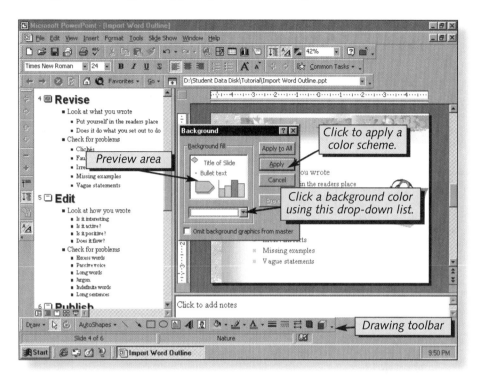

Adding Special Effects

To add the bold effect:

1. Select the text to change.

2. Click the Bold button.

To add the italic effect:

1. Select the text to change.

2. Click the Italic button.

To add the underline effect:

1. Select the text to change.

2. Click the Underline button.

To add the shadow effect:

1. Select the text to change.

2. Click the Text Shadow button.

18. In the Background dialog box, click the **Color sample drop-down arrow**, click the **olive sample**, and click **Apply**. Then save your changes.

The background of this slide changes to olive and is different from the other slide background colors in this presentation.

19. Navigate to slide 4, select the level 1 subtitles, and click the **Bold button** 🅱 on the Formatting toolbar.

PowerPoint adds bold to the selected text.

20. In the first subtitle, select the word *what.* On the Formatting toolbar, click the **Italic button** *I*.

PowerPoint changes the selected text from normal to italic, and the text remains selected.

21. Navigate to the Title slide. In the title, select *This.* On the Formatting toolbar, click the **Underline button** U.

PowerPoint underlines the word *This* in the title.

22. Switch to Slide Sorter View, change the magnification rate to 100%, save your changes, and close the file.

Changing Designs and Layouts

PowerPoint offers flexibility as you create your presentations. After you select a design template, for example, you can change this design, if desired, during development. Likewise, if you see that a different layout would work better for a particular slide, you can change that, too.

On more than one occasion you have clicked New on the File menu to select a design template for a new presentation. What if you chose a bright design, such as Citrus with its orange, bright green, and hot pink color scheme—and then you find out that you are expected to give a lecture-style presentation to a conservative audience. You certainly do not want to start over, but you surely would like to have a more modest design template. The Formatting toolbar contains a Common Tasks button [Common Tasks ▾] that holds a solution to your dilemma—an Apply Design Template command 🖹. When you click this command button, the list of design templates opens. As soon as you select and apply a new template, your presentation takes on a whole new look.

Each time you add a slide, you try to select an AutoLayout with the right kind of placeholders. As you develop the information, though, you may find that two text columns would look better than one; or perhaps a clip would be better than the graph you planned initially. You can use the Slide Layout command 🖾 on the Standard toolbar or on the Common Tasks menu. The text and object on your original slide appear automatically in the new layout. You may have to move objects, cut and paste text, or delete a text placeholder to complete the change.

Changing the Design Template and Slide Layouts

In this activity, you will open a file on your Student Data Disk. You will change the look of the presentation and select a different layout for a slide.

1. **Open *Rainfall* on your Student Data Disk and save the file as *Common Tasks* in the *Tutorial* folder. In the status bar, note the name of the design template on which this presentation is based—Japanese Waves. Then switch to Slide Sorter View to get an overall impression of the presentation.**

The presentation opens in Slide Sorter View, and the Slide Sorter toolbar displays.

2. **Click the Common Tasks button [Common Tasks ▾]. Then click Apply Design Template 🖹.**

The Apply Design Template dialog box displays. Notice this dialog box is similar to the New Presentation dialog box.

3. **Click Whirlpool to preview the design, and then click the Apply button.**

The new design is applied to every slide, and *Whirlpool* appears in the status bar.

4. **Select slide 7 and switch to Normal View. Click the Common Tasks button [Common Tasks ▾] and click Slide Layout 🖾. Click the 2 Column Text and click Apply.**

The new layout appears, with two text placeholders, but all the text remains in the text placeholder on the left.

5. **Cut the last three subtitles to the Clipboard. Then click the right-hand placeholder and paste the items there, as shown in Figure 2.8.**

6. **Save and close the presentation.**

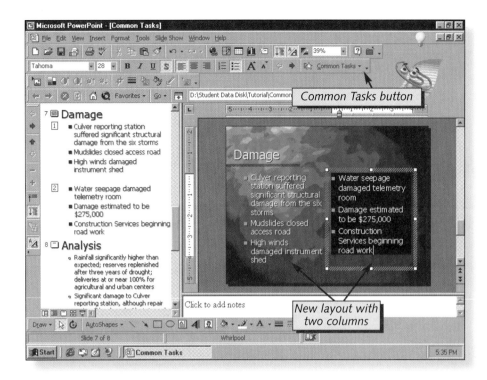

INSERTING CLIP ART

To maintain the attention of an audience, you will want to add more than text to your presentations. A quick way to emphasize a slide and add variety to your presentation is to use clip art. *Clip art* are ready-to-use graphic images that are installed with PowerPoint. The clips are stored in a special folder called the Clip Gallery. After you insert a graphic from the Clip Gallery, you can adjust the size and scale of the object.

Insert Clips With and Without a Placeholder

The fastest way to add clip art if you are creating a new presentation or adding slides to an existing presentation is to click one of the AutoLayouts in the New Slide dialog box that features a clip art placeholder. Double-clicking that placeholder opens the Clip Gallery. Once you select a picture, another click inserts the clip into your presentation. You can also add clip art to any slide that has adequate space by using the Insert Clip Art button 🔲; a slide does not need to have a clip art placeholder.

Inserting Clips

In this activity, you will reopen the *Transportation Projects* file and add a slide, using an AutoLayout that contains a clip art placeholder. You also will add a clip to the Title slide (no clip art placeholder).

1. **Open *Transportation Projects* in the *Tutorial* folder on your Student Data Disk and scroll to slide 2.**

Adding Clip Art

To add clip art with a placeholder:

1. Double-click the clip art icon.

2. Click the desired clip art category.

3. Click a picture and Preview Clip.

4. Click Insert Clip and the Close box.

To add clip art without a placeholder:

1. Click the Clip Art button.

2. Click the desired clip art category.

3. Click a picture and Preview Clip.

4. Click Insert Clip and the Close box.

Figure 2.9 ◀
The Microsoft Clip Gallery

The Transportation Projects presentation opens in tri-pane view.

2. On the Standard toolbar, click the New Slide button 🔲.

The New Slide dialog box opens.

3. Click the Text & Clip Art autolayout and click OK to add the new slide.

PowerPoint inserts the new slide immediately following slide 2.

4. In Slide View, click the slide title placeholder text and type Our Strengths **as the slide 3 title.**

The new text replaces the slide title placeholder text.

5. Click the subtitle placeholder text and type Industry leader in medium-size construction. **Then press** Enter⏎. **Then type** State-of-the-art project controls technology.

6. Double-click the clip art placeholder.

If you receive a message about additional clip art on the Microsoft Office CD-ROM, click OK. The Microsoft Clip Gallery dialog box opens, as shown in Figure 2.9.

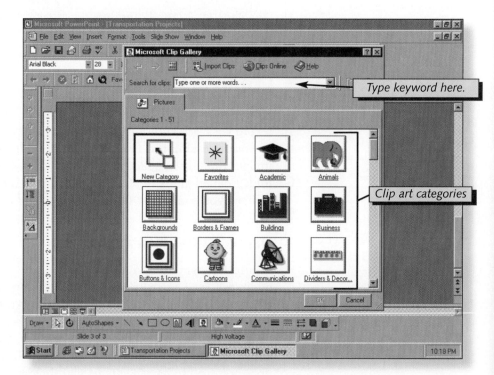

 *The categories and pictures in Microsoft Clip Gallery may vary on your computer from those displayed in Figure 2.9, depending on what has been imported or deleted by other users of the computer you are using.*

7. Scroll the list of categories and click the People at Work icon.

8. Scroll to find and select an icon of a steel beam.

If you do not find this clip in the displayed frame, click Keep Looking to search the next frame. Select a clip that you think represents *Our Strengths*.

9. Click the Insert Clip button 🔳.

The picture replaces the clip art placeholder, and the Picture toolbar displays. The Picture toolbar displays when a clip is inserted, or whenever you double-click existing clip art. You will use this toolbar to change the size and other attributes of the clip.

10. **Click the area surrounding the slide to deselect the placeholder.**

The box and white square around the clip disappear, showing that the clip is not selected.

11. **Using the Save As command, save the file in the *Tutorial* folder on your Student Data Disk by adding *with Clips* to the current file name.**

12. **Go to slide 1 and click the blank area below *Transportation Projects.* On the Drawing toolbar, click the Insert Clip Art button 🖼.**

PowerPoint opens the Clip Gallery.

13. **Click the Transportation category icon; then click the traffic light icon.**

If this frame does not contain a traffic light picture, search the next frame. If you do not find this particular clip, click another suitable image.

14. **Click the Insert Clip button 🖼 and close the dialog box. Then save the changes.**

The clip art inserts in the middle of the slide, as shown in Figure 2.10.

**Another Way**

To insert clip art without a placeholder, click Insert on the menu bar, click Picture, and then click Clip Art.

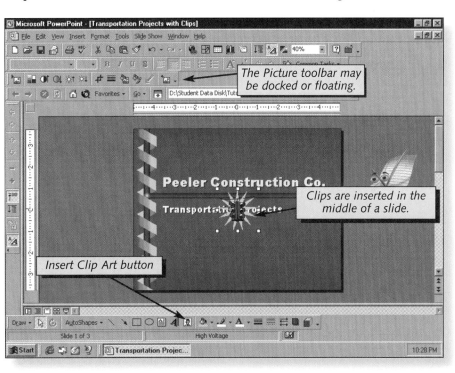

Figure 2.10
Clip art inserted without a clip art placeholder

Scaling and Sizing Objects

You can resize clip art in two ways. You can use the *sizing handles* (small white squares) surrounding the clip art. Drag the upper-left handle up and left to enlarge and down and right to reduce the size of the picture. In this process, the pointer first becomes a two-way arrow; then it changes to the crosshair pointer. Dragging the crosshair pointer up and left or down and right changes the height and width proportionately. Changing height in the same ratio as width prevents distortion of the image.

Another Way

To access the Format Picture dialog box, right-click the image and click Format Picture on the shortcut menu.

Another way to resize clip art is to use the Format Picture button 🖼️ on the Picture toolbar. The Format Picture dialog box includes a Size tab. Using this tab, you can change height and/or width in separate list boxes. To change height and width proportionately using this method, you must lock the *aspect ratio,* which refers to the height of the image in relation to the width. You lock the aspect ratio by selecting a check box. With the aspect ratio locked, you specify either the height or the width; the other dimension will be changed accordingly. If the aspect ratio is not locked when you change height or width, the image may be distorted.

You can move clips by dragging and by using cut and paste. However, using cut and paste to move clip art is not always the most effective means because precision pasting is not always possible. Place clip art at least 0.25" from the slide edges. You can apply the procedures for resizing and moving clip art to other graphical elements, such as objects, shapes, tables, and graphs.

Resizing and Moving Graphics

To resize a clip (sizing handles method):

1. Select the clip; point to the upper-left sizing handle.

2. Click the two-way pointer.

3. Drag the crosshair up to the left to enlarge the image or down to the right to reduce the image.

To move a clip:

1. Point to the picture (deselected).

2. Click and drag the four-way pointer.

3. Drop the clip in the desired location.

Resizing and Moving a Clip

In this activity, you will enlarge and move the clip on slide 1 of your presentation.

1. Verify that the clip art is selected on slide 1.

Handles appear around the clip art.

2. Click the Format Picture button 🖼️ on the Picture toolbar.

The Format Picture dialog box displays.

3. Click the Size tab. Verify that a check mark appears before the Lock aspect ratio option, as shown in Figure 2.11.

4. In the Size and rotate section, click the Height list box and type 2.5. Click OK and deselect the image.

PowerPoint increases the image size according to the instructions in the Height list box and adjusts the width proportionately.

5. Point to the clip.

The pointer changes to a four-way arrow.

6. Drag and drop the clip to the lower-right corner of the slide.

If you make a mistake, remember to click the Undo button 🔄. Then repeat steps 5 and 6 to place the clip art properly.

7. On slide 3, select the clip and point to the sizing handle in the upper-left corner. When the two-way pointer appears, click and drag the crosshair until the sizing handle is across from the words *medium-size.* Deselect the clip.

The clip has now changed in size.

8. Drag and drop the clip to the lower-right corner, at least 0.25" from the right and bottom edges. Then save your changes and close the file.

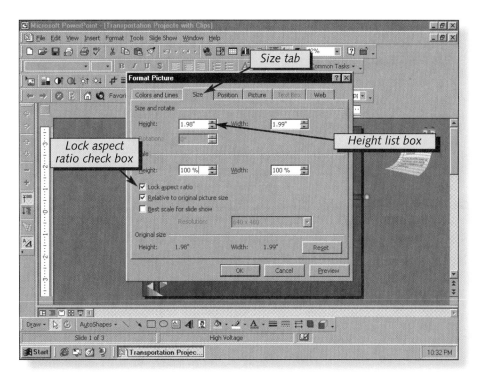

Figure 2.11
Format Picture dialog box

USING THE SLIDE MASTER TO CHANGE FORMATTING

Using the Slide Master, you will learn how to customize a presentation. A *master* is a special slide that includes a collection of placeholders for text and objects. The master allows you to change a slide in one place and reflect that change throughout a presentation.

The Slide Master lets you standardize the changes you make to a design template. All slides based on that master reflect the custom changes. Also, a Slide Master can incorporate custom repeating elements that occur in exactly the same location. For example, you can place a company name or logo on the Slide Master and that logo will appear on every slide. When you change the Slide Master, however, those changes do not affect the Title slide. The Title slide has a separate master, the *title master,* which controls the appearance of the title slide.

Every presentation has a Slide Master, a Title Master, a Handout Master, and a Notes Master. The Slide Master is actually another view. To display the Slide Master, you first press ⇧ Shift. Then the Slide View button □ becomes the Slide Master View button □. Clicking this button opens the Slide Master. When you open the Slide Master, text placeholders and sample text are visible, even if the Slide View contains actual text.

To make a change to the Slide Master, you first need to display it. One example of a change you can make to the Slide Master is to change the line spacing. You may want to do this if text looks too crowded on the slides in your presentation. To change line spacing, click inside a placeholder and click Line Spacing on the Format menu. In the Line Spacing dialog box, you can adjust line spacing before a paragraph, within a paragraph, and after a paragraph. Simply click the up and down arrows in each box, or enter a number in the boxes manually.

PowerPoint 2000 opens files created by other presentation programs; namely, Harvard Graphics and Lotus Freelance. PowerPoint's converter preserves much of the original content and formatting of these presentation types.

Changing Fonts and Bullets for an Entire Presentation

Sometimes you may like one of PowerPoint's design templates, but prefer a slightly different style for certain elements. Using the Slide Master, you can change font style, size, and/or color for all slides at once, instead of changing each slide individually.

Even though design templates include bullets for each subtitle level, you may want a different bullet design. In addition to the seven styles available in the Bullets and Numbering dialog box (on the Format menu), you can select bullet characters from a large number of symbols and icons called *Wingdings.* The Clip Gallery also contains a number of tiny pictures that you can insert as bullets.

Or, perhaps you prefer to make the bullets larger or smaller or a different color to enhance the presentation. Using the Slide Master, you can globally change the color and size of all the bullets in your presentation. In the Bullets and Numbering dialog box, you can select from PowerPoint's template colors, or you can select a color from the standard color chart. Bullet size is measured as a percentage of text size. The percentage may range from 25% (one-fourth the size of text) to 400% (four times the size of text). Bullet sizes of 50% and 100% are common.

Sometimes the text appears too close to the bullets, especially if you enlarge the bullets. In the Slide Master, you can increase (or decrease) the distance between the bullets and text for all subtitle levels at one time.

The Slide Master shows the effect of your work, but you cannot scroll an entire presentation while in Slide Master View. Therefore, a better way to review changes made in the Slide Master is to scroll the presentation in Slide View.

Using the Slide Master to Change Fonts

Peeler Construction has created a nine-slide presentation to explain the employee benefits. In this activity, you will open the **Benefits** presentation and display this presentation in Slide Master View. Then you'll make font changes to the entire presentation.

1. **Open *Benefits* on your Student Data Disk and save the presentation as *Benefits Customized* in the *Tutorial* folder.**

The presentation appears on the screen in Slide Sorter View.

2. **Double-click slide 2.**

PowerPoint changes to Slide View with slide 2 displayed.

3. **Click the title and look at the font shown in the Font list box** Times New Roman ▾ **. Then check the subtitle font. Next, navigate to slide 8 and check the title and subtitle font.**

The title font is Times New Roman; the subtitle font is Arial.

4. **Press** ⬆ Shift **and point to the Slide View button** ▭ **.**

The ScreenTip reveals a new name for the button.

5. **Press** ⬆ Shift **and click the Slide Master View button** ▭ **.**

The Slide Master for this presentation appears, as shown in Figure 2.12.

Figure 2.12
A Slide Master

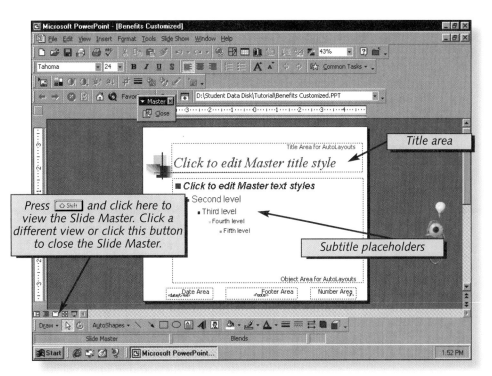

A Slide Master

Using the Slide Master

To display the Slide Master:

1. Press `⇧ Shift`.

2. Click the Slide (Master) View button.

Or

Click the View menu, point to the Master submenu, and then click Slide Master.

To change fonts in an entire presentation:

1. Select the placeholder text to change.

2. Click the desired font.

3. Click the desired special effects.

4. Click the Slide View button and verify the changes.

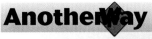

To change fonts, click the Format menu and click Replace Fonts. In the Replace Fonts dialog box, identify the font you want to replace, select a replacement font, and then click Replace.

6. Click the title placeholder text. On the Formatting toolbar, click the **Font drop-down arrow** `Times New Roman ▼`. Then click **Arial Narrow**. With the title area still selected, click the **Italic button** `I` to eliminate the italic effect. Now, click the area surrounding the slide.

The title placeholder text, *Click to edit Master title slide,* displays the style changes you made.

7. Click the bullet at the first-level subtitle to select all five subtitle levels.

8. Click the Font drop-down arrow `Times New Roman ▼` **and change the font to Times New Roman.** Then remove the italic effect and click the area surrounding the slide.

All text in the object area changes font. The text in the title area does not.

> *Note*  *Use one style for all subtitle levels. Different font sizes and indents distinguish the levels.*

9. Click the Slide View button `▢` **to close the Slide Master and display slide 8 in Slide View.**

10. Scroll to slide 6 and click the slide title; read the name of the font. (You changed the font to Arial Narrow.) **Click the subtitle text** and read the name of the font. (You changed the font to Times New Roman.)

11. Navigate to slide 3 and check the title and subtitle fonts. Click the area surrounding the slide. Then save the changes to the file.

All slides reflect the changes made in the Slide Master.

ADDING HEADERS AND FOOTERS

You can use the Slide Master to create text and objects that repeat in exactly the same location on every slide. Repeating elements are called **background items.** The Slide Master View includes placeholders below the object area that may be used as a **footer,** repeated text at the bottom of every slide. By default, the footer includes three parts: date area, footer area, and number area. To insert or change the information in any of these areas, use the Header and Footer dialog box from the View menu.

You can also add both **headers** and footers to outline pages. Header text appears at the top of each page. To do this, use the Header and Footer dialog box from the View menu, and click the Notes and Handouts Sheet tab. The header and footer information you enter there will display when you print pages in Outline View; it will not display on slides in your presentation.

Adding Headers and Footers

The company name, Peeler Construction, must appear in the footer area on every slide in the **Benefits Customized** presentation. In addition, each slide must show the presentation date and the slide number. In this activity, while in Slide View, you will open the Header and Footer dialog box and insert all three repeating elements at once. You'll also add a header and footer to outline pages.

Adding Headers and Footers

1. Click the View menu and click Header and Footer.

2. Click the Date and time check box.

3. Click the Update automatically button, if desired; click a date style in the list box.

4. Click the Slide number check box and the Don't show on title slide check box.

5. Click the Apply to All button.

1. In the **Benefits Customized** presentation, click **View** on the menu bar and click **Header and Footer**.

The Header and Footer dialog box appears, as shown in Figure 2.13.

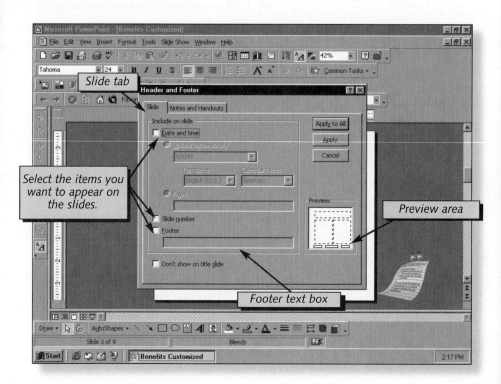

Figure 2.13
The Header and Footer dialog box

2. On the Slide tab, click the **Date and time check box** and the **Update automatically option**.

The current date will be displayed each time you show the presentation from a computer.

3. Click the **Update automatically drop-down arrow** and select this date style: *January 9, 2001*.

4. Then click the **Slide number check box** and the **Footer check box**. Type Peeler Construction in the Footer text box.

5. Click the **Don't show on title slide** check box.

6. Finally, click the **Apply to All button**.

The Header and Footer dialog box closes.

7. Scroll to slide 9, noting the footer on each slide.

8. Switch to Outline view.

9. Click **View** on the menu bar and click **Header and Footer**.

10. In the Header and Footer dialog box, click the **Notes and Handouts tab**.

11. Click the **Date and time check box** and the **Update automatically option**.

12. Click **Header**. In the Header text box, type Benefits with Header and Footer.

13. Click the **Page number check box** and click **Apply to All**.

14. Click **Print** on the File menu. In the Print what area of the Print dialog box, click **Outline View**. Then click **OK**.

Notice that the header you entered appears at the top of the page, and the date and page number appear at the bottom of the page.

15. Save your file as *Benefits with Header and Footer* in the *Tutorial* folder, and close the presentation.

ANIMATING PRESENTATIONS

As computer projection replaces traditional slide shows, presenters increasingly add *multimedia* effects to their presentations. For example, PowerPoint includes tools for adding motion to slides and lets you import photographs, movies, music, and voice clips. You will learn about the motion (*animation*) effects available in PowerPoint, which help information flow and audiences to focus. Both text and objects, such as clip art, can be animated.

Applying Slide Transitions

A *transition,* an eye-catching way to move from slide to slide, determines how one slide replaces another. PowerPoint has 42 different slide transitions. Transition effects have descriptive names such as: *Fly From Bottom, Checkerboard Across, Peek From Top, Stretch From Left, Swivel,* and *Zoom In.* Transition effects are applied in Slide Sorter View; they can be previewed there, too. A transition symbol appears under a slide when an effect is applied to it. Clicking the symbol gives you a general idea of the transition. Of course, you can see the full effect only in Slide Show. When you run a slide show that contains transition effects, PowerPoint displays the transition effect when you click to move to the next slide. In developing a presentation, you may apply a transition to one or two slides or a different transition to each slide. Transitions, though, like any other special effects, lose their ability to grab attention if overused. Therefore, your presentation plan should identify only a few slides to carry a transition.

Inserting WordArt

In this activity, you will search Help for information about WordArt.

1. Open *Congratulations* on your Student Data Disk and save the file as *WordArt* in your *Tutorial* folder. Click the **New Slide button** 🖫 and add a blank slide.

2. Click the **Office Assistant** and type the keywords insert WordArt. Find answers to these WordArt questions: Is WordArt text or an object, like clip art? How do you insert WordArt? How do you edit WordArt?

3. Click the **Insert WordArt button** 🖪 on the Drawing toolbar.

4. In the WordArt Gallery, click the **multicolored sample** (fourth square in the third row) and click **OK**.

5. In the Edit WordArt Text dialog box, type Congratulations! and click **OK**.

Your WordArt object and the WordArt toolbar appear (Figure 2.14). Sizing handles surround the selected object.

6. Drag the WordArt until the left and right edges read 3.5" on the horizontal ruler, the top reads 2" on the vertical ruler, and the bottom reads 2.5".

Figure 2.14
WordArt object and toolbar

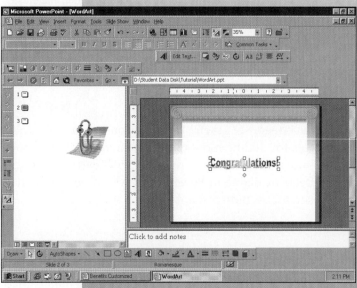

7. Click the **WordArt Character Spacing button** 🖾 and click **Loose** to add space between characters.

8. Click the **WordArt Shape button** 🖾. In the WordArt Shape dialog box, click the **Wave 1 option** and deselect the object.

9. Click the WordArt object to display the toolbar again and click the **WordArt Edit Text button** [Edit Text...]. In the Font list box, change the font to Times New Roman and apply the bold effect.

10. Right-click the bottom edge of the slide and click **Background**. Change the slide background to black. Then save your changes and close this file.

HANDS ON

Applying and Previewing Transitions

To apply a transition to one slide:

1. Select a slide and click the Slide Transition button.

2. Select an effect from the list box, and select a transition speed option.

3. Click the Apply button.

4. To preview the effect, click the transition symbol.

To apply the same transition to all slides:

1. Click the Slide Transition button.

2. Select an effect from the list box, and select a transition speed option.

3. Click the Apply to All button.

4. To preview the effect, click a transition symbol.

Figure 2.15
The Slide Transition dialog box

Applying Transition Effects

In this activity, you will open and enhance a presentation by adding transition effects.

1. Open *Moving* on your Student Data Disk and save the file as *Transition* in the *Tutorial* folder. Switch to Slide Sorter View.

The Slide Sorter toolbar displays.

2. Click **slide 3** and click the **Slide Transition button** .

The Slide Transition dialog box appears, as shown in Figure 2.15.

3. Click the **Effect drop-down arrow**, click the **Blinds Horizontal transition**, and preview the effect by clicking the preview area.

> *Note* *Transition speed may be set for Slow, Medium, or Fast. Also, a sound effect list box allows you to apply a sound to accompany a visual effect.*

4. Click the **Apply button** to add the transition to slide 3 only.

The transition is applied to the slide, and a transition symbol appears in the lower-left corner of the slide.

5. Click the **transition symbol** to preview the Blinds Horizontal effect again.

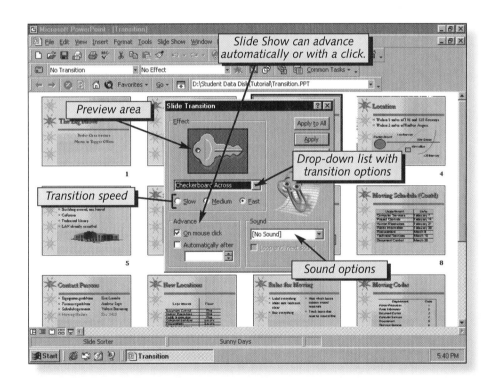

6. Select **slide 8**, click the **Slide Transition button** 🖼, and then click **Checkerboard Across**. Change the transition speed to **Medium** and apply the effect. Preview the transition by clicking the transition symbol.

7. Click the **Slide Transition button** 🖼; select the **Cover Right-Down transition**; change the transition speed to **Slow**; and click the **Apply to All button**.

Each slide now has a transition symbol, as shown in Figure 2.16.

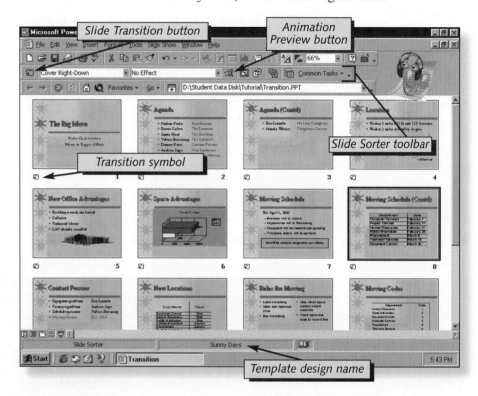

Figure 2.16 ◄
Transition effect applied
to an entire presentation

8. Click the **Edit menu** and click **Select All** to select all of the slides. On the Slide Sorter toolbar, click the **Animation Preview button** 🔆.

You have decided to eliminate the transition effect on slides 1, 4, 9, 10, and 14.

9. Click anywhere between two slides to deselect all of the slides. Select **slide 1** and then hold `Ctrl` while you click slides 4, 9, 10, and 14.

10. With slides 1, 4, 9, 10, and 14 selected, click the **Slide Transitions Effects drop-down arrow** `No Transition ▾` and click **No Transition**.

The transition symbol disappears from the selected slides.

11. Again, select all slides and click the **Animation Preview button** 🔆 to observe the transition effects.

12. Preview the slide show. Then save the revised presentation and close the file.

Applying Builds and Animating Clip Art

An effect called ***build text*** is an interesting way to move from subtitle to subtitle within a slide. With build text, text appears on a slide one portion at a time. You can add build text to one slide or to an entire presentation in Slide Sorter View. Many build effects have the same name as the transition effects, but you select builds from the Preset Animation list box. Besides building text, you can create interesting effects using ***build objects.*** As you might guess, build objects are graphics that appear in succession, rather than all at once. This work must be done in Slide View or Normal View. The Preset Animation command on the Slide Show menu contains some of the same animation effects as the Preset Animation list box used for build text.

In Slide Sorter View, a build icon appears under slides that contain build text or build objects. You can preview these animation effects by clicking the icon or by clicking the Animation Preview button 🔲 on the Slide Sorter toolbar. Of course, you can change any build, or eliminate it by choosing No Effect in the list box. When you review a presentation in Slide Show, the build effects require extra clicks. A slide containing three subtitles with text builds, for example, takes four clicks: one to advance to the slide and one to display each animated subtitle. Likewise, you would click the screen to display each build object. PowerPoint provides a timer option for displaying builds automatically during an actual slide show.

You can animate clip art in much the same way as you animate text. You can select an animation option from the Preset Animation list, or you can select animation options in the Custom Animation dialog box.

Animating Text and Objects

In this activity, you will open the ***Photo*** presentation and add animation effects to text, objects, and clip art.

1. **Open *Photo* on your Student Data disk and save the file as *Builds* in the *Tutorial* folder. In Slide Sorter View, select slides 5 and 6, to which you will add build text.**

2. **On the Slide Sorter toolbar, click the Preset Animation drop-down arrow**
No Effect **and select the Crawl From Right effect. Then watch as each subtitle crawls into place.**

When all subtitles appear, a build icon appears under the slide.

You will add text builds to slides 1 through 4. (Slides 5 and 6 already have special effects.) Then you will add a transition effect to all slides.

BASICS

Adding Text and Object Builds

To add text builds:

1. Select a slide and click the Preset Animation drop-down arrow.

2. Select the desired build effect and watch the selected slide.

3. To preview the effect, click the build icon.

To add object builds:

1. Select the object.

2. Click the Slide Show menu and click Preset Animation.

3. Click the desired build effect.

4. To preview the effect, click the build icon.

To become familiar with animation procedures, you are adding more effects than desirable in most cases. For presentations you make in school or business, animate selectively.

3. Select **slides 1–4** and click the **Preset Animation drop-down arrow**. Click **Dissolve**.

A build icon appears under each of the selected slides.

4. Click the **Animation Preview button** 🟦 to see the Dissolve effect on each selected slide.

5. Select **slides 1, 3, and 5**. In the Slide Transition Effects list box
`No Transition ▾`, select **Box In**. Then select **slides 2, 4, and 6** and apply the **Box Out transition**.

A build icon and transition symbol appear under each slide, as shown in Figure 2.17.

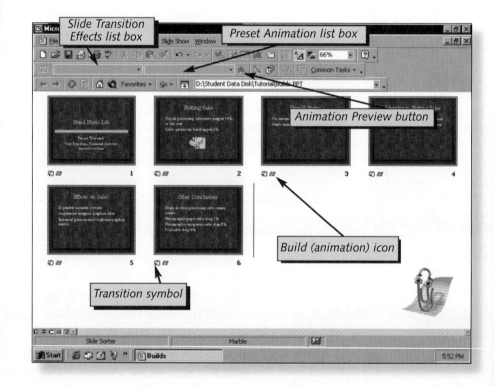

Figure 2.17 ◄
A build icon and transition symbol under each slide

6. Press ⟦F5⟧ and view the presentation in Slide Show View. Click the screen to run through the entire presentation, noting each transition and build.

7. Select **slides 1 and 4**. Click the **Preset Animation drop-down arrow** [No Effect ▾] and select **No Effect**.

8. Switch to Normal View, scroll to slide 2, and click the clip art.

9. Click **Preset Animation** from the Slide Show menu and select **Drive-In**.

The clip art will now be animated, along with the text on the slides.

10. View the presentation in Slide Show again, but focus this time on the *flow* of information. Then save and close the presentation.

Test your knowledge by matching the terms at the left with the definitions at the right. See Appendix B to check your answers.

TERMS	DEFINITIONS
1. AutoLayouts	**a. Collection of designs that can be applied to a presentation**
2. title master	**b. Space on a slide reserved for text or a graphic**
3. unfilled object	**c. An empty placeholder**
4. placeholder	**d. Controls the appearance of the title slide**
5. template	**e. Collection of formatted slides**

ON*the*WEB

PREVIEWING, CREATING, AND PUBLISHING WEB PAGES

You can save a PowerPoint presentation as a Web page without changing the way you work with the presentation in PowerPoint. If you use the AutoContent Wizard to create a presentation, you can select *Web Page* as the desired form of output. You can then preview your Web pages in the Microsoft Explorer browser.

For all the world—or even a few fellow students or coworkers—to see your Web presentations, you need to ***publish*** them. Publishing a presentation involves storing the Web page on a ***server*** that has a permanent connection to the Web or your school's intranet. Most people do not have their own Web server, so they choose to upload their page(s) to the Web server provided by their Internet service provider. Each Internet service provider charges a different fee (if any) and requires a different process to publish your page. Contact the ***sysadmin*** (system or network administrator) at your school to learn how to upload your Web presentation to a server, for publishing on the Internet or your intranet. For others to read a Web page you publish, they must know about it. Whatever methods you choose to publicize a Web page, the key to obtaining readers who will return regularly is to provide interesting, informative, accurate, up-to-date information on the page. Consider these methods to publicize a page on the World Wide Web:

■ Exchange links with other Web page owners.

■ Announce a new page at ***newsgroup*** (discussion group, forum, or chat group) sites.

■ Advertise in banners (long, narrow ad strips that scroll and blink at the top of many home pages).

■ Register your page with search engines or subject directories.

In this activity, you will display a presentation using the Microsoft Explorer browser.

   1. Open *Moving* on your Student Data Disk. Then click the File menu and click Web Page Preview.

The Explorer window appears.

   2. Maximize the browser window, shown in Figure 2.18.

The slide titles appear automatically as hyperlinks in the scrollable frame at the left. Now you will navigate the presentation and use other previewing features on the browser.

   3. Click the Moving Schedule hyperlink in the outline pane, which the status bar indicates is slide 7 of 14. Click the Next Slide button below the browser window; then click the Previous Slide button. Scroll to the *Moving Codes* title.

   4. Click the Full-Screen Slide Show button—the show begins with the Title slide—and click the screen to advance three slides. Then press ⌈Esc⌋ to exit the full-screen show.

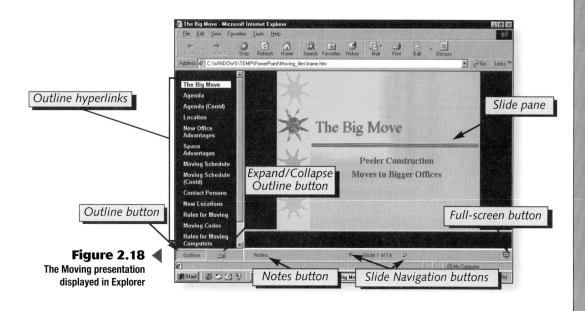

Figure 2.18 ◀
The Moving presentation
displayed in Explorer

5. Click the **Notes button** to hide the notes pane. Click the **Expand/Collapse Outline button** to see subtitles along with slide titles in the outline pane. Next, click the **Outline button** to hide the outline altogether.

6. Now display the outline and collapse it. Scroll to the *Agenda* title, jump to the slide, and display the notes pane.

7. Close your browser.

8. In PowerPoint, click the **File menu** and click **Save as Web Page**.

9. Click the **Change Title button** to open the Set Page Title dialog box. Type The Big Move **for the title.**

Visitors to the page will see this title in the title bar of their browsers. The Title slide will be unchanged.

10. Save the file as *Moving Web Page* in the *Tutorial* folder on your Student Data Disk. Close the presentation.

Now you will learn a different way to open the file in Explorer.

11. On the Standard toolbar, click the **Open button** 📂. In the Open dialog box, click *Moving Web Page.* Click the **Open button drop-down arrow** and click **Open in Browser**.

12. Maximize the browser and navigate to four slides by clicking outline links. Switch to a full-screen slide show and skim the entire presentation. Then close the browser. Disconnect from the Internet, close your PowerPoint files, and exit PowerPoint.

Warning *You may proceed directly to the exercises for this lesson. If, however, you are finished with your computer session, follow the "shut down" procedures for your lab or school environment.*

SUMMARY

Each time you start PowerPoint, you have the option of beginning a presentation with a design template. Each additional slide requires you to select an AutoLayout. Some AutoLayouts have a placeholder for clip art, a chart, or a table in addition to text. You can enhance a presentation by formatting the text (for example, different fonts, font sizes, font colors, effects, and alignments). Inserting a clip involves the Microsoft Clip Gallery. A master—a collection of placeholders for text and repeating objects—allows you to change a slide in one place and reflect that change throughout a presentation. You can change presentation design and slide layouts. Furthermore, you can apply finishing touches to your presentation by adding slide transitions, animating text, and animating objects. You can also publish your PowerPoint presentation on the Web and save files as a Web page.

Now that you have completed this lesson, you should be able to do the following:

- Create a presentation from a template. (PowerPoint-532)

- Open a template, add a slide, and add text to a slide. (PowerPoint-535)

- Insert notes in a presentation and print a notes page. (PowerPoint-536)

- Create slides by importing a Microsoft Word outline. (PowerPoint-538)

- Change the font, font size, and color for text on a slide, and emphasize text with other special formatting effects. (PowerPoint-540)

- Change presentation design and slide layouts. (PowerPoint-544)

- Insert clip art into a presentation. (PowerPoint-545)

- Scale and size objects. (PowerPoint-548)

- Use the Slide Master to make changes. (PowerPoint-550)

- Add a header and footer in a presentation. (PowerPoint-552)

- Add WordArt to a presentation. (PowerPoint-554)

- Apply and preview transition effects. (PowerPoint-555)

- Animate text, objects, and clip art. (PowerPoint-557)

- Save presentations as Web pages and preview them in your browser. (PowerPoint-560)

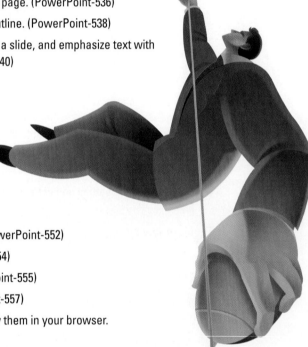

CONCEPTS REVIEW

1 TRUE/FALSE

Circle T if the statement is true or F if the statement is false.

T   F   **1.** An AutoLayout is a design template.

T   F   **2.** Clicking the New Slide button 🔲 gives access to the AutoLayouts.

T   F   **3.** Clip art can be inserted with or without a placeholder.

T   F   **4.** The Insert Clip Art button 🔳 is on the Drawing toolbar.

T   F   **5.** Move a clip when the pointer becomes the crosshair pointer.

T   F   **6.** You can use the Slide Master to change line spacing on all slides in the presentation.

T   F   **7.** Header and footer text will display in outline view on your screen.

T   F   **8.** A transition is the way a slide is replaced by another slide.

T   F   **9.** A sentence added to the screen one word at a time is an example of build text.

T   F **10.** Text and object builds are added in Slide View.

2 MATCHING

Match each of the terms on the left with the definitions on the right.

TERMS	DEFINITIONS
1. AutoLayouts	**a.** Represents a place for a graphic or text to be inserted
2. text object	
3. animation	**b.** A collection of preformatted slides
4. Header and Footer dialog box	**c.** Controls how one slide replaces another
	d. A filled object that contains text
5. transition	**e.** Gives access to the Select All command
6. Slide Show menu	**f.** Motion effects
7. Slide Sorter toolbar	**g.** Location of features for transitions and text builds
8. placeholder	
9. Edit menu	**h.** Contains a menu of object build effects
10. transition symbol	**i.** Indicates animated slides
	j. Place to add slide numbers

Lesson Summary & Exercises

3 COMPLETION

Fill in the missing word or phrase for each of the following statements.

1. Preformatted slides called AutoLayouts can be selected from the _____ dialog box.

2. A placeholder is a(n) _____, which is a single element on your PowerPoint slide.

3. Double-clicking a clip art placeholder opens the _____.

4. To make a change to the _____, you first need to display it.

5. To choose a new design template when you have an existing presentation open, click the _____ button on the Formatting toolbar.

6. To add a new slide with the same AutoLayout as the previous slide, press _____ and click the New Slide button.

7. The Header and Footer command is located on the _____ menu.

8. To display the Slide Master, press _____ and click the Slide View button.

9. To navigate from slide 12 to slide 11, for example, click _____ on the shortcut menu.

10. Select a build effect for an object from the Preset Animation menu, an option on the _____ menu.

4 SHORT ANSWER

Write a brief answer to each of the following questions.

1. Explain how to add slide numbers while omitting the date or other footer.

2. What are AutoLayouts and where can you find them?

3. Describe how the pointer changes in the process of moving an object, such as clip art.

4. Explain how to type a multi-level bulleted list.

5. What is the Auto-Fit feature, and how can you deactivate it?

6. Name three ways to publicize a just-published Web presentation.

7. Describe two ways to display a presentation in Explorer.

8. Give step-by-step directions for removing a transition from certain slides after applying it to all.

9. Explain the advantage of clip art placeholders. Then briefly explain how to insert clip art without placeholders.

10. Explain how to change line spacing on all slides in a presentation at one time.

5 IDENTIFICATION

Label each of the items of the PowerPoint window in Figure 2.19.

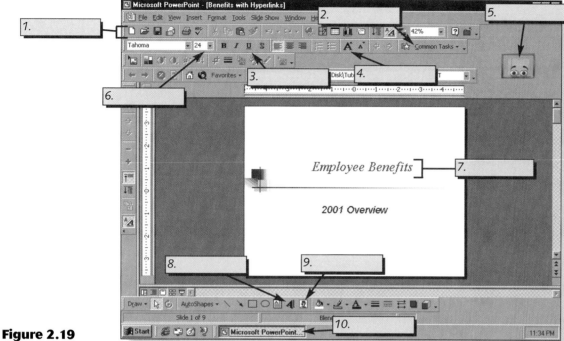

Figure 2.19

SKILLS REVIEW

Complete each of the Skills Review problems in sequential order so that you will review your PowerPoint skills to begin a presentation with a template; add slides, text, and notes; import and format text; insert clip art; add headers and footers; change design templates and slide layouts; and add transitions and animations.

1 Open a Template, Add a Slide, and Type Text

1. Start PowerPoint.

2. Click **Design Template** from the initial PowerPoint dialog box and click **OK**. If you already started PowerPoint, click the **File menu** and **New**. Click the **Design Templates tab**.

3. Open the **Notebook template**. Add the **Title slide AutoLayout**.

4. Save the file as *Writer's Friend* in the *Skills Review* folder on your Student Data Disk.

5. Click the **New Slide button** 🔲. Select **Text & Clip Art**. In Normal View, click the **slide pane**.

6. On slide 1, click the **title placeholder** and type A Writer's Friend. Click the **subtitle placeholder** and type Write Like a Pro.

7. On slide 2, click the **title placeholder** and type Just Checking. In the *Click to add text* box, type the following as a multi-level bulleted list. Make the second and fourth lines level 2 bullets by clicking the Demote ⬛ and Promote ⬛ buttons as necessary.

I said what I meant to say.
I gave enough details.
Details are in order.
Paper has a beginning, middle, and end.

2 Prepare and Print Notes

1. Click the **View menu** and click **Notes Page**. Click the **notes pane** and type the following text, checking spelling as you type:

   Cover one main idea in each paragraph.
   Double-check your facts.
   Use a style that's easy to read and understand.

2. Change magnification to the Fit setting. Then switch to Normal View.

3. Switch back to Notes Page View.

4. Click **File** on the menu bar and click **Print**.

5. Verify that the Number of copies is set to 1. Click **Notes Pages** in the Print what area. Click the **Pure black and white option**. Click **OK**.

6. Switch to Normal View.

3 Insert a Word Outline

1. Click **slide 1** in the outline pane.

2. Click **Insert** on the menu bar and click **Slides from Outline**.

3. Navigate to the Word file named **Write This Way** on your Student Data Disk.

4. Click the **Insert button**.

5. Save the updated file.

4 Format Text

1. Navigate to slide 7 and select the slide title.

2. Change the font to Arial Black. Change the font size to 54 points. Change the font color to blue-green (third square from right).

3. Select the subtitles. Increase the font size to the next size shown in the list box using the Increase Font Size button ⬛.

4. In the last subtitle, select *beginning* and apply italic.

5. Underline *middle*. Apply bold to *end*.

6. Navigate to slide 5 and select all subtitles.

7. Decrease the font size to the next size shown so all subtitles fit on the slide.

5 Change the Design Template and a Slide Layout

1. Switch to Slide Sorter View. Click the **Common Tasks button** `Common Tasks ▾` and apply the **LaVerne template**.

2. Switch to Slide View. Select slide 4, click the **Common Tasks button** `Common Tasks ▾`, and change the layout of slide 4 to **2 Column Text**.

3. Cut and paste the last six subtitles to the second column.

4. Save the updated file.

6 Insert, Resize, and Move a Clip

1. On slide 7, double-click the **clip art placeholder**.

2. In the Clip Gallery, click the **Animals icon**. Click the **Horses clip**.

3. On the shortcut menu, click **Insert Clip**. Then close the gallery.

4. At slide 1, click the **Insert Clip Art button** 🖼. Click the **Animals icon** and click the **veterinary medicine clip** (woman with dog). Insert the clip and close the gallery.

5. Click the **Format Picture button** 🖼 and click the **Size tab**.

6. Verify that Lock aspect ratio is selected. Change the Height to 2.5".

7. Deselect the clip art. Drag the clip to the lower-right corner of the slide when the four-way pointer appears.

8. On slide 7, select the clip art and point to the sizing handle in the upper-left corner.

9. Drag to decrease the size slightly. Move the resized clip art slightly.

10. Save your updated file.

7 Use the Slide Master to Change Fonts

1. Open *Annual Report* on your Student Data Disk and save the file as *Annual Report Customized* in the *Skills Review* folder.

2. In Slide View, scroll to slide 2. Determine the name of the title font and the subtitle font. Then scroll to slide 7 and verify that the same title and subtitle fonts are used on that slide.

3. Switch to Slide Master View. Select the **slide title text** and change the font to Arial and remove the italic effect. Then select **all subtitles** and change the font to Times New Roman.

4. Click the area surrounding the slide.

5. Save and close the file.

Lesson Summary & Exercises

8 Add Headers and Footers

1. In the *Writer's Friend* presentation, switch to Slide View. Click the **View** menu and click **Header and Footer**.

2. Select the **Date and time check box** and the **Update automatically option**.

3. Apply the footer to all slides.

4. Open the Header and Footer dialog box again and click the **Notes and Handouts tab**.

5. Select the **Date and time check box** and the **Update automatically option**. Type Writer's Friend as your header text.

6. Apply to all, and save your updated file.

9 Apply Transition Effects

1. In Slide Sorter View, select slides 2 and 3, click the **Slide Transition button** [icon], and apply the **Split Vertical Out effect**.

2. Apply the **Split Vertical In effect** to slide 4.

3. Click the **transition symbols** to preview the effects.

4. From the Edit menu, click **Select All**. Then apply the **Box Out effect**. Use the **Animation Preview button** [icon] to preview the effects.

5. Save the changes.

10 Animate Texts and Objects

1. In Slide Sorter View, select slide 3.

2. On the Slide Sorter toolbar, click the **Preset Animation drop-down arrow** [No Effect ▼] and select the **Fly From Left effect**.

3. Select slides 4 and 5, click the **Preset Animation drop-down arrow** [No Effect ▼], and select the **Peek from Left effect**.

4. Switch to Normal View and select the clip art on slide 1.

5. Point to **Preset Animation** on the Slide Show menu and click **Flying**.

6. Run your slide show.

7. Save and close your updated file.

LESSON APPLICATIONS

1 Moving and Sizing

Change the size of a clip. Move the object to balance the elements on the slide.

1. Open the *Ping Pong* presentation on your Student Data Disk. Save the file as *Moving and Sizing* in the *Lesson Applications* folder.

2. In Slide View, navigate to slide 6, enlarge the clip art by about one-third, and balance the position of the clip with the text on the left.

3. Save the changes and close the file.

2 Changing Times

Change font size and add special effects. Apply a new design template and a new layout.

1. Open *Benefits* on your Student Data Disk and save the file as *Changing Times* in the *Lesson Applications* folder.

2. On the Title slide, change the title font size to 60. Change the subtitle font size to 42.

3. Apply the Notebook design template.

4. Change the layout of slide 2 to 2 Column Text.

5. Adjust the bulleted text to fit attractively in two columns.

6. Save changes, but do not close the file.

3 Head to Foot

Insert footers on all slides and headers and footers on printed outline pages.

1. Add a date that will update automatically and slide numbers to all slides, except the title slide.

2. On printed outline pages, add a date that will update automatically and page numbers as a footer. Add Employee Benefits as a header.

3. Save the updated file as *Changing Times with Header and Footer* in the *Lesson Applications* folder.

4 Be Bold!

Open a presentation on your Student Data Disk and change the text style using the Slide Master.

1. Open the *Marketing* presentation on your Student Data Disk. Save the file as *Marketing Customized* in the *Lesson Applications* folder.

2. In the Slide Master, change the title font size to 44 and bold. Change all subtitle text to Times New Roman. Add bold to help the text stand out against the marble background.

3. Switch to Slide View and check the effect of these changes on each slide. Save the changes. Close the file.

Lesson Summary & Exercises

5 Transition Condition

Apply slide transitions. Insert clipart. Animate text and objects.

1. Open **Experience** on your Student Data Disk and save the file as **Transition Condition** in the **Lesson Applications** folder.

2. On slides 3 and 4, use the object placeholders to insert clip art that represents the slide titles.

3. Insert clip art on slide 7. Resize the clip art and center it attractively.

4. Add the Cut transition to even-numbered slides; apply the Dissolve transition to odd-numbered slides except for slide 1. Preview the animations.

5. Animate the clip art on slides 3, 4, and 7 with the Flying effect.

6. On slides 2 and 5, apply the Fly from Top build effect.

7. Run your slide show. Save and close the updated file.

PROJECTS

1 One-Minute Presentation

You belong to Toastmaster's International, a group whose goal is to develop the public speaking skills of the members. Members often volunteer to speak extemporaneously on relevant, interesting topics. In addition, big-name speakers are sometimes invited to demonstrate their skills to the group. Someone always introduces them, or presents them, to the audience. You have an idea that novice speakers (like you) would do better if someone presented them, too.

Create a presentation (two to four slides) for introducing a speaker—someone you know well (for example, instructor, close friend, parent). Plan first—text, graphics, and notes. Jot key words for these points, which you will include: topic, importance of the topic to the audience, speaker's name, and speaker's qualifications for addressing the topic. (Experts recommend ending with the speaker's name; therefore, you may plan to show the Title slide last; or you may plan to delete the Title slide.) Limit the content to a minute's worth of material, including comments (notes) not shown on the slides. Save the presentation as **Introduction** in the **Projects** folder on your Student Data Disk.

2 By Design

Your first trial with the one-minute presentation went rather well at the last Toastmaster's gathering. You've decided to keep using the concept. You realize, of course, that you will have to vary the look and feel of your presentation to fit your presenter, although you present the same type of information in each case.

Use *Introduction* in the *Projects* folder on your Student Data Disk as the basis for a new presentation and name this project *Introduction 2*. Select another person to introduce and plan the text, objects, clips, etc., that you will use. In addition to different graphics, special effects, etc., use a different template. Use a multi-level bulleted list on one of the slides. Insert appropriate headers and footers on slides and outline pages.

3 Old Favorite, New Look

You have used the *Agenda* presentation numerous times in presentations to different employee groups within Peeler Construction; in fact, some groups have seen and heard the presentation more than once. Most of the information is still current, and the Fireball template on which it's based still looks modern. You decide to customize the presentation, using the Slide Master to make most of the changes.

Open *Agenda* on your Student Data Disk and save the file as *New Look* in the *Projects* folder. Plan a complete (Slide Master) makeover of the presentation, using the information in the original. Changes to consider include changing the title font, size, and special effect; changing the subtitle font; changing the background color (use Format menu in the Slide Master); using different slide layouts; and inserting footers. Remember to check each change in Slide View before making the next change. Correct all spelling errors. Then save all changes and close the file.

4 New Template Design a Benefit

You will be showing the *Benefits* presentation to Peeler managers and superintendents in the near future. Two or more recent presentations to that group were based on the Blends design template, so you decide it's time for a change—and a more formal look.

Open *Benefits* on your Student Data Disk. View the entire presentation in Slide Show. Then attach a formal-looking presentation template to the presentation (Common Tasks button). On paper, note what changes the new template made. What did not change? Close the file without saving the changes.

5 I is for Interview

Training sessions about career planning are extremely popular, attracting varied audiences of career starters and changers. You have printed materials about job interviewing, but you would like a PowerPoint presentation to introduce or summarize the topic or reinforce main points. Here is what you have planned so far: Illustrate both incorrect and correct ways of behaving during a job interview. Illustrate just one point on each slide. Insert a title with the word *Don't* (incorrect way) or *Do* on each slide that relates to interview behavior. Use several pieces of clip art. Use appropriate animation, transition, and build effects. Start with just three points, plus a Title slide. Information about job interviewing may be obtained from sources listed in Table 2.1 or other sources available to you. Save the presentation as **Interview** in the **Projects** folder on your Student Data Disk.

TABLE 2.1	WEB SITES AND URL'S
Web Site	**URL**
Career Mosaic	http://www.careermosaic.com
Career Path	http://CareerPath.com
JobTrak	http://www.jobtrak.com
Monster Board	http://www.monster.com

6 Career Presentation

Since graduating from college several years ago, you have become well established in your chosen career. Now, you decided recently, would be a good time to publish a Web presentation, establishing your identity in your field and promoting the work that you do. Before planning your home page, you visit and evaluate several Web sites.

Search the Web, using the name of your career (for example, accountant, paralegal, printer, realtor) and related terms as keywords; then follow any of the first 20 links that appear helpful. In addition, examine two or more of these Web sites, noting features of the site and the presence of any banner ads and other publicity. Plan your Web presentation. First, on a separate sheet, describe in detail the method(s) you will use to publicize the new Web page. Then, sketch your presentation (three to six slides) on paper. One slide should contain FAQs (Frequently Asked Questions); that is, questions commonly asked of someone in your field. Another slide or slides should contain answers to those questions, and a hyperlink should allow Web users to jump from each question to its answer. (Remember to include links for jumping back to the FAQ slide.) Preview the file in Explorer. Save the file as a Web page named **Career Presentation** in the **Projects** folder on your Student Data Disk.

Project in Progress

7 Build Up

Your small business, I-Comm, provides various writing and editing services to small and medium-sized organizations. You wish to create new slides for your presentation to promote the Business Writer's Workshop. Open *I-Comm Title* in the *Projects* folder on your Student Data Disk and save the file as *Writer's Workshop*. Add a slide containing testimonials of business people who have taken the workshop. Add another slide depicting the workshop activities, which include hands-on practice in planning, drafting, editing, revising, and publishing (producing) documents, such as letters, memos, and short reports. Change the design template. Preview the slides and consider changing the layout of a few slides. Add clip art and move and size it appropriately. Include headers and footers on the slides and outline pages. Explore Help and consider experimenting with features you may not have used before, such as inserting graphs. Preview the file in Slide Sorter View (Figure 2.20), then animate the presentation and review the effects in Slide Show.

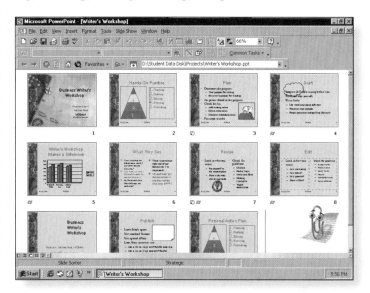

Figure 2.20

Overview: Congratulations! You have completed the lessons in the PowerPoint tutorial and now have the opportunity in this capstone project to apply the PowerPoint skills you have learned. You will create a slide show for young people who will soon apply for a driver's license in your state. The show, created as a community service project by a college student organization you belong to, will be presented at a local shopping mall, near a store where many teens like to shop. As you create the case study slide show, try to incorporate these skills:

- Create and save a presentation using different layouts and inserting second-level subtitles, WordArt, and clip art.

- Proofread and edit text. Use the spelling feature; use the Undo, Redo, and Find and Replace commands.

- Ask the Office Assistant for help as needed.

- Navigate the presentation efficiently.

- Apply templates as desired to create slides.

- Use the Office Clipboard to cut, copy, and paste text.

- Change page orientation and line spacing.

- Change font style, size, attributes, and color.

- Create headers and footers.

- Add formatting and special effects, including bold, italic, and underline.

- Use the Format Painter and apply styles.

- Create hyperlinks to pages, slides, and Web sites.

- Insert, resize, and position clip art.

- Add transitions and animations to your presentation.

- Use Print Preview; print all documents.

Instructions: Read all directions and plan your work before you begin. You will be evaluated on these factors: (1) the number of skills involved in completing the case; (2) creativity; (3) practical applications for the task; (4) appropriate use of presentation features; (5) quality of the presentation produced, including mechanical accuracy, format, and writing style; and (6) oral presentation of the case.

1. *Getting Started.* Search the Web, using keywords such as *the name of your state, bureau/department of motor vehicles, driver licensing, government agencies/offices, state licensing, traffic laws.* Add an informative site to your list of favorites/book-marks in case you need to go back to complete the research.

2. *Plan the Presentation.* Sketch a presentation plan. Represent each slide and show the type of information it will contain—bulleted text, clip art, etc. Write key words for the text on each slide, referring to information obtained from the Web. Strive for a smooth flow of information and a professional appearance. Include a list of credits at the end of the presentation.

3. *Design the Presentation.* Use the design template of your choice. Save the file as *Teen Presentation* in the *Projects* folder on your Student Data Disk.

4. *Add Data.* Type a title and subtitle on the title slide. Add one new slide (AutoLayout) and type the text planned for it. Continue, adding one new slide and title and subtitles on it before adding the next slide. Check the spelling throughout the presentation.

5. *Add Graphics.* Add WordArt, or clip art as appropriate throughout the presentation. Then insert a hyperlink.

6. *Modify the Slide Master.* Add a footer, slide numbers, and a date.

7. *Add Animations.* Add animation and build effects. Preview the slide show, focusing on the flow of information and the overall presentation. Adjust as needed.

8. *Request Reviewer Comments.* Ask one to five other students to review the presentation and to insert reviewer comments. Read the comments and take appropriate action.

9. *Present the Presentation.*

Managing Information

Outlook Basics

CONTENTS

OBJECTIVES

After you complete this lesson, you will be able to do the following:

- Describe what you can accomplish with Outlook.
- Start Outlook and navigate its window.
- Use the Inbox to create, send, read, and reply to mail messages.
- Explain the archiving process.
- Schedule appointments with the Calendar.
- Enter names and addresses as contacts, manipulate the contact information, and communicate electronically with contacts.
- Create and maintain an electronic to-do list with Tasks.
- Create, format, and sort Notes.
- Preview your day with the Outlook Today page.
- Record, view, and open Journal entries.

All the Office 2000 applications that you have learned so far help you create documents. Microsoft Outlook 2000 is a little different. It helps you manage information. Sometimes the result of your work in Outlook is a printed document; but oftentimes the result is an intangible one, such as improved productivity. With Outlook, you can manage telephone and e-mail messages, meetings and other appointments, tasks, and contacts. Outlook can also help you track activities, view Office documents, and share information with other users. In this lesson, you'll learn how to start Outlook and navigate around its window. Then you will learn how to use each of Outlook's main tools.

HANDS On

Office **BASICS**

Launching Outlook

1. Click the Start button and point to Programs.

2. Click Microsoft Outlook.

STARTING OUTLOOK AND EXPLORING THE OUTLOOK WINDOW

Microsoft Outlook is a personal information management program that helps you manage messages, appointments, contacts, and tasks. Like all Windows programs, you can launch Outlook 2000 several different ways; however, the most common method is clicking the Start button [Start].

The Outlook window contains several familiar objects, such as the title bar, menu bar, and toolbar. The main part of the window is composed of two frames. The main working area is the larger frame to the right. The bar at the top of this frame, called the folder banner, displays the name of the open folder. The smaller frame to the left is the Outlook Bar. The Outlook Bar contains group names and shortcut icons. The icons serve as shortcuts to frequently used folders. You can click a bar that contains a group name, such as Outlook Shortcuts, My Shortcuts, and Other Shortcuts, to see the shortcuts within that group.

Launching Outlook

In this activity, you will launch Outlook using the Start button and maximize its window.

1. Click the **Start button** [Start], point to **Programs**, and click **Microsoft Outlook**.

2. The Office Assistant may appear to provide helpful information and tips. If it appears, read the message displayed and click **OK**. Then, if the window is not maximized, click the **Maximize button** [□].

The Microsoft Outlook window will resemble the one shown in Figure 1.1.

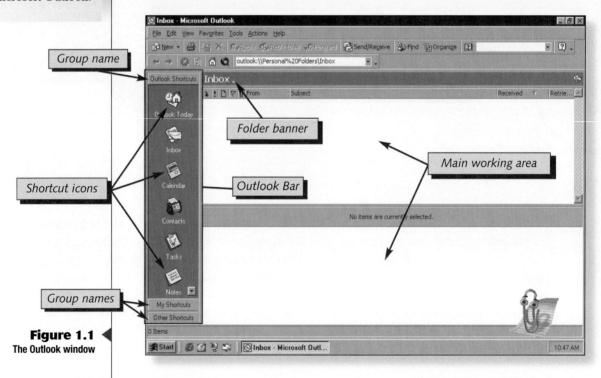

Figure 1.1
The Outlook window

Using the Outlook Bar

- Click a group name to open it.

- Click a shortcut icon to open its folder.

You can add a Web page to your Outlook Bar for quick access. First, display the Web toolbar in Outlook and type the Web page address in its Address bar. When the Web page appears in the main working area, point to New on the File menu and click Outlook Bar Shortcut to Web Page.

Using the Outlook Bar

In this activity, you will learn how to select the different groups in the Outlook Bar as well as the folders within a group.

1. If it is not already selected, click the Outlook Shortcuts group name in the Outlook Bar. A group name is selected if shortcut icons appear directly below it.

The Outlook tools appear as shortcut icons, as shown in Figure 1.1.

2. Click the Contacts shortcut icon.

The folder banner name changes to show the selected folder. Depending on whether other users of this computer have previously entered contacts, your main working area may contain names and addresses or it may be blank. You'll learn more about Contacts and the other Outlook tools later in this lesson.

3. Scroll the Outlook Bar if necessary to find and click the Tasks shortcut icon.

Again, the folder banner changes and the Task list is shown in the main working area, as shown in Figure 1.2. Now, you can find out what folders exist in some of the other groups.

Figure 1.2
The Task list

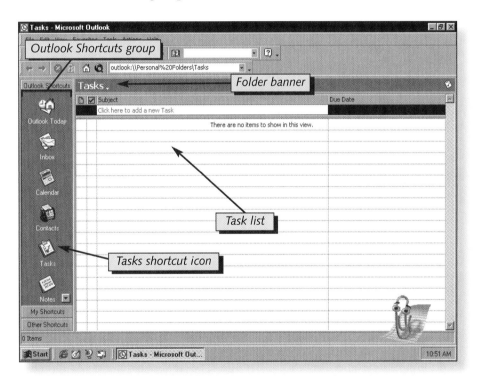

4. Click the My Shortcuts group name.

The bar that contains the My Shortcuts group name jumps to the top of the Outlook Bar, directly below the Outlook Shortcuts group name. The icons in the Outlook Shortcuts group are hidden and the icons in the My Shortcut group are displayed. The Tasks frame is still active in the right frame since you haven't yet selected a new icon.

Another Way

To move to another folder, such as Tasks, point to Go To on the View menu and click the folder name.

5. Click the **Sent Items shortcut icon**.

The Sent Items icon is selected and the folder banner and working area change to reflect the active folder.

6. Click the **Other Shortcuts group name to see the icons contained in that group.**

Now that you know how to switch from group to group, you're ready to learn about Outlook's tools. If you are using a computer that has been used by others, consult your instructor before continuing with this lesson. Your instructor may provide specific instructions about deleting existing Outlook entries.

USING THE INBOX

Electronic mail, also known as e-mail, is becoming a popular means of communication—for both work and personal use. You can send e-mail messages to anyone who has an e-mail account on the Internet or who has an account within the same network or intranet as you. The Inbox in Outlook allows you to send and receive messages electronically. You'll learn how to create, send, read, and reply to a mail message.

Creating and Sending a Mail Message

1. Open the Inbox folder.

2. Click the New Mail Message button.

3. Type the recipient's address in the To box.

4. Type a descriptive subject in the Subject box.

5. Type the message itself in the main area of the message box.

6. Proofread the message.

7. Click the Send button.

8. If necessary, click the Send/Receive button.

Creating and Sending a New Mail Message

The Inbox allows you to access messages that others have sent to you and to create and send new messages. To create and send a message, you must have the recipient's full e-mail address. In this activity, you act as an employee of The Pet Deli, Inc. First, you create a mail message informing a coworker of a change in a product release date. Then you will send the message to your instructor or a classmate.

1. Click the **Outlook Shortcuts group name to display the shortcut icons in this group. Then click the Inbox icon.**

The folder banner changes to indicate that the Inbox is active. The main working area of your window displays incoming messages or a message that you have no items.

2. Click the **New Mail Message button** .

As shown in Figure 1.3, the Untitled - Message window appears, ready for you to create a new mail message.

3. In the To box, type the e-mail address of your instructor or a classmate. (Your instructor will provide this information.)

Note *The Cc box allows you to send a copy of the same message to others.*

4. Press `Tab` twice to move to the Subject box.

5. Type New Product Release Date and press `Tab` to move to the message area.

Now you are ready to type the text of your message. You work for The Pet Deli, Inc., and want to inform the recipient, a coworker, of a new product release date.

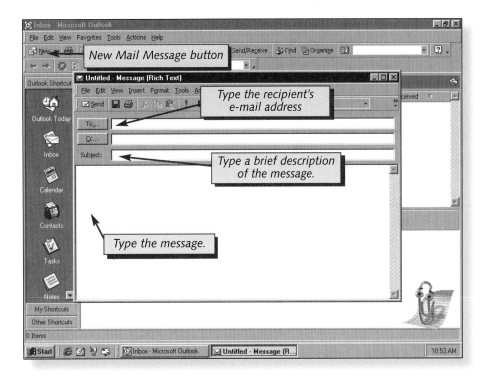

Figure 1.3
The Untitled - Message window

6. Type the following text:

The release date of our new nutritional supplement has been changed to April 26. As you know, we are still finalizing a name for the supplement. Any name suggestions are welcome.

7. Click the Importance: High button  **to indicate to the recipient that this message carries a high importance, as shown in Figure 1.4. (The address will be different.)**

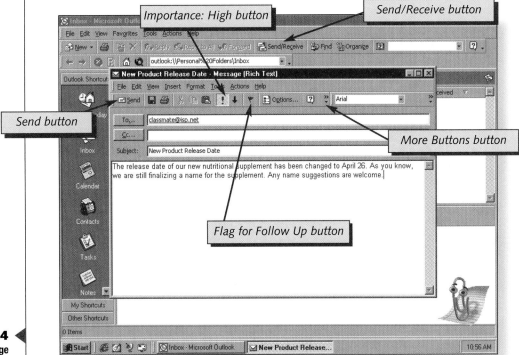

Figure 1.4
The finished mail message

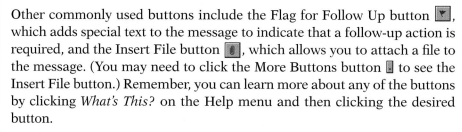

Another Way

- To create a new mail message, press Ctrl + N or point to New on the File menu and click Mail Message.

- To send your message and check for new messages, point to Send/Receive on the Tools menu and click the appropriate option.

Other commonly used buttons include the Flag for Follow Up button ⬛, which adds special text to the message to indicate that a follow-up action is required, and the Insert File button ⬛, which allows you to attach a file to the message. (You may need to click the More Buttons button ⬛ to see the Insert File button.) Remember, you can learn more about any of the buttons by clicking *What's This?* on the Help menu and then clicking the desired button.

8. Proofread your message. Once you are sure that it is error free, click the **Send button** ⬛Send.

In a typical Internet setup, Outlook connects to the Internet service provider, delivers the outgoing mail messages, checks for incoming messages, and then disconnects from the Internet service provider. A copy of the reply is stored in the Sent Items folder in the My Shortcuts group.

If you are not online or your mail was not sent because of your computer setup, click the Send/Receive button ⬛Send/Receive on the Standard toolbar. If clicking the Send/Receive button ⬛Send/Receive does not connect you to your Internet service provider, you may receive an Undeliverable Mail message. If so, you may need to change some Outlook settings so that it can recognize and communicate with your mail program. Ask your instructor for assistance.

Understanding Incoming Mail

Along the top of the Inbox window are several column headings. You can double-click any of these column headings to sort messages by that column. Table 1.1 provides a brief description of the Inbox column headings.

You can e-mail a Web page to another user. First, display the Web toolbar in Outlook and type the Web page address in its Address bar. When the Web page appears in the main working area, click Send Web Page by E-mail on the Actions menu.

TABLE 1.1	THE INBOX COLUMN HEADINGS
Column Heading	**Purpose**
!	Indicates importance of the message (high, normal, or low)
🗋	Indicates whether the message is read or unread
⬛	Indicates whether the message requires a follow-up action
📎	Indicates whether a file is attached to the message
From	Displays the e-mail address or name of the sender
Subject	Displays the text in the Subject line of the message
Received	Shows the date the message was received

Note   *Outlook uses many other symbols to indicate the characteristics of a message. To see a list of symbols, click the Office Assistant character, type* Inbox symbols, *and press* Enter⏎.

HANDS
On

**Reading a Mail
Message**

1. Open the Inbox folder
and click the
Send/Receive button.

2. Double-click the message you want to read.

3. Read the message.

Figure 1.5
An incoming message

Reading a Mail Message

If you sent a message in the previous hands on activity, the recipient may
have responded. In this activity, you'll check for new mail and read a message if one has arrived.

1. Click the **Inbox folder** in the Outlook Shortcuts group, if it is not active.

2. Click the **Send/Receive button** Send/Receive.

Clicking this button checks for new mail and sends any messages you've created. The messages you receive will appear as shown in Figure 1.5. The
sender's name, the subject line, and the date received appear in the top portion of the Inbox and the message itself appears at the bottom of the Inbox.

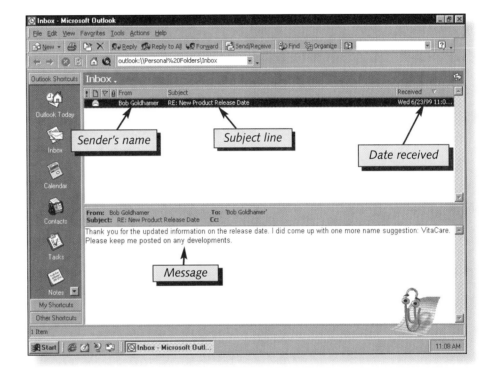

*Under perfect conditions, mail sent to you will take only a
few seconds to be delivered. However, depending on your
modem speed, traffic on the Internet, and other factors, a
message may take a few minutes, hours, or even days to be
delivered.*

You can open the message window to see more information.

3. Double-click the line of information at the top of the Inbox.

The message window appears, showing the sender's name and address, date
sent, the recipient, subject line, and the message itself.

4. Read the message.

Office BASICS

Replying to a Message

1. With the message you wish to reply to open, click the Reply button.

2. Type the desired reply.

3. Click the Send button.

4. If necessary, click the Send/Receive button.

Replying to a Mail Message

You can use the mail message window to reply immediately. Using the Reply button [Reply] saves you from typing the address of the person you are replying to and the subject line. You can also access the Reply button from the Inbox. In this activity, you will reply to the message you received.

1. Click the Reply button [Reply].

A window appears with the address and subject already filled in.

2. Type the following reply:

Thank you for the name suggestion. I will add it to the list of potential names. Will you be able to attend a team meeting on Wednesday at 1:00 p.m.? I hope to make a final decision during this meeting.

Your window will resemble the one in Figure 1.6.

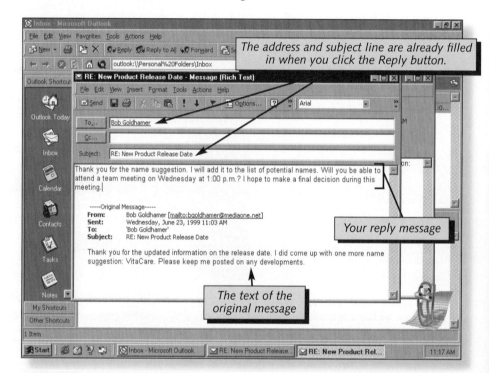

Figure 1.6
Replying to a mail message

3. Click the Send button [Send].

The original message that you received appears. A banner above the From line indicates the date and time you replied.

4. Close the mail message. If necessary, click the Send/Receive button [Send/Receive] to deliver your reply.

Your reply is sent. A copy of the reply is stored in the Sent Items folder in the My Shortcuts group.

Another Way

To reply to a mail message, press Ctrl + R or click Reply on the Actions menu.

Using HELP

Archiving Items

Depending on your Outlook settings, you may periodically be asked if you wish to archive old items. Use Help to better understand the archiving process.

1. Click the **Office Assistant**.

Figure 1.7
Learning about archiving

2. Type archive in the *What would you like to do?* box.

3. Click the **Search button**.

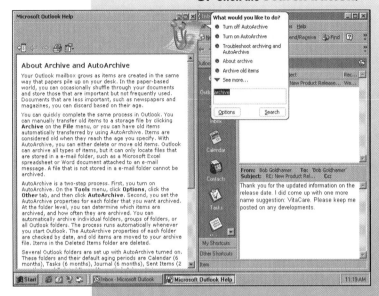

4. Click the **About archive link**.

5. Read the new text in the Help window, clicking any links to terms that you do not understand (Figure 1.7).

6. If the Help balloon next to the Office Assistant has disappeared, click the **Office Assistant** again.

7. Click the **Archive old items link**.

8. Read the text in the new Help window and click links to additional information about which you'd like to learn.

9. When you are finished exploring, close the Help window.

SCHEDULING WITH THE CALENDAR

The Calendar in Microsoft Outlook allows you to schedule appointments, meetings, events, and tasks. In this section, you'll learn how to set a new appointment, schedule an event, display the calendar window in a variety of views, and plan a recurring meeting.

HANDS On

Setting a New Appointment

Just as you can block time in a paper calendar, you can do the same in Outlook's Calendar. You can give the appointment a name to describe it and set the time and other characteristics of it. In this activity, you'll set a few appointments for your work at The Pet Deli.

1. Click the **Calendar shortcut icon** in the Outlook Shortcuts group of the Outlook Bar.

The main working area will display today's calendar, as shown in Figure 1.8. If your screen does not show the daily view, click the Day button 🔲Day. Also, if today's calendar is not shown, click the Go to Today button Go to Today.

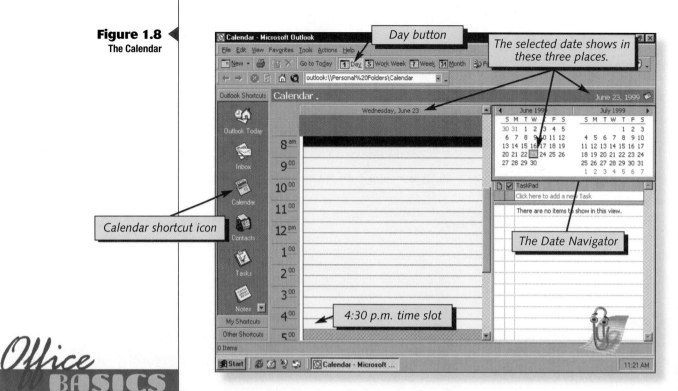

Figure 1.8
The Calendar

Day button

The selected date shows in these three places.

Calendar shortcut icon

The Date Navigator

4:30 p.m. time slot

Setting an Appointment

1. Click the Calendar shortcut icon.

2. To set an appointment, click the desired time slot (or drag to select a longer one), type a brief description of the appointment, and press ⏎Enter.

3. To switch to another day, click the date in the Date Navigator.

4. To set an appointment with more details, double-click the time slot. Type a description in the Subject box, type a location, and change the end time. Then click the Save and Close button.

2. Click the 4:30 p.m. time slot.

The section representing 4:30 to 5:00 is selected.

Note *If someone has previously used the Calendar tool to set appointments on the computer you are using, these appointments may interfere with the completion of this section. Ask your instructor whether you may delete the previously set appointments.*

3. Type Presentation by Leslie Adams **and press** Enter⏎.

The text that you typed appears in a highlighted bar with a bell icon that indicates that Outlook will remind you of your appointment 15 minutes before it occurs.

4. In the Date Navigator, click the date for next Wednesday.

The appointment book for next Wednesday appears in the center pane and the top of this pane shows the date of next Wednesday.

5. Double-click the 1:00 p.m. time slot.

The Untitled - Appointment dialog box appears. You can use this dialog box to set specific attributes for an appointment.

6. Type New Product Naming Meeting **in the Subject box and press** Tab **to move to the Location box.**

Your date will likely be different than the one shown in Figure 1.9.

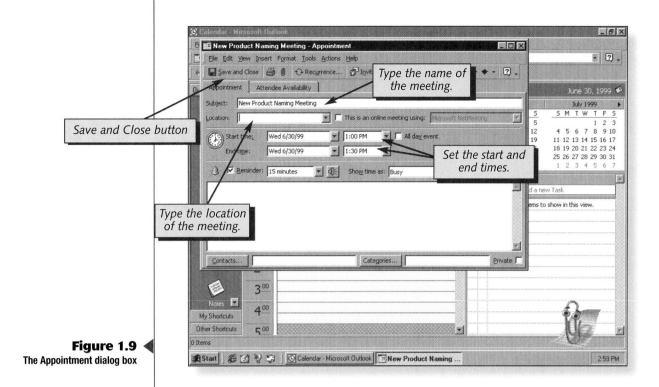

Save and Close button

Type the name of
the meeting.

Type the location
of the meeting.

Set the start and
end times.

Figure 1.9
The Appointment dialog box

7. **Type** Conference Room C **in the Location box.**

8. **Click the** **End time drop-down arrow** **and set the end time to 2:30 p.m. Then click the** **Save and Close button** .

The new meeting appears on Wednesday's appointment book, as shown in Figure 1.10.

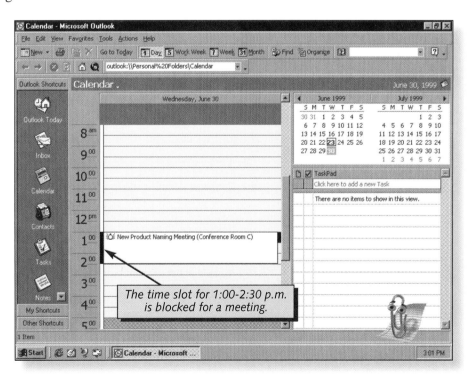

The time slot for 1:00-2:30 p.m.
is blocked for a meeting.

Figure 1.10
New appointment indicator

Another Way

To jump to today's date, point to Go To on the View menu and click Go to Today.

You have just been notified that the presentation by Leslie Adams has been rescheduled for next Friday and has been extended to an hour-long presentation. You need to mark the new presentation time and date on your calendar and then delete the notation for today.

9. **In the Date Navigator, click the date for next Friday.**

Notice that today's date and next Wednesday's date are shown in bold in the Date Navigator. The bold date indicates that you have an appointment or other activity scheduled during that day. Also notice that the Date Navigator encloses today's date in a box.

10. **Drag to select the time slot for 10:00 a.m. to 11:00 a.m., type** Presentation by Leslie Adams, **and press** Enter⏎ .

To set an appointment that blocks more than 30 minutes of time, click the beginning time and drag until the desired block of time is selected.

11. **Click the Go to Today button** Go to Today .

The Go To Today button Go to Today jumps to the current day on the calendar.

12. **Click the notation for the 4:30 p.m. presentation so that it is surrounded by a border and then click the Delete button** ✕ .

The appointment is deleted.

Scheduling an Event

1. Move to the day of the event.

2. Click New All Day Event on the Actions menu.

3. Type a subject and set the reminder time. If desired, type notes about the event.

4. Click the Save and Close button.

Scheduling an Event

An event is an activity that lasts one day or longer, such as vacations, seminars, and birthdays. Events are not indicated by blocks of time on the Calendar; instead they are indicated by a banner at the top of a day. In this activity, you'll set an event to remind you of a client's anniversary.

1. **Use the Date Navigator to move to December 19 of this year. If necessary, repeatedly click the right arrow in the Date Navigator to display the month of December.**

The date of December 19 appears above the daily calendar.

2. **Click New All Day Event on the Actions menu.**

The Untitled - Event dialog box appears.

3. **Type** First Anniversary of Dr. Dan's Animal Hospital **in the Subject box.**

4. **Click the Reminder drop-down arrow and set the reminder time to 2 days.**

5. **Click the notes section at the bottom of the dialog box and type** Deliver free sample of pet vitamins with a congratulations note.

The Event dialog box should resemble the one in Figure 1.11.

6. **Click the Save and Close button** 🖫 Save and Close .

A banner appears at the top of the appointment book for December 19.

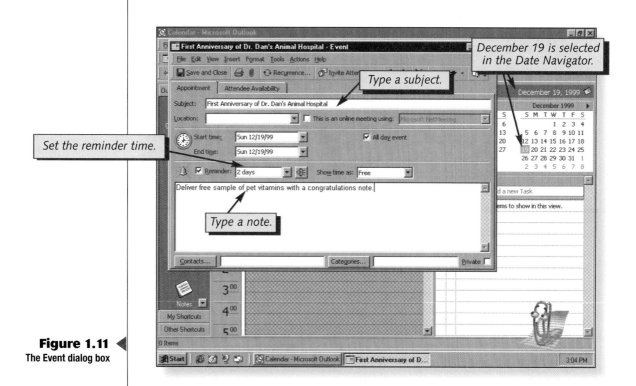

Figure 1.11 ◀
The Event dialog box

Changing Views

- Click the Day button to view one day.

- Click the Week button to view one full week.

- Click the Work Week button to view one work-week (Monday - Friday).

- Click the Month button to view one month.

- Click the Go To Today button to move to the current day in the existing view.

Changing Views

At times, you'll want to look at your calendar a day at a time. Other times, however, you'll want to look at a week or month as a whole. The Outlook Calendar allows you to do just that. In this activity, you'll change the view of your calendar to display different views of it. You'll view an entire week, an entire month, and a five-day workweek. Then you'll use the Go To Today button to return to today's date.

1. Click the Week button [7] Week.

The calendar for the week that includes December 19 appears in the center pane of the window with the event on December 19 displayed.

2. Click the Month button [31] Month.

The entire December calendar is shown.

3. Click the Work Week button [5] Work Week.

The view changes to display the days Monday through Friday with a time slot for each day.

4. Click the Go to Today button Go to Today.

The calendar for the current workweek is displayed in the center pane, and the week is selected in the Date Navigator.

No matter which view you are in, you can view details of a specific appointment by clicking the Preview Pane on the View menu to display the appointment.

Setting a Recurring Meeting

A recurring meeting is one that occurs at regular intervals. For example, if you have a project meeting on the first Wednesday of every month, you set one appointment and tell Outlook to automatically schedule the meeting for the same time each month. Your manager at The Pet Deli, Inc., holds a staff meeting every other Thursday. In this activity, you'll learn how to schedule these recurring meetings, without manually entering an entry for each meeting.

1. **In the center pane, drag to select the 9:30 to 10:30 a.m. time slot for Thursday of this week.**

2. **Click New Recurring Meeting on the Actions menu.**

The Appointment Recurrence dialog box appears.

3. **In the Recurrence pattern box, set the meeting to recur every 2 weeks on Thursday.**

The Appointment Recurrence dialog box should now resemble Figure 1.12.

Office
BASICS

Setting a Recurring Meeting

1. Select the meeting time of the first meeting to schedule.

2. Click New Recurring Meeting on the Actions menu.

3. Set the recurrence pattern in the dialog box that appears and click OK.

4. Type a description of the meeting in the Subject box and click Save on the File menu.

5. Click the Close button.

Figure 1.12 ◄
The Appointment Recurrence dialog box

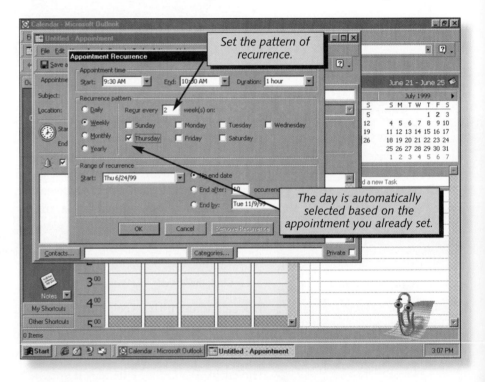

4. **Click OK.**

Outlook automatically assumes that you want to send a mail message to alert others of this meeting.

5. **Move to the Subject box in the Untitled - Appointment window, type Staff Meeting and then click Save on the File menu. Since you do not need to send a message at this time to notify others of the meeting, close the dialog box.**

As shown in Figure 1.13, the 9:30 a.m. meeting reminder appears in the box for Thursday in the center pane. Looking at the Date Navigator, you can see that every other Thursday date is bold, indicating that the meeting has been set on these dates.

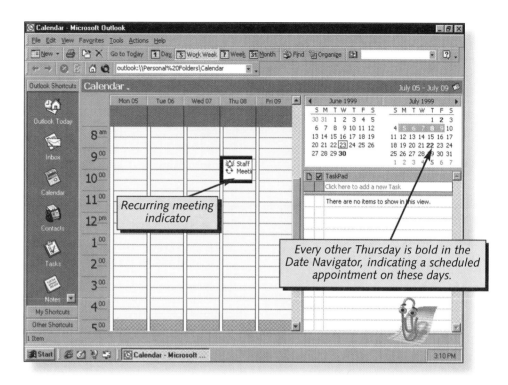

Figure 1.13
Setting a recurring meeting

Recurring meeting indicator

Every other Thursday is bold in the Date Navigator, indicating a scheduled appointment on these days.

6. Click the Month button 🗓Month **to switch to Month view.**

As you can see, the Staff Meeting title appears every other Thursday. You can scroll down to see the meeting reminders that occur in future months.

CREATING CONTACTS

The Contacts tool of Outlook acts as a personal and business address book. Outlook allows you to create and delete contacts; view, sort, and filter contacts; quickly send messages to a contact; and track activities entered in the journal (which you'll learn about later in this lesson) concerning the contact.

Creating a New Contact

You can store information about your contacts in the address book. For instance, you can store names, business and home addresses, e-mail addresses, and telephone numbers. To use information without retyping it each time, you can save the data for each contact. In this activity, you will create a few new contacts.

1. Click the Contacts shortcut icon in the Outlook Shortcuts group on the Outlook Bar.

The Contacts window will appear.

Note   *If someone has previously used the Contacts tool on the computer you are using, these contacts may interfere with the completion of this section. Ask your instructor whether you may delete the previously created contacts.*

2. Click the New Contact button 📇New ▾.

Another Way

To create a new contact, press Ctrl + N or point to New on the File menu and click Contact.

Creating a New Contact

1. Click the Contacts shortcut icon.

2. Click the New Contact button.

3. Type the desired information in the Contact window, pressing [Tab] to move among fields.

3. Enter the following information in the Untitled - Contact window.

Full Name:	Mr. Robert A. Aarons
Job Title:	Owner
Company:	Centerville Pet Shop
Business Phone:	(513) 555-1824
Home Phone:	(513) 555-8222
Business Fax:	(513) 555-9002
Mobile Phone:	(513) 555-2323
Business Address:	89 Centerville Avenue
	Cincinnati, OH 45222-8880

4. After entering the business address, click the **arrow next to the Business box** in the Address section and click **Home**.

5. Type the following home address for Robert Aarons: 1003 Savannah Court, Cincinnati, OH 45218-1255.

6. Type RAarons@mailrtw.com in the E-mail box, as shown in Figure 1.14.

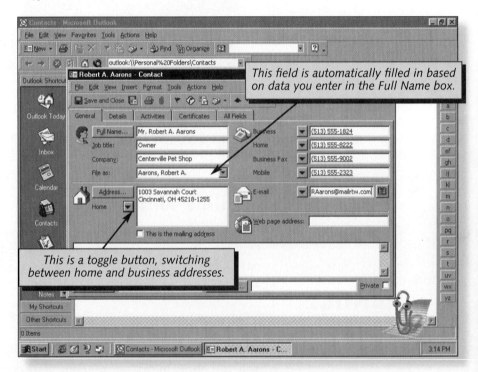

Figure 1.14
The completed Contact window

7. Click the **Save and Close button** [Save and Close]. (If you have Microsoft Small Business Customer Manager installed you may be asked if you want to include this contact in the program. If so, check the *Don't prompt me about this again* box and click No.)

The contact information appears in the Contact window.

8. Repeat steps 2 through 6 to create the following new contact:

Full Name:	Mrs. Rosa P. Lugo
Job Title:	Manager
Company:	The Doggie Den
Business Phone:	(606) 555-9222
Business Fax:	(606) 555-9223
Mobile Phone:	(606) 555-3400
Business Address:	2324 Grand Park Street
	Covington, KY 41011-2399
E-mail:	RLugo@mailrtw.com

Hints & Tips

- You can move from field to field by pressing `Tab`.

- If you don't type parentheses, hyphens, or spaces in telephone numbers, Outlook will add them for you.

9. Since you want to enter other contacts, click the **Save and New button** 🔲 to save the information for this contact and progress to a new, blank Contact window.

10. Create new contacts from the data in Tables 1.2, 1.3, and 1.4. When you save and close the last contact, the Contacts window reappears. The contacts appear in alphabetical order by the File As field (which displays each contact's last name, first name, and middle initial, if available).

TABLE 1.2	DATA FOR NEW CONTACTS 1-3		
	Contact 1	**Contact 2**	**Contact 3**
Full Name	Dr. Daniel Sweeney	Dr. Margaret Miata	Ms. Aileiah Smolty
Job Title	Owner		Manager
Company	Dr. Dan's Animal Hospital	Valley Emergency Animal Hospital	Alley's Pet Place
Business Phone	(513) 555-3000	(513) 555-8712	(606) 555-3112
Home Phone	(513) 555-1888		
Business Fax	(513) 555-3003	(513) 555-4322	(606) 555-6775
Mobile Phone	(513) 555-3009	(513) 555-2902	(606) 555-3337
Business Address	73 Petros Avenue Cincinnati, OH 45218-1899	13 South Street Cincinnati, OH 45220-9333	1892 Delgado Avenue Covington, KY 45011-7790
Home Address	9012 City Boulevard Amelia, OH 45102-2311		
E-mail	DrDan@ammt.com	Miata@mailrtw.com	Aileiah24@ammt.com
Web Page	www.DrDanSw.com		

TABLE 1.3	DATA FOR NEW CONTACTS 4-6		
	Contact 4	**Contact 5**	**Contact 6**
Full Name	Mr. Gunther Pratt	Mr. Alexander Hori	Ms. Marie Rolland
Job Title		Customer Service Representative	
Company		The Pet Deli, Inc.	
Business Phone	(513) 555-2190	(513) 555-3456	
Home Phone	(513) 555-5553	(513) 555-9026	(513) 555-7045
Business Fax		(513) 555-1899	
Mobile Phone		(513) 555-5477	
Home Address	1384 Safeway Court Cincinnati, OH 45255-7223	23 Pinnacle Way Cincinnati, OH 45255-1824	
E-mail		Type your instructor's e-mail address or a classmate's e-mail address.	
Web Page			

TABLE 1.4	DATA FOR NEW CONTACTS 7-9		
	Contact 7	**Contact 8**	**Contact 9**
Full Name	Mr. Patrick Perry	Mr. Andres Wallace	Mrs. Cindy Latty
Job Title		Sales Manager	
Company		The Pet Deli, Inc.	
Business Phone		(513) 555-0223	(513) 555-3390
Home Phone	(513) 555-0033	(513) 555-1234	(606) 555-0655
Business Fax		(513) 555-8235	
Home Address		89000 South Circle Drive Cincinnati, OH 45233-3344	17 Oak Street Covington, KY 41015-1382
E-mail		AWallace@petdeli.com	CLatty@mailrtw.com

Modifying a Contact

Outlook allows you to change contact information easily. In this activity, you will change the information for two contacts.

1. **Double-click the name bar for Robert Aarons.**

The Contact window for Robert Aarons appears. You want to add the pager number for Mr. Aarons.

2. **Click the arrow next to the Mobile box and click Pager on the list that appears.**

3. **Type (513) 555-1185 in the Pager box, as shown in Figure 1.15. Then click the Save and Close button** 💾 Save and Close .

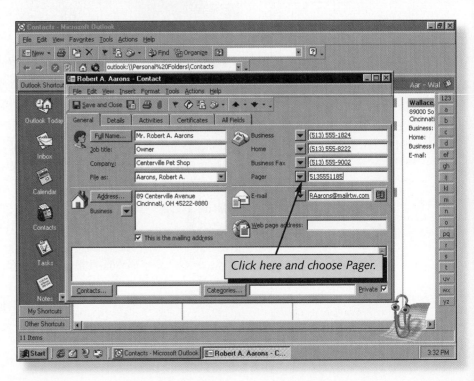

Figure 1.15
Typing a pager number

4. Double-click the **name bar for Daniel Sweeney**. If Daniel Sweeney's name does not appear in the window due to the number of contacts entered, click the button to the right of the window that contains the letter *S* to jump to the contacts last names that begin with the letter *S*.

5. When the Contact window appears, click the **Details tab**.

6. Click the **Anniversary drop-down arrow** and click **December 19** of the current year. Then click the **Save and Close button** [Save and Close].

HANDS On

Sorting and Finding Contacts

To sort contacts:

1. Point to Current View on the View menu and click Customize Current View.

2. Click the Sort button and select the sort criteria. Then click OK.

3. Click OK.

To find information:

1. Click the Find button.

2. Type the data for which you are searching and click the Find Now button.

3. Click the Find button again to hide the Find items in Contacts pane.

Sorting and Finding Contact Information

One advantage of storing your contacts in Outlook is the ability to quickly sort and find names, addresses, and other information. You can also view the contact information in various ways. In this activity, you will first sort the contacts by company name. Then you will find all of the contacts who are doctors.

1. Point to **Current View** on the View menu and click **Customize Current View**.

2. In the View Summary dialog box, click the **Sort button**.

3. In the Sort dialog box, click the **Sort items by drop-down arrow** and click **Company**. Click the **Ascending option** if it is not already selected and click **OK**. If a message appears asking if you want to show the Company field, click **Yes**. Click **OK** to close the View Summary dialog box.

The contacts are rearranged in ascending order by company name.

4. Using the scroll bar at the bottom of the window, scroll to the first contact.

As shown in Figure 1.16, those contacts that do not contain a company name are listed first. Your screen may contain more contacts if you did not delete entries made by previous users.

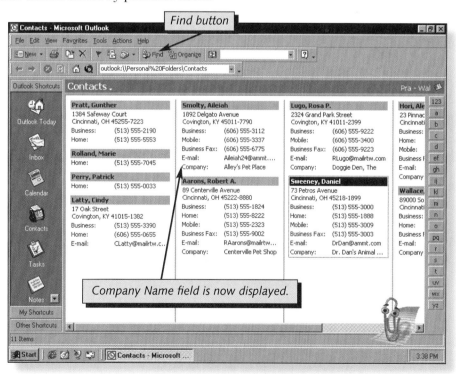

Figure 1.16
Sorted contacts

5. Point to **Current View** on the View menu and click **Customize Current View.** Click the **Sort button** and re-sort the contacts by the **File As field** in **Ascending order.**

You can also find contacts whose fields contain specific information.

6. Click the **Find button** 🔍Find .

The Find items in Contacts pane appears above the addresses.

7. Type Dr. in the Look for box and click the **Find Now button.**

The two records that contain the title *Dr.* in the Name field appear. Outlook can search for this title even though it does not appear on the screen. (If entries from previous users were not deleted, more than two names may appear.)

8. Click the **Find button** 🔍Find .

The Find items in Contacts pane disappears and all of the contacts reappear in the main working area.

Sending an E-Mail to a Contact

Using Outlook, you can send mail messages to contacts without typing their e-mail addresses, and you can call them without manually dialing the telephone. In this activity, you'll create and send an e-mail to one of your contacts without utilizing the Inbox.

1. Select the contact name for Alexander Hori. (If you can't see the name for Alexander Hori, click the button to the right of the window that contains the letter *H* to view the contact names that begin with the letter *H.*)

2. Click the **New Message to Contact button** 📇 .

A new mail message appears, with Alexander Hori's e-mail address automatically inserted in the To box.

3. Type and send an e-mail message asking Alexander to send a sample package of Tiny Paws food to Aileiah Smolty at Alley's Pet Place.

 *If your computer has a modem and telephone voice capabilities, you can call a contact by selecting the contact name, clicking the Dial button* 📞 , *and choosing the desired phone number.*

TRACKING TASKS

Outlook not only helps you track your mail messages, appointments, and contacts, but also lets you track things you need to do. The Tasks component of Outlook is an electronic to-do list. In this section, you'll learn how to create a new task, assign a priority to the task, sort tasks, and mark a task as complete.

Creating a New Task

1. Click the Tasks shortcut icon.

2. Click the New Task button.

3. Type a description of the task in the Subject box, select a due date if desired, and choose any other options you wish.

4. Click the Save and Close button.

Figure 1.17
The Task dialog box

Another Way

- To create a new task, press Ctrl + N or point to New on the File menu and click Task.

- To quickly add a task while in the task list, click the first line that reads Click here to add a new Task.

Creating a New Task

When you create a new task, it appears on your task list. You can assign a due date and a priority to any task. You can also give other details, such as a start date, percentage completed, and billing information concerning the task. In this activity, you'll create several new tasks, assigning priorities and due dates to most of them.

1. Click the Tasks shortcut icon in the Outlook Shortcuts group of the Outlook Bar.

The Tasks list appears in the main working area.

Note   *If someone has previously used the Tasks tool on the computer you are using, these tasks may interfere with the completion of this section. Ask your instructor whether you may delete the previously created tasks.*

2. Click the New Task button 🗹 New ▾.

3. When the Untitled - Task dialog box appears, type Send brochures to pet stores in the Subject box. Click the Due date drop-down arrow and click next Tuesday as a due date. Change the Priority to High.

As shown in Figure 1.17, an informational banner appears at the top of the tab telling you how many days you have to complete the task.

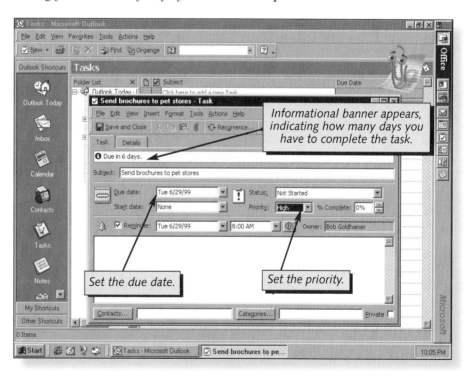

4. Click the Save and Close button 🔲 Save and Close.

The task appears on the task list.

5. Create the new tasks listed in Table 1.5. When you are finished, your screen may contain other tasks in the task list if you did not delete entries made by previous users.

TABLE 1.5	DATA FOR NEW TASKS			
	Task 1	**Task 2**	**Task 3**	**Task 4**
Task	Send birthday card to Gunther Pratt	Schedule dentist appointment	Make airline reservations for conference in Atlanta, GA	Create database of vendors
Due Date	October 14	July 2	April 24	None
Priority	Normal	Normal	High	Low

HANDS On

Arranging and Sorting Tasks

1. Point to Current View on the View menu and click Detailed List.

2. Click the heading of the column by which you want to sort.

Arranging and Sorting Tasks

No matter what order you add tasks to your list, if you view them in Simple List view, Outlook sorts the tasks by due date. In this activity, you will learn how to change the task list to view more information about each task and then change the sort order.

1. Point to Current View on the View menu and click Detailed List.

New columns appear in the task list showing new information including the priority and status of each task.

2. Click the Due Date column heading.

The tasks are sorted by due date in reverse order.

3. Click the Due Date column heading again.

The tasks are sorted by due date.

4. Click the Priority column heading.

As shown in Figure 1.18, the tasks are sorted by priority with the high priority tasks listed first and the low priority tasks listed last.

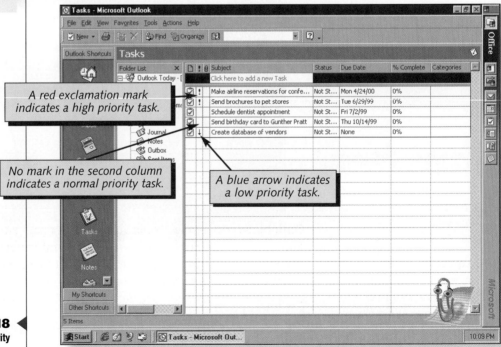

Figure 1.18 ◀
Sorting tasks by priority

5. Point to Current View on the View menu and click Simple List.

Figure 1.19
Marking a task as complete

Deleting and Marking Tasks

When you complete a task, sometimes you'll want to remove it from your task list. To do so, you can use the Delete button. Other times, you will want to keep it on your list but cross it off to remind you that it has been completed; this process is called marking the task as complete. In this activity, you'll first mark a task as complete. Then you'll delete another task.

1. Click the **check box** (in the second column) next to the Send brochures to pet stores task.

As shown in Figure 1.19, Outlook inserts a check mark in the box and draws a line through the task and its due date to indicate that you have completed the task.

2. Since your duties at work have increased, your manager decided to indefinitely postpone the creation of a database of vendors. To remove the task from your list, select it and then click the **Delete button** ⊠.

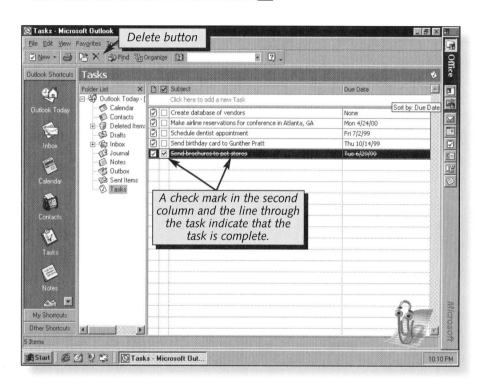

ORGANIZING WITH NOTES

Outlook Notes are electronic versions of paper self-stick, removable notes. You can use them to store any bits of information that you need. For instance, you might use notes to record ideas, questions, or comments. You can type any data you wish on notes. You can resize notes to fit the text on each and you can color code notes. Outlook allows you to view your notes as icons or as lists.

HANDS on

Creating and Opening Notes

1. Click the Notes shortcut icon.

2. Click the New Note button.

3. Type the desired data on the note.

4. Click the note's Close button.

Creating and Opening Notes

To create notes, you can start in the Notes folder of the Outlook Bar. If your defaults have not been changed, a new note appears yellow in color and medium in size. In this activity, you'll create three notes. In the first scenario, you are speaking with a travel agent on the phone to make arrangements for two trips. You'll jot down the notes electronically.

1. **Click the Notes shortcut icon** in the Outlook Shortcuts group of the Outlook Bar.

   If someone has previously used the Notes tool on the computer you are using, these notes may interfere with the completion of this section. Ask your instructor if you may delete the previously created notes.

2. **Click the New Note button . If the defaults have not been changed, a medium-sized yellow note will appear. The current date and time appear at the bottom of the note.**

3. **Type the following information on the note:**

   Flight #325
   Depart Cincinnati at 2:40 p.m. on 11/3
   Arrive in Boston at 4:50 p.m. on 11/3

   Flight #1288
   Depart Boston at 3:50 p.m. on 11/6
   Arrive in Cincinnati at 6:05 p.m. on 11/6

The note should resemble the one in Figure 1.20.

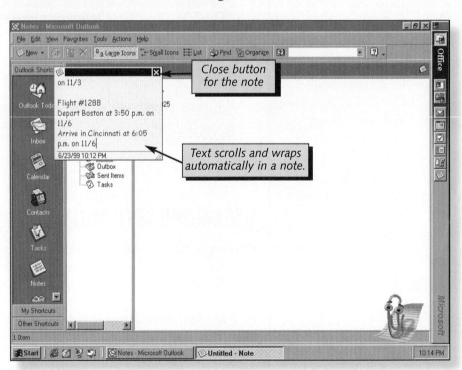

Figure 1.20
Creating a new note

4. Click the **Close button** ☒ on the note.

The note shrinks to an icon labeled Flight #325.

5. Create two more notes containing the information in Table 1.6. Then close the notes.

TABLE 1.6	DATA FOR NOTES
Note 1	**Note 2**
Hotel Arrangements in Boston	Flight #890
The Raven Inn	Depart Cincinnati at 6:42 p.m. on 12/10
395 Presser Blvd.	Arrive in Dallas at 7:52 p.m. on 12/10
$156 per night	Flight #211
Check in by 7:00 p.m. on 11/3	Depart Dallas at 8:39 p.m. on 12/16
Check out by 2:00 p.m. on 11/6	Arrive in Cincinnati at 11:45 p.m. on 12/16
Confirmation #12370	

You should now see three icons for the notes you created.

Changing the Size and Color of a Note

1. Double-click a note to open it.

2. Drag the bottom-right corner to resize the note. Then close it.

3. Right-click the note, point to Color, and click a color.

Changing the Size and Color of a Note

You can categorize your notes by changing their colors. You can also change the size of a note to fit the text in it. In this activity, you'll open the notes you created and change their sizes and colors.

1. Double-click the **Flight #325 note** to open it.

2. Drag the bottom-right corner down and to the right so that the text fits in the note, as shown in Figure 1.21. Then close the note to save it.

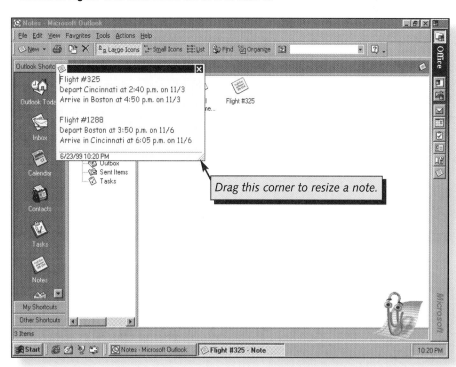

Drag this corner to resize a note.

Figure 1.21 ◀
Resizing a note

To organize your notes, you've decided to make all of your Boston trip notes yellow and your Dallas trip notes green.

3. Right-click the **Flight #890 note**, point to **Color**, and click **Green**.

4. Open the **Flight #890 note**.

The note now appears as green.

5. Resize the note so that all of the text fits on it and then close the note.

You can also set the color and size of a note before you create it.

6. Click the **Tools menu** and click **Options**.

7. In the Options dialog box, click the **Preferences tab** and click the **Note Options button**.

8. In the Note Options box, select **Green** as the color, **Large** as the size, and click **OK**. Then click **OK** to close the Options dialog box.

9. Create a new note with the changed color and size to record the following hotel arrangements for your Dallas trip and then close the note:

Hotel Arrangements in Dallas
The Portsmouth
1812 Chaplin Street
$169 per night
Late check in is okay on 12/10
Check out by 2:00 p.m. on 12/16
Confirmation #3GH77

10. Create a note to remind yourself to take the *Pet Deli* PowerPoint presentation and 100 sample variety treat packs to Boston. Use the appropriate color and resize the note, if necessary.

Changing the View and Sorting Notes

The Icons view of notes shows the first line of text as the note title. To view more text, you can change to a different view. In this activity, you will display the notes in a variety of views. You will also sort the notes by subject and then by color.

1. Point to **Current View** on the View menu and click **Notes List**.

The notes appear in a list.

2. To sort the notes in alphabetical order by subject, click the **Subject column heading**.

3. Click the **By Color option** on the Current View submenu to view the notes by color.

4. Click the + of each **color category** to view the notes within that category.

As shown in Figure 1.22, the notes are now sorted by color—thus separated into your two trips.

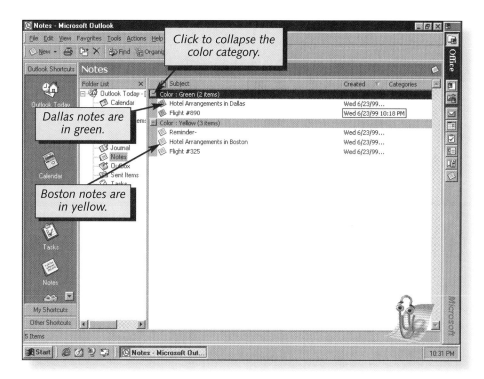

Figure 1.22
Sorting notes by color

5. Switch back to Icons view.

The notes in Icons view are arranged in reverse chronological order of the date and time they were created. You can sort the note icons by using the View menu.

6. Click Current View on the View menu and click Customize Current View. Then click the Sort button. Click the Sort items by drop-down arrow, click Color, and click OK. Click OK again.

The icons are rearranged by color.

Deleting a Note

At some point, each note you create will likely become obsolete. Rather than filling the Notes folder with notes that you no longer need, you can delete notes. You can delete notes one at a time or you can delete groups of notes. After you return from your Boston trip, you no longer need the notes for it. In this activity, you will delete all of the notes related to this trip.

1. Click the first yellow note related to your Boston trip.

2. Hold down [⇧ Shift] and click the last yellow note related to your Boston trip. If other yellow notes were previously created by another user and are highlighted by your actions, select only your three yellow notes by clicking the first note, holding down [Ctrl], and clicking each of the other notes.

All three of the Boston notes are selected.

3. Click the Delete button ☒.

The notes are removed from the window.

Deleting Notes

1. Select the note(s) you wish to delete.

2. Click the Delete button.

USING OUTLOOK TODAY

The Outlook Today page gives you a quick preview of your day. When you click its icon, the main working area of Outlook displays your appointments for the day, your complete task list, and a summary of e-mail messages.

Getting an Overview of Your Day

In this activity, you will view the Outlook Today page to review your day at a glance. You will then learn how to mark a task as complete from the Outlook Today page and move to another part of Outlook.

1. Click the **Outlook Today shortcut icon** in the Outlook Shortcuts group of the Outlook Bar.

The Outlook Today page appears. It should resemble the one in Figure 1.23. If other users have set additional appointments, tasks, or messages, some of the data on the page may vary.

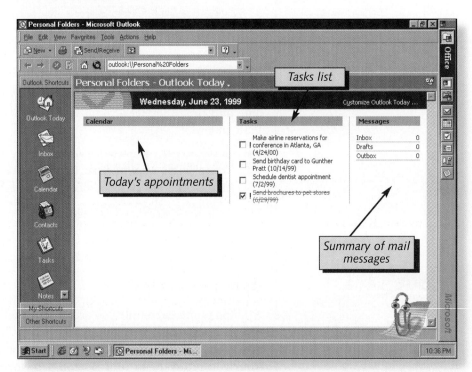

Figure 1.23 ◄
The Outlook Today page

Since you called your dentist yesterday to schedule an appointment, you can mark this task as complete. Rather than switching to your task list to do so, you can mark the task on the Outlook Today page.

2. Click the **check box** in front of the dental appointment task.

To indicate that the task has been completed, a check mark appears in front of the task and a line is drawn through its description. From the Outlook Today page, you can move to other areas of Outlook without using the shortcut icons.

Using Outlook Today

1. Click the Outlook Today shortcut icon.

2. Review the Outlook Today page.

3. Click an item to review, modify, or delete it.

4. Click the Outlook Today shortcut icon to return to the Outlook Today page.

You can click a task's description to open the window that contains its details.

Creating Journal Entries

1. Click the Journal shortcut icon in the Outlook Bar.

2. If desired, click the activities in the Journal Options dialog box that you wish to track.

3. Click the New Journal Entry button and specify the characteristics of the new journal entry.

4. Click the Save and Close button.

3. Click Inbox in the Messages column.

Outlook opens the Inbox, displaying any messages in it. If you have new mail, you may read it.

4. Click the Outlook Today shortcut icon on the Outlook Bar.

Outlook returns you to the Outlook Today page.

USING THE JOURNAL

The Journal tracks the history of various activities. Some activities, such as opening an Office document, are automatically tracked. You can instruct the Journal to track other activities, such as mail messages sent to specific contacts. You can even create Journal entries to track non-computerized activities, such as placing a phone call.

Creating Journal Entries

When you start Outlook for the first time, a dialog box appears asking what types of activities you wish to record. The activities you choose are automatically recorded in the journal. You can manually track other activities as well. In this activity, you will first specify the types of activities to be recorded. Then you will create manual journal entries for a phone call and fax. Another entry will be recorded automatically when you create a new Word document.

1. In the Outlook Bar, click the Journal shortcut icon. The Journal icon may be in the Outlook Shortcuts or the My Shortcuts group.

2. If you see a message telling you that you don't need the Journal to track e-mail and confirming that you want to turn the Journal on, click Yes. If you don't recieve a message about turning on the Journal, click Options on the Tools menu. Then click the Journal Options button.

The Journal Options dialog box appears in which you can specify the types of activities you want to track.

3. Click the necessary options so that your dialog box looks like Figure 1.24. Then click OK.

4. Click OK to close the Journal Options dialog box.

The journal, which appears as a timeline, appears in the main working area.

5. Click the New Journal Entry button ⬚ New ▾.

6. Type New Product Name in the Subject box in the Untitled - Journal Entry window. If it is not already selected, click the Entry type drop-down arrow and click Phone call.

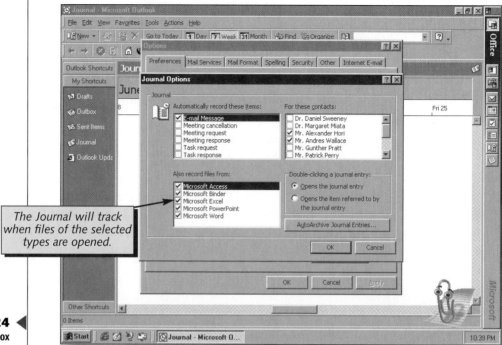

The Journal will track when files of the selected types are opened.

Figure 1.24 ◀
The Journal Options dialog box

7. **Click the Contacts button**, click **Alexander Hori** in the Select Contacts dialog box, and click **OK**.

8. Set the **Start Time** to 7:30 a.m. and the **Duration** to 30 Minutes. In the Notes box, type Discussed names for the new nutritional supplement. I will fax the top seven names to Alexander at the Cincinnati office today.

9. Click the **Save and Close button** .

You return to the Journal window. A category named *Phone Call* is added to the window.

Note — *If other phone calls were previously recorded, the category existed before you created the new journal entry. Later in the lesson, you'll find your entry within that category.*

10. **Open Word and use a template to create a fax to send to Alexander. Switch to your Contact list to find Alexander's phone and fax numbers and include them in the document. Make up and include the seven potential names for the new nutritional supplement product. Save the Word document as *New Product Names Fax* in the *Tutorial Solutions* folder in the *Tutorial* folder on your Integration Student Data Disk. Then close the document and exit Word.**

11. **Return to Journal and create another journal entry recording the fax that you sent to Alexander. Use the same name (New Product Name) in the Subject box and select Alexander as the contact. Set the time as the time of day now and the duration as 5 minutes. Provide a description of the document in the Notes section. Then, save and close the journal entry.**

When you return to the Journal window, three categories of entries are shown: *Fax, Microsoft Word,* and *Phone Call.*

Every time you delete an Outlook item, whether it's a mail message, journal entry, or other item, it is transferred to the Deleted Items folder.

HANDS On

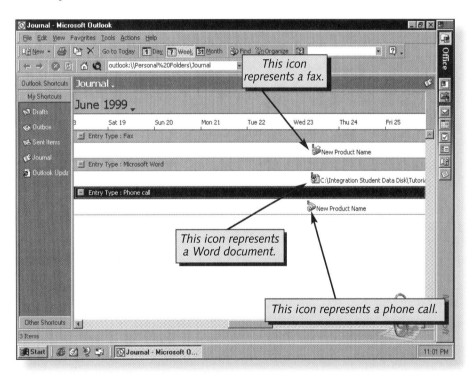

Office BASICS

Viewing and Opening Journal Entries

1. Click the + next to the category in which the journal entry was made.

2. If desired, change the view to the Day or Week view.

3. Scroll to find the entry for the activity.

4. Double-click the entries icon to open it and see the details.

Figure 1.25
Viewing the phone call journal entry

Viewing and Opening Journal Entries

After you create journal entries, you can use the journal to view them. Using the journal is an excellent way to track activities. For instance, you might need to recall the date and details of a phone call that you made regarding a specific issue. If you tracked the activity, you can look through your journal to see the date and time of the phone call as well as specifics of the conversation itself. In this activity, you'll view journal entries.

1. **If necessary, click the Week button [7 Week] to view the Journal in Week view.**

2. **Click the + next to the Fax category.**

The category opens and the *New Product Name* fax icon and name appear under today's date. This indicates that the fax was sent today.

3. **Click the + next to the Microsoft Word category.**

The path and file name *C:\Integration Student Data Disk\Tutorial\Tutorial Solutions\New Product Names Fax* appear under the Microsoft Word category. This entry indicates that the file was opened today.

4. **Finally, click the + next to the Phone Call category.**

As shown in Figure 1.25, the *New Product Name* phone call entry appears under today's date.

5. **Click the Day button [1 Day] to change to Day view.**

6. **If necessary, use the bottom scroll bar to scroll to the location on the time line that shows 7:30 a.m. today.**

The phone call entry appears. The small gray bar at the top of the entry indicates the start time, and its length indicates the duration of the call.

Another Way

To expand all groups at once, point to Expand/Collapse Groups on the View menu and click Expand All.

7. Double-click the **phone call icon**.

The Journal Entry dialog box appears, listing the details of your conversation.

8. Close the dialog box and scroll to the time that you opened the Word document.

You should see the icons and names for the Word document and fax, as shown in Figure 1.26. Your manager would like a copy of the fax that you sent to Alexander, but you didn't keep the printout. However, Outlook will allow you to reopen the document.

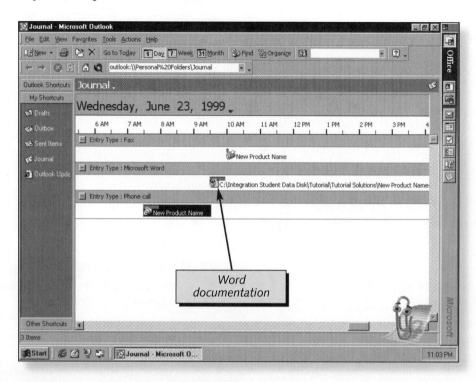

Figure 1.26
Icons for the Word document and fax journal entry

9. Double-click the **Word document icon** called *New Product Names Fax*.

The New Product Names Fax - Journal Entry window appears, as shown in Figure 1.27. Notice that an icon representing the document appears in the bottom section of the window. Double-clicking this icon opens the document.

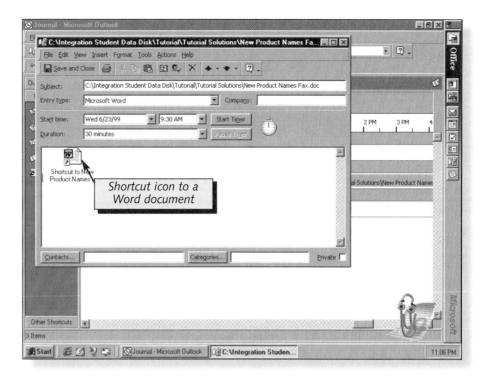

Figure 1.27
The New Product Names Fax -
Journal Entry window

10. Double-click the **New Product Names Fax icon**. Print, close the file, and then exit Word.

11. When you return to Outlook, close the New Product Names Fax - Journal Entry window. Then close Outlook.

Test your knowledge by answering the following questions. See Appendix B to check your answers.

1. The _____ folder lists a summary of appointments, mail messages, and tasks.

2. You can store addresses, phone numbers, and other information on various people in the _____ folder.

3. The _____ folder tracks computerized and non-computerized activities specified by you.

4. You can use the _____ folder to send and receive electronic mail messages.

5. You can keep track of things you need to do and their due dates in the _____ folder.

Lesson Summary & Exercises

SUMMARY

Microsoft Outlook is Office 2000's personal information manager program—an application that keeps track of your daily personal and/or business activities. Outlook organizes these activities into folders, and can display one or more of these folders on your desktop. The Inbox is where you read, compose, and send e-mail messages. In the Calendar, you make, view, and edit appointments and other events. You enter information about people—addresses, phone numbers, birthdays, and so on—in the Contacts folder. By entering Tasks as a to-do list, you make sure that your most important obligations are done on time. You can jot down information that doesn't fit into one of the other categories as an entry in the Notes folder. Using Outlook Today you can view a summary of all the information on today's activities, including appointments, tasks, and mail messages. Finally, the Journal keeps track of the times, durations, and other facts of various activities.

Now that you have completed this lesson, you should be able to do the following:

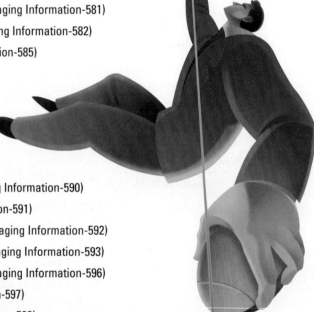

- Describe how Microsoft Outlook helps you manage personal information, track activities, and share information with others. (Managing Information-580)
- Launch Microsoft Outlook. (Managing Information-580)
- Display the contents of Outlook folders. (Managing Information-581)
- Create and send an e-mail message. (Managing Information-582)
- Read an e-mail message. (Managing Information-585)
- Reply to an e-mail message. (Managing Information-586)
- Explain the archiving process. (Managing Information-587)
- Schedule an appointment in the Calendar. (Managing Information-587)
- Schedule an event in the Calendar. (Managing Information-590)
- Change Calendar views. (Managing Information-591)
- Set a recurring meeting in the Calendar. (Managing Information-592)
- Create a contact in the Contacts folder. (Managing Information-593)
- Modify a contact in the Contacts folder. (Managing Information-596)
- Sort and find contacts. (Managing Information-597)
- Send e-mail to a contact. (Managing Information-598)
- Create a new task in the Tasks folder. (Managing Information-599)
- Arrange and sort tasks. (Managing Information-600)
- Delete and mark tasks as complete. (Managing Information-601)
- Create and open a note in the Notes folder. (Managing Information-602)
- Change the color and size of a note. (Managing Information-603)
- Change the view or sort order of notes. (Managing Information-604)
- Delete a note. (Managing Information-605)
- View a summary of the current day's activities by using the Outlook Today folder. (Managing Information-606)
- Record entries in the Journal folder. (Managing Information-607)
- View and open Journal entries. (Managing Information-609)

Lesson Summary & Exercises

PROJECTS

You should complete all of these projects in sequence; they build upon each other and demonstrate integration among the Outlook tools.

1 Create a New Contact

Add a classmate's name, address, phone number, and e-mail address as a new contact. Assume that your classmate works at The Pet Deli, Inc., as a production manager and include that information in the company and job title boxes. Set the Outlook options so that e-mail messages with this contact are recorded automatically. Then send a mail message to this contact asking for information about the recommended daily serving sizes for Kibble Senior dog food.

2 Create a Journal Entry

A few hours after sending the e-mail message in Project 1, your coworker responds with the information in Table 1.7.

TABLE 1.7	KIBBLE SENIOR DOG FOOD
Weight of Dog	**Amount of Food**
5 lbs.	1/2 cup
10 lbs.	7/8 cup
20 lbs.	1 1/2 cups
40 lbs.	2 1/2 cups
60 lbs.	3 1/4 cups
80 lbs.	4 1/4 cups
100 lbs.	5 cups

Since you are not sure whether the measurements of food are per meal or per day, you stop by your coworker's office to ask. You learn that the food measurements provided are the total amounts for one day. Record the five-minute conversation in your journal. Create a new Excel workbook and type the information about food amounts. Save the workbook as *Daily Serving Sizes* in the *Projects Solutions* folder in the *Projects* folder on your Integration Student Data Disk. Close the file and exit Excel.

3 Create a Task and Appointments

You are preparing to hire a new assistant. First, add a task to your task list to call the human resources department; you need four brochures that explain the company's benefits to your potential assistant candidates. Then, mark next week's calendar with the interview times shown in Table 1.8. Assume that each interview will last one hour. View your appointments in Day, Week, and Month views. On a separate sheet of paper, describe the advantages and disadvantages of each of the views.

TABLE 1.8	INTERVIEW TIMES	
Candidate	**Day**	**Time**
Mauricio Espino	Tuesday	2:00 p.m.
Penny Appleton	Thursday	2:00 p.m.
Tyler Jacobs	Thursday	3:30 p.m.
Mary Ellen Zickerman	Friday	8:00 a.m.

4 Create a Note, Create a Recurring Appointment, and Complete a Task

You just learned that a new pet store is moving into the area. Create a note to record the name and location of the store, Pet Boutique in the West Square Mall. The expected opening date is November 30 of this year. Change the color of the note to pink, since this is the color you use to indicate that a note contains information to include in your monthly report. Resize the note if necessary. Send a copy of the note to a classmate without retyping it; use Help if you can't figure out how to do this. Next, set a recurring event in your calendar to remind you that your monthly report is due on the last Friday of each month. Set the event so that you are reminded one day in advance. Lastly, since you received the brochures from human resources, mark this task as complete while you are in the Outlook Today window.

5 Write Journal Contents and Print a Mail Message from a Journal

Look at the journal for today (or the days that you worked on this lesson). On a separate sheet of paper, list the entries made, the category of each entry, and whether the entry was automatically or manually entered. From the Journal window, open and print the mail message that you sent to your coworker asking about recommended serving amounts for Kibble Senior dog food (Project 2).

6 Send a Web Page by E-mail

One of your customers owns a shop that specializes in products made for cats. You want to tell them about a Web site that you found for cat fanciers. With the Web toolbar displayed, type www.fanciers.com in the Address bar and press Enter←. The Cat Fanciers page will be displayed in the main working area. Then click Send Web Page by E-mail on the Actions menu. When the new mail message appears, type the address of your instructor or a classmate and type a brief message explaining that you are sending a link to a Web page in which they might be interested. Send the e-mail and then close Outlook.

LESSON 2

Integrating Office 2000

CONTENTS

OBJECTIVES

After you complete this lesson, you will be able to do the following:

- Set appointments in the Calendar and copy them into an Excel worksheet.
- Enter new contacts and create a letter automatically addressed to one of them.
- Embed an Excel worksheet into a Word letter.
- Import a database of names, addresses, and numbers into the Contacts folder.
- Copy text from a Word document into an Outlook journal entry.
- Send a PowerPoint document to Word.
- Create a new form letter and merge it with selected Outlook contacts.
- Use Word as your e-mail editor link.
- Add a Web page shortcut to your Outlook Bar.

As you have learned in this tutorial Office 2000 provides many ways to integrate data among the Office 2000 programs. Although the results of Outlook often do not result in printed documents as in the other programs, you can still integrate data from Outlook with the other Office programs. In this lesson, you will create various documents that combine data from the Calendar, Contacts, and Journal tools of Outlook with Word, Excel, PowerPoint, and Access.

OFFICE in the workplace

In this lesson, you'll integrate several aspects of Outlook with other Office 2000 programs, thus further increasing your productivity in the workplace.

HANDS On

Office BASICS

Setting Appointments

1. Open the Calendar folder in Outlook.

2. Click the date on which to set the appointment.

3. Switch to the view you wish to use.

4. Double-click the desired time slot and enter the appointment data.

5. Click Save and Close.

INTEGRATING CALENDAR DATA INTO A WORKSHEET

As you know, you can view the Outlook Calendar in several views. You can copy data from your Calendar using any view; however, certain views allow you to see and copy more data at one time. For instance, using one view, you can display all your active appointments in a table format; you can easily copy this data to an Excel worksheet.

As you work through the activities in this lesson, assume that you work for Parker Consultants, a company that helps other companies increase their sales. As your first task as an associate for Parker Consultants, you will integrate information that you've entered in your Outlook Calendar into an Excel worksheet.

Setting Appointments

In this activity, you work for Parker Consultants, a company that helps other companies increase sales. You are traveling to meet with several prospective clients next month and need to mark your appointments in the Calendar.

1. **Launch Outlook and click the Calendar shortcut icon.**

2. **Click the first Wednesday of next month in the Date Navigator and switch to Work Week view. (If appointments that you or another user set during completion of Lesson 1, *Outlook Basics* appear, ask your instructor if you may delete them.)**

3. **Double-click the 1:00 p.m. time slot on Wednesday and set an appointment with the following information:**
   Subject: Mabel Corporation - prospective client appointment
   Location: San Diego, CA
   Start time: 1:00 p.m.
   End time: 3:00 p.m.
   Reminder: 1 hour

4. **Save and close the Appointment dialog box.**

5. **Use the Calendar to set the additional appointments in Table 2.1.**

TABLE 2.1	ADDITIONAL APPOINTMENTS					
Day	**Subject**	**Location**	**Start Time**	**End Time**	**Reminder**	
First Thursday of month	Crosley Mortgage Co. - prospective client appointment	San Diego, CA	9:00 a.m.	11:00 a.m.	1 hour	
First Friday of month	Potter & Newman, Attorneys at Law - prospective client appointment	San Diego, CA	1:00 p.m	3:00 p.m	1 hour	
Second Wednesday of month	Maplewood Retirement Community - prospective client appointment	Los Angeles, CA	2:00 p.m.	4:00 p.m	1 hour	

TABLE 2.1	**ADDITIONAL APPOINTMENTS—cont.**					
Day	**Subject**	**Location**	**Start Time**	**End Time**	**Reminder**	
Second Friday of month	Bright Beginnings, Wedding Consultants - prospective client appointment	Los Angeles, CA	3:00 p.m.	5:00 p.m.	1 hour	
Third Monday of month	Universal Moving Company - prospective client appointment	San Francisco, CA	10:00 a.m.	12:00 p.m.	1 hour	
Third Tuesday of month	United Bank of San Francisco - prospective client appointment	San Francisco, CA	9:00 a.m.	11:00 a.m.	1 hour	

HANDS

Copying Your Appointments to Excel

In a meeting with your manager, she asked you to provide a list of your prospective client meetings scheduled for next month. Rather than retyping all of the information, you can copy the data from your Calendar. In this activity, you will first view your Calendar appointments in Active Appointments view. Then you will copy the appointments and paste them to a new Excel worksheet.

1. **While viewing the Outlook Calendar, point to Current View on the View menu and click Active Appointments.**

The appointments you have scheduled appear in a list, similar to the one shown in Figure 2.1. (If the list is not expanded, click the plus sign in front of the category name. If you did not delete previous appointments, other appointments may appear on the list.)

Copying Calendar Data to Excel

1. While in the Calendar, switch to the Active Appointments view.

2. Select the appointments you wish to copy.

3. Click Copy on the Edit menu.

4. Switch to a blank Excel worksheet.

5. Click the Paste button.

6. Format the worksheet as desired.

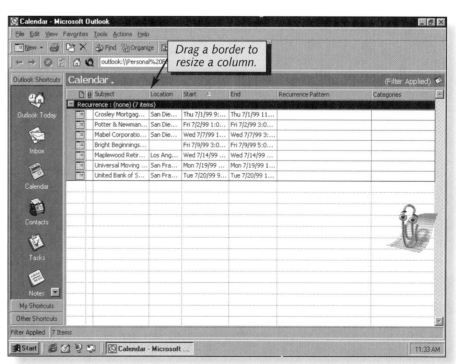

Figure 2.1
Active Appointments view
of the Calendar

You can save any part of your Calendar as a Web page. Simply click Save as Web Page on the File menu and choose the desired options in the Save as Web Page dialog box.

2. Click anywhere in the first appointment row, hold down ⇧ Shift , and click anywhere in the last row. Or, if more appointments appear than your prospective client appointments, click the first one, hold down Ctrl , and click each prospective client appointment.

All of the pertinent appointments are selected.

3. Click **Copy** on the Edit menu.

4. Launch Excel so that a new workbook is opened. Click **cell A1** of the new worksheet and click the **Paste button** 📋.

The selected appointments are pasted to the worksheet.

5. Format the worksheet as desired to improve its appearance.

6. Delete the Recurrence Pattern and Categories column labels if they appear. Save the workbook as *Prospective Client Appointments* in the *Tutorial Solutions* folder of the *Tutorial* folder on your Integration Student Data Disk.

CREATING A WORD LETTER FROM AN OUTLOOK CONTACT ENTRY

Usually, the people that you enter as contacts in Outlook are those with whom you communicate on a regular basis. For that reason, Outlook allows you to start a Word letter directly from the Contacts folder. When you create a letter from the Contacts folder, you don't need to retype the name and address of your contact; Outlook does it for you.

Entering Contacts

In this activity, you will enter names, addresses, and telephone numbers for a few contacts.

1. Switch to Outlook and click the **Contacts shortcut icon**.

2. Click the **New Contact button** 🔲 New ▾ and add the contacts in Table 2.2 to your address book.

Entering Contacts

1. Click the New Contact button in the Contacts folder.

2. Type the desired contact information into the dialog box.

TABLE 2.2	DATA FOR NEW CONTACTS		
Field	**Contact 1**	**Contact 2**	**Contact 3**
Full Name	Ms. Alicia Rodriguez	Mr. Jonathon Martin	Ms. Carol Potter
Job title	Manager	Vice President	Senior Partner
Company	Parker Consultants	Crosley Mortgage Co.	Potter & Newman, Attorneys at Law
Business address	2447 5th Avenue San Diego, CA 92101-9344	2845 Adams Avenue San Diego, CA 92116-8777	1069 Front Street San Diego, CA 92101-6933
Business phone	(619) 555-9322	(619) 555-1189	(619) 555-2222
Business fax	(619) 555-9111	(619) 555-7330	(619) 555-2223
Home phone	(619) 555-1729		
E-mail	arodriguez@parker.com	jmartin@caonline.com	cpotter@caonline.com

Creating a Letter Using a Contact

In this activity, you'll use Outlook's ability to address a letter automatically. Rather than simply providing her with a printout of your worksheet, you've decided to write a letter to your manager, Alicia Rodriguez, to provide her with information about your upcoming appointments with potential new clients.

1. While viewing the Contacts folder, click the **name bar for Alicia Rodriguez.**

2. Click the **Actions menu** and click **New Letter to Contact.**

Microsoft Word is automatically launched and the Letter Wizard appears to help you create a new letter.

3. Click the **Date line option** in the first dialog box and click **Next.**

The second Letter Wizard dialog box appears. Notice that Alicia Rodriguez's name, title, and address are automatically inserted.

4. Continue to click **Next** until you reach the fourth dialog box. If your name does not appear in the Sender's name box, select it from the drop-down list or type it. Click the **Complimentary closing drop-down arrow** and click **Sincerely.** Then click **Finish.**

5. If the Office Assistant asks if you want to do more with the letter, click **Cancel.**

The beginning and ending of your letter are automatically generated, as shown in Figure 2.2. Your manager's name, title, and address are at the top and the closing you selected and your name are at the bottom. You can type the text of your letter to replace the selected text.

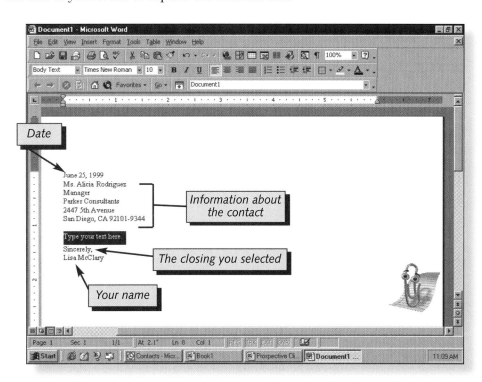

Figure 2.2
The letter generated by the Letter Wizard

6. Type the following text to replace the selected text:

Dear Alicia,

The following table shows the appointments that I have set for the month of (list the name of next month). As you can see, I will be traveling in the San Diego, Los Angeles, and San Francisco areas throughout the month. I am especially hopeful about the appointments that I have with Potter & Newman, Attorneys at Law and Universal Moving Company.

7. Save the letter as *Letter to Rodriguez* in the *Tutorial Solutions* folder in the *Tutorial* folder of your Integration Student Data Disk.

HANDS On

Office BASICS

Copying a Worksheet into a Word Document

1. Select the Excel cells to copy and click the Copy button.

2. Switch to the Word document.

3. Place the insertion point where you want to paste the data and click the Paste button.

4. Reformat the pasted data if desired.

Integrating the Excel Worksheet Data into the Letter

In this activity, you will copy the data from the *Prospective Client Appointments* workbook to your Word document.

1. Switch to Excel. If the *Prospective Client Appointments* workbook is not still open, open it from the *Tutorial Solutions* folder.

2. Select the cells that contain the data on your appointments and click the **Copy button** .

3. Switch back to the *Letter to Rodriguez* document, place the insertion point below the first paragraph, and click the **Paste button** .

4. If necessary, format the pasted data and any other part of the letter to improve its appearance.

Your letter may resemble the one in Figure 2.3.

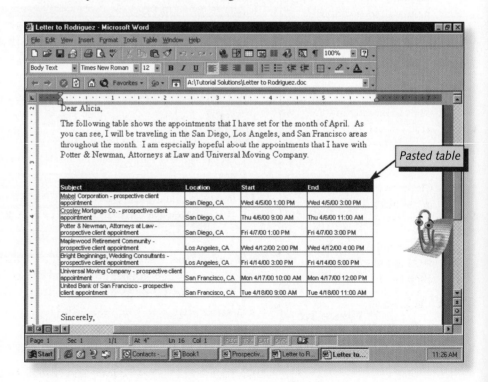

Figure 2.3
Copying a worksheet into a letter

5. Save, print, and close the letter. Then close Excel without saving any changes.

INTEGRATING ACCESS DATA WITH OUTLOOK

You have learned that Access database tables and Outlook's Contact folder often store names, addresses, and telephone numbers. At times, you may want to share data between Outlook and Access. When you use the Export command, Office automatically sets up the needed fields and transfers the contact information.

Importing Database Data into the Contacts Folder

1. Open the Contacts folder in Outlook.

2. Click Import and Export on the File menu.

3. Click Import from another program or file in the dialog box and click Next.

4. Click Microsoft Access in the next dialog box and click Next.

5. Use the Browse button to locate and select the database to import. Click OK.

6. Click the desired option in the next dialog box and click Next.

7. Click Contacts as the destination folder and click Next.

8. Click Finish.

Importing Database Data into the Contacts Folder

Two weeks after your meeting with Potter & Newman, Attorneys at Law, you find that you've landed an account with them. The law firm wants you to help them find ways to attract new clients. One of your first projects is to create a PowerPoint presentation that will introduce the firm to potential new clients. As soon as you were awarded the account, one of the partners at the firm provided an Access database that contains the names, phone numbers, and addresses of the key people at the firm. In this activity, you will transfer the data from Access to your Contacts folder in Outlook.

1. Launch Access and open the database called *Potter & Newman* in the *Tutorial* folder on your Integration Student Data Disk.

2. Open the Key Staff Members table and scroll the data. Notice the names in the table. Then close the table, the database, and Access.

3. Switch to Outlook and open the Contacts folder if it is not already active.

4. Click **Import and Export** on the File menu.

The Import and Export Wizard appears.

5. If the Office Assistant asks if you want help with this feature, click either choice you desire. If you choose help from the Office Assistant, you will see explanatory tips for each dialog box in the Import and Export Wizard.

6. In the Import and Export Wizard dialog box, click **Import from another program or file** and click **Next**. (If you see a message that this feature is not installed, ask your instructor for help.)

7. In the next dialog box, click **Microsoft Access** and click **Next**. (If you receive a message informing you that this feature is not installed, ask your instructor for help.)

8. In the next dialog box, click the **Browse button** and then locate and select the *Potter & Newman* database in the *Tutorial* folder on your Integration Student Data Disk. Then click **OK**.

The name of the *Potter & Newman* database appears in the File to import box. Because you previously entered Carol Potter as a contact and she is included in this database, Outlook will create two Contact entries for her if you leave the default setting in this dialog box.

9. Select the **Replace duplicates with items imported option**, and click **Next**.

10. Click **Contacts** as the destination folder, if it is not already selected, and click **Next**.

The name of the table from which you are exporting (Key Staff Members) and the name of the Contacts folder appear in the next dialog box.

11. Click Finish.

The Import and Export process begins. When it is finished, the Contacts folder will reappear and the names, addresses, and telephone numbers of the Potter & Newman staff members are added as contacts. If you deleted contacts created in Lesson 1, *Outlook Basics,* your folder should resemble the one shown in Figure 2.4.

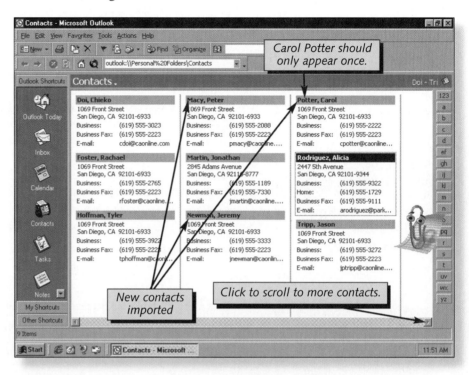

Figure 2.4
New contacts added

12. If spelling, spacing, or punctuation differences cause Carol Potter to appear twice in the Contacts folder, select the one without an e-mail address and click the Delete button.

SHARING TEXT BETWEEN WORD AND OUTLOOK

You can use the Copy and Paste commands to copy data from Word to just about any folder in Outlook. For instance, you can copy text from Word to the body of a new e-mail message, to a note, to a task, or to a calendar entry. Likewise, you can copy text from any of these tools to a Word document.

Copying Text from Word to the Journal

In this activity, you'll copy text from a Microsoft Word document and paste it into a journal entry. You met with Carol Potter, one of the senior partners of the Potter & Newman law firm to discuss the objectives of the firm. You'll be incorporating the information she provided during this meeting into the

PowerPoint presentation that you are creating for them. While talking to Ms. Potter, you took notes on your laptop computer using Microsoft Word. To better track the conversation, you will copy some of the text into a journal entry in Outlook.

1. Click the **Journal shortcut icon** on the Outlook Bar.

2. Create a new journal entry to record a meeting with Carol Potter. The entry should indicate that the meeting took place last Friday at 1:00 p.m. and lasted for two hours.

3. In the Notes section of the entry, type Met with Carol to discuss the law firm's objectives that should be placed in the PowerPoint presentation. The key objectives include the following:

4. Switch to Word without closing the journal entry. Open the document called *Objectives Meeting with Potter* in the *Tutorial* folder on your Integration Student Data Disk.

This Word document contains the notes you took during your meeting with Ms. Potter.

5. Select all the text in the document *except* for the centered title. Then click the **Copy button** 🖺.

6. Switch to the journal entry and press Enter twice to insert a blank line. Then click the **Paste button** 🖺.

The bulleted list is pasted into the journal entry, as shown in Figure 2.5.

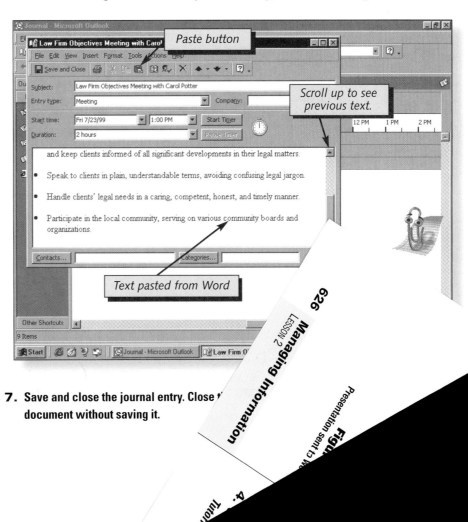

7. Save and close the journal entry. Close document without saving it.

USING MAIL MERGE THROUGH OUTLOOK

Outlook provides a mail merge feature that allows you to create a document addressed to several contacts. You can create a new letter or use an existing one and create a mail merge document that is addressed to all or selected contacts in Outlook.

Sending a PowerPoint Document to Word and Composing a Letter

1. Open the PowerPoint document.

2. Point to Send To on the File menu and click Microsoft Word.

3. Click the desired option in the Write-Up dialog box and click OK.

4. Move to the top of the letter and insert a page break.

5. Move to the top of the first page and type the desired text for the letter.

6. Save and close the document.

Sending a PowerPoint Document to Word and Composing a Letter

You've started a PowerPoint presentation for the Potter & Newman law firm that includes a title slide, the firm's objectives, their areas of practice, and a brief introduction of each partner. Before you continue with the presentation, Carol Potter wants you to send a printout of the partial presentation to each partner, asking each to verify the information in his or her introduction. In this activity, you will open the PowerPoint presentation and send it to Word. Later, you'll use this Word document as the beginning of a letter to send to each partner and insert mail merge fields to automatically address the letters.

1. **Launch PowerPoint and open the *Potter & Newman Introduction* presentation in the *Tutorial* folder on your Integration Student Data Disk.**

2. **Point to Send To on the File menu and click Microsoft Word.**

3. **Click the Blank lines next to slides option in the Write-Up dialog box and click OK.**

Your new Word document should look like the one in Figure 2.6.

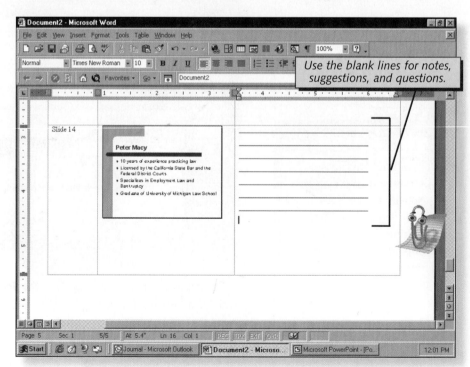

Use the blank lines for notes, suggestions, and questions.

Figure 2.6 ◄
Word

Save the Word document as *Initial Review of Potter & Newman Presentation* in the ...ial Solutions folder in the *Tutorial* folder on your Integration Student Data Disk.

5. With the *Initial Review of Potter & Newman Presentation* letter still open, press Ctrl + Home to move to the top of the document. Insert a page break above the first slide.

6. Compose a letter on the first page of the document that asks each partner to review the printout of the presentation. Ask the partners for feedback about the overall presentation as well as the accuracy of the information about the partners. Then save and close the document.

 Warning

You must close the letter to use it in the mail merge process.

 **HANDS On**

 **Office BASICS**

Mail Merging with Contacts

1. Select the contacts that you wish to use in the merge.

2. Click Mail Merge on the Tools menu.

3. Use the Browse button to find and select the document you wish to merge with and click OK. Click OK again.

4. Choose to edit the document.

5. Insert merge fields.

6. Save the document.

7. Issue the desired merge command.

Merging with Contacts

In this activity, you will create a mail merge document using Outlook.

1. Switch to Outlook and click the **Contacts shortcut icon**.

2. Click the name bar of the first firm partner listed in the Address book, Chieko Doi, to select the contact. Hold down Ctrl and click the names of each of the other partners in the firm. The partners include Chieko Doi, Tyler Hoffman, Peter Macy, Jeremy Newman, and Carol Potter.

3. Click **Mail Merge** on the Tools menu.

The Mail Merge Contacts dialog box appears.

4. In the Document file section, click the **Browse button** next to the Existing document box.

5. Use the Open dialog box to find and select the *Initial Review of Potter & Newman Presentation* document and click **OK**.

6. Make sure that all the options in each section match Figure 2.7. Then click **OK**.

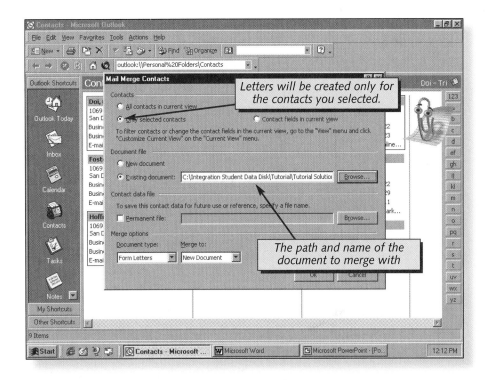

Figure 2.7
The Mail Merge dialog box

After a few moments, your Word letter is opened so that you can insert the necessary merge fields.

7. If the Office Assistant or a message box appears asking you what to do next, click the **Edit MailMerge document option**.

8. Place the insertion point where you want to insert the first line of the addressee, and click the **Insert Merge Field button** `Insert Merge Field ▾` on the Mail Merge toolbar.

A list of merge fields appears.

9. Click the **Title merge field** from the list that appears.

The Title placeholder appears in your letter.

10. Press `Spacebar` and continue to add merge fields so that the beginning of your letter resembles the one in Figure 2.8. Remember to add spaces, hard returns, and punctuation as needed between merge fields.

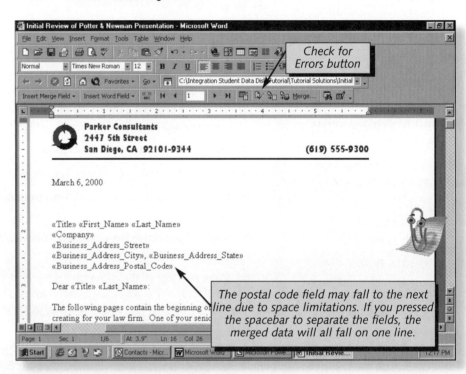

Figure 2.8
The letter with merge fields added

The postal code merge field may fall below the city and state fields because all three field names do not fit on one line. However, if you pressed `Spacebar` to separate the fields, the merged data will all fall on one line.

11. Save the document. Then click the **Check for Errors button** 🔄 on the Mail Merge toolbar.

12. When the Checking and Reporting Errors dialog box appears, click the **Complete the merge, pausing to report each error as it occurs option**. Then click **OK**.

Word checks for mail merge errors and merges the letter with the selected contacts in Outlook.

13. Print one of the merged letters, including the pages that contain the PowerPoint presentation. Then close the merged document without saving it.

14. Close the *Initial Review of Potter & Newman Presentation* letter. Exit all open programs.

Using HELP

Using Word as Your E-mail Editor

Outlook works very well to store incoming and outgoing mail messages, but did you know that you can create an e-mail message using Microsoft Word as well? When you use Word as your e-mail editor, you can take advantage of its powerful features such as spell and grammar checks, AutoCorrect, and tables. You can also use Word to send an existing document to someone. Use Help to learn how to use Word as your e-mail editor.

1. **Launch Word, if it is not already open.**

2. **Click the Office Assistant. Type** e-mail using Word **in the *What would you like to do?* box.**

3. **Click the Search button.**

4. **Click the E-mail messages and documents link.**

Figure 2.9
Learning how to use Word as your e-mail editor

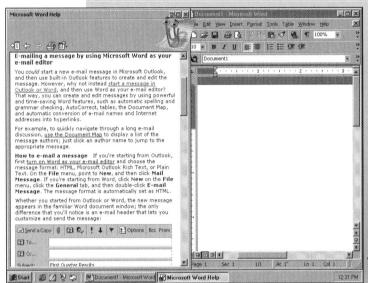

5. **Read the new text in the Help window and click the E-mail a message by using Word as your e-mail editor link.**

6. **Read the new text in the Help window and then click the using Microsoft Word as your e-mail editor link.**

7. **Read the new text to learn even more about using Word as your e-mail editor (Figure 2.9).**

8. **Click any other links in which you are interested.**

9. **If time permits, send a mail message to your instructor or a classmate using Word as your e-mail editor.**

10. **When you are finished exploring, close the Help window.**

Test your knowledge by answering the following questions. See Appendix B to check your answers.

T   F   1. You can copy data from the Contacts folder to an Access database but you cannot copy data from a database to the Contacts folder.

T   F   2. When you use Outlook's mail merge feature, you can create a new letter or use an existing Word document.

T   F   3. One of the best ways to view your Calendar in order to copy it to a worksheet is Active Appointments view.

T   F   4. One of the drawbacks of Outlook's mail merge feature is that you can only use it when you are addressing documents to all contacts; you cannot use it to select specific contacts.

T   F   5. To embed a worksheet into a Word document, use the Copy and Paste Append commands.

ON*the*WEB

ADDING A WEB PAGE SHORTCUT TO YOUR OUTLOOK BAR

You've worked with several of the default shortcut icons on the Outlook Bar to access the Outlook tools such as the Calendar, task list, and more. Outlook also allows you to add your own shortcuts. One special type of shortcut you can add links you to a Web page of your choice. In this activity, you continue to act as an associate at Parker Consultants working to help a law firm gain new clients. To learn more about the law industry, you will use Outlook to navigate to a specific Web page that features several law journals. Since you plan to visit the site on a regular basis, you will add a shortcut to your Outlook Bar that jumps directly to the page.

1. **Launch Outlook. If the Web toolbar is not displayed, right-click any toolbar and click Web.**

2. **In the Address bar of the Web toolbar, type** dir.yahoo.com/government/law/journals **and press** Enter←┘.

As shown in Figure 2.10, the Yahoo! Government Law Journals page appears in the main working area of the Outlook window. (If this page no longer exists, click the Search the Web toolbar button and search for any page that contains a list of law journals.)

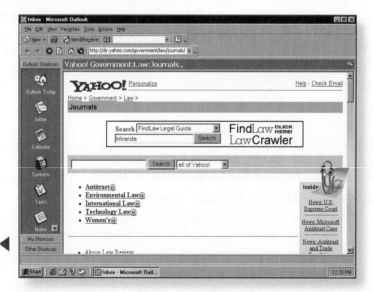

Figure 2.10 ◀
The Yahoo! Government
Law Journals page

Reproduced with permission of Yahoo! Inc. © 1999 by Yahoo! Inc. YAHOO! and the YAHOO! logo are trademarks of YAHOO! Inc.

3. Scroll down the page and click the **In Brief Law Journal link**. (If this link no longer exists, click a link to another law review or journal.)

4. Click the **Legal News link**, click the **LawJournal Directory link**, and finally click the **Articles Online** link.

5. Click the links to read any of the articles.

6. Click the **Back button** on the Web toolbar repeatedly until you return to the original Yahoo! Government Law Journals page (or the home page of another journal).

So you can return to this page quickly, you want to create a shortcut to the page.

7. Point to **New** on the File menu and click **Outlook Bar Shortcut to Web Page**.

A message appears indicating that the new shortcut will be added to the bottom of the My Shortcuts group.

8. Click **OK** to remove the message.

You need to change the display in your main working area so that you can test your new shortcut.

9. Click the **Inbox shortcut icon**.

The main working area changes to display your inbox.

10. Click the **My Shortcuts group**. If necessary, scroll down in the Outlook Bar to find the shortcut you added and then click it.

The Yahoo! Government Law Journal page reappears in the main working area (or another page for the shortcut you added). Now you can click this shortcut anytime you wish to redisplay the page.

11. Ask your instructor whether you should remove the shortcut from the Outlook Bar. If so, right-click the shortcut. Click **Remove from Outlook Bar** and click **Yes** to remove the shortcut.

12. Disconnect from the Internet if your instructor tells you to do so.

You may proceed directly to the exercises for this lesson. If, however, you are finished with your computer session, follow the "shut down" procedures for your lab or school environment.

Lesson Summary & Exercises

SUMMARY

Lesson 2 allowed you to integrate data from all the Office 2000 tools that you have learned about in the integration lessons and in the Office 2000 tutorials. You had a chance to work with the Calendar, Contacts, and Journal tools of Outlook and integrate data with Word, Excel, PowerPoint, and Access.

Now that you have completed this lesson, you should be able to do the following:

■ Schedule appointments using the Calendar. (Managing Information-618)

■ Display appointments in the Active Appointments view and copy them to an Excel worksheet. (Managing Information-619)

■ Enter names, titles, addresses, phone numbers, and e-mail addresses for new contacts. (Managing Information-620)

■ Use Outlook to automatically address a letter to a selected contact. (Managing Information-621)

■ Copy an Excel worksheet and paste it into a Word document. (Managing Information-622)

■ Import a database of names, addresses, and numbers into the Contacts folder. (Managing Information-623)

■ Copy selected text from a Word document and paste it into the Notes box of an Outlook journal entry. (Managing Information-624)

■ Use the Send To command to copy the contents and design of a PowerPoint presentation to Word. (Managing Information-626)

■ Create a new form letter and use Outlook to merge it with selected contacts. (Managing Information-627)

■ Use Help to learn how to use Word as your e-mail editor. (Managing Information-629)

■ Add a Web page shortcut to your Outlook Bar. (Managing Information-630)

CONCEPTS REVIEW

1 TRUE/FALSE

Circle T if the statement is true or F if the statement is false.

T   F   **1.** When importing database data into the Contacts folder, the *Replace duplicates with items imported* option allows you to create multiple contact entries for the same person.

T   F   **2.** To use Outlook's mail merge process with an existing document, the existing document must be open.

T   F   **3.** You can use Microsoft Word to create an e-mail document.

T   F   **4.** When you click the Week button in Calendar, the calendar for only Monday through Friday of the current week appears in the main working area.

T F **5.** To embed Excel data into a Word document, use the Copy and Paste commands.

T F **6.** Office allows you to copy data from Word to a note or task.

T F **7.** Click Mail Merge on the Actions menu to begin the merge process in Outlook.

T F **8.** When you export data from a database table to the Contacts folder, you must make sure the database field names exactly match those used in the Contacts folder.

T F **9.** Outlook allows you to issue a Mail Merge command.

T F **10.** You can create a mail merge document that is addressed to all or selected contacts in Outlook.

2 MATCHING

Match each of the terms on the left with the definitions on the right.

TERMS

1. Check for Errors

2. shortcut icons

3. mail merge

4. Control key

5. Shift key

6. Letter Wizard

7. Insert Merge Field

8. Send To

9. export

10. Contacts

DEFINITIONS

a. The command that transfers the contents and design of PowerPoint slides to a Word document

b. Press this key to select a group of adjacent contacts

c. Press this button to insert placeholders for information from the Contacts folder

d. The process used to transfer information from an Access database to the Contacts folder in Outlook

e. Press this button to begin the mail merge process in Word

f. The buttons that appear in the Outlook Bar that allow you to switch between tools

g. Press this key to select a group of non-adjacent contacts

h. An Outlook feature that allows you to create a document addressed to several contacts

i. The folder that contains names and addresses of people you communicate with on a regular basis

j. Tool that appears when you select the command to automatically address a letter to one contact

Lesson Summary & Exercises

3 COMPLETION

Fill in the missing word or phrase for each of the following statements.

1. You can jump quickly to any date in the Calendar by clicking the day in the _____.

2. Click the _____ box when creating a contact to specify the address to be used as the main address.

3. When a contact is selected, its name bar appears in _____.

4. The results of Outlook often appear in the form of increased productivity, rather than actual _____ like most of the other Office 2000 tools.

5. Using _____ as your e-mail editor allows you to take advantage of features such as grammar and spelling checks and tables.

6. To start the transfer of data from a database to the Contacts folder, click _____ on the File menu.

7. You can use the _____ and _____ commands to copy data from Word to most Outlook tools.

8. To automatically address a letter to one contact, select the contact and click _____ on the _____ menu.

9. Before copying appointments to a worksheet, you can display them as a list in Outlook in _____ view.

10. You may need to add _____, _____, or _____ between merge fields for the final merged data to appear correctly.

4 SHORT ANSWER

Write a brief answer to each of the following questions.

1. Describe the appearance of a Word document when you send a PowerPoint presentation to it using the *Blank lines next to slides* option. What is the purpose of the blank lines?

2. Why might you copy Calendar data into an Excel or a Word document?

3. How do you set the duration of an appointment in the Calendar?

4. What is the benefit of creating a letter within the Contacts folder?

5. Which parts of a letter does the Letter Wizard help you create?

6. Explain the process you use to bring names and addresses from a database into the Contacts folder.

7. Why might you copy data from Word into a journal entry? a task list? an e-mail message? Give at least one example of each.

8. Describe the process of using Outlook's mail merge feature to address letters to several contacts.

5 IDENTIFICATION

Identify each element of the Outlook window in Figure 2.11.

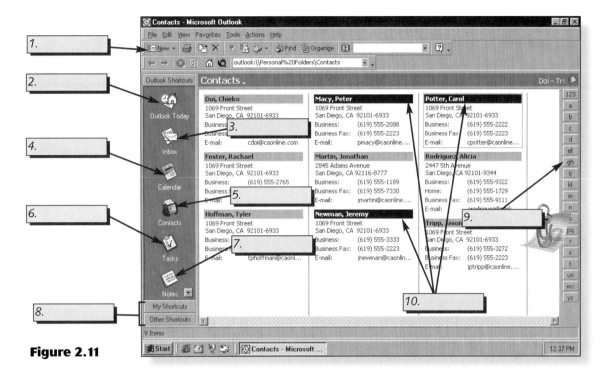

Figure 2.11

SKILLS REVIEW

Complete each of the Skills Review problems in sequential order to review your Office 2000 integration skills.

1 Set Appointments in the Calendar

1. Launch Outlook and click the **Calendar shortcut icon**.

2. In the Date Navigator, click the **date for next Tuesday**.

3. Switch to **Work Week view**.

4. Double-click the **8:00 a.m. time slot** and set an appointment for a golf lesson with the following information:

Subject:	Golf lesson with Grant Tomas
Start time:	8:00 a.m.
End time:	9:30 a.m.
Reminder:	1 hour

5. Click the **Recurrence button** in the Appointment dialog box and set the appointment to recur each week on the same day for a total of eight weeks.

6. Set the additional appointments in Table 2.3.

Lesson Summary & Exercises

TABLE 2.3		DATA FOR NEW APPOINTMENTS			
Day	**Subject**	**Start Time**	**End Time**	**Reminder**	**Recurrence**
Wednesday	Golf lesson with Marta Phillips	8:00 a.m.	9:30 a.m.	1 hour	8 weeks
Thursday	Golf lesson with Oscar Jimenez	8:00 a.m.	9:30 a.m.	1 hour	8 weeks
Thursday	Golf lesson with Sandra Wagner	3:00 p.m.	4:30 p.m.	1 hour	8 weeks

2 Copy Appointments to Excel

1. While in the Calendar, point to **Current View** on the View menu and click **Active Appointments**.

2. Click the first golf lesson appointment, hold down ⇧ Shift, and click the last golf lesson appointment. (If the appointments are not adjacent, click each appointment while holding down Ctrl.)

3. Click **Copy** on the Edit menu.

4. Launch Excel and click **cell A1** of the active worksheet. Then click the **Paste button**.

5. Format the data in an attractive manner.

6. Delete the **Location** and **Categories columns** if they appear.

7. Save the workbook as *Golf Lessons* in the *Skills Review Solutions* folder in the *Skills Review* folder on your Integration Student Data Disk.

3 Enter a Contact

1. Switch to Outlook and click the **Contacts shortcut icon**.

2. Click the **New Contact button** New and type the following information in the New Contact dialog box:

Name:	Mr. Eric Sims
Job title:	Golf Pro
Home address:	1824 Garden View Court
	Marina del Rey, CA 90292-9705
Home phone:	(310) 555-0832
E-mail:	eric_sims@caonline.com

3. Save and close the contact.

4 Address a Letter to a Contact

1. In the Contacts folder, click the **name bar for Eric Sims**.

2. Click **New Letter to Contact** on the Actions menu.

3. Click the **Date line option** in the dialog box and click **Next**.

4. Click **Next** until you get to the dialog box that has sender information.

5. Click the **Complimentary closing drop-down arrow** and click **Sincerely yours,** and then click **Finish**.

6. If the Office Assistant asks if you want to do more to the letter, click **Cancel**.

7. Type the following text:

    Dear Eric,

    Congratulations! All of your time slots have been filled with customers anxious to start their lessons. As you are aware, golf lessons begin next Tuesday and last eight weeks. We are now accepting reservations for the next session of lessons. The following table contains the customers who have signed up for the first session.

8. Type your name below the closing.

9. Save the letter as *Letter to Sims* in the *Skills Review Solutions* folder in the *Skills Review* folder on your Integration Student Data Disk.

5 Copy a Worksheet into the Letter

1. Switch to Excel and open the *Golf Lessons* workbook in the *Skills Review Solutions* folder, if it is not still open.

2. Select the cells that contain the golf lesson appointments and click the **Copy button** 📋.

3. Switch to the *Letter to Sims* document. Place the insertion point below the first paragraph and click the **Paste button** 📋.

4. If necessary, format the table and the letter to improve its appearance.

5. Save, print, and close the letter. Close the *Golf Lessons* workbook.

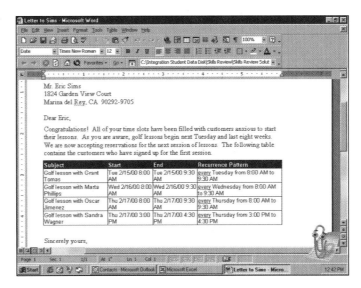

Figure 2.12

Lesson Summary & Exercises

6 Import a Database into the Contacts Folder

1. Launch Access and open the *Marina Golf Course* database in the *Skills Review* folder on your Integration Student Data Disk.

2. Open the Session 1 Golf Lessons table and read the names in the table. Close the table and the database. Exit Access.

3. Switch to Outlook and open the Contacts folder.

4. Click **Import and Export** on the File menu.

5. Click **Import from another program or file** in the dialog box and click **Next**.

6. In the next dialog box, click **Microsoft Access** and click **Next**.

7. In the next dialog box, click the **Browse button** and find and select the *Marina Golf Course* database in the *Skills Review* folder on your Integration Student Data Disk. Click **OK**.

8. Click **Next** in the next dialog box.

9. Click **Contacts** as the destination folder and click **Next**.

10. Click **Finish**.

11. Check the Contacts folder to make sure the four new contacts have been added.

7 Copy Text from Word to the Journal

1. Click the **Journal shortcut icon** on the Outlook Bar.

2. Click the **New Journal Entry button** and record a journal entry for a phone conversation with Eric Sims, the golf pro who works at your golf course. The entry should indicate that you talked to Eric today from 9:30 to 10:00 a.m.

3. Switch to Word without closing the journal entry.

4. Open the *Conversation with Eric Sims* Word document in the *Skills Review* folder on your Integration Student Data Disk.

5. Select the text in the document and click the **Copy button**.

6. Switch to the journal entry and click the **Notes section**. Click the **Paste button**.

7. Save and close the journal entry. Close the *Conversation with Eric Sims* document without saving it.

8 Send a PowerPoint Presentation to Word

1. Launch PowerPoint and open the *Bobcat Golf Clubs* presentation in the *Skills Review* folder on your Integration Student Data Disk.

2. Point to **Send To** on the File menu and click **Microsoft Word**.

3. Click the **Notes below slides option** in the Write-Up dialog box and click **OK**.

4. Save the Word document as *Bobcat Discount Letter* in the *Skills Review Solutions* folder in the *Skills Review* folder on your Integration Student Data Disk.

9 Compose a Letter

1. With the *Bobcat Discount Letter* still open, move to the top of the document.

2. Insert a page break above the first slide.

3. Compose a letter on the first page of the document that tells customers that since they signed up for golf lessons at your golf course, they are entitled to receive a 10 percent discount on any purchase of Bobcat golf clubs they buy at your pro shop.

4. Save and close the letter.

10 Merge a Letter with Contacts

1. Switch to the Contacts folder of Outlook. Click the name bar of the first golf lesson student (Oscar Jimenez). Hold down `Ctrl` and click the names of the other students (Marta Phillips, Grant Tomas, and Sandra Wagner).

2. Click **Mail Merge** on the Tools menu. Click the **Browse button** in the Document file section of the Mail Merge Contacts dialog box. Find and select the *Bobcat Discount Letter* document in the *Skills Review Solutions* folder and click **OK**.

3. Click **OK**.

4. When asked, click the **Edit MailMerge document option**.

5. Place the insertion point where the first merge field should be placed.

6. Click the **Insert Merge Field button** `Insert Merge Field ▾` on the Mail Merge toolbar. Click the appropriate merge field from the list that appears.

7. Continue adding appropriate merge fields for the inside address and salutation.

8. Save the document and click the **Check for Errors button** 🖳.

9. Click the **Complete the merge, pausing to report each error as it occurs option**.

10. Print one of the merged letters, including the pages that contain the PowerPoint presentation.

11. Close the merged document without saving it. Close the *Bobcat Discount Letter*.

Lesson Summary & Exercises

LESSON APPLICATIONS

1 Setting and Printing Dental Appointments

You work as the office manager for Dr. Susan Beauchere, a dentist. Your staff has taken several phone calls this week for various appointments that you need to enter into the Outlook Calendar. Dr. Beauchere wants a printout of the appointments at the beginning of the week so she can carry a copy with her.

1. Launch Outlook and start the Calendar.

2. In the Date Navigator, click the date for two Mondays from now.

3. In Day view, set the appointments in Table 2.4 for two weeks from now. Set all reminders to 0 minutes.

TABLE 2.4	DATA FOR NEW APPOINTMENTS			
Day	**Subject**	**Location**	**Start Time**	**End Time**
Monday	Ashton Meijer: cleaning and checkup	Room 1	9:00 a.m	9:30 a.m
Monday	Lois Graves: cleaning and checkup	Room 2	9:30 a.m.	10:00 a.m.
Monday	Bob Clary: root canal	Room 1	10:00 a.m.	11:15 a.m.
Monday	Benito Rios: cleaning, checkup, and x-rays	Room 2	11:30 a.m.	12:15 p.m
Monday	Sally Manchester: two fillings	Room 1	2:00 p.m.	3:00 p.m.
Monday	Parker Koenig: cleaning and checkup	Room 2	3:00 p.m.	3:30 p.m.
Monday	J.T. Stevens: crown	Room 1	3:30 p.m.	4:45 p.m.
Tuesday	Jim Doyle: cleaning, checkup, and x-rays	Room 1	9:30 a.m.	10:15 a.m.
Tuesday	Ashley Baker: two fillings	Room 2	10:30 a.m.	11:30 a.m.
Tuesday	Carl Mansberg: cleaning and checkup	Room 1	2:00 p.m.	2:30 p.m.
Tuesday	Evan West: root canal	Room 2	2:30 p.m.	3: 45 p.m.
Tuesday	Umeko Shinoda: one filling	Room 1	4:00 p.m.	4:45 p.m.

4. Switch to Active Appointment view and select the dental appointments.

5. Use the Copy command to copy the appointments.

6. Launch Excel and paste the appointments into a new workbook.

7. Format the workbook as desired and delete extra column headings.

8. Save the workbook as *Dental Appointments* in the *Lesson Applications Solutions* folder in the *Lesson Applications* folder on your Integration Student Data Disk.

9. Print a copy of the worksheet for Dr. Beauchere. Then close the workbook.

Lesson Summary & Exercises

2 Entering Dental Patients in Outlook and Sending a Letter

Your next duty as office manager is to enter patient information in the Contacts folder. You are also responsible for sending welcome letters to new patients.

1. Switch to the Contacts folder of Outlook and use the New Contact button to create a new entry.

2. Enter the patient information in Table 2.5.

TABLE 2.5	DATA FOR NEW APPOINTMENTS			
Name	**Home Address**	**Business Phone**	**Home Phone**	**Notes**
Ms. Ashton Meijer	9 Bigelow Terrace Watertown, MA 02172-2532	(617) 555-1200	(617) 555-6917	
Ms. Lois Graves	27 Irma Ave. Watertown, MA 02172-3530		(781) 555-1749	
Mr. Bob Clary	69 Parker St. Watertown, MA 02172-3913	(617) 555-3099	(781) 555-3165	Allergic to penicillin
Mr. Benito Rios	64 Union St. Watertown, MA 02172-2525	(781) 555-8800	(781) 555-0026	
Ms. Sally Manchester	708 Mt. Auburn St. Watertown, MA 02172-1522		(781) 555-4361	
Mr. Parker Koenig	24 Whites Ave. #5 Watertown, MA 02172-4314		(781) 555-7550	
Ms. J.T. Stevens	158 Waverley Ave. Watertown, MA 02172-1105	(781) 555-1608	(781) 555-1304	
Mr. Jim Doyle	71 Putnam St. Watertown, MA 02172-1980	(617) 555-8332	(617) 555-0812	
Ms. Ashley Baker	239 Warren St. Watertown, MA 02172	(781) 555-8223	(781) 555-6090	
Mr. Carl Mansberg	8 Summer St. #2 Watertown, MA 02172-3468		(781) 555-7958	
Mr. Evan West	53 Boylston St. Watertown, MA 02172-1971	(781) 555-6506		
Ms. Umeko Shinoda	212 Bellevue Rd. Watertown, MA 02172-4907	(617) 555-3828	(781) 555-0034	

3. Since Jim Doyle is a new patient, you need to send him a welcome letter. Use the Outlook command to automatically address a new letter to a contact. In the letter, welcome the new patient and refer to a table that you will insert that contains fees for common procedures.

4. Open the *Dental Fees* workbook in the *Lesson Applications* folder on your Integration Student Data Disk and copy the services and fees information in it.

5. Paste the data to your letter and format it appropriately.

6. Save the letter as *New Patient Welcome* in the *Lesson Applications Solutions* folder in the *Lesson Applications* folder on your Integration Student Data Disk. Print and close the letter.

7. Close the *Dental Fees* workbook without saving it.

3 Importing New Contacts from a Database

Dr. Beauchere recently attended a dental conference where she met several other dentists who practice in Massachusetts. She created a database while she was at the conference and wants you to transfer the database data to Outlook.

1. Open the **Dentists** database in the **Lesson Applications** folder on your Integration Student Data Disk. Open the Contacts table and note the names of the dentists in it. Close the database and exit Access.

2. Open the Contacts folder in Outlook and issue the Import and Export command.

3. Click the selections that allow you to import the **Dentists** database to the Contacts folder. Then click Finish.

4. Check to make sure the contacts were imported correctly.

4 Copying Information into a Journal Entry

After the dental conference, Dr. Beauchere asks you to call one of the dentists that she met. Dr. Garvin Nickell gave you the name of a Web site where you can find the Principles of Ethics and Code of Professional Conduct for dentists. You'd like to share this site with your staff, but you lost the note where you wrote the address. You call Dr. Nickell's office and make a note in a Word file. Now you want to create a journal entry to record the phone call.

1. Switch to the Journal in Outlook and issue the command to create a new journal entry.

2. Create an entry that records a ten-minute conversation with Dr. Nickell yesterday at 1:30 p.m.

3. Open the **Ethics and Conduct** file in the **Lesson Applications** folder on your Integration Student Data Disk in Word to see the notes you took during the conversation.

4. Copy the text from the Word file and paste it to the Notes section of the journal entry.

5. Save and close the journal entry. Then close the **Ethics and Conduct** file.

5 Sharing a PowerPoint Presentation with Other Dentists

Dr. Beauchere mentioned to the other dentists that she met at the dental conference that she has created a PowerPoint presentation for use by her new staff members. She wants you to send a printout of the presentation to these dentists.

1. Open the **Dental Staff Training** presentation in the **Lesson Applications** folder on your Integration Student Data Disk.

2. Send the presentation, including its contents and design, to a Word document.

3. Compose a letter before the first slide informing the dentists that the following pages contain the PowerPoint presentation.

4. Save the letter as **Sharing Staff Training Presentation with Dentists** in the **Lesson Applications Solutions** folder. Close the file and return to Outlook.

5. Select Drs. Cranley, Coith, Rabkin, Nickell, Feng, and Polasky in the Contacts folder.

6. Issue the Mail Merge command to merge the selected contacts with the **_Sharing Staff Training Presentation with Dentists_** document.

7. Edit the document to add appropriate merge fields.

8. Resave the document and then issue the merge command.

9. Print one copy of the letter and then close the merged document without saving it. Close the **_Sharing Staff Training Presentation with Dentists_** letter.

PROJECTS

1 Keeping Track of Classes

Anthony Chao has expanded his personal training and health counseling business. He has a new partner, additional locations, and the company name is now Fitness Plus. His partner, Linda Prescott, uses Outlook and Anthony would like to start using it as well. Your first project as an employee of Fitness Plus is to enter the karate, judo, and kung-fu classes into the company's Outlook calendar.

The next session of classes starts the second full week of June and lasts for 10 weeks. All youth classes last 45 minutes and adult classes last 60 minutes. Use the Calendar to schedule the classes in Table 2.6.

TABLE 2.6		DATA FOR NEW APPOINTMENTS				
Class Type	**Age**	**Level**	**Day**	**Start Time**	**Instructor**	**Location**
Karate	Youth	Beginner	Monday	1:30 p.m.	Perry	Plymouth
Karate	Youth	Intermediate	Thursday	10:30 a.m.	Samantha	Shaker Heights
Karate	Youth	Advanced	Wednesday	1:30 p.m.	Perry	Plymouth
Karate	Adult	Beginner	Tuesday	4:30 p.m.	Samantha	Wellfleet
Karate	Adult	Intermediate	Monday	7:30 p.m.	Allison	Montgomery
Karate	Adult	Advanced	Thursday	7:00 p.m.	Allison	Wellfleet
Judo	Youth	Beginner	Tuesday	9:30 a.m.	Scott	Wellfleet
Judo	Youth	Intermediate	Tuesday	1:30 p.m.	Allison	Montgomery
Judo	Youth	Advanced	Wednesday	11:30 a.m.	Allison	Wellfleet
Judo	Adult	Beginner	Friday	6:30 p.m.	Rosa	Plymouth
Judo	Adult	Intermediate	Wednesday	7:00 p.m.	Scott	Shaker Heights
Judo	Adult	Advanced	Friday	7:30 p.m.	Rosa	Wellfleet
Kung-fu	Youth	Beginner	Friday	2:00 p.m.	Scott	Wellfleet
Kung-fu	Youth	Intermediate	Wednesday	3:30 p.m.	Perry	Plymouth
Kung-fu	Youth	Advanced	Monday	10:30 a.m.	Samantha	Shaker Heights
Kung-fu	Adult	Beginner	Tuesday	7:30 p.m.	Scott	Plymouth
Kung-fu	Adult	Intermediate	Thursday	8:00 p.m.	Rosa	Montgomery
Kung-fu	Adult	Advanced	Monday	5:30 p.m.	Rosa	Plymouth

Lesson Summary & Exercises

After you enter all of the classes in the Calendar, the partners want you to copy them to a worksheet and print a copy to post at each studio. Transfer the information about classes to an Excel workbook, format as desired, and save the workbook as *New Class Schedules* in the *Projects Solutions* folder in the *Projects* folder on your Integration Student Data Disk. Print and then close the workbook.

2 Tracking Your Employees

Anthony and Linda have asked you to add all employees of Fitness Plus to the Contacts folder. Use Outlook to add the information in Table 2.7 as contacts.

TABLE 2.7	**DATA FOR NEW CONTACTS**			
Name	**Job Title**	**Company**	**Home Phone**	**Home Address**
Ms. Rosa Aponte	Instructor	Fitness Plus	(602) 555-1824	8330 N. 19th Ave. Phoenix, AZ 85021-1233
Mr. Anthony Chao	Co-owner	Fitness Plus	(602) 555-8232	2201 E. Cactus Rd. Phoenix, AZ 85022-6508
Ms. Samantha Deitschel	Instructor	Fitness Plus	(602) 555-7124	2333 E. Devonshire Ave. Phoenix, AZ 85016-4322
Ms. Allison Faulkner	Instructor	Fitness Plus	(602) 555-0342	4630 E. Thomas Rd. Phoenix, AZ 85018-2388
Mr. Scott Jacobs	Instructor	Fitness Plus	(602) 555-8245	6131 N. 27th Ave. Phoenix, AZ 85017-1749
Mr. Perry Kahn	Instructor	Fitness Plus	(602) 555-7139	2813 W. Colter St. Phoenix, AZ 85017-2932
Ms. Linda Prescott	Co-owner	Fitness Plus	(602) 555-0498	938 W. Glenrosa Ave. Phoenix, AZ 85013-2808
Mr. Brent Varley	Instruction Supervisor	Fitness Plus	(602) 555-2843	350 E. Eva St, #215 Phoenix, AZ 85020-2564

3 Reporting Information to the Supervisor

You've been asked by Brent Varley, the instruction supervisor, to provide a list of all the names, phone numbers, areas of expertise, and hire dates of the instructors who work for Fitness Plus. You'd like to have the instructors' names in a workbook so that you can easily add and delete information. View the Contacts folder in By Company view and highlight the instructors' names. Copy this information and then paste it to a new workbook. Save the workbook as *Fitness Plus Instructors* in the *Projects Solutions* folder in the *Projects* folder on your Integration Student Data Disk. Delete any columns or rows that you don't need and add a column called *Expertise* and another named *Start Date*. Add data that indicates the areas of expertise and hire dates for each instructor as shown in Table 2.8. Sort the worksheet in ascending order by the dates in the Start Date column.

TABLE 2.8	INSTRUCTOR DATA	
Name	**Area(s) of Expertise**	**Start Date**
Rosa Aponte	Judo and Kung-fu	3/15/97
Samantha Deitschel	Karate	2/1/99
Allison Faulkner	Karate and Judo	8/15/94
Scott Jacobs	Judo and Kung-fu	12/1/92
Perry Kahn	Karate	5/1/95

Save the changes to the workbook and switch to Outlook. Use the Contacts folder to automatically address a letter to Brent Varley. In the letter, tell him that you are providing the information he requested and that you have sorted the instructors by the length of time they have worked for the company. Embed the data from the *Fitness Plus Instructors* workbook in the letter. Save the letter as *Instructor Information* in the *Projects Solutions* folder in the *Projects* folder on your Integration Student Data Disk. Print and close the letter. Close the workbook and exit Excel.

4 Attracting New Customers

Many customers call and ask about the services that Fitness Plus can provide. Although many set an appointment for a tour of the facilities, some of them just wish to have information sent to them. Although Fitness Plus has not finalized its company brochures, it does have a PowerPoint presentation for customers to view. You can mail a printout of the presentation to those customers who cannot visit for a tour and live presentation.

Recently, some customers have requested information by mail. Since you'll send them information now and later follow-up with a phone call or letter, start by entering the data provided in Table 2.9 into the Contacts folder.

TABLE 2.9	DATA FOR POTENTIAL CUSTOMERS	
Name	**Home Address**	**Home Phone**
Mr. Davis Ramos	5023 N. 18th St. Phoenix, AZ 85016-4041	(602) 555-0344
Ms. Judith Zawbraski	7728 W. Crittenden Ln. Phoenix, AZ 85033-4204	(602) 555-4002
Mr. Rinji Saga	12810 N. Cave Creek Rd. Phoenix, AZ 85022-5879	(602) 555-2749
Ms. Abigail Freemont	9923 W. Madrugada Ave. Phoenix, AZ 85037-5251	(602) 555-3383
Ms. Madison Alexander	1737 E. Pinchot Ave. Phoenix, AZ 85016-7623	(602) 555-6399
Mr. Raymond Hanson	8738 W. Lewis Ave. Phoenix, AZ 85037-3653	(602) 555-1648
Mr. Ryan Telpon	5608 W. Verde Ln. Phoenix, AZ 85031-3327	(602) 555-7133

After entering the contacts into Outlook, open the *Fitness Plus* presentation in the *Projects* folder on your Integration Student Data Disk in PowerPoint. Send the presentation to Word and compose a letter as page 1 of the document. Target the letter to the potential customers and mention that you will call them in a week to answer any questions they might have. Save the letter as *Potential Fitness Customers* in the *Projects Solutions* folder in the *Projects* folder on your Integration Student Data Disk. Use Outlook's mail merge feature to insert merge fields and then merge the letter with the contacts you just entered. Print one copy of the letter with the presentation pages. Then close the merged letters without saving the file. Close the *Potential Fitness Customers* letter.

5 Noteworthy Impressions

Fitness Plus has an opening for an instructor trainee. Last week you interviewed three candidates. Create journal entries in Outlook to record the following interviews.

- David Campbell—interviewed at 3:00 p.m. on Tuesday. The interview lasted one hour.
- Sara McAllister—interviewed at 8:00 a.m. on Wednesday. The interview lasted one hour.
- Pat Burbank—interviewed at 2:00 p.m. on Friday. The interview lasted 45 minutes.

Immediately following each interview, you typed some notes into a Word file. Open the **Interview Notes** Word document in the **Projects** folder on your Integration Student Data Disk. Copy the appropriate information from the Word file into the Notes section of each journal entry. Close all of the entries and close the **Interview Notes** file without saving it.

APPENDICES

CONTENTS

Portfolio Builder

WHAT IS A PORTFOLIO?

A *portfolio* is an organized collection of your work that demonstrates skills and knowledge acquired from one or more courses. The materials included in a portfolio should pertain to a specific educational or career goal. In addition to actual assignments, a portfolio should contain your self-reflection or comments on each piece of work as well as an overall statement introducing the portfolio.

Two types of portfolios exist. The first, which shows progress toward a goal over a period of time, is called a *developmental portfolio.* Developmental portfolios help you become more aware of your strengths and weaknesses and assist you in improving your abilities. The second type, called a *representational portfolio,* displays a variety of your best work. You can show a representational portfolio as evidence of your skills and knowledge. While you may use either type of portfolio when you are seeking employment, a representational portfolio is more effective.

WHY USE PORTFOLIOS?

Portfolios offer great advantages to you, your instructor, and potential employers. They allow you to reevaluate the work you have created, by determining which assignments should be included in the portfolio and analyzing how you can improve future assignments. If the goal of the portfolio is career related, portfolios also help you connect classroom activities with practical applications. A wide variety of genuine work is captured in a portfolio, rather than a snapshot of knowledge at a specific time under particular circumstances. Presenting a portfolio of your work to your instructor and potential employers gives them the opportunity to evaluate your overall skills and performance more accurately.

CREATING A PORTFOLIO

Creating a portfolio involves three steps—planning, selecting work to include, and providing comments about your work.

First, you should plan the overall purpose and organization of the portfolio. After you plan your portfolio, you can begin selecting pieces of work to include in it. Ideally, you should select the work as you complete each document; however, you can review prior work to include as well.

Table A.1 recommends documents from *Managing Information Lesson 2* that you may want to consider for inclusion in your portfolio; however, you should also choose additional documents of which you are proud, especially from the *Word 2000, Excel 2000, Access 2000,* and *PowerPoint 2000* tutorials included in the *Office 2000: Brief Edition* tutorial. If two documents demonstrate identical Office 2000 skills, choose only one for your portfolio. If you apply your Office 2000 skills in another course or elsewhere, include a sample in your portfolio.

TABLE A.1	POSSIBLE DOCUMENTS TO INCLUDE IN YOUR PORTFOLIO
FILE NAME	**ACTIVITY**
Letter to Rodriguez	Managing Information Lesson 2: Integrating Office 2000
Bobcat Discount Letter	Skills Review 9 in Managing Information Lesson 2: Integrating Office 2000
Dental Appointments	Lesson Application 1 in Managing Information Lesson 2: Integrating Office 2000

Create a list or log that provides a summary of the contents of your portfolio. (Your instructor may provide a preformatted log that you can complete.) The log can include columns in which you can list the file name, description of the file, when and by whom the file was reviewed, whether the file was revised, and the grade you received on the assignment.

Lastly, you should prepare comments for each piece of work included in the portfolio. As you add work to your portfolio, generate comments about each piece. You may want to reflect on the skills used to create the document, or you can explain how the document is applicable to a specific job for which you are interviewing. Your instructor may provide you with a preformatted comments form or you may type your comments.

HANDS On

Building Your Portfolio

In this activity, you will plan your portfolio, select the documents to include in the portfolio, and prepare written comments about each piece of work included in the portfolio.

1. Using Word, answer the following questions to help you plan your portfolio:

   ■ What is the purpose of your portfolio?

   ■ What criteria will you use in selecting work to include in the portfolio?

   ■ What is the overall goal that your portfolio will meet?

   ■ How will you organize your portfolio?

2. Using Word, create a log that provides a summary of the contents of your portfolio. Follow the guidelines given by your instructor or provided in this appendix.

3. Remember the purpose and goal of your portfolio and select and print one document that you have completed to include in your portfolio. Enter information about the document in your log.

4. Prepare comments about the selected document and attach them to the printout.

5. Repeat steps 3 and 4 to select and prepare comments for other documents to include in your portfolio.

6. Using Word, write a paragraph or two introducing your portfolio. Include some of the information considered in step 1.

7. Gather the documents to include in your portfolio and place them in a binder, folder, or other container in an organized manner.

ANSWERS TO *Self* ✓CHECK

Lesson	Question 1	Question 2	Question 3	Question 4	Question 5
Getting Started Lesson 1	copies	booting	read-only	dialog	Folders
Getting Started Lesson 2	true	true	false	false	true
Getting Started Lesson 3	Microsoft Excel	Microsoft Access	Microsoft Word	Glossary terms	Microsoft PowerPoint
Word 2000 Lesson 1	true	false	true	true	false
Word 2000 Lesson 2	d	e	c	a	b
Excel 2000 Lesson 1	Ctrl + Home	the position of the cell cursor and the cell address in the Name Box	cell address	Glossary terms	menu bar; Close
Excel 2000 Lesson 2	two	5	arguments	relative references	Chart Wizard
Access 2000 Lesson 1	fields, records	Objects	Design	primary key	Captions
Access 2000 Lesson 2	Zoom	referential integrity	recordset	AutoForm	group
PowerPoint 2000 Lesson 1	true	false	false	true	false
PowerPoint 2000 Lesson 2	e	d	c	b	a
Managing Information Lesson 1	Outlook Today	Contacts	Journal	Inbox	Tasks
Managing Information Lesson 2	false	true	true	false	false

Glossary

A

accessory A small program built into the Windows 98 operating system.

action An instruction or a command that you can combine with other instructions in a macro to automate a task.

active (program) The application that is currently running.

active cell The cell you are entering data into; the active cell contains the cell cursor.

Active Desktop A Windows 98 interface option that sets up your desktop to work like a Web page and to receive and display information from Internet content providers. Compare with *classic style desktop* and *Web style desktop*.

adaptive menu A feature that allows each user to customize menus. When you select a less frequently used command from an expanded menu, you automatically add that command to the short menu. Compare with *short menu* and *expanded menu*.

alignment The position of text, objects, or graphs in relation to the top and bottom or left and right margins.

animation Motion effects available with PowerPoint.

application Specialized software program used to create or process data, such as creating text in a word processing document, manipulating financial information in a worksheet, tracking records in a database management file, or creating a presentation with a presentation or graphics program. Also called *application program*.

application program See *application*.

application software See *application*.

application window A rectangle on the desktop containing the menus and document(s) for an application.

argument In Excel, a variable upon which a function operates. An argument appears between parentheses and may be a number, text, values, cell reference, formula, or other function.

Arial A common font for headings; a sans serif font.

article A message, also known as a post, distributed on a newsgroup.

ascending See *ascending sort*.

ascending sort A sort that arranges letters from A to Z, numbers from smallest to largest, and dates from earliest to most recent. Also called *ascending*. See also *sort*. Compare with *descending sort*.

aspect ratio The width-to-height ratio of an image.

attribute Characteristic of a file or folder controlling how the file is or should be used.

AutoCalculate area The area of the Excel window located in the middle of the status bar that can be used for calculating sums, averages, and other values of a range of cells.

AutoComplete tip

AutoComplete tip An Office feature that automatically tries to complete what the user is typing. Press or ⌐ to accept the tip.

AutoForm A form that Access builds automatically; the AutoForm gathers the information it needs by examining the selected table or query.

AutoFormats Ready-made worksheet designs provided by Excel.

AutoLayout Predesigned slide layouts you use to develop a PowerPoint presentation.

automatic page breaks See *soft returns*.

automatic recalculation An Excel feature that recalculates the results of formulas when the value in any referenced cell changes.

AutoReport A report that Access builds automatically, based on the selected table or query.

B

background items Repeating elements that are placed on the slide master in a PowerPoint presentation.

bold Thick, heavy effect applied to text or tables for emphasis.

booting the system Another expression for starting up, which the computer often accomplishes by loading a small program, which then reads a larger program into memory. Also called *system boot*.

border An edging around a paragraph, page, graphic, or table.

bottom aligned Page alignment in which text is even with the bottom margin regardless of the amount of text on the page.

browser A software package that lets the user access the major components of the Internet, such as the World Wide Web, e-mail, and so on.

build object An object that appears in a sequence on a PowerPoint slide. See also *animation*.

build text Text that appears one portion at a time on a PowerPoint slide. See also *animation*.

bullet A character, typographical symbol, or graphic used as a special effect.

C

calculated field In Access, a field that contains an expression as the data source and displays the computed result.

caption (1) A title, an explanation, or a description alongside an illustration; (2) in Access, words or phrases used to abbreviate or clarify field names; used as labels in forms and tables.

cell A box formed by the intersection of a column and a row. Each cell can hold a single value or text entry.

cell address The column letter and row number combination that identifies each individual cell.

cell cursor In Excel, a black border surrounding a single cell indicating that the cell is active.

cell reference A cell address in a formula that tells Excel to perform calculations using the value currently in the designated cell.

center aligned Centered; paragraph alignment in which each line of text or an image is midway between the left and right margins; also, page alignment in which text or an image is midway between the top and bottom margins.

channel A Web site that is updated on a regular basis by the owner.

Channel bar A bar that includes a series of icons that lets you receive information from Web sites automatically.

character spacing The amount of space between characters; e.g., normal, expanded, condensed, or kerned.

chart A picture that displays data from an Excel worksheet or a PowerPoint datasheet in the form of circles, lines, bars, or other shapes.

chart sheet A special sheet in Excel that shows only your chart, not the worksheet data upon which it is based.

Chart Wizard A special tool in Excel that helps you build a chart by asking a series of questions and generating a chart based upon your responses.

check box A square box in a dialog box that contains a ✓ when an option is selected or appears empty when the option is not selected.

choose See *select*.

classic style desktop The Windows 98 default desktop setting that gives the user interface the same look and feel as Windows 95. Compare with *Active Desktop* and *Web style desktop*.

click The technique of quickly pressing and releasing the left button on a mouse or trackball.

Click and Type An Office feature that allows you to double-click a document anywhere and insert text or an image at that point.

clip See *clip art*.

clip art A graphic file made of lines and curves that you can insert into a file and then resize, move, and modify as desired. Also called *clip*. See also *Clip Gallery* and *graphic file*.

Clipboard An area in memory used by all Windows 98 applications for temporarily storing up to 12 pieces of text or graphics to be placed in a new location. Also a toolbar (in Word, Excel, and PowerPoint) for controlling and clearing items from Clipboard memory; the Office Clipboard.

Clip Gallery A Microsoft Office folder that has professionally designed images (pictures, photographs, sound, and video clips) from which you can choose an illustration to complement many different subjects.

close To remove a file, a dialog box, or a window from the screen or desktop and the computer's memory.

column heading The gray area at the top of an Excel worksheet area that contains a letter identifying each column.

columnar report An Access report that displays all fields in a single column with field labels or captions to their left as identifiers.

command An instruction given to a computer by clicking a menu option, clicking a toolbar button, or pressing a combination of keys.

command buttons Small, labeled rectangles in a dialog box that perform actions such as accepting or canceling changes.

Comma Style A predefined numeric format in Excel that inserts commas as thousands separators and displays negative numbers in parentheses.

common field In Access, a field that has the same name and data type as a field in one or more other tables. You need to set up common fields in preparation for sharing data between tables. The common field is what lets Access find matching data in different tables.

compact To rearrange how a fragmented database is stored on disk, improving performance and reducing size.

comparison operator (1) In Access, a symbol that is used to compare a value or text in the table to characters that you enter; (2) In Excel, special symbols used to test a condition in an IF function (> greater than, < less than, = equal to, for example).

conditional formatting Specified formatting applied to cells that meet certain criteria.

Contents tab One of the three tabs in the Help window; this option provides a list of Help topics.

copy To place a copy of text or graphics on the Clipboard.

crop To trim an image.

Currency Style A predefined numeric format in Excel that precedes values by a currency symbol (usually the dollar sign), inserts commas as thousands separators, and displays negative numbers in parentheses.

current record In Access, the record that is active. In Datasheet view, the current record is the row that contains a triangle or pencil icon in the record selector.

customize To make or alter to individual or personal specifications.

cut To remove text or a graphic and to place it on the Clipboard.

Glossary

D

data access page A database object designed to be viewed in a Web browser.

database An organized collection of data about similar entities—such as employees, customers, or inventory items. In Access, a database also means a collection of objects—such as reports, forms, tables, queries, and data access pages—associated with a particular topic.

database management system See *DBMS*.

Database window A window that lets you gain access to all the objects (tables, forms, reports, and so on) in a particular database.

data point One value in a data series in Excel.

data series A set of related values that you want to plot on an Excel chart.

datasheet (1) In PowerPoint, a grid of columns and rows for entering, viewing, and editing data, used in PowerPoint to create graphs; (2) In Access, a tabular layout of rows and columns that allows you to add, edit, and view data in a table immediately.

Datasheet view In Access, a view that permits you to view, add, delete, and edit the actual information in a table.

data type In Access, a designation that determines the type of data that can be entered into a field, such as text, numbers, and dates.

DBMS (database management system) A system for storing and manipulating the data in a database.

default A preset condition in an operating system or application that remains in effect unless canceled or overridden by an operator.

delete Remove text or graphics from a file.

demote On a PowerPoint slide, move a subtitle to the next lowest indent level.

descending See *descending sort*.

descending sort A sort that arranges letters from Z to A, numbers from largest to smallest, and dates from most recent to the earliest. Also called *descending*. See also *sort*. Compare with *ascending sort*.

deselect To return an object to its original color or turn off an option, indicating that an item will not be affected by the next action taken or that an option will no longer be in effect.

design template A collection of designs that you can apply to a PowerPoint presentation. See also *template*.

Design view In Access, a view that permits you to set up and modify the structure and appearance of database objects.

desktop (1) The working area of the screen that displays many Windows tools and is the background for computer work; (2) the most common PC model, sized to fit on a desk, with separate units for the CPU and the monitor.

developmental portfolio An organized collection of your work that demonstrates your progress toward a goal over a period of time. Developmental portfolios help you become more aware of your strengths and weaknesses and assist you in improving your abilities. See also *portfolio* and *representational portfolio*.

dialog box A rectangle containing a set of options that appears when the application requires more information from the user to perform a requested operation.

document A computer file consisting of a compilation of one or more kinds of data; a file that stores the work you have created with the computer. Document types include text documents, worksheets, graphic files, HTML files, and so on. A document, which a user can open and use, is different from a program file, which is required by a software program to operate. Also called *document files*.

document files See *document*.

document window A rectangle within an application window for viewing and working on a document.

domain name The address of a Web site's computer.

double-click The technique of rapidly pressing and releasing the left button on a mouse or trackball twice when the mouse pointer onscreen is pointing to an object.

drag The technique of moving an object onscreen by pointing to the object, pressing and holding the mouse button, moving the mouse to a new location, and then releasing the mouse button. Also called *drag-and-drop* and *dragging*.

drag-and-drop See *drag*.

dragging See *drag*.

drive icon A small icon or image that represents a storage device.

drop-down list A list of options displayed when you click a triangle button.

E

ellipsis A series of three dots that indicates a dialog box will display when this option is clicked.

e-mail The exchange of messages and computer files through the Internet and other electronic data networks; electronic mail.

embed To paste text or an object from the Clipboard in the form of a static picture that cannot be edited as text (only as an object).

embedded chart In Excel, a chart that is displayed on the same worksheet that contains the numeric data used to create the chart.

end mark A short horizontal bar that marks the end of a document.

endnote Supporting or additional information that appears on a separate page at the end of a document. Compare with *footnote*.

expanded menu A list of all commands available on a menu that displays when a user clicks the double arrow at the bottom of a short menu. Compare with *short menu*.

expression In Access, a combination of field names, values, and comparison operators that can be evaluated as criteria for most types of filters.

Expression Builder An Access tool that allows you to build complex expressions by choosing the fields on which you want to perform calculations and the operators you want to use in those calculations. See also *expression*.

F

field In Access, a column in a table that contains a category of data.

field properties In Access, field settings that control the way a field looks and behaves.

field selector In an Access table, the field names or captions that appear at the top of each column in Datasheet view.

filled object A placeholder on a PowerPoint slide that contains text or graphics.

fill handle In Excel, small square at the bottom-right corner of the cell cursor used to fill a range with values.

first-line indentation The conventional paragraph indentation style in which the first line is indented from the left margin by .15" to 1" (standard is .5").

folder A named location on a drive or disk for storing and organizing files and programs.

font The design of a set of characters. Also called *typeface*.

font size The size of text characters, measured in points; also called *point size*. See also *point*.

footer Information that appears at the bottom of each page.

footnote Supporting or additional information that appears at the bottom of a page. Compare with *endnote*.

foreign key In Access, a field in a related table that has the same name and data type as the primary key in the primary table.

foreign table See *related table*.

form In Access, windows that present a custom layout for your data, enabling you to view, edit, and enter data.

format A conventional arrangement of text on a page; also, the act of arranging text (aligning, indenting, spacing, etc.).

formatting Changing the alignment, indentations, line spacing, margins, and/or paragraph spacing of text.

formatting marks The nonprinting characters that display onscreen but are not visible on a printout.

formula A group of instructions that performs a calculation and displays the result.

formula bar In Excel, the bar immediately below the toolbars that displays the contents of the active cell. You can enter and edit data in the formula bar.

Form view In Access, a view that can be used to see only one record at a time and display only pertinent fields in a record, if desired. Form view is often used to enter and edit records in a database.

frame One of several sections or panels on a Web page or on a window. See *frames page*.

frames page The container that holds a group of frames or panels. See *frame*.

function A predefined formula that performs specialized calculations.

G

glossary term A word or phrase appearing in blue (not underlined) on a Help screen that, when clicked, shows the definition of the word or phrase.

graphic A picture, drawing, photograph, or WordArt that can be inserted into a file. Also called *image* and *object*.

graphical user interface (GUI) An operating environment in which controls and data are visible on screen so you can select items with a pointing device.

graphic file A file made up of dots (called a bitmap type file), as in a photograph, or lines and curves (called a metafile type file) as in clip art. See also *clip art*.

grayscale A printer option that represents PowerPoint slide colors with black, white, and varying shades of gray; a black-and-white-and-gray image. Compare with *pure black and white*.

group (1) Multiple worksheets in an Excel workbook file that you can work on simultaneously; (2) to associate objects together so they can be manipulated as one object; (3) categories of information from an Access table or query that you can use to arrange records and show subtotals in a report.

GUI See *graphical user interface*.

H

handle Squares that surround an object and allow you to move or resize the object. Also called *selection handle*. See also *move handle* and *resize handle*.

hanging indentation A paragraph indentation style in which the first line of text is flush with the left margin and succeeding lines are indented.

hard return Pressing to end a short line of text and force the insertion point to the next line. Also called *manual page break*.

header Text that appears at the top of each printed page.

hide To temporarily remove columns and/or rows from view.

Glossary

highlight   An enhancing Word tool that allows you to place color over text to appear much like a highlighter; can be used to emphasize important text or to mark text to be reviewed.

home page   The first page of a Web site, used as a starting point for Web browsing.

horizontal alignment   The arrangement of text or an image in relation to the left and right margins.

horizontal scroll bar   Scroll bar at the bottom of the screen that scrolls documents from side to side. Compare with *vertical scroll bar*.

HTML   See *Hypertext Markup Language*.

HTTP   See *Hypertext Transfer Protocol*.

hyperlink   Text or a graphic inserted in a Help frame, a file, or a Web page that links to another frame, a document, an Internet address, a page on the World Wide Web, or an HTML page on an intranet. Also called *link* or *jump*.

hypertext   Text that contains a hyperlink; also displays text.

Hypertext Markup Language (HTML)   The language used to tag a document with codes so the document can be viewed on the World Wide Web. HTML includes the capability that enables Web page creators to insert hyperlinks (links to other resources) into their documents.

Hypertext Transfer Protocol (HTTP)   The set of rules that defines the way hypertext links display Web pages.

hyphenate   To divide words at line breaks by inserting a hyphen; automatic hyphenation, a Word language tool.

I

I-beam pointer   Pointer in the shape of the capital letter "I" when moved over text.

icon   A small image that represents a device, program, file, or folder.

image   See *graphic*.

import   (1) To insert or add into a file; you can add a graphic file to a document or to the Clip Gallery; (2) in Access, the operation in which data from outside a database is brought into the database.

indentation   Distance of text from the left or right page margins.

indent level   Number that describes the position of a subtitle on a PowerPoint slide.

Index tab   One of the three tabs in the Help window; this option provides an alphabetical listing of Help topics.

insertion point   The flashing, vertical line within a document that indicates where text will appear when typing begins.

Insert mode   Mode in which typed text is inserted into existing text, pushing the characters after it to the right.

Internet   A worldwide network of computers that connects each Internet user's computer to all other computers in the network and allows users to exchange digital information in the form of text, graphics, and other media.

intranet   A network within an organization allowing users to exchange messages and data with other users in the organization.

italic   Thin, right-slanted effect applied to text for emphasis.

J

join   A method of notifying Access how to match up records from one table with the appropriate records from any other tables.

joystick   An input device used to control the onscreen pointer; a small joystick is often found in the middle of keyboards on laptop computers.

jumps   Also called *link*; see *hyperlink*.

justified   Paragraph alignment in which both the left and right edges of text are perfectly even. Also page alignment in which text is distributed among the top, middle, and bottom.

K

keyword   A word or phrase that defines or narrows the topic for which you are searching in Help or on the World Wide Web.

L

landscape orientation   Layout that prints data horizontally across the page on paper that is wider than it is long.

large icon   An icon displayed at full-size.

launch   To enter a command that runs an application program.

layout   The process of arranging graphics and text; specifically, the horizontal alignment and the wrap style.

leaders   Dots, dashes, or other characters between tab stop positions for leading readers' eyes from left to right.

left aligned   Paragraph alignment in which text is perfectly even at the left margin; the standard (default) paragraph alignment.

level   Number that describes the position of a bullet on a PowerPoint slide.

line spacing   The number of blank lines between text lines; e.g., double spacing leaves one blank line below each line of text.

link   Also called *jump;* see *hyperlink*.

M

macro A series of stored commands that you can play back all at once by issuing a single command.

major key See *primary sort key*.

manual page break See *hard return*.

many-to-many relationship In Access, a relationship between tables in which each record in each table may have many matches in the other table.

margins Blank areas bordering text on a page, a slide, or within an Access label.

master The primary background slide, used to make changes to the entire PowerPoint presentation. Also called *Slide Master*.

menu A list of commands or options displayed on an application window from which you can choose.

menu bar An area below the title bar of all application windows, containing menu names that, when clicked, display a list of commands.

minor key See *secondary sort key*.

moderated newsgroup A newsgroup whose messages are screened by a host to ensure their content relates to the topic of the newsgroup.

module In Access, a set of programmed statements that are stored together as a unit; a module is used to automate a task.

mouse A hand-held, button-activated input device that when rolled along a flat surface directs an indicator to move correspondingly about a computer screen, allowing the operator to move the indicator freely, to select operations, or to manipulate data or graphics.

mouse pointer See *pointer*.

move handle A large square with a four-way arrow (at the top-left corner of a table), used to drag an object.

multi-level bulleted list slide A PowerPoint slide with more than one level of bulleted text.

multimedia The combined use of several media, such as movies, slides, music, and lighting, for educational or entertainment purposes.

multitasking The ability of an operating system to carry out multiple operations at the same time; for example, running more than one program.

N

Name Box The box to the left of the formula bar that identifies the cell address of the active cell in an Excel worksheet.

navigate To move about on the Windows desktop in a planned or preset course.

nested parentheses Parentheses within parentheses used to regulate the precedence of Excel calculations. The operations in the innermost sets of parentheses are performed first.

newsgroup A public discussion containing a set of articles about a single topic.

news reader An application program used to send and receive online news articles from newsgroups.

news server A computer that supplies news articles to a news reader program.

Normal style The base style for the Normal template in Word. See *style*.

numeric format A format that stipulates how Excel displays numbers in the worksheet area; used to add commas as thousands separators, to add currency symbols, and more.

O

object (1) An element in a document, a chart, or a worksheet that you can manipulate independently, such as clip art, photos, sound files, or video clips; (2) in Access, the major components of a database, including tables, queries, forms, reports, data access pages, macros, and modules; (3) in PowerPoint, a single element on a slide. See also *graphic*.

object area The dotted line area below the Title Area on a PowerPoint slide. It can be a placeholder for text or graphics.

Office Assistant An animated character that can answer specific questions, offer tips, and provide help.

Office Clipboard See *Clipboard*.

one-to-many relationship In Access, a relationship between two tables in which each record in the primary table can have no records, one record, or many matching records in the related table, but every record in the related table has one—and only one—associated record in the primary table.

one-to-one relationship In Access, a relationship between two tables in which every record in each table can have either no matching records or only a single matching record in the other table.

online Help system An onscreen, electronic manual that provides assistance with the features and operations of a computer program. Also called *onscreen Help*.

onscreen Help See *online Help system*.

open To copy a file from disk into the computer memory and display it on screen; to start an application; to access the contents of an icon in a window.

operating system A collection of programs that allows you to work with a computer by managing the flow of data between input devices, the computer's memory, storage devices, and output devices. Also called *operating system software*.

operating system software See *operating system*.

option button A small circle filled with a solid dot when selected; only one in a set of option buttons can be selected. Sometimes called *radio button*.

Glossary

orphan The first line of a paragraph printed by itself at the bottom of a page. Compare with *widow*.

overhead transparency A transparent 8.5" by 11" page that is enlarged and projected for audience viewing by light from an overhead projector shining through it.

Overtype mode Mode in which text replaces existing text as it is typed.

P

Pack and Go Wizard A PowerPoint feature that allows you to pack a presentation and all associated elements to run on another computer. See also *PowerPoint Viewer*.

page (1) An area equivalent to dimensions and text capacity of standard-sized paper (8.5" x 11"); (2) another name for *Web page*.

page break The point at which a page ends and another begins, inserted automatically or manually.

pane A bordered area within a window. Also called *windowpane*.

paragraph mark In Word, an onscreen symbol (¶) marking the end of a paragraph; also a proofreading symbol indicating to begin new paragraph.

paragraph spacing The amount of white space, measured in six-point increments, above and/or below paragraphs.

paste To insert cut or copied text or a graphic from the Clipboard.

path The exact location of a file or Web page.

Percent Style A predefined numeric format in Excel that changes values into percentages, multiplying the value by 100 and appending a percent sign.

placeholders In PowerPoint, text, object, or graphic boxes in a preset location in the AutoLayout slides.

point A unit of measure for text and white space, equivalent to 0.01384 inch.

pointer An arrow or other onscreen image that moves in relation to the movement of a mouse or trackball. Also called *mouse pointer*.

pointing Moving the mouse pointer over an onscreen object.

point size See *font size*.

portfolio An organized collection of your work that demonstrates skills and knowledge acquired from one or more courses. The materials included in a portfolio pertain to a specific educational or career goal. See also *developmental portfolio* and *representational portfolio*.

portrait orientation Layout that prints data vertically across the page on paper that is longer than it is wide; the default orientation.

POST See *Power On Self Test*.

post To create and send a message to a newsgroup.

Power On Self Test A program that checks a computer system's memory, keyboard, display, and disk drives. Also called *POST*.

PowerPoint Viewer A program used to run slide shows on computers that don't have PowerPoint installed. See also *Pack and Go Wizard*.

precedence The order in which operators are evaluated. Operators with a higher level of precedence are evaluated first.

presentation Series of PowerPoint slides shown to relay information.

presentation program Program, such as PowerPoint, that provides tools to create presentations using text, animation, charts, clip art, pictures, shapes, and sounds.

primary key In Access, a field or set of fields that uniquely identifies each record in the table.

primary sort key When you sort records in an Access database using multiple fields, the more important field used in the sort is called the primary sort key. Also called *major key*.

primary table In Access, a table in a one-to-many relationship that can have zero, one, or many matching records in the related table; but every record in the related table has exactly one matching record in the primary table. You can think of a primary table as the "one" side in a one-to-many relationship.

printout A printed copy of a file.

print preview An accurate image of the printed output—including headers, footers, page breaks, and print titles—displayed on the screen. A print preview lets you see on the screen what you will be printing before you send the output to the printer.

print scaling An Excel option that allows you to enlarge or reduce printed output without changing font sizes in order to better fit data on the page.

program files The application software that lets you perform tasks on the computer.

promote In PowerPoint, to move a subtitle to the next highest indent level.

proofread To verify that a document is accurate and error free.

protocol A set of signals and commands computers use to communicate with each other.

publish To allow others access to your Web page by storing it on a server that has a permanent connection to the Internet.

pure black and white A printer option that saves printer memory and time by ignoring colors, printing all PowerPoint slides in black and white only. Compare with *grayscale*.

Q

query   In Access, a question to the database, asking for a set of records from one or more tables or other queries that meets specific criteria.

query design grid   In Access, the grid in the Query Design view window that you use to make decisions about how to sort and select your data and which fields to include in the recordset.

R

radio button   See *option button.*

range   A group of adjacent cells in a worksheet.

range address   The cell addresses of the upper-left and lower-right cells in a range, separated by a colon. A range address tells the location of the range within the window. See also *range.*

readability   A rating of text in terms of how easy it is to read and understand, often stated as a grade (school) level.

record   In Access, a row in a table that contains the set of fields for one particular entity.

record selector   In Access, the box in Datasheet view to the left of a record. You can click the record selector to highlight the entire record.

recordset   In Access, a subset of your data sorted and selected as specified by a query. Recordsets change to reflect modifications to the data in your tables, and you can often make changes to recordsets that are reflected in the underlying table(s).

Redo   A command that reverses the effect of the previous Undo command.

redundancy   Duplication of data; storing the same information in more than one place. When creating Access tables, you want to avoid redundancy in order to conserve storage space, minimize keystroking, and decrease the likelihood of data-entry errors.

referential integrity   A set of rules that Access can enforce to preserve the defined relationship between tables.

related table   In Access, a table in a one-to-many relationship in which every record has exactly one matching record in the primary table. Also called *foreign table.*

relational database   A database program that lets you link, or relate, two or more tables to share data between them.

relationship   In Access, the connection between two or more tables. If tables contain a common field, they can be linked through this field. When tables are related in this way, reports and other objects created can combine data from both tables.

relative reference   A cell reference that changes to correspond to its new location when copied.

report   Database objects that permit you to produce polished printed output of the data from tables or queries. Some Access reports automatically generate totals of the values in particular fields.

report header   In Access, text information that is printed at the top of only the first page. Compare with *header.*

representational portfolio   An organized collection of your work that displays a variety of your best work. You can present a representational portfolio as evidence of your skills and knowledge. See also *developmental portfolio* and *portfolio.*

resize   To change the height and/or width of a graphic.

resize handle   A square at each corner and along the sides of a selected clip or object (or a square in the lower-left corner of a table) that may be used for expanding or contracting the object (or table). See also *sizing handle.*

reverse video   White text against a dark background.

right aligned   Text alignment in which the right edge is perfectly even.

right-click   The technique of quickly pressing and releasing the right button on a mouse or trackball.

root folder   The top level of a disk icon, which contains files and folders that are not nested within any other folder.

row heading   The gray area on the left side of an Excel worksheet that contains a number identifying each row.

row selector   In Access, a small box to the left of a field (in Table Design view) that you can click to select the entire field.

ruler   A display of numbered tick marks and indent markers that indicate measurements across a document used to format paragraphs and to position objects.

S

sans serif   A font without serifs (e.g., Arial); a gothic typeface.

save   To transfer a file from computer memory to a storage disk—either a floppy or hard disk.

ScreenTip   A text box showing the name and description of elements on the screen.

scroll arrows   Buttons at each end of a scroll bar that scroll a window in small increments when clicked—for example, scrolling text line by line.

scroll bar   A rectangular bar that appears along the right or bottom side of a window when not all the contents of the window are visible; used to bring hidden contents into view.

scroll box   Control within the scroll bars that allows quick navigation within a document.

scrolling   Using a scroll bar, scroll box, or scroll arrows to move through a document.

Glossary

search engine An Internet tool that allows a user to search for information on a particular topic. See also *Search Page*.

Search Page The Web page used as a starting point for an Internet search or a Web page which uses a search engine or subject directories to hunt for information on the Web. See also *search engine*.

Search tab One of the three tabs in the Help window; this option allows you to type words to search for in the Help system.

secondary sort key When you sort records in an Access database using multiple fields, the less important field used in the sort is called the secondary sort key. Also called *minor key*.

section break In Word, a way to subdivide a document (next page break) or page (continuous break) so that each defined section may have distinctive formatting.

select (1) To designate or highlight (typically by clicking an item with the mouse) where the next action will take place, which command will be executed next, or which option will be put into effect; (2) to extract specified subsets of data based on criteria that you define.

selection bar The left margin in the Word window that responds to the pointer by selecting the line of text.

selection criteria Instructions that tell Access exactly which records you want to extract from the database.

selection handles Black boxes that surround a selected area, such as a chart, a portion of a chart, or an object. The area surrounded by selection handles will be affected by any commands you issue. You can drag a selection handle to resize the selected area. Also called *handles*.

select query In Access, a query that you can use to sort, select, and view records from one or more tables.

Select Query window An Access window that displays the structure of a select query. You use the Select Query window to create a query by choosing the fields to be displayed, determining the order in which the fields will appear, and selecting the criteria to be used.

serif Finishing strokes on the characters of some fonts (e.g., Times New Roman) that form a fine line.

server A computer that supplies data or services to another (client) computer.

shading Color or gradations of gray applied to cells, paragraphs, and pages, often in combination with a border.

shadow A decorative effect for emphasizing large-font headings.

sheet tab A tab at the bottom of an Excel worksheet area that you can click to select a specific sheet in the workbook.

shift-click To press and hold ⇧Shift while clicking the left mouse button.

shortcut menu A context-sensitive menu that appears when you right-click certain screen elements.

short menu A list of the most commonly used commands that appears when you click a menu name on the menu bar. Compare with *expanded menu*.

size (1) To change the dimensions of a window so that its contents remain visible, but the window occupies only a portion of the desktop; (2) to change the dimensions of an object.

sizing handles Small white squares surrounding a selected object, used for changing the height and width of the object proportionately. See also *resize handle*.

slide In PowerPoint, an image of text and graphics shown on a computer, a slide projector, an overhead projector, or on paper.

Slide Master See *master*.

Slide Navigator dialog box PowerPoint dialog box available in Slide Show that allows you to move to any slide in a presentation.

slider control An indicator that you drag along a vertical or horizontal line. Dragging the indicator increases or decreases the value shown on the line.

small icon An icon displayed at quarter size.

soft return A line break that Office inserts automatically as copy wraps to the next line. Also called *automatic page break*.

software A collection of electronic instructions that directs the CPU to carry out a specific task. Software usually resides in storage.

sort To rearrange records, text, or table data into alphabetical, numerical, or chronological order. See *descending* and *ascending*.

sort key The field on which you sort records in an Access database. Compare with *primary sort key* and *secondary sort key*.

spinner buttons A pair of controls used to change a numerical setting, consisting of an up arrow above a down arrow. Clicking the up arrow increases the setting; clicking the down arrow decreases it.

spreadsheet The name for a workbook file in some worksheet programs other than Excel.

start value A beginning number or entry that you specify when using the Fill, Series command in Excel. Compare with *step value* and *stop value*.

statistical functions Excel functions that perform statistical analysis on ranges of data, such as the AVERAGE function, the COUNT function, the MAX function, and the MIN function.

status bar Bar at the bottom of the document window that indicates information about a command or toolbar button, an operation in progress, the location of the insertion point, or other information.

status indicators Buttons on the status bar that turn special keys or modes on and off; they display darkened when turned on and dimmed when turned off.

step value   A number by which to increment that you specify when using the Fill, Series command in Excel. Compare with *start value* and *stop value*.

stop value   An ending number or entry that you specify when using the Fill, Series command in Excel. Compare with *start value* and *step value*.

structure   The underlying design of an Access table that describes the characteristics of each field in the table. The structure controls the kind of information that can be entered into a table.

style   (1) In Excel, a combination of formats that has a specific name, such as Comma Style, Currency Style, and Percent Style; (2) in Word, a named set of character and paragraph attributes; and (3) in PowerPoint, preset options for a specific template or layout.

subdatasheet   In Access, a datasheet within a datasheet that allows you to view and edit related or joined data in another table.

subform   In Access, a form within a form that displays related records.

subject directory   A list of links to topics arranged alphabetically to facilitate browsing for a specific topic.

submenu   Indicated by an arrow on a menu, another list of commands, or options.

subscribe   (1) To activate a channel, telling the browser to periodically check for updated material; (2) to designate a newsgroup as one you may read on a regular basis.

subscript   A font that prints small characters below and immediately to the right of the body text.

subtitle   Any text under the title of a PowerPoint slide, except text appearing in an object.

superscript   A font that prints small characters above and immediately to the right of the body text.

sysadmin   A system (network) administrator; a person who manages a multi-user computer.

system boot   See *booting the system*.

T

tab   A control at the top of some dialog boxes that displays different screens within the dialog box.

table   A format having data arranged in columns and rows of cells in Word, Excel, and PowerPoint and in fields and records in Access.

table of contents   Listing of chapter and headings and (usually) their page numbers. Also called *TOC*.

tab split box   The box to the right of the sheet tabs, which can be dragged to increase or decrease the view of the sheet tabs.

tab stop   A preset (default) or user-set position on the horizontal ruler that defines the beginning of text columns and the size of paragraph indentations.

tabular form   In Access, a form that displays all the fields for a single record in one row, field names or captions as column headings, and data in the table or query as a tabular arrangement of rows and columns.

taskbar   An area on the Windows 98 Desktop that displays a button for the Start menu, icons for commonly used Windows 98 features, a button for each application running, and a button for the clock.

template   Master copy of a type of document; a model document that includes standard and variable text and formatting and may include graphics. Also called *design template*.

text   Data, such as descriptive labels, titles, and headings, on which you cannot perform calculations. Text is one of the two types of data Excel recognizes; the other is values. Compare with *values*.

text box   (1) In Office 2000 applications, a box used to hold text (or a graphic) in an object; (2) In Windows 98, a rectangular control that displays the name or value of a current setting and in which you can type a different name or value to change the setting.

text object   A filled object on a PowerPoint slide that contains text.

Thesaurus   A Word reference tool containing synonyms, often including related and contrasting words and antonyms.

Times New Roman   The standard, or default, font in Word 2000 for paragraph copy; a serif font.

title   First line of text in a PowerPoint slide.

title area   The dotted line area labeled *Click to add title* on a PowerPoint slide. It is the location of the text placeholder where you will type the main title of the slide.

title bar   Bar at the top of the screen containing application and file names.

title master   Controls the appearance of a PowerPoint title slide.

title slide   The first slide in a new PowerPoint presentation; it introduces the presentation to the audience.

TOC   See *table of contents*.

toggle key   A key that turns on and off.

toolbar   A row of icons representing frequently used commands, used to execute commands quickly.

top aligned   Page alignment in which text is even with the top margin regardless of the amount of text on the page; the default vertical alignment in Word.

touch-sensitive pad   An input device used to control the onscreen pointer by pressing a flat surface with a finger; usually found on laptop computers.

trackball   An input device that functions like an upside-down mouse, consisting of a stationary casing containing a movable ball that is rolled by the thumb or fingers to move the onscreen pointer; used frequently with laptop computers and video games.

Glossary

transitions In PowerPoint, visual effects that determine how one slide is replaced by another on the screen during a presentation; each slide can have its own transition.

triangle button A button in the shape of a small downward-pointing triangle, which displays a menu of options when clicked.

typeface See *font*.

U

underline A line under characters added for emphasis; numerous underline style options are available.

Undo A command that restores your file to the condition it was in before the previous action.

unfilled object An empty placeholder on a PowerPoint slide.

Uniform Resource Locator (URL) The address of a Web site. A URL can be made up of letters, numbers, and special symbols that are understood by the Internet.

URL See *Uniform Resource Locator*.

user interface The rules and methods by which a computer and its users communicate. See also *graphical user interface*.

V

values Numbers, dates, times, and formulas on which you can perform calculations. One of the two types of data Excel recognizes is values; the other is text. Compare with *text*.

variable information In a Word template, placeholder text in brackets.

vertical alignment The arrangement of text in relation to the top and bottom margins.

vertical scroll bar Scroll bar at the right side of the screen that scrolls documents from beginning to end. Compare with *horizontal scroll bar*.

W

Web See *World Wide Web*.

Web page A parcel of information located on the World Wide Web that may contain text, graphics, animation, sound, and video. The terms *Web page* and *Web site* are often used interchangeably. Also called *page*. See also *Web site*.

Web query An Excel feature that allows you to retrieve external data from a site on the World Wide Web.

Web site Specific location on the World Wide Web, accessible by means of a unique address, or URL. See also *Uniform Resource Locator* and *Web page*.

Web style desktop A Windows 98 desktop setting that gives the user the same look and feel as when on the Internet. Compare with *Active Desktop* and *classic style desktop*.

Web support An Office feature that allows you to save entire documents or parts of a document in Hypertext Markup Language (HTML).

widow The last line of a paragraph printed by itself at the top of a page. Compare with *orphan*.

wildcard character In Access, a character used in searches and filters to find a variable string of characters. For instance, *we** would find all words that start with *we*, such as *weather, well,* and *weekday*.

window A rectangular area that displays information, such as the content of a document or the controls of an application; you can open, close, move, size, maximize, and minimize a window.

windowpane See *pane*.

Wingdings A font consisting solely of iconic and symbolic characters.

wizard An interactive help tool that guides a user through an operation step by step.

WordArt Decorative text that you can stretch, skew, or rotate to fit a particular shape. See also *graphic*.

word processing program Computer program for creating word-based documents that are changed and stored easily.

word wrap Word processing feature that automatically moves the insertion point to the next line when text reaches the right margin.

workbook A collection of related worksheets and chart sheets saved as an Excel file.

workbook pages In Excel, the worksheets and chart sheets that can make up a single workbook.

worksheet In Excel, a grid of columns and rows for entering, viewing, and editing data; used most often for entering numbers and performing calculations.

worksheet area The area of the Excel window that contains a grid of columns and rows and occupies most of the screen. This is where your data appears and where you generally enter and edit data. The column and row headings, the scroll bars, and the sheet tabs are considered to be part of the worksheet area.

World Wide Web An Internet service that allows users to view documents containing jumps to other documents anywhere on the Internet. The graphical documents are controlled by companies, organizations, and individuals with a special interest to share. Also referred to as the *Web* or *WWW*.

wrapping style In Word, the way in which lines of text break in relation to an object on the same page; styles include In line with text, Square, Tight, Behind text, and In front of text.

WWW See *World Wide Web*.

WYSIWYG An acronym for *What you see is what you get*, a GUI characteristic in which documents appear on screen much as they will appear on a printed page or on a Web page.

Index

Index

Index

Index

Index

Index

Index